Your *Flower Garden*

Your Flower Garden

ROB HERWIG

foreword by Roy Hay

Mitchell Beazley

First published in the Dutch language in 1977
under the title:
TUINPLANTEN-ENCYCLOPEDIE
by Rob Herwig

© 1977 Zomer & Keuning Boeken BV.,
Wageningen, Holland

English text and additional material © 1979
by Mitchell Beazley Marketing Limited

First published in Great Britain in 1979
by Mitchell Beazley Marketing Limited,
Artists House, 14–15 Manette Street,
London W1V 5LB

Edited by Michael Leitch
Production Barry Baker and Bob Towell

Technical consultant: Kenneth A Beckett
Translator: Arnold J Pomerans

ISBN 0 85533 159 3

Filmset in 'Monophoto' Plantin by
Servis Filmsetting Limited, Manchester
Printed in England by Balding + Mansell

CONTENTS

FOREWORD by Roy Hay MBE, VMH

Too many inexperienced gardeners invite disappointment by trying to grow plants where they do not want to grow, and so they end up running a plant hospital or even a plant mortuary. There are plenty of plants that will grow in any garden—the problem is to discover which they are. This book enables the gardener to identify them in an easier and simpler way than I have seen in any other book. The 25 symbols used to indicate the needs of individual plants give an "at a glance" assessment of their suitability for the conditions in a particular location.

To make the best use of this book, which is the result of extraordinary attention to detail, we have to answer some preliminary questions. What kind of garden is it? Is it exposed to cold easterly or northerly winds, perhaps on a hillside on poor soil, or is it lying snug in a sheltered valley on rich loamy soil with an abundant water supply? Is the soil acid or alkaline? (A simple soil testing kit provides the answer.) Is it light, quick-drying soil, or is it heavy and perhaps rather badly drained?

All that plants need to grow is fertile soil, adequate light and sufficient water. The soil, no matter whether it is sandy, loamy, chalky or pure clay, can be improved. Sunlight plants normally have in good measure. Water they receive from rain, although there is usually some period in the year, be it in spring, summer or even autumn, when not enough rain falls and we have to resort to watering.

Once we have made a realistic assessment of our garden's advantages and disadvantages, we can begin to do something about its shortcomings. Provision of shelter is perhaps the most important improvement a gardener can make. Hedges are an obvious solution, but it may well be necessary in very exposed locations to provide temporary shelter—for example, wattle hurdles or the like to enable hedging plants to become established. Perhaps better than hedges, which need regular clipping, is a screen of shrubs in depth, provided there is enough room.

Light soils can be made more fertile by the addition of peat, organic fertilizers, garden compost, hop manure, bark fibre and various other materials. Heavy soils can also be improved by digging in such materials, and by adding lime if they are acid. Soils that lie too wet may often be much improved by installing some form of drainage.

For most of the plants we wish to grow an acid soil is best. There are very few plants that must have an alkaline soil, and for most of them we can make special provision, as indeed we can for acid-loving plants on alkaline soils. For example, to grow acid-loving rhododendrons or azaleas on an alkaline soil, dig a hole say 2 ft deep and line it with plastic sheeting. Fill this with acid compost, a good peaty soil mix, and once the plants are established feed them with an acid fertilizer such as sulphate of ammonia.

Or the gardener can make raised beds (say 2 ft high) with bricks, stone, peat blocks or old railway sleepers, fill them with the appropriate soil (acid or alkaline) and grow the chosen plants in these beds.

Even moist shady parts of a garden can be infinitely rewarding. There we can grow some of the loveliest of plants—primulas, meconopses, astilbes, trollius and many more. And if there is a supply of water to hand, even dry shade need be no problem. Most of these moisture-loving plants will thrive if we can turn on a sprinkler two or three times a week during dry spells. With modern plastic equipment, it is also possible to install a permanent irrigation system.

Next, having done all we can to make the garden as hospitable as possible for our plants, we have to decide what kind of a garden we really want. Most of us like to use flowers as a framework to enhance the house and here there is ample opportunity for the gardener to express his or her personality and there is unlimited scope for original planting ideas. With some forethought in planning, the home need never be short of cut flowers—even in the depths of winter posies can be gathered from a very modest garden.

All the basic information about a vast range of plants can be found in the pages that follow, whether they are rock plants, water plants, plants with attractive foliage—indeed any particular type of plant.

There are various ways in which the gardener can put this book to practical use. The plant tables enable appropriate flowers of any colour, height, habitat or type to be identified and selected as required. Or the index and the 190-page A–Z section can provide information on growing a particular flower or shrub, with advice on how to choose the most suitable varieties of each plant. And, of course, the book with its 500 colour pictures is the ideal guide for planning colour and contrast in both large and small gardens.

By taking time to study the list of plants and then checking by means of the symbols in the A–Z section the gardener should be able to select the plants that will thrive in any particular garden and avoid disappointing and expensive failures.

This book is a mine of information and I make no apology for using this overworked phrase. I would have been very proud if I had written it and I offer my warmest congratulations to Rob Herwig. Thousands of garden owners, many of whom have yet to take their first faltering footsteps on that most rewarding, but often exasperating, road to success with gardening, will have good cause to thank him for this book which he has so painstakingly produced.

Roy Hay

5

INTRODUCTION

Give fools their gold, and knaves their power:
Let fortune's bubbles rise and fall;
Who sows a field, or trains a flower,
Or plants a tree, is more than all.

(J. G. Whittier)

Your Flower Garden was first published in the Netherlands as the successor to a great gardening classic, *Herwig's Practical Garden Encyclopaedia*. The author of this famous work was A. J. Herwig. His son, Rob Herwig, decided to produce an updated book on garden plants to succeed his father's encyclopaedia and *Your Flower Garden* is the result.

Rob Herwig explains: "When my publisher and I decided to publish the *Herwig Tuinplanten-encyclopedie*, as *Your Flower Garden* is called in Holland, we quickly realized that it would be an expensive, almost élite, work. But at the same time we were aware that a growing number of amateur gardeners are devoting more and more time, attention and money to their hobby. It was with these people in mind that this book was written.

"Many garden-lovers over the age of 40 remember, and indeed still use, *Herwig's Praktische Tuin-encyclopedie*. This book was first published in instalments in 1937 by my father, A. J. Herwig. Its 788 pages contained all the garden plants mentioned in Dutch catalogues and moreover a great number of house plants, vegetables and fungi. After the Second World War some reprints appeared and, in 1967, I revised it and divided it into two volumes, an encyclopaedia of house plants and an encyclopaedia of garden plants. These volumes too were once more reprinted but were completely sold out by 1973. This book is intended as a new edition of the volume on garden plants."

Your Flower Garden consists of four parts. The first part, illustrated with colour photographs, deals with the use of plants in the garden, and discusses the effects produced by the groupings of form and colour. The second part is the actual encyclopaedia of plants. More than 1,500 garden plants are described in alphabetical order. This section also contains hundreds of colour photographs of different garden plants. The third part of the book discusses the propagation of plants and is illustrated with drawings. Finally, the fourth part contains tables of plants by type, colour and height, and an alphabetical index of common names. This index allows the reader to look up a plant under its common name and find the Latin name under which it is listed in the main A–Z encyclopaedia section.

The author doubled as photographer in the preparation of *Your Flower Garden*. "Taking the photographs for this book proved to be a very rewarding experience," he says. "My trips took me through Belgium, the Netherlands, Britain and West Germany. I was greatly impressed by the number of beautiful gardens which are still not well known. I discovered also that the finest gardens are to be found in England—a fact acknowledged by many Dutch experts—and I would strongly advise all European garden-lovers to visit this beautiful country.

"For present-day garden designs, however, we should look eastwards. From Denmark, Germany and Switzerland come inspiring and creative efforts that are well worth visiting. If in my country of the Netherlands we could find a synthesis between "eastern" design and "western" love for plants, then it might be possible to create the ideal garden.

"Inspired as I was by the beauty of English gardens, I resisted the temptation to have too great an English bias in this book. It is designed for the European gardener."

Knowing what you want to grow is one thing. Finding somewhere to obtain the plants is another. Unfortunately not all nurseries are able to supply all the plants described in this book. However, there will always be somebody who stocks the plant you want. Often it will be a specialist or it may be a small firm.

Rob Herwig adds: "Finally I would like to thank a number of people who contributed to this work; in particular my former collaborators Ines Girisch, who researched the text, and Esther van Duyvendijk, who assisted especially with taking the photographs. Ellen Lubbers-de Beer helped with the compilation of the index and tables. I would also like to thank the highly experienced Harry van de Laar, who checked the precise names of many of the plants that appear in the photographs and corrected them if necessary. Without the help of these and many more people—in particular those who allowed me to photograph their gardens—I would never have been able to compile this book."

The technical consultant for this English edition was Kenneth A. Beckett, the well-known horticultural writer and journalist. He added many new plants to Rob Herwig's list in order to adapt *Your Flower Garden* to the needs of British gardeners.

Rob Herwig and the publishers would be glad to receive any remarks from readers that might enhance the usefulness of this book.

FORM AND COLOUR IN THE GARDEN

What is colour?

When we consider colour in the garden we are not so much referring to its physical causes as to its physiological effects. What we see, and what colours we see, varies from person to person and is also dependent on many factors beyond our control.

Everyone will probably have taken a colour photograph of a garden or a figure in the evening light, only to be surprised by the yellowish-red tones of his snapshot. To the physicist, the light was exactly as the photograph shows it to have been, but our eyes did not see it that way. Our sense tends always to shift the overall impression towards the neutral, in this case towards white. This is called colour adaptation, and if we are aware of it at work it is possible to observe the difference in colour between morning, noon and evening light. In the garden, colour adaptation produces greater problems than it does indoors where the artificial light is more or less constant. The colour impression depends on the colour of the rays that impinge on a particular object. A series of photographs of a group of red, blue and yellow flowers, taken every hour throughout a single day, will demonstrate this fact.

Every photographer also knows that it makes a difference whether an object is lit by the sun or by reflection from the blue sky. The bluish tinge in the shadows constitutes a notorious trap for the beginner.

The colours of plants

The natural function of coloured flowers is to attract insects, while the green pigment in the leaves plays an important role in the plant's metabolism. The fact that the colours also appeal to our aesthetic sense is the most important reason for displaying plants in our gardens.

When talking about plant colours we come up against a language problem. The basic colours like red and green are based on a consensus. Everyone knows what they are, and everyone agrees which is which. Even terms such as "yellow ochre" are generally understood. However, things become more difficult when we speak of, say, the colour of *Amaranthus*, since many people do not know what precise colour that plant is. Even "grass green" is a vague term, for there are at least ten types of grass in an ordinary lawn, all of which have different tints.

Another example: the term "rose" is well known but nevertheless confusing. Rose is a light shade of red, purple or violet, with varying overtones of blue. To be absolutely correct, we should therefore speak of "light red", "light purple", "light violet", instead of "rose-red", etc.

In professional circles a successful attempt has been made to do something about this confusion. By colorimetric methods it is possible to identify and reproduce colours and shades very precisely. The best colour chart for gardeners is that prepared by the Royal Horticultural Society. It comes in the formula of a system of fans with 202 colours, each in four different densities, making 808 tints altogether. With this chart it is possible to find the colour of almost

every flower and leaf and to link it with a number.

In this system, the circle of colours is logically divided into segments—yellow, orange, red, purple, violet, blue and green—each with intermediate tints. These fans are particularly useful for judging competitions, exhibitions and so on, and with their help it is possible, even when plants are not in flower, to arrive at attractive colour combinations using the code number.

When we look at the colours of flowers and leaves, it is as well to remember that plants look quite different in reflected light to the way they do if the light shines on them directly from behind the observer. Some petals are so glossy that from certain angles they reflect light, without revealing much of their own colour. This is a factor that should be taken into account when positioning plants in the garden.

The importance of colour in your garden
Because colours make so strong an impression on us, colour plays a crucial role in the overall impact of a garden. That impact creates certain moods and these moods may affect your own. So do not underestimate the importance of colours in the garden. Naturally, colour is not our only concern. The shape of plants and flowers is important as well, and so is the balance between plants and buildings. But two identical gardens with different approaches to colour make quite distinct impressions. The same thing happens with clothing: the first thing we notice about a person is the colour of his clothes. Other characteristics are noticed later.

In the garden all colours play some part, and not just those of flowers. First of all there is the house. The smaller the garden the more the house is noticed, and its colours too: bricks of a certain shade, wood painted in various hues, curtains, outside lights, balcony or terrace furniture. All these elements tend to disturb the colour scheme of the garden as such, which is why so many people like to paint their house and everything attached to it in neutral black and white. This also applies to garden furniture, awnings and so on. Only if colour makes an essential contribution to the architecture is it allowed to stay and the plant life adapted accordingly.

If we want to be successful with colours we must be as consistent as possible. Everything put in the garden introduces its own colour. Stones, paving slabs, garden lamps, the swimming pool, the wooden fences—if all are allowed their own colour the garden will look a hotch-potch even before we grow any plants. The most sensible thing is therefore to choose all the colours deliberately and even then to plump for black and white wherever possible.

Most plants differ not only in the colour of their flowers but also in the colour of their foliage. Green, we call it, but have you ever noticed how very different the leaves of various shrubs can be? And how each differs from season to season? Conifers, too, display an endless variation of colours, which also change with the seasons. Grass, too, may be green, but its colour changes almost daily.

Luckily the many green tints do not readily clash; hence we do not have to consider whether the foliage of each plant will fit in with the rest of the garden. But do pay attention to plants with variegated leaves or foliage in unusual colours for they may quickly dominate less conspicuous vegetation.

Colour sense
Colour sense has to be learnt. Most people have an underdeveloped colour sense. Even the average designer, architect or interior decorator will often show exceedingly bad taste.

The same is true of most garden designers. A garden must be colourful, so most people believe, planting brilliant red salvias right next to orange African marigolds. Even profusion of colour is treated as a status symbol, for the greater the number of colours in your flower beds the more likely they are to catch the eyes of your neighbours.

Better gardening sense often leads to a healthy improvement of the colour sense. The more one looks around, travels and reads about gardening, the more subdued the colours one tends to choose. Professional gardeners are remarkable for their conscious use of subtle colour. And if we visit some of the most famous

The colour of a subject is partly determined by the light that shines on it. The long shadows of the evening sun lend a golden glow to this *Catalpa* and its surroundings.

Deliberate choice of colour led to the emergence of the 'colourless' or white garden, here shown at Hidcote Manor, Gloucestershire. Note the small red flowers in the hedge.

A colour combination like the above does not add greatly to the beauty of a garden. Such borders are usually planted by those with a poorly developed colour sense.

Sissinghurst Castle in Kent is a garden in which colour has been used very deliberately and to most striking effect. The combinations were devised by Vita Sackville-West.

gardens then we are often struck by their extreme refinement. The fact that so much has been written about them (often with colour photographs) naturally helps the reader to develop his appreciation of colour.

It should be mentioned that not all professional gardeners agree with the manipulation of colour to produce a certain effect. This is particularly true of those who advocate a "natural" garden. Such gardens are based on artificially created differences in level and filled with naturalized and wild plants. All weeding and hoeing is eschewed, along with the creation of formal lawns and colour manipulation.

Gardens in special colours
It is interesting to find that warm colours usually predominate in fairly "primitive" gardens, with red and yellow in the lead, balanced with green and blue. But bedding plants in particular have relatively little green foliage and are very rarely blue, often producing a surfeit of red and yellow. The addition of blue will help to redress the balance.

Even professional borders often have this kind of surfeit, sometimes deliberately introduced. It is not a bad thing to have, say, a large green hedge behind the border, or to have lots of blue sky reflected in the pool. But when the wall of the house is yellow, the paths are made of yellow brick and the garden umbrella is a gay red and orange, then there is a most disturbing excess of colour.

It is perfectly possible to make a garden without conspicuous colours. As we said earlier, no shade of green is like any other, and it is precisely the combination of various greens that can provide a splendid spectacle. Your garden does not, however, have to become like a cemetery, in which the greens are particularly sombre. It is possible to achieve a vivid effect with ornamental grasses, which come in all tints from bluish to yellowish green. If you now set a pink azalea in this sea of green, everyone who comes into the garden at flowering time will notice it. Even if the visitor has just as fine an azalea himself, he will exclaim at yours with surprise, because his is hidden

Ornamental grasses in the garden of the Royal Horticultural Society at Wisley in Surrey. Photograph taken on 25 October. Note the combination of brown and green tints.

In this masterfully composed border at Great Dixter you can see how yellow and red can be used close to each other if they are connected with the right tints.

amidst dozens of other flowering shrubs, herbaceous perennials and trees.

This is just one example, but it is a good idea to start with: build up your garden from a neutral colour and treat every new shade as a concession. In any case you will achieve a special effect more quickly and effectively than by scattering colours about. When we look at gardens that are famous for their particularly beautiful colour combinations—and the best of these gardens are in Britain—then we are struck by the fact that they owe their distinction to their severe limitation of colours. Very unusual but nevertheless greatly admired are the white gardens, for instance, at Hidcote Manor and Sissinghurst Castle. They are stocked exclusively with white and cream-coloured flowers and abound in silver-leaved plants. And yet these are not uniformly coloured, for quite apart from the various shades of white and silver there is still a great deal of green. Moreover supplementary colours are often provided, say by a brick path. In Hidcote Manor bright red *Tropaeolum speciosum* grows amidst

the dark green *Taxus* hedges.

Gardens with two or three colours are much more common. Thus there are "blue" gardens, very cool and reserved, with shades of blue and violet alternating with silver and a little purple here and there. Things become quite a lot easier when we add a little violet and bright red. These are the so-called red, white and blue borders. But there are other possibilities. Crimson, orange and light yellow make excellent combinations that are set off most effectively with bluish-green foliage plants such as conifers. An entirely yellow garden is easily planted but it will not be to everyone's taste. If you like the somewhat sweetish combination of soft yellow and rose-red, then it is best to confine it to the border. The range of colours is easily extended to comprise combinations of yellow, white, blue and orange. We must be particularly careful with red, because pure red is very rare and the various shades of red rarely mix well. An attractive but difficult shade of red is best isolated from another with white flowers.

Another possibility is to plant a border with silver as the main colour and to dot it with dabs of light red, soft blue, purple and violet.

Depending on personal preferences, you can extend any particular combination. But do remember that you are more likely to produce striking effects with few colours than with many.

Special colour effects

If we combine specific colours we do not need to take equal numbers of each. Thus, a single bright rose will balance a whole field of lavender blue. The brightness of a given colour must therefore be our measure of the quantity that we use: this is a rule that is often broken to the detriment of the garden.

Because plants in warm colours appear to be closer together, and those with cool colours seem further apart than they are, we can use this rule for playing optical tricks. Thus a garden will look longer if it has bright blue flowers in the distance and bright red flowers in the foreground.

Shadows can be lightened with white flowers and even a sombre background can be made to look brighter with plants in white, silver and cream.

Deliberate choice of colours

You are standing in front of an empty garden, or your own garden which you want to change. You accept the fact that the choice of colour must not be arbitrary. But how do you go on from there?

First of all, establish your personal preferences. Do you like soft shades that gradually merge, or do you prefer stark contrasts? What is your favourite colour scheme?

The next problem is to choose plants with flowers and leaves in the particular colours you want. All these details are set out in the A–Z entries and to make things even easier you will find several colour tables at the end. However these are not precise enough to tell exactly what shade a particular flower will have; hence it is best to inspect your potential purchases at close quarters. This can be done in any nursery or public garden, and by paying attention as you walk through your own neighbourhood or travel about. Do not forget that many garden plants come in countless varieties, each in shades of their own. Thus it is not enough to know that a plant is called *Phlox paniculata*; you must also know the name of the particular variety you prefer—for instance 'Star Fire'. If you want to check on precise colours then it is a good idea to carry a colour chart with you on your travels. You can do no better than use the Royal Horticultural Society's colour fans, but you may prefer to make do with a simpler system.

Another important point to bear in mind is that the colours chosen to blend or contrast with one another must flower at roughly the same time. You will have achieved very little if your beautiful red poppy has faded before the blue aster next to it has come into flower. You must also pay attention to the height of the plants and to their particular needs, lest you plant shade-loving plants and sun-worshippers, or plants that need a different pH, side by side.

If you have selected an attractive colour scheme no one will expect perfect results overnight—there are too many unpredictable factors for that to happen.

But do not despair. Let everything take its natural course for two years and then on a nice summer's day when your garden is in full flower sit down and take a critical look at your creation. Take pen and paper and make a note of what you want to change. Take colour photographs, preferably slides, for their colours are generally closest to nature. Without this preparation, in the winter, when you come to order and plan your next move, everything will be flat, and some of the worst features will have gone from your mind. And so your garden will grow a little more beautiful every year, since naturally you will continue to make changes. That is the most wonderful thing about gardening: anyone can sweep, rake, edge prune and weed, but only the truly creative gardener can create a satisfying colour spectacle.

Which plants for your garden?

On hearing the word "garden" most people think primarily of plants. However, it is only when everything else is ready that plants are introduced. Nevertheless plants largely determine the character of the garden. Consider the difference between an English garden, full of colours, and a Japanese garden made of pebbles and a few green plants. In a harmonious garden, architecture and plants will have been blended most carefully.

In this chapter we shall first divide plants by their botanical characteristics and next on the basis of purely practical considerations.

Annuals

Annuals are herbaceous plants that usually grow from seed, and that flower and die in one season. This is not always so by nature. Many so-called annuals are perennials in their homeland but are cultivated as garden annuals because our winters are too severe.

Annuals may also be grown from cuttings taken from older plants in the autumn, protected from frost during the winter, and allowed to come into bloom during the following year.

The seed of many annuals can be sown under glass as early as December or January. Other annual plants, by contrast, must be sown outdoors in May. There are, of course, many sorts of intermediate types.

There is no reason why you should grow all your annuals from seed. Nurseries provide cheap bedding plants, which may be bought in May when they are in flower. Favourite bedding plants include marigolds, salvias and petunias. If you want to grow these plants yourself from seed, you will need a heated greenhouse, for they cannot be sown outside before April for flowering in June–July.

Do not assume that all annuals can be bought as bedding plants. Good catalogues list hundreds of species and varieties that can never be bought ready-made. The reason may be that they are not widely known or that they are late-flowering and hence are not an economic proposition for nurseries. Many gardeners feel that the best annuals cannot be bought as bedding plants and accordingly prefer to raise their annuals from seed in the greenhouse or under frames. **The use of annuals** In the garden bedding plants are often used to fill in the empty spaces left by the removal of bulbs. Some species are suited for leading a modest existence in the perennial border, where it is particularly important to pay very careful heed to their colours. Other bedding plants are excellent for cutting in the summer, and may be grown in a special bed set aside for that purpose.

It should be said that bedding plants are a garden designer's *bête noire*. He invariably prefers perennial plants and bulbs suitable for naturalization, and considers the annual putting in and lifting of bulbs and summer plants a certain way of ruining a good garden.

Plants grown from seed can, of course, be used for similar purposes. Because the choice is much larger the possibilities are much wider, particularly when it comes to combinations. A special shade of, say, antirrhinums may be the missing link in your herbaceous border, and in your cut-flower corner annuals are indispensable: think of asters, cosmeas, sweet peas and ornamental tobacco plants.

An annual border is one of the most attractive

features to create with flowers grown from seed in the flowering position. It is essential to plan everything on paper first, making sure that all the colours and sizes go well together. Then the border is dug and raked and the design copied on the ground. The different flowers are then sown in their various outlined areas, preferably in rows or in groups so as to make weeding easier. Approximately three months after sowing the border will begin to come into flower.

The right mixture of annuals can also produce a magnificent flowering meadow, or wild garden, and whenever a piece of ground lies fallow these seeds may be lightly raked in to produce a fine spectacle later. For covering ugly sheds and fences we can use various annual climbing plants such as nasturtiums, hops or cathedral bells. Bees are strongly attracted by the nectar of various annuals.

Many annuals are self-seeding. This may sometimes be a real nuisance, but it can also be a boon to see promising seedlings spring out of the ground when you least expect them. It is important to identify the various species lest they be weeded by accident. According to experts this method of "seed control", which can also be practised with biennials, is one of the secrets of the successful, natural-looking garden.

Biennials

Biennials—just like annuals—are usually grown from seed. They cannot complete their full growing cycle within a single growing season—after developing in the summer, they then overwinter without flowering, return to life in the early spring, and usually come into flower between February and June.

However this cycle is not followed by all biennials. Thus some will not flower until the third year, while others send up so many basal shoots that they look deceptively like perennials. Finally, but very exceptionally, the whole biennial cycle may be completed within a single year.

By sowing at various times, it is possible to vary the flowering period, but in general it is true to say that biennials should be sown in June or July to produce flowers the next spring—at a time, that is, which is most propitious, for few annuals are out by then.

The use of biennials Biennials are often much taller than annuals; they are proud and highly ornamental plants with a conspicuous appearance and a fairly long flowering period. Mullein, Scotch thistle and foxglove are three good examples. After flowering biennials usually produce seed in profusion, the seed germinating very easily. As a result, the garden tends to become swamped with seedlings, which should be thinned out (bearing in mind the correct distance apart) or lifted in the summer or in the autumn and replanted to flower the next year. Some species will deteriorate if they are allowed to seed themselves. In

Typical example of how to build up a mixed border, using herbaceous perennials, shrubs and conifers. The main colours are blue, violet and red, with a little yellow in the foreground and background.

Even in the small garden it is possible to grow a large assortment of annuals. Here they are arranged neatly in rows, as in a nursery.

Above top: A larger garden with borders made up exclusively of annuals. The cost is minimal. (RHS Garden, Wisley.)
Above: The meadow-flower mixture so popular on the Continent (Hortus De Uithof, near Utrecht).

that case it is best to remove all seedlings and sow new plants every year. If the new plants are dead-headed in time they will have no chance of running to seed.

Some biennials can be bought as bedding plants, such as pansies, which begin to flower in the winter, and giant-flowered daisies, which become available in the early spring. Other popular biennial bedding plants are sweet Williams, wallflowers, forget-me-nots and hollyhocks. But the beautiful mullein (*Verbascum*), the imposing Scotch thistle (*Onopordum*), the familiar foxglove (*Digitalis*), the fragrant damask violet (*Hesperis*), the charming honesty (*Lunaria*) and the admirable Himalayan blue poppy (*Meconopsis*) are all plants you will have to grow from seed.

Herbaceous perennials

Herbaceous perennials are plants that lack the permanent woody branches of shrubs and trees. They die down to the ground in the winter but the roots and growing points stay alive. Thus though the root system grows bigger every year, the plants do not grow taller and taller because they have to start all over again from the beginning every year. In theory, perennial plants could therefore continue indefinitely, but in practice they have a life expectancy of from one to twenty years. They are threatened by all sorts of dangers, of which decay and frost are probably two of the greatest.

In discussing annuals and biennials, we noticed that some were really perennials. Similarly many perennials are really shrubs, for they produce woody branches that do not completely die back. We call these plants sub-shrubs. In addition there are several evergreen perennials in which the leaves do not have to be shed, although they usually are during severe European winters. In many cases these sub-shrubs and evergreen perennials recuperate in the spring, although often with great difficulty.

Perennial plants may be bought at garden centres or by mail order, often from specialist nurseries. Many perennial plants can also be propagated from seeds ordered by post. Most perennials will only flower during the second year, but if fairly substantial quantities of one plant are required, sowing is nevertheless worthwhile.

Perennial plants are easily propagated by root division. This is best done in autumn or in spring, and provides a simple method of stocking the garden with a little help from your friends.

Many rock plants are perennials, generally requiring a dry, sunny position. Marsh plants, which must be kept in moist soil throughout the year, such aquatic plants as water lilies, and lawn and ornamental grasses are all perennials.

The use of perennials It is obvious that the applications of perennial plants will be very extensive. Indeed, it is almost impossible to have a beautiful garden without perennial plants; when a garden seems to be lacking something, this may often be put down to a shortage of perennials.

Because many perennials are so floriferous and also because their height ranges between 2 in (5 cm) and 10 ft (3 m), the correct juxtaposition of colour, height and flowering period is an important matter. The right combination can make up a mixed perennial border, but the plants may also be limited to a few species, in which case we speak of a group. If the group is free-standing it may be termed a bed. Perennials can also be combined with shrubs, biennials and annuals. Their range has been vastly extended by hybridization, a technique that has been developed into a fine art, especially in Britain.

Perennials are ideal for planting over larger areas; they can be used to stop banks from eroding, as edging plants, and some species are particularly attractive when used as solitary plants. There is one problem: weeds grow easily between perennial plants and must be removed by hand.

Bulbous and tuberous plants

Bulbous and tuberous plants resemble perennial plants in many ways, but differ from them in that they have underground storage organs which maintain the plant when it dies down to the ground. This may happen at various times of the year so that these plants, unlike herbaceous perennials, cannot be said

Planting an annual border is not difficult. First, the whole border is designed on paper, attention being given to the colour, height and flowering period of the annuals. Next the design is copied to scale on the raked soil. All divisions, solitary plants, etc., are marked with string, and nameplates, prepared previously, are placed in the appropriate places. The required species are then planted in their

compartments, preferably in rows so as to facilitate weeding—the seedlings are hard to distinguish from weeds. Once the plants have been thinned out, the linear pattern disappears automatically. If the soil is very sandy, it is better to make 2 in (5 cm) deep drills instead of rows, and to fill them with a good-quality peat or seed compost before the species are planted.

to "hibernate". Thus all spring-flowering bulbs and tubers rest in the summer. The aim of this very clever system is to help the plant survive periods of severe drought, common in their countries of origin. The tulip, for instance, will suffer very little harm from June onwards, by which time it is completely dead above ground. In its original home, Turkey, it comes back into flower and sends up young leaves only when it starts to rain again. In wet summers it is often a good idea to store bulbs above ground for a few months.

Not all underground bulbs and tubers play the same botanical role. We distinguish four groups:

Bulbs These consist of fleshy scales which grow out of a solid piece of tissue known as the basal plate. The scales may be considered as leaves. Example: hyacinth, tulip, narcissus, lily.

Corms These are swollen underground stems which are solid throughout and are not made up of separate layers of scales. Each corm produces only one bud. Examples: crocus, gladiolus.

Tubers The difference between tubers and corms is sometimes difficult to tell, although tubers usually have several buds each. A tuber is really a thickened underground stem; in the case of the dahlias we can speak of thickened roots, just as in potatoes.

Rhizomes These consist of thickened and usually horizontal underground stems, to which the actual roots are attached. All vegetation above ground dies down every year. Examples: the bearded iris.

In practical gardening we have to deal with:

Spring-flowering bulbs These include tulips, narcissi, hyacinths, etc. They are planted in the autumn and flower in the early spring. The foliage dies down around June, when the bulbs must be lifted and stored in a dry place until planting time in October–November (the soil in summer is often a little too wet for them). Bulbous plants suitable for naturalization (e.g. narcissi) may be left in the ground throughout the year, provided the soil and the position are suitable.

Summer-flowering bulbs The lily is a well-known summer-flowering bulb. Most of the bulbs are planted in March–April, but there are a few exceptions which must be planted in the autumn. Many species can be treated as perennial plants and do not need to be lifted, although they do need at times to be covered with straw or litter in the winter. However there are some summer-flowering bulbs which are tender, for instance the summer hyacinth (*Galtonia*). It should be lifted in October, and stored in a frost-proof and dry place until planting time.

Spring-flowering corms and tubers As far as their cultivation is concerned there is no difference between corms and tubers on the one hand and bulbs on the other—so much so that corms such as crocuses are usually referred to as bulbous plants. Their hardiness differs and it is advisable to cover spring-flowering anemones, for instance, with a good layer of leaf mould. The corms need not be lifted. After flowering, the leaves should be allowed to develop and die off naturally.

Summer-flowering corms and tubers This group contains a great many well-known plants including begonias, cannas, dahlias and gladioli. None of them are hardy, so that they can be placed outdoors only after the beginning of May. It is a good idea to transfer the corms, etc. to boxes or pots of potting compost at the beginning of April and to start them off in a fairly warm corner at 15°C (59°F). By the middle of May you will then have an attractive plant that can be planted out.

After the first autumn frosts, when the foliage has turned brown, the plants should be lifted, the stems cut off slightly above the corms or tubers and the plants tied up in small bunches, labelled, and hung up in a dry, frost-proof place. After about a month the corms or tubers should be further cleaned and then stored in boxes with dry peat at a temperature of between 5° and 12°C (41° and 54°F). At the beginning of January check that the corms are neither too dry nor too moist. If they are too dry transfer them to slightly moister peat, and if too moist cut off the rotten parts and store them in absolutely dry peat. Dried bulbs stored in plastic bags are likely to rot.

Spring and summer-flowering rhizomes This group includes most irises and *Polygonatum*, which

One of the most attractive biennials in semishaded positions: *Digitalis* or foxglove.

Below: Perennial grasses can be very decorative, not only in the summer but also when they change colour in the autumn.

Below right: Rock plants are easily grown in well-drained basins.

Biennials often seed themselves, so that it pays to be able to identify the seedlings. Top left: *Lunaria* (honesty); top right: *Digitalis* (foxglove); centre left: *Viola*; centre: *Verbascum* (mullein); centre right: *Cheiranthus* (wallflower); bottom left: *Hesperis*; centre: *Dianthus*; right: *Myosotis* (forget-me-not).

Many herbaceous perennials like slightly calcareous soil that does not become too moist in the winter. Clearly, a loosely stacked and well-drained rock wall provides these plants with optimal conditions. It is possible to substitute concrete elements in modern rockeries.

Above left: Water lilies are the most popular of all aquatic plants. They are suitable for large and small ponds. The species depicted here will only grow in a heated pool.

Above right: *Peltiphyllum peltatum* is a typical marginal plant. The flowers appear before the leaves in April.

can, to all intents and purposes, be treated as herbaceous perennials. The rhizomes are generally completely hardy. Bearded irises prefer to be transplanted in August–September. In the winter most of the foliage dies down, new leaves appearing in the spring.

Sources of supply Bulbous and tuberous-rooted plants may be acquired in various ways. The spring-flowering types (tulip, narcissus, hyacinth, etc.) are usually bought by mail order. Garden shops, too, stock the best-known species, although for unusual bulbs you will probably have to go to the specialist nurseries. Avoid offer of inferior products (out-of-date or bad strains, undersized, damaged or diseased bulbs). Summer-flowering bulbs are not so common and are generally not available except by mail order from specialists. Begonias, cannas, dahlias and gladiolis are still great favourites and are therefore stocked by most garden centres. But they, too, are best acquired from reputable mail order concerns. Some firms sell nothing but dahlias and gladioli and these naturally offer the widest choice. Every year scores of new dahlias come on to the market and many gardeners consider it a challenge to be one of the first to have an example. Naturally, the price of such novelties is very high.

With cannas and begonias, new varieties are much rarer, gardeners usually confining themselves to standard mixtures without a name. In garden shops bulbous plants can be bought that have already begun to make new growth and are ready for the garden.

Bearded irises, the best-known rhizomatous plants, can also be bought by mail order, from nurseries and from garden centres. Specialists will also supply the latest varieties from the USA, and though prices are very high, the gardener will get something very special for his money.

The uses of bulbs, corms and tubers The uses of bulbs, corms and tubers for the garden are highly diversified. Spring bulbs that do not lend themselves to naturalization are usually planted in beds which, once the bulbs have died down, are filled with annual bedding plants. The bulbs are then thrown away. This is a very expensive and quite unnatural way of gardening. True, it has the advantage of allowing one to grow bulbs in otherwise quite impossible places (for instance in deep shade), since, after all, the flower is waiting to come out inside the bulb and very little can go wrong.

Spring-flowering bulbs that do lend themselves to naturalization ought to be used much more often than they are, especially in not-too-tidy gardens looked after by those who do not want to spend all their time raking and hoeing. These little bulbs will usually make a fine show in the shade of deciduous shrubs, under trees and between ground-covering plants. The vegetative cycle of these bulbous plants is over as soon as the foliage begins to fade, so that the shade does not greatly affect them, nor, for that matter, the lack of moisture that often prevails around the bottom of trees in the summer. Snowdrops, winter aconites, wild crocuses, chionodoxas, scillas, erythroniums, wild narcissi—all of these little plants will spread gradually through the garden and beautify it in the spring.

In the lawn, too, early-flowering bulbs and corms will make a fine show, though if you want to enjoy them for more than a year the first mowing must be delayed until their foliage has died off, or else rather unsightly clumps of grass must be left around them. They can however be grown in a wild garden, or on a bank that is only mown a few times in the summer. Bulbous plants—the "once only" varieties no less than those suitable for naturalization—can also be grown in herbaceous borders or amidst other groups of plants. It is precisely in the spring when the perennials have been trimmed, that the herbaceous border may become a sad spectacle unless there are bulbs to fill the gap. The perennials usually come into flower by the time the foliage of the bulbs has begun to die off. However, try to avoid digging the soil between the plants in the summer or autumn, for bulbs do not like such treatment. Nor do they like fresh manure; they greatly prefer blood-meal or other slow-working fertilizers.

Summer-flowering bulbs such as begonias, cannas, dahlias and gladioli are often found in borders by the side of annuals, or in special beds. The colour range is

Above: Perennial borders were introduced in Britain at the end of the last century. They are said to have been based on road verges, though most of the plants in them are cultivated species. The most beautiful borders are still found in Britain. As these and other photographs show, it is obvious that such borders are man-made, and yet the whole strikes most observers as being exceedingly attractive.

Below: Bulbous and tuberous-rooted plants occur in countless forms and can be used in the garden throughout the year. From right to left: a spring-flowering cormous plant, *Crocus tomasinianus*; a spring-flowering bulb, the Cottage tulip 'Groenland' (syn. 'Greenland'); a summer-flowering bulb, *Galtonia candicans*, also known as the giant summer hyacinth; and a rhizomatous plant, *Polygonatum* or Solomon's seal.

extremely wide, so much so that most garden designers will use them very sparingly, if at all. If you take the same view you can nevertheless grow dahlias and gladioli in a special corner set aside for cut flowers and away from the rest of the garden. These plants are best grown under wide-mesh netting, at least 4 in × 4 in (10 cm × 10 cm) stretched between sticks 12 in (30 cm) above the ground. The flowers grow through the netting and are supported by it.

Some rhizomatous "bulbs" thrive in moist, others in dry, soil. Bearded irises, to mention the most important, like a dry, sunny position and are therefore often grown in rock gardens or in raised beds. Solomon's seal, on the other hand, likes moist soil and a shady position.

Woody perennials

Woody perennials are plants that do not die back to ground level after flowering but continue to make new growth every year. In other words their shoots are hardy and grow thicker and longer every year unless they are damaged by severe winter frosts. While some bear flowers on the current season's growth, others bear flowers on the last season's or earlier growth. These differences play an important role in the overwintering process and also during pruning. Woody perennials are divided into trees and shrubs, each group comprising species that retain their leaves in the winter (evergreens) and species that shed their leaves (deciduous).

Trees Trees usually have their trunks clear of branches to a height of 6–7ft (2m). Natural trees grow this way from seed; "artificial" trees are grafted on to the stock of another species. There can be various reasons for grafting, the most important being a desire for more vigorous growth or better fruit. Grafting may also be the easiest way of propagating a particular tree, and sometimes the only one. Moreover grafting can be used to produce a particular ornamental form (e.g. weeping trees). It is not always easy to tell whether a tree has been grafted; the graft union may be variously under the ground or 10ft up the stem, or anywhere in between. Shrubs can also be grafted.

Although most non-coniferous trees shed their leaves in the winter, there are also some that remain evergreen. A well-known example is the holly, and there are also evergreen oaks such as the holm oak. All evergreen species should be given some protection during very severe frosts.

Shrubs Shrubs usually develop several woody stems. It goes without saying that there are many intermediate forms between trees and shrubs.

Shrubs are, of course, woody perennials. They are often referred to as bushes, although they include 15ft (5m) high elders and the 2in (5cm) high creeping cotoneaster. Roses, too, are shrubs, and so are bamboos.

Many shrubs, for instance rhododendrons, laurels and several barberries, retain their leaves in winter. This means that the vital processes, including transpiration, continue quite normally during that season. If evergreen shrubs are exposed too much to the wind, if the ground freezes up or contains too little moisture, then the plants may become desiccated, which is reflected in the appearance of crinkled and discoloured leaves. If something is not done quickly the plant may die from too much loss of water.

Conifers Conifers have needle-like foliage instead of leaves, though the "needles" may assume very strange forms, as for instance in the *Ginkgo*. There are tree-like and shrub-like conifers, their heights varying from a few inches to scores of feet. Most conifers are evergreen and retain their needles in the winter, when they may suffer the same problems as evergreen foliage plants, leading to total desiccation. This condition is particularly marked in conifers that have just been transplanted. Some species lose their needles in the winter, among them larches and swamp cypresses, so that transpiration is slowed down and assimilation comes to a stop. In purely physiological terms, such conifers are comparable in many ways to deciduous trees.

Obtaining shrubs Shrubs can be bought in garden centres and by mail order. Salesmen sometimes call on new housing estates with a car full of shrubs and conifers, but however persuasive a salesman may be, never buy anything from him, for his stock is more

Garden shrubs come in innumerable shapes and forms, as these photographs clearly show. *Prunus padus*, bird cherry (top left), makes a good filler and it also attracts birds. Smaller rhododendrons and azaleas feel particularly at home in the shrub border (top right). Ground-covering shrubs, such as the evergreen creeper *Pachysandra terminalis*, save a great deal of labour (centre left). The most beautiful of shrubs, such as

Magnolia stellata, are often planted as specimens (centre left). Heathers, too, are shrubs; they cover the ground densely, come in various colours and flower at various periods (bottom left).
Housefronts and trees can be completely covered with climbers such as the *Hedera* (ivy) depicted here (bottom middle). Other climbing shrubs, e.g. *Wisteria sinensis*, will cover walls with flowers for weeks at a time (bottom right).

than likely to consist of the rejects of a *bona fide* nurseryman, and your choice is, moreover, severely restricted. For the same reason it is best not to buy shrubs from market stalls. When it comes to rare shrubs, turn to the few specialists in the field; you will find that some offer you a choice of, say, no less than 140 different maples, all ready for immediate delivery.

Others specialize in conifers, others again in tall trees of various types. A customer may want to buy a whole garden all at once, or a completely grown stout hedge; these wishes can be met if the money is available. Needless to say, such desires are expensive to fulfil.

For roses, too, no matter whether they are novelties or old-fashioned species, you can do no better than go to specialist rose nurseries. Most of the trade is done by mail order, but all the leading rose growers have show gardens in which you can admire their products in full bloom.

Roses offered at cut prices are almost inevitably unnamed varieties and the chances are that they are sensitive to diseases. It is best to pay the full price and not to run any risks.

Heathers, too, are shrubs and there are quite a few nurseries that specialize in them. It is advisable to buy from them for that is the best chance of acquiring excellent named varieties.

There are even specialist clematis nurseries, from which scores of different varieties can be bought, and other specialities are being created all the time. In Britain we are fortunate indeed in having nurserymen with extremely wide selections to choose from, many being willing to deliver to the door.

It can be quite an achievement for the gardener to track down exactly the right shrub for his garden; his satisfaction will be great years later when it is still in place and flourishing.

There is yet another way of acquiring shrubs that are difficult to obtain: by propagation. Perhaps a friend will give you a cutting or a few seeds; perhaps a grower will bud some roots for you. Sometimes propagation is very difficult but more often than not it is easy. In the A–Z section, the correct method of propagation for every genus is given.

When you collect your evergreen shrubs or conifers, or when the nurseryman delivers them to you, it is most important to ensure that the foliage is properly packed and covered so that the wind cannot dry it out. All too often one sees precious plants being transported without cover, mostly by ignorant laymen, but sometimes by a nurseryman or a gardener who should know better. As a general rule, an evergreen shrub carried on an open truck for one hour at 40 mph will have suffered so much that most of the leaves will have dried out. Refuse to accept shrubs that have been transported in this way, and make sure that you have enough plastic sheeting when you go to fetch shrubs that may make the journey home sticking out of your car windows.

Evergreen trees and shrubs, as well as some of the more expensive deciduous ornamental shrubs, are usually sold with a soil ball wrapped in a container. This is done because washing the earth off the roots often causes irreparable damage. Never buy shrubs that have had this done to them, for the result is always bad or abortive growth and you will have wasted your money.

The uses of shrubs Shrubs form the backbone of your garden. Without them a garden is static and must be started from scratch every year. Use shrubs for a growing framework that stays in place even in the winter and that charms precisely by its constant increase in size.

In larger gardens foliage trees and conifers form the background against which to offset the more delicate shrubs and other garden plants. They afford a splendid protection to everything living and everyone in the garden. In small modern gardens there is rarely room for such large plants; just one large deciduous tree or conifer is welcome, and then it is unlikely to be a beech or a Douglas fir, but rather a sumach, a small elm, a juniper or a Serbian spruce.

Smaller gardens are usually protected or divided by means of hedges. If the wind is very strong belts of poplars and alders will be needed, which, of course, will not grow more than a few feet wide while

Top left: The splendid Rhododendron shown here is called 'Insel' (syn. 'Island').

Above: Here a wild variety of *Prunus* (with white flowers) has been grafted on to an ornamental cherry (with red flowers).

Left: Conifers can grow to a considerable height and are therefore more suitable for parks than private gardens.

Below: *Ginkgo biloba*, the maidenhair tree, is a unique deciduous tree bearing cones.

attaining heights of up to 30 ft (9 m).

More common are clipped or loose hedges with a height of 4–10 ft (1.5–3 m). They take up little room and afford a great deal of protection. They will only rob border plants of food if they themselves are not fed properly and regularly.

Hedges may be started by buying fairly tall (and expensive) plants, however the end result may well turn out a disappointment. It is best to choose plants 2½–4 ft (80–120 cm) high and to allow 5–10 years for the hedge to grow to 6 ft (2 cm) high and form a dense barrier. Privet (*ligustrum*) grows quickly but is unsightly in the winter. Much more beautiful hedges are those grown from beech (*Fagus*), hornbeam (*Carpinus*), ornamental thorn (*Crataegus*), field maple (*Acer campestre*); yew (*Taxus*) and arbor-vitae (*Thuja*) are highly recommended for evergreen hedges. If there is enough space then it is well worth while to consider various cypresses (*Chamaecyparis*) or the recently introduced *Cupressocyparis*. If the site is not exposed and the soil is suitable, then the holly (*Ilex*), too, will make a beautiful dense hedge.

All these plants can be pruned and kept to a height of 6 ft. There are many others, of course, that will make good hedges, but they are more compact or cannot be cut back as severely. A beautiful but loose hedge can be grown from climbing roses, and the Cornelian cherry (*Cornus mas*) can also be shaped into a hedge.

All the most important hedging plants are listed in one of the tables found at the end of this book.

Shrubs can also be used as temporary fillers for

screening ugly objects and for sound insulation, for which their dense foliage and branches make them eminently suitable, as anyone who has walked through the same deciduous wood in the summer and in the winter knows well. In the small private garden, however, a wall or an embankment is a much better solution to the noise problem, and the space is better devoted to more delicate ornamental shrubs. They may be combined in beds (roses) or borders and form the nucleus of many groups and other formations. Used as low hedges and edging plants they also add shape to the garden.

Beautiful shrubs are particularly effective as specimen plants in solitary positions. This does not necessarily have to be in the lawn; specimen plants can also be surrounded with ground-covering plants or rise up from terraces or pavements. They must be chosen with particular care, for they will catch the eye all year.

There are also many special shrubs for the rock garden, for window boxes or for raised flower beds. There are many creeping shrubs, too, which cover the ground in such a way that no weeds can grow between. These shrubs must, of course, be evergreen.

A special group of such shrubs are the heaths and heathers—particularly the callunas and ericas. Thanks to the great popularity of heather gardens there now exist nurseries that specialize in this field.

It is also, of course, possible to attract birds or bees by choosing to plant shrubs that appeal to them.

Most of the groups mentioned above are combined into special tables at the end of this book.

THE PLANTS

In the A-Z section beginning on page 18, the plants have been listed alphabetically by their Latin names. In order to find a plant you know by its English name, an older name, or synonym, use the index at the end of the book. The photographs may provide you with further means of identification.

The naming of cultivated plants
People often wonder why it is necessary to use long and unfamiliar Latin words to refer to plants, when they all have perfectly good, straightforward English names. This is because not all plants do have an English name, and therefore any such listing must be incomplete. Secondly, the English names of many plants vary from region to region, and to include all these would introduce a further complication.

Although the Latin names are the best means of description, it can also be difficult to establish which Latin name is the correct one. You may notice that several of the names given in this book differ from those in others. The Latin nomenclature which the botanist uses is far from static. Every year, quite a few names are changed. The difficulty is that we have been encumbered with the so-called priority rule of the Swiss classifier A. de Candolle (1806–93), according to which the oldest designation is the correct one. Now and then an ancient plant description is rediscovered, with the result that the time-honoured but younger name has to be dropped.

Moreover, the systematic division of plants is rearranged from time to time, so that certain genera may be moved abruptly to a different position. We shall have to put up with this irritating habit for quite some time to come, although the growing improvement in scholars' ability to communicate with each other may in the end put a stop to it.

There are several scientific works listing the most recent names of almost every plant. For this volume we have followed Zander's *Handwörterbuch der Pflanzennamen* (10th edition). As a further aid to identification, most of the synonyms listed in the leading plant catalogues have been included as well. The most usual English names are mentioned in the headings or in the text. In addition, they are also listed in the index, and so it is unlikely that you will be unable to find a given plant in one section or the other.

Family, genus, species and variety
The plant kingdom is subdivided into divisions, classes, sub-classes, orders, families, genera, species, subspecies and varieties. In this book, we shall be ignoring divisions, classes and orders because they have very little relevance to everyday gardening practice.

Every plant has been listed by its generic name, eg *Aster*, followed by its specific name, eg *amellus*. In this respect, the classification of plants may be compared to that of persons in official documents, where a man may be listed as Smith, John. When we have a string of plants in one and the same genus the generic name is usually abbreviated, eg *A. amellus*. This particular species is the one found in nature and has light blue flowers. However, over the past hundred years or so nurserymen have been successful in growing a number of varieties of *Aster amellus* in various shades of blue, violet and lilac. These cultivated varieties, or cultivars, must not be confused with the varieties produced by nature herself (which are known as sports). In this book the names of cultivars appear in Roman letters, starting with a capital and placed in inverted commas, eg *Aster amellus* 'Blue King'. In the A-Z section you will find descriptions of many hundreds of names varieties or cultivars, for nurserymen have engaged in so much selective breeding that more than half the garden plants they now offer are cultivars. You need only think of roses: hybrid tea roses and floribundas are all nursery-bred.

Whenever there is mention of a natural variety, we use the abbreviation 'var.', coupled to the Latin name in italics. Sometimes reference is also made to a subspecies, which is rendered as 'ssp'. Very occasionally a variety is further subdivided into a form, 'f'. Thus we may find *Hydrangea macrophylla* ssp *macrophylla* f *otaksa*. (This, incidentally, is the plant from which the indoor hortensia has been developed.)

From time to time a nurseryman will succeed in crossing two species in one and the same genus. In that event we speak of a hybrid, not a variety. Such crosses are indicated by the symbol '×' preceding the new specific name. Thus *Forsythia* × *intermedia* is a cross between *F. suspensa* and *F. viridissima*. Very occasionally it has even been possible to cross plants in two distinct genera. For example, × *Heucherella* is a cross between *Heuchera* and *Tiarella*. Alphabetically this cross is listed under 'H'.

Headings and descriptions
The most important needs, properties and uses of each of the plant species listed on pages 18–208 are represented by means of 25 symbols, whose meaning is explained in the table on this page. The name of the first species in each section is followed on the next line by all the symbols appropriate to it; if the next species has no symbols, this is because the symbols describing the first species apply to it as well. When a difference next occurs, the appropriate symbols are given in full.

The following summary is intended to give a brief account of the systematic classification of plants used in the book. Every entry begins with a heading, which starts with the Latin name of the genus. This is followed by another Latin name, indicating to which family this particular genus belongs. Next comes the 'official' English name; but since some plants have more than 20 such names, only the most popular one has been listed. In some instances there is no English name, and the third line of the heading is omitted. Most headings look like the following example:

Digitalis
Scrophulariaceae
Foxglove

The heading is followed by a short introductory text discussing how the plant may best be used in the garden. The more important the genus, the longer the introductory text. Then under separate headings are some general comments about cultivation, the soil needed by that group of plants and recommended methods of propagation. Next come the descriptions of the species arranged alphabetically by their Latin names. The name of the species is followed by the symbols appropriate to it, and perhaps also to other species listed immediately after it. If a plant has a Latin synonym, this is given as 'syn.' at the beginning of the text describing it. The species may also have a common English name; if so, that name is listed next. There follows the country of origin, if known, and concise information about the plant; usually this deals with its height, flowering period, appearance of the flower, its foliage, etc., concluding with a summary of the most important garden varieties. The Latin synonyms of species are also listed separately with a cross-reference to the main entry.

○	Requires full sun (at least 7 hours per day in summer)
◐	Requires a semi-shaded position (3–5 hours' full sun in summer)
◑	Will grow in a shaded position (less than 3 hours' full sun in summer)
⊖	Requires very dry, calcareous soil
≋	Requires moist, acid soil
∧	May require protection against frost in severe winters
→	Wind-resistant
→|	Requires protection from the wind
·	Annual, or cultivated as an annual
··	Biennial, or cultivated as a biennial
○	Herbaceous perennial
◌	Bulbous plant
⊗	Tuberous or rhizomatous plant
⫲	Shrub
✳	Tree
✿	Particularly beautiful flowers
✤	Particularly beautiful foliage
✲	Evergreen
⁙	Produces attractive fruits or berries
☠	Partly or wholly poisonous
⊥	Suitable as a solitary, or specimen, plant
⬙	Suitable for rock and paved gardens
⦀	Suitable as a hedging plant
⌒	Suitable for carpeting or ground cover
✂	Good for cut flowers

Abies
Pinaceae
Silver fir

A genus of evergreen coniferous trees, most species of which are hardy but too large for the small garden. If space is available, the silver firs make fine background trees and are often effective on their own, particularly as a lawn specimen. There are several dwarf varieties.

The silver firs (*Abies* spp) bear a striking resemblance to the firs (*Picea* spp). The easiest way to distinguish the two is by pulling off a leaf. In *Abies* the leaf comes away with a small basal disc; *Picea*, by contrast, has no disc, and the leaf comes away, leaving a small "peg" of hard tissue. The cones of *Abies* are erect while *Picea* cones are pendulous.
Soil Most silver firs prefer a fairly acid soil. *A. grandis* and *A. pinsapo*, however, tolerate, and *A. cephalonica* thrives on, chalk and limestone soils.
Propagation From seed.

Abies arizonica, see *A. lasiocarpa* var. *arizonica*.
Abies balsamea
○ ❀ ❀
Balsam fir. A tree from North America with a conical habit that in the wild reaches heights of 50–80ft (15–25m) with a spread of 12–18ft (4–6m), but rarely grows well in Britain. Balsam firs generally require an open position. The variety 'Nana', however, is a small globe-shaped bush that only reaches a height of 32in (80cm), and 'Hudsonia', which has a more spreading habit and grows up to 2ft (60cm), are both suitable for rock gardens. The name balsam fir refers to its dark green aromatic leaves.
Abies cephalonica
Greek fir. A tree with a conical habit and dark green leaves. Height 35–65ft (10–20m).
Abies concolor
White fir. A tree from mid-California with a pyramidal habit that reaches heights of 80–150ft (25–45m) and spreads 12–16ft (4–5m). The horizontal branches carry blue or grey-green leaves. The variety 'Candicans' has silvery white leaves that eventually assume a bluish tint. The exceptionally attractive variety 'Violacea' has glaucous-blue leaves, and helps to create striking contrasts in the garden.
Abies grandis
Giant or grand fir, also known as the Oregon or white fir, originally from British Columbia, California and Vancouver Island. A tree reaching heights of 100–300ft (30–90m), with a spread of 12–18ft (4–6m), the giant fir is easily identified by its shiny, bright green leaves which lie flat on the horizontal branches. The leaves are alternately long and short, and have two silver bands beneath. It is wind tolerant and will flourish in harsh conditions provided the soil is fairly moist and not too poor.
Abies homolepis
Nikko fir. A broad, columnar tree from Japan that reaches a height of 80ft (25m). It has dark green leaves with two broad silver bands beneath.
Abies koreana
○ ❀ ❀ ⊕
Korean fir. One of the smaller firs, only reaching up to 50ft (15m) in western Europe. The bristly leaves point up-

A young specimen of *Abies concolor*

wards; they are dark green on top, with soft bright silver undersides. Korean fir is planted in many gardens for its attractive violet-purple young cones.
Abies lasiocarpa
○ ❀ ❀
Alpine fir. A medium-sized tree from North America that grows up to 60ft (18m) in height, with pubescent young shoots. The flowers are very attractive, the male being dark blue to violet, and the female a deep purple-red. The cones are purple. The best-known variety is *Abies lasiocarpa* var. *arizonica* (Arizona cork bark fir), which has beautiful blue leaves.
Abies nordmanniana
Caucasian fir. A handsome fir that reaches 80–115ft (25–35m) and spreads 12–18ft (4–6m). It thrives in the west and north of Great Britain but also grows well, though more slowly, in other parts of the country. It grows best in rich soil. The dark glossy leaves have two white bands beneath.
Abies pinsapo
Blue Spanish fir. A tree with radially spreading leaves, 35–65ft (10–20m) tall, and with a spread of 15–25ft (5–7m). The variety 'Glauca' is often chosen for its striking glaucous-blue leaves.

The leaves of the Spanish fir, *Abies pinsapo*

Abies procera
Noble fir or red fir, from western USA. A conical tree up to 65 ft (20 m) high, with thick branches and densely set blue-green leaves that curve upwards. The variety 'Glauca' has glaucous-grey leaves.

Abies veitchii
From Japan, this tree is found in mountainous regions above 6,500 ft (2,000 m), where it grows up to a height of 80 ft (25 m) with a spread of 12–15 ft (4–5 m). It is a beautiful, fast-growing tree with leaves that are dark green on top, silver-white underneath.

Acaena
Rosaceae

New Zealand bur or bidi-bidi. Hardy trailing perennials, effective as ground cover and in rock gardens.
Soil *Acaena* will grow in all well-drained soils.
Propagation By division or seed.

Acaena buchananii
A plant with greyish green, compound leaves just under ¾ in (2 cm) long, each having 3–6 pairs of leaflets. It has amber-brown burrs.

Acaena microphylla
This plant has olive-green leaves and is more vigorous than *A. buchananii*. The crimson burrs are very ornamental.

Acaena novae-zelandiae
Taller and stronger than *A. buchananii* and *A. microphylla*. The leaves are bright green with purple-red burrs.

Abies grandis, the giant fir

Burrs of *Acaena microphylla*

Abies lasiocarpa var. *arizonica*

Acaena novae-zelandiae, which makes excellent ground cover for dry places

Acanthus spinosus demands sun and a great deal of warmth

Acanthus
Acantheae
Bear's breeches

The leaf of this hardy herbaceous perennial plant was the usual motif on Corinthian columns. In winter, *Acanthus* will tolerate fairly dry soil, but when it is in bud it needs moisture.
Soil The plants thrive in any fertile well-drained soil.
Propagation From seed, by division or from root cuttings.

Acanthus mollis
This plant comes from southern Europe, the Near East and North Africa. It will grow to a height of 3 ft (1 m), and in early to midsummer bears tubular flowers with white lips and purple veins in long, fairly loose spikes. The variety 'Latifolius' grows to a height of 4 ft (1.2 m) and is most effective when grown in front of a group of shrubs.

Acanthus spinosus
A summer-flowering plant from Italy and Greece that grows 4–5 ft (1.2–1.5 m) high. The dark green, glossy leaves, have narrow, spiny lobes, and the whitish and purple flowers are carried in erect spikes.

Acer
Aceraceae
Maple

This genus includes many fine shrubs, trees and hedging plants, whose appeal lies in their delicate shape and lovely foliage. It is quite common for the leaves to change colour from one season to the next. Several species develop into large, strong trees that will grow anywhere; the Japanese species, however, are smaller and much more demanding.

Most maples have attractive small flowers that are borne in racemes or corymbs, which are mostly green or yellow, and some are highly orna-mental. The seeds have prominent wings. Some species, such as *A. negundo* and *A. rubrum*, are dioecious, i.e. they have male and female sex organs on separate plants.
Soil Many maples will grow in any soil, but most prefer a moist, slightly acid, well-drained position. Sandy soil rich in humus suits them well. *A. campestre*, *A. griseum*, *A. negundo*, *A. platanoides*, *A. pseudoplatanus* and *A. saccharinum* will tolerate chalk.
Propagation Most named garden varieties are propagated by grafting. Species such as *A. negundo* and *A. palmatum* can also be propagated by layering. All species can be grown from seed, but the seeds are not viable for more than six months. They should be sown in October.

Acer campestre
Field maple. A European tree or shrub that reaches heights of 15–65 ft (5–20 m). As a tree, it has a spread of 18–25 ft (6–8 m). It grows well in shady positions, and is often planted beneath larger trees; it also makes a good hedge. The leaves turn butter-yellow in late autumn.

Acer cappadocicum
Syn. *A. laetum*. From China, this tree reaches heights up to 65 ft (20 m) and flowers in spring. The glossy leaves turn yellow in autumn; in the variety 'Rubrum' the shoots and young leaves are blood-red. The young leaves of 'Aureum' are yellow, turning green later in the season and then yellow again in the autumn.

Acer dasycarpum, see *Acer saccharinum*.

Acer ginnala
A bushy and picturesque large shrub or small tree from China and Japan that grows 10–15 ft (3–5 m) high and spreads 10–12 ft (3–4 m). It flowers in early summer and the bright green leaves turn to crimson and orange in autumn. The plant bears fruit in great profusion.

Acer griseum

○ ◐ ❋ ⊛

Paper bark maple, originally from China. In Europe, this maple is considerably smaller than in its country of origin where it can reach a height of 40ft (12m). Old bark on the trunk and primary branches peels back to reveal a glossy cinnamon-coloured underbark. The leaves are grey-green on top and downy grey underneath. It flowers in clusters in late spring, and makes an excellent specimen for a lawn.

Acer japonicum

○ ◐ ⊛ ⊛ ❋ ⊛

Japanese maple. A shrub or small tree from Japan, growing up to 15ft (5m), with a spread of 6–10ft (2–3m). It has attractive, soft green, deeply divided leaves that in autumn turn various beautiful shades of crimson. All the many named varieties prefer moist positions and shelter from the wind. 'Aconitifolium' has notably large, deeply toothed leaves. 'Aureum', with soft yellow leaves, is slow growing and well suited to rock gardens but needs partial shade.

Acer laetum, see *A. cappadocicum*.

Acer negundo

Box elder. This North American shrub or tree grows up to 50ft (15m) high, and

Field maple leaves

spreads 25–35ft (8–10m). It flowers in spring. The variety 'Auratum' has yellow leaves and red stalks; 'Elegans' has leaves with yellow margins; 'Variegatum' has white-edged leaves, while var. *violaceum* has twigs with a violet bloom and dark green leaves.

Acer palmatum

○ ◐ ⊛ ⊛ ⊛

Syn. *A. polymorphum*. Japanese maple. A shrub or small tree from Japan reaching heights of 6–20ft (2–7m) and with a spread of 6–10ft (2–3m). This most attractive spring-flowering maple should be sheltered from cold winds,

The rare *Acer japonicum* 'Aureum'

Acer japonicum 'Veitchii'

and is better grown as a shrub and not as a tree (the same is true of *A. japonicum*). Propagation should be by layering, not from seeds or seedlings. One of the most popular of the cultivars is 'Dissectum Atropurpureum', which has dark purple, finely divided leaves, while 'Senkaki', the coral bark maple, has red stems and soft yellow autumn foliage.

Acer pensylvanicum

○ ◐ ⊛ ❋ ⊛

Syn. *A. striatum*. Snake bark or moosewood maple, from North America. A shrub or tree reaching heights of 10–25ft (3–8m) and spreading as a tree 15–18ft (5–6m). Suitable for large to medium-sized gardens, it flowers in May and has a very attractive greenish, white-striped stem. The three-lobed leaves turn bright yellow in autumn.

Acer platanoides

Norway maple, originally from central and southern Europe. This tree usually reaches heights of 50–65ft (15–20m) with a spread of 35ft (10m). It produces an abundance of bright greenish-yellow flowers in spring and makes an attractive addition to parks and streets. Many named varieties are slow growing and so are suited to being grown in gardens. 'Crimson King', one of the smaller varieties, has deep crimson-purple, smooth leaves with a silvery sheen, and bears a strong resemblance

The silhouette of the field maple, *Acer campestre* 'Elsrijk', wreathed in autumn mists

Acer polymorphum, see *A. palmatum*.

Acer pseudoplatanus

Sycamore. From central and southern Europe, this tree has a regular crown and grows to heights of 65–100ft (20–30m), spreading to 35ft (10m). It is spring-flowering, and ideal for parks and streets. Several varieties are more compact and can be planted in medium-sized gardens. The variety 'Brilliantissimum' is the best-known cultivar: a large shrub or small tree, it produces a dense, spherical crown. A tree that prefers shade, it is most striking in the spring, when its shrimp-pink leaves come out. The variety 'Leopoldii' has a very broad, pyramidal crown, and leaves that are yellowish-pink at first, becoming green and speckled with yellow and pink. 'Prinz Handjery' bears a strong resemblance to 'Brilliantissimum', but its leaves are light purple underneath; it is also more tolerant of bright sunlight. 'Worleei', the golden sycamore, grows 18–40ft (6–12m) high and has an asymmetrical crown, with leaves that turn from light orange to golden, and finally to green, usually by July. This is another variety of sycamore that does not like direct sunlight.

Acer pensylvanicum with striped bark

A large specimen of the Japanese maple, *Acer palmatum* 'Atropurpureum', in Sheffield Park

Acer palmatum 'Dissectum Ornatum'

Acer palmatum 'Dissectum'

to 'Faassen's Black', which has very dark brown, glossy leaves. 'Drummondii' has yellowish-green leaves with a very broad white marginal band. 'Globosum' has a distinctive mushroom-shaped head and green foliage, while 'Lorbergii', with its circular crown and deeply divided, light green leaves, makes a good specimen tree. 'Columnare' is cylindrical to conical in shape and better suited to small gardens and also to narrow streets. 'Schwedleri' grows vigorously: it has rich crimson-purple leaves that turn green in summer and bronze in autumn.

Acer platanoides 'Globosum'

Acer platanoides, the Norway maple, in the autumn

21

Acer platanoides 'Drummondii'

Acer pseudoplatanus 'Brilliantissimum'

The red maple, Acer rubrum

Acer saccharinum, the silver maple

Acer rubrum

Red or Canadian maple. A North American tree reaching heights of 35–50ft (10–15m), and spreading 20–35ft (7–10m). It flowers in spring, and forms a circular crown with brilliant red and scarlet foliage in autumn, especially during dry, sunny seasons. Because its flowers are also scarlet, *Acer rubrum* is one of the most ornamental of garden trees. It demands a moist position, and grows very well on soil deficient in chalk.

'Schlesingeri' has a broad crown, but is a slow grower; in autumn it often turns a deep and brilliant red.

Acer saccharinum

Syn. *A. dasycarpum*. Silver maple, originally from eastern North America. A broad-crowned tree reaching heights of 80–100ft (25–30m), and spreading 35–50ft (10–15m). It flowers in spring and is an excellent tree for parks, flourishing in any well-drained but moisture-retentive soil. 'Pyramidale' has a slender crown and smallish, deeply cut leaves.

Acer striatum, see *A. pensylvanicum*.

Achillea
Compositae
Yarrow

A genus of hardy herbaceous perennials characterized by flat-topped flower clusters and, in many species, dissected ferny leaves. Plants are suitable for rock gardens, borders and cutting.
Soil The plants will grow in any well-drained garden soil.
Propagation By division or from seed.

Achillea chrysocoma

This plant only grows 2–4in (5–10cm) high. Yellow flowers form in early to midsummer in loose clusters of tightly packed heads.

Achillea clavennae

From Austria and the eastern Alps, this rock plant grows to a height of 4in (10cm) and has silver-green tufted leaves. Its white, daisy-like flowers are borne in May–June.

Achillea clypeolata

This hybrid of unknown origin grows to heights of 18–24in (45–60cm). It has grey foliage and produces yellow flowers in summer. If the plants are cut back after flowering, they will flower again in early autumn. *A. clypeolata* is more tolerant of moisture than *A. chrysocoma*. The variety 'Coronation Gold', probably a cross between *A. clypeolata* and *A. filipendulina*, grows 28–32in (70–80cm) high; it too bears yellow flowers, in tightly packed heads, but has greyish-green foliage.

Achillea eupatorium, see *A. filipendulina*.

Achillea filipendulina

Syn. *A. eupatorium*. From the Near East, this excellent and vigorous border plant grows to 3ft (1m) high and bears clusters of lemon-yellow flowers in midsummer. The plant grows best in an open, sunny position, and looks well with delphiniums and other blue flowers. The flowers, cut in their prime (not too late!), may be stored for winter

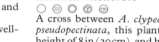
Achillea taygetea, a yarrow suitable for borders

decoration; hang them up in a dry but draught-proof place, away from sunlight. The best varieties are 'Gold Plate', which has deep yellow flowers, and 'Parker's Variety', whose flowers are bright yellow.

Achillea × kellereri

A cross between *A. clypeolata* and *A. pseudopectinata*, this plant grows to a height of 8in (20cm), and has elongated greyish-green leaves. It produces fairly large white flowers in late spring and summer.

Achillea millefolium

Milfoil, a European native. Not an outstandingly attractive border plant, it will grow to a height of 12–28in (30–70cm), and flowers in early summer. 'Red Beauty' has dark red flowers, and those of 'Cerise Queen' are bright pink.

Achillea ptarmica

Sneezewort. A European plant that thrives in a moister soil than most species, it grows to a height of 30in (75cm), and bears white flowers in midsummer. 'Perry's White' has small double white flowers and is one of the best garden cultivars.

Achillea taygetea

A useful plant in rock gardens, reaching a height of 16in (40cm). It also grows in borders, and bears lemon-yellow flowers in midsummer and early autumn.

Achillea tormentosa

A native of Europe and northern Asia, this species grows to a height of 6–9in (15–25cm) and is useful as ground cover for the border or a rock garden. Its long narrow leaves are grey-green and it bears tightly-packed yellow flowers in July–September.

Achillea millefolium 'Red Beauty'

Achillea filipendulina 'Gold Plate'

Aconitum
Ranunculaceae
Monkshood

A genus of hardy herbaceous perennials with a most attractive appearance. They are best planted in small groups in largish borders, and, because they are fairly tolerant of shade, they can also be planted near the edges of spinneys or in clearings. The entire plant is poisonous.
Soil These plants grow in moist but well-drained soil.
Propagation Plants are very easily divided or grown from ripe seed.

Aconitum × cammarum

Probably a cross between *A. napellus* and *A. variegatum*. It grows 2½–4ft

(80–120 cm) high and its leaves are shiny green, five lobed and deeply cut. In summer it bears blue and white flowers. The variety 'Bicolor' is 35 in (90 cm) high and bears white and light violet flowers. 'Sparks' is 4 ft (1.2 m) high and produces a profusion of deep blue flowers.

Aconitum carmichaelii

This plant grows to heights of 3–4 ft (1–1.2 m), has leathery leaves, and produces violet-blue flowers in late summer. The variety 'Wilsonii' grows to a height of 6 ft (2 m), has brighter green leaves, and bears its violet-blue flowers in autumn. 'Barker's' is equally tall and has very attractive amethyst-blue flowers.

Aconitum napellus

A European and Asian plant that grows to 3 ft (1 m) high. Its deep blue flowers appear in summer. Aconitum napellus ssp pyramidale bears violet flowers in branching spikes.

The common horse chestnut, Aesculus hippocastanum, in full bloom

Aconitum napellus ssp pyramidale

The rock plant, Adonis vernalis

The red-flowering Aesculus × carnea

Adonis
Ranunculaceae
Pheasant's eye

Rock-garden plants conspicuous for their brightly coloured flowers, especially when planted in small groups; the finely dissected foliage is most attractive. The genus includes annuals as well as herbaceous perennials.

Soil Adonis will grow in any fertile, well-drained soil.

Propagation Annual species are best sown in the open during the autumn. Germination may be poor, and ideally seeds should be sown as soon as they are ripe. Perennial species are propagated by division or seeds; with the latter method plants take two years to reach flowering size.

Adonis aestivalis
○ ◐ ⊛ ⊗ ⊘

A summer-flowering plant 12–20 in (30–50 cm) high. The flowers are scarlet or red, with a central black spot. The variety 'Citrina' is straw coloured.

Adonis amurensis
○ ◑ ◐ ⊗ ⊘

A small plant with large yellow flowers that come out in February–April while

Aconitum × arendsii with Hosta fortunei 'Hyacinthina' in the foreground

the leaves are young. Several cultivars of Japanese origin are sometimes available, among them: 'Fukujukai', with larger golden-yellow flowers; 'Nadeshiku', petals fringed, satiny lime-green; 'Pleniflora' ('Flore-pleno'), double flowered.

Adonis vernalis

A rock plant, 6–12 in (15–30 cm) high, with bright yellow flowers up to 2 in (5 cm) across which open out flat in bright sunlight.

Adonis pyrenaica

This native of the Pyrenees is similar to A. vernalis but more robust and somewhat taller. The flowers are bright golden-yellow.

Aesculus
Hippocastanaceae
Horse chestnut

These trees are magnificent planted either singly or in rows. A. parviflora is a low shrub suited to smaller gardens, while the most attractive horse chestnut for medium-sized gardens is A. × carnea and its several cultivars. Pruning should be avoided or kept to a minimum.

Soil Grows in any fertile garden soil.

Propagation Garden varieties must be increased by grafting on to stocks of A. hippocastanum grown from seed. A. parviflora can be propagated from root cuttings, by layering or by division, and can also be grown from seed; the latter lose their germinating power if stored dry for more than a few months.

Aesculus × carnea
○ ◐ ⊛ ⊗ ⊗ ⊘

Red horse chestnut. A hybrid between A. hippocastanum and A. pavia, growing to heights of 35–50 ft (10–15 m) and spreading 35–40 ft (10–12 m). Its rose-pink flowers are borne in panicles in late spring to early summer. The variety 'Briotii' has deeper pink flowers, in larger panicles.

Aesculus hippocastanum

Common horse chestnut, originally from Greece and Albania. A large tree, up to 100 ft (30 m) high, and with a spread of 35–50 ft (10–15 m), it bears white flowers, blotched red at the base, in spring. The cultivar 'Baumannii' has double white flowers and bears no fruit.

Aesculus indica

The Indian horse chestnut is native to the north-west Himalayas. It is a handsome tree 65 ft (20 m) or more tall, not unlike A. hippocastanum but with slimmer stems and narrower often lanceolate leaflets.

Aesculus macrostachya, see A. parviflora.

Aesculus parviflora
○ ◑ ⊛ ⊗ ⊗ ⊘

Syn. A. macrostachya. A bushy suckering shrub from the United States that grows 4½–10 ft (1.3–3 m) high, bearing small white flowers in panicles. It flowers in mid- to late summer, and is a very attractive plant for parks and larger gardens.

Aesculus pavia
○ ◑ ⊛ ⊗ ⊗ ⊘

Syn. Pavia rubra. Red buckeye. A North American tree growing up to 50 ft (15 m) high with a spread of up to 40 ft (12 m). It flowers in late spring to early summer. 'Humilis' is shrubby in habit with dark red sepals and yellow-red petals, while 'Atrosanguinea' has dark red flowers.

Agapanthus
Liliaceae
African lily

Perennial plants of African origin with fleshy roots. African lilies can be grown in tubs, and this is a good method in cold areas since they are not fully hardy. The tubs should be moved to a frost-free light garage or shed in winter. In sheltered sites and in coastal regions they may be grown outside, if necessary protected with a layer of straw or bracken.

Soil African lilies thrive on fertile, well-drained garden soil.

Propagation By division. They can also be grown from seed, but it takes two to three years before the seedlings come into flower.

Agapanthus campanulatus

○ ○ ⊛ ⊥ ⊗

The stem of this plant rises to 3 ft (1 m), and its deciduous leaves grow to 18 in (45 cm). The mid-blue to white flowers are 1½ in (4 cm) long and open in midsummer.

Agapanthus 'Headbourne Hybrids'

○ ○ ⊛ ⊥ ⊗

A surprisingly hardy group basically derived from crossing *A. campanulatus* and *A. inapertus*. Plants grow 2–4 ft (60–120 cm) tall, with deciduous leaves, and produce umbellate flowers in shades of blue, purple and white in July and September. There are many cultivars available.

Agapanthus praecox

○ ⌢ ○ ⊛ ⊥ ⊗

Syn. *A. umbellatus*. A 16 in (40 cm) tall plant with strap-shaped, curving leaves and tall stalks bearing crowded umbels of blue flowers. There are numerous cultivars in various colours.

Agapanthus umbellatus, see *A. praecox*.

Ageratum
Compositae
Floss flower

These profusely flowering ornamental plants are much used in groups at the front of borders and as bedding plants; they are also suitable for window boxes, tubs and other containers.

Soil Ordinary garden soil is adequate.

Propagation Seeds should be sown from February onwards under glass. Seedlings can be pricked off as soon as they are large enough, preferably into peat pots, and hardened off slowly. Use any good proprietary potting compost.

Ageratum conyzoides

A plant growing to a height of 2 ft (60 cm) having mid-green, serrated leaves and blue or white flowers.

Ageratum houstonianum

○ ◐ ⊙ ⊛

Syn. *A. mexicanum*. This is the most popular garden species, giving profusely blooming plants that remain in flower from late spring until the first frosts. The best-known F₁ hybrids are 'Blue Blazer', 'Blue Chip', 'Blue Mink' and 'Blue Mist'. White hybrids include the rarely used 'Summer Snow', and pink varieties such as 'Fairy Pink' are also available.

Ajuga
Labiatae
Bugle

These are hardy annuals and herbaceous perennials that prefer moist positions.

Soil Ordinary garden soil containing humus.

Propagation By division.

Ajuga reptans

◐ ○ ⊛ ⊛ ⊜

Common bugle. The plant grows up to 8 in (20 cm) high, and has a creeping habit. The most popular cultivar is 'Atropurpurea', with purple-flushed leaves and dark blue flowers. 'Multicolor' has bronze, pink and yellow variegated leaves; 'Variegata' has grey-green leaves with white markings.

Alcaea
Malvaceae
Hollyhock

Perennial herbaceous plants, mostly grown as biennials because they may lose their vigour after the second year; they can then be replaced cheaply. Where more than a year's growth is wanted, it is advisable to cut down the plants to 6 in (15 cm) after flowering. Hollyhocks are seen to best advantage from a distance. Their bright colours make them stand out particularly well against dark shrubs.

Soil Any fertile, well-drained soil.

Propagation Annual strains are sown in February in a temperature of 13°C (55°F). The first flowers will appear within four months. Although this method of cultivation is the simplest, the annuals thus cultivated lack the character of such perennials as 'Chater's Double', a cultivar that remains as popular as ever. Perennial cultivars are grown from seed sown outdoors in May–June. As soon as the seedlings have 2–3 leaves, they are transplanted to 6 in (15 cm) apart, the long roots first having been trimmed back. In late summer or in spring, the plants are transferred to their permanent flowering positions, being set out about 2½ ft (75 cm) apart.

Diseases Hollyhocks are frequently attacked by rust, which shows on the stem and leaves as orange pustules. The disease is encouraged by moist, warm air. Infected plants should be destroyed as soon as possible. In areas where rust is prevalent, grow only those cultivars known to be rust resistant.

The half-hardy *Agapanthus praecox*

Light blue flowers of *Ageratum*

The bugle, *Ajuga reptans*

Alcaea rosea, the biennial, single form

Alcaea rosea, semi-double form

Alcaea rosea
○ ⊗ ⊛ ⊙ ⊗ ⊥ ⊗

Hollyhock, from China. A plant growing up to 10 ft (3 m) high, and flowering in mid- to late summer. Flowers are borne singly or in pairs on the rigid stems, and may be white, yellow, red, pink, purple or brown in a variety of shades, as well as striped, mottled or marbled. The various cultivars can be classified as follows:

1 *Biennials or perennials*
a Single-flowered, with large, single flowers.
b Double-flowered, with very large double flowers.
c Double-mixed, with all the petals roughly the same size—up to 5 in (12 cm) across.
d 'Chater's Double', with very large double flowers up to 6 in (15 cm) across, and available in separate colours or as a mixture. This is the most popular variety.
e 'Keizer', with very large semi-double flowers.
f 'Fimbriata', with semi-double flowers, with fringed or ruffled petals, up to 7 in (18 cm) across.

2 *Annuals*
a Single-flowered.
b Double-flowered.

Annual hollyhocks are enjoying increasing popularity. 'Indian Summer' is a slightly older variety; 'Silver Puffs' and 'Summer Carnival' were introduced more recently.

Alchemilla
Rosaceae
Lady's mantle

Hardy herbaceous perennials with attractive foliage, often used for flower arrangements.
Soil Grows in almost any moist garden soil.
Propagation By division or from seed.

Alchemilla conjuncta
A densely leafy clump-forming plant 6 in (15 cm) or more tall. The leaves are deeply lobed, dark green above, with silky silvery hairs beneath. Tiny yellow-green flowers appear in summer. It is sometimes offered by nurserymen under the name of *A. alpina*, but that species is smaller and less effective as a garden plant.

Alchemilla mollis
○ ◐ ⊜ ○ ○ ⊗

Growing up to 20 in (50 cm) high, this

Allium giganteum—giant onions in the garden

The lady's mantle, *Alchemilla mollis*

Allium moly

Allium christophii

Allium ursinum

plant from Europe and Asia Minor has light grey-green palmate leaves with rounded lobes and serrated edges, and bears tiny yellow flowers in branched fluffy heads. It makes a useful addition to the front of borders.

Allium
Liliaceae

Bulbous plants comprising approximately 450 known species, most of which smell of onions, and are sometimes referred to as ornamental onions. In general, those with large bulbs produce tall stems and are useful for borders and for cutting; those with smaller bulbs produce shorter stems and are

recommended for rock gardens. Hardy and easily cultivated, they should be planted in autumn, the larger bulbs to a depth of 4 in (10 cm), the smaller to a depth of 2 in (5 cm). The bulbs may be left undisturbed for several years.
Propagation From seed or by division of the bulbs.

Allium aflatunense
○ ⊜ ⊚ ⊗ ⊗

This Central Asian plant grows to heights of 2½–3 ft (75–100 cm), and bears rose-purple flowers in late spring to early summer. It needs a fairly sheltered position.

Allium caeruleum
Syn. *A. azureum*. From Turkestan and Siberia, this plant grows about 2 ft (60 cm) high, and produces sky-blue

flowers in umbels in late spring to early summer.

Allium christophii
Syn. *A. albopilosum*. A plant from Persia that grows up to 2 ft (60 cm) high, it flowers in early summer with umbels up to 8 in (20 cm) across that are packed with glossy lilac-pink flowers.

Allium cowanii, see *A. neapolitanum*.

Allium cyathophorum farreri
Syn. *A. farreri*. A densely tufted almost bulbless species from western China with grassy foliage and winged or angled stems growing to 10 in (25 cm) tall which bear heads of red-purple pendent bells in early summer.

Allium flavum
This somewhat neglected plant from South and East Europe produces tufts of chive-like foliage and heads of small pale yellow bells on stems up to 12 in (30 cm) high in late summer. Small forms growing to half this height are sometimes offered by nurserymen under the names of *A. nanum*, *A. pumilum* and *A. minus*.

Allium giganteum
○ ⊜ ⊜ ⊚ ⊗ ⊥ ⊗

A Himalayan plant that reaches a height of 5½ ft (1.75 m). It produces deep lilac flowers in umbels about 4 in (10 cm) across in early summer.

Allium karataviense
○ ⊜ ⊜ ⊚ ⊗ ⊗

From Turkestan, this is one of the most beautiful of the *Allium* spp. It is very hardy, grows 8–12 in (20–30 cm) high and has broad leaves with a metallic sheen. The small whitish or purplish flowers appear in late spring.

Allium moly
◑ ⊜ ⊚ ⊗ ⊗

From southern Europe, this plant grows 10 in (25 cm) high and is suitable for rock gardens. In late spring to early summer it bears bright yellow star-shaped flowers with a green stripe, in umbels.

Allium narcissiflorum
Syn. *A. pedemontanum*. This curiously named species is clump-forming and barely bulbous. The leaves are narrowly strap shaped, 8 in (20 cm) or more long, and are just over-topped by pendent umbels of rose-purple bell-shaped flowers. Each flower is ½ in (12 mm) long and opens in summer.

Allium neapolitanum
○ ⊜ ⊜ ⊚ ⊗ ⊗

From Italy, Spain and southern France, this plant grows 8–12 in (20–30 cm) high, bearing brilliant white flowers in spring. Unlike most other species, *A. neapolitanum* does not smell of onions.

Allium pulchellum
○ ○ ⊚ ⊗ ⊗ ⊗

Originally found from south-western Europe to western Asia, this is one of the most colourful and graceful of the smaller alliums. It grows 1–2 ft (30–60 cm) in height, and produces its bright purplish-red, bell-shaped flowers in late summer, the leaves dying just as the flowers open.

Allium roseum
○ ⊜ ⊜ ⊚ ⊗ ⊗

From southern Europe, this plant grows 2 ft (60 cm) high, and bears bright pink, bell-shaped flowers in umbels in early summer.

Allium schubertii
○ ⊜ ⊜ ⊚ ⊚ ⊗ ⊗ ⊗

From Israel, this plant grows 1–2 ft (30–60 cm) high, and in early summer bears very wide umbels with long- and short-stemmed flowers.

Alnus
Betulaceae
Alder

A familiar tree, but because of its size not suited to smaller gardens.

Soil Most species will grow on any soil provided it is moist. The grey alder also flourishes on dry soil, while the common alder prefers wet soil.

Propagation Species are grown from seed and hybrids by layering.

Alnus cordata
○ ◑ ✳ ⊖ ✳ ⊗

Italian alder, from Italy and Corsica. A tree suitable for parks and streets, growing to a height of 50ft (15m). It has dark green heart-shaped leaves and an oval crown.

The common alder, young specimen

Alnus glutinosa
○ ◑ ⊗ ⊖ ✳ ⊗

Common alder, found from Europe to Siberia. A tree with egg-shaped doubly serrated leaves that grows up to 80ft (25m) high. It requires a moist, fertile soil, and though slender stands up well even to onshore winds. The variety 'Aurea' has pale yellow leaves that eventually turn bright green, and 'Imperialis' has deeply and finely cut leaves.

Alnus incana
○ ◑ ⊗ ⊖ ✳ ⊕

Grey alder. This species has downy buds and twigs. Although it stands up badly to the wind it does grow well on poor soil. The variety 'Aurea' does not exceed a height of 18ft (6m) and bears yellow-green leaves, its yellowish branches and reddish-brown catkins being particularly conspicuous in spring. This cultivar is well suited to smaller gardens with a sandy soil. 'Pendula' is a weeping variety that looks picturesque at the side of pools.

Alstroemeria
Amaryllidaceae
Peruvian lily

Attractive herbaceous perennials, well suited to borders, where they combine well with late-flowering delphiniums. The tuberous roots must be planted to a depth of about 6in (15cm), preferably in autumn but also in early spring.

Soil Peruvian lilies need a well-drained and fertile soil; if the ground is too wet or the water cannot drain away, they will make no progress.

Propagation Most species can be

Alnus glutinosa in the winter. Immature male flowers in drooping catkins and last year's seeding cones

Yellow-orange Peruvian lily

grown from seed sown in pots from spring to early summer, but a much simpler method is to propagate the plants by root division.

Alstroemeria aurantiaca
○ ◈ ○ ⊕ ⊗

From Chile, this plant ranges from 2–4ft (60–120cm) high, and produces clusters of 10–30 bright yellow to orange-scarlet flowers. Well-known varieties are 'Orange King', which has large, deep orange flowers; 'Concolor', whose flowers are orange-yellow; 'Aurea', its yellow flowers veined with pink, and 'Moorheim's Orange' with dark orange flowers.

Alstroemeria ligtu
A plant with pink flowers, it is seldom grown today, its place having been taken by pink to orange-red hybrids.

Alstroemeria ligtu hybrid

Alternanthera
Amaranthaceae

Perennials, usually treated as annuals or biennials, they are grown for their coloured leaves and used effectively in summer bedding schemes. The flowers are insignificant, and if required the plants can be trimmed with shears to keep them compact. They grow best in full sunlight. The genus is native to the Americas, most species being tropical plants.

Soil Ordinary garden soil.

Propagation By cuttings taken in late summer or spring, or they may be propagated by division. Plants must be overwintered with a minimum temperature of about 15°C (60°F).

Alternanthera dentata
○ ○ ⊗

Found from the West Indies to Brazil, this plant grows to a height of 18in (45cm). The 2in (5cm) wide leaves are sometimes green, but often coloured. 'Rubiginosa', a very common variety, has striking red or purple leaves.

Alternanthera ficoides
○ ○ ⊗

Found from Mexico to Argentina, this very variable plant ranges from 2 to 4ft (60 to 120cm) in height, and its many varieties differ widely in the colouring of their leaves. Those of 'Amoena' are veined and blotched red, orange and yellow, while 'Bettzickiana' has narrow green, red and yellow leaves. 'Versicolor' has bronze-green leaves with coppery or red shading.

Althaea
see Alcaea

Alyssum
Cruciferae

This genus includes many evergreen sub-shrubs. They should be cut back directly after flowering, or else they may become straggly.

Soil Ordinary well-drained garden soil is adequate.

Propagation Species are grown from seed. Named sorts are best propagated from cuttings of lateral shoots.

Alyssum montanum
○ ⊖ ○ ⊕ ⊗

A European herbaceous perennial

Gold dust, *Alyssum saxatile*

The Cornflower, *Centaurea moschata*

reaching 4–8in (10–20cm) in height. Grey, hairy and mat-forming, it bears yellow flowers in June–August.

Alyssum argenteum

A shrubby perennial reaching a height of 12in (30cm), with oblong leaves that are silver-grey underneath. Blooming slightly later and often more profusely than *A. saxatile*, it produces yellow flowers in May–July.

Alyssum saxatile

Syn. *Aurinia saxatile*. Golden tuft, from central Europe. The most common of all Alyssums, this evergreen shrubby perennial grows 6–12in (15–30cm) high. It has woolly grey-green leaves, and bears yellow flowers in spring. The best-known cultivars are 'Citrinum', with lemon-yellow flowers; 'Dudley Neville', with pale biscuit-coloured flowers; 'Plenum', with yellow double flowers; and 'Tom Thumb', which is dwarf and compact.

Amaranthus
Amaranthaceae

Half-hardy annuals, some with very colourful leaves.
Soil Ordinary garden soil, well drained; for best results add garden compost or decayed manure.
Propagation By seed sown at 15–18°C (59–64°F) in spring.

Amaranthus caudatus
○ ☉ ⊗ ⊛

Love-lies-bleeding. A tropical plant growing to a height of 3–5ft (1–1.5m), it produces catkin-like tails of deep red flowers in mid- to late summer.

The flowers of the shadbush come out in April–May

Amaranthus tricolor
○ ☉ ⊛

Joseph's coat. An excellent tropical plant for summer bedding, ranging in height from 1–4ft (30–120cm). The oval to willow-shaped leaves exhibit splendid colours from yellow through orange and bronze to red.

Amberboa
Compositae
Knapweed

The species listed below is often assigned to the genus *Centaurea*, but is treated as *Amberboa* by most modern taxonomists.
Soil Normal, well-drained garden soil.
Propagation Seeds can be sown from February onwards in heated frames; prick out into pots, and plant out in late May. Alternatively, sow seeds in the flowering site in March or April. The plants grow to full size within about 10 weeks.

Amberboa moschata
○ ⊛ ☉ ⊛ ⊗

Syn. *Centaurea moschata, C. odorata, C. suaveolens*. Sweet sultan, from the Near East. Growing up to 32in (80cm) high, it flowers in midsummer to autumn, usually bearing yellow flowers though blue, red or white are now also available. The flowers are always scented, and very suitable for cutting.

C. suaveolens is available in larger-flowered selections, known as *A. m. imperialis*, in shades of white, pink, lavender, red, purple or yellow.

Amelanchier
Rosaceae
Snowy mespilus

A genus of shrubs or small trees, admired for their early and profuse flowers, and best suited to larger shrubberies. The foliage turns red and yellow in autumn.
Soil Any well-drained but moisture-retentive soil is suitable; a good autumn

colour is best achieved in acid to neutral soils.
Propagation From seeds, layering, and rooted suckers, and by grafting on to stocks of *Crataegus monogyna* or *C. laevigata*.

Amelanchier canadensis
○ ⊕ ⊕ ⊛ ☉ ⊛ ⊛

Syn. *A. oblongifolia*. Shadbush. Often

The flowers of *Anaphalis margaritacea*

confused with *A. lamarckii*, this shrub grows up to 10ft (3m) high, with ovate leaves and masses of pure white flowers borne on erect racemes.

Amelanchier laevis

A shrub, 12–18ft (4–6m) high with a large spread. The best garden species, it produces white flowers up to 2in (5cm) across in April. The purplish-brown, edible fruits ripen in June.

Amelanchier lamarckii

Snowy mespilus or June berry. This slender shrub has been naturalized in western Europe. The leaves are coppery-red, turning to scarlet in autumn. It is spring-flowering with white flowers in loose clusters, and later forms bluish-black edible berries.

Amelanchier oblongifolia, see *A. canadensis*.

Amelanchier lamarckii, a large specimen of the shadbush in the autumn

Anaphalis
Compositae
Pearl everlasting

Popular herbaceous perennials much admired for their silver-grey foliage and white flowers. They are particularly striking in borders by the side of blue or purple plants. If the flower heads are cut before they are fully grown and then dried away from the sun, they make excellent winter decorations. For best results, the plants should be given a sunny position, but they will also grow fairly well under trees, provided the canopy is not too dense.

Soil Any well-drained soil is suitable.
Propagation By division or from small cuttings of basal shoots in spring. *Anaphalis* can also be grown from seed, sown in cold frames in spring.

Anaphalis margaritacea
○ ⊜ ○ ⓨ ⊛

Originally from North America, now naturalized in Great Britain. Plants are 1–2ft (30–60cm) high, and produce pearly white flowers in summer. They have creeping roots and grey foliage, and are excellent for the border, where they may be used to support taller but less sturdy plants growing behind them. For the best effect, plant them out in elongated groups beside blue flowers.

Anaphalis triplinervis
○ ⊜ ○ ⓨ ⊗

A plant growing 12–18in (30–45cm) high, it bears woolly white leaves with prominent triple veins about 3–5in (8–12cm) long, and silvery white flower heads in terminal clusters. *A. nubigena* is similar but grows no taller than 8in (20cm).

Anchusa
Boraginaceae
Alkanet or bugloss

Most attractive annuals and herbaceous perennials. The pure blue sorts make very useful border plants, especially when combined with bright red flowers. A clump of red poppies in front of the blue *A. italica* makes a most effective grouping.

Soil Easily grown in any part of the garden, but prefers well-drained, fertile soil in a sunny position.
Propagation From root cuttings or by division in spring for perennials. *Anchusa* can also be grown from seeds in spring either *in situ* or in a nursery bed, and planted out in its permanent site in autumn. See also *A. capensis*. The seeds germinate in about two weeks and remain viable for two years.

Anchusa azurea, see *A. italica*.
Anchusa cespitosa
○ ⊜ ○ ⓨ

A compact plant with a bushy habit growing up to 16in (40cm) high. It has bristly linear leaves and bears bright blue flowers in clusters from May to September on branching stems.

Anchusa capensis
○ ⊜ ⊙ ⓨ

A South African plant growing to heights of 1–2ft (30–60cm), it produces beautiful red, mauve-purple and brilliant blue flowers in midsummer. The sprays of the variety 'Blue Bird' resemble forget-me-nots; this plant is a

Anchusa italica 'Loddon Royalist'

Anemone coronaria, Caen single

Anemone × hybrida, a beautiful autumn-flowering anemone

tender biennial grown as an annual. Sow in spring in a greenhouse or frame, or in late spring to early summer in the flowering position.

Anchusa italica
Syn. *A. azurea*. From southern Europe, Siberia and North Africa, this large herbaceous perennial or biennial plant reaches heights of up to 5ft (1.5m), and flowers in early to midsummer. Especially recommended are the garden varieties 'Dropmore', 'Little John' and 'Loddon Royalist', which have a spread of up to 3ft (1m) and bear glorious blue flowers in large panicles.
Anchusa myosotidiflora, see *Brunnera macrophylla*.

Anemone
Ranunculaceae
Windflower

A large genus of hardy herbaceous perennials ranging from the simple, short-stemmed wood anemone to the stately Japanese anemone. Anemones can be divided into three groups: the spring-flowering, non-tuberous species; tuberous-rooted; and summer- and autumn-flowering species.

The first group includes *A. nemorosa*

Anemone blanda in mixed colours

and *A. sylvestris*; the second *A. apennina*, *A. blanda*, *A. coronaria* and *A. pavonina*; and in the third group are *A. japonica × hybrida*, *A. hupehensis* and *A. vitifolia*.
Soil Any well-drained, moisture-retentive fertile soil is suitable.
Propagation Spring-flowering anemones are grown from seed, by separation of the offsets or by division of the rhizomes, the latter preferably after the top growth has died down. Summer- and autumn-flowering plants are best propagated by division; *A. × hybrida* may also be raised from root cuttings.

Anemone alpina, see *Pulsatilla alpina*.
Anemone apennina
○ ◐ ○ ⓐ ⓨ ⊛

Italian anemone, from southern Europe. A tuberous-rooted plant reaching 6–8in (15–20cm) high, spectacular in rock gardens either in sunny or semi-shaded positions, and flowering in spring. The flowers are usually sky-blue, but those of 'Rosea' are bright pink and of 'Alba' pure white.

Anemone blanda
○ ◐ ⓐ ⓨ ⊛

Mountain windflower, from south-eastern Europe and Turkey. This tuberous-rooted plant resembles *A. apennina*, but the leaflets are almost hairless and have no stalks. It bears deep blue, pink or white flowers in early spring.

Anemone japonica 'Honorine Jobert'

Anemone coronaria
○ ⌃ ⓐ ⓨ ⊗

Poppy anemone, originating in southern Europe and Turkey. A tuberous-rooted plant reaching heights of 10–14in (25–35cm) and producing white, red or blue flowers in spring, or in summer if planted in the spring. Members of this species vary greatly in size and in the number and colour of flowers, which may be single or double. The single cultivars tend to be more vigorous. Named cultivars include:

De Caen single. These have large single flowers on stout stems, and include 'The Bride' (white), 'Mr Fokker' (blue), and 'Hollandia' syn. 'His Excellency' (scarlet).

De Caen double. These are of the same habit, but with double flowers.

St Brigid. These are semi-double flowers with fairly small petals. They are available in scarlet, white and blue.

All three types are best planted out in spring to flower in summer, or in summer to flower in autumn, or in autumn to bloom the following spring. Cultivars tend to deteriorate fairly quickly, and it is advisable to replace them every two years.

Anemone hupehensis
○ ◐ ○ ⓨ ○ ⊗

Syn. *A. japonica* var. *hupehensis*. A short autumn-flowering anemone which comes out somewhat earlier than other species and bears red-flushed buds opening into lilac-pink flowers.

Anemone × hybrida
○ ◐ ⌃ ○ ○ ⓨ ⊗

Syn. *Anemone japonica* Japanese anemone. Garden plants are 1½–3ft (50–100cm) high and flower in late summer to autumn with large, single or

The yellow flowers of *Anthemis*

A strain of *Antirrhinum majus*

Penstemon-flowered snapdragon

tuberous-rooted plant about 6–10in (15–25cm) high that grows best in woodlands and in the shade of trees and shrubs. Spring-flowering, it bears white flowers flushed with pink, and, more rarely, with red or blue. 'Alleni' has soft purple-blue flowers; while those of 'Blue Bonnet' are pale blue; 'Robinsoniana' has large lavender-blue blossoms, while 'Royal Blue' is much deeper in hue. 'Vestal' is white with a double centre.

Anemone pavonina
Peacock anemone. A hardy perennial covered with fine hair and bearing finely divided foliage. It grows 8–12in (20–30cm) high. The best-known form is 'St Bravo', whose flowers have 6–10 fairly broad petals in various colours. Plant *A. pavonina* in autumn.

Anemone pratensis, see *Pulsatilla pratensis*.

Anemone slavica, see *Pulsatilla halleri* spp *slavica*.

Anemone sylvestris
○ ◑ ○ ⊕ ◉
Snowdrop windflower. A herbaceous perennial from Europe and western Asia, it grows 8–16in (20–40cm) high. In spring it produces fragrant white flowers that are silky on the outside; the fruits are covered with silvery hairs. 'Plena' is a less attractive double-flowered form. When planted in fairly cool, rich soil, these plants will often flower again from midsummer to late autumn.

Anemone vitifolia
This species can be distinguished by its undivided leaves. It also grows slightly taller, ranging between 1½–3ft (50–100cm) in height. *A. vitifolia* is recommended as a border plant, but only for sheltered sites.

Anthemis
Compositae
Camomile or chamomile

Perennial plants for rock gardens and borders. *A. nobilis* (syn. *Chamaemelum nobile*), the common chamomile, is grown for its medicinal properties, and is also planted to make lawns.
Soil Chamomile grows best on well-drained and not too rich soil.
Propagation From soft cuttings in the spring, and by division.

Anthemis tinctoria
○ ⊖ ○ ⊗
Ox-eye chamomile, from Europe and the Near East. A herbaceous perennial reaching heights of 2–3ft (60–100cm) and producing fairly large, long-stemmed flowers in summer. Those of 'Grallagh Gold' are glorious deep golden-yellow, and 'Kelwayi' bears darker flowers.

Antirrhinum
Scrophulariaceae
Snapdragon

Although 30 species from western Europe and western North America are known, only one, *A. majus*, the common snapdragon, is commonly grown. It has given rise to many cultivars in a range of heights, habits and flower colours, all but a few with the small quaint tubular dragon-mouthed flowers so beloved by children.
Soil Well-drained, light to medium soil, ideally enriched with manure.

Propagation Cultivars grown as biennials are best sown in August and early September, then pricked out into cold frames no later than mid-October, and planted out in spring. They will come into flower in May and continue to bloom until the first frosts of autumn, provided faded spikes are removed before seeds can form. Antirrhinums can also be grown from seeds sown in pans in February or March at a temperature of 16–18°C (61–64°F), or in late April in the open. The later they are sown, of course, the later they will come into flower. The growing points should always be pinched out when the plants are 3–4in (7.5–10cm) high or when they are established in the flowering position. This will encourage bushy growth.

Antirrhinum majus
○ ☉ ⊕ ⊗
A perennial plant from southern Europe and North America, often grown as an annual and reaching 9–36in (22–100cm) high. It flowers approximately 10 weeks after sowing; the flowering period is in early to mid summer. Available in nearly every colour and shade, the plants are usually divided into three groups, based on height:
1 Tall or giant cultivars, up to 3ft (1m) high, known as 'Grandiflorum'. Catalogues usually list them together with 'Maximum', which has even larger flowers but is of the same height.
2 Medium cultivars, up to 2ft (60cm) high, which are known as 'Nanum Grandiflorum'. This group includes the 'Majestic' class, in which the side shoots tend to come into flower at the same time as the central spike, which is visually an asset, particularly in flower beds. The stems are, moreover, just tall enough to provide good cut flowers.
3 Dwarf cultivars, often described as 'Tom Thumb', and ranging in height up to 8in (20cm). These are mainly used as bedding and edging plants.

The taller cultivars are grown chiefly for cut flowers, and are invariably raised under glass. Most important for the amateur are the shorter bedding forms, generally F₁ hybrids such as the 'Coronette' strain, which flower profusely and grow to an even height.

A recent addition is the Penstemon-flowered group. Here the flowers have an open trumpet-shaped form. The first to be introduced was 'Bright Butterflies', up to 2½ft (75cm) high, and grown in various colours. This trumpet-shaped form is also available with double flowers, which are known as 'Madame Butterfly'. A very beautiful member of the same group is called 'Little Darling'; only 15in (40cm) high, it too occurs in a variety of colours.

Aquilegia
Ranunculaceae
Columbine

Hardy herbaceous perennials for the border, for cutting and for the rock garden. The long-spurred sorts are considered exceptionally attractive and ornamental.
Soil Ordinary garden soil, moist but well-drained, is suitable.
Propagation By division or from seed. Selected individuals must be propagated by division, but flowers for general use are easily grown from seed,

preferably in spring in boxes of seed compost placed in a cold frame.

Aquilegia alpina
○ ◑ ○ ⊕ ⊗
These Swiss plants grow to a height of 1ft (30cm), and produce blue flowers in midsummer; white or light wine-red forms, probably of hybrid origin, also occur. Particularly attractive is 'Hensol Harebell', which has larger, violet-blue flowers.

Aquilegia caerulea
○ ◑ ○ ⊼ ○ ⊕
A useful border plant from the North American Rockies, growing 1–2ft (30–60cm) high and bearing blue flowers. Garden selections include 'Alba', which has pure white flowers and 'Plena' in which the stamens have been modified into white petals.

Aquilegia hybrids
Obtained from *A. alpina*, *A. caerulea*, *A. formosa* and *A. vulgaris*, the hybrids are mostly grown from seed. The flowers have long spurs and occur in various colours. 'Crimson Star' is crimson with a white centre; 'Mrs Nichols' is blue and white; 'Mrs Scott Elliot's Strain' occurs in a variety of soft shades; and 'McKana's Giant Hybrids' have very large flowers. All these plants should be dead-headed.

Aquilegia skinneri
○ ⊖ ○ ⊕
Ranging from 2–2½ft (60–75cm) in height, these plants flower in late spring to early summer, but come back into flower in autumn. The flowers have green sepals, greenish-orange petals, and 1¼in (3cm) scarlet or purple spurs, and combine well with the blue-green foliage.

A graceful columbine hybrid

Aquilegia vulgaris
○ ○ ⊕ ◉
Granny's bonnet, from Europe. A plant growing 1½–2½ft (45–75cm) high and flowering in late spring to early summer with attractive, nodding blue or purple flowers. 'Nivea Grandiflora' has large white blooms; 'Multiplex' and 'Flore Pleno' have double flowers in many shades; 'Clematiflora' and 'Stellata' have spurless star-shaped flowers in various colours. 'McKana Hybrids' and 'Mrs Scott-Elliot's Strain' bear long-spurred flowers in May–June. They may be white, yellow, pink, red or blue and grow to 3ft (1m).

double blooms that can be white, pink or flesh coloured. Among the many good-looking cultivars are 'Honorine Jobert', with white single flowers; 'Queen Charlotte', a semi-double with white flowers flushed with pink; and 'Whirlwind', a semi-double with white flowers. All these medium-sized, autumn-flowering hybrids are seen to good advantage in the centre of borders, and are also highly prized for their very long flowering periods.

Anemone japonica, see *A. hupehensis* var. *japonica* and *A. × hybrida*.

Anemone japonica var. *hupehensis*, see *A. hupehensis*.

Anemone montana, see *Pulsatilla montana*.

Anemone nemorosa
○ ◑ ⊼ ⊕ ◉
Wood anemone, from Europe. A

Arabis
Cruciferae

Widely distributed, found throughout Europe, the mountains of Africa and temperate parts of Asia and North America.
Soil Ordinary, well-drained garden soil.
Propagation Usually best grown from seed in spring. The double and variegated types, however, should be propagated by division or, better still, from cuttings of non-flowering rosettes in summer.

Arabis albida, see A. caucasica.
Arabis × arendsii
○ ⊜ ○ ⊛ ⊗ ⊖
A cross between *A. aubrietioides* and *A. caucasica*, this plant has hoary, serrated leaves. It bears pink flowers in terminal clusters; 'Coccinea' has purple-pink flowers, while those of 'Rosabella' are slightly darker.

Arabis blepharophylla
This mat-forming species comes from the rocky places of northern coastal California and needs a sheltered sunny site to thrive outside. It has hairy obovate leaves and spikes of rose-purple flowers 6 in (15 cm) or more tall in spring and early summer.

Arabis caucasica
○ ⊜ ○ ⊛ ⊖ ⊗
Syn. *A. albida*. Originally from the Caucasus, and naturalized in western Europe, this plant grows 4–8 in (10–20 cm) high. It makes an excellent edging plant and has greyish, hoary leaves. It produces white flowers in early spring. 'Flore Pleno' has double white flowers and is recommended for cutting.

Aralia
Araliaceae
Angelica tree

Suckering shrubs or small trees with large compound leaves and small flowers in globular clusters that make handsome specimens for a lawn or corner site.
Soil Aralias prefer fairly moist soil, rich in humus.
Propagation From small suckers in autumn or spring.

Aralia elata
○ ⊕ ⊛ ⊛ ⊛ ⊗ ⊗ ⊕
Japanese angelica tree. Usually seen as a large, tall shrub, up to 15 ft (5 m) high, with stout, rather spiny stems. The leaves are long and hang in a ruff-like arrangement. In late summer, creamy flower clusters are borne in panicles up to 15 in (40 cm) long, and are followed by black berries. 'Variegata' has white-edged leaves, while 'Aureovariegata' has green leaves with yellow margins.

Araucaria
Araucariaceae

A genus of evergreen coniferous trees, native to the Southern Hemisphere, of which the monkey puzzle tree is the best-known garden species.
Soil Any well-drained fertile soil.
Propagation From seed sown in March, or cuttings.

Araucaria araucana
○ ⊜ ⊛ ⊛ ⊕
Syn. *A. imbricata*. Monkey puzzle tree or Chilean pine. An attractive medium-sized to large coniferous tree, popular as a single ornament on a lawn; the curving branches, with their green scaly leaves, have a sinuous, beckoning appearance. It is one of the few South American trees to grow well in Europe.

Arabis caucasica

Arbutus
Ericaceae
Strawberry tree

Evergreen trees and shrubs which brighten the winter scene; many have a reddish-brown peeling bark.
Soil A humus-rich, neutral soil is best, but the species mentioned below all tolerate lime.
Propagation From seed sown when ripe in a cold frame, or from cuttings rooted under glass in summer bottom heat.

Arbutus andrachne
A native of southeast Europe to Turkey. This small tree can attain a height of 40 ft but is usually grown as a large bush. It has oblong, sometimes toothed leaves up to 4 in (10 cm) long and white flowers in compact panicles in spring. The globular fruits are orange.

Arbutus × andrachroides
Syn. *A. × hybrida*. This hybrid between *A. unedo* and *A. andrachne* blends the characters of its parents but ultimately is often more tree-like, with eye-catching cinnamon-red bark. It bears white flowers in compact panicles and rarely fruits.

Arbutus unedo
○ ⊕ ○ ⊛ ⊛ ⊕
A small tree or shrub from the Mediterranean and western Europe. It is often many stemmed, growing to 33 ft (10 m) and spreading to 12 ft (4 m), with glossy green leaves up to 4 in (10 cm) long. The flowers are small white and pink bells, and form in drooping clusters; the fruits are red, like round but sadly insipid strawberries. The flowers of the variety 'Rubra' are a deeper pink.

Arctostaphyllos
Ericaceae

A genus of evergreen shrubs and small trees, some of which have decorative flowers, bark, foliage or fruits.
Soil A neutral to acid, preferably peaty soil that is moist but well aerated.
Propagation Increase can be effected by layering in spring, by cuttings with a heel in a cold frame in later summer or by seeds when ripe, also in a frame.

Arctostaphyllos manzanita
The common manzanita of California makes a shrub 6 ft (2 m) or more tall with attractively crooked smooth red-

Aralia elata 'Aurovariegata', a Chinese angelica tree with variegated leaves

Monkey puzzle tree, at least a hundred years old

brown branches and broadly elliptic bright green leaves 1–1¾in (2.5–4.5 cm) long. The white or pink spring-borne flowers are followed by deep red berries ½in (12 mm) wide.

Arctostaphyllos nevadensis

The pine-mat manzanita is native to the West Coast mountains of the USA. It forms a wide mat, sometimes with semi-erect stems 1–2 ft (30–60 cm) tall. The generally narrow leaves are variable in shape, up to 1 in (2.5 cm) long and bright green. In spring white flower clusters appear and are followed by carmine berries.

Arctostaphyllos uva-ursi

This prostrate shrub comes from the far north and is very hardy. It forms wide mats of somewhat glossy, narrow, rich green leaves and bears small clusters of white-flushed pink flowers on the stem tips from late spring to late summer. The globose berries are bright glossy red.

Arctotis
Compositae
African daisy

Annuals suitable for fairly dry positions such as rock gardens.
Soil Ordinary, well-drained, fertile garden soil.
Propagation Sow under glass in spring at 18–21°C (64–70°F). Plant out 1 ft (30 cm) apart when fear of frost has passed.

Arctotis stoechadifolia grandis

○ ◐ ○

This South African plant grows 2–2½ft (60–75 cm) high and bears flowers that

are silvery-white inside and shiny violet outside, on elongated and downy stems; the flowers open in sunlight. The leaves too are downy and most attractively shaped.

Arenaria
Caryaphyllaceae
Sandwort

A large genus of mostly small tufted or mat-forming plants suitable for the rock garden or as small-scale ground-cover. They have tiny leaves in pairs and 5-petalled, mainly white, starry flowers. Most species are best in sun, but see *A. balearica*.
Soil Any well-drained soil is suitable. However soils should have grit or coarse sand added.
Propagation Division in spring or early autumn is the easiest means of increase, but seeds may also be sown in a cold frame in spring.

Arenaria balearica
From the western Mediterranean, this attractive plant forms wide mossy mats spangled with solitary pure white flowers from spring to summer. It needs a shaded site that never dries out to thrive happily.

Arenaria montana
A loosely mat-forming plant from Western Europe having narrow grey-green leaves ½–¾in (12–20 mm) long and solitary or small clusters of sizeable white flowers, often in profusion, from spring to summer.

Thrift, *Armeria maritima*

Aristolochia
Aristolochiaceae
Dutchman's pipe

Soil Grows in any well-drained garden soil.
Propagation From seeds or cuttings.

Aristolochia macrophylla

○ ◐ ○ ◉ ⊘ ⊛

Syn. *A. durior, A. sipho*. A vigorous climber, originally from North America, this shrub grows 15–30ft (5–10 m) high, and has heart-shaped leaves up to 10in (25 cm) long; it is excellent for covering summer houses and walls. In late spring to early summer it bears green and brown flowers on long pendulous stems.

Armeria
Plumbaginaceae
Thrift

Attractive edging plants forming hummocks or mats from which innumerable flowers rise on leafless stems.
Cultivation Thrift can be planted to form a fairly wide edge at the front of a border, or as ground cover for sunny dry areas; to obtain this effect, plant in rows 6in (15 cm) apart. Remove faded flower heads to tidy up the otherwise neat hummocks.
Soil Ordinary garden soil.
Propagation Easily propagated from cuttings in autumn or spring.

Armeria alliacea
Syn. *A. plantaginea*. This species grows much taller than *A. maritima*, reaching 1½–2ft (45–60 cm), and has blue-green leaves 1–2in (2.5–5 cm) wide; the flower heads measure 2–3in (5–7 cm) across. The best known variety is 'Bees Ruby'.

Armeria juniperifolia

○ ◐ ⊖ ○ ⊙ ⊘ ⊛ ⊗ ⊖

Syn. *A. caspitosa*. Growing to a height of 1 in (2.5 cm), this low, hummock-forming plant from Spain has grey-green leaves and bears bright pink flowers in late spring to early summer. The variety 'Bevan's' is 2–3in (5–7.5 cm) tall and has rose-red flowers, while 'Six Hills', also a recommended variety, has pale pink flowers.

Armeria maritima

○ ◐ ⊖ ○ ⊙ ⊘ ⊛ ⊗ ⊖

Sea pink. This plant grows 6in (15 cm) or more high and bears flowers in various shades of pink in late spring to early summer. The variety 'Laucheana' is smaller in all respects, and 'Alba' bears white flowers.

Dutchman's pipe, *Aristolochia macrophylla*

Artemisia
Compositae

A genus including a number of attractive herbaceous perennials and shrubs with handsome silvery-green leaves. In some of the taller species, the flowers are also attractive, and the plants make a useful addition to the border. It is a peculiarity of *Artemisia* that garden pests seem to shun it; humans grow it for its medicinal properties.

Soil The shrubby varieties do well in normal garden soil, provided it is well drained. Herbaceous types require a light, drier soil, except for *A. lactiflora*.

Propagation Shrubby species are propagated from cuttings; herbaceous perennial species by division.

Artemisia ludoviciana

Shrubby species include:

Artemisia abrotanum
○ ◉ ◎

Growing to a height of 3 ft (1 m), this plant produces yellow pendulous flower heads in late summer to late autumn. It has grey-green foliage, and the leaves give off a lemon smell when rubbed between the fingers.

Artemisia absinthium
Wormwood. This plant is used in the preparation of absinth.

Artemisia stelleriana
○ ◉ ◎ ◎

A creeping sub-shrub that has to be pruned regularly to produce a compact plant with numerous silvery-grey tips. If pruning is neglected, the plant becomes straggly and unsightly with bare stems. It is excellent in borders, especially if placed behind blue flowers.

Herbaceous perennial species include:

Artemisia dracunculus
○ ◐ ⊖ ◎ ◎

French tarragon. A herb used to flavour salads, poultry, fish, etc., it grows up to 3 ft (1 m) high. Loose panicles of tiny globular flowers appear in late summer to early autumn.

Artemisia lactiflora
○ ◐ ◎ ⊖ ◎

White mugwort. A robust, aromatic border plant reaching heights of 4 to 5 ft (1.2–1.5 m) and bearing milky white flowers in autumn. Unlike the other herbaceous species, this plant demands a fairly moist soil.

Artemisia ludoviciana
○ ◐ ○ ◎

White sage. A spreading sub-shrubby plant suitable for large sandy tracts that grows 1–3 ft (30–100 cm) high. It has grey foliage and yellowish flowers.

Artemisia ludoviciana gnaphalodes 'Silver Queen'
○ ◐ ○ ◎

A silvery-grey cultivar 2½–3 ft (75–100 cm) high. Plants may be dried for decorative purposes.

Aruncus
Rosaceae
Goat's beard

A genus of very attractive herbaceous perennials which take some years to become established but then grow vigorously on moist ground. *A. dioicus* is often misnamed *Spiraea aruncus* and is sometimes confused with *Astilbe* (see under these headings).

Soil Deep moist loam.

Propagation By division in March or April, and again in October.

Aruncus dioicus
◐ ○ ⊛ ⊕

Syn. *A. vulgaris*, *A. sylvester*. Goat's beard, from Europe. A dioecious plant (having the male and female flowers on separate plants), it grows to heights of 3–6 ft (1–2 m). The flowering period is in early to midsummer when creamy white flowers are borne in long plumes. With its large and feathery foliage, it is excellent in solitary positions, especially on lawns and near water. 'Kneiffii' has smaller, narrower, pointed leaflets.

Aruncus sylvester, see *A. dioicus*.
Aruncus vulgaris, see *A. dioicus*.

Asclepias
Asclepediaceae
Milkweed

These perennials and shrubs are strong-growing and their flowers are often striking, but only a few are hardy in cool climates.

Soil Any light soil without lime.

Propagation By seed sown in spring.

Asclepias tuberosa
○ ⊖ ⊜

A North American plant that grows 12–24 in (30–70 cm) high. The stems appear above ground in late spring, bearing narrow oblong leaves; in midsummer orange flowers appear in erect, flat-topped clusters. Once planted, do not disturb them.

Aster
Compositae

It is difficult to think of another genus to which we owe so many garden plants, especially if we also consider the annual China aster (treated here under *Callistephus*). In this section we look at perennial asters only. All species are very easy to grow. The late-flowering species and cultivars, which come into bloom in autumn, must be planted in a sunny position and in well-drained ground. The other types grow better in slightly moist soil.

Because asters are so robust and so easily divided, there is a temptation to plant them over-profusely. The result can then be that a border ends up with very little else in it but asters, all the weaker plants having been killed off. However beautiful asters may be, most gardeners prefer to see other plants in the border as well.

Asters can be divided into spring-, summer- and autumn-flowering plants.

Aruncus dioicus planted near a pond

The first group includes *A. alpinus*, *A. × alpellus*, *A. farreri*, *A. tongoiensis* and *A. yunnanensis*. In the second group are *A. amellus*, *A. cordifolius*, *A. dumosus* hybrids, *A. ericoides*, *A. × frikartii*, *A. linosyris*, *A. novae-angliae*, *A. novi-belgii* and *A. sedifolius*.

Autumn-flowering asters may develop black leaves during their later years, when they should be transplanted. For the rest, the vigorous older clumps tend to produce the most attractive flowers.

Soil Asters grow well in any garden soil, but thrive in light calcareous conditions.

Propagation Very easily propagated by division. With older plants, discard the centre of the clumps and use only the outer parts.

Diseases Asters are very prone to

Aster novi-belgii 'Harrison's Blue'

Aster farreri 'Berggarten'

attack by mildew, fusarium wilt and aster wilt (verticillium wilt). The affected plants should be uprooted and burned.

Aster × alpellus
○ ○ ⊛

A cross between *A. alpinus* and *A. amellus*, also known as 'Triumph', this plant bears a profusion of purple flowers with an orange centre, and grows up to 6 in (15 cm) high. It makes a good edging plant.

Aster alpinus
Rock aster, from the Alps, central and southern Europe and Russia. Growing 4–8 in (10–20 cm) high, it flowers from June to July during the first year, and from May onwards in subsequent years. With its blue or red-purple flowers, it is attractive as an edging plant, or it can be planted out in larger groups at the front of the border, set 8 to 10 in (20–25 cm) apart. 'Albus Giganteus' has large white flowers; those of 'Dunkle Schöne' are deep

Aster sedifolius

Aster amellus 'King George'

Aster novae-angliae 'Harrington's Pink'

Autumn asters stand out well

violet, and those of 'Wargrave Pink' are lilac-pink with a yellow centre.

Aster amellus

○ ○ ⊛ ⊗

Italian aster, found in central and southern Europe, and the Near East. An exceptionally attractive garden plant, it grows 1–2 ft (30–60 cm) high, flowering between midsummer and early autumn according to the variety. The wild species bears lilac-blue flowers for about one month. Highly recommended cultivars are 'Lac de Genève', 2½ft (75 cm) high, with lavender-blue flowers; 'King George', 2 ft (60 cm) high, with violet-blue flowers; 'Lady Hindlip', a 2 ft (60 cm) plant with rose-pink flowers; 'Sonia', which has the same characteristics as 'Lady Hindlip'; and 'Sternkugel', which grows 1½ft (45 cm) high and has lavender flowers. Because of their compact habit, most cultivars need not be staked.

Aster chinensis, see *Callistephus chinensis*.

Aster cordifolius

From North America, this 2–5 ft (60–150 cm) plant produces small pale violet flowers in autumn. It is a very attractive ornamental plant and has splendid foliage.

Aster dumosus hybrids

Raised by crossing *A. dumosus* with *A. novi-belgii*, these late autumn-flowering plants grow between 6 in and 2 ft (15–60 cm) in height. Some of the best-known cultivars are 'Alice Haslam', 1 ft (30 cm) high with deep pink flowers; 'Diana', 8 in (20 cm) high with light pink flowers; 'Herbstfreude', 2 ft (60 cm) high with lavender flowers; 'Lady in Blue', 1 ft (30 cm) high with pure blue flowers; 'Peter Harrison', 1½ft (45 cm) high with pink flowers; 'Professor Anton Kippenberg', 1–1½ft (30–45 cm) high with lavender flowers; and 'Schneekissen', which grows up to 1 ft (30 cm) and has pure white flowers.

Aster ericoides

Syn. *A. multiflorus*. Heath aster, from North America. This species grows to heights of 2–3 ft (60–100 cm) and flowers into late autumn, its branching stems densely covered with small white or pink flowers. 'Golden Spray' has creamy flowers.

Aster farreri

A spring-flowering aster from China and Tibet that grows up to 2 ft (60 cm) high with hairy stems. It produces deep violet flowers with an orange centre.

Aster × frikartii

Raised by crossing *A. amellus* with *A. thomsonii*, its flowers, sky-blue with an orange eye, are larger than those of *A. amellus* and are produced from late summer to early autumn. 'Wonder of Stafa' bears extra-large violet-blue flowers, and grows to a height of 2½ft (75 cm).

Aster linosyris

Syn. *Linosyris vulgaris, Crinitaria linosyris*. Goldilocks, from Europe. Growing to heights of 1½–2 ft (45–60 cm), this plant bears bright yellow flowers in compact terminal clusters in late summer.

Aster multiflorus, see *A. ericoides*.

Aster novae-angliae

Michaelmas daisy or New England aster. This popular autumn-flowering plant from North America ranges between heights of 4–6 ft (1.2–2 m). It has hairy stems and its flowers are purple or dark blue with a yellow, reddish-white or purple centre. Many cultivars are listed in catalogues: the best known include 'Barr's Pink', 4–5 ft (1.2–1.5 m) high with bright rose-pink flowers; 'Harrington's Pink', 4–5 ft (1.2–1.5 m) high with clear rose-pink flowers; 'Lye End Beauty', 4–5 ft (1.2–1.5 m) tall bearing phlox-purple flowers of great charm; 'September Ruby', 3½–4 ft (1.1–1.2 m) high with deep rosy-red flowers; and 'Treasure', which grows to 5 ft (1.5 m) high and has violet flowers.

Aster novi-belgii

Michaelmas daisy or (USA only) New York aster. Its height is from 6 in to 6 ft (15 cm–2 m), and it flowers in autumn. The original species bears purple or dark blue flowers but has been superseded by numerous cultivars, several of which are listed below, by colour:

Violet: 'Eventide' and 'Harrison's Blue'.

Light blue: 'Marie Ballard', 'October Dawn' and 'Plenty'.

Purple-pink: 'Fellowship', 'Lassie' and 'Tapestry'.

Ruby-red: 'Winston Churchill' and 'Crimson Brocade'.

Purple-red: 'Melbourne Bell' and 'Twinkle'.

White: 'White Ladies'.

For dwarf cultivars, see under *A. dumosus* hybrids.

Aster sedifolius

From south-eastern Europe and western Asia, this is a plant which grows 2–3 ft (60–100 cm) high and produces lavender-blue flowers with a yellow centre in late summer to early autumn. The most popular cultivar, 'Nanus', is a neat and compact plant, 10 in (25 cm) high with bright mauve flowers.

Aster subcaeruleus, see *A. tongolensis*.

Aster tongolensis

Syn. *A. subcaeruleus*. Originating in north-western India, this is the earliest flowering aster. It bears dark blue flowers with a yellow centre in late spring to early summer. The variety 'Berggarten' is 1½ft (45 cm) high with violet-blue flowers; 'Napsbury' is 1½ft (45 cm) high and has blue flowers.

Aster yunnanensis

A bushy plant from western China, growing 9–12 in (23–30 cm) in height, it produces large, dark blue flowers with a dark brown centre; these are borne on erect stems during May–July.

Astilbe
Saxifragaceae
False goat's beard

These are attractive garden plants for moist ground. If the soil starts to dry out, the leaves of *Astilbe* soon begin to curl up. The only exception is *A. chinensis* var. *pumila*, which is drought resistant.

Soil Any garden soil will do as a basis, enriched if necessary in early spring with a mixture of leaf-mould and well-

Astilbe arendsii hybrid cultivar

rotted manure. Remember to keep the ground moist at all times.

Propagation Astilbes are propagated in spring by division of the rootstock. This is not as easy as it is with most perennial plants: a sharp knife must be placed between two "eyes" and pressed down quickly or hit with a mallet.

Astilbe × arendsii hybrids

○ ◑ ⊛ ○ ⊛ ⊗

A group of hybrid cultivars resulting from crosses between various *Astilbe* spp, these make most attractive garden plants, particularly in groups beside water. They grow 2–4 ft (60–120 cm) high and in summer bear flowers in loose panicles in various shades of crimson, pink, rosy-lilac and white. Among the recommended cultivars are the following, arranged by colour:

Garnet-red to salmon pink: 'Fanal', 'Fire' and 'Venus'.

Light to dark purple: 'Amethyst' and 'Federsee'.

White: 'White Gloria'.

Astilbe arendsii hybrids, excellently suited to the banks of pools and ponds

Astilbe chinensis pumila

Astilbe chinensis var. **pumila**
Ⓘ ⊖ ⊗ ◐ ⊖
A 1 ft (30cm) high, spreading plant that bears plumes of pink flowers from mid-summer to autumn. This variety is fairly drought resistant.

Astilbe japonica
○ Ⓘ ⊗ ◐ ⊖
Growing 1½–3ft (45–100cm) high, this species has reddish leaf stalks and produces white flowers in late spring to early summer. All garden varieties are hybrids, and include 'Red Sentinel', 2 ft (60cm) high with bright red flowers; 'Mainz', 1½–2ft (45–60cm) high, and 'Koblenz', 2ft (60cm) high, both with bright red to violet-pink flowers; and 'Deutschland', which is 2 ft (60cm) high and bears white flowers.

Astilbe thunbergii
Growing to heights of 2–3ft (60–100cm), the entire plant is covered with brownish hair. It is not widely cultivated. In midsummer it bears white or lilac-pink blooms.

Astrantia
Umbelliferae
Masterwort

These are beautiful border plants with distinctive flower shapes.
Soil They will grow in any garden soil, but although they are easily cultivated, they should be kept out of the midday sun.
Propagation From seed sown in September. Overwinter in a cold frame and transplant in spring; keep them in a nursery bed for one year. Plants may also be propagated by division in spring.

Astrantia **helleborifolia**, see *A. maxima*.
Astrantia major
Ⓘ ⊗ ◐ ⊗
Widely distributed in Europe and the Near East, this herbaceous perennial grows 1–2ft (30–60cm) high, and in early to midsummer bears attractive

Astrantia maxima, Masterwort

clusters of small white flowers tinged with a pink to purple-red shade.
Astrantia maxima
Syn. *A. helleborifolia*. From the Caucasus and Turkey, this plant is more graceful than *A. major* with trifoliate leaves and rose-pink flower heads in summer.

Athyrium filix-femina, lady fern

Aubrieta hybrids

Athyrium
Athyriaceae

Hardy garden ferns, easily cultivated in a sheltered position, *Athyrium* spp should be transplanted every three or four years because some species tend to become invasive.
Soil Plant in humus-rich garden soil.
Propagation Can be either from spores or by division in spring.

Athyrium filix-femina
Ⓘ Ⓘ ⊗ ◐ ⊗
Lady fern. A clump-forming fern with elongated, bipinnate green fronds, growing 2½–3½ft (75–115cm) high. The shape of the fronds varies among the several cultivars. This fern will tolerate a great deal of sunlight, provided the soil is kept moist, but it prefers partial shade.

Aubrieta
Cruciferae

Exceptionally attractive plants that form graceful mats of spring-flowering rock plants, and make a colourful display in sites such as dry-stone walls or when grown between paving stones. They are seen to good advantage when planted out in large groups; and they combine most attractively with *Alyssums*.

Soil A well-drained, calcareous garden soil is preferred, not too loose or dry, lest the roots become overheated. An addition of sandstone rubble will help to reduce the temperature of the soil. They grow best in a sunny situation.

Propagation By division or by cuttings. Good results can also be obtained by sowing in spring in a cold frame, but cultivars do not breed true when grown from seed.

Aubrieta × cultorum, see *Aubrieta* hybrids.

Berries of *Aucuba japonica*

Aubrieta hybrids
○ ⊖ ○ ⊛ ⊗

Syn. *A. × cultorum*. This name covers the only cultivars of interest to gardeners. The plants flower in spring and are low-growing, only 2–4 in (5–10 cm) high. Well-known cultivars include 'Ashtead Purple', which has dark violet-purple flowers; 'Blue King', a pure blue variety; 'Double Pink', with lilac-pink double flowers; and 'Lavender', which has lavender-blue flowers.

Aucuba
Cornaceae

Ornamental plants well suited to growth in tubs and boxes in shady courtyards, in conservatories, and indoors as house plants. *Aucuba* spp are content with very little light and are prized for their most attractive leaves and berries. They are not completely hardy, but will tolerate normal winters, especially when sheltered against the morning sun.

Soil Humus-rich, fertile and moist garden soil.

Propagation From cuttings taken in autumn and overwintered in a cold frame.

Aucuba japonica
○ ◑ ◔ ◍ ⊛ ⊗

An evergreen shrub from Japan that grows 6–12 ft (2–4 m) high. The flowers, borne in spring, are inconspicuous, but the female plants bear most attractive clusters of bright scarlet berries. The plant is variable in leaf

shape and glossiness. There are two cultivar groups, those with lustrous plain green leaves and those variably yellow flecked or spotted by a benign virus infection. Among the latter, often known as spotted laurels, the following are recommended: 'Crotonifolia' and 'Speckles' (both male clones) and 'Gold Dust' and 'Variegata Maculata' (both females). The two best green-leaved cultivars are 'Longifolia', a free-fruiting female, and 'Lance Leaf', the male equivalent.

Begonia
Begoniaceae

Two *Begonia* spp are of particular importance to the gardener: *B. semperflorens* cultivars provide some of the most popular summer bedding plants, while the tuberous species can also be grown in tubs and pots. The second group lasts longer because the tubers survive the winter.

Soil *Semperflorens* begonias require humus-rich soil that must never be allowed to dry out; it is advisable to mix in large quantities of peat. The tuberous types also grow best in humus-rich soil; if necessary, add a good layer of peat.

Propagation *Semperflorens* begonias are grown from seed, generally in late winter to spring under glass at a temperature of 16°C (61°F), then hardened off, and planted out May–June, when they will flower until autumn. Tuberous begonias can be propagated from seed, from stem cuttings or by division of the tubers. Seed does not

always produce plants that are true to type. The tubers should be divided in the spring after they have sprouted, each section having at least one "eye". The wound must be allowed to dry and dusted with a mixture of sulphur and charcoal to prevent bleeding and fungus attack. Stem cuttings are taken when young growths are visible. It is usual to leave a small section or heel of the tuber attached to the young shoot.

Diseases Powdery mildew is the most troublesome disease to attack begonias. It can be prevented by regular applications of fertilizer and by keeping the soil sufficiently moist.

Begonia semperflorens
○ ◑ ⊙ ⊛

These well-known perennials are usually cultivated as annuals, and make popular bedding plants in either tall (1½ ft/45 cm), medium-sized (10 in/25 cm) or dwarf (6–8 in/15–20 cm) cultivars. Flowers are white, pink, orange or red, and foliage green or bronze. The better cultivars will stand up to fairly bad weather; most of them are F_1 hybrids. Because there are so many different sorts, the reader is advised to consult the appropriate catalogues. The plants are usually sold ready for planting in late spring to early summer, and are set out while in bloom. They should be shaded from the midday sun and, to obtain the best results, grown under glass.

Tuberous begonias
◑ ⊛ ⊗

This group includes all the species and varieties whose top growth dies in the autumn. There are several groups, the best known being the camellia-

flowered (*camelliaeflora*) and rose-flowered (*rosaeflora*) cultivars and 'Bertinii', a profusely flowering plant with bright orange-red, pendulous and elongated flowers. There are also the cultivars of pendulous habit, well suited for growing in hanging baskets. If tuberous begonias are planted out, they should be shaded from the midday sun. The plants will continue to flower until the first frosts, when the top growth should be cut off and the tubers lifted and dried, preferably in the sun. Place them in dry peat and store in a dark dry place at a temperature of about 5°C (40°F). In January–March, set the tubers into pots in a frame or greenhouse at a minimum temperature of 13°C (55°F); do not move them to their flowering positions until the danger of night frosts is over.

In addition, the following are hardy in sheltered sites. In cold areas they should be mounded over with 4–6 in (10–15 cm) of coarse sand or peat in autumn. Alternatively, the tubers may be lifted when growth is killed by the first frost and stored in barely damp peat in a frost-free, but not warm, place. Do not let them dry out.

Begonia evansiana

This attractive east Asian species grows 1 ft (30 cm) or more tall with somewhat lobed leaves flushed red beneath. The pure pink flowers open from late summer to autumn.

Begonia sutherlandii

Surprisingly hardy considering its South African homeland, this 6 in (15 cm) tall species has an arching habit of growth, reddish-veined pale green leaves and orange flowers from summer to autumn.

Mixed tuberous begonias, *Begonia × tuberhybrida*

Garden daisies, double forms of *Bellis perennis*

Bellis
Compositae
Daisy

The common daisy is widespread and not very popular among gardeners, who consider it an aggressive weed. Good lawns can be ruined, it is true, by daisies spreading from nearby beds. On more natural grassland, however, by the side of shrubs and trees, daisies can make a most attractive picture, for example in combination with narcissi. The large-flowered double cultivars are less invasive and much more showy than the wild species. Although perennials, they flower best when young and are grown as biennials. Daisies can be transplanted even in full bloom.

Soil Daisies grow in every type of adequately moist garden soil.

Propagation Double cultivars can only be cultivated from the seed of flowers that still have some normal, tubular flowers. Sow in midsummer in the open or in a cold frame. Keep the soil moist and partly shaded. The seeds will germinate in a week and will retain their germinating power for three years. Young seedlings should be transplanted several times and later moved to their flowering position and planted out 6 in (15 cm) apart.

Bellis perennis
○ ◑ △ ○ ○
Common meadow or lawn daisy. This species grows up to 6 in (15 cm) high and flowers from March to June. All named varieties belong to the 'Hortensis' group. In practice they are subdivided into (1) small-flowered strains, with flower heads smaller than $1\frac{1}{4}$ in (31 mm) and numerous rolled ray florets in colours ranging from red to white; (2) large-flowered strains, with flower heads larger than $1\frac{1}{4}$ in (31 mm) and names such as 'Enorma', 'Monstrosa', etc. There are several F_1 hybrids that are valued for their uniformity.

Berberis
Berberidaceae
Barberry

Attractive garden shrubs, both deciduous and evergreen, and usually spiny, barberries are simple to cultivate even in fairly poor, dry soil. The ornamental effect of these plants varies and depends on the combined colours of flowers, foliage and fruit. The sun has a marked effect on the colour of the berries which may also vary according to their position at the top or the bottom of the shrub.

Soil Although most species are undemanding, they respond well to doses of fertilizer and humus.

Propagation All botanical species can be grown from seed. Sow in cold frames immediately the berries are ripe; this is usually in November. Garden varieties must be propagated from cuttings of lateral shoots if they are to come true. This is best done from late summer to early autumn. The cuttings should be about 4 in (10 cm) long, and inserted in a cold frame in equal parts (by volume) of peat and sand. It is advisable to dip the cuttings in rooting hormone. Line them out in a nursery row in spring. Suckering species are easily divided during the winter.

Pruning Barberries should be cut back from time to time, otherwise they may become straggly, especially in shady sites. Prune the oldest branches every two to four years, cutting them just above a young lateral shoot near ground level. Shrubs intended for hedging should be cut back to half-size immediately after planting, and trimmed to the required shape every year.

Pests and diseases The leaves of some species may be attacked by rust; *B. vulgaris* is the worst sufferer. Since no cure is known, it is wiser to cultivate resistant species, such as *B. koreana*; however, many gardeners prefer to go ahead with their chosen species and hope for the best. *B. gagnepainii* is attacked by red spider mites. Honey fungus may also occur.

a. Evergreen species

Berberis aquifolium, see *Mahonia aquifolium*.

Berberis buxifolia
○ ◑ ⊕ ⊕ ⊛ ⊛ ⊕ ⊕
Syn. *B. dulcis*. An evergreen shrub from southern Chile reaching a height of 6 ft (2 m). In spring it produces long-stemmed, pendulous, yellow flowers; the berries are large and an attractive blue colour. If planted in sunny positions, this shrub may shed all its leaves in the winter, and it is not recommended for rockeries. It is, however, suitable for clipping into ornamental shapes, much like *Buxus* (q.v.). The variety 'Nana' forms a dense evergreen mound about $1\frac{1}{2}$ ft (45 cm) high and rarely flowers.

Berberis calliantha
A native of Tibet, growing to a height of 3 ft (1 m), this is a compact and hardy plant. Its narrow, glossy leaves are dark-green above and white beneath. It bears small, pale yellow flowers in May. The berries are very dark blue.

Berberis candidula
○ ◑ ⊕ ⊕ ⊕ ⊕
A low-growing, evergreen, dome-shaped shrub from China that is ideal for the larger rock garden, it attains heights of $1\frac{1}{2}$–3 ft (50–100 cm). The leaves are dark green above and white underneath, and the single flowers, which are borne in spring, are large and yellow. The berries are bluish-black and have a waxy bloom.

Berberis darwinii
A profusely flowering shrub that grows to heights of 3–10 ft (1–3 m), it is one of the most beautiful *Berberis* spp. The leaves are dark green above and light green underneath. The shrub is spring-flowering, bearing golden-yellow flowers in dense pendulous clusters. Varieties include 'Firefly', bearing deep-red flowers; and 'Prostrata', which is a dwarf form.

Berberis dulcis, see *B. buxifolia*.

Berberis gagnepainii
From China, this very hardy, rather sombre-looking shrub grows $4\frac{1}{2}$–6 ft (1.3–2 m) high, with dark green leaves that turn reddish-brown in winter. The blue-black berries have a waxy bloom. See also *Berberis* × *hybrido-gagnepainii*.

Berberis hookeri
○ ◑ ⊕ ⊕ ⊛ ⊕ ⊕
A Himalayan shrub with somewhat angular, reddish to brownish branches, reaching a height of $4\frac{1}{2}$ ft (1.3 m). It has yellow to reddish spines up to 6 in (15 cm) long, and glossy, dark green, holly-like leaves that are powdery white underneath. The shrub partly changes colour in autumn, which creates a striking effect. In spring, bright yellow flowers are followed by deep blue berries. *B. hookeri* var. *viridis*, the most common variety, has a somewhat more robust habit and leaves that are green to yellowish-green underneath. Other varieties include 'Nana', a dwarf form height 2–3 ft (60–90 cm).

Berberis × *hybrido-gagnepainii*
A hybrid of *B. gagnepainii* var. *lanceifolia* and *B. verruculosa*. This shrub has a compact habit, and is prized for its magnificent, glossy dark green leaves. It is fairly tolerant of shade, but grows more vigorously and produces more fruit in a sunny position; the berries are bluish-purple. A well-known cultivar is 'Chenaultii', growing up to $1\frac{1}{2}$ ft (1.3 m) high with a broad and compact habit.

Berberis japonica, see *Mahonia japonica*.

Berberis japonica var. *bealii*, see *Mahonia bealii*.

Berberis julianae
○ ◑ ⊕ ⊕ ⊛ ⊕
A fairly tall shrub, up to 5 ft (2 m) high, it has yellow-brown, somewhat angular branches. From late spring to early summer it bears yellow flowers in clusters; the leaves are rather glossy and dark green, some turning bright red in autumn. Its berries are blue with a waxy bloom.

Berberis linearifolia
From Argentina and Chile, and growing no taller than 3 ft (1 m) this shrub is not hardy throughout Great Britain, but grows well in the south and other mild areas. Large orange flowers appear in spring in long clusters. The variety 'Orange King' has orange and apricot flowers.

Berberis × *hybrido-gagnepainii* 'Chenault', a floriferous hybrid

Berberis lologensis

From Chile, a natural hybrid between *B. linearifolia* and *B. darwinii*. It grows to a height of 8–10 ft (2.5–3 m) and has a similar spread. Its leaves and habit are similar to *B. darwinii* and its apricot-coloured flowers are borne in March and April. They are followed by purple berries.

Berberis manipurana

○ ◐ ◑ ⊛ ⊛ ⊕ ⊗

A robust shrub with angular branches that attains heights of 3–4 ft (1–1.2 m) and is good for hedging. It is often listed as *B. hookeri* or *B. xanthoxylon*.

Berberis pinnata, see *Mahonia pinnata*.

Berberis × stenophylla

◔ ◐ ◑ ◐ ⊛ ⊕ ◑

A hardy hybrid of *B. darwinii* and *B. empetrifolia*, this very attractive shrub, up to 6 ft (2 m) high, has graceful arching branches and is most effective when planted in groups near steps and small walls. Because of its spread, up to 10 ft (3 m), it should be planted at least 4½ ft (1.3 m) away from a path or else it will have to be cut back and will lose its attractive shape. It bears golden yellow flowers in spring, followed by round, black berries with a blue-white waxy bloom. The variety 'Autumnalis', a 3 ft

The fruits of *Berberis vulgaris*

Berberis gagnepainii var. *lanceifolia*

(1 m) plant, bears yellow flowers both in spring and autumn. 'Coccinea' has pink flowers and 'Corallina' yellow flowers. 'Crawley Gem' is 2 ft (60 cm) high with a loose habit, and produces yellow flowers (red on the outside) from late spring to early summer and again in autumn. 'Gracilis' is 3 ft (1 m) high and has arching branches and 'Irwinii' is almost spherical, grows up to 2½ ft (75 cm) high, and is very attractive.

Berberis verruculosa

◐ ◑ ◐ ⊛ ⊛

From central China, a very attractive shrub growing up to 5 ft (1.5 m) high, it has spine-toothed leaves, elliptical in

Berberis thunbergii in glorious autumn colours

shape, glossy dark green above and blue-white underneath. The older leaves turn a reddish colour. Large yellow flowers appear from late spring to early summer. The branches of *B. verruculosa* are covered with warts; it is an exceptionally hardy shrub, and is tolerant of shade.

b. Semi-deciduous species
Berberis jamesiana

○ ◑ ⊛ ⊕

A vigorous Chinese shrub up to 10 ft (3 m) high, with leaves that are usually slightly spine-toothed and colour well in autumn. The hanging clusters of small flowers are followed by chains of round, coral-red translucent berries—the plant's chief attraction.

Berberis × mentorensis

○ ◐ ◑ ⊛ ⊕

A cross between *Berberis julianae* and *Berberis thunbergii*, it grows to a height of 4½ ft (1.3 m). Its dull green leaves, which partly turn orange-yellow to red in the autumn, are shed late in the year.

c. Deciduous barberries
Berberis aggregata

○ ◑ ⊛ ⊕

From western China, this fairly low shrub, up to 4½ ft (1.3 m) high, has

narrow leaves and bears long racemes of yellow flowers from late spring to early summer. The beautiful translucent berries are yellow-orange to salmon pink and appear in autumn. See also *Berberis × rubrostilla*.

Berberis chillanensis, see *Berberis montana*.

Berberis dictyophylla

○ ◔ ◔ ◑ ⊛ ⊕

An attractive Chinese shrub up to 4½ ft (1.3 m) high with reddish-brown, rather angular stems covered with a waxy white bloom and with single to triple yellowish-brown spines. The leaves are slightly rounded on top, toothed at the tip and finely veined above, with a white bloom underneath, and are no more than ¾ in (19 mm) long. Bright yellow flowers appear in May, followed by red, almost spherical berries with a white bloom.

Berberis koreana

○ ◑ ⊛ ⊕

This very hardy Korean shrub grows stiffly upwards to a height of 4½ ft (1.3 m). Its spines are very variable in shape; the leaves are dull green and turn deep red in autumn. The bright red berries are retained for a very long period. *B. koreana* is resistant to the fungus wheat rust.

Berberis montana

Syn. *Berberis chillanensis*. Native to Chile, this plant grows to a height of 6 ft (2 m) with a spread of 4–6 ft (1.2–2 m). Its angular branches bear mid-green leaves and, in April and May, solitary yellow and orange flowers 1 in (2.5 cm) across appear. They are followed by black berries.

Berberis × ottawensis

○ ◑ ⊛ ⊕ ◑

A cross between *B. thunbergii* and *B. vulgaris*, this shrub is often confused with *B. thunbergii*. It has robust reddish-brown branches and rounded leaves; the yellow flowers, borne in clusters, generally have pink sepals, and are followed by red berries. The variety 'Decora' has dull purple-blue leaves, while those of 'Superba' are purple-red.

Berberis × rubrostilla

○ ◔ ◔ ◑ ⊛ ⊕

This is the collective name of *B. aggregata* and *B. wilsoniae*, and includes a host of generally unfamiliar cultivars. The best known is 'Buccaneer', an attractive plant that bears large red, orange-red and partly greenish-white berries in profusion. 'Barbarossa' bears clusters of scarlet berries. It grows vigorously.

The salmon-pink fruits of *Berberis wilsoniae* in the autumn

Berberis candidula

Berberis sieboldii
A Japanese berberis of compact habit, with a height and spread of 3–4 ft (1–1.2 m). The bright green, elliptic leaves turn a vivid crimson in autumn and are borne on dark red shoots. The flowers are yellow and appear in May; they are followed by spherical bright red berries.

Berberis thunbergii
○ ⊕ ⊛ ⊛ ⊙

From Japan, this low, branching shrub grows up to 4½ ft (1.3 m) tall. From late spring to early summer it produces yellow flowers, followed by the striking scarlet berries that make this one of the most beautiful of all the barberries. Particularly handsome is the variety 'Atropurpurea', whose magnificent reddish-purple leaves make the plant a blaze of colour, especially in autumn. It bears relatively few berries. 'Atropurpurea Nana' is a dwarf variety no taller than 1½ ft (45 cm) with a spread of 2–3 ft (60–100 cm). 'Erecta', by contrast, is an upright variety, as is 'Red Pillar', which has red leaves; both are excellent for low hedges.

Berberis vulgaris
◑ ◐ ⊛ ⊙ ⊙

Common barberry. A dense shrub that will tolerate a great deal of shade, growing to heights of 6–7 ft (2 m). It will flourish under large trees and is useful for hedging; the roots are poisonous. Light yellow flowers are borne in dense clusters during May–June, followed by dark red berries. The variety 'Atropurpurea' has wine-purple foliage.

Berberis wilsoniae
A very compact shrub with a spreading habit that grows up to 3 ft (1 m) high. The sea-green leaves turn soft shades of red in autumn; the berries are round and coral-red. *B. wilsoniae* var. *stapliana* has a more erect habit, bluish-green leaves and oval berries.

Bergenia × schmidtii with evergreen foliage

Bergenia
Saxifragaceae

These attractive, hardy herbaceous perennials (formerly known as *Megasea*) with their large ornamental leaves and dense clusters of flowers are particularly useful beside pools. They should be planted out 1–1½ ft (30–45 cm) apart, preferably in large groups.

Soil A moist but well-drained soil fairly rich in humus is preferred, but almost any garden soil will do, either in sun or, preferably, in partial shade.

Propagation By division.

Bergenia cordifolia

This spring-flowering plant, from the Altai Mountains of the USSR, grows 12–18 in (30–45 cm) high and has heart-shaped leaves. The flowers are usually lilac-rose, but white in 'Alba' and purple-pink in 'Purpurea'. Some of the most recent hybrid cultivars include 'Abendglut', syn. 'Evening Glow', which has bright purple-red flowers; 'Morgenröte', syn. 'Dawn', having pale pink flowers; and 'Silberlicht', syn. 'Silver Light', whose flowers are white, ageing to pink.

Bergenia crassifolia

From the Altai Mountains, USSR, *B. crassifolia* flowers from winter to spring and bears fairly large, pale pink blooms; it has large ovate leaves.

Bergenia delavayi, see *B. purpurascens*.

Bergenia purpurascens

Syn. *B. delavayi*. A plant growing 8–15 in (20–38 cm) high, in spring it bears bell-shaped purple flowers in loose panicles. It has large, ovate, dark green leaves with an attractive autumn colouring.

Bergenia × schmidtii

A cross between *B. crassifolia* and *B. ciliata*. The leaves are fringed and wedge-shaped at the base; tall, flat-topped clusters of violet-pink flowers are produced from February onwards. The plant is sensitive to late frosts.

Betula
Betulaceae
Birch

Ornamental trees for medium-sized and larger gardens. The beautiful white bark of many species makes them exceptionally attractive; in young trees the bark is often green before it changes colour. In general, the poorer the soil, the whiter the stem will be. Because of its open crown, the birch does not make nearly as much shade as many other trees. Those species which come into growth early should be planted where they are protected against wind and frost.

Soil Birches are best suited to poor sandy soil or peat (that is, an acid soil), but they also thrive on good loam. *B. pubescens* and *B. nigra* will also grow on a moister type of acid soil.

Propagation From seed.

Diseases Honey fungus and bracket fungi of various types, rust, and witches' brooms are the most prevalent diseases.

Betula alba, see *B. pendula* and *B. pubescens*.

Betula alleghaniensis, see *B. lutea*.

Betula costata

A fine tree for parks, it reaches up to 40 ft (12 m) in height and has a fairly firm, yellow-brown bark. The catkins are always erect, and the leaves are firm and narrow with a rounded base.

Betula ermanii

This tree is sometimes multi-stemmed, and grows up to 65 ft (20 m) high. It has a very attractive orange-brown bark that changes to creamy white as the tree gets older. It can be damaged by spring frosts.

Betula jacquemontii

A birch tree that strongly resembles *B. utilis* but with a vivid white trunk. It reaches a height of 40 ft (13 m). The leaves are smooth on both surfaces and are usually doubly serrated.

Betula lutea

Syn. *B. alleghaniensis*. A tall, robust tree growing 50–65 ft (15–20 m) high with a spread of 20–25 ft (7–8 m). The peeling bark is amber coloured and the leaves dark green.

Birches are loved mainly for their winter colours. *Betula costata* after shedding its leaves

Betula medwediewii
A very hardy shrubby tree with a yellow-grey bark.

Betula nana
Dwarf birch. A compact, dome-shaped shrub, no taller than 3 ft (1 m), with thin, downy branches. This plant looks well on slopes, in low hedges or the rock garden.

Betula nigra
○ ⊗ ❋ ⊘ ⊥

River birch. A large tree growing up to 65 ft (20 m) high with hairy branches spreading 25–30 ft (8–9 m). Its reddish-brown, peeling bark later turns somewhat lighter; the leaves are 1–3 in (25–27 cm) in length, diamond-shaped, pointed and wedge-shaped at the base, and covered with white down underneath. The river birch thrives on moist soil.

Betula papyrifera
○ ⊖ ❋ ⊘ ⊥

Paper birch. A tall tree that grows up to 80 ft (25 m) high with a spread of 35–40 ft (10–12 m). It has an attractive crown, with pendulous, rather hairy branches and white papery bark over a beautiful browny-red stem. The leaves are 4–8 in (10–20 cm) long, ovate, rounded at the base, and at first hairy underneath, later becoming hairless.

The catkins of *Betula nigra*

Betula medwediewii, a shrubby tree with a lovely autumn colour

The common white birch, *Betula pubescens*, in a heather garden

Betula pendula
Syn. *B. alba*, *B. verrucosa*. Silver birch. A distinctive tree with white peeling bark that grows up to 80 ft (25 m) high and spreads up to 35 ft (10 m). Its twigs are covered with warts, and the leaves are 1–2½ in (25–63 mm) long, diamond-shaped, pointed, and wedge-shaped at the base. The cultivar 'Dalecarlica', or 'Swedish birch', has prettily cut leaves and resembles 'Laciniata', although the buds on its young shoots are flattened whereas those of 'Laciniata' are pointed. 'Laciniata', too, has a deeply cut leaf, and while highly ornamental is not as robust as 'Dalecarlica'. 'Fastigiata' has an erect crown, and 'Gracilis' has low, arching branches; 'Purpurea' has purple leaves that eventually turn bronze-green; 'Tristis' is a weeping birch with slender pendulous branches and a narrow symmetrical head. 'Youngii' (Young's weeping birch) has a dome-shaped head and is often planted at the edge of pools; it is more suited to smaller gardens since it does not grow as large as that great waterside favourite, the weeping willow.

Betula populifolia
Grey birch. This tree is the American counterpart of the British silver birch. It grows up to 65 ft (20 m) high with an

Betula jacquemontii

irregular crown, and is mainly planted in parks.

Betula pubescens
Syn. *B. alba*. Common white birch. In height this tree reaches up to 65 ft (20 m), and has a variable spread of 25–65 ft (8–20 m). The bark is white and peeling, the branches downy and rather pendulous. Leaves are ¾–1½ in (19–38 mm) long, diamond-shaped,

Betula pendula is always attractive but never more so than in the winter

pointed, generally wedge-shaped at the base, and hairy at first on the underside then later chiefly in the nerve axils. The variety 'Urticifolia' has pointed, very deeply cut leaves.

Betula utilis
Himalayan birch. An erect, fairly tall tree suitable for parks and larger gardens, with very beautiful white bark.

Betula verrucosa, see B. pendula.

Bilderdykia
Polygonaceae
Knotweed

These climbing plants, more commonly described as *Polygonum*, are highly rampant and vigorous and can very quickly cover unsightly walls, sheds, etc.
Soil It grows on all soils, including calcareous types.
Propagation In July–August from heel cuttings or from seed.

Bilderdykia aubertii
Syn. *Polygonum aubertii*. A vigorous climbing shrub producing reddish young shoots and in late summer a profusion of greeny-white flowers borne in rough pendulous panicles. It is much confused with *B. baldschuanica*.

Bilderdykia baldschuanica
Syn. *Polygonum baldschuanicum*. Russian vine. Less vigorous than *B. aubertii*, with which it is often confused, the young shoots of this plant do not have a reddish tinge, while the flowers are less profuse, pink in colour and borne in smooth, erect panicles.

Brunnera
Boraginaceae

Hardy herbaceous perennials, highly recommended for planting at the front of borders.
Soil They prefer a rich garden soil.
Propagation By division, from seed or from root cuttings.

The fast-growing *Bilderdykia*

Brunnera macrophylla

Brunnera macrophylla
Syn. *Anchusa myosotidiflora*. A hardy herbaceous perennial from the sub-alpine forests of the western Caucasus. It grows 12–18in (30–45cm) high, flourishing in light shade, though it is fairly tolerant of deep shade. It has large leaves and in spring bears flowers in blue sprays reminiscent of forget-me-nots. 'Variegata', whose leaves are variegated, looks most attractive in shady parts of the garden.

Buddleja (Buddleia)
Buddlejaceae

A genus of attractive spring- and summer-flowering shrubs. Many are hardy; half-hardy species are best grown against a warm, preferably south- or west-facing wall. Even if the branches should be killed by frost, most will send up new shoots from the base and come into flower on the annual wood. All branches of *B. davidii* should be cut back severely in spring. A charming aspect of these plants is the large number of butterflies that the purple flowers attract.
Soil Buddlejas thrive on rich loam, and are tolerant of lime. Add well-rotted stable manure every year.
Propagation From cuttings with a heel, grown in a cold frame, or from seed sown under glass.

Buddleja alternifolia
A hardy shrub from China that grows up to 10ft (3m) high with long, thin, arching branches. The alternate leaves are 2–4in (5–10cm) long and narrowly lanceolate. The violet, sweet-scented flowers are borne in clusters in early summer on the previous year's growth. This species should be pruned after flowering, not in spring. 'Argentea' has silvery leaves.

Buddleja colvilei
This Himalayan species has the largest flowers of all buddlejas, individual flores being up to ¾in (2cm) wide and of a deep rose shade. The shrub, which can grow 15ft (4.5m) or more tall, is somewhat tender when young but reasonably hardy when mature. It is best against a sunny wall, where it flowers more freely. *B. c.* 'Kewensis' has red flowers.

Buddleja crispa
Syn. *B. paniculata*. A liberal coating of

white woolly hairs on the stems and leaves renders this one of the most conspicuous of buddlejas when out of bloom. The leaves are cordate at the base and 2–5in (5–13cm) long. Fragrant, white-eyed lilac flowers in panicles up to 4in (10cm) long open from summer to early autumn. It is best in a sunny sheltered site.

Buddleja davidii
Syn. *B. variabilis*. Butterfly bush, from China. This shrub reaches heights of up to 9ft (2.7m) with long, spreading branches and leaves 6–10in (15–25cm). The scented flowers are borne in slightly arching, plume-shaped clusters. Its numerous varieties include 'Black Knight', which has dark violet-purple flowers in magnificent long trusses; 'Border Beauty', bearing deep crimson trusses, is not as tall as 'Black Knight' and is particularly recommended; 'Empire Blue' has rich violet-blue flowers with an orange eye, and is fairly compact in its habit. *B. davidii* var. *nanhoensis* is a compact and spreading shrub with cylindrical panicles of mauve flowers; 'Royal Red' is a tall shrub that bears massive panicles of purple-red flowers and 'White Profusion' produces large panicles of white flowers with a yellow eye.

Buddleja davidii 'Empire Blue'

Buddleja alternifolia

Buddleja davidii × fallowiana hybrids

○ ⊘ ⊞ ⊥

These vigorous hybrids are similar to *B. davidii* but are more white and woolly on the stems and leaf undersides. Best known is 'Lochinch', which grows to a height of 6 ft (2 m), has a wide spread and bears violet-blue scented flowers.

Buddleja fallowiana

A native of China, this 6–10 ft (2–3 m) tall shrub has willow-like, long pointed leaves densely white felted beneath. The many fragrant lavender flowers are carried in cylindrical, tapered panicles to 8 in (20 cm) or more long in summer. *B. f.* 'Alba' has orange-eyed, milk-white blossoms.

Buddleja farreri

This tall Chinese species is one of the

Bulbocodium vernum, an early bloomer

Buphthalmum salicifolium

finest of the spring-flowering group of buddlejas, producing fragrant rose-lilac blossom as early as April. The large almost triangular leaves are densely white and woolly beneath and velvety above. It needs a sheltered position in full sun to thrive and flower well.

Buddleja globosa

○ ⊞ ⓨ ⊗ ⊥

From Chile and Peru, this is a partly evergreen shrub, 10–16 ft (3–5 m) high, with leaves that are dark green above, buff and felted beneath. Usually it is grown for its loose clusters of globose heads of orange flowers which open in midsummer.

Buddleja officinalis

Regrettably, this autumn- and winter-flowering species is only half-hardy and requires the most sheltered site to

Butomus umbellatus, flowering rush, indispensable in the pond

thrive. It is worth trying however, even if the floral display is spoilt by frost or completely ruined in cold winters. The flowers are a light mauve and delightfully fragrant. The leaves are grey woolly beneath and semi-evergreen.
Buddleja variabilis, see *B. davidii*.
Buddleja × weyeriana
A cross between *B. davidii* and *B. globosa*. This unusual-looking hybrid has spherical heads of orange, mauve-tinted flowers borne in elongated panicles.

Bulbocodium
Liliaceae

A genus of small, poisonous, bulbous plants, suitable either for naturalizing in grass or on the rock garden.
Soil A moist soil is preferred.
Propagation From offsets every 2–3 years.

Bulbocodium vernum

○ ⓐ ⓨ ⊘ ⊗

Syn. *Colchicum bulbocodium*, *Colchicum vernum*. From the Caucasus and the Alps, this plant is 8 in (20 cm) high and produces its violet-purple flowers from February to April. The leaves start to develop at approximately the same time as the flowers.

Buphthalmum
Compositae

Pleasant perennial plants for the front row of the border.
Soil They grow on any garden soil that is kept moist.
Propagation By division, and also from seed. Sow from early spring to summer. The plants will come into flower during the second or third year.

Buphthalmum salicifolium

○ ⊗ ○ ⓨ ⊗

Ox-eye. A plant growing 1½–2 ft (45–60 cm) high and bearing flowers

with yellow heads in summer. Unless these are dead-headed regularly, the plants start to look untidy. They are excellent for cutting.

Butomus
Butomaceae
Flowering rush

A rush-like plant with sword shaped leaves that grows wild by the waterside. It is suitable for planting beside large garden ponds.
Soil It will grow on any soil covered with water to a depth of up to 16 in (40 cm).
Propagation From seed or by division.

Butomus umbellatus

○ ⊗ ⓐ ⓨ ⓨ

Flowering rush. It grows 2–4 ft (60–120 cm) high, and bears dense umbels of pink, red or white flowers from May to September.

Buxus
Buxaceae
Box

A genus of hardy evergreen shrubs used for hedging and often for ornamental clipping or topiary. Most species reach a very old age. The foliage, which is poisonous, has a characteristic sweet smell.
Soil Any good, fairly moist garden soil will do, preferably in a sunny or not too shaded position.
Propagation From cuttings taken in late summer. Insert them in a cold frame, and when rooted line out in nursery rows in spring, and grow them for two years before setting them out in their permanent position.

Buxus sempervirens is easily clipped

Calceolaria × fruticohybrida

Buxus sempervirens 'Handsworthensis'

Buxus microphylla

○ ⓘ ⓐ ⊗ ⊛

A dwarf shrub with narrow oblong leaves.
Buxus microphylla ssp. koreana
Korean boxwood, an extremely hardy dwarf shrub, more commonly planted than *B. microphylla*. Its evergreen leaves are ½–1 in (6–12 mm) long.
Buxus sempervirens

○ ⓘ ⊗ ⓐ ⊗ ⊛ ○ ⓓ ⓘ

A plant widely distributed in southern Europe, North Africa, the Near East and China. In its natural habitats they make a green undergrowth in open forests. As shrubs or small trees they can grow up to 25 ft (8 m) high. Some of the best-known cultivars include 'Aureovariegata', with yellow-green variegated leaves; 'Elegans', a dwarf variety with small, white-edged leaves;

'Handsworthensis', a robust shrub with 1 in (25 mm) long, dark green leaves; 'Latifolia', which has a vigorous spreading habit and is suitable for hedges up to 6 ft (2 m) tall; 'Marginata', a large variety with an erect habit and possessing yellow-edged leaves; and 'Suffruticosa', a dwarf shrub with small, ovate leaves, also known as 'edging box'.

Calendula officinalis in the border

A red variety of the summer-flowering China aster, *Callistephus chinensis*

grown alongside other shrubs. Plants often die down in severe winters, but generally produce new shoots and flower again next summer, though perhaps later than usual. The most striking features are the beautiful lilac berries.
Soil They like a humus-rich, moist but well-drained garden soil.
Propagation From seed or from cuttings grown under glass.

Callicarpa bodinieri var. *giraldii*

Syn. *C. giraldii*. A fairly hardy shrub from western China that grows up to 8 ft (2.4 m) high with dull green leaves that take on beautiful autumn tints. They produce a lavish display of lilac flowers in early to mid-summer followed by round violet-purple berries in autumn and winter.

Blue and white-flowered China asters

Callicarpa dichotoma

Syn. *C. koreana*. A hardy, compact shrub, up to 5 ft (1.5 m) high, bearing deep lilac berries.
Callicarpa giraldii, see *C. bodinieri* var. *giraldii*.
Callicarpa koreana, see *C. dichotoma*.

Callistephus
Compositae
China aster

A single species of half-hardy annual, popular for bedding and also grown for cutting. It is easily cultivated provided gardeners remember that asters can be attacked by wilt disease and ideally should not be grown in the same ground for more than two years in succession.
Soil Any fertile, moisture-retentive but well-drained soil is suitable.
Propagation Sow in early spring in a frame or greenhouse at 15–18°C (60–65°F) and plant out in the flowering position a month or so later. Plant the smaller cultivars 6–8 in (15–20 cm) apart, and the taller 1 ft (30 cm) apart.
Pests and diseases China asters are susceptible to various diseases. Young plants may be attacked and killed off by seedling blight; mature plants are often infected with callistephus wilt, but more often than not only when the plants are not in peak condition, usually because they have been crowded together, given too little light, too much moisture, etc. Quite often the leaves of young China asters will begin to curl up: the culprits are usually aphids.

Callicarpa bodinieri var. *giraldii*

Calceolaria
Scrophulariaceae
Slipperwort

Some of the annuals in this genus, which is also known as pouch flower, are particularly useful garden plants, admired for their profuse and highly ornamental flowers. They look at their best planted together in large groups. The plants are suitable for growing in rockeries as well as flower beds.
Soil Plants grow best in humus-rich garden soil.
Propagation From seeds, sown in March or early April under glass. Transplant to their flowering position in May or sow in late April in the flowering position and thin out to 6 in (15 cm) apart.

Calceolaria × *fructicohybrida*

The collective name for a group of hybrids generally listed as *C. rugosa* or *C. integrifolia*. Generally cultivated as annuals, these plants are very effective in window boxes and tubs. Their leaves are oval, and they bear small yellow or red flowers in dense clusters. If plants are to flower in mid-May, seed must be sown in late autumn.

Calceolaria polyrrhiza

A perennial creeper from Chile, growing up to 1 ft (30 cm) high. Its lanceolate leaves are 2 in (5 cm) long, and its slipper-shaped flowers, yellow with purple-brown spots, appear in early to midsummer.

Calceolaria scabiosifolia

This is one of the most attractive of all

the annual slipperwort species and comes from Peru and Chile. It is an easily cultivated plant and grows to a height of 2 ft (60 cm). In summer or autumn, depending on the sowing time, it produces yellow flowers.

Calendula
Compositae
Marigold

A modest, brightly coloured flower, easily cultivated and very effective in large or small groups.
Soil Marigolds grow in any kind of soil, however poor, but like some lime.
Propagation From seed sown in the flowering position, from April onwards, or in September for June flowers.
Diseases Powdery mildew.

Calendula officinalis

Growing up to 2 ft (60 cm) high, these plants from southern Europe flower 8–10 weeks after sowing and remain in flower until autumn. The yellow and orange blooms should be dead-headed regularly. Very beautiful cultivars are 'Ball's Long Orange', growing 2–2½ ft (60–75 cm) high with large orange double flowers; 'Ball's Gold', of similar size but with pure yellow flowers; 'Golden Emperor', 2 ft (60 cm) high, has very large yellow flowers; those of 'Radio' are orange with rolled margins, a characteristic shared by 'Radio Goudstraal', whose flowers are yellow; 'Tangerine' has dark orange double flowers. New varieties include 'Geisha Girl', which has deep orange, chrysanthemum-shaped flowers, and 'Golden Princess', which has golden-yellow aster-shaped flowers.

Callicarpa
Verbenaceae

A genus of summer-flowering deciduous shrubs that look splendid when

A typical heather garden

Calluna
Ericaceae
Ling, Heather

A widespread genus of hardy ever-greens containing just one cultivated species but with hundreds of named varieties.

Soil Plants grow best in peaty, acid soils.

Propagation From cuttings of young side-shoots taken in late summer and rooted in cold frames.

Pruning Trim the taller varieties lightly with shears before new growth starts in the spring.

Calluna vulgaris

The height and habit, and the colour of flowers and foliage of this plant are very variable. The leaves, however, are uni-versally very small and scale-like, and most species flower between late summer and autumn. The number of cultivars is very large and is being extended all the time. Some of the best known are: 'Alba Erecta', 1½ft (45cm) high, with white flowers and bright green foliage; 'Alba Plena', which is 1–1½ft (30–45cm) high with a spreading habit and bears double white flowers; 'Alportii', growing 2–3ft (60–100cm) high, produces crimson flowers; 'C. W. Nix', a 2ft (60cm) plant, has crimson flowers and thus strongly resembles 'Alportii', but is somewhat less sturdy; 'Elegantissima', which grows up to 2ft (60cm) high, bearing flowers with greyish-green foliage; 'Elsie Purnell', 2½ft (75cm) high, has silvery-pink flowers and is very ornamental; 'Flora Pleno' grows up to 2ft (60cm) high and produces lilac-pink double flowers; 'Gold Haze' is a 2ft (60cm) plant with white flowers and yellow foliage; 'H. E.

Calluna vulgaris 'Gold Haze'

Callistephus chinensis

Syn. *Aster chinensis*. This very popular annual is available in so many cultivars that a full description would fill many more pages than we have to spare. They are grouped according to flower shape: Ball, neat round heads of quilled petals; Chrysanthemum flowered, a self-explanatory group; Ostrich Plume, large heads of long waved petals; Peony flowered, compact heads of incurved petals; and Pompon, small dense heads on dwarf plants. Some of the best-known strains are 'Giants of California', growing 2½ft (75cm) high with a spreading habit and producing flowers mainly in shades of white, blue and pink; 'Bouquet Powder Puffs', 2ft (60cm) high and available in a great variety of shades including fiery red

and bright yellow; 'Dwarf', growing 8in–1ft (20–30cm) with a spreading habit and flowers in shades of red, white and blue; 'Duchess', up to 2½ft (75cm) high, a late-flowering strain with chrysanthemum-shaped flowers measuring 4–6in (10–15cm) across; 'Lilliput', growing 15in (40cm) high with small flowers on long stems; 'Meteor', a strain 2½ft (75cm) high that produces semi-double flowers with tubular ray florets in white, blue, red and yellow shades; 'Pompon', growing to a height of 1½ft (45cm) with spherical flower heads in a great variety of colours; 'Princess', a 2–2½ft (60–75cm) high strain with large double flowers and robust stalks; 'Rose', which grows 2ft (60cm) high with fairly large flowers having loose, curly petals; and 'Ostrich Plume', a 2ft (60cm) high strain with large feathery flowers in red, blue and white shades. In addition, there is 'Unicum Mixed' (spider aster), a plant 1½ft–2ft (45–60cm) high with long, slender, quilled petals in all colours; 'Waldersee Mixed', which reaches a height of 1ft (30cm) and bears a profusion of strangely shaped flowers. Apart from these various groups, all of which have more or less double flowers, there are also some asters with contrast-ing centres. Many of the above-mentioned groups have been carefully selected to be almost immune to disease.

Marsh marigold, *Caltha palustris*

Camellia japonica

Camellia
Theaceae

A genus of mostly hardy evergreen trees and shrubs, best grown in sheltered positions, and also favoured for indoor use. Camellias are among the most popular evergreen shrubs, thanks to their attractive, glossy foliage and to the cup- or bowl-shape of their blooms. These may be single, semi-double, anemone-flowered, peony-flowered, double and formal double.

Soil They need fertile, humus-rich, moist but well-drained lime-free soil.

Propagation From cuttings, layers or from seed.

Camellia japonica

Common camellia, from Japan and Korea. A shrub with glossy, dark green leaves that flowers from February to June; the blooms are red, pink, white or bi-coloured, and occur in many shapes and sizes.

Campanula
Campanulaceae
Bellflower

An important genus of garden plants, most of which are herbaceous perennials, though some species are cultivated as biennials. The genus ranges from small, creeping rock plants to tall flowers usually found in the back row of the border; in short, they offer something for everybody, the more so since they are generally easy to grow.

Soil The soil should not be too dry except for the rock plants in this genus, which are more tolerant of drought. Too much moisture in winter should also be avoided lest the plants rot, and

good drainage is essential. If signs of deterioration appear, it is a good idea to lift and divide the plants if necessary, then replant in fresh soil or the same site after enriching with humus and fertilizer.

Propagation All wild species come true from seed. Perennials can be sown either in autumn or early spring; biennials must be sown in June. Many perennials can also be propagated by division, and all can be grown from cuttings in spring; this is particularly important when it comes to the propagation of garden varieties. Further hints on propagation may be found below.

Campanula caespitosa

An Alpine plant, found in clefts of calcareous rocks where it grows 3–6 in (7.5–15 cm) high. It produces a mat of small tufts, and flowers in summer, bearing light blue bell-shaped flowers, usually one or two on each stem.

Campanula glomerata

From Europe and Asia, a hardy border plant growing 10–24 in (25–60 cm) high. In summer it bears dense heads of erect purple bell-shaped flowers.

Campanula carpatica cultivar

Campanula medium

Campanula persicifolia

Beale' is also 2 ft (60 cm) high, and has rose-pink, double flowers; 'J. H. Hamilton', a 6–9 in (15–23 cm) high plant, has large pink double flowers and green foliage turning bronze in winter; 'Mrs Ronald Gray' is a small plant 2 in (5 cm) high with a creeping habit that has bright green foliage and bears purple flowers; 'Peter Sparkes', 1½ ft (45 cm) high with deep pink double flowers, is a fairly new strain, useful for cutting; 'Rannoch' is 1 ft (30 cm) high with foliage that is bright green, turning yellowish-red at the base; 'Robert Chapman' grows up to 1½ ft (45 cm) with soft purple flowers and orange foliage; and finally 'Tib', 1½ ft (45 cm) high, which bears rosy-red double flowers in great profusion earlier than most other cultivars, from June to September.

Caltha
Ranunculaceae
Marsh marigold

These are hardy herbaceous perennials for moist or marshy ground. They look most attractive round the edges of pools or in shallow water. The single-flowered *C. palustris*, which is common in marshes, is more attractive than the double variety.

Soil Rich, neutral or slightly acid soil is preferred.

Propagation From seeds when ripe, or by division in spring or after flowering.

Caltha palustris

Marsh marigold; kingcup. An attractive European plant with a robust stem, growing to heights of 10–20 in (25–50 cm). It flowers from spring to early summer and often comes back into flower in autumn. The flowers are deep golden-yellow and the foliage is deep green. Garden varieties include 'Multiplex' (syn. 'Plena'), which has double flowers, and 'Monstrosa', whose larger flowers are more fully double.

Campanula persicifolia

Campanula portenschlagiana

'Dahurica' ('Superba') is the most common garden variety, and thrives on rich, calcareous soil. Propagation is by division or from seed (in the open).

Campanula grandis

Syn. *C. latiloba*. This Siberian species is much like the better known *C. persicifolia* and is sometimes confused with it in gardens. In habit it is a stiffer plant with slightly larger stalkless flowers which face outwards.

Campanula lactiflora

From the Caucasus and Armenia, this attractive, clump-forming plant for the border grows 1½–3 ft (45–100 cm) high

Campanula lactiflora, a glorious border plant

Campanula latifolia

Campanula cochleariifolia, ideal for rock gardens

and produces white flowers in summer. 'Lodden Anna' is one of the taller cultivars and bears pink flowers in clusters; 'Pouffe' is 1 ft (30 cm) high with bright blue flowers, and 'Pritchard's Variety', a 2 ft (60 cm) variety, has lavender-blue flowers.

Campanula latifolia
Great bellflower, from central and southern Europe. A robust plant, 2–6 ft (60 cm–2 m) high, with sturdy stems and large ovate to oblong leaves. The flowering period is in mid summer, when it bears 1½–2 in (4–5 cm) long light violet to dark blue flowers; the cultivar 'Alba' has white flowers. The blooms are carried on long, leafy spikes, and are usually nodding. A good border plant requiring little attention, it is also suitable for clearings in copses where it will readily seed itself.

Campanula medium
Canterbury bell. Originally from southern Europe, this is a robust, summer-flowering plant with a pyramidal habit. It grows to heights of 2–3 ft (60–100 cm) and produces large, pendant, bell-shaped violet flowers. Garden varieties are also available in blue, white, pink, carmine, lilac and also in white with blue stripes. An unusual cultivar is 'Calycanthema' ('cup and saucer'), in which the leaf-shaped sepals are the same colour as the petals. Seeds should be sown May–June; prick out young plants in pans or boxes as soon as possible, then into nursery rows and plant out in autumn.

Campanula muralis, see *C. portenschlagiana*.

Campanula persicifolia
This glorious border plant, native to Europe and Siberia, grows 1½–3 ft (45–100 cm) high and flowers in early to midsummer. It has very large, short-stemmed, soft purple-blue, saucer-shaped flowers, and peach-like leaves. The flower stems are sufficiently robust not to need support. Exceptionally beautiful cultivars are 'Alba' with large white flowers, and 'Grandis', with blue. 'Planiflora' and the white 'Planiflora Alba' are dwarfs 9–12 in (23–30 cm) tall. Of confused naming, they are still sometimes listed as "Campanula nitida", a name of no botanical standing. Propagation is by division; these plants thrive in fertile, humus-rich soil.

Campanula portenschlagiana
Syn. *C. muralis*. One of the most beautiful and graceful of the creeping bellflowers, and very easily cultivated, this species of Dalmatian origin is particularly suited to the rock garden. It grows about 4 in (10 cm) high and yields an abundance of deep blue-purple flowers in summer. The attractive 'Birch Hybrid', which has larger, purple-blue flowers, grows 6 in (15 cm) high and flowers June–September. All cultivars provide rapid ground cover and are excellent for garden walls and semi-shady positions. They grow in any well-drained soil. Propagation is easiest by division.

Campanula poscharskyana
A quick-growing plant, it bears star-shaped, lavender-blue flowers on 1½ ft (45 cm) stems in summer. The sepals are downy white. The species resembles a vigorous *C. garganica*, and flourishes on walls and in well-drained positions.

Campanula pusilla, see *C. cochleariifolia*.

Campanula pyramidalis
A half-hardy border perennial from southern Europe, usually grown as a biennial, it flowers in midsummer and grows up to 6 ft (2 m) high. Light blue or violet flowers are borne in groups of three on broad spikes. If grown from seed, this species will flower just over a year later, and thereafter seed itself. Care must be taken to identify the seedlings so that they are not weeded by accident.

Campanula rapunculoides
A profusely flowering, fast-spreading plant, 1–3 ft (30–100 cm) high, that produces small violet flowers borne on short stems in late spring to midsummer. Once established, it is almost ineradicable, and while excellent suited to naturalization it can degenerate into an undesirable weed.

Campanula rotundifolia
Harebell or bluebell of Scotland. Growing up to 8 in (20 cm) high, it bears nodding, bell-shaped blue flowers in midsummer.

Campanula thyrsoidea
This 1–1½ ft (30–45 cm) Alpine plant produces a single rosette in the first year, followed during the second year by a leafy stem with sulphur-yellow flowers in a dense pyramidal spike. It thrives on calcareous soil.

Campsis
Bignoniaceae
Trumpet creeper

A genus of attractive climbing plants with striking pinnate leaves and trumpet-shaped flowers that flourish in sheltered sites in full sun. They are very attractive when grown against walls, to which they will cling like ivy, though extra support should be provided in the form of vertical wires. Flowers may not emerge for several seasons. During the

Flowers of *Campsis radicans*

first few years, the plants should be cut back hard so that they bush out from the base. Later, it is enough to cut them back to last year's wood; the flowers are then carried on the current year's growth.

Soil They prefer a calcareous, well-drained and rich garden soil.

Propagation This can be from root cuttings, layering or seed.

Diseases If the roots become too dry or the night temperature too low, buds may drop off, and sometimes whole branches will die.

Campsis radicans
Syn. *Bignonia radicans*. A climbing plant from North America (Canada to Virginia). It has clinging roots and grows up to 35 ft (10 m) high, and in midsummer produces flowers that are orange on the outside and yellow within. The cultivar 'Praecox' bears scarlet flowers in early June.

Campsis × tagliabuana
A cross between *C. grandiflora* and *C. radicans*, this plant bears larger flowers, orange-red on the inside and salmon-pink on the outside, but unfortunately is not so hardy. The best-known garden variety is 'Madame Galen'.

Canna indica hybrids as summer bedding plants, edged with fuchsias

Canna
Cannaceae

If the cultivation of this plant were somewhat simpler it would surely be found in every garden. The foliage is exceptionally ornamental, and when its beautiful flowers appear in summer the plant is a joy to behold.

Cultivation In March the fleshy rhizomes should be cleaned, divided, planted in boxes and covered with a rich peaty compost. They are then placed in a frame or greenhouse at a temperature of 16–18°C (61–65°F). As soon as the first leaves unfurl, the plants can be hardened off. Plant out during the second half of May, or when fear of frost has passed, 1½–2ft (45–60cm) apart in a sunny, sheltered spot that has been well manured. During droughts water well and in summer add liquid fertilizer at frequent intervals. Flowers are produced from the end of June until autumn. Before the autumn frosts and in any event not later than early November the plants should be lifted and stored in dry sand in a frost-free place, for instance under a cool greenhouse bench, the loose earth having first been shaken off and the foliage cut off 4in (10cm) above the roots.
Soil A rich garden soil is needed.
Propagation This is done by division of the rhizomes. These plants can also be grown from seed but will not then come true.

Canna edulis
Although less spectacular than the hybrid cultivars of *C. × generalis*, this 4–6ft (1.2–2m) tall plant has a quiet distinction graced by spikes of 1½in (4cm) long red and yellow flowers from summer to early autumn.

Canna indica hybrids

Syn. *C. × generalis*. There are two main groups: the dwarf, which grows 20–30in (50–75cm) high, and the normal, which can reach 3½–5ft (1–1.5m). The ovate-lanceolate leaves are up to 20in (50cm) long and 10–12in (25–30cm) wide. The colour of the leaves may be green or browny-purple, and the colour of the flowers rich yellow, orange, salmon-pink or red. Among green-leaved cultivars are 'Bonfire', which bears scarlet flowers with an orange glow; 'Louis Cayeux', which has rose-red flowers; 'President', a scarlet-flowered variety, and 'R. Wallis', whose flowers are bright yellow. The brown-leaved cultivars include 'America', which has dark red flowers; 'Hercules', with purple-red flowers; 'Tyrol', with salmon-pink flowers; and 'Wyoming' which has bronze flowers.

Canna inidiflora
This Peruvian species is the giant of the cannas, well-grown plants attaining heights of 6–9ft (2–3m). The oblong leaves range from 1–2ft (30–60cm) long and the stems are tipped by clusters of nodding rose-pink to rose-red flowers, each one rather orchid like and up to 5in (13cm) in length. This canna is more tender than others mentioned here and needs a very warm sheltered site outside. It is better suited to culture in large pots or tubs stood outside on sheltered patios for the summer. Treated in this way it can add a real touch of the tropical to the summer garden.

If cannas are to be planted in groups, careful attention must be paid to their respective heights. They generally seem out of place in borders, and are seen to best advantage when grown in combination with suitable annuals in special beds. Cannas are increasingly grown for cutting.

Carpinus
Betulaceae
Hornbeam

The common hornbeam grows as a tree throughout the Northern Hemisphere, but gardeners are more interested in it as a hedging plant. Provided the ground is not too dry, it will prosper where little else will grow. As a hedging plant, the common hornbeam is often confused with the common beech (see under *Fagus*), but they belong to two distinct genera and differ in both the size and shape of their leaves; those of the hornbeam are narrower and much more clearly ribbed. A hornbeam hedge grows quickly, but sheds most of its leaves in winter. By contrast the beech grows a little more slowly and retains its dead foliage throughout the winter, thus forming a more lasting barrier.
Soil Hornbeams grow in almost any moderately fertile soil.
Propagation Species may be grown from seed, and named varieties from cuttings.

Carpinus betulus
○ ◐ ✳ ◎ ▥
Common hornbeam. A tree growing up to 65ft (20m) high, with a spread of up to 40ft (12m). The variety 'Columnaris' has a columnar habit, while 'Fastigiata' is more pyramidal, broadening out more and more as it matures. 'Incisa' has deeply toothed leaves; 'Purpurea' is a small tree bearing young leaves with a purple tinge that shortly turn green; 'Quercifolia' is a very broad tree with leaves reminiscent of the oak; the leaves of 'Variegata' are splashed with creamy-white.

Carpinus caroliniana
○ ◐ ✳ ◎ ◎
American hornbeam. A tree over 20ft (7m) high whose branches spread out, arching at the tips. The leaves are bluish-green and turn orange in autumn.

Carpinus japonica
This species grows 20–40ft (6–12m) high, and has heart-shaped leaves.

The hornbeam, *Carpinus betulus*, pruned to perfection

A large specimen of *Caryopteris × clandonensis*

Caryopteris
Verbenaceae

A genus of hardy and half-hardy shrubs that flower in late summer and bear aromatic leaves.

Soil Any ordinary well-drained garden soil will be adequate, possibly with some extra humus. These plants thrive in chalky soils.

Propagation Take cuttings in midsummer from half-ripened lateral shoots. Plants can also be grown from seed, but the garden varieties will not come true using this method.

Caryopteris × clandonensis

A small shrub raised by crossing *C. incana* with *C. mongolica*. It has rather small, narrow-toothed or entire leaves, and bears blue flowers in clusters in autumn. Plants may die back in winter but will come up again in spring. 'Heavenly Blue' has deep blue flowers.

Caryopteris incana

Syn. *C. mastacanthus*. A shrub from China, Japan and Korea that grows up to 20in (50cm) high, it has narrow leaves with blunt teeth that are covered with a greyish felt-like growth underneath. Fragrant violet-blue flowers bloom from mid- to late summer.

Caryopteris mastacanthus, see *C. incana*.

Catalpa
Bignoniaceae

These are unusual trees with very large leaves. In maturity they produce rich clusters of beautiful flowers in summer and slender seed pods in autumn. Young branches may die back in severe winters, especially in exposed positions, and it is advisable to plant this tree only in sheltered and sunny places.

Soil Ordinary garden soil is adequate.

Propagation From cuttings of half-ripened wood.

Catalpa bignonioides

Indian bean tree. A small- to medium-sized tree, originally from eastern North America, it reaches a height of 35ft (10m) with a spread of 20–25ft (7–8m), it can also be grown as a shrub up to 15ft (5m). White flowers with yellow and purple markings are borne in loose panicles in early summer. The leaves are up to 8in (20cm) long and ovate-lanceolate in shape, some forms having several lobes. 'Aurea' has yellow leaves.

Catalpa × erubescens

Syn. *C. × hybrida*. A cross between *C. bignonioides* and *C. ovata*, this tree usually has purplish leaves when young. The best cultivar is 'Purpurea', which has purple-black young leaves and white flowers with yellow stripes and violet spots.

Catalpa × hybrida, see *C. × erubescens*.

Catalpa ovata

From China, this tree is 35ft (10m) or more in height and bears small white flowers with yellow and red markings in panicles in midsummer.

Catalpa speciosa

A fairly large tree from the central United States, the peeling bark of *C. speciosa* makes it conspicuous. Purple-spotted white flowers appear in June or July.

Catalpa bignonioides, a large specimen of the Indian bean tree

Catalpa ovata

Ceanothus 'Gloire de Versailles'

Ceanothus
Rhamnaceae

A genus of mainly deciduous shrubs, also known as California lilac, that bears beautiful small flowers in autumn. Some species are hardy in southern areas, but elsewhere need the protection of sunny walls, against which they can be trained.

Soil A well-drained, moderately fertile soil is required.

Propagation This can be by layering in spring or from cuttings in summer. Seeds may also be sown, but germinate erratically and the resulting plants vary in flower shade and vigour.

Ceanothus americanus

A shrub from the eastern and central United States that grows up to 3ft (1m) high and flowers in mid- to late summer, it produces minute white flowers in dense panicles.

Ceanothus dentatus floribundus, see *C. × veitchianus*.

Ceanothus hybrids

The most common garden form, these long-stemmed shrubs are raised from various crosses with *Ceanothus × delilianus* and *Ceanothus × pallidas*. The *delilianus* group includes 'Gloire de Versailles', with large sky-blue flowers; 'Indigo', a less robust variety which has indigo-blue flowers; and 'Topaz', whose flowers are soft indigo-blue. Of the evergreen hybrids, the most hardy and free-flowering are: 'Autumnal Blue', which produces mid-blue flowers from July onwards; 'Burkwoodii', whose flowers are a brighter blue but carried in small clusters; and 'Cascade', which has powder-blue flowers.

Ceanothus impressus

One of the hardiest species, it grows up to 10ft (3m) with small, deep green corrugated leaves and a profusion of small clusters of mid-blue flowers.

Ceanothus thyrsiflorus

A fairly tall evergreen shrub, reaching a height of 30ft (9m), it has glossy green leaves and large clusters of pale blue flowers. 'Repens' is prostrate and mat-forming; its branches must not be overshadowed by any other plant or they will die back.

Ceanothus × veitchianus

Syn. *C. dentatus floribundus*. A 10ft (3m) shrub with leaves that are glossy green above and greyish beneath. It is one of the hardiest sorts and produces abundant clusters of bright, deep blue flowers.

Cedrus
Pinacea
Cedar

Cedars are attractive, evergreen conifers. Most are hardy and long-lived and grow to considerable heights. They are at their most effective when planted as solitary specimens, for instance on a lawn, where they can develop freely. Do not cramp these magnificent trees by tucking them between rival plants. They should not be pruned, and need to be planted at least 12–15 ft (4–5 m) from paths; *C. libani* should be positioned still farther away.

Soil A well-drained, slightly alkaline soil is best.

Propagation This can be from seed or by grafting.

Cedrus atlantica

○ ❋ ❋ ❋ ⊥

Atlas cedar. From North Africa, this tree reaches a height of 130 ft (40 m), with a spread of 30 ft (10 m) or more. Its branches grow mainly upwards, forming a conical crown that broadens with age. The leaves are usually blue-green or silver-grey. 'Aurea', the Golden Atlas cedar, is commonly found in gardens: this is a stocky cultivar some 10–15 ft (3–5 m) high, with distinctly golden-yellow leaves. 'Glauca', the Blue Atlas cedar, has attractive blue-green to silver-grey leaves and barrel-shaped cones 2–3 in (5–7.5 cm) long. 'Glauca Pendula', the most beautiful of all the cedars, is a weeping variety of the Blue Atlas.

Cedrus deodara

Deodar. A tree from the western Himalayas that reaches a height of 100 ft (30 m) or more and a spread of 30 ft (10 m). It has an attractive pendulous habit with drooping branches and glaucous green leaves.

Cedrus libani

Cedar of Lebanon. A slow-growing tree that eventually reaches heights of 75–120 ft (23–36 m) with a spread of 30–40 ft (9–12 m). The young tree's broadly pyramidal shape later takes on a flatter crown, the branches growing out almost horizontally.

Cedrus deodara

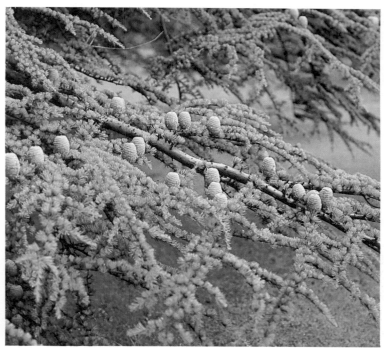

Cedrus atlantica seen in detail

The blue cedar requires a great deal of space

Celastrus
Celastraceae
Staff vine,
Climbing bittersweet

These hardy deciduous shrubs are useful for covering walls, fences, etc. They should not be allowed to climb on healthy, actively growing trees because they wind round the trunk and as they grow in thickness, they exert a throttling pressure on the tree.

Soil Almost any soil will do, though preferably it should not be too chalky.

Celastrus fruits

Propagation By layering, from seed, or from cuttings of half-ripe shoots.

Celastrus hypoleucus

Syn. *C. hypoglaucus*. A handsome climber reaching 40 ft (12 m) under good conditions having young shoots covered with a distinctive purplish patina. The small fruits are yellow and red.

Celastrus orbiculatus

○ ◐ ⊕ ❉ ◍ ⊛ ❀

Growing up to 30 ft (9 m) high, this species originates from China and Japan. It has variably shaped but usually oval leaves. It bears yellow-green flowers and attractive orange fruits.

Celastrus scandens

A North American climber reaching a height of about 20 ft (7 m). It produces orange and scarlet fruits.

Celosia
Amaranthaceae

These striking annuals make useful bedding or pot plants. They have a long flowering period and should be watered regularly and treated with liquid fertilizer from time to time.
Soil Celosias require a rich, not-too-heavy soil, preferably well drained.
Propagation Sow in pans in early spring at a temperature of 18°C (64°F). Prick off the seedlings as soon as possible into boxes. To ensure sturdy growth, the seedlings should be potted into a good proprietary compost and grown on under glass until ready to harden off in late May. Plant out 10–14in (25–35cm) apart.

Celosia argentea
○ ⊙ ⊛
From eastern India, this summer-flowering plant ranges between 6–20in (15–50cm) high, and produces flowers that are silvery to whitish. It is the parent of the two most popular cultivar groups. The first, *C. argentea cristata*, is the cockscomb, which grows 1–2ft (30–60cm) high and bears crested heads of red, white, yellow and orange flowers from July to September. *C. argentea plumosa* is taller (up to 2ft/60cm) and produces feathery plumes of yellow, red, violet and white flowers, and looks more attractive in flower beds than 'Nana'. 'Thompsonii Magnifica' is the most attractive of all the cultivars: it grows 1–2ft (30–60cm) high with a fairly broad spread, and can be dried for decorative purposes. 'Lilliput' has a more compact habit.

Centaurea
Compositae

The genus *Centaurea*, which is also mentioned under *Amberboa*, supplies gardeners with various attractive annuals and herbaceous perennials both for the border and for cutting. Thanks to numerous crosses, most species can now be obtained in almost every colour.
Soil All species grow in every kind of garden soil, provided it is moderately fertile and well drained.
Propagation Annuals are grown from seed. Sow from late spring directly into the open ground. Perennials can be propagated from seed, from cuttings or by division in spring.

Centaurea cineraria
○ ⊗ ⊚ ⊛
Syn. *Centaurea gymnocarpa*. Dusty Miller. An Italian plant some 2½ft (75cm) high that is grown for its intensely grey-white fern-like leaves, and is much favoured as a bedding plant. The purple flowers are rarely seen.
Centaurea cyanus
Cornflower. A very popular European garden plant ranging from 1–3ft (30–100cm) high, it flowers some 10 weeks after sowing, i.e. May–July, or August–October. Cultivars can now be obtained in all colours and sizes (the latter down to 8in/20cm), and also with double flowers. Cornflowers should not be sown too early; dry sunny positions tend to restrict growth and shorten the flowering period, and may encourage black fly.

Celosia argentea var. *plumosa*

Centaurea cyanus

Typical site for *Cerastium*

Centaurea macrocephala

Centaurea dealbata
○ ⊖ ⊚ ⊛
From the Caucasus and Persia, the varieties of this plant are available from 8–24in (20–60cm) high, while the main species grows up to 3ft (1m). The flowers, rose-pink with very pale centres, appear in midsummer. Leaves are green above and covered with white down beneath. 'Steenbergii' has rose-crimson flowers.
Centaurea gymnocarpa, see *C. cineraria*.
Centaurea hypoleuca
This species resembles *C. dealbata*, but is more compact and has lilac-pink flowers.
Centaurea macrocephala
○ ⊖ ⊚ ⊛ ⊗
A plant some 15in–3ft (38–100cm) high, with thick leafy stems that pro-

duce spherical flower heads up to 4in (10cm) across in midsummer. The golden yellow petals make a striking contrast with the brown calyx.
Centaurea montana
○ ⊖ ⊚ ⊚ ⊗
Originally from the Pyrenees, Alps and Carpathians, these summer-flowering plants grow 1–2ft (30–60cm) high, and bear blue flowers with a purple centre. The most attractive cultivars are 'Alba', which has pure white flowers, and 'Grandiflora' with large blue flowers. Another, 'Carrea', is pink.
Centaurea moschata, see *Amberboa moschata*.
Centaurea odorata, see *Amberboa moschata*.
Centaurea suaveolens, see *Amberboa moschata*.

Centranthus
Valerianaceae
Valerian

These are outstanding border plants that make a particularly fine show when grown in combination with grey or purple plants.
Soil *C. macrosiphon* will grow in any garden soil, but *C. ruber* likes a little lime.
Propagation Plants may be grown from seed; perennial species may also be produced by division or basal cuttings in spring.

Centranthus macrosiphon
○ ⊖ ⊚
From Spain, these plants grow 8–16in (20–40cm) high, and in early to midsummer bear dark red flowers in dense clusters. Named varieties are sometimes available in many different shades.
Centranthus ruber
○ ⊚ ⊛
Red valerian. Growing up to 3ft (1m) high, these plants from southern Europe flower in late spring to early summer, sometimes longer. The flowers are pale red in the species and dark red in the much more beautiful 'Coccineus'. The white A. biflorus' is also very attractive and can be used with 'Coccineus' to emphasize the latter's fine colour.

Cerastium
Caryophyllaceae

A genus of spreading plants that are excellent for covering banks, for edging and for rock gardens. The grey-leaved species are generally preferred, and all are rapid growers; if they spread too far, the unwanted areas are easily removed with a spade. It is advisable anyway to cut the plants back slightly after flowering, and so keep them in check. In sunny positions, cerastiums look very attractive on walls, or when spilling out from tubs or other plant containers.
Soil Any well-drained garden soil will suffice; poor soil serves to enhance the grey of the leaves.
Propagation Plants are easily propagated by division.

Cerastium alpinum lanatum
Alpine mouse-ear chickweed. A densely white woolly mat-former of great hardiness from arctic regions. It is

A mixture of pink and white *Centranthus ruber* plants on a sunny, calcareous terrace

China, admired for its long-lasting, late-summer blue flowers. Growing no higher than 3 ft (1 m), it is very suitable for small gardens. In severe winters it can be cut back to ground level, and will grow again from the base.

Cercidiphyllum
Cercidiphyllaceae

The leaves of this tree or shrub strongly resemble those of *Cercis*, but the flowers are quite distinct. Both genera flower in spring, when it is easy to tell the difference between them.

Soil These plants like slightly acid, moisture-retaining soil.

Propagation From seed.

Cercidiphyllum japonicum

A tree originally from Japan, where it grows up to 100 ft (30 m); in Europe it is rarely higher than 30 ft (9 m). The young leaves are a beautiful red colour, assuming a bright green tint in the summer and a yellow tint in the autumn. The red-petalled flowers are inconspicuous and appear in spring, but only on mature trees. Its branching habit and the beautiful colour changes of its foliage make this species extremely attractive not only in the shrubbery but also when planted as a specimen.

Ceratostigma willmottianum

mainly grown as a foliage plant for gritty soil in a raised bed or on a scree. Small starry white flowers are usually rather sparingly produced in summer.

Cerastium biebersteinii

Syn. *C. repens.* Snow-in-summer. Originally from southern Europe, this is a vigorous, white-flowering plant up to 1 ft (30 cm) high that flowers in late spring to early summer. It has woolly, silver-grey foliage, and is suitable for cultivation in tubs or other containers.

Cerastrium repens, see *C. biebersteinii.*

Cerastium tomentosum

The leaves of this plant are silver-grey, but less woolly than those of *C. biebersteinii*; its height of 1 ft (30 cm) and white flowers are not dissimilar. *C. tomentosum* var. *columnae* has a more compact habit. The species comes from southern Europe.

Ceratostigma
Plumbaginaceae

In Italy, these attractive plants can often be seen growing on old walls. They are recommended for sheltered shrubberies or mixed borders, but are not hardy enough for gardens in the northeast of Britain.

Soil Both species listed below require alkaline soil.

Propagation They may be grown from cuttings or by division.

Ceratostigma griffithii

From the eastern Himalayas and China, this species forms a spreading bushy shrub 2 ft (60 cm) or more tall. The stems are bristly and the obovate leaves about 1 in (2.5 cm) long. In autumn the latter take on tints of red. During late summer and autumn a succession of $\frac{3}{4}$ in (2 cm) wide blue flowers open in spiky clusters. Although less easily obtainable, this is as good and marginally hardier than *C. willmottianum.*

Ceratostigma plumbaginoides

Syn. *Plumbago larpentae.* An almost hardy sub-shrub, 8–12 in (20–30 cm) high, that creeps underground and dies back each winter. Cobalt-blue flowers are borne in small terminal clusters in autumn.

Ceratostigma willmottianum

An exceptionally attractive shrub from

The young foliage of *Cercidiphyllum japonicum*

The Judas tree, *Cercis siliquastrum*

Cercis
Leguminosae

A genus of small trees producing clusters of beautiful pea-shaped flowers in spring.

Soil A fertile, well-drained, preferably slightly calcareous soil is required.

Propagation Plants may be grown from seed. It is advisable to protect young plants against frost.

Cercis canadensis

○ ◐ ⊛ ⊛ ⓨ ⓛ

A North American tree growing to a height of 20ft (7m) in gardens, and up to double that in the wild. The leaves are heart-shaped and the clusters of pink pea-flowers open in spring.

Cercis siliquastrum

○ ⊝ ⊛ ⓨ ⊛ ⓛ

Judas tree, originally from southern Europe and the Near East. Reaching a height of 20ft (7m), and spreading to about 15ft (5m), this smallish tree favours sheltered positions and can be trained against a wall. Rose-purple flowers are borne in clusters in spring, before the leaves have come out; they are followed by flattened, bean-like seed pods which ripen in August–September.

Chaenomeles
Rosaceae
Ornamental quince, Japonica

The red-flowering species of this genus of shrubs make glorious garden plants, and are also admired for their yellow fruits, which appear in summer. These shrubs may be grafted to the stems of pears to make weeping trees, and they look most attractive when fan-trained against a white wall. Many gardeners place them at the front of borders, as groups or solitary plants, or in the larger rock gardens. Pruning should be minimized because these shrubs flower on shoots of the previous year.

Fruits of the Japanese quince

Soil These plants thrive in moderately fertile, well-drained soil, preferably in a sunny position.

Propagation They may be grown from cuttings or by layering, and are also easily raised from seeds, but cultivars do not come true to type. Plants only flower after 3–5 years.

Chaenomeles japonica

○ ◐ ⊛ ⓦ ⓨ ⊛ ⊙

Syn. *Cydonia japonica*. Maule's quince. A hardy shrub from Japan that reaches a height of about 3ft (1m) and has a slightly wider spread. It bears rose-pink flowers in spring. 'Sargentii' is 2½ft (75cm) high and bears salmon-pink flowers in great profusion.

Chaenomeles lagenaria, see *C. speciosa*.

Chaenomeles speciosa

Syn. *C. lagenaria*. Japanese quince or japonica. Growing to a height of 6ft (2m), this shrub sometimes has robust spines and flowers in spring. The variety 'Brilliant' produces an abundance of deep red flowers and grows 4½ft (1.3m) high; 'Nivalis', a 6ft (2m) plant, has pure white flowers; 'Simonii' has a dwarf habit (1½ft/45cm) and blood-red flowers, while those of 'Umbilicata' are deep salmon-pink.

Chaenomeles japonica, flowers

Chaenomeles × superba

A cross between *C. japonica* and *C. speciosa*. Cultivars include 'Boule de Fer', which is 6–8ft (2–2.4m) high, with orange-red flowers; 'Crimson and Gold', a 3ft (1m) plant of broad habit with dark red petals and golden anthers; 'Fascination', which is 3ft (1m) high with wide-spreading branches and scarlet flowers; 'Pink Lady', which has rose-pink flowers; and 'Vermilion', a 3ft (1m) plant bearing a profusion of orange flowers.

Chamaecyparis
Cupressaceae
False cypress

These popular conifers differ from ordinary cypresses (*Cupressus*) in that their leaves are flattened and they have smaller cones. If false cypresses are grown from seed, some of the resulting plants will show considerable variation. Nurserymen have taken full advantage of this to develop hundreds of different cultivars, especially from *C. lawsoniana*. A special feature of some cultivars is that they keep their young foliage, which disappears in the normal species. There are differences, too, in

habit of growth, and sometimes the leaves are combined into densely packed sprays.

Soil Ordinary well-drained soil.

Propagation The species can be propagated from seed, but the cultivars must be grown from cuttings. It is possible to root the cuttings in a cold frame, but a far more reliable method is to use a mist propagator.

Chamaecyparis lawsoniana

○ ◐ ⊛ ⊛ ⊛ ⊙ ⓛ ⊜

Lawson cypress. A tree from California with a pyramidal crown capable of attaining heights of up to 200ft (60m) in its natural habitat. The crimson male flowers make a most striking effect in May. There are so many cultivars that there is space here only to mention a few of the most popular. Unless stated otherwise, the trees described below grow to heights of 15–30ft (5–10m). 'Alumii' has a narrow, conical habit and can also be used for hedges. Its dark green leaves are covered with a blue bloom when young. 'Columnaris' has a columnar habit and bluish-green leaves. 'Ellwoodii', a conical tree 6–10ft (2–3m) high, has bluish juvenile foliage. 'Erecta Viridis' has a compact columnar habit and bright green

Chamaecyparis lawsoniana 'Lanei'

The filigree effect of *Chamaecyparis pisifera* 'Filifera Aurea'

foliage. 'Filiformis' has a pyramidal habit, drooping branches and dark green leaves. 'Fletcheri' is compact, and its juvenile leaves are covered with a bluish-green bloom.

'Forsteckensis' is a small bush with a globular habit, useful for rock gardens. 'Fraseri' resembles 'Alumii' but has darker leaves. 'Lutea' has golden-yellow leaves, a broad columnar habit and drooping branches. 'Minima Glauca', with bluish-green leaves, has a dense globular habit and is suitable for rock gardens. 'Silver Queen' is a large tree with creamy-white leaves and a pyramidal habit. 'Stewartii' has golden-yellow leaves and a pyramidal habit. 'Triomph van Boscoop' has silvery leaves with a blue bloom and a columnar habit, and stands up well to wind. 'Wisselii' has bluish-green leaves in tapered sprays, a dense pattern of branches and a columnar habit. In addition, there are several excellent recent cultivars, including 'Delorme', a broad spherical tree with green foliage; 'Golden Wonder', an erect tree whose foliage is golden-yellow; 'Pembury Blue', also erect but with very thin branches and bluish-grey foliage; and 'Stardust', a narrow conical tree with broad sulphur-yellow leaves.

Chamaecyparis nootkatensis 'Pendula'

Mature *Chamaecyparis lawsoniana* cultivar at Blenheim Palace, Winston Churchill's birthplace

Chamaecyparis nootkatensis

○ ◐ ◉ ⊛ ⊛ ⊛ ☺ ⊥

Nootka cypress. A tree from western North America that grows up to 125 ft (38 m) high, with a pyramidal habit and yellow-brown, generally angular branches bearing dark green resinous foliage without stripes or spots. The cultivar 'Aurea', often called 'Lutea', is an erect tree or a very large shrub with yellow leaves that later turn green. 'Glauca' has leaves with a blue waxy bloom; 'Pendula' is a weeping form 15–30 ft (5–10 m) high.

Chamaecyparis obtusa

○ ◐ ⌂ ⊛ ⊛ ⊛ ☺ ⊥

Hinoki cypress. This Japanese tree grows up to 130 ft (40 m) high and has bright green, blunt-tipped leaves with blue marks on the undersides. It does not have resin glands. The variety 'Crippsii' is a 10–15 ft (3–5 m) tree with golden-yellow leaves and a spreading habit. 'Filicoides' does not grow much taller than 4½ ft (1.3 m) and has pendulous sprays of feathery leaves and a somewhat straggly habit. 'Gracilis' has light green leaves, a globular or slightly pyramidal habit, and a height of up to 6 ft (2 m). 'Pygmaea' is 4½–6 ft (1.3–2 m) high and has bluish-green leaves and a flat top; both this cultivar and 'Gracilis'

Chamaecyparis obtusa 'Tetragona Aurea'

are suitable for the larger rock garden. 'Tetragona Aurea' is a large shrub with golden-yellow leaves and an angular habit.

Chamaecyparis pisifera

○ ◐ ⊛ ⊛ ⊛ ☺ ⊥

Sawara cypress. A Japanese tree growing up to 100 ft (30 m) high with horizontally flattened sprays of dark green leaves marked with characteristic blue-white stripes underneath. The variety 'Aurea' has golden-yellow leaves. 'Boulevard' is a juvenile form with unusual steel-blue leaves and a pyramidal habit. 'Filifera' has spreading branches which carry long drooping branchlets. 'Filifera Aurea' is more compact and has bright yellow leaves. 'Filifera Nana' is a flat-topped dwarf bush, suitable for rock gardens, as is 'Nana Aureovariegata', another dwarf bush, which has greenish-yellow foliage. 'Plumosa' has feathery branches, a pyramidal habit and grows to heights of 15–30 ft (5–10 m). 'Plumosa Aurea' has golden-yellow leaves. 'Plumosa Flavescens' has branches with sulphur-yellow tips and a very compact habit. 'Squarrosa' bears bluish, billowing sprays of foliage and has a dense spreading habit and a height of up to 30 ft (10 m).

Cheiranthus
Cruciferae
Wallflower

Wallflowers are usually grown as biennials either in beds among late tulips, or in borders, where they flower in late spring and early summer.

Soil Wallflowers prefer calcareous, well-drained soil. Acid soils should be dressed with ground chalk, limestone, hydrated lime or rubble. Wallflowers—as the name indicates—can make do with very little top-soil. They will often grow on old, weathered walls where lack of food impedes leaf production but where they flower all the more profusely.

Propagation Sow seeds in open seed beds during May and June and thin out

Cheiranthus cheiri

Chelone obliqua

Chionodoxa gigantea

Chionodoxa luciliae
Only 5–6 in (10–12 cm) high, this hardy plant from Asia Minor is very useful in the front row of mixed borders and also in large groups on the lawn. The flowers are mostly blue with a white eye, but can be obtained in various shades of white and pink. Plant them 1 in (25 mm) or so apart, at a depth of 2 in (50 mm). Other well-known species are *C. gigantea*, which has violet-blue flowers, and *C. sardensis*, producing dark blue flowers.

Choisya
Rutaceae
Mexican orange blossom

Evergreen shrubs from Mexico and southern USA. *C. ternata*, described below, is generally hardy and deservedly popular.

Soil Any well-drained garden soil will suffice, preferably in a position sheltered from strong, cold winds.

Propagation Plants are grown from cuttings taken with a heel in late summer.

Choisya ternata
From Mexico, a shrub growing 6–10 ft (2–3 m) high, with glossy trifoliate leaves that set off the strongly fragrant, white, starry flowers. These appear mainly in late spring, then sporadically until autumn.

Chrysanthemum
Compositae

This large genus can be divided into (a) annuals, (b) half-hardy perennials and (c) hardy perennials.

Soil Most light soils will do, but outdoor chrysanthemums should not be planted in acid soil. *Pyrethrum* hybrids demand a spongy, fertile and humus-rich soil.

Propagation The annuals are grown from seed. Those in the second group, the half-hardy perennials, are grown from cuttings taken in spring or in August. These are placed in a propagator or a box covered with glass; a gentle bottom heat is beneficial. They can also be sown from February to May under glass at a minimum temperature of 10°C (50°F), but cultivars do not come true from seed. Hardy perennials, the third group, are propagated by

Chrysanthemum lacustre

division. *C. leucanthemum* can also be propagated from seed. Hints on the propagation of garden chrysanthemums are given in the section (d) below. *C. indicum* and *C. koreanum* hybrids must be propagated by division or from cuttings.

a. Annual species
Chrysanthemum carinatum
Growing 1½–2 ft (45–60 cm) tall, this plant flowers about 10 weeks after sowing. It has delicate, bipinnate leaves with angular lobes. The central disc of the flower is purple surrounded by ray petals banded with white, yellow, copper or brown, depending on the variety. There are also double varieties.
Chrysanthemum coronarium
A plant 1–3 ft (30–100 cm) high that flowers June–September or even later, bearing large cream to golden yellow flowers.
Chrysanthemum multicaule
With its bluish-green foliage and bright golden-yellow flowers borne on long stems, this 10 in (25 cm) annual plant from Algeria is suitable for growing in rock gardens and at the fronts of borders.
Chrysanthemum parthenium
Syn. *Matricaria parthenioides*. Feverfew. Although really a perennial, this plant is usually grown as an annual. It reaches heights of 1½–2½ ft (45–75 cm) and flowers through the summer, its small blooms having a yellow disc and white ray petals. The plant has a strong smell of camomile. Its numerous cultivars include 'Golden Ball', which has

A bed filled with mixed wallflowers and forget-me-nots

to about 2 in (5 cm) apart. When the seedlings are large enough they should be set out 6–9 in (15–23 cm) apart in the nursery row, and transferred to the flowering site in October.

Cheiranthus cheiri
A plant from southern Europe. Flowering in spring or summer, this species grows 10–24 in (25–60 cm) high and its cultivars are available in various colours including ivory, yellow, golden-yellow flushed or striped with brown or violet, chestnut brown and purple. Several fully double-flowered cultivars are known, but only the yellow 'Harpur Crewe' is generally available. This is a good shrubby perennial suitable for the rock garden. It can only be propagated by cuttings in late summer.

Chelone
Scrophularaceae
Turtle-head

These fairly uncommon herbaceous perennials are best suited to being planted out in groups in a natural setting.

Soil A moist, humus-rich soil.

Propagation Sow in spring in the open and prick out the seedlings into seed beds for planting out during the next year. Mature plants may be divided in spring

Chelone barbata, see *Penstemon barbatus*.
Chelone obliqua
Growing up to 2 ft (60 cm) high, this North American plant has spear-shaped leaves, serrated at the margins with prominent veins and very short or no leaf stalks. The deep rose, tubular flowers are borne in dense terminal spikes in summer.

Chionodoxa
Liliaceae
Glory of the snow

A genus of hardy bulbous perennials with most attractive small flowers that follow snowdrops in early spring.

Soil Any well-drained garden soil is adequate.

Propagation These plants are self-seeding when suitably situated. Cultivars do not come true from seed and must be grown from offsets.

double flowers, and 'Snowball'.

Chrysanthemum segetum
○ ⊙ ⓨ ⊗

Corn marigold. Growing 1–2 ft (30–60 cm) high, its golden-yellow flowers appear in midsummer. It is more robust than *C. carinatum* and *C. coronarium*, and in appearance its bluish-green foliage is coarser and less deeply indented than that of *C. carinatum*. The varieties 'Eldorado', with dark yellow flowers, and 'Helios', with golden-yellow flowers, are recommended for cutting.

b. Half-hardy perennials for outdoor pots and beds

Chrysanthemum frutescens
From the Canary Islands, this sub-shrubby species is 1–3 ft (30–100 cm) high, and flowers in summer and

Chrysanthemum coronarium

winter. It has deeply lobed leaves and a succession of daisy flowers. The ray petals are pure white in the species, golden-yellow in 'Etoile d'Or', and white in most other cultivars, while the central disc is always yellow.

c. Perennials for the border and for cutting

Chrysanthemum coccineum
○ ○ ⓨ ⊗

Syn. *C. roseum, Pyrethrum roseum*. The wild species, a parent of the *Pyrethrum* cultivars, is no longer grown. The cultivars, however, have become increasingly popular not only because they are excellent for cutting but also because the more sturdy ones look so splendid in the June border. Available in both single- and double-flowered forms, the pink, red and white flowers combine especially well in groups. The plants should be moved immediately after flowering. Every three years they should be lifted, divided and replanted; if this is not done then the flowers will deteriorate. Recommended cultivars include 'Avalanche', with single white blooms; 'Eileen May Robinson', which has salmon-pink flowers; 'Kelway's Glorious', with deep scarlet flowers; 'Madeleine', which bears large double pale pink blooms; and 'Mont Blanc' with white flowers.

Chrysanthemum indicum hybrids
These garden or autumn chrysanthemums are crosses between *C. indicum* and *C. morifalium*. They grow 1½–3 ft (45–100 cm) high, and from August to November produce mostly single and some double flowers in white, yellow, purple, dark red and brown.

A cream coloured hybrid of *Chrysanthemum rubellum*

Chrysanthemum koreanum hybrids
These strongly resemble the *C. indicum* hybrids but are hardier. Flowering August–October, they are available in single and double forms.

Chrysanthemum lacustre, see *C. maximum*.

Chrysanthemum maximum
Syn. *C. lacustre*. Shasta daisy. The parent of many attractive cultivars, most of which are white with a central yellow disc. The flowering period extends from June to late autumn. Many of the taller cultivars need staking in the border. Popular cultivars include the white-flowering 'Everest', which is 3 ft (1 m) high and produces single flowers; 'Esther Read', with double white flowers, grows 1½ ft (45 cm) high; 'Juno' is single and white-flowering, 2½ ft (75 cm) high; and 'Wirral Supreme' is a 3 ft (1 m) plant bearing double white flowers.

Chrysanthemum roseum, see *C. coccineum*.

Chrysanthemum rubellum
○ ○ ⌃ ⓨ ⊗

A good border plant with stiff stems that grows 1½–2½ ft (45–75 cm) high. 'Clara Curtis' and 'Duchess of Edinburgh' are two well-known cultivars, probably of hybrid origin. The first produces deep pink flowers and blooms from September to October, the second bears velvet-red flowers some 10 days earlier.

Chrysanthemum uliginosum
○ ○ ⓨ

Syn. *Tanacatum serotinum*. A tall and fairly sturdy plant for the back of the border, it produces flowers with a yellow disc and white ray petals in autumn.

d. Cultivation of garden chrysanthemums (*C. indicum* and *C. koreanum* hybrids)
All garden chrysanthemums are propagated from cuttings or by division. Cuttings provide a large number of specimens from a single plant. When the plant has stopped flowering in autumn, the main stem is cut down to 9–12 in (23–30 cm). The plants or stools are lifted in November and stored away from frost. The best method is to plant them in a ventilated cold frame when there is no frost. In March some of the basal growths are broken off as far from the old main stem as possible to provide 2–3 in (5–7.5 cm) cuttings that are planted in trays of equal parts peat and sand. The trays are placed in a box covered

The annual *Chrysanthemum carinatum* is easily grown for cutting with glass. A gentle heat will encourage growth; the boxes may also be kept indoors near a south-facing window. As soon as the cuttings show signs of having rooted, they are transferred separately to 3 in (7.5 cm) pots and put straight into a cold frame. During sunny weather they require a great deal of ventilation; later the glass cover should be removed permanently so that the plants are hardened off. It is essential to ensure regular development until the middle of April, when the young plants can be moved to their flowering position or potted up in 5 in (12 cm) pots.

If you do not want to grow your own cuttings, you can buy well-rooted cuttings in April, the younger and sturdier the better. Old spindly plants generally have a woody stem and are worthless. These remarks apply to all garden chrysanthemums. In their subsequent treatment we must distinguish between early-flowering cultivars (before the beginning of October), and late-flowering cultivars (after the beginning of October). The first group can flower out of doors; the second blooms under glass. The outdoor cultivars are planted in rows about 15–18 in (38–45 cm) apart, and the second grow and flower

Chrysanthemum coccineum generally known as *Pyrethrum*

Chrysanthemum frutescens

in 8–10 in (20–25 cm) pots. The latter are stood outside in a sheltered site at 1 ft (30 cm) apart for the summer. They are moved indoors when the buds show colour, and in any event before night frosts set in. To obtain more profuse sprays, the plants may be pinched back until late June. The more often they are stopped, the more branches they will produce, although the branches will be shorter. For cut flowers it is best to make do with just one stopping, directly after the plant has been established outside. For larger individual blooms the bud clusters must be thinned to the largest terminal one (disbudding) while still small. All *C. indicum* hybrids like liquid fertilizer in the summer, and they must be watered frequently in dry weather.

Cultivation of florists' chrysanthemums

Florists' chrysanthemums are grown for their large flowers. They are not allowed to form sprays but are sold as single-flowered stems. Hence the best cultivars are those derived from large-flowered parents. These include a few which flower so early that they may easily be grown in the open. Others flower too late and must be covered with glass in the autumn. Most large-flowered florists' chrysanthemums produce the best flowers from the first crown bud. When the young plants are 6–8 in (15–20 cm) tall, pinch out the tip

and allow up to six lateral shoots to develop, later reducing to the strongest three or four. Each of these stems can now be allowed to grow naturally (apart from pinching out any axillary shoots) until the flower bud cluster shows. Once the cluster is big enough to handle, disbud. However some produce the best flowers on the second crown bud. These plants must have the first laterals pinched back to 5 or 6 leaves. All but the strongest side shoot on each stem is removed and these are allowed to grow on and flower, disbudding as before. Good catalogues always state which crown bud must be secured. When cutting chrysanthemums, care should be taken to discard all flowers that have been bruised, however slightly. Many growers protect large-flowered chrysanthemums with plastic bags well before their flowers open.

Cimicifuga
Ranunculaceae
Bugbane

These herbaceous perennials grow naturally in woods and will therefore tolerate a fair amount of shade. They will also do well in the sun provided the ground is not too dry. They are good border plants.

Soil Bugbanes like rich, neutral to acid soil. Mulch with leaf-mould or compost during March.

Propagation By division or from fresh seeds sown under glass.

Cimicifuga cordifolia (*C. racemosa cordifolia*)

○ ◑ ⊛ ⊝ ⊙ ⑦
A North American plant, growing to heights of 2–4 ft (60–120 cm). In late summer it bears white flowers in erect spikes.

Cimicifuga dahurica

Growing up to 6 ft (2 m), this is the most attractive of the autumn-flowering species. The flowers are white and appear on numerous large, densely branched spikes. They appear in August and September.

Cistus
Cistaceae
Sun rose

These are attractive shrubs for sunny sites. They flower in late spring to early summer and must be kept away from freezing winds, which can damage or kill them.

Soil Any well-drained garden soil is adequate.

Propagation They can be grown from seed in spring or from cuttings (with a heel) in late summer.

Cistus × corbariensis

○ ⊛ ⊝ ⊙ ⑩ ⑦
A hybrid between *C. populifolius* and *C. salvifolius*, first found in the wild. This bushy shrub grows 2–3 ft (50–100 cm) high, bearing small, dark green leaves and white flowers with a yellow eye.

Cistus crispus

A bushy shrub from the western Mediterranean, growing up to 2 ft (60 cm) high with grey-white hairy leaves up to 1¾ in (4 cm) long. The flowers are red-purple.

Cistus × cyprius

A hybrid between *C. ladanifer* and *C. laurifolius* that occurs in the wild. It is a

Cimicifuga racemosa

Cimicifuga racemosa

○ ◑ ⊛ ⊝ ⑦ ⊗
Snakeroot, from Canada. It grows 3–4½ ft (1–1.3 m) high, and in early summer bears white flowers on long, branching spikes. A very attractive border plant and the best of the summer-flowering species.

Cimicifuga racemosa cordifolia, see *C. cordifolia*.

Cimicifuga simplex

Syn. *Cimicifuga foetida simplex*. Originally from eastern Asia, this plant grows up to 4 ft (1.2 m) high. Its yellow-green star-shaped flowers appear in late summer to autumn.

Clarkia unguiculata

vigorous shrub, up to 6ft (2m) high, with narrow leaves that are dark green above and greyish beneath. The flowers are white, each petal having a central dark red blotch.

Cistus ladanifer
An erect shrub found in southwestern Europe that grows up to 6ft (2m) high. It has dark green, narrow, leathery leaves, and white flowers with a maroon blotch at the base of each petal.

Cistus launifolius
Similar to *C. ladanifer* in most respects, but the leaves are broader and the pure white flowers smaller.

Cistus parriflorus
A compact shrub up to 3ft (90cm) with ovate grey downy leaves and clear rose-pink flowers about 1in (2.5cm) wide. Some forms are remarkably hardy.

Cistus × purpureus
A hybrid between *C. ladanifer* and *C. creticus*, this rounded shrub grows to heights of 3–4ft (1–1.2m). It has grey-green leaves and light crimson flowers with a maroon blotch at the base of each petal, and is less hardy.

Cistus × 'Silver Pink'
Probably a cross between *C. laurifolius* and *C. creticus*, this shrub grows 2–2½ft (60–75cm) high with narrow grey-green leaves and silvery pink flowers.

Clematis 'Nelly Moser'

Clarkia
Onagraceae

Attractive annual plants for the border, they are suitable for cutting and for pots indoors.

Soil This plant grows in every kind of garden soil.

Propagation Sow in the flowering site March–April and thin out the seedlings to 10in (25cm) apart. Flowering lasts from the beginning of July to the middle of August.

Clarkia concinna
○ ⊙ ⊛ ⊗
Syn. *Eucharidium concinnum*. An uncommon annual that grows 8–12in (20–30cm) high with branching, reddish stems and ovate-lanceolate leaves. The flowers, which open in summer, have dark pink to lilac, ribbon-like petals and bright red sepals.

Clarkia elegans, see C. unguiculata.
Clarkia unguiculata
Syn. *C. elegans*. Originally from California, this plant grows to 2ft (60cm) high and flowers in summer, according to the sowing time. Double cultivars may be grown in carmine, pink, red,

The early-flowering *Clematis montana* is a most floriferous species

Clematis macropetala

Clematis 'Ville de Lyon'

scarlet, violet and white; all come fairly true from seed. The single sorts are also attractive but are less commonly seen.

Clematis
Ranunculaceae

A large genus of climbing plants and several herbaceous perennials.

Cultivation Many of the climbing species and especially the large-flowered hybrids do not grow well on dry ground, but it is a great help to plant them so that the roots are shaded, perhaps by positioning a small shrub such as *Lavandula*, *Euonymus fortunei* or *Santolina* on the sunny side. It is also possible to improve the soil with leaf-mould and peat; indeed an annual

mulch is indispensable with the large-flowered hybrids. *C. montana*, *C. vitalba* and other small-flowered species are relatively tolerant of drought conditions and make few other demands on the soil. All species should be planted at a good depth.

The more freely and naturally a clematis is allowed to grow, the more beautiful it will turn out to be. Young plants will have to be trained up against trellises or wire supports, but older plants should be allowed to cascade down. Some winter protection, above all for young plants and early-flowering species, is recommended. Spring-flowering species should only be pruned after flowering; the summer-flowering species should be pruned in the spring.

Soil Clematis will grow in any soil that

is not too acid, provided the roots can obtain sufficient air. They do best in humus-rich, calcareous soil. Before planting, dig out a hole about 1½ft (45cm) square and fill to a good depth with rich soil. In autumn, dress with manure or garden compost and dried blood.

Propagation Herbaceous perennials can be propagated by division or from seed. The woody climbers are propagated from layers in spring or cuttings in late summer. The species can be grown from seed sown in a cold frame as soon as it is ripe. Germination takes place the following spring.

Clematis × durandii
○ ◑ ⊚ ◐ ⊗
A cross between *C. integrifolia* and *C. × jackmanii*, this is a low climbing plant, no more than 4½ft (1.3m) high, suitable for training on low fences. In summer it produces dark violet flowers measuring 3–4in (7.5–10cm) across.

Clematis flammula
○ ◑ ⊚ ⊛ ⊚ ⊚
Found from the Mediterranean to Persia, this plant climbs to a height of 13ft (4m), bearing fragrant, creamy-white flowers in summer.

Clematis heracleifolia
○ ◑ ⊚ ⊚ ⊚ ⊚
Originating in eastern Siberia, northern China and Japan, this summer-flowering plant produces hyacinth-like, indigo-blue flowers.

Clematis hybrids
⊚ ⊚ ⊚ ⊚
Among the large-flowered hybrids are some of the best-known garden cultivars. The five most important groups are:

Lanuginosa. A group including 'Lilacina Floribunda', which has deep purple-blue flowers; 'Lincoln Star', whose flowers are rose with a purple-brown centre; 'Madame le Coultre', with white flowers; 'Nelly Moser', which has pale mauve-pink flowers, each sepal having a carmine central bar; 'Prins Hendrik', whose lavender flowers have pronounced bars; 'The President', which has dark violet-blue flowers; and 'William Kennard', with dark lavender-blue flowers.

Patens. In this group are 'Lasurstern', with very large dark blue flowers; 'Miss Bateman', a white-flowering variety with brown stamens; and 'Vyvyan Pennell', which has violet-blue generally double flowers.

Florida group. This includes 'Duchess of Edinburgh', which has double white flowers.

Jackmanii group. Among the cultivars are 'Comtesse de Bouchard', with soft satin-pink flowers; 'Gypsy Queen', which has dark red flowers with pink bars; 'Jackmanii-Superba', with larger flowers than *C. × jackmanii*; 'Madame Baron Veillard', with reddish-purple flowers; 'Perle d' Azure', which has light blue flowers; and 'Sealand Gem', whose heliotrope

Clematis 'Lady Betty Balfour'

Clematis 'Barbara Jackman'

Clematis 'Comtesse de Bouchaud'

flowers have a pink glow.

Viticella. This group includes 'Ernest Markham', a red-flowering variety; 'Lady Betty Balfour', which has velvety purple flowers; and 'Ville de Lyon', which bears an abundance of carmine flowers.

Pruning. In restricted areas on walls or pergolas, hybrids that come into flower after June should be cut down to the last pair of buds in early spring. Alternatively, they may be cut back before winter to clear away the dead wood in good time (this is why many people prefer late-flowering hybrids). If grown naturally in trees, pruning is not necessary. Late-flowering hybrids include 'Prins Hendrik' and all hybrids in the *Jackmanii* and *Viticella* groups.

Clematis × jackmanii

○ ◑ ◒ ◓ ◔ ◕

A cross between *C. lanuginosa* and *C. viticella*, this is a fast-growing climber, generally with triple leaves and 4 in (10 cm) purple-blue flowers. See also under *Clematis* hybrids.

Clematis macropetala

○ ◑ ◒ ◓ ◔

A very hardy climber, growing up to 10 ft (3 m) high and bearing bowl-shaped flowers in late spring to mid-summer.

Clematis montana

A vigorous climber from the Himalayas that flourishes on dry ground and is one of the easiest flowering climbers to grow. It may be trained against a north wall. In late spring to early summer it bears a profusion of white flowers (pink in 'Rubens'). The new 'Tetrarose' variety is generally larger, its rose-red flowers growing up to 3 in (7.5 cm) across.

Clematis orientalis

Native to Iran, the Himalayas and China, a vigorous plant growing to a height of 20 ft (6 m). The foliage is pale green and fern-like. Its yellow, star-shaped flowers appear in August–October. They are followed by silvery-grey seed heads in October–November.

Clematis recta

○ ◑ ◒ ◓ ◔ ◕

A herbaceous plant of floppy habit from Europe, Asia and North America, that grows up to 4½ ft (1.3 m) high with a support of pea sticks. In early to mid-summer it produces white flowers, sometimes with a touch of yellow.

Clematis tangutica

○ ◑ ◒ ◓ ◔

A vigorous climber to 20 ft (6 m) or more with solitary yellow lantern-

Clematis recta, an attractive creamy-white border plant

shaped flowers. Its late flowers are followed by attractive silvery seed heads.

Clematis × violacea

A hybrid of *Clematis flammula* and *Clematis viticella*, this deciduous plant reaches a height of 12 ft (4 m). It bears dark green leaves and pale violet flowers which appear in August–September. The variety 'Rubromarginata' has white flowers with a red edging.

Clematis viticella

A plant of southern Europe, climbing to a height of 10 ft (3 m), it bears violet-pink flowers in summer. Cultivars include double forms in numerous colours: 'Kermesina', which has crimson flowers, is the best known. See also under *C.* hybrids.

Cleome
Capparidaceae
Spider flower

An annual with a pronounced bushy growth, bearing spider flowers so striking in appearance that it is often used as a specimen plant.

Soil A fertile, well-drained soil is needed, enriched with humus

Propagation Sow from March onwards under glass at 18°C (64°F), then prick out into pots and plant out in late May, 1½ft (45 cm) apart.

Cleome spinosa

○ ⊙ ⊛

Spider flower. An attractive plant, 3–4ft (1–1.2 m) high, it bears profuse clusters of purple-red flowers in July–September. The cultivar 'Cerise' has beautiful cherry-red flowers; those of 'Pink Queen' are pink and white, and 'Helen Campbell' has white flowers.

Clematis tangutica

Cleome spinosa 'Cerise', an attractive spider flower

Cobaea
Polemoniaceae
(*Cobaeaceae*)

Half-hardy climbers, these plants are often grown as annuals to provide quick cover for pergolas, while the hardy climbers are still very small.
Soil They will grow in all types of well-drained soil.
Propagation Sow February–March. Place one or more of the large seeds in a pot and keep in a warm place. Plant out in late May.

Cobaea scandens

○ ⊙ ⦾

Cup and saucer creeper, from South America. It provides useful quick cover for pergolas, trelliswork, etc. The main growing period is July–August, when development is so vigorous that the plant quickly reaches a height of 10ft (3m). From August to September, bell-shaped flowers appear, yellowish-white maturing purple.

Colchicum
Liliaceae
Autumn crocus

A genus of bulbous species with crocus-like flowers, produced direct from the corms. The flowers are mainly larger and the leaves much longer and broader than those of the crocus. Plant in a sunny or only lightly shaded position, in any well-drained fertile soil, at a depth of about 4in (10cm). Alternatively place the corms in a bowl indoors August–September; they need no watering before coming into flower. Immediately after flowering, the corms must be planted outside. From June to July, after the leaves have died down, the bulbs may be lifted again and potted if required. In the garden, they are seen to best advantage at the front of the shrubbery or as edging plants or in lawns. They should be planted 8in (20cm) apart.
Soil They prefer a well-drained but

Cobaea scandens

moisture-retentive fertile soil.
Propagation Plants can be grown from seed, but are best increased by offsets.

Apart from a few attractive hybrids such as 'Lilac Wonder' (lilac-pink flowers), 'Lilac Queen' (purple-violet), 'The Giant' (dark lilac), and 'Water Lily' (lilac-mauve double flowers), the forms most commonly seen in gardens are:

Colchicum autumnale

○ ◑ ⦾ ⦿ ⦾ ⊗

Meadow saffron. A 6–8in (15–20cm) high plant that grows wild in meadows. It flowers in late summer to autumn, after the leaves have died down, producing pink, lilac or pale purple blooms. 'Albiflorum' has white flowers; 'Plenum', with red double flowers,

looks less attractive outdoors, while 'Purpureum' has dark purple flowers and is very suitable for the garden.
Colchicum bornmuelleri (*C. speciosum bornmuelleri*)
This plant produces large, pale violet flowers with a white centre in mid-summer.
Colchicum bulbocodium, see *Bulbocodium vernum*.
Colchicum byzantinum
An excellent indoor plant, it bears lilac-pink flowers.
Colchicum speciosum
This species bears large pink flowers September–October. The variety 'Album' has pure white flowers and is exceptionally beautiful. *C. s. bornmuelleri*, see above.
Colchicum vernum, see *Bulbocodium vernum*.

Colutea arborescens, bladder senna

Colutea
Leguminosae
Bladder senna

A genus of large deciduous flowering shrubs suitable for medium to large gardens. These plants can grow to a height of 10ft (3m) and have a similar spread. Coluteas are sometimes used as hedge fillers, being planted between less vigorous shrubs. After four years or so, when the rest of the hedge has caught up, the coluteas may be discarded.
Soil Any ordinary garden soil.
Propagation Sow seeds in May in the open and transplant the seedlings to their permanent position as soon as possible, having first trimmed the tap-roots to encourage more vigorous growth. Seeds germinate within a month.

Colutea arborescens

○ ◑ ⦾ ⦿ ⊗ ⊗

Originally from southern Europe and the Near East, these plants have a height and spread of 6–10ft (2–3m). They flower in late spring to early autumn, producing yellow pea-shaped flowers in racemes.

Colchicum speciosum, an autumn crocus

Convallaria majalis, lily of the valley

Convolvulus tricolor curling its petals in the sunlight

Colutea × media
○ ◑ ◍ ⊛ ⊛

An attractive cross between *C. arborescens* and *C. orientalis*, it bears orange to yellow-red flowers in summer, followed by bladder-shaped pods.

Colutea orientalis
○ ◑ ◍ ⊛

A broad and erect shrub with bluish-green foliage. It grows to a height of 6 ft (2 m), and bears reddish-brown flowers June–September.

Convallaria
Liliaceae
Lily-of-the-valley

Its delicious fragrance and attractive flowers have earned the lily-of-the-valley long-lasting popularity as a garden plant. It makes a delightful contribution to small flower arrangements, and is often used in wedding bouquets.

Cultivation Lily-of-the-valley does best under light shrubs or trees. It has underground stems (rhizomes) that bear buds. The best planting time is in November, when the buds are ready to open.

Soil Plants grow in any humus-rich soil.

Propagation This can be done by division of the rhizomes. They can be grown from seed, but it is very slow.

Convallaria majalis
○ ◑ ◍ ⊛ ⊛ ⊛ ⊛ ⊝ ⊗

Found in Europe and neighbouring areas of Asia, this plant, 6–10 in (15–25 cm) high, grows mostly in fairly open, deciduous woods. White flowers appear in late spring. Cultivars include 'Plena', with double white flowers; 'Rosea', which has pale pink flowers; and 'Variegata', with white flowers and creamy-white striped leaves.

Convolvulus
Convolvulaceae

This genus comprises annuals, perennials, sub-shrubs and shrubs, many of them climbers. The majority of the 250 known species are either tropical or have little garden-worthiness. Of the species mentioned below, the annual *C. tricolor* is the most colourful and suitable for growing in annual and mixed borders.

Soil This should not be too acid, nor too rich. It must be well drained.

Propagation Sow in April. Convolvulus is difficult to transplant, hence the seed is best sown in the flowering position and the seedlings thinned out 8–10 in (20–25 cm) apart. Convolvulus may also be sown earlier under glass in peat pots and transplanted later. Shrubby species can also be increased by semi-hardwood cuttings in a propagating case with bottom heat in late summer.

Convolvulus althaeoides
A hardy herbaceous perennial from southern Europe with twining or trailing stems. The grey-green basal leaves are roughly triangular, but higher up the stems they become deeply lobed in a pinnate or pedate fashion. In summer 1–1½ in (2.5–4 cm) wide pink flowers open in succession from the upper leaf axils. *C. a. tenuissimus* (syn. *C. elegan-*

tissimus) is densely silky, silvery hairy, and with more deeply cut leaves. It is the most attractive form but can be invasive in some light soils.

Convolvulus cneorum
From the western and central Mediterranean, this half-hardy species is one of the finest of all silver-leaved shrubs. The 1–2½ in (2.5–6 cm) long evergreen leaves are hairy and make an excellent foil for the pink-budded white flowers, which are usually borne in quantity from late spring to autumn. This shrub needs a sunny sheltered site but is only badly damaged in continental-type winters.

Convolvulus elegantissimus, see *C. althaeoides tenuissimus*

Convolvulus mauritanicus, see *C. sabatius*

Convolvulus sabatius
Syn. *C. mauritanicus*. This delightful half-hardy sub-shrub forms mats of prostrate slender stems set with small, hairy, obovate leaves. During the summer and autumn silky purple ¾ in (2 cm) wide flowers open in succession and often in profusion. It needs a sunny sheltered site, for example a dry wall.

Convolvulus tricolor
○ ○ ⊛

Dwarf convolvulus, from the Mediterranean region and Portugal. At first recumbent, it then grows erect 8–16 in (20–40 cm) high. In summer it produces flowers that are blue, white and yellow in that order from the edge of the petals to the throat. Cultivars include white, dark blue, pink and red sorts, of which 'Monstrosus' is particularly attractive, 'Royal Flag' has cherry red flowers with a white centre.

Coprosma
Rubiaceae

A genus of berrying evergreen trees and shrubs from the Pacific region. The majority need greenhouse treatment but the following New Zealand species make interesting additions to the rock garden and patio. The tiny insignificant flowers are unisexual and carried on separate plants. To ensure a crop of berries, therefore, at least two individuals, ideally several females to one male, are required.

Soil Any well-drained but not dry soil is suitable, ideally enriched with peat or leaf-mould. Grit or coarse sand should be added to the heavier soils.

Propagation Increase is not difficult by semi-hardwood cuttings with a heel in a case with bottom heat. Seeds should be sown when ripe in a cold frame.

Coprosma acerosa
A spreading mat-forming shrub with narrow yellow-green leaves and intriguing translucent blue fruits.

Coprosma petrei
An Alpine shrublet forming dense mats of small, dark green, narrowly elliptic leaves which, under ideal conditions, become thickly studded with purplish to blue-white fruits.

Coprosma repens 'Variegata'
Although too tender for outside culture all year, this striking shrub makes a splendid container subject for the summer patio, its dense, glossy, obovate leaves being boldly margined creamy-yellow.

The hoop petticoat growing in the alpine meadow at Wisley, Surrey

Coreopsis tinctoria

Yellow *Coreopsis verticillata*

Corbularia, see
narcissus

Cordyline
Agavaceae

Evergreen trees and shrubs mainly originating in warmer regions of the Southern Hemisphere. They have one or more stems terminating in a sheaf-like rosette of long, narrow leaves, creating a palm-like appearance.
Soil They will grow in any well-drained garden soil.
Propagation This can be by seed, from stem section cuttings or suckers.

Cordyline australis
Cabbage tree, from New Zealand where it grows up to 65 ft (20 m); in cooler areas it does not usually exceed 35 ft (10 m). Unbranched when young, it makes a good accent plant for summer bedding. Provided severe frosts are not encountered, plants will grow to tree size, branching and producing leaves up to 3 ft (1 m) in length. The fragrant flowers are borne in large clusters and are followed by white fruit. The varieties 'Purpurea' and 'Rubra' have coloured foliage.

Cordyline indivisa
Syn. *Dracaena indivisa*. Usually single stemmed, this robust New Zealander is probably the most imposing of all cordylines. It has a stem up to 9 ft (3 m) and a massive head of lanceolate leaves. Each leaf is 3–6 ft (1–2 m) long, purple flushed above and often with a blue-

white patina beneath. Mature specimens may produce large compact panicles of small white flowers, which are followed by bluish berries. It stands shade much better than *C. australis* but is somewhat more tender.

Coreopsis
Compositae
Tickseed

A genus containing many attractive annuals and perennials for the garden. All are excellent in borders and the annual species also make splendid cut flowers.
Soil Plants will grow in any ordinary garden soil, however, a light soil gives the best results.
Propagation Annual species are sown in the open in spring, and thinned out to 10 in (25 cm) apart. Perennial species are easily divided or grown from seed. In either case, the plants should be lifted every three years, divided and replanted.

Annual species
Coreopsis basalis
From North America, this plant grows to a height of about 1½ ft (45 cm) and flowers 10–12 weeks after sowing, producing ray florets that are dark yellow, and brownish-purple underneath with a brownish-yellow to purple disc. Double-flowered strains are available.
Coreopsis bigelovii
This plant is characterized by its alternate leaves and yellow flowers, measuring 1½ in (38 cm) across, that open in early to midsummer.

Coreopsis grandiflora, a very attractive plant for the border

61

Cornus kousa var. *chinensis* in the autumn

Flowers of *Cornus mas*

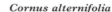

Coreopsis tinctoria
A plant from North America, whose taller cultivars grow up to 3 ft (1 m) high and shorter cultivars up to 1 ft (30 cm). Flowering takes place 10–12 weeks after sowing, when dark yellow ray florets appear, with purple or brown underneath. Numerous cultivars are available in many different colours.

Perennial species
Coreopsis grandiflora
○ ⊖ ⊖ ⊛ ⊗
A plant growing 2–3 ft (60–100 cm) high, producing yellow flowers on long stems in midsummer, and winged fruits. 'Badengold' is a very attractive cultivar, 3 ft (1 m) high, with dark golden-yellow flowers.

Coreopsis verticillata
○ ⊖ ○ ⊛
From North America, this slender but sturdy attractive border plant can grow to a height of 2 ft (60 cm). The foliage is cut into thread-like segments and its flowering period stretches from June to September, when clear yellow, star-shaped blooms are borne. 'Grandiflora' is slightly taller and has slightly larger flowers.

Cornus
Cornaceae
Dogwood, Cornel

This genus includes many attractive herbaceous perennials and shrubs for semi-shady and sunny places. They can be divided into several groups. The more attractive species such as *C. kousa* (the best known), *C. florida* and *C. nuttalli* (the rarest, but most beautiful of all), bear their flowers in clusters surrounded by large cream-coloured bracts. Rather different is the densely branched *C. mas* (Cornelian cherry), which is often grown as a solitary specimen and produces an abundance of small yellow flowers on bare twigs as early as February. A striking winter effect is provided by species with coloured twigs, such as *C. alba* and *C. stolonifera*.

Soil Cornels grow on any normal garden soil that is adequately moist. *C. mas* and *C. sanguinea* also do well on dry ground. *C. canadensis*, *C. florida*, *C. nuttallii* and *C. suecica* thrive on slightly acid soil.

Propagation *C. canadensis* and *C. suecica* are propagated by division; *C. alba* and *C. stolonifera* by division and also by layering. *C. florida*, *C. kousa*, *C. mas* and *C. sanguinea* can be grown from seed. Garden varieties must be grown from layers if they are to keep their fine shape. *C. sanguinea* and *C. stolonifera* are frequently propagated from heeled cuttings.

Cornus alba
○ ◑ ◐ ⊗ ○ ⊗
Red-barked dogwood, from northern China. Growing up to 10 ft (3 m) high and having a similar spread, this spring-flowering tree produces white, rather inconspicuous flowers. Its leaves are green on top, and bluish-grey underneath; the stems are red in autumn and winter. Those of 'Sibirica' are bright crimson. 'Gouchaultii' is a spreading shrub with yellow and pink variegated leaves. 'Kesselringii' has black-purple branches, puts out red leaves and demands a moist position. 'Spaethii' has bronze-green variegated leaves that turn gold at the edges. 'Westonbirt' has bright red stems in winter. The species and varieties are deciduous.

Cornus alternifolia
○ ◑ ⊗ ◑ ⊥
Not often seen in gardens this large shrub has reddish-brown branches and bears white flowers in small clusters. Its fruits are round and dark blue.

Cornus canadensis
◑ ○ ⊛ ⊛ ⊗ ⊗ ⊖
A spreading herbaceous perennial from North America. Growing 4–8 in (10–20 cm) high, it forms attractive carpets of mid-green ovate leaves that are tightly crowded together. Greeny-purple flowers surrounded by four large bracts appear in June. The berry-like fruits are bright red and edible.

Cornus controversa
○ ◑ ◐ ⊗ ◑ ⊛ ⊘ ⊥
A shrub closely resembling *C. alternifolia*, but the branches of this species are strongly tiered. *C. c.* 'Variegata' (wedding cake tree) leaves are boldly variegated creamy-white.

Cornus florida
○ ◑ ◐ ⊛ ⊗ ⊗ ⊖
Originally from the eastern United States, this plant generally reaches heights of 12–18 ft (4–6 m) in Europe and has a spread of 6–12 ft (2–4 m). In May, shortly before the leaves come out, yellow flowers are borne in clusters, surrounded by four white bracts.

Cornus alba has a red bark in winter

Cornus stolonifera 'Flaviramea'

Cornus canadensis which makes outstanding ground-cover

*The beautiful flowers of *Cornus kousa*

The fruits are scarlet, and the leaves turn beautiful shades of red in autumn. 'Rubra' has most attractive rose-pink and white bracts but flowers less profusely. 'Cherokee Chief' has deep rose-red bracts.

Cornus kousa
○ ◑ ◐ ⊛ ⊗ ⊘ ⊗ ⊖
From Japan and China, this tree reaches a height of approximately

Corydalis lutea

Corydalis solida

Cortaderia selloana, pampas grass, looks most beautiful in the autumn

12–18ft (4–6m), with a spread of 10–12ft (3–4m). In late spring to early summer it produces very large creamy-white bracts; the fruits are strawberry-like. *C. kousa* var. *Chinensis* has larger bracts.

Cornus mas
○ ◐ ◑ ◒ ⊕ ⊗ ⊥ ⊞

Cornelian cherry, from central and southern Europe, the Near East, Caucasus and Armenia. A shrub or small tree reaching heights of 10–22ft (3–7m) with a spread of 6–12ft (2–4m). From March to April, bright yellow flowers appear in clusters on the naked twigs. There are several cultivars, one of the best being 'Variegata', with leaves that are conspicuously white margined.

Cornus nuttallii
○ ◐ ◑ ⊗ ◒ ⊕ ⊗ ⊥

A very attractive tree with a strong resemblance to *C. florida*. Its leaves turn bright red in autumn, and the creamy-white bracts later become flushed with pink.

Cornus sanguinea
○ ◐ ◑ ◒ ⊕ ⊗ ⊞

Common dogwood, from Europe and the Near East. It grows to heights of 10–15ft (3–5m), with a spread of 6–10ft (2–3m). In late spring to early summer small inconspicuous white flowers appear, followed by purple fruits. The leaves are bright red in autumn; in winter the twigs turn red.

Cornus stolonifera
○ ◐ ⊗ ◒

A North American shrub growing 6ft (2m) or more high. It produces white flowers followed by white fruits in early to midsummer. The branches turn blood-red to brownish-red in autumn and winter. The best-known cultivar is 'Flaviramea', which has yellow to olive-green shoots in winter.

Coronilla
Leguminosae

Pea-flowered perennials and shrubs from Europe and the Mediterranean.
Soil Any well-drained garden soil.
Propagation By seed or spring cuttings.

Coronilla varia
○ ○ ⊗ ⊖

Crown vetch, from central and southern Europe. This vigorous, semi-prostrate perennial growing up to 1ft (30cm) high makes good ground cover in a sunny site. The leaves have up to 12 pairs of leaflets; light purple, pink or white flowers are borne in clusters of 10–20 from August to October.

Cortaderia
Gramineae
Pampas grass

One of the most impressive of all ornamental grasses.
Cultivation Plant in April in well-drained, fertile soil, choosing a sheltered and sunny spot. If required, remove the dead leaves carefully when the young foliage expands in May. Feed every 14 days.
Soil Plants will grow in any well-drained garden soil.
Propagation Division of established plants gives much better results than propagation from seeds. The plant is dioecious, i.e. the male and female sex organs are on separate individuals. The plumes of the female specimens are more attractive and retain their silvery glow longer. If grown from seed, it is best to select good female plants—the difference is apparent only when they flower—and to divide them in April.

Cortaderia selloana
○ ○ ⌂ ◒ ⊕ ⊥ ⊗

Syn. *Gynerium argenteum* and *Arundo sellowana*. A densely tufted species from temperate South America. It has arching slender leaves 3–6ft (1–2m) long, each with finely serrated hard margins that can easily cut a finger if carelessly handled. In autumn stems grow rapidly reaching 5–10ft (1.5–3m), topped by silvery-white plumes 1½–3ft (45–90cm) long. Several worthwhile cultivars are available: 'Aureolineata' has the leaves striped with yellow; 'Monstrasa' is the tallest, well-grown plants always exceeding 10ft (3m), it also has more spreading plumes; 'Pumila' only grows to 5ft (1.5m) and is ideal for the small garden; 'Rendatleri' is tall, its large plumes arching and tinted rose-purple; 'Sunningdale Silver' has feathery white plumes.

Corydalis
Papaveraceae
(*Fumariaceae*)

A genus of hardy perennials, suitable for naturalization in shady positions.
Soil A neutral to slightly acid soil is preferred.

Propagation The grasses are grown from seed. Sow either in the autumn or in early spring.

Corydalis cashmeriana
◐ ⌂ ⊕ ◒

Originally from Kashmir, plants grow to a height of 8in (20cm) and bear brilliant blue flowers from late spring to midsummer. Undoubtedly this is the most beautiful of the *Corydalis* spp, but it is difficult to cultivate outdoors in areas where summers are warm and dry. It is best grown in an alpine house that should be well-aired in summer. Avoid calcareous soil.

Corylopsis pauciflora in March

Corylopsis
Hamamelidaceae

A genus of compact shrubs, hardy and very suitable for the ornamental garden. They flower early on the leafless stems.

Soil These plants like a humus-rich, well-drained soil, preferably lime-free. Calcareous soil should be liberally enriched with peat or leaf-mould.

Propagation They can be grown from cuttings in July or August but are not easily rooted; hormone treatment and bottom heat are necessary. Layering in October is the surest method of propagation.

Corylopsis pauciflora
○ ◑ ⊛ ⊗ ⊙ ⊛

A wide-spreading shrub from Japan that grows to a height of 4ft (1.2m). It strongly resembles *C. spicata* but bears smaller flowers in great profusion and for a longer period.

Corylopsis spicata
○ ◑ ⊛ ⊗ ⊙ ⊛

A Japanese shrub growing 3–6ft (1–2m) high and flowering in March, before the leaves come out. Bright yellow, cowslip-scented flowers are borne in pendant racemes. The leaves have a metallic sheen that makes the shrub stand out even after flowering; in autumn it takes on a most attractive coloration.

Corylus
Betulaceae
Hazel

Hazel trees are grown for their attractive appearance as much as or for their nuts, which are borne late in the year in variable quantities according to the weather conditions.

Soil A neutral or slightly alkaline soil is preferable.

Propagation Plants can be grown from seed or from layers in spring.

Corylus avellana
◑ ◑ ⊛ ⊗ ⊛

Hazel. A shrub very suitable for planting in the shade of larger shrubs or trees. In winter, flowers appear in catkins. 'Aurea' has soft yellow leaves; 'Contorta' ('Corkscrew hazel' or 'Harry Lauder's walking stick') has curiously twisted branches; 'Fuscorubra' has a compact habit and resembles the more

Corylus avellana 'Contorta'

Corydalis cheilanthifolia
◑ ◑ ⊛ ⊗ ⊛ ⊙ ⊛

A plant from China with fern-like foliage that bears numerous yellow flowers from late spring to early summer. It grows to a height of 1ft (30cm).

Corydalis lutea

Yellow corydalis from Europe. A densely branched plant up to 1ft (30cm) high that in summer produces lemon-yellow flowers, paler at the tips. Seeds prolifically and can become a weed.

Corydalis nobilis

Originally from Siberia, this plant flowers somewhat earlier (April–June), and grows slightly taller than other *Corydalis* spp. The flowers are slightly darker at the tips than those of *C. lutea*, and are flushed purple on the inside.

Corydalis solida
◑ ◑ ⊛ ⊗ ⊛

Purple corydalis. A plant growing 6–10in (15–25cm) high and bearing violet-purple flowers March–April. It is very suitable for naturalization in open woods, where it may seed itself.

Corylus avellana 'Pendula', a rarely seen weeping form of the common hazel

Cosmos bipinnatus

common *C. maxima* 'Atropurpurea' though the leaves are paler; 'Pendula' is a weeping form.

Corylus colurna
🔵 ❀ 🌳 ✿

Turkish hazel. Eventually a large tree, up to 65 ft (20 m) high, that is profusely clothed in yellow-brown catkins in early spring, followed by nuts in late autumn. The leaves remain on the stem for a long time in autumn. The crown is oval at first but becomes more pyramidal with age; the bark is somewhat corky. This species may also be grown as a large bush.

Corylus maxima
🔵 ❀ 🌳 ✿

Filbert. A large shrub with striking purple leaves. 'Atropurpurea' ('Purple-leaf filbert') is the only ornamental form seen in gardens.

Cosmos
Compositae

A genus of annuals, excellent for cutting and for growing in borders. The large flowers bear some resemblance to dahlias. The plants must be staked in the summer.

Smoke tree *Cotinus coggygria* in the summer, full of feathery panicles

The smoke tree in the autumn

Soil An ordinary garden soil is adequate; it should not be too rich.

Propagation Sow in April under glass; prick out the seedlings into boxes before they have a chance to become straggly. Plant out in May in a warm, sheltered position, some 2 ft (60 cm) apart. In good weather it is possible to sow the seeds outside in May. For early flowering, sow under glass in February or March.

Cosmos bipinnatus
⊙ ⊙ 🌳 ✾ ⊗

Purple Mexican aster. This plant grows up to 3 ft (1 m) high, and flowers in July–October; the blooms are rose or pink. Catalogues usually list the early-flowering Praecox cultivars, also known as 'Sensation'. Other attractive sorts include 'Dazzler', with dark crimson flowers; 'Gloria', whose flowers are dark pink with a central red ring; and 'Versailles', which has rose flowers with a purple ring.

Cosmos sulphureus
⊙ ⊙ 🌳

A Mexican plant bearing pure orange flowers, 1–2 in (2.5–5 cm) across, and growing to a height of 2 ft (60 cm). 'Klondyke' is a late-flowering cultivar with golden-orange flowers.

Cotinus
Anacardiaceae
Smoke tree

A striking shrub for the medium-sized and larger garden. The dark-leaved forms in particular can provide beautiful colour contrasts.

Soil These shrubs grow in any reasonably well-drained garden soil.

Propagation They can be raised by layering or from cuttings in summer.

Diseases The dark-leaved cultivars are very susceptible to mildew; little can be done to prevent attacks.

Cotinus coggygria
⊙ 🌙 ✾ ✿ ☺ ①

Syn. *Rhus cotinus*. A shrub widely distributed in southern Europe, and through the Himalayas to China. It grows to heights of 6–10 ft (2–3 m), with a spread of 6 ft (2 m). Flowering in early to midsummer, it produces greenish, inconspicuous flowers that mostly drop off unfertilized. A peculiar feature of the smoke tree is that many of the flower stalks are covered with pinkish hairs and turn smoky-grey in late autumn. 'Purpureus' ('Burning bush') is a fairly common variety with green

Cotoneaster × watereri

Cotoneasters are usually grown for the sake of their fruits, though the flowers, too, can be very attractive

followed by brilliant red fruits each with two seeds. 'Little Gem' is a dwarf form that does not bear fruit.

Cotoneaster apiculatus

○ ◐ ⊛ ⊛ ⊛

A Chinese shrub, growing 3–6ft (1–2m) high with arching branches that bear rounded leaves and white flowers followed by bright red fruits.

Cotoneaster applanatus, see *C. dielsianus*.

Cotoneaster bullatus

○ ⊛ ⊛ ⊛

A broad, evergreen, vigorous shrub with wide-spreading twigs. The leaves are 2–3in (5–7.5cm) long and conspicuously corrugated. It flowers in late spring to early summer bearing pink followed by orange-red fruits.

Cotoneaster conspicuus

○ ⊛ ⊛ ⊛ ⊖

The best-known of these shrubs is *C. conspicuus* 'Decorus', a low, arching, wide-spreading and profusely flowering shrub. It produces white flowers followed by orange-red fruits. The species has white flowers and red fruits.

Cotoneaster dammeri

○ ⊛ ⊛ ⊛ ⊖

Never growing taller than 6–8in (15–20cm) and usually prostrate, this shrub is seen to best advantage when trailing over a wall. It has dark green leaves, solitary white flowers, and scarlet fruits. 'Major' is an exceptionally vigorous selection, as is 'Skogholm', probably a hybrid, which grows to a maximum height of 18in (45cm).

leaves and panicles resembling, from a distance, puffs of pink smoke. 'Red Beauty' has exceptionally large leaves that turn from light red to deep purple, though not so deep a shade as those of 'Royal Purple', a very beautiful and vigorous cultivar having maroon-red foliage. 'Rubrifolius' has deep wine-red leaves. Smoke trees that become thin-bottomed may safely be cut back hard.

Cotinus obovatus

Syn. *Cotinus americanus* and *Rhus cotinoides*. This native of the south-east USA makes a large shrub or small tree 16ft (5m) or more high. It has inferior floral panicles to those of *C. coggygria* but has larger and more decorative leaves. These are bronze-pink when young, orange, scarlet and purple in autumn. It thrives best on acid soil.

Cotoneaster
Rosaceae

Although the flowers of these ornamental shrubs are not very spectacular, they attract bees in large numbers. Their chief attractions for the gardener are the elegant habit of many species and the magnificent fruits, which per-

sist deep into winter, or as long as the birds allow. Cotoneasters are grown for various special purposes, as follows:

1 For ground cover. Species include *C. dammeri* and *C. salicifolius* 'Repens'. Both are evergreen.

2 For growing against walls. Species include *C. horizontalis* and *C. salicifolius* var. *floccosus*.

3 For informal hedging. Among these species are *C. acutifolius* and *C. simonsii*.

Soil Cotoneasters do well in any garden soil.

Propagation Plants can be grown by layering and from seed sown in autumn and placed in a cold frame.

Cotoneaster acutifolius

○ ⊛ ⊛ ⊞

A deciduous, wide-spreading shrub that grows up to 10ft (3m) high with hairy branches, pinkish flowers, black berries and leaves which turn red in the autumn.

Cotoneaster adpressus

○ ◐ ⊛ ⊛ ⊛ ⊖

A low, deciduous, creeping shrub growing up to 1ft (30cm) high. Its leaves, dull green on the upper side, are hairy when young. Small red flowers appear in late spring to early summer,

Cotoneaster horizontalis, its branches arranged in herringbone fashion

Cotoneaster salicifolius in good fruit

'Coral Beauty' resembles 'Skogholm' but bears many more fruits.

Cotoneaster dielsianus

Syn. *C. applanatus*. An ornamental, vigorous shrub with arching branches that grows to a height of 6 ft (2 m). The leaves are dark green on the upper side, and greyish-yellow and hairy underneath. The white flowers are followed by solitary scarlet fruits, which remain on the shrub for a long time. Good orange- to red-tinted foliage in late autumn.

Cotoneaster divaricatus

A shrub that grows up to 6 ft (2 m) high with thin, drooping branches and shiny green, almost round leaves. It bears pink flowers followed by red fruits.

Cotoneaster franchetii

A very graceful, semi-evergreen plant with drooping branches that grows to a height of up to 6 ft (2 m), with a spread of 10 ft (3 m). Its shiny leaves, pale sage-green on top, darken in maturity; underneath they are downy, sometimes with a yellowish tinge. The flowers are pink and borne in June, the fruits orange-red. This is a most attractive plant to grow as a solitary or specimen tree on the lawn.

Cotoneaster franchetii var. ster-nianus, see C. sternianus.

Cotoneaster horizontalis

A deciduous shrub with flattened branches resembling fronds, invaluable for growing against north- and east-facing walls or as ground cover. The short stem bears horizontal branches and may reach a height of 3 ft (1 m). Branches may be pruned. The plant has glistening leaves and bright red fruits with three stones. 'Robusta' is a very hardy, vigorous selection showing attractive colour changes in autumn.

Cotoneaster lacteus

An evergreen shrub from China that grows 6–12 ft (2–4 m) high. The arching branches carry oval, leathery leaves which are paler and downy beneath.

and arching branches. It grows up to 10 ft (3 m) high, and bears white flowers in profusion followed by masses of scarlet fruits.

Cotoneaster praecox

Excellent on banks, this shrub resembles *C. adpressus* but is generally larger, growing to a height of 2 ft (60 cm). Dark pink solitary flowers are followed by a brief show of red fruits that appear as early as August.

Cotoneaster racemiflorus

A tall deciduous shrub with hairy twigs and leaves that are 1–2 in (2.5–5 cm) long and almost circular, dull green on top and greyish underneath. It bears white flowers and red fruits with two stones. *C. racemiflorus* var. *soongoricus* has oval leaves and carries much heavier crops of fruit.

Cotoneaster salicifolius

A shrub that grows up to 11 ft (3.3 m) high with hairy twigs clothed in lanceolate leaves, covered with bluish down underneath. It bears masses of red fruits. Var. *floccosus* has graceful, drooping branches, long and slender dark green leaves white woolly beneath, and bears a profusion of scarlet fruits.

A hedge of *Cotoneaster simonsii*

Clusters of white flowers appear in July and are followed by red fruits, which ripen late and remain on the plant through the winter.

Cotoneaster microphyllus

A low, arching shrub reaching heights of 1½–3 ft (45–100 cm). The young branches are downy, and the leaves dark green above and hairy beneath. Solitary white flowers are followed by small numbers of large red fruits. *Cochleatus* is a charming, carpet-forming, prostrate variety.

Cotoneaster moupinensis

A shrub that strongly resembles *C. bullatus*. It has black fruits and is very tolerant of semi-shade.

Cotoneaster multiflorus

A deciduous shrub with an erect habit

Cotoneaster dammeri

'Autumn Fire' is a vigorous grower, with large leaves and red fruits. 'Park-teppich' resembles 'Repens' but is wider spreading and taller, has small leaves and a relatively small number of red fruits. 'Repens' (syn. 'Avondrood') is a prostrate shrub with narrow leaves and small red fruits, excellent for ground cover.

Cotoneaster simonsii

A shrub of erect habit, growing up to 10 ft (3 m) high and suitable for hedging. Its hairy branches carry glossy leaves with hairs on the ribs underneath (young leaves are completely covered in hair). Pale pink flowers are followed by masses of coral fruits.

Cotoneaster sternianus

Syn. *C. franchetii* var. *sternianus*. A very sturdy, deciduous shrub, up to 3 ft (1 m) high, which strongly resembles *C. franchetii* but has glossier leaves and produces fruits in greater abundance.

Cotoneaster × watereri hybrids

Many of these are crosses between *C. frigidus*, *C. salicifolius* and *C. henryanus*. They resemble the latter, but the leaves are generally broader and smoother above. 'Cornubia' has an

Cotula squalida for moist sites

erect habit; 'Exburiensis', another erect shrub, has large, strongly corrugated leaves and apricot-yellow fruits; and 'Pendula' is a weeping form with drooping branches.

Cotoneaster zabilii

A shrub growing up to 6 ft (2 m) high that bears red fruits. The branches are densely covered with hair in the young plant, but later become smooth. The ovate leaves are dull green on top, and are covered with yellow hair underneath.

Cotula
Compositae

A genus of mat-forming perennial plants that are not completely hardy. The flowers of the species described have no ornamental value.

Soil They thrive in any soil.

Propagation Plants are grown by division.

Cotula atrata

This New Zealander forms small mats of somewhat fleshy lobed leaves that are flushed copper to purple. The button-shaped flower heads are $\frac{1}{2}$–$\frac{3}{4}$ in

Crataegus × prunifolia is one of several ornamental thorns with an attractive autumn colour

Crataegus monogyna 'Pendula'

Crataegus laevigata 'Paul's Scarlet'

(1.2–2cm) wide, black-crimson with pin-like white stigmas. *C. a. luteola* has the flower heads burnt crimson when in bud, which then open wine-red and fade to pink.

C. coronapifolia

Brass buttons. A waterside perennial 4–12 in (10–30cm) tall having very slender leaves and a profusion of bright yellow flower heads in summer.

Cotula dioica

○ ◑ ⊗ ◠ ○ ⊛ ⊗ ⊖

A vigorous species from New Zealand, growing 2–3 in (5–7.5 cm) high. It has dark green leaves and yellowish button-like flower heads.

Cotula squalida

The most common garden form, this species is also from New Zealand and has hairy bronze-green leaves and greenish-yellow flower heads that appear in midsummer. Often planted between paving stones, *C. squalida* likes moist ground.

Crataegus × grignonensis

Crataegus
Rosaceae
Hawthorn, May

Those who know the hawthorn as a hedging plant only have not seen it at its finest. For it is when it is left unpruned that the hawthorn attains its most beautiful shape. It flowers most abundantly when planted in a sunny position. Single-flowered hawthorns are more fragrant than the double cultivars.

Soil Hawthorns prefer soil that is not too dry, but they can withstand long periods of drought in summer and wet in winter; if the soil contains some lime, so much the better.

Propagation Species can be propagated from seed, but this may take as long as two years to germinate. Harvest the seeds as soon as they are ripe, remove the pulp and sow in pots. Keep in a cold frame or sheltered spot outside and keep moist. Cultivars must be grafted on to stocks of *C. monogyna*.

Diseases Occasionally hawthorns are attacked by mildew and rust; fire blight causes a gradual dieback of branches. Leaf spot may also occur.

Crataegus × carrierei, see *C. × lavallei*.

Crataegus crus-galli

○ ◑ ⊕ ⊛ Ⓨ ⊘ ⊛

Coxspur thorn, from America. A wide-spreading tree with sharp, thorny branches. White flowers appear in spring in clusters of 15–20, followed by red fruits. Nurseries usually prefer *C. × prunifolia* which resembles *C. crus-galli* but has hairy flower clusters.

Crataegus × grignonensis

○ ◑ ⑩ ⚛ ⓨ

A hybrid of *C. stipulacea* and similar to *C. × lavallei*. It is a slow-growing tree with a dense crown. Excellent for streets and parks, it has green branches and leathery leaves with 2–4 pairs of short lobes that remain green until winter. It flowers in late spring to early summer and bears reddish-brown fruits.

Crataegus laevigata

○ ◑ ⑩ ⑩ ⚛ ⓨ ⊛

Syn. *C. oxyacantha* and *C. oxyacanchoides*. This shrub grows up to 12 ft (4 m) high with downy, reddish-brown twigs and thorns up to 1 in (2.5 cm) long. It bears flowers like *C. monogyna*, the common hawthorn, but with two or three styles. It can be distinguished from *C. monogyna* by its more shallowly lobed glossier leaves. *C. monogyna* produces fruits with one stone, while those of *C. laevigata* have up to 3 stones. Named cultivars include 'Alboplena', which has a wide-spreading habit and double white flowers fading to pink; 'Paul's Scarlet', with double scarlet flowers, which is highly recommended as a specimen tree; and 'Punicea', which with its large, single scarlet flowers and dull red fruits makes an excellent specimen shrub.

Crataegus × lavallei

Syn. *C. × carrierei*, a cross between *C. crus-galli* and *C. stipulacea*. A small, dense-headed tree with reddish-brown branches and 2 in (5 cm) spines. Its glossy dark green leaves are reddish in spring. In late spring to early summer it bears white flowers that are larger than those of the common hawthorn; the fruits, also larger, are orange in colour. A glorious tree for streets, this species is also excellent for medium-sized to large gardens.

Crataegus monogyna

Common hawthorn, from Europe. A tree or shrub, growing to a height of 25–30 ft, and flowering in early summer, about two weeks later than *C. laevigata*. It has long, straight spines and ovoid haws containing one seed each. 'Stricta' has a columnar habit, white flowers and edible red fruits.

Crataegus phaenopyrum

○ ◑ ⚛ ⊚ ⊛

Washington thorn, from the United States. A round-headed tree that grows up to 30 ft (9 m) high with large thorns and maple-like leaves which colour well in autumn. The clusters of white flowers are followed by crimson fruits.

Crataegus × prunifolia

○ ◑ ⚛ ⊚ ⊛

A cross between *C. crus-galli* and *C. macracantha* or *C. succulenta*, this hybrid resembles *C. crus-galli* but has olive-brown branches and broader, glossy, oval leaves. Flowers are borne in downy clusters, and are followed by crimson fruits. 'Splendens' is the most popular cultivar: it has a very broad crown and bears red fruit in November and December.

Crocosmia
Iridaceae

Bulbous plants, with long sword-shaped leaves. The beautiful flowers last well in floral arrangements.
Soil A rich, moist soil is preferred. Plant the corms to a depth of 2 in (5 cm) in spring.

Crocosmia × crocosmiiflora, commonly known as *Montbretia*

Propagation Plants are usually grown from seeds collected in autumn and sown immediately in pots placed in a cold frame. Garden varieties may be grown from bulbils.

Crocosmia × crocosmiiflora

○ ◑ ⊛ ⊛ ⊛ ⊛ ⊛

Syn. *Montbretia crocosmiiflora*. A cross between *C. aurea* and *C. pottsii* that grows to heights of 2–3 ft (60–100 cm). In mid- to late summer it bears bright orange-red, trumpet-shaped flowers in two rows running up the stems.

Crocus
Iridaceae

This genus of well-known garden bulbs is divided into autumn-flowering and spring-flowering species.
Cultivation Spring-flowering crocuses are planted in lawns, and are also used as edgings for flower and mixed borders, in rock gardens and in naturalized groups in orchards and meadows. They make splendid combinations with *Eranthis*, *Galanthus*, *Leucojum* and *Scilla*. In lawns, they should be planted early and be of very good quality.

Remove the turf, loosen the soil and plant the crocuses to a depth of 2–3 in (5–7.5 cm), replace the turf and lightly firm. Plant in informal groups, for instance under a tree. Crocuses may be left undisturbed for years but the foliage must then be allowed to die naturally; if a lawn containing them is mown too early, the bulbs quickly become exhausted and will not produce flowers in subsequent years. In borders and rock gardens, the bulbs should be planted to depths of 2–3 in (5–7.5 cm) and 3 in (7.5 cm) apart. Do not feed them with fresh manure, and do not lift them.

For cultivation in pots or bowls and for lawns, choose the largest bulbs; for borders, choose medium to large sizes.
Soil They thrive on any garden soil.
Propagation They are raised by replanting the numerous small cormlets or by seeds when ripe.

a. Autumn-flowering crocuses

Crocus byzantinus

○ ◑ ⚛ ⓨ ⊛

Syn. *C. iridiflorus* and *C. banaticus*. Flowering September–November, its outermost petals are light purple; the innermost ones, half as long, are white to pinkish-mauve. The styles are violet.

Crocus iridiflorus, see *Crocus byzantinus*.

Crocus kotschyanus

Syn. *C. zonatus*. A Turkish and Syrian crocus that flowers in autumn, bearing pinkish-lilac flowers having a ring of orange spots in the throat. See also *C. speciosus*.

Crocus longiflorus

A crocus from Sicily and Italy. Its fragrant flowers, appearing from October to November, are orange at the throat with a lilac exterior, often striped.

Crocus medius

From the western Alps, this crocus flowers October–November. It has violet petals and a white throat with violet veins.

Crocus pulchellus

From Yugoslavia to Turkey, an autumn-flowering crocus with blue-violet or white petals with five intertwining veins. This species has an elongated orange throat. Its leaves appear after the flowers.

Crocus sativus

Saffron crocus, found from the Mediterranean to India. From September to November it bears purple flowers with darker veins and an orange style.

One of the most beautiful crocuses is *Crocus tomasinianus*. A few snowdrops appear on the right

Crocus speciosus
Distributed through Persia, Asia Minor and southern Russia, this crocus bears lilac-blue flowers and, with *C. kotschyanus*, is one of the two most popular autumn crocuses. It comes into flower in early autumn. If they are placed in a dish or bowl of gravel or compost they will flower without water, but must be planted outside immediately afterwards. *C. s. Oxonian* has rich purple-blue flowers. It is advisable to stand them in dry sand or broken crocks. After flowering they may be planted out. If they are to flower in the garden, the bulbs must be planted out before the beginning of September.

Crocus zonatus, see *C. kotschyanus*.

b. Spring-flowering crocuses
Crocus aureus, see *C. flavus*.

Crocus angustifolius
Syn. *C. susianus*. 'Cloth-of-gold', from southern Russia. In March it bears orange-yellow flowers with brown streaks on the outside.

Crocus biflorus
Dutch yellow crocus. It has very narrow leaves $\frac{1}{10}$ in (3 mm) wide, and flowers February–March. The flowers are white with five feathery purple streaks on the outside of the outermost petals; the throat is yellow, and there are yellow anthers and red stigmas.

Crocus chrysanthus
The best-known wild crocus, having many cultivars. The most beautiful include 'Blue Bird', which is pure white inside with a bluish-grey exterior; 'Cream Beauty', with cream-yellow flowers; 'Lady Killer', which is shining white inside and dark purple

Crocus chrysanthus 'Blue Bird'

Crocus neapolitanus with *Crocus flavus*

Crocus longiflorus flowers in the autumn

edged with white outside. Slightly less impressive are 'Blue Pearl', which is light blue; 'E. A. Bowles', sulphur-yellow; and 'Saturnus', yellow with olive stripes.

Crocus etruscus
From Italy, this crocus produces bright lilac flowers with a yellow throat in March. 'Zwanenburg' is blue-violet on the outside and golden-yellow within.

Crocus flavus
Syn. *C. aureus*. From Yugoslavia to Turkey, this crocus has large flat corms producing orange-yellow flowers March–April. Most yellow cultivars are derived from this species. There are also several wild sorts in different shades of yellow.

Crocus imperati
Originating in Italy, this crocus flowers January–February or March in cold winters. Its inner petals are satin-purple, the outside ones buff tinged or feathered with purple; it has an orange throat.

Crocus napolitanus
Syn. *C. vernus*. An alpine species having purple or white flowers in February–March. Among the blue cultivars are 'Early Perfection'. with purple-blue flowers; 'Flower Record', which is light violet with a dark base;

'Queen of the Blues', soft blue; and 'Remembrance', purple with a silvery sheen. In the white group are 'Jeanne d'Arc', which is pure white, and the ivory 'Peter Pan'. 'Pickwick' is multi-coloured, being purple-grey with dark purple stripes.

Crocus susianus, see *C. angustifolius*.

Crocus tomasinianus
From Yugoslavia, this species bears slender flowers in a variety of blue shades, all with a white throat. 'White-well Purple' is a beautiful deep mauve.

Crocus vernus, see *C. napolitanus*.

Crocus versicolor
Originating in the southwestern Alps, this plant flowers March–April, producing white or violet blooms, many having violet stripes.

Cryptomeria
Taxodiaceae
Japanese cedar

An attractive genus of conifers that consists of a single species.
Soil A neutral soil is best, but it will grow in any soil rich in humus.
Propagation Species may be raised from seed, and cultivars from cuttings taken in September.

Cryptomeria japonica 'Elegans'

Cryptomeria japonica 'Cristata'

Cryptomeria japonica

A handsome conifer from Japan and China that attains a height of up to 50ft (15m). It has a broadly columnar habit and is easily cultivated, but does best in moist soils. The narrow leaves are densely crowded on the slender branches. The best-known cultivars are: 'Bandai-Sugi', a dwarf form with an irregular habit and green leaves that turn a bronze colour in winter; 'Compacta', with a compact habit, bluish-green leaves and a height of up to 50ft (15m); 'Cristata', whose branches are flattened into cockscomb-like growths; 'Elegans', which has a bushy habit and soft foliage turning bronze in winter—the commonest crytomerid in Britain; 'Jindai-Sugi', with bright green twisted leaves, a compact habit and a height of up to 8ft (2.4m); and 'Vilmoriniana', which grows to a height of 3ft (1m) only, forms a dense globe, and turns reddish-purple in winter.

× Cupressocyparis
Cupressaceae

An interesting hybrid, already very popular as a hedging plant.
Soil Any type of well-drained soil.
Propagation From cuttings.

× Cupressocyparis leylandii
Leyland cypress. This conifer is a cross between two plants of different genera, *Chamaecyparis nootkatensis* and *Cupressus macrocarpa*. A vigorous, quick-growing tree of dense columnar habit and a height of up to 65ft (20m), its foliage is light green to grey-green. The branches droop slightly and resemble those of *Chamaecyparis nootkatensis*. It is easily pruned. 'Leighton Green' is one of the most commonly propagated cultivars, with bright green leaves in fern-like sprays.

Cupressus
Cupressaceae
Cypress

Evergreen, coniferous trees with plume-like sprays of tiny, scale-like leaves and small, rounded, woody cones.
Soil Any well-drained garden soil.
Propagation Raise from seed in spring, or from cuttings in late summer.

A × *Cupressocyparis leylandii* hedge

Cynoglossum nervosum, hound's tongue

Cupressus macrocarpa
Monterey cypress, from California. This tree grows in a dense broad column up to 100ft (35m) high; when mature it becomes broad and flat-topped. It is often grown as a screening plant but resents being cut back; the foliage may also be damaged by severe frosts. Cultivars have golden-yellow foliage, and dwarf forms are available.

Cyclamen
Primulaceae
Cyclamen

Small perennials growing from woody corms and producing long-stalked leaves and small, shuttlecock-shaped flowers. Many species flower in winter and early spring and these are often grown under glass. Cool nights are essential for their successful cultivation, and an annual mulch of leaf-mould is very beneficial.

Cyclamen coum
Originally found in southeastern Europe and southwestern Asia, this species has rounded leaves that are either plain dark green or variously marked with silver patterning. The flowers are usually pale pink but can be darker or white. They appear in late winter or early spring.

Cyclamen cyprium
From Cyprus, this plant grows to 4in (10cm) high and bears white or pale pink flowers in October.

Cyclamen hederifolium
Syn. *C. neapolitanum*. A species from southeastern Europe and Turkey with lobed leaves, often rather like ivy (*Hedera*) with silver patterning. The flowers, which open in autumn, vary from carmine-red to mauve. 'Album' is pure white.

Cyclamen purpurascens
Syn. *C. europaeum*. This plant, from southeastern Europe, has rounded to heart-shaped leaves, either unmarked or with silver patterning. The pale pink flowers open from late summer to autumn and are very fragrant.

Cynoglossum
Boraginaceae
Hound's tongue

A genus of herbaceous perennials and biennials. The two species listed here are hardy.

Cytisus × *praecox* surrounded by heathers

Soil Any normal garden soil will suffice.

Propagation Seeds of *C. amabile* should be sown in an outdoor nursery bed in May or June, thinned and planted out from October onwards. To flower in the same year, the seeds can be sown at a temperature of 13–16°C (55–61°F) during February and March, pricked out into boxes, hardened off and planted out in May. Seeds of *C. nervosum* may be sown in the flowering position April–May, to flower in the same year, or in a cold frame March–April, then planted out in autumn. Plants may also be divided and replanted between October and March.

Cynoglossum amabile

○ ◐ ⊙ ⊙ ☉

A plant from China, growing 16–24 in (40–60 cm) high with sky-blue flowers. A particularly beautiful cultivar is 'Firmament', which has indigo-blue flowers.

Cynoglossum nervosum

○ ◐ ○ ☉

From the Himalayas, this plant grows 3 ft (1 m) high and bears intensely blue flowers in midsummer.

Cytisus
Leguminosae
Broom

A genus of attractive, mainly hardy shrubs for the border or less formal parts of the garden. Because most brooms tend to grow thin-bottomed and straggly, it is advisable to plant shrubs or perennials in front of them.

Cultivation All brooms are difficult to transplant, especially older ones, and it is best to buy pot-grown brooms only, and to ensure that the rootball is intact.

Brooms flower on shoots of the previous season and should only be pruned if absolutely necessary, and then immediately after flowering and never in autumn or spring, which inevitably leads to a loss of flowers.

Soil Most brooms like a light, well-drained soil, not too rich. *C. purpureus* prefers a limy soil. Most other species are indifferent, but see comments under individual species. They should be planted in a sunny position.

Propagation Species may be grown from seed in spring and cultivars from lateral cuttings in late summer to early autumn.

Pink garden variety of *Cytisus scoparius*

Cytisus albus

○ ◍ ☉ ⊗

Syn. *C. leucanthus*. White broom, an upright summer-flowering species with long, arching, hairy branches that grows to a height and spread of up to 6 ft (2 m). The flowers are white to creamy. This species is often confused with *C. multiflorus*.

Cytisus alpinus, see *Laburnum alpinum*.

Cytisus battandieri

○ ○ ◍ ☉ ⊗

A plant from Morocco that grows 10–16 ft (3–5 m) high. Its silky white hairy leaflets, borne in threes, make an interesting feature in all but the hardest winters, and in June erect golden-yellow clusters of pea-shaped flowers appear. These have a strong pineapple fragrance.

Cytisus × beanii

A dwarf hybrid resulting from a cross between *C. ardoini* and *C. purgans*. The plant, which grows up to 1½ ft (45 cm) high with a spread of 3 ft (1 m), strongly resembles *C. decumbens*, but is not quite so prostrate. Deep yellow flowers open in May.

Cytisus decumbens

○ ⊖ ⌃ ◍ ☉ ⊗ ⊖

Syn. *Sarothamnus decumbens*. A shrub that grows close to the ground with hairy twigs, bearing golden-yellow flowers in groups of 1–2 in late spring to early summer.

Cytisus hirsutus

○ ◍ ☉

Syn. *Chamaecytisus hirsutus*. An upright, small, hairy shrub of loose habit, tolerant of shade, that produces yellow or buff pea-shaped flowers in late spring to early summer

Cytisus purpureus (extreme left)

Cytisus × kewensis

○ ◍ ☉ ⊗

A cross between *C. multiflorus* and *C. ardoini*, this semi-prostrate shrub grows to a height of 1 ft (30 cm), with a spread of 5 ft (1.5 m). It bears cream-coloured flowers in spring.

Cytisus leucanthus, see *C. albus*.

Cytisus multiflorus

○ ⌃ ◍ ☉

A fairly large shrub with light green hairy drooping branches. In late spring to early summer it produces small, creamy-white flowers. In many catalogues this species is wrongly listed as *C. albus*.

Cytisus nigricans

○ ◍

Syn. *Lembotropis nigricans*. A plant of shrubby habit that grows to a height of 2½ ft (75 cm) and has greyish-brown branches. Yellow flowers are borne in midsummer in long terminal racemes.

Cytisus × praecox

○ ◉ ⊙ ⊛ ⊞

A cross between *C. multiflorus* and *C. purgans*, this plant grows up to 6 ft (2 m) high, and is generally wider than it is tall. One of the most beautiful of garden brooms, it has an attractive, arching habit. It flowers in spring with yellow buds and creamy-white flowers. 'Allgold' has a sulphur-yellow standard and darker wings.

Cytisus purgans

○ ◉ ⊙

Syn. *Sarothamnus purgans, Genista purgans.* A spring-flowering plant up to 3 ft (1 m) high with golden-yellow flowers.

Cytisus purpureus

○ ◠ ◉ ⊙ ⊛ ⊗

Syn. *Chamaecytisus purpureus.* From central and southern Europe, this plant grows 1–2 ft (30–60cm) high and looks most attractive in front of taller shrubs. Its flowers, appearing in early to midsummer, are usually purple-red, but white in 'Albus' and dark purple in 'Atropurpureus'. This species may be forced under glass.

Cytisus scoparius

○ ◉ ⊙

Syn. *Sarothamnus scoparius.* Common broom, growing up to 6 ft (2 m) high and bearing yellow flowers in late spring to early summer. Large-flowered hybrids include 'Andreanus Splendens', golden-yellow with dark crimson wings; 'Burkwoodii', with a light violet standard and yellow-edged red wings (an improvement of 'Dorothy Walpole'); 'Dukaat', which has a light yellow standard and deeper

Daboecia cantabrica (foreground)

yellow wings; 'Fulgens', whose standard is orange-yellow and wings deep crimson; 'Golden Sunlight', with a golden-yellow standard and orange-yellow wings; 'Luna' which has a light yellow standard and deep yellow wings; 'Maria Burkwood', with a standard that is white on the inside and crimson on the outside, has crimson, yellow-edged wings; 'Newry Seedling', which has a purple-yellow standard and brownish-red wings; 'Palette', with a yellow-white standard and dark red wings; 'Red Wings', with a crimson standard and dark red wings, and 'Roter Favorit', with a light red standard and dark red wings.

'Kinky', an outstanding pompon dahlia

Daboecia
Ericaceae

A genus of evergreen sub-shrubs that are grown in very much the same way as heathers and are often used in combination with them. The species listed is hardy in Britain.
Soil A light, peaty, acid soil is preferred.
Propagation Plants may be raised from cuttings or from seed.

Daboecia cantabrica

○ ◉ ◠ ◉ ⊙ ⊛

St Dabeoc's heath or Irish heath. Originally from Ireland, France and Spain, this evergreen shrub grows to a height and spread of up to 3 ft (1 m), with narrow, dark green leaves, $\frac{1}{4}$–$\frac{3}{4}$ in (6–19mm) long. Light violet urn-shaped flowers are borne during July–October. The many cultivars include 'Alba', with white flowers; 'Bicolor', which has pink and white flowers; 'Praegerae', with deep pink, and 'William Buchanan' with rosy crimson flowers.

Dahlia
Compositae

These popular tuberous-rooted perennials originated in Mexico, the first seeds reaching Spain in 1789 and Great Britain in 1802. Soon afterwards various species, among them probably *D. coccinea* and *D. pinnata*, were crossed to produce the so-called garden hybrids.

A classification of these hybrids is given overleaf.
Cultivation Garden dahlias are not difficult to grow. The most important thing to remember is to enrich the soil with well-rotted manure, garden compost, hop manure or peat and a general fertilizer. Although dahlias may be returned to the same position year after year, it is advisable to rotate them with other plants to avoid the possibility of virus infection.

Young plants grown from cuttings should not be planted out before 15 May, as even the slightest frost can destroy them. Since frosts may also occur after that date, it is advisable to keep some large flower pots ready to cover the tender plants if it is necessary. After planting out, the young dahlias should be watered thoroughly. The planting distances vary according to type: Lilliputs should be spaced 9–12 in (23–30cm) apart, dwarf bedders 15 in (38cm) apart and all other types 2½ ft (75cm) apart.

If dahlias are to be grown for cut flowers, plant a few tubers 3 ft (1 m) apart, or plant out rooted cuttings 1 ft (30cm) apart in special beds, each bed being divided into two or three rows also 1 ft (30cm) apart. Stakes are driven into the ground and garden twine stretched between them at heights of 1 ft, 2 ft and 3 ft (30cm, 60cm and 1 m). Because they are so close together, the individual dahlias support one another and do not need to be tied separately, which makes cutting much easier. If the tubers are planted 3 ft (1 m) apart, then every plant has to be tied, which is a laborious process. Each tuber is allowed to produce three shoots at most.

If only one shoot appears, then it must be "stopped", i.e. pinched out, some 8 in (20cm) above the ground to encourage branching. Rooted cuttings must be stopped as well, but only when established. During the growing period a dressing with well-rotted stable manure, or artificial fertilizer, can do wonders, particularly on poorer soils.

If large cut flowers are wanted, then the side shoots must be thinned—snapped off sideways as soon as they can be held between thumb and fore-finger. Disbudding is also necessary, e.g. removing the two smaller buds beneath the main terminal one. The flowers should only be cut after they have opened and before the rear petals have begun to fade. If they are cut too soon, the flowers will wither prematurely. They should be cut in the early morning as soon as they are dry, or in the evening, and the stems plunged immediately into water and allowed to soak for a few hours.

The tubers should be lifted immediately after the first frosts blacken the foliage, and in any event not later than 15 November. Before lifting the tubers it is customary to attach a label giving their name. Next, the stem is severed with secateurs about 6 in (15cm) above ground and the tubers lifted very carefully. They must be dried before they are stored, preferably in dry peat, in a frost-proof place. The tubers should be inspected in mid-January. If they show signs of rotting, then the peat was too moist and must be immediately replaced; if they have shrivelled badly then the store-room was too dry and the tubers should be placed in slightly moist peat.

'Baudelaire', a semi-cactus dahlia

'Trendy', a decorative dahlia

An anemone-flowered dahlia

A collerette dahlia

Soil Any fertile garden soil can be used.
Propagation Cultivars may be raised by division or from cuttings, as follows:
a By division of old tubers.
This is by far the simplest method for amateur gardeners. In early March, the tubers are cleaned before being placed in shallow wooden boxes filled with light soil that should be kept fairly moist. In a warm room, young shoots will appear soon afterwards and must be allowed to grow to a length of about 2 in (5 cm). Next the tubers must be removed from the boxes and divided with a sharp knife in such a way that each division has at least one eye or shoot. The cuts can be sprinkled with a fungicide or flowers of sulphur and the divisions potted separately in 5–6 in (12–15 cm) pots and placed in a light but not too warm place, if possible in a frost-free cold frame. The more light and air they are given, the earlier they will come into flower. Plant out in late April, placing a flower pot over every young plant if night frosts are expected. If the weather is unfavourable, it is best to defer planting-out until after mid-May.

b Propagation from cuttings.
This method gives quicker results and generally yields better flowering plants,

but requires a greenhouse and a cold frame. Towards the end of February, the tubers from which the cuttings are to be taken are placed in boxes on the greenhouse staging, close to the glass. Make sure the labels can be seen easily, and that the temperature is about 18°C (65°F). Keep slightly moist. The first shoots generally produce inferior plants and, if propagation on a large scale is not required, it is best to discard them. For the rest, every shoot appearing on a tuber can be used for cuttings. Once they are 2–3 in (5–7.5 cm) long, the shoots are cut off close to the tuber. If a large number of cuttings of new cultivars is needed, the shoots are allowed to grow a little longer and cut off a few eyes higher up, thus allowing the lowest eyes to produce further cuttings. Cuttings taken close to the tuber (with or without a heel) must have the lowest leaves removed. Cuttings taken higher up must be severed just beneath a leaf pair and also have their lower leaves removed. Place several cuttings round the edge of a 3½ in (9 cm) pot or singly in 2½ in (6 cm) containers of rooting compost and place in a propagating frame or in the warmest part of the greenhouse, where they should be kept shaded from the sun. In the mornings spray with tepid water, and ventilate well to prevent fungus infections. As soon as the cuttings have rooted, they are potted up singly in 3½–4 in (9–10 cm) pots, and placed in a frost-proof frame. If the weather is favourable, always remove the top. Dahlia cuttings must not be planted out before mid-May because of night frosts, but growth must not be halted in the meantime, and the first cuttings may have to be potted on into 5 in (13 cm) pots.

Dahlias can also be propagated from seed, but cultivars will not reproduce true to colour or type. The seeds are sown thinly in seed pans from mid-March onwards and covered with compost. The temperature should be about 18°C (65°F). As soon as the seedlings are large enough to handle, they are pricked out into boxes or individually into 3 in (7.5 cm) pots. They are grown

on as coolly as possible and planted out in late May or early June. The plants with the best flowers are marked and the tubers set aside for reproduction the following year.
Pests Dahlias are subject to severe attacks by greenfly and blackfly.

Dahlia hybrids

All garden dahlias are hybrids. Their heights vary widely, from 8 in–6 ft (20 cm–2 m), and they flower from late June to October. The leaves are pinnate; most are green, and some are suffused purple brown.

It is impossible here to list and describe all the cultivars available, since they run into thousands. Even if we mentioned only the most popular ones, our list would be out of date within a few years. The National Dahlia Society divides modern hybrid dahlias into 10 classes with some of the larger classes subdivided into sections:

Class 1. Single-flowered, with a single row of outer petals and an open centre.

Class 2. Anemone-flowered, with a dense group of tubular petals in the centre surrounded by one or more rings of flat outer petals.

Class 3. Collarette, with a ring of small petals (the "collar") surrounding an open centre and an outer ring of flat petals.

Class 4. Peony-flowered, similar to the singles but with two or more rings of outer petals.

Classes 5–9 are all doubles, i.e. the flowers have a closed centre instead of the open disc.

Class 5. Decorative, with broad, flat petals.

Class 6. Ball, with a spherical or slightly flattened shape and petals that point inwards for more than half their length.

Class 7. Pompon, with smaller, more globular blooms than the Ball class, the petals folding inwards for the whole of their length.

Class 8. Cactus, with narrow petals the edges of which are rolled back for more than half their length.

Class 9. Semi-cactus, with petals mostly narrower than those of Decoratives and broader than those of Cactus.

Class 10. Miscellaneous. All varieties whose shape cannot be fitted into any other category.

Because of numerous crossings it is not always easy to decide to which particular class an individual dahlia belongs, but with practice even the novice should be able to distinguish most types by class.

Daphne
Thymelaeaceae

A genus of small shrubs for garden and rockeries with attractive small flowers.
Soil A humus-rich, acid soil is needed.
Propagation From seed.

Daphne alpina
From the Alps, this deciduous species is not unlike a compact version of *D. mezereum*. It grows 6–12 in (15–30 cm) or more tall and bears fragrant white flowers in terminal clusters in early summer.

Daphne arbuscula
This charming evergreen bushlet from the Carpathian mountains seldom exceeds 6 in (15 cm) tall. The lustrous dark green thickly set leaves are linear to oblanceolate, about 1 in (2.5 cm). In early summer, all the shoot tips bear clusters of slender bright pink flowers.

Daphne blagayana
A spreading almost prostrate shrub from southeast Europe of rather gawky appearance but bearing a profusion of strongly fragrant white flowers in spring. It looks neater if all the stems are pegged down or held to the ground by stones once they are about 6 in (15 cm) long.

Daphne × burkwoodii
A semi-evergreen cross between *D. caucasica* and *D. cneorum* that grows up to 3 ft (1 m) high with downy branches and rather leathery leaves. Fragrant white or pink flowers are borne in

'Fascination', an attractive bedding dahlia

Daphne cneorum, the garland flower

groups of 15–20 in dense terminal clusters, from late spring to early summer. 'Somerset' grows to well over 3 ft (1 m) and has rich pink flowers appearing in May.

Daphne cneorum
○ ◑ ◒ ⊗ ◍ ⊕ ⊛ ⊗
Garland flower, from southern Europe. Generally no taller than 10 in (25 cm), it produces dense terminal clusters of fragrant rose-pink flowers from late spring to early summer; white flowers are rarer but do occur. The variety 'Alba' has white flowers and 'Eximia' is larger than the species.

Daphne genkwa
Considered by some to be the most desirable of all the larger daphnes, this Chinese species grows 3 ft (90 cm) or more tall. It is deciduous, the lanceolate to oval leaves being 1–2 in (2.5–5 cm) long and silky beneath. Unlike on most daphnes the leaves tend to be borne in opposite pairs. The blue-lilac flowers wreath the naked stem, as do those of *D. mezereum*. It is not an easy species to please, needing a well-drained soil with abundant moisture and fairly warm summers.

Daphne mezereum
○ ◑ ◒ ◍ ⊕
Mezereon, from Europe and northern Asia. Growing up to 3 ft (1 m) high, it is well suited to small gardens. In spring it bears deep rosy-purple fragrant flowers followed by scarlet fruit. Young plants have an upright habit, growing more globose in maturity. Prune sparingly, and only if absolutely necessary, immediately after flowering. 'Alba' has white flowers and yellow fruit; 'Grandiflora', also known as 'Autumnalis', has larger bright purple flowers and often begins to flower in autumn; 'Ruby Glow' produces dark purple-red flowers March–April and is highly recommended.

Daphne pontica
○ ◑ ◒ ⊗ ◍ ⊕ ⊛ ⊗
A wide-spreading shrub from Asia Minor that does very well on heavy ground. Yellow-green flowers appear April–May, followed by blue-black fruits.

Daphne mezereum, mezereon

Daphne retusa
From the eastern Himalayas to western China, this species forms a dense, rounded, evergreen shrub up to 2 ft (60 cm) tall. The 1–2 in (2.5–5 cm) long leaves are deep, lustrous green and of leathery texture. In late spring rose-purple budded white flowers open in terminal clusters.

Davidia
Davidiaceae
Handkerchief tree, Dove tree, Ghost tree

This genus has only a single but most unusual species. In spring, the tiny flowers are surrounded by a pair of large white bracts resembling pocket-handkerchiefs. The tree is sometimes jokingly described as the "Kleenex tree".
Soil Any ordinary garden soil will do, provided it is not too dry. They make excellent specimen trees.
Propagation Plants are raised by layering long shoots in October and severing from the parent plant two years later. They can also be grown

Daphne × burkwoodii 'Somerset'

from seed: germination usually takes 1½–2½ years.

Davidia involucrata
○ ◑ ◍ ⊛ ⊕ ⊕
A tree from western China that grows up to 30 ft (9 m) high and tends to branch from the base. It has an unpleasant smell. The leaves are ovate, pointed, toothed and hairy on the underside. Tiny purplish flowers appear in clusters May–June, borne at the base of white bracts up to 6 in (15 cm) long. The oval fruits are 2 in (5 cm) long, and contain very hard seeds like nuts. The species is largely represented in gardens by *D. i.* var. *vilmoriniana*, in which the underside of the leaf is smooth.

Decaisnea
Lardizabalaceae

A genus of medium-sized deciduous shrubs, particularly beautiful when in fruit.
Soil Any ordinary garden soil is suitable.
Propagation It may be raised from seed, from suckers or from summer cuttings.

Decaisnea fargesii
○ ◑ ◍ ⊛ ⊕ ⊕
A shrub from the mountains of western China that grows up to 8 ft (2.4 m) high with large, bluish-green pinnate leaves. Yellow-green flowers in large pendulous racemes appear May–June, followed by fleshy bean-like blue pods.

Davidia involucrata

Fruits of *Decaisnea fargesii*

Delphinium
Ranunculaceae

This genus includes annuals (of which *D. ajacis* and *D. orientale* are described below) and perennial species. The best-known delphinium is *D. × cultorum*.

Soil The plants like any rich, well-drained soil.

Propagation Annuals may be raised from seed sown in the flowering position September–October or in spring. Perennials may be divided, or raised from cuttings. They may also be raised from seed sown from February onwards under glass and in the open from April to July.

Diseases On dry soil, *D. ajacis* is often attacked by mildew; in too moist a site it may suffer from crown rot and root rot in winter.

Delphinium ajacis and *Delphinium consolida*

○ ⊙ ⓨ ⊚ ⊗

Larkspur. Both species grow $1\frac{1}{2}$–3 ft (45–100cm) high, and are generally alike with finely cut, fern-like leaves and flowers borne in loose racemes. Catalogues often distinguish between such strains as 'Giant Imperial', which branches from the base and bears double flowers in various shades, and the hyacinth-flowered types. These produce double flowers in spikes that tend to branch less than the others. In addition there are the dwarf cultivars that grow no taller than $1\frac{1}{2}$ft (45cm); they also bear double flowers.

Delphinium brunonianum

An intriguing dwarf species which rarely exceeds 10in (25cm). Found throughout the great Himalaya range and into Afghanistan and China, it is a tufted perennial with hairy, 5-lobed, kidney-shaped basal leaves which are somewhat musk scented when bruised. The hooded flowers have purple-tinted blue sepals and smaller almost black petals. A moist but very well-drained site is needed.

Delphinium cardinale

From California and Mexico, this fleshy rooted perennial is surprisingly handy in a sheltered well-drained site though tending to be short lived. It has deeply 5-lobed leaves and branched racemes of scarlet, cupped blossoms, each one $\frac{3}{4}$–$1\frac{1}{4}$in (2–3 cm) wide. It can be grown as an annual if sown under glass in early spring. The flowering period is July and August.

Delphinium × cultorum, see *D. hybrids*.

Delphinium grandiflorum

○ ⊚ ⓨ ⊚ ⊗

Syn. *D. grandiflorum* var. *chinense*. Plants grow 2–3ft (60–100cm) high and in summer bear flowers in various shades of blue and lilac. They are best planted in large groups.

Delphinium hybrids

○ ⊛ ⊚ ⓨ ⊚

Syn. *D. × cultorum* (*D. hybridum*). This group includes the Belladonnas, the Elatums and Pacific Giants. Growing up to 6ft (2m) high, they flower in early to midsummer in shades of blue, white, cream, pink, lilac and purple. While there are innumerable cultivars, those with sturdy stems and mildew resistance are to be preferred. Because the stems are not generally strong enough to carry the very heavy flower spikes in wet windy weather, it is advisable to

Delphiniums are the pride of every old-fashioned gardener. An attractive group of Pacific Giants 'Galahad'

support them. Do not drive a stake into the centre of a group of delphiniums, but a slim, strong bamboo cane into the ground at the base of each flowering stem in such a way that the tops of the canes are just below the flower spikes. Then tie the stems to the canes with raffia. If this is done, the delphiniums will retain their graceful habit. Cut the stems back after flowering to encourage the production of fresh blooms. The border will look bare once the flowering period is over, and it is therefore a good idea to plant some slightly later-flowering, shorter plants in front of the delphiniums.

The Belladonna cultivars are a relatively small type, growing $3\frac{1}{2}$–$4\frac{1}{2}$ft (1.1–1.4m) high with wiry stems and looser spikes. Well-known sorts are 'Capri', light blue; 'Lamartine', dark blue; 'Moerheimii', white; and 'Pink Sensation', bright pink.

The Elatum cultivars reach heights of up to 8ft (2.5m), and bear flowers in long spikes from late spring to midsummer. Many dozens of cultivars are available in shades of blue, purple and white; red ones also have recently been developed.

The Pacific Giants have large, loose spikes with large, generally semi-

'Blue Triumphator' is one of many Elatum varieties of Delphinium

A beautiful light blue delphinium of the Elatum variety

The annual *Delphinium ajacis*

double flowers, and grow 4–6ft (1.2–2m) high. They are generally grown as mixed colours from seed.

Delphinium menziesii
California to Alaska is the home territory of this tuberous rooted perennial. It has deeply cleft basal leaves and stems up to 18in (45cm) tall bearing rich deep-blue flowers from late spring to summer.

Delphinium nudicaule
○ ⌃ ◇ ⍟ ⊛
This species produces small red or orange-red flowers that are cup-shaped and spurred. Flowers appear in June and July.

Delphinium tatsienense
Akin to *D. grandiflorum*, this slender tufted perennial has hairy more dissected leaves and flowers with long spurs twice the length of the sepals. (The spurs of *D. grandiflorum* are the same length as the sepals.) Easily grown as an annual if sown under glass in early spring.

Deutzia
Philadelphaceae
(Saxifragaceae)

A genus of attractive, popular flowering shrubs. They are hardy, although the young growth may be damaged by late frosts, especially when followed by bright sunshine. In such instances, screen them from the sun with sacking. To encourage new growth, cut back the stems immediately after flowering (the flowers are borne on last year's or older wood). *Deutzia* strongly resembles *Philadelphus*, but whereas *Deutzia* has hollow branches, those of *Philadelphus* have a white pith.

Soil Though *Deutzias* are content with any ordinary garden soil, they will flower more profusely on heavy, fertile ground.

Propagation Plants should be raised from cuttings.

Deutzia corymbosa
This vigorous Himalayan species grows 6–10ft (5–10m) tall and is crowded with corymbs of pure white flowers around midsummer.

Deutzia crenata, see *D. scabra*.

Deutzia gracilis
○ ⍟ ◐ ⍟
A bushy shrub generally no taller than 3ft (1m), bearing white flowers in erect racemes or panicles 4in (10cm) high in late spring to early summer.

Deutzia × hybrida
A cross between *D. discolor* and *D. longifolia* that includes a number of medium-sized cultivars, all of which have large flowers with lilac-red petals, often with a lighter edge. 'Contrast' has drooping branches, while 'Mont Rose' is an upright shrub. 'Perle Rose' bears soft rose-pink flowers in June.

Deutzia × kalmiiflora
A cross between *D. parviflora* and *D. purpurascens* that grows up to 6ft (2m) high with drooping branches and white flowers, pink on the reverse, borne in clusters of 5–12.

Deutzia × lemoinei
A cross between *D. parviflora* and *D.*

gracilis. This group includes a number of attractive, generally white-flowered hybrids, taller than *D. gracilis*, that look splendid in front of other shrubs. 'Boule de Neige' has round clusters of white flowers resembling snowballs.

Deutzia × magnifica
A cross between *D. scabra* and *D. vilmorinae* with an erect habit, peeling branches and clear white flowers carried in broad panicles. 'Erecta' has finely toothed leaves and bears erect white panicles of most attractive, large single flowers. 'Magnifica' has densely filled double flowers.

Deutzia monbeigii
An uncommon Chinese species growing 5ft (1.5m) tall, with compact clusters of glistening white flowers.

Deutzia × rosea
A cross between *D. gracilis* and *D. purpurascens*, this compact shrub has brown, peeling bark and produces graceful flowers, white inside and purple on the reverse, that are borne in short, broad panicles in early to midsummer. 'Campanulata' has long, purple sepals and pure white petals; 'Carminea' has light pink petals.

Deutzia scabra
Syn. *D. crenata*. Probably the best-known species, this is an upright shrub

growing 6–10ft (2–3m) high. White or light pink flowers are carried in small, erect panicles in early to mid-summer. 'Candidissima' has white double flowers; 'Plena' has double white flowers with a central red stripe on the reverse of the petals; 'Pride of Rochester' is similar to 'Plena' but has a less pronounced pink stripe.

Deutzia × magnifica

Deutzia × hybrida 'Mont Rose'

Deutzia × rosea 'Campanulata'

Dianthus plumarius, pink

Dianthus deltoides, maiden pink

Dianthus
Caryophyllaceae
Pinks and Carnations

This genus includes many important garden species, some grown as annuals, others as perennials. The smaller species are used frequently in rock gardens or as edging plants, the taller ones in borders or cut-flower beds. One species has a drooping habit and may be planted in hanging baskets.

Soil Sandy loam is preferred. Most species are lime loving, but *D. deltoides* requires a slightly acid soil.

Propagation Annuals and biennials should be raised according to their group, as follows:

Dianthus barbatus (Sweet William). Sow April–July, preferably early in a cold frame, or from late May in a sheltered seed bed. Transplant once or twice, and move to the flowering position August–September 8–12 in (20–30 cm) apart. If the ground is not free by then, plants may be moved there in mid-October or in early spring, but those that are established in the final position in August–September are stronger and more floriferous. Although Sweet Williams may be grown as hardy perennials, they are not nearly so beautiful in consecutive years. There are also double cultivars many of which come true from seed. Double and single sorts can also be propagated by division, by layering and from cuttings. In the past, multicoloured cultivars used to be the most popular, but today there are very attractive single-coloured strains.

Dianthus caryophyllus (Carnation). Sow 'Chabaud' January–February in a moderately heated greenhouse or frame. The soil must be sandy, and the seeds, as with all types of *Dianthus*, must not be buried too deeply. Sprinkle regularly with a very fine rose. As soon as the seedlings can be handled they should be pricked out into boxes, hardened off in a cold frame and planted outdoors in fertile but not too heavy soil in May. Cover the flowers with cloches in autumn to prolong the display. Seed-sown plants invariably produce a number of single blooms of little value, but reliable seed should give an 85%–90% yield of double flowers.

Annual and biennial species:
Dianthus barbatus

○ ⊙ ⓨ ⊗

Sweet William. A perennial herbaceous plant, usually grown as a hardy biennial, that grows 6–16 in (15–40 cm) high and flowers June–July, bearing purple-pink flowers in flattened heads. There are a great many strong cultivars that can make do with most soils, but they grow better and flower longer in rich soil. Some recent cultivars come into flower the year they are sown. 'Wee Willie', 6 in (15 cm) high, offers a mixture of white, pink and red flowers. The scarlet 'Red Monarch' is slightly taller at 8 in (20 cm).

Dianthus caryophylus

○ ⊙ ⓨ ⊗

Carnation. A herbaceous perennial plant that reaches heights of 1½–2 ft (45–60 cm). Its fragrant flowers appear in various colours, and in single and double forms, in the midsummer months. There is also a group grown as annuals, the 'Chabaud' type whose large double flowers are reminiscent of florists' carnations but are less artificial in appearance.

All carnations should be sown very early or they will be too small when winter comes. Ideally sow under glass in warmth in February. Alternatively sow in a cold frame from April onwards (or in the open provided the young plants are protected with mats against night frosts). Prick out into boxes and plant out May–July. Cover with cloches during the winter in cold areas; the plants will come into flower during the next summer.

Dianthus chinensis

○ ⊙ ○ ⓨ

Indian pink. A herbaceous perennial, usually cultivated as an annual or biennial, growing 6–20 in (15–50 cm) high, with pale to mid-green leaves. Flowers are solitary or borne in small groups, with indented or fringed petals. Pinks come in many colours, but are not fragrant. There are numerous single and double-flowered varieties of which 'Imperialis' is one of the best known. 'Heddewigii' has blue-green leaves and large flowers, and 'Baby Doll' is a dwarf cultivar of mixed colours.

Perennial species:
Dianthus alpinus

From the Alps, a short-lived species reaching a height of 4 in (10 cm). The flowers are pink to purple with a white centre, appearing in May–August. The variety 'Albus' has white flowers.

Dianthus arenarius

A mat-forming plant growing to a height of 8–12 in (20–30 cm). The leaves are grey-green and the flowers are 1 in (2.5 cm) across and white with a green centre. They appear in May–August.

Dianthus × auvernensis

First developed in Auvergne, France, this hybrid grows to a height of 6 in (15 cm). It is very similar to *D. caesius* and bears numerous pink flowers in May–August.

Dianthus × calalpinus

A hybrid resembling *D. alpinus* from which it was derived. It grows to 3 in (7.5 cm) high and has pink flowers with white dots in the centre appearing in June–August.

Dianthus carthusianorum

From central Europe, this species grows to a height of 1–3 ft (30–90 cm). The leaves are mid-green and the flowers are pink and small, about ½ in (1 cm) across. They appear in June–September.

Dianthus deltoides

○ ⊝ ○ ⓨ ⊗

Maiden pink. Originally from Europe, this species grows 6–12 in (15–30 cm) high and flourishes in the south in sandy clearings. It flowers in summer, its pink petals marked with white spots and a purple ring.

Dianthus gratianopolitanus

Syn. *D. caesius*. Cheddar pink. This mat-forming grey-green-leaved plant is 4–6 in (10–15 cm) high and produces pink, red or white flowers in June.

Dianthus haematocalyx

A native of Greece, growing to a height of 6–12 in (15–30 cm). The leaves form a grey-green mat and the flowers are pink above and yellow underneath. They appear from early to late summer.

Dianthus knappii

From Hungary, a species growing to a height of 10–15 in (25–35 cm). Useful as either a border plant or in the rock garden, it has pale, grey-green leaves and bright yellow flowers with a purple spot at the base, borne in June.

Dianthus neglectus

From southwest Europe, growing 4–9 in (10–20 cm) high. The flowers, whose colours vary from pink to deep red, appear in July and August.

Dianthus plumarius

○ ⊝ ○ ⓨ

Wild pink, the ancestor of the garden pink. The true wild form is no longer grown, but cultivars make excellent bedding and edging plants forming loose mats of colour. 'Duchess of Fife' is 6 in (15 cm) high, with pink flowers; 'Maggie' is a double pink with a darker centre, also 6 in (15 cm) high.

Dianthus superbus

A species found throughout Europe and northern Asia, growing to a height of 9–18 in (20–45 cm). Shorter forms may be planted in a rock garden and taller varieties are more suitable in a herbaceous border. The latter need to be staked. The leaves are mid-green and the flowers white to mauve. They appear in midsummer.

Dianthus chinensis, Indian pink

Dianthus barbatus, sweet william

Dicentra
Papaveraceae
Bleeding heart

Also known as Lock-and-keys and Teardrops, this is one of the most old-fashioned perennials and is often found in country gardens. It may be listed as Dielytra.

Soil Humus-rich, ordinary garden soil is preferred.

Propagation Plants are raised by division or from cuttings.

Dicentra formosa

◑ ⊕ ○ ⊕ ⊕ ⊕ ⊜ ⊗

California bleeding heart. A North American plant growing 8–12 in (20–30 cm) high and bearing flowers June–October in pendulous clusters, rose-red to pale pink in colour. Its sturdy stems, long flowering period and beautiful pinnate, light green leaves make *D. formosa* a particularly good border plant, even though its colour may make it difficult to combine with others. The answer is to surround it with white-flowering plants, so that the pink is greatly intensified.

Dicentra spectabilis

◑ ⊕ ○ ⊛ ⊗ ⊘ ⊜ ⊗

Bleeding heart, or Dutchman's breeches, is from China and has a graceful habit, growing 2–3 ft (60–100 cm) high and flowering April–June, sometimes later. Bright pink to rose-red flowers are borne in arching racemes, and the blue-green leaves are also attractive. Because the plant takes up some 10 sq ft (3 sq m) of space and looks considerably less attractive after flowering, it is not well suited to the border, but is seen to best advantage when planted among shrubs and is best in partial shade. An alternative method of raising this species is by forcing in pots. Pot up in autumn, and plunge the pots into outside beds, protecting them with leaves against frost. Plants may be forced into flower from mid-January if taken to a very light, moderately warm place in the house; after flowering, they are taken outdoors again. Even when planted normally, bleeding heart will come into flower quite early in the year.

Dictamnus
Rutaceae
Burning bush

The common name reflects the fact that the flowers, the stems, and above all the old flower heads are covered in tiny glands containing volatile oils.

These highly ornamental plants should be used more frequently in the border. They take some time to mature, and quick results cannot be expected.
Soil *Dictamnus* will grow in any ordinary fertile well-drained soil.
Propagation Plants are raised from seeds sown when ripe, or by division in spring.

The flowers of *Dicentra spectabilis*, bleeding heart

Dictamnus albus

○ ⊜ ○ ⊛ ⊗

Syn. *D. fraxinella*. A plant growing 2–3 ft (60–100 cm) high and producing purple-pink, red-veined flowers in erect spikes June–July. 'Albiflorus' is sturdier and has white flowers.
Dictamnus fraxinella, see *D. albus*.

Dierama
Iridaceae
Wand flower

These very decorative plants have long, narrow, sword-shaped leaves which last through the winter. The flowers open from late July into August, dangling from very slender, arching stems which wave in the slightest breeze.
Soil Any well-drained, but not dry, fertile soil.
Propagation Plants may be raised by seeds sown in spring or by division.

Dierama pulcherrimum

○ ⊙ ⊛ ⊛ ⊕

A South African plant that flowers up to 6 ft (2 m) high, its stems hung with blooms up to 1¼ in (3 cm) long that emerge from papery bracts in shades of purple, red, pink and also white. This is an eyecatching plant for a sheltered, sunny site.

Digitalis
Scrophulariaceae
Foxglove

Most foxgloves are grown as biennials. They are very tolerant of shade and are often planted to add colour to shady spots, to the north edge of shrubberies, for instance, where the tall flower spikes of the lighter or multicoloured cultivars, such as *D. purpurea* 'Excelsior', look particularly impressive. Foxgloves will even flower under deciduous trees, if the crown is not too dense, and in very poor soil, although they may not reach anything like their

Dictamnus albus 'Albiflorus'

full height of 6 ft (2 m), and the flowers and spikes will also be much smaller.
Soil *Digitalis* will grow in any ordinary garden soil that does not dry out in summer. It appreciates humus.
Propagation Sow the very fine seeds in early summer in cold frames or in shady seedbeds, not too close together. Move to the flowering position in early autumn and plant 2½ ft (75 cm) apart.

D. purpurea is self-seeding, which has two disadvantages: firstly, too many young plants may be crowded together in the wrong places; secondly, cultivars do not always come true from seed. Hence it is better to remove the dead spikes when they have flowered and to grow new plants each year from freshly bought seed.

Perennial species can also be propagated by division.

Dicentra formosa

Digitalis purpurea

Foxglove. Normally grown as a biennial, this plant originates from western and southern Europe, and grows up to 5 ft (1.5 m) high, flowering in early to midsummer. The flowers of the species are red, often maroon-spotted on the inside. 'Gloxiniaeflora' is an improved variety with a sturdier habit and extra large flowers in colours ranging from purple to white that open in early to midsummer. In 'Excelsior' the flowers are carried horizontally all round the 5 ft (1.5 m) spike. 'Foxy' is similar to 'Excelsior' but not so tall, growing to a maximum of 2½ ft (75 cm); if sown under glass in February, it will flower the same summer. Perennial species of foxglove include:

Digitalis grandiflora

From Europe and the Caucasus, this plant grows 2–4 ft (60–120 cm) high and in early to midsummer produces flowers that are soft ochre yellow on the outside and brown-veined inside.

Digitalis × mertonensis

A cross between *D. grandiflora* and *D. purpurea*. The leaves and flowers of this perennial are larger than those of the parents. Crushed strawberry-pink blooms appear in early summer.

Foxgloves proliferate in the light shade of trees

Dodecatheon
Primulaceae
Shooting star

The flowers of these herbaceous perennials resemble those of cyclamens when inspected at close quarters. They are most attractive in raised positions in the rock garden, and beside a path. If the ground does not dry out too much in summer, they can also be planted in sunny positions. Nurserymen now generally offer hybrids. The flowers are mostly shades of red-purple or white.
Soil A humus-rich soil is needed, preferably with added leaf-mould or manure. Plant in a shaded position in moist soil.
Propagation Plants are raised by division in August. All the stronger roots have one or two little buds. These, together with segments of the root, are severed with a sharp knife and placed into seed boxes and kept fairly moist in a greenhouse or cold frame. It is also possible to grow shooting stars from seed sown in September or in March under glass in the cold frame. It takes a few years before the seedlings come into flower.

A strain of the common foxglove

'Gloxiniaeflora'

Propagation Sow in June in a moist, shady seed bed. Prick out and transfer to the flowering position in September, at least 1½ ft (45 cm) apart.

Dipsacus fullonum, see *D. sativus*.
Dipsacus sativus

Syn. *D. fullonum*. The common teasel, originally from southern Europe, a 3–6 ft (1–2 m) plant bearing tiny lilac flowers in dome-shaped heads. Its elongated leaves broaden out at the base and are slightly spinous along the edges.

Dipsacus sativus, teasel

Dimorphotheca
Compositae
Star of the veldt

These are most attractive annuals which demand a warm and sunny position.
Soil Any fairly light, well-drained soil will do; if necessary, improve drainage by adding a little sand.
Propagation Plants are raised from seed. For early flowers, sow under glass in March at a temperature of 18°C (65°F). Prick off the seedlings into boxes, harden off and plant out 6–8 in (15–20 cm) apart when the danger of frost is past. The young seedlings are very tender and must be handled very carefully.

Dimorphotheca annua, see *D. pluvialis*.
Dimorphotheca aurantiaca

Syn. *D. sinuata*. Of South African origin, this summer-flowering plant grows about 10 in (25 cm) high and produces bright orange flowers. Gardeners generally prefer the many hybrids ranging from white through yellow and salmon-pink to orange.

They all combine exceptionally well and make a fine display in the front row of the mixed border.
Dimorphotheca barbariae

A South African shrub 18 in (45 cm) high, bearing rosy-purple flowers from May to September. 'Prostrata' is lower growing and reaches only 6 in (15 cm).
Dimorphotheca pluvialis

Syn. *D. annua*. A plant growing 8–16 in (20–40 cm) high and flowering in midsummer, the blooms having a deep golden-brown central disc with a purple ring and creamy-white ray petals, purple on the underside.
Dimorphotheca sinuata, see *D. aurantiaca*.

Dipsacus
Dipsacaceae
Teasel

An ornamental plant grown as a biennial. The dead flower heads were used in the past for carding wool; their main use today is in dried flower arrangements.
Soil This plant will grow in any well-drained soil.

Dimorphotheca sinuata, the Cape marigold

Dodecatheon meadia, shooting star

Dodecatheon jeffreyi

This species grows 1–2 ft (30–60 cm) and bears purple-red to lavender flowers in May and June. It is downy and so is easily distinguished from *D. meadia*.

Dodecatheon meadia

Syn. *D. pauciflorum*. The leaves of this plant form in rosettes close to the ground. The purple-red flowers droop gracefully. They are borne in April and May.

Dodecatheon pauciflorum, see D. meadia.

Doronicum
Compositae
Leopard's bane

These attractive plants have daisy-like flowers. Cut flowers tend to curl up unless they are picked the day before use and soaked in water for 24 hours. The earliest cultivars can be forced in cold frames.

Cultivation The taller cultivars tend to topple over and should therefore be supported. Dead-head immediately after flowering to prevent seed formation.
Soil Any type of soil will do provided it is not too poor.
Propagation Plants are raised by division after flowering.

Doronicum caucasicum, see D. orientale.

Doronicum columnae

Syn. *D. cordatum*. A spring-flowering plant originally from the E. Alps to the Balkans, rarely growing above 6–8 in (15–20 cm) high.

Doronicum cordatum, see D. columnae.

Doronicum orientale

Syn. *D. caucasicum*. A Caucasian plant that grows 1–2 ft (30–60 cm) high and in spring produces yellow flowers with flat orange-coloured discs about 2 in (5 cm) across. 'Frühlingspracht' (syn. 'Spring Beauty') is a floriferous double cultivar; 'Goldzwerg' (syn. 'Golden Dwarf') has golden-yellow flowers, and those of 'Miss Mason' are a paler yellow.

Doronicum pardalianches

An invasive plant from western Europe, growing 2½–3 ft (75–100 cm) high and bearing yellow flowers in groups of 2–3 in early to midsummer. It is only suited to larger gardens.

Doronicum plantagineum

From western Europe, this plant grows 2½ ft (75 cm) high and produces dark yellow flowers April–June. A popular cultivar is 'Harpur Crewe' (syn. 'Excelsum'), which is excellent for cutting: it grows 4½ ft (1.3 m) high and tends to droop in the border.

Dryas
Rosaceae

A genus of hardy prostrate evergreen sub-shrubs, excellent for the rock garden and for growing between paving stones.
Soil A humus-rich, well-drained limy soil is needed.
Propagation By division or seed when ripe.

Dryas octopetala

Originally from northern and western Europe, this plant grows up to 6 in (15 cm) and has a creeping habit with prostrate, woody stems carrying dark green, shallowly lobed, glossy leaves. The eight-petalled white flowers appear July–September, producing attractive, fluffy seed heads in autumn.

Dryopteris
Aspidiaceae
Buckler fern

Perennial ferns for the garden.
Soil These plants require a loamy soil.
Propagation They may be raised by division of the crowns or from spores.

Dryopteris filix-mas

Male fern, growing up to 3 ft (1 m) with deep green lanceolate fronds. There are several cultivars, differing in leaf shape.

Dryopteris goldieana

Syn. *Aspidium filix-mas* var. *goldieana*. Sometimes confused with *D. filix-mas*, this plant has larger fronds.

Echinacea
Compositae
Purple cone flower

These attractive herbaceous perennials are closely related to *Rudbeckia*, with which they are often confused.
Soil They grow in any fertile soil.
Propagation By division.

Dryas octopetala

Echinacea purpurea

Syn. *Rudbeckia purpurea*. From North America, this plant grows 2–3 ft (60–100 cm) high and flowers in August–October, bearing flesh-coloured reddish-purple to crimson ray petals; at first these project horizontally, later they droop. 'The King' is dark crimson. Cultivars do not come true from seed.

Echinops
Compositae
Globe thistle

Herbaceous plants with strikingly handsome spherical flower heads. They make highly ornamental dried flowers, and in the garden attract bees in large numbers. Each plant needs 2–3 sq ft (60–100 sq cm) of space depending on its height.
Soil Any well-drained soil is suitable.
Propagation Plants may be raised by division, seed or root cuttings.

Echinops banaticus

From southeastern Europe, this plant grows to 3 ft (1 m) and more. It has thick, downy stems and slender, spiny, dark green leaves, downy underneath. Blue flowers appear in July–August.

Echinops humilis

An Asian species, 3–4 ft (1–1.2 m) high, flowering in late summer to early autumn. The flower heads are small and dark blue; another attractive feature are the lyre-shaped, wavy-edged, blue leaves, cobwebby on top and downy white underneath. 'Taplow

Doronicum orientale, leopard's bane in striking contrast to the blue *Anemone blanda* growing to the rear

Echium lycopsis

Echinops ritro

Dryopteris filix-mas, male fern

Echinacea purpurea 'The King'

Blue', 2½–3 ft (75–100cm), is exceptionally floriferous.

Echinops ritro
From southern Europe and the Near East, this plant grows 1½–3 ft (45–100cm) high and produces steel-blue flower heads from midsummer to early autumn. The leaves are divided, and smooth on top and downy underneath.

Echium
Boraginaceae
Viper's bugloss

This genus comprises hardy and half-hardy annuals and biennials. The best-known species is *E. lycopsis*, which provides excellent food for bees.
Soil The plants prefer a light dry soil.

Propagation They may be raised from seeds sown under glass in March and planted out at the end of May.

Echium lycopsis
○ ⊜ ☉ ⊗
Syn. *E. plantagineum*. A plant growing up to 15in (38cm) high and bearing purple flowers with a blue throat. Cultivars include 'Blue Bedder', which has pale blue flowers.
Echium plantagineum, see *E. lycopsis*.
Echium rubrum
Syn. *E. russicum*. Related and similar to *E. lycopsis* but with shorter leaves and red flowers. Well-grown plants grow 20in (50cm) tall. *E. r.* 'Burgundy' has dark red blooms. A useful hardy biennial which can be grown as an annual if sown earlier under glass.

Edraianthus
Campanulaceae

A genus of small plants closely allied to and resembling *Campanula*. All are of tufted growth, sometimes forming small mats, and are eminently suitable for the rock garden or raised bed in sunny sites.
Soil A well-drained rooting medium is essential, but apart from this proviso almost any soil type is suitable.
Propagation Seed is the usual means of increase, but cutting of non-flowering basal shoots can be taken as cuttings in late summer. Insert them in sandy or gritty soil in a cold frame.

Edraianthus dalmaticus
From the Jugoslav coast, this species forms tufts of short almost grassy leaves 2in (5cm) long. In summer, erect to ascending stems reach to 3in (7.5cm) long and bear blue-violet bell flowers in small clusters.
Edraianthus graminifolius
As its name suggests, this is a truly grassy leaved plant, with the narrow foliage 4in (10cm) long in compact tufts. The purple flowers are ¾in (2cm) long and carried in clusters on stems 4in (10cm) or more tall.
Edraianthus pumilio
This native of Jugoslavia is one of the most distinctive and desirable. It forms low, dense hammocks of tiny, narrow, grey-green leaves. In summer very short, slender, densely leafy stems arise, each one bearing a solitary blue-purple bellflower.

Edraianthus serpyllifolius
From Albania and Jugoslavia this is undoubtedly the showiest specimen in the genus. It forms small mats of narrow spoon-shaped leaves bearing stems up to 2in (5cm) long which in summer end in relatively large up-turned deep violet-purple bells.

Eichhornia
Pontederiaceae
Water hyacinth

A genus of tropical aquatic plants with attractive flowers of unusual shape.
Cultivation These plants flower in sunny, relatively shallow ponds during the summer provided the temperature does not drop below 18°C (65°F). In autumn, transfer into bowls containing loam covered with water ½in (12mm) deep, and place in a heated greenhouse. Store in the light, and bring out again in May.
Soil These plants are truly aquatic and do not root in the soil.
Propagation New plants are produced on the stolons in spring, and thrive at high temperatures. As soon as a young plant has produced several well-formed leaves, it is ready to be detached.

Eichhornia crassipes
○ ⊗ ⊘ ○ ⊗
Floating water hyacinth, originally from tropical and sub-tropical America. Its leaves grow on inflated petioles, in rosettes and the beautiful lavender-blue flowers are borne in spikes throughout the summer.

Elaeagnus
Elaeagnaceae
Oleaster

Attractive shrubs for fairly large gardens and parks. Old shrubs that grow straggly may safely be cut back and will quickly recover.
Soil The plants will grow in any well-drained ordinary garden soil.
Propagation They may be raised from seed, cuttings and layers.

Elaeagnus angustifolia
○ ◑ ◍ ⊛ ⊛
A deciduous shrub with lanceolate leaves that are greyish-green on top and silvery beneath. It bears pale amber-yellow fruit with a silver sheen, and grows up to 15ft (5m) high, with a spread of 15ft (5m).

Elaeagnus × ebbingei

Eichhornia crassipes, floating water hyacinth

Elaeagnus angustifolia, oleaster

Elaeagnus pungens 'Maculata'

Elaeagnus argentea, see *E. commutata*.

Elaeagnus commutata

○ ◐ ⦾ ⊛

Syn. *E. argentea*. The silverberry, a deciduous spineless shrub that grows slowly to a height of 7½ft (2.2m). The most beautiful of the silvery shrubs, it combines very well with other silvery shrubs or bluish-grey grasses. Silver flowers appear in May.

Elaeagnus crispa, see *E. umbellata*.

Elaeagnus × ebbingei

○ ◐ ⊖ ⦾ ⊛

A cross between *E. macrophylla* and *E. pungens*, it grows to a height and spread of up to 15ft (5m), and has brown branches turning to grey, with elliptical leaves. This is an ideal plant for hedges and screens, especially along the coast.

Elaeagnus edulis, see *E. multiflora*.

Elaeagnus glabra

This evergreen shrub from China and Japan rather resembles *E. pungens*, but when happily situated it develops a semi-climbing habit up to 20ft (6m) or so. A further distinction is the glossy metallic brown leaf undersides. Silver flowers are borne in autumn.

Elaeagnus multiflora

○ ◐ ⦾ ⊛

Syn. *E. edulis*. A thornless deciduous shrub, growing to a height and spread of up to 10ft (3m), with oval leaves that are green on top and silvery-grey underneath. Yellow-white flowers are borne in spring, followed by edible but sour, oblong red fruits.

Elaeagnus pungens

○ ◐ ⌒ ⊖ ⦾ ⊛ ▦

A vigorous, evergreen shrub with stems clothed in brown scales; some cultivars

have thorns. Its autumn flowers are fairly inconspicuous. Much more attractive are the cultivars, above all 'Maculata', which has yellow leaves with a dark green edge. Twigs with plain leaves, which often occur, should be removed immediately. The leaves of Variegata have cream margins.

Elaeagnus umbellata

○ ◐ ⊖ ⦾ ⊛ ▦

Syn. *E. crispa*. A vigorous deciduous shrub with yellowish, generally thorny branches. The leaves are narrowly oval, and light red, small fruits are borne in autumn.

Elsholtzia
Labiatae

About 35 shrubs and perennials make up this genus but only one shrubby member is usually available.

Soil Almost any well-drained soil is suitable, ideally enriched with peat, leaf-mould, or compost.

Propagation The usual means of increase is by cuttings in summer, ideally with bottom heat. Seeds may also be sown in spring in a greenhouse or cold frame.

Elsholtzia stauntonii

This deciduous sub-shrub is a native of China. It can reach 5ft (1.5m) in height, rarely more, as much of each season's growth dies back each winter. The leaves are lanceolate and toothed and borne in pairs. They smell of mint when bruised. In autumn, each stem terminates in a dense spike-like panicle of tubular, 2-lipped, lilac-purple flowers. It grows best in a sunny site and needs pruning hard back each spring. The plant is particularly useful for its autumn display.

Elymus
Gramineae

A genus of perennial ornamental grasses.

Soil Even the poorest soil will do.

Propagation By division.

Elymus arenarius

○ ⊖ ◐ ⊗

Lyme grass. Found on sand dunes on the North Sea and Baltic coasts, it grows 3–4½ft (1–1.3m) high and is bright blue-green, with gracefully drooping leaves.

Elymus arenarius a particularly attractive ornamental grass

Emilia
Compositae

A group of plants from the tropics, one of which is in general cultivation.
Soil A well-drained and moderately fertile soil is needed.
Propagation Plants are raised from seed, either under glass in spring in cold areas or outside where they are to grow in late spring, early summer.

Emilia flammea
○ ⊙ ⑰
Tassel flower, from tropical America, a colourful annual with long-stalked, flattened clusters of small scarlet to yellow pompon-shaped flowers that open in summer and autumn. Plants grow 1–2ft (30–60cm) high.

Enkianthus
Ericaceae

These attractive, fairly hardy shrubs are liked not only for their profuse flowers but also for the beautiful autumnal shades of their leaves. They require a sheltered position in sun or partial shade and are particularly effective in Japanese gardens when combined with primulas, ferns and rhododendrons.
Soil Acid humus-rich soil is essential.
Propagation They may be grown from seed in spring or cuttings of lateral shoots taken in autumn.

Enkianthus campanulatus
○ ◑ ⑱ ⑲ ⑰ ⑳
A spring-flowering shrub from Japan, growing up to 8ft (2.4m) high, and bearing pink flowers with dull red stripes. 'Albiflorus' has almost pure white flowers.

Epimedium
Berberidaceae
Barrenwort

A genus of hardy perennials with orchid-like flowers, giving excellent ground cover under a tree canopy.
Soil *Epimedium* is very vigorous and will grow on almost any soil provided it is kept sufficiently moist.
Propagation Plants may be raised from seed, by division or from cuttings of the rhizomes.

Epimedium × warleyense, one of many hybrids

Epimedium alpinum
○ ◑ ⑱ ⑳ ○ ⑰ ⑳ ⑳ ⊖ ⑳
From central and southern Europe, a spring-flowering plant growing up to 8in (20cm) high and producing sprays of dark red flowers with small yellow spurs.
Epimedium grandiflorum
Syn. *E. macranthum*. A Japanese plant, 8in (20cm) high and spring-flowering. The comparatively large flowers vary from pink to purple and white and have long slender spurs. 'Rose Queen' bears crimson flowers.
Epimedium macranthum, see *E. grandiflorum*.
Epimedium pinnatum
Of Persian origin, this plant bears bright yellow flowers with short brown spurs in spring. Its leaves take on red tints in autumn.
Epimedium × rubrum
A cross between *E. alpinum* and *E. grandiflorum*, this hybrid resembles *E. alpinum* but has larger flowers in greater profusion and is more attractive. The flowers are crimson with white spurs and appear in spring. The young leaves are red.
Epimedium × versicolor
A cross between *E. grandiflorum* and *E. pinnatum*. A spring-flowering plant growing 10–20in (25–50cm) high, whose flowers resemble those of *E. grandiflorum* but are smaller and have shorter spurs. The sepals are rose-pink in colour, the petals yellow and the somewhat twisted spurs reddish. 'Sulphureum' has sulphur-yellow flowers.
Epimedium × warleyense
A cross between *E. alpinum* and *E. pinnatum*. A spring-flowering plant up to 20in (50cm) high, producing flowers in a variety of colours; copper-red with a little yellow is the most common.
Epimedium × youngianum
A cross between *E. diphyllum* and *E. grandiflorum*, growing 4–12in (10–30cm) high and flowering in spring, when clusters of 3–8 pendulous, bell-shaped white blooms, with a little green, appear. 'Roseum' has lilac-pink flowers, and those of 'Niveum' are pure white.

Flowers of *Enkianthus campanulatus* look best when seen from below

Enkianthus campanulatus in autumn

Epimedium × rubrum

Eranthis hyemalis in February

Eranthis
Ranunculaceae

A genus of hardy, tuberous-rooted perennials that may come into flower as early as January, though February is more usual. The yellow flowers resemble short-stemmed buttercups.
Cultivation *Eranthis* should be planted in early autumn at a depth of just under 2in (5cm) and no more than 2in (5cm) apart. The tubers are small and dark brown.
Soil Plants grow in any garden soil provided it is kept adequately moist.
Propagation By division; in some gardens *Eranthis* is self-seeding.

Eranthis cilicica
○ ◑ ⑳ ⑳ ⑰ ⑳
Usually flowering in March, this species has darkish yellow flowers and coppery tinted foliage.
Eranthis hyemalis
Winter aconite. The most prevalent of the *Eranthis* spp, it grows 4–6in (10–15cm) high, and flowers from January to March. The flowers are pale yellow.

Eremurus himalaicus

Eranthis × tubergenii

A cross between *E. cilicica* and *E. hyemalis*. The plant is more robust and the flowers a little larger and more rounded than the parents'. The flowering period is March.

Eremurus
Liliaceae
Foxtail lily

Herbaceous perennials with octopus-like, fleshy roots.

Cultivation The fleshy roots must be treated with care, lest they snap off and rot. All wounds must be dusted with flowers of sulphur powder. If grown on poor, sandy soil, *Eremurus* should be mulched with rotted manure annually. The plants need a great deal of water in spring but dry conditions after they have flowered. Set out 20–30 in (50–75 cm) apart. If moved later than October, *Eremurus* may not flower during the next year.

Soil A fertile, well-drained, soil is needed. Dig a hole, fill it with a mixture of well-rotted manure and good loam, and top up with a layer of sandy soil. Spread out the roots carefully and bury the crown to a depth of 4–6 in (10–15 cm). Make sure that the hole is sufficiently wide. On wet and badly drained soil, it is advisable to place a 1½ft (45 cm) layer of rubble in the bottom of the hole before filling it up with manure, etc.

Propagation Plants are raised from careful division or ripe seeds. The latter will flower in 3–4 years.

Ememurus bungei, see *E. stenophyllus* ssp *stenophyllus*.
Eremurus elwesianus, see *E. elwesii*.

Eremurus elwesii

Syn. *E. robustus* var. *elwesii* and *E. elwesianus*. Growing to heights of 6–10 ft (2–3 m), with leaves up to 3½ft (1 m) long, the flower spikes of this species are longer than those of *E. robustus*. Soft lilac-pink flowers appear in late spring to early summer.

Eremurus himalaicus

A plant from the western Himalayas that grows 3–6 ft (1–2 m) high and flowers in early summer, producing 2 ft (60 cm) spikes of white flowers having brown stripes on the outside.

Eremurus robustus

From Turkestan, this plant grows 3–6 ft (1–2 m) high and flowers in early to mid-summer. The leaves are longer and narrower than those of *E. him-*

alaicus, and the peach-pink flowers are borne on 1½–2 ft (45–60 cm) spikes.
Eremurus robustus var. *elwesii*, see *E. elwesii*.

Eremurus stenophyllus

A plant from central Asia that grows 1½–2½ft (45–75 cm) high and flowers in early to mid-summer. The dense flower spikes are 6 in (15 cm) or more long, and the blooms are yellow with orange stripes on the outside.

Eremurus stenophyllus ssp stenophyllus

Syn. *E. bungei*. This sub-species is more attractive than the parent form. Plants are 2½ft (75 cm) tall and have 1 ft (30 cm) spikes, sometimes longer.

Erica
Ericaceae
Heath, Bell heather

Several species are native to Europe. Heaths are best grown in peaty and acid soils and should be trimmed after flowering. See also under *Calluna*.
Soil Ericas thrive on acid soil, and calcareous soils should be avoided except for *E. carnea*, *E. erigena* and *E. × darleyensis*.
Propagation Plants are raised by division or layering and from cuttings or seed. Take cuttings in the first half of August. Cuttings about 1 in (2.5 cm) long are placed in shallow boxes or pans, covered with glass and placed in the greenhouse or garden frame. To avoid fungus infection, the cuttings should not be crowded too closely together, and the glass covers should be dried every morning. The cuttings root in just over a month. Pot up in spring and plant out in the flowering position the following May.

Erica arborea var. alpina
○ ◑ ⌂ 🌢 🌢 🍂 🏵 🙂 ⊗
Tree heath. A fairly rare alpine heather growing to a height of 4½ft (1.3 m), with erect branches and fragrant white globular flowers in long plumes. This makes a splendid addition to any heather garden.

Erica carnea
○ ◑ 🌢 🌢 🍂 🏵 🙂 ⊖ ⊗
Syn. *E. herbacea*. Winter heath, a completely hardy, wide-spreading shrub from the European Alps, growing up to 1 ft (30 cm) high. The flower buds appear in autumn, and in mild winters the plant will produce flowers in January and even earlier, though the usual flowering period is from March to

May. The urn-shaped flowers are flesh-coloured. There are a number of attractive cultivars, including 'James Backhouse', 10 in (25 cm) high, producing rose-purple flowers March–April; 'Praecox Rubra', an 8 in (20 cm) plant bearing light rose-purple flowers November–March; 'Ruby Glow', 8 in (20 cm) high with rose-purple flowers February–April; 'Springwood White' with 4 in (10 cm) high spreading white

Erica vagans 'Mrs D. F. Maxwell'

An attractive heather garden with various species of *Erica* and a weeping birch in the background

Erica arborea var. *alpina* is a most striking plant

flowers December–March; 'Vivellii', an 8in (20cm) plant producing carmine flowers March–April; and 'Winter Beauty', 6in (15cm) high, whose rose-pink flowers appear December–March.

Erica ciliaris

○ ◑ ◬ ⬡ ✳ ☺ ⊗

Dorset heath. Native to southern England, Portugal and Spain, this highly recommended garden plant is greyish-green in colour and 12–18in (30–45cm) high, and bears large rose-purple flowers from late summer to early autumn.

Erica cinerea

○ ◬ ⬡ ✳ ☺ ⊖

Bell heather. A hardy native of western Europe, it grows 9–12in (23–30cm) high with mats of wiry stems. Flowers appear June–September. Recommended cultivars include 'Alba', 10in (25cm) high, with pure white flowers August–September; 'Atrosanguinea', 8in (20cm), whose reddish-purple flowers appear July–October; 'C. D. Eason', 14in (35cm) high, with rosy-red flowers June–September; 'Cevennes', 10in (25cm), bears lavender-rose flowers August–October; 'Pallas', 1ft (30cm), has purple flowers June–September; 'Pallida', 1ft (30cm), has light lavender-pink flowers July–September; 'P. S. Patrick', 16in (40cm), with bright purple flowers, and 'Rosea', a 10in (25cm) plant bearing bright rose flowers June–September.

Erica × darleyensis

○ ◑ ◬ ⬡ ⬡ ✳ ☺ ⊖

A cross between *E. carnea* and *E. erigena*, this plant is wide-spreading and twice as tall as *E. carnea*, and also has larger flowers.

Erica erigena

Syn. *E. mediterranea*. Found in W. Ireland, Portugal, Spain and France, this shrub grows up to 4½ft (1.3m) high, and opens out from March to May to produce purple-pink urn-shaped flowers in great profusion.

Erica herbacea, see *E. carnea*.
Erica hibernica, see *E. erigena*.
Erica mediterranea, see *E. erigena*.
Erica tetralix
Cross-leaved heath. A plant originally

Erica carnea 'Springwood White'

from western Europe that grows to a height of more than 1ft (30cm). Soft pink flowers are borne in terminal clusters July–September. 'Alba' is a white variety, and 'Con Underwood', 1ft (30cm), is crimson, and flowers June–September.

Erica vagans

Cornish heath. A native of W. France, C. Spain, Portugal and S.W. England

Erica cinerea 'Pallas' (centre) and the white flowers of Erica tetralix 'Alba'

that grows to a height of 1–2ft (30–60cm), and flowers in late summer, bearing numerous lilac pink to purple blooms. Cultivars include 'Diana Hornibrook', 1ft (30cm) high, with red flowers July–September; 'Lyonesse', 1ft (30cm), with creamy-white flowers; 'Mrs D. F. Maxwell', 14in (35cm) high, with deep cerise flowers August–October; and 'St Keverne', 14in (35cm) high, with clear rose-pink flowers August–September.

Erigeron
Compositae
Fleabane

Medium-sized herbaceous plants that flower in exceptional profusion and are firm favourites for the border. The flowers strongly resemble asters but have a larger number of narrower ray florets.
Soil Any moist but well-drained soil.
Propagation Plants may be grown from seed sown from April to May, or by division.

Erigeron hybrids

○ ○ ⓨ ⊗

Many of these crosses are between *E.*

An *Erigeron* cultivar

aurantiacus and *E. speciosus*. They grow 20–30in (50–75cm) high with spatulate to sword-shaped leaves. The daisy-like flowers have 00–150 very thin ray florets, the double varieties an even greater number; the centres are yellow. The best-known cultivars are 'Dainty', a dark purple single with a short stem; 'Fairy' (syn. 'Die Fee'), a light reddish-purple single; 'Dignity', a

Erigeron flowers have more ray florets than asters

dark purple single; 'Darkest of All' (syn. 'Dunkelste Aller'), a very dark purple semi-double with a short stem; 'Mrs E. H. Beale', a light violet single with a very short stem; 'Quakeress', a very light purple single; 'Red Beauty' (syn. 'Rote Schönheit'), a purple-red double; 'Serenity', a violet-purple single; 'Violetta' a purple double, and 'Wuppertal', a light purple semi-double.

There are several species in addition to these hybrids but only the following are easily obtainable: *E. aurantiacus* from Turkestan, which grows to a height of 1ft (30cm) and bears bright red flowers July–August, and *E. compositus*, an 8in (20cm) rock plant from North America that bears white purplish flowers June–July.

Bees love the beautiful flowerheads of the blue thistle, *Eryngium planum*

Eryngium
Umbelliferae
Sea holly

These ornamental plants are best grown in groups in the border. The smaller cultivars can be grown in the larger rock garden. All make excellent dried flower arrangements.
Soil Any well-drained and not too rich soil is suitable.
Propagation Plants are grown from seeds sown outside at the end of May or the beginning of June.
Diseases On very moist soils, *Eryngium* often suffers from root rot.

Eryngium alpinum
○ ⊖ ⊚ ⊛ ☺ ⊚ ⊗ ⊗
An Alpine plant growing 18–24 in (45–60 cm) high and bearing glorious steel-blue flowers July–August; the flower stems are similarly coloured. The basal leaves are heart-shaped, and those on the stems are deeply cut.

Eryngium × oliverianum
○ ⊕ ⊛ ☺ ⊚ ⊗
A hybrid of uncertain parentage, said to have originated from seed of *E. alpinum*. It grows 3–4 ft (1–1.2 m) high, and July–September produces beautiful steel-blue flowers.

Eryngium planum
From France, Austria and Eastern Europe, this plant grows 24 in (60 cm) high, flowering in early to midsummer. The blooms are smallish and deep blue; the basal leaves, borne on long petioles, are heart-shaped and toothed.

Eryngium tripartitum
○ ⊖ ⊚ ⊛ ⊗
Perhaps a hybrid, this plant grows 30 in (75 cm) high and flowers from July to September. Its three-lobed, grey-blue leaves provide as much attraction as the small, rounded, light blue flower heads.

Eryngium × zabelii
A cross between *E. alpinum* and *E. bourgatii*, growing up to 3 ft (1 m) high with branching stems and spherical heads of blue flowers appearing from July to September. 'Violetta' has violet blue flowers.

The outstandingly attractive *Erythronium* × 'Pagoda'

Erythronium
Liliaceae
Dog's tooth violet

A genus of hardy bulbs with exceptionally beautiful spring flowers, ideal for the mixed border.
Cultivation The bulbs should be planted August–September about 3 in (7.5 cm) apart. Failure is generally due to two causes; planting the bulbs too late, and in too dry sandy soil. In moist, cool ground the bulbs may be left undisturbed for years. They will not tolerate fresh manure. They grow well on a north-facing slope.
Soil Any humus-rich garden soil is adequate.
Propagation Bulbs are grown from seeds or offsets.

Erythronium dens-canis
◐ ⊚ ◔ ⊛ ⊚
An Alpine bulb resembling a dog's tooth, hence the Latin name, that grows 4–8 in (10–20 cm) high and flowers in spring. The leaves are spotted and the stems bear one or more small, nodding, violet flowers somewhat resembling a small cyclamen. Several cultivars are available in different colours.

Erythronium grandiflorum
Glacier lily from northwestern America, this plant is 1–2 ft (30–60 cm) high, and bears yellow, solitary, nodding flowers in spring.

Erythronium revolutum
American trout lily, from California. A spring-flowering plant with pink flowers it grows up to 6 in (15 cm) high. 'White Beauty' has heavily mottled leaves and white flowers.

Erythronium dens-canis

Escallonia hybrid 'Donard Seedling'

Erythronium tuolumnense
A spring-flowering Californian species that includes the cultivar 'Pagoda', a 10 in (25 cm) plant with bronze foliage and deep yellow flowers having brown basal rings that are borne 3–4 to the stem.

Escallonia
Saxifragaceae

A genus of flowering shrubs. Most species are slightly tender but grow well in southern and western counties of Britain.
Soil Any well-drained garden soil will do.
Propagation Plants are raised from cuttings.

Escallonia virgata
○ ⊚ ⊛ ⊛ ⊕ ☺
A hardy deciduous shrub with very small leaves and white flowers, often crossed with the less hardy *E. rubra* form *E.* × *rigida*. The best cultivars include 'Donard Seedling', a vigorous grower with flesh-pink flowers, most suitable as a hedging plant; 'Donard Star', of erect compact habit with large deep rose-pink flowers; and 'Edinensis', with light carmine flowers borne on graceful branches, most suitable for growing against a south-facing wall.

Eschscholzia
Papaveraceae

A genus of herbaceous plants with bright flowers suitable for growing in poor sandy ground in a sunny position.
Soil *Eschscholzia* makes no special demands.
Propagation Sow the seeds in the flowering site from March to June and thin out to 18in (45cm) apart. Plants sown in autumn will survive mild winters and come into flower in late spring.

Eschscholzia caespitosa
Syn. *E. tenuifolia*. A plant with almost thread-like leaves and yellow flowers measuring about 1in (2.5cm) across. 'Sundew' is the best-known cultivar.

Eschscholzia californica
○ ○ ⊛ ⊚
Californian poppy, from North America. A plant reaching a spread and heights of 1–2ft (30–60cm). The taller cultivars must be thinned out vigorously if the plants are to be sturdy and bushy. The flowering period is from May onwards for plants sown in autumn, and from July to October for those sown in spring. Masses of yellow

Habit and autumn colour of *Euonymus alatus*, spindle tree

Eschscholzia californica

Seed coats and fruits of *Euonymus*

saucer-shaped flowers are borne, each with an orange throat. There are numerous cultivars in various colours. The most outstanding are 'Ramona', 'Robert Gardner' and 'Toreador', the last two bearing double flowers. 'Erecta Compacta' grows to a height of 1ft (30cm) and bushes out most attractively. It bears single or double flowers in red, buff, orange, scarlet, white, pink and carmine. 'Aurantiaca' is a most beautiful orange-yellow variety; 'Red Chief' is brownish-red, and 'Golden Glory' bears large, single yellow flowers with an orange centre.

Eschscholzia tenuifolia, see *E. caespitosa*.

Euonymus
Celastraceae
Spindle tree

A genus of deciduous and evergreen shrubs and trees, many of which make excellent additions to the garden. The evergreen *E. japonicus* and *E. fortunei* are sometimes grown as indoor plants but much more often as ornamental shrubs outside. The deciduous species are usually cultivated for their remarkably beautiful fruits borne in late summer and autumn. They will tolerate semi-shade, but flower and fruit much more profusely in full sunlight. The autumn coloration of the foliage, too, is more intense if the plants are not

grown in the shade.
Soil Ordinary garden soil will do, but a moisture-retentive fertile one is ideal.
Propagation Plants may be grown from basal cuttings, by layering and from seeds. The latter have a very short life and must therefore be sown as soon as they are ripe.
Pests On dry and poor soil, *Euonymus* is liable to attack by aphids and caterpillars.

Euonymus alatus
○ ⊕ ⊛ ⊚
From Japan and China, this shrub grows up to 6ft (2m) high and has corky wings on the branchlets. The leaves are narrow, oval and finely serrated. The fruits are purplish with scarlet seeds.

Euonymus europaeus
○ ⊕ ⊛ ⊛ ⊚ ⊚
Common spindle tree, originating in Europe and Asia. It grows up to 12ft (4m) high with spreading branches and narrow, oval leaves. The pink fruits contain orange seeds. 'Atropurpureus' has purplish foliage and 'Red Cascade' bears a profusion of rose-red fruits.

Euonymus fortunei
⊕ ⊛ ⊛ ⊛ ⊚
A prostrate or climbing evergreen shrub, whose long stems root at intervals. When used as a self-clinging climber, it will reach heights of 15–25ft (5–8m). The most important cultivars are *E. fortunei* var. *radicans*, a climbing form with dark green leaves, often

Euonymus europaeus 'Red Cascade', an attractive form of the spindle tree

listed as *E. radicans*; 'Colorata', a wide-spreading shrub with large leaves that turn a beautiful red shade towards autumn; 'Silver Queen', a small shrub reaching 10ft (3m) on a wall, with white margined leaves; and 'Vegetus', a bushy creeping form which also climbs. It has glossy green leaves, and is becoming increasingly popular as ground cover.

Euonymus hamiltonianus maackii
From eastern Asia, this uncommon plant has long, narrow leaves and bears an abundance of pink fruits with orange seeds.

Euonymus japonicus
○ ⊕ ⊛ ⊛ ⊛
An evergreen from Japan that grows up to 10ft (3m) high but can also be cultivated as a wide-spreading bush. It

has large, somewhat angular branches, and narrow, oval leaves. There are several cultivars with variegated leaves.

Euonymus nanus
○ ⊕ ⊛ ⊛ ⊛ ⊘ ⊖
A semi-evergreen shrub reaching a height of 1½ft (45cm) with smooth, angular branches and leaves with incurling margins. It produces brown flowers and pink fruits. *E. nanus* var. *turkestanica* has flat leaves.

Euonymus phellomanus
○ ⊕ ⊛ ⊛
An attractive shrub reaching a height of up to 20ft (7m). The branches have broad, corky wings and oval leaves. It bears pink fruits with red seeds.

Euonymus planipes, see *E. sachalinensis*.

Euonymus radicans, see *E. fortunei* var. *radicans*.

Euonymus sachalinensis

Syn. *E. planipes*. A large, handsome shrub with oval leaves, best planted in groups and very colourful in autumn. The flowers are green and inconspicuous, appearing in May. The seeds are orange-red.

Euonymus verrucosus

○ ⦻ ⊛

From Europe and the Near East, this shrub grows up to 10ft (3m) high and has densely warted branches with oval, pointed leaves. The seeds are black, and partly surrounded by blood-red capsules.

Euphorbia
Euphorbiaceae
Spurge

This widespread genus includes succulent and shrubby indoor plants and several annual and perennial species for the garden. The generally insignificant flowers are sometimes surrounded by large red, green or yellow bracts.
Soil Plants grow well in ordinary garden soil. The colour of the foliage is greatly enhanced if grown on poor, dry soils.
Propagation Annuals are grown from

Euonymus fortunei 'Silver Queen'

Corky wings of *Euonymus alatus*

seed, perennials by division or from seed.

Annuals include:
Euphorbia heterophylla
○ ⊙ ⊛ ◉

Painted spurge. From the USA, a plant growing 24in (60cm) high and July–September producing crimson-orange bracts. Sow in March at a temperature of 16°C (61°F). Prick out the seedlings into boxes and harden off in a cold frame before planting out in May.

Euphorbia marginata
○ ⊙ ⊛ ◉

Syn. *E. variegata*. An autumn-flowering plant from North America that grows 24in (60cm) high and is chiefly cultivated for its ornamental green leaves; these become edged and veined with white as the plant matures.

It flowers in September.
Euphorbia variegata, see *E. marginata*.

Perennials include:
Euphorbia characias
○ ⊜ ○ ⊛ ⊛ ⊗

A Mediterranean plant growing 2–6ft (60–180cm) high with narrow grey-green leaves that persist through the winter. The flowering bracts are yellow-green with small, dark, central flowers and are borne in wide, dense clusters up to 1ft (30cm) long. The sub-species *wulfenii* (syn. *E. veneta*) is more statuesque with lime green flowers. Although they start blooming in March, the spikes remain attractive to midsummer.

Euphorbia cyparissias

A compact species useful as ground cover, growing to a height of 1ft (30cm). It has pale green leaves and yellow-green flowers which are borne in April and May. It can be invasive.

Euphorbia epithymoides
○ ⊜ ○ ⊛ ⊛ ⊗

Syn. *E. polychroma*. From southern Europe, this is a very attractive plant for growing on walls or for border edges. It grows 12–16in (30–40cm) high, and in spring to early summer produces bright chrome-yellow bracts.

Euphorbia griffithii

This hardy herbaceous perennial from the Himalayas forms widening clumps of erect stems up to 3ft 4in (1m) tall. The ample leafage has attractive reddish veins. In summer, spreading terminal clusters of light red bracts light up each clump. 'Fireglow' is the cultivar which is most commonly seen and has bright brick-red bracts.

Euphorbia myrsinites
○ ⊜ ○ ⊛ ⊛ ⊗

From southern Europe, a 4–8in (10–20cm) plant whose trailing stems are clothed in blue-green leaves. Yellow-green bracts appear May–July.

Euphorbia palustris

A marsh plant that grows in water up to 8in (20cm) deep but will also grow in any moist soil. It has creeping roots and hollow, blue-green stems, often red at the base. Stems and leaves turn purple in autumn, and yellow-green bracts are borne May–June.

Euphorbia polychroma, see *E. epithymoides*.

Euphorbia rigida

Syn. *E. biglandulosa*. A near ally of *E. myrsinites* but with narrower longer leaves and erect stems.

Euphorbia robbiae
◑ ⦿ ⊜ ○ ⊛ ⊛ ⊜

From Turkey, this plant reaches heights of 9–18in (25–45cm). The deep evergreen leaves show up the contrasting clusters of yellow-green bracts. It makes an excellent but invasive ground cover, and is tolerant of deep shade.

Euphorbia sikkimensis

A hardy herbaceous perennial from the eastern Himalayas forming clumps of erect stems 4–6ft (1.2–1.8m) high. The leaves have white mid-ribs and the bold terminal clusters of bracts are yellow. Added attractions are the ruby-red young shoots and colouring autumn leaves.

Euphorbia veneta, see *Euphorbia wulfenii*.

Euphorbia wulfenii

An evergreen sub-shrub growing to a height of 4ft (1.2m). It possesses blue-green leaves and green-yellow bracts appearing in May–July.

Euphorbia myrsinites, an attractive plant for the rock garden

Exochorda racemosa

Exochorda
Rosaceae
Pearl bush

A genus of beautiful shrubs having long arching branches festooned with large white flowers in conspicuous racemes. These are followed by a profusion of fruits that greatly enhance the plant's winter appearance. It likes full sun and is seen to best advantage when planted as a specimen, e.g. on a lawn, to be admired from all sides. To prevent solitary shrubs from becoming too spindly, it is advisable to cut back the long shoots every year to roughly half their length.
Soil Any well-drained soil is recommended, preferably rich in humus.
Propagation Plants are grown from

seeds, by root grafting or from cuttings taken in June. Use rooting hormone, *E. racemosa* may also be propagated from suckers.

Exochorda grandiflora, see *E. racemosa*.

Exochorda × macrantha
○ ⊘ ⊛ ⦿ ⊜ ⊕

A cross between *E. korolkowii* and *E. racemosa*, this is a beautiful shrub with abundant racemes of large flowers. 'The Bride' is a compact arching 3ft (1m) cultivar whose paper-white flowers are borne May–June.

Exochorda racemosa

Syn. *E. grandiflora*. A shrub from China that grows 10–12ft (3–4m) high, with elegantly arched branches and oval leaves. Flowers appear in clusters May–June.

Fagus
Fagaceae
Beech

A tree native to Europe that grows up to 100ft (30m) in height and develops a spread of up to 50ft (15m). The larger leaved American beech (*F. grandifolia*) rarely thrives in Britain.

Cultivation In addition to being planted as a large tree, the common beech is often used for hedging. Planting is done in autumn and the roots must not dry out during the operation. Dig a large hole and fill with a layer of well-rotted beech leaves mixed with soil. Beeches do best on ground on which they can send their roots down to the water table.

Propagation Sow seeds outdoors as soon as they are ripe and carefully transplant the seedlings two years later. Cultivars must be propagated by grafting on to seedlings of *F. sylvatica*.

Fagus sylvatica

Common beech. A European tree up to 100ft (30m) high with a smooth grey trunk and a broad crown. The leaves are bright green at first, broadly ovate, pointed, wavy margined and have 5–9 pairs of prominent veins; in autumn they turn a rich shade of bronze-yellow. The best known of the many cultivars are 'Asplenifolia', the fern-leaved beech, which has deeply cut leaves; 'Atropurpurea' ('Riversii'), the purple beech, a magnificent tree with dark purple leaves, best planted in a solitary position; 'Cristata', with clustered leaves that are deeply lobed and curled; 'Fastigiata', which has a tall, columnar habit; 'Lanciniata', with deeply cut leaves; 'Pendula', a green weeping variety with enormous pendular branches; 'Purpurea pendula', the weeping purple beech, which has dark purple leaves, a small crown and overhanging branches; 'Roseomarginata', with pink-edged purple leaves; 'Rotundifolia', a smaller tree with small round leaves, and 'Zlatia', a large tree with

A mighty specimen of the purple beech, *Fagus sylvatica* 'Atropurpurea Macrophylla' flanked by cedars

golden-yellow leaves that can turn yellowish-green in summer.

Fatsia
Araliaceae

An evergreen shrub often grown as a house plant, but also excellent in the garden.

Soil Any well-drained garden soil is adequate, preferably rich in humus.

Propagation From seeds or cuttings.

Fatsia japonica

A shrub growing up to 15ft (5m) but usually less. The leaves are deeply lobed and glossy, and the rounded heads of the white flowers rather resemble those of the ivy in shape. They are borne in late summer.

Festuca
Gramineae

A genus of ornamental grasses forming dense tufts and capable of withstanding long dry spells.

Festuca glauca, blue fescue

Soil *Festuca* does best on fairly poor, well-drained soil.

Propagation The species are grown from seed (*Festuca* can be self-seeding) and by division. Cultivars must be propagated by division.

Festuca amethystina

A native of central Europe, growing 1½ft (45cm) high or more and suitable for heather and rock gardens. It has narrow amethyst-blue leaves and produces narrow dark violet panicles in early summer.

Fagus sylvatica 'Zlatia' in the spring

Festuca glacialis

Syn. *F. ovina frigida*. A close ally of *Festuca ovina*, from the Alps and Pyrenees. It is smaller and more densely tufted, with grey-green leaves and flowering stems to 6 in (15 cm) tall.

Festuca glauca

○ ◑ ◉ ⊖ ⊘ ⊛ ⊗

A small plant 4–6 in (10–15 cm) high with thin leaves that form thick tufts. Oval, purplish spikelets appear in early to mid-summer.

Festuca ovina

Sheep's fescue. A stiff erect plant up to 10 in (25 cm) high and excellent for the heather garden; it has green to greyish-green leaves.

Festuca punctoria

Syn. *F. acerosa*. From the mountains of Turkey, this attractive grass has dense tufts of glistening grey-green bristle-like leaves with prickle tips. The flowering stems rise to 1 ft (30 cm) in height, bearing narrow panicles of grey spikelets.

Festuca rubra

○ ◑ ◉ ⊖ ⊘ ⊗

Creeping fescue or red fescue. Frequently used in lawn-seed mixtures for dry ground, where it forms a serviceable carpet.

Festuca scoparia

○ ◑ ⊖ ⊘ ⊛ ⊖

No taller than 6 in (15 cm), this species has light green, almost cylindrical leaves, and is the most suitable one for the rock garden.

Filipendula purpurea

Filipendula
Rosaceae

A genus of hardy herbaceous perennials closely related to *Spiraea*. Although excellent for waterside planting, they should only be placed in positions sheltered from the fierce rays of the midday sun.

Soil *F. purpurea* and *F. rubra* like moist, well-manured soil; *F. vulgaris* prefers drier, calcareous soil.

Propagation Plants are raised by division or from seed sown in autumn in pots or pans and overwintered in a cold frame.

Filipendula hexapetala, see *F. vulgaris*.

Filipendula purpurea

◑ ⊖ ⊘ ⊛ ⊗

A plant up to 2½ ft (75 cm) tall with leafy stems and purple-pink flowers that appear June–August. 'Elegans' is snowy-white with red stamens.

Filipendula rubra

A North American herbaceous perennial that grows 3–4½ ft (1–1.3 m) high, and June–July produces soft pink to flesh-coloured flowers. 'Venusta' is a

very decorative perennial cultivar with graceful leaves and blood-red flowers borne in August.

Filipendula vulgaris

◑ ⊖ ⊘ ⊛ ⊗

Syn. *F. hexapetala*, *Spiraea filipendula*. A European herbaceous perennial, up to 1 ft (30 cm) tall and producing white flowers June–July. The most popular cultivar is 'Plena', which has double white flowers and ornamental leaves. The stems are unfortunately too weak to keep the heavy flowers upright at all times; particularly during and after rain, the flowers tend to droop and become spattered with mud.

Forsythia
Oleaceae

A genus of beautiful and very rewarding spring-flowering shrubs. Try to content yourself with one specimen if your garden is small, or the yellow colour may become too overpowering. Moreover, once the flowers have faded in early spring, the garden may look rather bare. Species with drooping branches can be trained against walls or fences. In rural areas of Britain, bullfinches eat the flower buds and unless the bushes are netted there is no point in planting these shrubs.

Soil Forsythias grow in any garden soil, but dry conditions are better than wet. They will tolerate some shade but flower much more profusely in sunny positions.

Propagation Plants are grown by layering, by division and from cuttings. Seeds may also be sown when ripe and overwintered in a cold frame, but are seldom worth while.

Forsythia × intermedia

○ ◑ ◍ ⊛ ⊕ ⊞ ⊗

A shrub up to 6 ft (2 m) high, a cross between *F. viridissima* and *F. suspensa*. The flowers are a brighter yellow colour than those of either parent. The branches have the airy look of *F. suspensa*, but are much stouter and droop in graceful curves. The best cultivars are 'Beatrix Farrand', a fairly recent introduction with exceptionally large flowers up to 1½ in (4 cm) across; 'Lynwood Gold', with large bell-shaped and broad-petalled flowers; 'Spectabilis', an older form but still unexcelled in the profusion and colour of its large flowers; 'Spring Glory', which bears masses of large golden-yellow flowers and resembles 'Spectabilis' except for its colour.

Forsythia ovata

This species flowers earlier than the others but is less attractive. The cultivar 'Tetragold' is a bushy shrub up to 3 ft (1 m) tall with amber-yellow flowers.

Forsythia suspensa

○ ◑ ◍ ⊛ ⊕

A shrub from China, growing up to 10 ft (3 m) high and March–April bearing yellow flowers. The young branches are upright, but the older branches droop and may trail across the ground, and are often trained against walls, etc. 'Fortunei' differs from the species in the brown colour of its stems and also by flowering on the current year's shoots. 'Nymans' is a vigorous shrub with very dark branches, red when young, and pale yellow flowers.

Forsythia × intermedia 'Spectabilis'

Flowers of *Fothergilla major* in April

Fothergilla
Hamamelidaceae

A genus of hardy deciduous shrubs.
Soil A light soil is preferred, rich in peat or humus.
Propagation Plants are grown from seeds or cuttings.

Fothergilla alnifolia, see *F. gardenii*.
Fothergilla gardenii

○ ◑ ◉ ⊛ ⊘ ⊛ ⊕ ⊗

Syn. *F. alnifolia*. A shrub, up to 3 ft (1 m) tall, from Virginia and Florida, with dull green, oval leaves turning red in autumn. Tiny white flowers appear in erect catkin-like spikes in spring.

Fothergilla major

○ ◑ ◉ ⊛ ◍ ⊛ ⊗ ⊕

Syn. *F. monticola*. This shrub grows to a considerably greater height than *F. gardenii*; its leaves are larger, and its autumn colour is orange-yellow. White flowers are borne in spikes April–May. *F. m. monticola* (syn. *F. monticola*) is more spreading and less hairy, up to 3 ft (1 m) high, with foliage that turns orange-red in autumn.

Fraxinus ornus in the spring

Fraxinus
Oleaceae
Ash

A genus of popular trees and shrubs, often seen in large gardens and parks and along paths and drives.

Soil *Fraxinus* develops into a stout and long-lived tree in any ordinary garden soil. Because of its size it is not recommended for the smaller garden.

Propagation Species can be grown from seed in autumn; cultivars are raised by grafting.

Fraxinus americana

○ ⊖ ❀ ⊘ ⊕

White ash. A deciduous tree up to 60ft (18m) high with a spread of up to 30ft (9m) and an oval crown. It has olive-green to brown branches, often with a slight bloom, and black-brown buds; the pinnate leaves usually consist of 7, and sometimes 5–9, leaflets. Leaflets are pointed, almost entire, but with fine teeth at the tip, glossy dark green on top, whitish underneath, turning yellow and purple in autumn. The tree produces green flowers with very short stamens, and narrow winged fruits known as keys.

Fraxinus excelsior

Common ash from Europe to the Caucasus. A tree up to 120ft (36m) high with a spread of about 30ft (9m). It has hairless, greyish-green branches with black, angular buds. The pinnate leaves have 9–13 leaflets, the upper side dark green, the lower side paler; the autumn colour is yellow. The tree flowers in spring before the leaves are out, and bears pendulous winged fruit. The many cultivars include 'Diversifolia', the one-leaf ash, a large, slim tree with a pyramidal crown and simple leaves; 'Eureka', a large tree with a conical crown; 'Jaspidea', which has a broad, pyramidal crown, yellow leaves and branches that turn bronze-yellow in winter; 'Monophylla' has one or three roughly serrated leaflets; and 'Pendula', the weeping ash, with pendent branches.

Fraxinus ornus

○ ⊜ ❀ ⊗ ⊘ ⊕

Manna ash, from southern Europe. Growing up to 30ft (9m), with a spread of 10–18ft (3–6m). In May and June it produces frothy white flowers followed by 1in (2.5cm) long fruits. The branches are greyish-green and either hairless or covered with very fine hair. Buds are greyish-brown, and the compound leaves consist of pointed, finely serrated leaflets. This species needs a well-drained soil.

Fraxinus pennsylvanica

○ ❀ ⊘ ⊕

A beautiful tree from Canada, Dakota, Florida and Louisiana, growing up to 60ft (18m) high, with a spread of up to 30ft (9m). The branches are usually covered with hair, but can be hairless. The buds are rust-coloured, and there are 5–9 leaflets, finely serrated or entire, and hairy underneath. The green leaves turn purplish in autumn. This species will grow on a somewhat drier soil than *F. excelsior*.

Fritillaria
Liliaceae

A genus of bulbous plants of widely differing appearance. Some are obviously attractive and showy, others are more intriguing than beautiful. Most of the 85 species are best grown in pots in a cool or frost-free greenhouse, but those described below all thrive outside in sunny sheltered sites.

Soil Of the species described here, all but *F. meleagris* thrive in a moist soil at least during the growing period.

Propagation Plants are grown from seeds immediately they are ripe (August); seedlings take several years to flower. Fritillarias can also be grown from offsets.

Fritillaria assyriaca

From Iraq and western Persia, this species grows to 8in (20cm) or more tall, the slender stems bearing green or greyish lanceolate leaves. The solitary flower is pendent and narrowly bell-shaped, maroon with yellow tips, opening in late spring.

Fritillaria imperialis

○ ⊗ ⊘ ⊘ ⊘ ⊗

Crown imperial. A herbaceous perennial from Persia and Turkey, growing up to 3ft (1m) or more. The bulb is large with loose, yellowish scales and an unpleasant smell. In spring sturdy leafy stems appear bearing a terminal cluster of large pendent yellow to red flowers crowned by a whorl of leaves. 'Rubra Maxima' bears dark red-orange flowers; 'Lutea Maxima' has yellow flowers, and those of 'Orange Brilliant' are bright orange. Plant in September to a depth of 4in (10cm), spacing the bulbs 10–12in (25–30cm) apart. Given suitable conditions, the bulbs will flower in the same position for many successive years.

Fritillaria meleagris

○ ◑ ⊗ ⊘ ⊘ ⊘ ⊗

Snake's head. A European perennial herbaceous plant, growing to a height of 8–16in (20–40cm) and producing broad, bell-shaped, pink flowers with purple chequered markings in the species. Plant in early autumn (September–October), placing the bulbs 2in (5cm) deep and 3in (7.5cm) apart.

Fritillaria meleagris, snake's head

They may be left undisturbed in the garden for several years, or naturalized. In England snake's head grows wild in damp meadows, and it is also very suitable for a rock garden, particularly in the vicinity of a small pond. The bulbs are almost spherical, 3–6in (7.5–15cm) across, whitish, and with an unpleasant aroma. The cultivar 'Alba' is white.

Fritillaria pallidiflora

This attractive fritillary comes from the Tien Shan and Ala-Tan mountains in the USSR. It is usually about 1ft (30cm) tall but can reach 1½ft (45cm) or more. The broadly lanceolate leaves are blue-green and the nodding flowers a luminous pale yellow. The latter are about 1½in (4cm) long and either solitary or in clusters of up to 4. Late spring is the usual flowering time.

Fritillaria persica

○ ⊗ ⊘ ⊘ ⊘

A species from Turkey that is becoming more popular. 'Adiyaman' is an exceptionally beautiful cultivar with dark purple bells on hairless green stems. It grows 2½–3ft (75–100cm) high and flowers in May.

Fritillaria pyrenaica

From the Pyrenees, this is one of the easiest of *Fritillarias* to please, growing both in light and heavy soils, sun and partial shade. It grows to 1ft (30cm) or more tall, with grey-green lanceolate leaves and usually solitary bells to 1½in (4cm) long. The petals are purplish-brown chequered with deeper crimson-purple without, and glossy yellow green within; they expand in late spring.

Fuchsia
Onagraceae

A genus of deciduous shrubs and trees, of which few species are still cultivated; most modern forms are hybrids. The plants are slightly tender and are usually grown indoors or placed outdoors during the summer in hanging baskets. They are also used in summer bedding.

Fuchsia magellanica, the hardiest of fuchsias

Although the cultivars of *F. magellanica* mentioned below are hardy, it is advisable to give them some protection in winter. The extra work is well worth the trouble, because fuchsias will flower throughout the summer. They are particularly effective when planted in groups or as a small hedge.

Cultivation In mild areas, fuchsias can be grown as shrubs; elsewhere cut them down to the ground in winter and cover the roots with a thick mulch of bracken, etc.

Soil A light, well-drained soil is required, enriched with peat or leaf-mould.

Gaillardia hybrids

Propagation Plants are raised from cuttings in late summer or spring.

Fuchsia magellanica

○ ◑ ⬡ ⬤ ⬤ ⬤

This species has two popular cultivars. 'Gracilis' reaches a height of 4½ft (1.3m), with scarlet sepals and violet petals. 'Ricartonii' has drooping branches and flowers with scarlet sepals and purple petals. Many showy hybrid cultivars are listed in catalogues, some of them as hardy as the wild *magellanica*.

Gaillardia
Compositae
Blanket flower

A genus of very beautiful hardy annual and perennial herbaceous plants with an exceptionally long flowering period.
Soil Gaillardias thrive in light, well-drained and preferably dryish soil.
Propagation Perennial gaillardias can be grown from basal cuttings in spring, or by division, or from seed. Sow perennials outdoors April–May, or in March to have flowers the same year. Sow annual gaillardias in late March to early April in pans or pots at 15°C (59°F). Prick off the seedlings into boxes, harden off and plant out 1ft (30cm) apart.

Gaillardia hybrids

○ ⊖ ⬡ ⬤ ⬤

These crosses between *G. aristata* and *G. pulchella* form a group whose flowers are very much larger than those of the species. Many will come fairly true from seed. If the seeds are sown in March to flower in late summer, it is possible to weed out specimens with an unsatisfactory colour. However, there is no need to be quite so selective in the border or with flowers for cutting, for which it is better to sow a little later to obtain better plants the following year. The vivid colours of the flowers range from bright red to bright yellow. Some of the most beautiful cultivars are 'Dazzler', yellow with red, and 'Cobalt', red with yellow. All these are

highly recommended. Cover the roots during severe frosts.
Gaillardia picta, see *Gaillardia pulchella*.

Gaillardia pulchella

○ ⊖ ⬤ ⬤ ⬤

From North America and Mexico, this annual, sometimes grown as a perennial, reaches heights of 1–2ft (30–60cm). It flowers July–September, its ray florets reddish-purple with a yellow edge, and the central disc orange-yellow, later turning dark purple. Some hybrids of *G. pulchella* are listed in seed catalogues under *G. picta*, and produce fairly pure colours from seed. 'Picta' is one of the best annuals for cutting and is also most suitable for planting in groups in a warm sunny position. There are also double-flowered cultivars of *G. picta*, such as 'Lorentziana', in which all the ray flowers are tubular and the flowers have the shape of powder puffs, which makes them look quite unlike any other gaillardia. The doubles are usually sold in mixed colours including cream, red with yellow, red with white spots, and yellow. Single varieties come in various shades of yellow, white with yellow, scarlet, salmon-pink, burgundy and rust. All are about 1½ft (45cm) high.

Galanthus
Amaryllidaceae
Snowdrop

Early-flowering bulbs that are well suited to woodlands and grassy banks, to rock gardens, and above all to naturalization.
Cultivation Snowdrops tolerate shade and will even thrive between light shrubs. They should be planted in the grass under trees or shrubs in random groups rather than in geometrical patterns. Do not stint on quantity, for these flowers are small and seen to best advantage when massed together. When planting beneath the grass in autumn, it is advisable to lift the turf and loosen the earth underneath. Plant the bulbs 2–3in (5–7.5cm) deep and no

Galanthus nivalis, snowdrop

more than 2in (5cm) apart.
Soil Snowdrops do best in moist, heavy loam. They dislike fierce sunlight, especially when the soil is sandy and there is no grass to screen the sun's rays.
Propagation Plants are grown by division. Lift the clumps July–August, separate the bulbs carefully and replant together with the parent bulbs either immediately or no later than the beginning of October. They may also be lifted and divided immediately after flowering.

Galanthus elwesii

◑ ⬤ ⬡ ⬤ ⬤

From the mountains of Asia Minor, this snowdrop grows 6–8in (15–20cm) high, flowering in February. The blooms are larger than those of *G. nivalis* and slightly more globular, and deep green on the inner petals.

Galanthus nivalis

Common snowdrop. A native of central and southern Europe, where it grows under shrubs and in meadows, this perennial reaches heights of 4–8in (10–20cm) and produces white flowers in February and later, depending on the weather. 'Plenus' is a double cultivar, its inner petals covered with numerous green flecks. *G. nivalis* ssp. *reginae-olgae* (syn. *G. octobrensis*) is the autumn snowdrop, producing its flowers before the leaves in October.

Galium
Rubiaceae
Bedstraw

These versatile plants are used as culinary herbs, and may also be planted as ground cover under deciduous trees that do not come into leaf before May, and for edging and as rock plants.
Soil They thrive in semi-shade under trees. A humus-rich soil is ideal.
Propagation By division.

Galium odoratum

◑ ⬤ ⬤ ⬤ ⬤ ⊖

Syn. *Asperula odorata*. Sweet wood-

ruff, a herbaceous perennial growing 4–10in (10–25cm) high and producing pure white flowers in small terminal clusters May–June. It has a glorious aroma and is used as a flavouring in some German wines.

Garrya
Garryaceae

A genus of shrubs, one species of which is commonly grown for its evergreen foliage and long male catkins.
Soil Any well-drained garden soil.

Galium odoratum, sweet woodruff

Gaultheria procumbens, partridge berry

Propagation By seed or from cuttings. The latter method is necessary if plants of a specific sex are required.

Garrya elliptica

○ ◑ ⬤ ⬤ ⬤ ⬤

A North American shrub growing 15–35ft (4.5–10.5m) high and flowering February–April. The small, wavy edged leaves are dark green above, grey beneath, and set off the male catkins which can be up to ¾in (2cm) in length. The females are much less decorative, and as they are borne on separate bushes, the male form should be obtained for the best effect. If both are grown, the female plant will carry brown-purple berries in early autumn.

Gaultheria
Ericaceae

A genus of evergreen flowering shrubs with beautiful berries.
Soil A peaty, acid soil is needed. The plants will not tolerate lime.
Propagation Plants are grown by division, from cuttings or from seed sown in autumn.

Gaultheria procumbens

⊙⊞⊞ ⊕ ⊛ ⊗ ⊖

Partridge berry, wintergreen or checkerberry. A small creeping shrub from North America with hairless branches that grows 3–6in (7.5–15 cm) high. The leaves are 2 in (5 cm) long, oval to circular, blunt, leathery, often slightly red and finely serrated at the edges. The solitary bell-shaped flowers are white to pinkish, and appear in June, followed by berry-like red fruits.

Gaultheria shallon

A shrub from North America growing up to 3 ft (1 m) high with tufted branches and broad, oval, brownish-green leaves that are more or less heart-shaped or rounded at the base. Flowers are borne in axillary racemes, and are pendent and white, and sometimes slightly pink. Fruits are a dark purple-black. This species is very suitable for growing under light trees.

Gazania
Compositae

A genus of very beautiful herbaceous perennials that must be grown as annuals except in the mildest areas. The

Gazania hybrids

magnificent large flowers only open in full sunlight. Gazanias are excellent for pot plants or for containers in which the beauty of the plant can be admired at close quarters.

Soil Well-drained fertile soil.

Propagation They are usually grown from cuttings in autumn or spring or by seed sown in February under glass.

Gazania hybrids

○ ⊖ ⊙ ⊛ ⊗

Many seedsmen offer the beautiful larger-flowered hybrids—generally under the name of *Gazania × splendens* or just "gazania hybrids"—that will flower the year they are sown. They grow to a height of about 8 in (20 cm).

Genista
Leguminosae
Broom

A genus of floriferous shrubs closely related to *Cytisus*.

Soil Plant in sandy soil. The shrubs will also do well on a clay soil provided it is well-drained and lime free. Very difficult to transplant, they are best grown in pots or containers.

Propagation They are grown from seeds sown outdoors in spring or cuttings in late summer. Seedlings and rooted cuttings must be placed into separate pots as soon as they can be handled.

Genista lydia hanging over a small wall in the magnificent gardens of Alan Bloom, near Diss, Norfolk

Genista anglica

○ ⊖ ⊛ ⊚ ⊚ ⊗

Needle furze. A dwarf shrub growing up to 1½ ft (45 cm) but broader than it is tall. It has spiny branches and bears yellow flowers May–July and sometimes in September. It requires a moist, humus-rich soil.

Genista hispanica

○ ⊖ ⊛ ⊚ ⊚ ⊗

Spanish gorse. This plant grows 1–2 ft (30–60 cm) high in prickly mounds, and bears terminal clusters of golden-yellow flowers June–July. Hardy in the south only; it tolerates dry conditions.

Genista lydia

○ ⊘ ⊛ ⊚ ⊚ ⊗

A most attractive shrub, 2 ft (60 cm) high with a spreading, arching habit that bears profuse golden-yellow flowers in June.

Genista pilosa

○ ⊘ ⊛ ⊚ ⊚ ⊗

A low hardy shrub native to W. and C. Europe that grows up to 1½ ft (45 cm) high. Yellow flowers open May–June and often again in autumn. *G. p.* 'Procumbens' is prostrate and bears masses of golden-yellow flowers May–June.

Genista purgans, see *Cytisus purgans*.

Genista sagittalis

○ ⊖ ⊛ ⊚ ⊚ ⊗ ⊖

An attractive dwarf shrub having prostrate, hairy green stems with broad wings. Yellow flowers are borne in small

Gentiana verna, one of many species of gentian

clusters May–June. This is a good plant for ground cover.

Genista tinctoria

Dyer's greenweed. A variable species ranging from prostrate shrubs to erect bushes 6 ft (2 m) high. Yellow flowers appear June–August, and the branches are usually hairy. 'Plena' grows to a height of 1 ft (30 cm) and produces golden-yellow double flowers June–

July. It is good for ground cover and in the rock garden. 'Royal Gold' has dense racemes of yellow flowers, up to 10 in (25 cm) long.

Gentiana
Gentianaceae
Gentian

A genus of beautiful perennials, prized for the attractive and rare blue of their magnificent flowers.

Cultivation Not all species are easy to cultivate: some gentians will tolerate semi-shade but will flower much more profusely in the sun, provided the soil is kept adequately moist.

Soil Most gentians thrive in deep well-drained soil enriched with leaf-mould or peat.

Propagation Sow ripe seeds in pots of sandy loam and plunge the pots in a shady bed. Move to a cold frame in winter. The seeds will germinate in spring. Prick out into separate pots and plant out in a semi-shady position but away from dripping trees. As soon as the seedlings are well-rooted, move the plants to a sunny position, and make sure they have sufficient moisture at all times.

Gentian acaulis, see *G. clusii*.
Gentiana asclepiadea
○ ⊛ ⊗ ⊘ ○ ⊗
A true shade-loving plant from southern and central Europe that grows 1–2 ft (30–60 cm) high. The blue flowers are borne singly or in groups of 2–3 all along the upper arching stems July–September.
Gentiana clusii
Syn. *G. acaulis*. From the Alps, Carpathians, Balkans and Pyrenees, these small evergreen plants grow 2–4 in (5–10 cm) high and bear blue flowers with olive-green longitudinal stripes in late spring to midsummer. This species thrives best in soils that lack lime.
G. lagodechiana, see *G. septemfida* var. *lagodechiana*.
Gentiana septemfida
○ ⊗ ⊗ ○ ⊘ ⊗
From Asia Minor. One of the easiest gentians growing 8–12 in (20–30 cm) high and producing blue flowers with brown spots inside in midsummer. *G. septemfida* var. *lagodechiana* (often listed as a true species *G. lagodechiana*) has prostrate stems, no basal rosette, and is the most beautiful variety.
Gentiana sino-ornata
A Chinese plant 6–8 in (15–20 cm) high with a prostrate habit that makes excellent ground cover. The flowers are 2 in (5 cm) long, and deep blue with 5 greeny-yellow stripes, and appear September–October. This species is not tolerant of lime.

Geranium
Geraniaceae
Crane's-bill

A genus of hardy herbaceous perennials suitable for rock gardens and herbaceous borders. This genus should not be confused with the bedding and pot "geraniums", which are treated under *Pelargonium*.

Soil Geraniums grow in any fertile garden soil, but do best in loamy sand enriched with humus. They can tolerate a fair amount of shade.

Propagation Plants are raised by division or from seed sown in a seed bed in the open. The seeds retain their germinating power for several years.

Geranium psilostemon

Geranium platypetalum

Geum with *Brunnera*

Geranium cinereum
○ ◑ ○ ⊘ ⊗
A Pyrenean plant growing 6 in (15 cm) high and flowering May–July. It has a tufted appearance with silvery leaves and pink flowers. The best-known form is 'Ballerina', which has white flowers so heavily marked with crimson as to appear entirely that colour.
Geranium cinereum var. *subcaulescens*, see *G. subcaulescens*.
Geranium dalmaticum
○ ○ ⊘ ⊗
A mat-forming plant from Yugoslavia–Albania that grows up to 5 in (12 cm) high, and flowers June–July. The clear pink flowers are up to 1 in (2.5 cm) wide and are held well above the leaves, which often turn red in autumn.
Geranium endressii
○ ◑ ○ ⊘
A floriferous species with prostrate to erect, slightly hairy stems, originally from the Pyrenees and growing 10–12 in (25–30 cm) high. In summer it bears pink flowers with darker veins.
Geranium grandiflorum, see *G. himalayense*.
Geranium himalayense
○ ◑ ○ ○ ⊗
Syn. *G. grandiflorum*, *G. meebaldii*. A plant from northern Asia growing 12–18 in (30–45 cm) high and bearing large, light lilac flowers with dark veins in early to midsummer. The stems and leaves are covered with glandular hair.

'Alpinum' is bright purple-blue, floriferous and grows up to 1 ft (30 cm) high.
Geranium platypetalum
○ ○ ○ ○
A Caucasian plant, 1½–3 ft (45–100 cm) high that flowers in summer, producing beautiful large violet-blue flowers, excellent for the border. Avoid too rich a soil, or the bushy plants will fall over.
Geranium 'Russell Prichard'
An 8–12 in (20–30 cm) hybrid between *G. endressii* and *G. traversii*, that bears bright pink flowers above silvery leaves June–September.
Geranium sanguineum
○ ◑ ○ ⊘ ⊗
Bloody crane's-bill. A European plant growing 6–10 in (15–25 cm) high and flowering May–August, producing large blood-red flowers in great profusion. It is an excellent plant for the front of herbaceous borders. The sub-species *lancastrense* is prostrate with smaller leaves and pale pink flowers marked by darker veins.
Geranium subcaulescens
Syn. *G. cinereum* var. *subcaulescens*. A 4–8 in (10–20 cm) high plant of tufted habit with greyish-green, hairy leaves and red to dark violet flowers. It grows in sun or semi-shade.

Geum
Rosaceae
Avens

Attractive hardy herbaceous perennials for the border and the rock garden. The beautiful foliage forms mounds which have a very attractive appearance even after flowering, and the flowers of the taller cultivars are also good for cutting, provided the cut stems are first dipped in boiling water and then trimmed.

Soil Geums grow in any ordinary garden soil that has been enriched with leaf-mould or peat and kept moist.

A *Geum chiloense* cultivar thrives near water

Propagation Plants may be raised by division or from seed, but cultivars do not come true from seed. Seeds will germinate in 2–3 weeks and retain their germinating power for 2 years.

Geum × borisii

A hybrid, probably between *G. coccineum* and *G. bulgaricum*, growing to 1 ft (30 cm) tall bearing bright orange flowers in early summer.

Geum chiloense

○ ◑ ○ ⊕

Syn. *G. quellyon*. A perennial herbaceous plant from Chile, growing 1–2 ft (30–60 cm) high, and bearing scarlet flowers June–August. This species strongly resembles *G. coccineum*, from the Balkans but has taller stems that branch more and leaves with a larger number of leaflets (10–12). For the cultivars listed under this name see *Geum* hybrids.

Geum coccineum (of gardens) see *G. chiloense*.

Geum hybrids

○ ◑ ○ ⊕

A group of cultivars, perhaps of hybrid origin, derived from *G. chiloense*, producing compact plants with a low habit about 1½ ft (45 cm) high. Their long flowering period begins in June, when orange-red flowers appear. These are among the best and most attractive geums for the border. Recommended cultivars include 'Dolly North', a semi-double with pure orange flowers; 'Fire Opal', orange with a touch of yellow;

Gillenia trifoliata

'Lady Stradheden', a double with yellow flowers; 'Mrs Bradshaw', bright brick red; 'Princess Juliana', bright orange-yellow and 'Red Wings', scarlet.

Gillenia
Rosaceae

A genus of lesser known shrub-like herbaceous perennials for the border.
Soil A fairly moist soil is preferred in summer, but a well-drained soil in winter.
Propagation Plants are grown by division in spring.

Gillenia trifoliata

◑ ◒ ◒

From the eastern United States, this perennial grows 2–2½ ft (60–75 cm) high, and June–July bears flowers with white petals and red sepals in loose panicles.

Ancient *Ginkgo* specimen in the Botanical Gardens, Leiden

The strange foliage of *Ginkgo biloba*

Ginkgo
Ginkgoaceae
Maidenhair tree

A genus consisting of a single species, distantly related to the conifers but, in fact, a primitive deciduous tree.
Soil Any ordinary garden soil will do.
Propagation Plants are grown from imported seeds in autumn in a cold frame. Sow singly in 4 in (10 cm) pots and plant out in a nursery bed from the following October to March. Grow on for 2–3 years, then move to their permanent positions.

Ginkgo biloba

○ ⊕ ✳ ⊗ ⊛ ⊥

Syn. *Salisbura adiantifolia*. A tree reaching a height of 80 ft (25 m) and a spread of 20 ft (6 m) or more. It assumes a pyramidal habit at first, then acquires a broader crown as the tree matures. It has greyish branches. The striking, fan-shaped green leaves turn a bright golden colour in autumn and are shed in winter. Inconspicuous flowers open in spring, followed, on female trees, by plum-shaped, creamy-yellow fruits. However, female flowers and fruits only appear after hot summers.

Gladiolus
Iridaceae
Sword lily

A genus of flowering plants having sword-shaped leaves and flowers in brilliant colours carried on long spikes that appear mostly July–August.
Cultivation Gladioli are half-hardy and should be lifted every autumn and overwintered in a dry and frost-proof place. In all but the coldest parts of Britain corms can be left in the ground if planted at least 4–5 in (10–13 cm)

deep. To obtain earlier flowers, plant out the corms from mid-November to mid-December, during frost-free weather, and cover with a thick layer of dry leaves weighed down with soil. The corms should be planted 4 in (10 cm) deep on dry soil. Alternatively, plants coming early into flower may be overwintered in a frost-free cold frame aired regularly in warmer weather. The taller cultivars should be tied to slim strong canes and sheltered from the wind.
Soil Gladioli prefer a rich, well-drained soil.
Propagation Plants may be grown from cormlets round the base of the old corm, and also from seed. The cormlets are the size of peas when the old corms are lifted in autumn. They are stored separately in dry sand, overwintered in a frost-proof place and planted out in drills in spring. They are lifted in autumn, tended as before and replanted the following spring. Many will reach flowering size the first year.

Sow seeds thinly in drills on rich soil in spring. Cloche protection will aid early germination. Some seedlings will flower the first autumn, the rest should do so the following year. Seeds do not breed true to colour and often not even to type.

Gladiolus × childsii, see *G.* hybrids.
Gladiolus × colvillei, see *G.* hybrids.
Gladiolus × gandavensis, see *G.* hybrids and *G. primulinus*

Gladiolus hybrids

○ ◑ ⊕ ⊗

These are large-flowered crosses between *G. × childsii*, *G. × gandavensis* and others. Such hybrids used to be divided into various groups, but recent crosses have led to the emergence of so wide a range of overlapping types that the old divisions have ceased to make much sense. Nor is there much point in naming particular examples since all selections tend to get out of date quickly. The hybrids reach heights of 3–4½ ft (1–1.3 m) and flower from late July to August. They should be planted 3–4 in (7.5–10 cm) deep and spaced 4 in

A small-flowered and graceful *Gladiolus primulinus* hybrid

Butterfly-flowered gladiolus

(10 cm) apart. Because the large-flowered, long-stemmed hybrids are not very sturdy, nurserymen have gone out of their way to develop shorter types of which the 'Butterfly' hybrids are perhaps the best examples. They reach heights of 2–4ft (60–120cm) and bear smaller flowers. Among the early-flowering types special mention should be made of the 'Nanus' hybrids, miniature types that flower in early July. For colours and names refer to any good catalogue.

Gladiolus primulinus
From tropical Africa, a plant growing $1\frac{1}{2}$–$2\frac{1}{2}$ft (45–75cm) high and flowering July–September. The flowers are attractive and variously coloured, but smaller than those of "common" gladioli. This species is frequently crossed with *G.* × *gandavensis* and it is these crosses that are usually sold as *G. primulinus*.

Gleditschia
Leguminosae

A genus of trees with beautiful foliage also formidably armed with long spines.
Soil Any garden soil will do, but the plant should not be exposed to too much wind.
Propagation Plants are raised from seed, soaked for 24 hours in water. Cultivars must be grafted.

Gleditschia triacanthos
Honey locust. A tree that grows up to 60ft (18m) high with a spread of up to 20ft (6m). The crown is broad, and grows umbrella-shaped in old trees; the leaves are mostly doubly pinnate with 30–32 leaflets. Pale yellow flowers are borne in clusters on short stems June–July. Sickle-shaped seed pods, up to 1ft (30cm) long, remain on the tree all winter; the spines are either simple or branched, and grow 4–8in (10–20cm) long. There are several cultivars, including 'Inermis', a tree without spines, and 'Sunburst', which has bright yellow young leaves that eventually turn pale green.

Godetia
Onagraceae

Hardy annuals, easy to cultivate in the border or as edging plants.

Gleditsia triacanthos in the autumn

Soil A light sandy soil, not too rich, is preferred, since otherwise the plant will make too much leaf.
Propagation The shorter cultivars can be planted in the flowering position as early as March. The taller types can be sown outside in September, or in cold frames in March to be moved out in April. Distance apart is 6–8in (15–20cm) for the shorter plants and 10–12in (25–30cm) for the taller ones.

***Godetia* hybrids**
A group of hybrids derived from cross-

A graceful *Godetia* hybrid

ing *G. amoena* with its variety *whitneyi* (*G. grandiflora*). Normal height is 1–$1\frac{1}{2}$ft (30–45cm), and purple-rose flowers appear in summer. Good seed catalogues list numerous cultivars in various shades of red, pink, purple, white and violet. They are divided into dwarf and tall types with single and double flowers respectively, and azalea-flowered types with semi-double flowers having frilled petals.

Gunnera
Haloragaceae

The species mentioned are majestic foliage plants that look like gigantic rhubarbs and are best grown as solitary plants on large lawns or beside water.
Soil Gunneras demand rich, fairly moist soil with plenty of humus. Before planting, dig a 3ft (1m) hole and fill it with leaf-mould mixed with half-rotted horse manure, then turfy loam to within 1ft (30cm) of the surface. Top with leaf-mould mixed generously with cow manure and garden soil. Stamp down but leave a raised mound because the filling will subside quite considerably. The site may be semi-shaded or in full sun, and should be kept moist in dry spells. In autumn cover with their dying leaves weighed down with stones or soil.
Propagation Gunneras are raised by division in spring.

Gunnera manicata
Growing up to 12ft (4m) high, this plant has massive leaves up to 6ft (2m) long and 6–10ft (2–3m) across. The leaves are a lighter green and less leathery than those of *G. tinctoria*, and the plant is less hardy, but where space permits this is the more attractive of the two species.

The impressive appearance of the gigantic *Gunnera tinctoria*

Gunnera tinctoria

Syn. *G. chilensis.* A hardy perennial plant, growing to a height of 4½ft (1.3m) or more with a spread of 10ft (3m). This is the more common of the two gunneras. The dark green leaves are palmate, lobed and toothed, and measure 4–5ft (1.2–1.5m) across. Inconspicuous reddish flowers are borne in long, heavy spikes, followed by fruits that turn red as they mature.

Gypsophila
Caryophyllaceae
Baby's breath

A genus of hardy annuals and herbaceous perennials with a bushy habit, suitable for borders and rock gardens. Mature perennials are rather difficult to transplant.

Soil These plants grow in any well-drained fertile soil.

Propagation Crown-graft the double gypsophilas on to rootstocks of single gypsophilas under glass. Of the annuals, *C. elegans* can be sown outside as early as March, whereas *G. muralis,* which needs warmth to germinate, is usually grown from seeds sown in pots in a heated frame.

Perennial species include:
Gypsophila paniculata
○ ⊖ ⊕ ⊙ ⊘ ⊗

Baby's breath. A Mediterranean plant with a height and spread of about 3ft (1m). It has a shrubby appearance with a profusion of small white flowers born in midsummer. The panicles may be dried and used for winter decoration. Very beautiful are 'Bristol Fairy

Gypsophila elegans

Perfect', 3ft (1m) high, a double white; 'Flamingo', 3½ft (1.1m) high, a double pink; and 'Plena', 2½ft (75cm) high, a double white. 'Pink Star' is an improved, larger and darker variety of 'Rosenscheyer', which grows to a height of 1½ft (45cm), has a wide-spreading habit, and bears double pink flowers.

Gypsophila repens
○ ⊖ ⊕ ⊙ ⊘ ⊗ ⊚

A creeping perennial from the limestone Alps. Growing only 4in (10cm) high, it bears relatively large white flowers from July until autumn. 'Rosea' has pink flowers. These plants are very suitable for the rock garden provided there is some lime in the soil.

Hamamelis mollis, Chinese witch hazel

Annual species include:
Gypsophila elegans
○ ⊖ ⊕ ⊙ ⊗

Very suitable as a filler in the border and also excellent for cut flowers, these plants produce white or pink flowers in summer.

Hamamelis
Hamamelidaceae
Witch hazel

Because it flowers so very early, this shrub is often planted close to the house so that its blooms may be admired from indoors. It will tolerate semi-shade and, since it flowers on the naked wood, it should be grown against a suitably dark background, such as a cherry laurel. Twigs placed in water will

Hamamelis × intermedia 'Jelena'

flower indoors January–February. In summer, the shrub strongly resembles the hazel and is not particularly ornamental.

Soil It grows best on well-drained acid soil enriched with humus.

Propagation Layering is the easiest method; but it is also possible, though much more difficult, to use heel cuttings taken in September. Plants may also be grown from seed sown in autumn. Cultivars must be grafted on to rootstocks of *H. virginiana.*

Hamamelis × intermedia
◐ ⊕ ⊛ ⊘ ⊗ ⊚ ⊙ ⊗

A cross between *H. japonica* and *H. mollis* that blends properties of both parents. The most attractive cultivar available is 'Jelena' (syn. 'Copper Beauty'), producing masses of large, coppery-red to orange flowers December–January. It was originally bred at Kalmthout Arboretum in Belgium and is named after the owner. 'Ruby Glow' is less floriferous and produces slightly smaller copper-coloured flowers in February. It is a fairly large and wide-spreading shrub. 'Winter Beauty' is a robust shrub with masses of deep yellow flowers.

Hamamelis japonica
Japanese witch hazel. A 10ft (3m) high shrub with slanting branches. The small flowers have crimped and twisted yellow petals tinged brownish-red at the base, and appear from January onwards. The best cultivar is 'Zuccariniana', which has sulphur-yellow flowers and blooms later than other witch hazels.

Hamamelis mollis
Chinese witch hazel. A most attractive shrub up to 12ft (4m) high, showing masses of deep yellow fragrant flowers from the end of December. 'Brevipetala', 10ft (3m) high, bears short-petalled buttercup-yellow flowers January–February; 'Pallida' has large sulphur-yellow flowers with a most delightful fragrance.

Hamamelis vernalis and Hamamelis virginiana
◐ ⊕ ⊛ ⊘ ⊙ ⊗

Ozark witch hazel and common witch hazel. Because of their smaller flowers these two species are not as ornamental as the others. The common witch hazel flowers in autumn just before and during the shedding of its beautifully coloured autumn foliage.

Gypsophila paniculata planted with lavender

The leaves of *Hamamelis virginiana* change colour just before the flowers come out

leaves and a profusion of white flowers.

Hebe buchananii
A perfect shrublet for the rock garden of bushy rounded shape up to 8 in (20 cm). It can be likened to a miniature *H. pinguifolia*, with grey-green leaves only $\frac{2}{10}-\frac{3}{10}$ in (5–7 mm) long. *H. b.* 'Minor' is even smaller, usually less than 4 in (10 cm) tall.

Hebe bulkeana
Very distinct from other hebes, this forms an open bush under 2 ft (60 cm) tall with glossy toothed leaves and erect 6–12 in (15–30 cm) long panicles of lavender to lilac flowers. A bush in full bloom is a sight to behold. It is not fully hardy and needs a sunny sheltered site, preferably at the foot of a wall.

Hebe buxifolia, see *H. odora*.

Hebe 'Carl Teschner'
A cross between *H. elliptica* and *H. pimelioides*, this nearly prostrate plant, 4–8 in (10–20 cm) high, makes good ground cover. In June and July it is covered with short spikes of violet, white-centred flowers.

Hebe cupressoides
Looking very much like a 1–2 ft (30–60 cm) high rounded cypress thanks to its slanting branches and scale-like grey leaves, this plant bears blue or white flowers in short spikes. In winter, especially if it is really cold, the foliage turns grey-purple.

Hebe × franciscana
A cross between *H. elliptica* and *H. speciosa*, growing 3–5 ft (1–1.5 m) high with glossy elliptical leaves and long clusters of white to purple flowers. 'Blue Gem' is probably the best form, having violet flowers. Although widely grown, it is not fully hardy in cold areas.

Hebe
Scrophulariaceae

This genus is often confused with *Veronica*. The latter, however, are herbaceous perennials while *Hebe* is a genus of evergreen shrubs. Some species have closely overlapping, scale-like leaves and are known as "whipcord" hebes.

Soil Any well-drained fertile soil is suitable.

Propagation Plants are raised from cuttings taken from midsummer to autumn.

Hebe albicans
A plant with glaucous leaves and a rounded habit growing 2 ft (60 cm) high or more. The white flowers open from a pink bud.

Hebe × andersonii
A hybrid of *H. salicifolia* and *H. speciosa* that grows 5 ft (1.5 m) high and is less hardy in cold areas. The leaves are narrow and up to 4 in (10 cm) long, and the lavender-blue flowers are borne in spikes. 'Variegata' has creamy-white margined leaves.

Hebe armstrongii
A moderately hardy shrub growing 2–3 ft (60–100 cm) high, with fan-shaped branches and tiny, closely overlapping, yellow-green scale-like leaves pressed close against them. White flowers are borne in terminal clusters.

Hebe brachysiphon
Often mistaken for *H. traversii*, a distinct species, this plant grows 4–6 ft (1.2–2 m) high and bears small, neat

Hebe pinguifolia in flower

Hebe armstrongii in flower

A good spot for *Hedera colchica* 'Sulphur Heart'

A cultivar of *Hedera helix*

Hebe glauco-caerulea

Syn. *H. pimelioides* var. *glauco-caerulea*. A semi-prostrate shrub with greyish-blue leaves and pale lavender flowers.

Hebe pimelioides var. glauco-caerulea, see H. glauco-caerulea.

Hebe 'Great Orme'

A hybrid derived from *H. speciosa* but hardier than that species. The flowers are deep pink at first, fading to white. They open from July to September.

Hebe macrantha

The largest-flowered *Hebe*, with white blooms up to $\frac{3}{4}$in (2cm) across and set off well by the dark green, glossy toothed leaves.

Hebe 'Midsummer Beauty'

A hybrid of *H. salicifolia* with narrow leaves that are often purple flushed, and long clusters of lavender flowers. It grows up to 3ft (1m) high, sometimes more.

Hebe ochracea

An attractive whipcord species much confused with *H. armstrongii* in gardens. It is easily separated from that species however by its more bronzy-yellow winter foliage and almost flat-topped habit.

Hebe odora

Syn. *H. buxifolia* of gardens. A moderately hardy shrub, to 3ft (90cm) high, with small, overlapping leaves. White flowers in dense 1in (2.5cm) spikes are produced in summer.

'Symbol' one of many *Helenium* hybrids

Hebe pinguifolia

A prostrate shrub bearing $\frac{1}{2}$in (12mm) blue-grey leathery leaves, often tinged with red, and white flowers. 'Pagei', with blue-green glaucous leaves and white flowers, is a hybrid of this species.

Hebe propinqua

A whipcord species not unlike *H. cupressoides* but smaller and more compact and staying green in winter. The flowers are white.

Hebe rakaiensis

A dome-shaped shrub 3ft (1m) high, with elliptical, bright green leaves and white flowers. This species makes excellent ground cover. Confused with the true *Subalpina* in British gardens.

Hebe recurra

This species is allied to *H. albicans* but has slender stems and narrower spreading to reflexed leaves, which are usually less glaucous. In addition, the flower spikes are longer and more tapered. Broader-leaved hybrid forms are sometimes seen in gardens and nurseries.

Hebe salicifolia

A shrub, 6–12ft (2–4m) high, with long, bright green leaves and lilac flowers tinged with white. Less hardy than some species, it withstands moderate frosts, and is much used in hybridization.

Hebe speciosa

A shrub growing 3–6ft (1–2m) high with dark green, leathery leaves and reddish-purple flowers. It withstands only moderate frost, but many of the cultivars derived from it are hardier. 'Alicia Amherst' has deep violet-blue flowers, and those of 'Simon Delaux' are crimson.

Hebe subalpina

Much confused with *Hebe rakaiensis*, this 3ft (1m) shrub has longer, more pointed, darker green leaves.

Hedera
Araliaceae
Ivy

The best climbing plant for shady positions, ivy is also excellent for ground cover.

Cultivation Ivy is very suitable for covering dark walls, screens, fences, etc. When trained against walls, the plants must always be cut back close to the support lest birds and rats be encouraged to nest inside. In variegated types, all branches bearing green leaves must be regularly removed since they will otherwise swamp the variegated leaves.

Soil It grows in almost any soil that is not too dry, but thrives in humus-rich soil.

Propagation Plants are grown from 3–5in (7.5–12.5cm) cuttings taken in July or August. Root in pots placed in a closed frame.

Hedera canariensis

From northwest Africa and adjacent islands, this robust plant has large, three-lobed leaves which sometimes turn a fine bronze in autumn. It needs to be grown on a sheltered wall as it does not tolerate severe frosts. 'Variegata' (syn. 'Gloire de Marengo') has silvery-white margined leaves.

Hedera colchica

Persian ivy, from the Caucasus to N. Iran. A rapid climber with large, leathery, thick, glossy green leaves. 'Arborescens' is a shrubby form up to 3ft (1m) or more high derived by rooting the non-climbing flowering shoots. Flowers in greenish-yellow umbels are borne in September and followed in October by small black berries. 'Dentata' has leaves with a few sharp teeth, as does 'Dentata Variegata', which is distinguished by its broad white edges.

Hedera helix

Common ivy. Growing to heights of 50–100ft (15–30m), this ivy occurs in many varieties differing in habit, shape and in the colour of the leaves and fruits. *Hibernica*, the Irish ivy, has 4in (10cm) leaves with shallow lobes; 'Sagittifolia' has arrow-shaped, five-lobed leaves, the central lobe being long and triangular; 'Argenteovariegata' has

Helenium hybrid

A hybrid rock rose

leaves shot with silver; 'Aureovariegata' has leaves shot with soft yellow; 'Aurantiaca' has yellow fruits; 'Arborescens' forms a densely leaved mound in shady parts of the garden; 'Conglomerata' forms low hummocks, and is excellent in rock gardens, as is 'Erecta', a slow-growing shrub with stiffly erect shoots.

Hedera helix makes ideal ground cover under trees

Helianthus annuus, sunflower, a giant among annuals

Mid-August to late September: 'Kanaria', 3ft (1m), golden-yellow flowers with a yellow centre; 'Karneol', up to 3ft (1m), copper with a brown centre. Late August to early October: 'Baudirektor Linne' 4ft (1.2m), having soft red petals with a brown centre; and 'Gold Rush', golden-yellow with brown markings.

Helianthemum
Cistaceae
Rock rose

Beautiful plants for sunny corners in the rock garden or the south-facing edge of the mixed border. Rock roses are exceptionally tolerant of dry conditions, and most averse to moist ground. Rock roses are attractive plants both before and after flowering.

Cultivation Most rock roses are sub-shrubs and tend to become straggly, and they should be pruned from time to time, in particular soon after the flowering period is over. For the rest, these plants are undemanding. They are fairly hardy, provided the ground is not too moist in winter, and are best planted on slopes. Some cultivars need sheltered sites in cold areas.

Soil Any well-drained soil is suitable.

Propagation Plants are easily propagated from cuttings of non-flowering lateral shoots taken in summer. Use rooting hormone and overwinter in a cold frame.

Helianthemum alpestre

A shrub from the Alps and southern Europe, growing to a height of 3in (8cm) with a spread of up to 2ft (60cm). It bears elliptic leaves and vivid yellow flowers which appear in June–July. The flowers are less than 1in (2.5cm) across. The variety 'Serpyllifolium' is smaller than the species.

Helenium
Compositae

A genus of vigorous and quickly spreading hardy herbaceous annuals and perennials. Care must be taken to restrict their number: if gaps in the border left by weaker plants are filled with surplus stock, and this principle is followed for several years, then the border will be overrun with *Helenium*, *Solidago*, *Phlox*, *Saponaria* and other strong plants. *Helenium* is not unattractive, however, and cultivars flower for a very long time. These plants make valuable additions to any border and the taller sorts are also useful both for planting between, or in front of, shrubs, and for cut flowers. One disadvantage of *Helenium* is that, just at the beginning of the flowering period, the lowermost leaves dry up, giving the plants a straggly appearance. If the plants are cut back in May, then the stems will remain in leaf and be sturdier, and the flowers will appear slightly later. Certain varieties that flower in early summer will produce a second crop if they are cut back after the first flowering. All *Helenium* species should be cut back in the autumn. The quality of the flowers is improved if the plants are divided and moved every three years.

Soil *Helenium* will grow in any garden soil that is not too dry. They prefer a sunny situation; if the situation is also exposed they should be given some support.

Propagation Plants are grown by division.

Helenium autumnale

○ ➔ ○ ⓨ ⊗

A North American herbaceous perennial reaching a height of 4–6ft (1.2–2m). Flowering August–October, it produces numerous dark yellow flowers which have almost spherical, brownish-yellow centres. The erect stems are crowded with masses of mid-green leaves.

Helenium bigelovii

From California, a plant growing 2–4ft (60–120cm) high and bearing flowers with yellow ray petals and brown to brownish yellow centres in summer.

Helenium hybrids

Although the precise origin of these plants is unknown, all have arisen from crosses with *H. autumnale*. They flower in three main periods:

Helianthus × laetiflorus is an attractive perennial sunflower

Helianthemum hybrids

○ ⊜ ∧ ⊕ ⑩ ⑨ ☀ ⊗

Crosses between *H. appeninum* and *H. nummularium*. These wide-spreading plants grow 4–6 in (10–15 cm) high and have greyish-green, elliptical foliage. Masses of flowers are borne in early to mid-summer but open in sunny weather only. The most attractive cultivars are: 'Ben Heckla', single, bronze-gold with a red centre; 'Ben Mare', single, dark orange; 'Cerise Queen', double, cerise-red; 'Golden Queen', single, lemon-yellow; 'Ruth', single, copper-red; and 'The Bride', single, white.

Helianthus
Compositae
Sunflower

A genus of hardy annuals and perennials.

Soil Any ordinary garden soil is adequate.

Propagation Sow the seeds of annuals in the flowering position during April and May, choosing a sunny place. Set three seeds together in groups 1½–2 ft (45–60 cm) apart, according to the size of the species, and later thin out to leave the best seedling of the three. Young plants may be moved, but should then be well watered-in. Perennial species are propagated by division.

Annual species include:

Helianthus annuus

○ ⊙ ⑨ ⑳ ⊗

Common sunflower. An annual from North America attaining a height of approximately 6 ft (2 m), although it will grow taller on good soil. In summer and autumn it bears golden-yellow flowers, 6–8 in (15–20 cm) across, sometimes up to 20 in (50 cm) high. Well-known cultivars include 'Golden Robe', 1½ ft (45 cm) high with double yellow flowers; 'Mammoth', 6 ft (2 m), a single having very large yellow flowers; 'Sanguineus', 5 ft (1.5 m) high with single blood-red flowers; and 'Tubulosus', which has tubular flowers carried in a spherical head.

Helianthus cucumerifolius, see *H. debilis* ssp. *cucumerifolius*.

Helianthus debilis ssp. *cucumerifolius*

A North American plant growing 3–5 ft (1–1.5 m) high and producing yellow to brownish-red flowers from July to September, smaller than those of *H. annuus* but borne in greater profusion and eminently suitable for the herbaceous border. Attractive cultivars include 'Diadem', which is 4 ft (1.2 m) high and has sulphur-yellow flowers with a dark centre; 'Purpureus', a 4 ft (1.2 m) plant with purple flowers; and 'Stella', 4 ft (1.2 m) high with large golden flowers.

Perennial species include:

Helianthus atrorubens

○ ∧ ○ ⑨ ⑳ ⊗

Syn. *H. sparsifolius*. Most attractive of the perennial species, and excellent for cutting, it can reach a height of 6 ft (2 m) and flowers in late summer to autumn. Cut the plant nearly to ground level after flowering and, in very cold localities, cover the crowns with leaves in winter. Divide in March–April, ensuring that each section has roots and dormant buds. Pot up and keep under glass until late spring, then plant out 2–2½ ft (60–75 cm) apart.

Helictotrichon sempervirens, in the foreground

Helianthus decapetalus

A North American perennial that grows 3–6 ft (1–2 m) high, and in late summer to autumn produces medium-sized yellow flowers. 'Multiflorus' has larger flowers and 'Soleil d'Or' bears double golden-yellow flowers for a longer period; both these cultivars require a very rich soil and are propagated by division.

Helianthus × laetiflorus

A cross between *H. rigidus* and *H. tuberosus* that grows up to 6 ft (2 m) high with large leaves and an erect habit like *H. rigidus*, which is not quite so tall and flowers from midsummer to early autumn.

Helianthus orgyalis, see *H. salicifolius*.

Helianthus salicifolius

○ ⊗ ∧ ○ ⑳

Syn. *H. orgyalis*. A plant from North America that grows 3–8 ft (1–2.4 m) high and flourishes best after growing in rich soil for several successive years. The flowers, which are produced very late in the season, are not as ornamental as the plant's willow-like habit might suggest. The leaves grow to a length of up to 1½ ft (45 cm) but have a maximum width of less than ½ in (12 mm), and droop decoratively from the upright stems.

Helianthus sparsifolius, see *H. atrorubens*.

Helichrysum
Compositae
Everlasting

A genus of shrubs, herbaceous perennials and annuals that includes one very popular species for winter flower arrangements.

Cultivation Flowers for winter decoration should be cut shortly before the flowers open fully, tied up in bunches and hung upside down in a dry airy place.

Soil Any ordinary well-drained soil will do. Do not over-fertilize.

Propagation Sow seeds of annuals in March in a cool greenhouse or heated frame. Prick out the seedlings into boxes and plant out in May 10–12 in (25–30 cm) apart.

Helichrysum bracteatum

○ ⊙ ⊗

An Australian plant growing 3–4 ft (1–1.2 m) high that flowers from midsummer to autumn. The best cultivar is 'Monstruosum', which bears 3 in (7.5 cm) spherical flowers in all colours except blue. Cultivars vary in the shades they produce.

Helictotrichon
Gramineae

A genus of perennial grasses of which only one species is in general cultivation. It is a hardy, very ornamental grass producing a profusion of flowers in spikelets. The arching leaves are a pretty sight even in autumn and winter. Useful among paving stones and in rock gardens, it also looks well in the mixed border where it combines most happily with roses.

Soil It thrives in any well-drained garden soil.

Propagation The simplest method is by division, but plants are also raised from seed.

Helictotrichon sempervirens

○ ⊜ ○ ⊕ ⊗

Syn. *Avena sempervirens*. A herbaceous perennial reaching a height of 12–18 in (30–45 cm) with erect to arching bluish-green foliage. Flowers are borne in drooping panicles up to 6 in (15 cm) long.

Heliopsis
Compositae

All the garden plants in this genus of annuals and herbaceous perennials look very much alike. They make outstanding additions to the border.

Soil Plant in any well-drained garden soil.

Propagation They may be raised by division or from cuttings.

Heliopsis helianthoides

A North American plant growing 3–4 ft (1–1.2 m) high and bearing yellow flowers midsummer to early autumn. The best-known species is *H. helianthoides* var. *scabra* (syn. *H. scabra*), from which a number of hybrids have been derived, including 'Golden Plume' with double yellow flowers up to 4 in (10 cm) across; 'Goldgreenheart', whose flowers are lemon-yellow tinged with green in the centre; and 'Incomparabilis', with double zinnia-like orange flowers.

Heliopsis scabra, see *H. helianthoides* var. *scabra*.

Heliopsis helianthoides 'Coldgreenheart'

Heliotropium arborescens, heliotrope

Helipterum roseum, everlasting

Helleborus showing frost damage

Day lily, a hybrid of *Hemerocallis*

Helipterum
Compositae
Everlasting

A genus including several most attractive annuals that are simple to grow, and also make long-living, straw-textured dried flowers.

Soil The plant thrives in humus-rich, well-drained sandy soils.

Propagation Sow seeds in early spring in a cold frame, or *in situ* in late spring. Set out frame-grown plants after mid-May, 6–8 in (15–20 cm) apart.

Helipterum humboldtianum

Syn. *H. sandfordii*. An annual from Australia that grows to a height of 10–16 in (25–40 cm). Chrome-yellow flowers appear 10–12 weeks after sowing; after drying, they assume a metallic green sheen.

Helipterum manglesii

Syn. *Rhodanthe manglesii*. A 15 in (38 cm) plant with glaucous leaves partly clasping the stem; its flowers are pink with silvery bracts. 'Plenum' has an unusually large number of bracts, giving the flower a double appearance. Other recommended cultivars are 'Al-bum', 'Maculatum' and 'Sanguineum'.

Helipterum roseum

Syn. *Acroclinium roseum*. This plant resembles *H. manglesii*, but its green leaves do not clasp the stem. 'Album' has white flowers.

Helipterum sandfordii, see *H. humboldtianum*.

Helleborus
Ranunculaceae
Hellebore

A genus of winter-flowering plants suitable for mixed borders and excellent for cutting.

Cultivation Hellebores are long lived and as long as they thrive are best left undisturbed. An annual mulch of leaf-mould or well-decayed manure each spring is very beneficial.

Soil Hellebores thrive in any well-drained but moist fertile soil, preferably deeply dug.

Propagation Plants may be raised from ripe seed sown in summer in boxes of sandy soil placed in a cold frame. They may also be propagated by division after flowering.

Helleborus atrorubens, see *H. pur-purascens*.

Helleborus foetidus

Stinking hellebore. A semi-shrub growing 1½ ft (45 cm) high and bearing green, purple-edged bell-shaped flowers from late winter to late spring.

Helleborus hybrids

Crosses between *H. abchasicus* and *H. guttatus*, *H. cyclophyllus* and possibly *H. purpurascens*, their colours range from pink to green and dark purple.

Helleborus lividus

This species, from Majorca, is not often grown, but the sub-species *corsicus* (syn. *H. corsicus*) is not uncommon. It has a vigorous habit growing to 2 ft (60 cm) in height with trifoliate, spiny-toothed, glossy-green leaves and bright, chartreuse-green flowers.

Heliotropium
Boraginaceae
Heliotrope, Cherry pie

Heliotropes are really shrubs, but because most species are half-hardy or tender they are usually cultivated as annuals.

Soil Any ordinary, well-drained fertile soil is suitable.

Propagation Plants are mainly raised from cuttings, which can be taken throughout the year but are best obtained in February to yield sturdy plants by May. (If cuttings are taken in midsummer, then the plants will flower indoors in the winter.) For February cuttings, lift the mother plants in late autumn, pot up, cut back hard, and overwinter at a temperature of 7–10°C (45–50°F). The air must not be too humid and the plants should not be watered too often. The young shoots are severed from the branches with a sharp knife and inserted in a propagator. After they have rooted they are potted up in 2–3 in (5–7.5 cm) pots and later potted on in 4 in (10 cm) pots. Stop young plants several times to encourage a bushy habit. During the growing period, water generously and feed often with liquid fertilizer. Harden off and plant out at the beginning of June. Heliotropes can also be grown from seed but the resulting seedlings do not have nearly so attractive a fragrance. Sow seeds in pots, germinate at 16–18°C (61–64°F) and screen seedlings from bright sunlight. Harden off and plant out in late spring to early summer.

Heliotropium arborescens

Syn. *H. peruvianum*. A sub-shrub from Peru that flowers from summer to autumn, bearing bluish-purple to violet flowers with a vanilla fragrance. There are many garden cultivars, perhaps of hybrid origin with the larger flowered *H. corymbosum*, all with flowers ranging from dark violet to lavender and white. Particularly attractive are 'Madame Bruant', with its soft blue-violet flowers, and 'Marine', blooming in violet-blue clusters.

A pink *Hemerocallis* hybrid

The plantain lily thrives on wet ground and a moist atmosphere. The species shown is *Hosta sieboldiana*

growing 8–10ft high, its branches usually spiny and silvery scaly. The leaves, too, are silvery, especially on the underside. Inconspicuous yellowish-green flowers are borne in late March in sessile clusters. Bright orange berries are borne by female plants (if fertilized) during the autumn and winter.

Hippuris
Hippuridaceae

An easily cultivated aquatic plant with a distinctive, spiny appearance.
Soil Plant in mud or any other type of soil covered with up to 12in (30cm) of water.
Propagation By division.

Hippuris vulgaris
Mare's tail, from Europe, North America, Greenland, etc. A herbaceous perennial with hollow stems that grows 1½ft (45cm) high with horizontally protruding, grey-green leaves. The flowers are inconspicuous.

Holodiscus
Rosaceae

A genus of very attractive flowering shrubs, of which only one species is in cultivation. It is a pity that this shrub, which is a useful addition to gardens of all sizes, should be so rarely seen—it looks glorious not only in summer when it is in full flower, but also in winter when the fruits are covered with a silvering of frost.
Soil It thrives in any well-drained soil that does not dry out.
Propagation Plants are raised from suckers, by layering or from cuttings taken in spring and rooted under glass.

Holodiscus discolor
Syn. *Spiraea discolor*. A plant from North America growing 6–12ft (2–4m) high with overhanging branches and doubly serrated or slightly lobed leaves, densely covered with hair underneath. In midsummer, small, creamy-white flowers appear in large plumey panicles.

Hosta
Liliaceae
Plantain lily

A genus of hardy herbaceous perennials grown chiefly for their unusually attractive leaves and trumpet-shaped flowers. Because these foliage plants provide landscape gardeners with such choice material for shaded parts of the garden and for ground cover, they have been crossed and selected over the years to yield a large number of cultivars.
Cultivation After a few years, hostas begin to lose their attractiveness and it is advisable to lift them at least once every four or five years and to replant the younger parts of the crown after the ground has been well dug-over and manured. This may be done in spring or autumn. Hostas are tolerant of shade but the green-leaved sorts also do well in the sun. Variegated plants, however, retain a better colour if they are planted in partial shade.
Soil Hostas like moist, rich soil that has been improved with leaf-mould, peat, well decayed compost or manure.
Propagation Division is the simplest method since the plants have to be lifted anyway. This may take place before the plants have begun to fade, but only in spring or autumn. Species and green-leaved cultivars can also be propagated from seed. Variegated plants do not come true from seed and must therefore be divided. Sow seed in pots as soon as it is ripe. Other seeds may lie dormant for a long time before they germinate.

Hosta albo-marginata, see *H. sieboldii*.
Hosta crispula
This species has 8in (20cm) long, 4in (10cm) wide leaves with a white wavy edge. The lilac flowers protrude high above the leaves in August but may not come into flower every year.
Hosta fortunei
Resembling *H. sieboldiana*, this plant has shorter, rounder, and less bluish-green leaves. The lilac flowers appear in early summer. Of the cultivars, 'Aurea' produces beautiful foliage in spring but it quickly loses its colour, 'Albopicta' has yellow leaves with an initially green border; 'Aureamarginata' is entirely yellow when it is young then becomes green with a yellow margin; 'Hyacinthina' has fairly large, glaucous leaves and masses of flowers, and 'Obscura' has dark green oval leaves.
Hosta glauca, see *H. sieboldiana*.
Hosta lancifolia
From Japan, this 1½–2½ft (45–75cm) plant has narrow leaves and flowers from midsummer to early autumn, when drooping lilac, or more rarely white, flowers appear.
Hosta plantaginea
A species with bright green, very glossy, heart-shaped leaves. It has pure

Hosta crispula

Hosta sieboldiana in the autumn

Garden hyacinths under a Japanese flowering cherry

white fragrant flowers, up to 4 in (10cm) long, in autumn.

Hosta sieboldiana
Syn. *H. glauca*. A Japanese plant with grey-blue leaves up to 1 ft (30 cm) long. Lilac flowers open in early to mid-summer. 'Aureomarginata' has yellow-edged leaves; 'Elegans' has glaucous leaves with corrugations between the veins.

Hosta sieboldii
Syn. *H. albo-marginata*. Growing up to 1½ ft (45 cm), this plant has narrow lanceolate leaves with a silver-white margin. Lilac flowers are borne in July–September in slender spikes borne well above the leaves. 'Alba' has light green leaves and white flowers.

Hosta undulata
A species that does not grow wild and may be of hybrid origin. Plants grow 1½–2 ft (45–60 cm) high with dark green leaves variegated with a central white line or splash and rather wavy at the edges. Pale violet to lavender flowers appear in July–September on stems up to 3 ft (1 m) long. 'Erromena' has plain bright green leaves with only slightly wavy margins.

Hosta ventricosa
A species with lilac flowers in long spikes, up to 3 ft (1 m) high, that flowers in late summer. *H. v.* 'Aureomaculata' has yellow centred leaves, while *H. v.* 'Variegata' has yellow margins.

Hyacinthus
Liliaeceae
Hyacinth

A popular genus of bulbous plants with fragrant flowers suitable for a spring bedding display.

Cultivation Hyacinths are apt to be top-heavy when in full bloom. To prevent this it is best not to plant over-large bulbs and to combine with other bedding plants that help to support them. Gardeners who fail to lift the plants after flowering, trusting that they will bear equally fine flowers the following year, will often be disappointed. Once the foliage has died down it is advisable to lift the bulbs and to store them in a dry place until October, when they should be planted out again.

Soil Do not manure the soil just before planting hyacinths, and in any case do not feed them liberally, for the bulb itself contains quite enough food. If it is considered absolutely essential, some artificial fertilizer may be added. For the rest, the soil should be well turned over and must not be allowed to dry out. Plant at a depth of 6 in (15 cm), preferably in October. Small bulbs should be set out 4 in (10 cm) apart, and larger bulbs at 6 in (15 cm). If other plants are grown between them, then of course, the hyacinths must be planted further apart.

Propagation The propagation of the large-flowered cultivars is so complicated that it is hardly worth the amateur's while. The process involves using a special knife on the growing point to encourage the bulb (at a given temperature and humidity) to form bulblets. It then takes a few years before these develop into flowering bulbs. The amateur is advised to buy new stocks of bulbs as and when they are needed.

Hyacinthus orientalis
○ ◐ ⊘ ⊚ ⊛ ⊗ ⊗
This species is the parent form of all the popular hyacinths grown in homes and gardens. The following are among the best-known cultivars, arranged according to colour:

Blue: 'Delft Blue', with light blue, very large flowers; 'King of the Blues', a late-flowering plant with dark blue, finely scented blooms; 'Ostara', with dark blue flowers and dense spikes; and 'Queen of the Blues', pale blue.

White: 'Carnegie'; 'L'Innocence'.

Yellow and orange: 'Orange Boven', with salmon-orange flowers; and 'City of Haarlem', with yellow blooms.

Pink and red: 'Anna Marie', with light pink flowers; 'Jan Bos', whose flowers are light red; 'Lady Derby', which has soft pink flowers; 'La Victoire', which has rose-red blooms appearing extra early; 'Pink Pearl', with pink flowers; 'Queen of the Pearls', which has bright pink flowers; and 'Tubergen's Scarlet', which bears blooms of intense scarlet.

Some special cultivars include:

Double hyacinths: 'Chestnut Blossom', with soft pink flowers; and 'Madame Sophie', with pure white.

Miniature hyacinths: Small bulbs with small spikes. These should be planted close together.

Multiflora hyacinths: Very large, specially treated bulbs that produce several small spikes.

Fairy hyacinths: These produce smaller-than-usual clusters of flowers. The only cultivar is 'Borah', which has light-blue flowers.

Hydrangea
Saxifragaceae

This genus includes various beautiful garden shrubs with striking flowers. The inflorescences contain fertile and infertile flowers, often arranged in flattened to hemispherical patterns.

Cultivation and soil See under the various species.

Propagation Climbing species are raised from cuttings of side growths taken in June or July, and shrubby species from cuttings of non-flowering shoots taken in August or September.

Hydrangea anomala ssp. petiolaris
○ ◐ ⊘ ⊛ ⊚ ⊗ ⊗
Syn. *H. petiolaris*, *H. scandens*. A glorious hydrangea with flat corymbs of sterile and fertile flowers that grows up to 6 ft (2 m) when planted as a solitary shrub but up to 20 ft (7 m) when trained against a wall and much taller up a tree. White flowers appear in midsummer. Completely hardy, it is one of the few climbers to do well against a northern wall. Prune the shrub very little if at all, and shape the climber by trimming off straggly branches, but not more. Vigorous growth begins in the second or third year.

Hydrangea arborescens
○ ◐ ⊘ ⊛ ⊛ ⊚ ⊗ ⊗
A North American shrub reaching a height of 6–10 ft (2–3 m). It must be cut back strongly every spring to a height of no more than 3 ft (1 m). In midsummer it bears white flowers in flat corymbs: there are few or no sterile outer florets. Completely hardy and tolerant of shade, the plant requires rich, calcareous soil, and should be propagated from cuttings. 'Grandiflora' has large, pure white flowers, all sterile and borne in rounded clusters.

Hydrangea aspera
A shrub reaching a height of up to 6 ft (2 m) with bristly branches and 4–6 in (10–15 cm) long leaves, downy on the underside. The flowers are borne in summer in 4 in (10 cm) wide corymbs containing lilac sterile blooms.

Hydrangea aspera ssp. sargentiana
○ ◐ ⊘ ⊚ ⊗ ⊗
Syn. *H. sargentiana*. A shrub from China reaching a height of 4½ ft (1.3 m), and in midsummer bearing flowers in 5–6 in (12.5–15 cm) wide corymbs. The sterile outer florets are white or pink tinted, the fertile inner florets violet; leaves are large, ovate and pointed, and bristly beneath. A highly ornamental and completely hardy garden plant, it thrives in semi-shaded positions and demands moist soil. It may be cut back hard in spring.

Hydrangea aspera ssp. strigosa
◐ ⊘ ⊚ ⊗ ⊗
Syn. *H. strigosa*. A shrub growing to a height of 8 ft (2.4 m) with large leaves, downy beneath, and lilac and white flowers borne in large corymbs in early to midsummer. A very attractive species, it tolerates partial shade.

Hydrangea bretschneideri, see H. heteromalla.

Hydrangea heteromalla
○ ◐ ⊘ ⊚ ⊗ ⊗
Syn. *H. bretschneideri*. A very hardy shrub that grows up to 10 ft (3 m) high with reddish-brown branches, peeling bark, and 3–7 in (7.5–18 cm) long, ovate leaves with a pointed tip. The flowers are borne in 4–6 in (10–15 cm) wide flat

'Lilacina', an attractive lace-cap form of *Hydrangea macrophylla*

Hydrangea aspera ssp. *sargentiana* thrives in moist positions under a canopy of tall trees

or arched corymbs with sterile outer florets.

Hydrangea macrophylla

A popular species suitable as a pot plant or for a garden decoration. If fed with aluminium sulphate, the pink flowers will generally turn blue, but this is not always completely successful in chalky soils. It is advisable to use the cultivars, these being much hardier than the species which flowers on the previous year's wood and whose buds are therefore liable to suffer frost damage. The only remedy then is to cover up the entire plant. *H. macrophylla* also has different pruning requirements from other hydrangeas: if cut back severely in spring, it will be stripped of its buds. To prevent it from growing thin-bottomed, no more than a few branches

should be removed; the young shoots produced afterwards will supply flower buds for the following year. The plant thrives on humus-rich soil, preferably well-manured. The best cultivars are 'Blue Wave', with blue, fertile florets and pink outer florets; 'Manchurica', which has very dark branches and pink florets, all sterile; 'Mariesii', with very large lilac-pink outer florets; 'Rosalba', with red or blue fertile florets and off-white outer florets, later turning a vivid rose; and 'White Wave', which has blue inner and sharply contrasting white outer florets.

Hydrangea macrophylla ssp. *serrata*

Syn. *H. serrata*. A shrub that grows up to 3 ft (1 m) high with thin, upright branches and smaller, thinner and less

glossy leaves than *H. macrophylla*. It bears large pink or blue outer florets. 'Acuminata' has pink fertile flowers, bluish-pink outer florets and very dark twigs, and grows to a height of 4½ft (1.3 m). 'Blue Bird' is more compact and has blue flowers. 'Preziosa' is a tall shrub with salmon-pink flowers.

Hydrangea paniculata

This hardy species is usually represented by 'Grandiflora', the most common outdoor hydrangea, with very large, somewhat pear-shaped terminal panicles. It flowers in summer, bearing sterile white blooms that turn pink. 'Grandiflora' requires rich, moist soil; it must be pruned hard every year, but will quickly spring back to a height of 8 ft (2.4 m) or more on rich soil. 'Praecox' flowers six weeks earlier and is more compact. 'Floribunda', with large inflorescences, is a fairly recent introduction that can be highly recommended.

Hydrangea petiolaris, see *H. anomala* ssp. *petiolaris*.

Hydrangea quercifolia

A species with foliage not unlike large red oak leaves. The plant grows to a height of about 6 ft (2 m), and in summer bears white flowers in erect panicles; the outermost blooms are large and infertile.

Hydrangea sargentiana, see *H. aspera* ssp. *sargentiana*.

Hydrangea scandens, see *H. anomala* ssp. *petiolaris*.

Hydrangea serrata, see *H. macrophylla* ssp. *serrata*.

Hydrangea strigosa, see *H. aspera* ssp. *strigosa*.

Hydrangea paniculata in summer and in autumn

Hypericum
Guttiferae
St John's wort

A genus of predominantly shrubby plants which, though hardy, may not live long in cold areas. While tolerant of shade, they also thrive in the sun. *H. olympicum* and *H. polyphyllum* are particularly suitable for rock gardens.

Soil A well-drained garden soil is needed, rich in humus.

Propagation Plants are raised from cuttings of soft basal growth taken in late spring or early summer or of firmer growth in late summer. *H. calycinum* can also be increased by division of the spreading rhizomes.

All the following are shrubby plants:

Hypericum androsaemum

From southern Europe, this hardy and highly recommended shrub grows up to 3 ft (1 m) and from midsummer to early autumn bears golden-yellow flowers followed by ½in (12 mm) fruits which are red at first and then turn black. The leaves are aromatic.

Hypericum calycinum

Rose of Sharon, or Aaron's beard, a sub-shrub from Bulgaria to Turkey that forms a thick carpet with its rhizomes. It grows to a height of about 1 ft (30 cm) and flowers from midsummer to early autumn, bearing large, solitary golden-yellow blooms. The leaves are leathery, dark green, oval and blunt, and are carried on short stalks; they are generally evergreen. This plant requires a sunny or lightly shaded position.

Hypericum hircinum

A compact shrub reaching a height of 2½ft (75 cm), bearing small golden-yellow flowers from midsummer to early autumn. The sepals are shed soon after flowering, and elongated brownish-red, later brownish-black, fruits are produced.

Hypericum forrestii

Syn. *H. patulum forrestii*. A hardy, deciduous shrub up to 5 ft (1.5 m) high with stout rounded branchlets and cup-shaped flowers borne solitarily or in clusters of three. The flowers appear from midsummer to autumn and are golden-yellow. 'Hidcote' is a semi-evergreen attractive cultivar probably of hybrid origin with *H. calycinum* bearing 3 in (7.5 cm) wide flowers having orange stamens.

Hypericum kalmianum

A narrow-leaved shrub growing up to 3 ft (1 m) high. The main stems are often gnarled, and from midsummer to early autumn it bears small, lemon-yellow flowers with golden-yellow stamens.

Hypericum × moserianum

A cross between *H. calycinum* and *H. patulum*, this semi-evergreen, low-spreading bush with angular branches bears large, golden-yellow flowers in clusters of 1–3, with rose-red anthers, from midsummer to autumn. A very beautiful shrub, it is also useful as an edging plant and as ground cover, and will tolerate long dry spells and shaded positions. The variety 'Tricolor' has variegated green and white leaves with red margins.

Hypericum hookerianum

Hypericum calycynum

Hypericum olympicum
○ ◑ ⊖ ⊘ ⍉ ⊗ ⊖

A small sub-shrub, 4–8 in (10–20 cm) high with erect stems, small grey-green leaves. Masses of golden-yellow flowers measuring 1–2 in (2.5–5 cm) across are borne in July and August. The variety 'Citrinum' has pale yellow flowers.

Hypericum patulum var. henryi
A shrub up to 3 ft (1 m) high with gracefully arching branches. The 2 in (5 cm) golden-yellow flowers have curved petals and are followed by reddish fruits that turn greener as they mature.

Hypericum × persistens
○ ◑ ⊖ ⊘ ⍉ ⊗ ⊛ ⊖

A cross between *H. androsaemum* and *H. hircinum*. A dense, erect, semi-evergreen shrub with reddish-brown angular branches that grows up to 3 ft (1 m) high. The leaves have an unpleasant odour; the flowers measure 1 in (2.5 cm) across and are golden-yellow, and the fruit is brownish-red, turning black. 'Elatum' is very hardy, producing golden-yellow flowers from midsummer to early autumn; the sepals do not fall off after flowering, as they do in *H. hircinum*, and the fruits are black. 'Elstead' has bright red fruits, and is slightly more compact than 'Elatum'.

These plants require a rich well-drained loam. The next species are eminently suitable for rock gardens. They thrive in full sun and do best on well-drained, clay soil.

Hypericum polyphyllum
○ ◑ ⊖ ⍉ ⊗ ⊗

This species is a sub-shrub or woody based perennial forming a dense carpet of glaucous leaves, and bears golden-yellow flowers in midsummer. The variety 'Sulphureum' bears paler coloured flowers.

Hypericum prolificum
○ ◑ ⊖ ⍉ ⊗ ⊗

A hardy but rare plant resembling *H. kalmianum*, it grows to a height of 3 ft (1 m), and bears lemon-yellow flowers with golden-yellow stamens from midsummer to early autumn.

Iberis
Cruciferae
Candytuft

A genus of exceptionally floriferous annual and perennial garden plants.
Cultivation Annuals: The more compact cultivars make excellent edging plants, the others look best when massed together at the front of the border. They can also be grown as pot plants, where they will remain in flower for many weeks. They are often sown in late September or early October, the seedlings being covered with cloches during the winter in cold areas.

Perennial species: These retain their leaves in winter and are therefore more liable to frost damage in severe winters. For this reason they are best planted in sunny sheltered sites in areas that are cold.
Soil All species thrive on well-drained calcareous soil. They will also grow on poorer quality soils.
Propagation Sow the seeds in the flowering site in spring, later thinning the seedlings to 3–4 in (7.5–10 cm) apart each way. Perennial species are propagated from soft-wood cuttings taken in June–August, by division or from seed in spring.

Iberis amara, candytuft

Iberis sempervirens 'Snowflake'

Annual species:
Iberis amara
○ ⊖ ⊙ ⊗ ⊗

Syn. *I. coronaria*. A southern European annual reaching a height of 8–12 in (20–30 cm). White flowers with a pleasant fragrance appear in April to June for seed sown in autumn, and in June–July for seed sown in March–April. The most popular sort is 'Coronaria', which has large racemes; recommended cultivars are the hyacinth-flowered 'The Empress'; 'Tom Thumb', a dwarf; and 'Pumila', which has a still more dwarfish habit.
Iberis coronaria, see Iberis amara.
Iberis umbellata
An annual, originally from southern Europe, that reaches a height of 6–18 in (15–45 cm) and produces pale purple flowers like those of *I. amara*. Cultivars are available in white, flesh-colour, carmine and scarlet. 'Mercury' is specially recommended for its very large flowers in mixed colours, and 'Dwarf Fairy Mixed' is also very popular.

Perennial species:
Iberis sempervirens
○ ⊖ ⊛ ⊘ ⊗ ⊗ ⊛ ⊗ ⊖
From southern Europe, a sub-shrub that grows up to 8 in (20 cm) high and

bears white flowers in May–June. This is the most common of the perennial *Iberis* spp. Attractive cultivars include the floriferous 'Snowflake'.

Ilex
Aquifoliaceae
Holly

Wild holly is common in woods and thickets in Europe and western Asia. Some species are sensitive to severe frost when planted in dry, sunny positions, and very sharp winds may damage the leaves and outer branches, particularly during the first year following transplantation. If the branches stay green, however, the plant will recover.
Soil Holly thrives in any well-drained but not dry fertile soil, ideally where the roots are shielded from the sun either by ground-covering plants or by thick layers of leaf-mould. Holly also grows well in partial shade. Transplant in spring, with the soil ball intact.
Propagation Cultivars must be budded or grafted on to stocks of *I. aquifolium*, or grown from cuttings taken in late summer and rooted in a cold frame. Plant out in May.

Ilex × altaclarensis
○ ◑ ⊕ ⊛ ⊕ ⊘ ⊛ ⊛ ⊛ ⊙ ⊕ ⊡ ⊗
A cross between *I. aquifolium* and *I. perado* that resembles *I. aquifolium* but has larger and often less spiny leaves. Cultivars include 'Camellifolia', which has shiny dark green leaves, mainly without spines; 'Golden King' having yellow margins to the leaves and the striking 'Lawsoniana' having each leaf with a central yellow splash. Large berries are borne during winter.

Ilex aquifolium
○ ◑ ⊕ ⊛ ⊕ ⊘ ⊛ ⊛ ⊛ ⊙ ⊕ ⊡ ⊗
Common holly, growing up to 40 ft (12 m) and bearing small white flowers in May–June followed by magnificent berries in autumn. Since the male and female flowers are borne on separate trees, it is advisable to grow the two sexes side by side. This species has

given rise to numerous forms differing in leaf shape and colour. The variegated forms are particularly attractive. 'Argenteomarginata' is prized for its silver-edged foliage and profuse berries. It is very vigorous, and has a broad pyramidal habit. 'Aureomarginata' has gold-edged leaves but it produces no berries; 'Bacciflava' has yellow fruits that distinguish it from the rest; 'Handsworth Silver' has creamy-edged leaves and attractive red berries; 'Madame Briot' has leaves with a broad golden edge and orange-red berries; 'Pyramidalis' has bright green glossy leaves, bears red berries in profusion, and is often used for Christmas decoration; 'Silver Queen' is a particularly attractive variegated holly, with creamy-white leaf edges and purplish branches. It and other white-variegated forms are also known as 'Albomarginata'.

Ilex bioritsensis, see *I. pernyi* 'Veitchii'.

Ilex crenata
○ ◐ ⦶ ⊛ ⊛ ❋ ❀ ☺ ⊜

Japanese holly. A shrub growing up to 12–18ft (4–6m) high with small, generally crinkled leaves and black berries. The following cultivars seldom exceed 3ft (1m). 'Convexa' has glossy convex

Ilex aquifolium 'J. C. van Tol' produces a host of berries

Ilex aquifolium 'Madame Briot'

leaves, is very hardy and ideal for compact hedges; 'Golden Gem' has golden-yellow leaves and also makes a compact shrub; and 'Stokes' is a dwarf shrub forming a dense mound of tiny leaves.

Ilex glabra
Inkberry. A shrub growing up to 8ft (2.4m) high, it has oval leaves with a few spines at the tip. The fruits are small and red, changing to black.

Ilex opaca
○ ◐ ⦶ ⊛ ≈ ⊛ ⊛ ❋ ❀ ⊗

American holly. An evergreen shrub with leaves that are olive-green on the topside. Flowers appear on young shoots only, and the fruits are red. This species requires moist neutral to acid soil.

Ilex pernyi
A dense, pyramidal shrub with spinous leaves and red fruit borne in great abundance. *I. p.* 'Veitchii', this shrub grows up to 15ft (5m) high and has a pyramidal habit. The 2in (5cm) long leaves have 4–5 protruding spines on either side, and the fruit is red with 3–4 seeds.

Ilex serrata
○ ◐ ⦶ ⊛ ⊛ ❋ ❀ ① ⊗

Syn. *I. sieboldii*. A dense, deciduous, dioecious shrub with finely serrated

leaves, rounded at the base, and dull green in colour. The female plants bear red berries.

Ilex sieboldii, see *Ilex serrata*.

Ilex verticillata
An attractive deciduous shrub up to 10ft (3m) high with oval leaves, singly or doubly serrated. This shrub is dioecious, and female plants produce masses of beautiful berries if they are planted beside males.

Impatiens glandulifera

Impatiens balsamina, a bedding plant

Impatiens
Balsaminaceae
Busy Lizzie

A genus of hardy, half-hardy and tender annuals and evergreen subshrubs including two species that are popular as bedding plants. They remain in flower for a very long time, the blooms being thought garish by some people and most attractive by others.
Soil Plant in fertile, not too moist garden soil in a sunny position. On drier sites, water regularly and on poorer soil feed generously during the growing season.
Propagation Sow *I. balsamina* and *I. wallerana* in late March or early April in a moderately heated frame or indoors. Harden off and plant out in late May spacing the young plants at 10–12in (25–30cm) apart each way. Sow *I. glandulifera in situ* in April, thinning seedlings to 18in (45cm) apart.

Impatiens balsamina
○ ⊖ ⊝ ⊙ ⊛

Common balsam. A plant growing 8–24in (20–60cm) high and producing white, crimson, blue, lilac and purple flowers, both singles and doubles, in autumn. Catalogues generally distinguish between ordinary cultivars ranging in height from 20–28in (50–70cm) and dwarf cultivars 8–16in (20–40cm) high. In addition there are the F_1 hybrids which flower more profusely and are more disease resistant.

Impatiens biflora
A hardy annual native to North America that grows to a height of 3ft (1m). It has serrated, mid-green leaves and orange flowers with brown spots borne in 1in (2.5cm) long panicles from July to October. It grows well in a moist, shaded position.

Impatiens glandulifera
Himalayan touch-me-not. A hardy annual with succulent red branches and ovate leaves that grows up to 6ft (2m) high. The flowers are red or pink, sometimes spotted. This species seeds freely and can become a weed.

Impatiens wallerana
○ ◐ ⊛

Usually seen as a greenhouse plant, this species, of East African origin, can be used with success in summer bedding schemes. Its flat flowers have a short spur and come in a wide range of reds, oranges, purples and white.

Incarvillea
Bignoniaceae
Chinese trumpet-flower

A genus of fairly uncommon herbaceous perennials, often difficult to keep alive for more than a few years, particularly in very moist soils. The flowers are slightly reminiscent of gloxinias.
Soil These plants require a sheltered, sunny place and humus rich, well-drained soil. Apply a mulch of peat or compost in the autumn.
Propagation From seed. Seeds germinate within a week of sowing and retain their viability for three years. Established plants may be divided and replanted in autumn, but the crowns are tough and difficult to split.

Incarvillea brevipes, see *I. mairei*.

Incarvillea delavayi

Incarvillea delavayi
The best-known *Incarvillea*, this is a perennial herbaceous plant with fleshy roots. The leaves rise in a tuft or clump from ground level and grow up to 1 ft (30 cm) in length. The flower stems are 16–24 in (40–60 cm) high and in late spring to midsummer produce 2–12 large, funnel-shaped gloxinia-like rose-pink flowers with a yellow throat. The plant is hardy, but the fleshy roots must never be allowed to become water-logged. Sow in March in a moderately warm frame, or in April in a cold frame, and plant out in May; flowering begins in the second year. When transplanting in spring, be careful not to damage the roots. It is also possible to pot up the plants in autumn and to use them indoors.

Incarvillea mairei
Syn. *I. brevipes*. A plant growing 6 in (15 cm) or more high and bearing deep rose-red flowers in late spring to early summer.

Incarvillea mairei var. grandiflora
A plant with long, dark green leaves that grows 6–12 in (15–30 cm) high and produces crimson flowers in clusters of 2–3 in late spring to early summer.

Indigofera
Leguminosae

A genus of perennials and shrubs, most of which produce pink pea-flowers and leaves divided into many small leaflets. The shrubs can be pruned hard, almost to ground level each spring.
Soil Any well-drained garden soil is adequate.
Propagation Plants are raised by seed in spring or from cuttings taken with a heel in late summer. Young plants are frost-tender.

Indigofera heterantha
Syn. *I. gerardiana*. A Himalayan plant growing up to 9 ft (3 m) high, but only to 3 ft (1 m) or so if pruned hard annually. Its grey-green leaves are divided into

up to 20 small leaflets, while the purplish-pink flowers are carried in loose clusters from June to September.

Inula
Compositae

A genus of hardy herbaceous perennials. They thrive on drier sites, but do fairly well in any ordinary garden soil. The taller species make good border plants and the more compact ones are suitable for use in rock gardens. The flowers open in a remarkable way (see photographs below).
Soil A fairly dry, slight calcareous soil is required.
Propagation Plants may be raised by division or from seed.

Inula ensifolia
From central and southern Europe, a hardy perennial attaining a height of 1–2 ft (30–60 cm). In midsummer it produces golden-yellow flowers, 1–2 in (2.5–5 cm) across. These make beautiful bushy additions to the first row of the border or the larger rock garden.
Inula glandulosa, see *I. orientalis*.

The unusual manner in which an *Inula* flower opens

Inula orientalis

Inula magnifica
A hardy perennial reaching a height of 4–6 ft (1.2–3 m). The basal leaves can grow up to 3 ft (1 m) long, although the stem leaves are much shorter. The flowers are borne in clusters in mid-summer, with narrow golden-yellow ray florets and an orange disc.

Inula orientalis
Syn. *I. glandulosa*. A hardy perennial from the Caucasus reaching a height of 1½–2 ft (45–60 cm) and flowering in mid-summer with very large blooms measuring 4–5 in (10–12.5 cm) across with narrow, orange-yellow ray florets. The most common cultivar is 'Compacta', a bushy plant that grows to a height of 8 in (20 cm).

Ipomoea
Convolvulaceae
Morning glory

A genus of tender and half-hardy annuals and perennials including several quick-growing climbers, and some that make fine pot plants.
Soil A very rich soil is needed.
Propagation Sow under glass from March onwards, at a temperature of

Morning glory, *Ipomoea violacea*

18°C (64°F). Allow the seeds to soak for a day before sowing. Move to pots, harden off and do not plant out before late May.

Ipomoea purpurea
Syn. *Pharbitis purpurea*. A Central and South American annual, one of the most widely cultivated species of this genus. Its fast-growing, twining branches and slightly hairy stems climb up to a height of 12 ft (4 m) and flower from midsummer to early autumn, coming into bloom roughly ten weeks after sowing. The flowers are large and funnel-shaped, reddish-purple in the species and available in various colours in the cultivars.
Ipomoea rubrocoerulea, see *I. tricolor*.

Ipomoea tricolor
Syn. *I. rubrocoerulea*. Red to purple-blue flowers are borne in clusters of 3–4 on fairly long stems. 'Praecox' is an early-flowering cultivar with very beautiful but short-lived flowers; 'Heavenly Blue' is deep sky-blue.

Iris
Iridaceae
Iris

The iris is one of the most important genera for the gardener. Their forms, cultivation and flowering periods are so diverse that it is possible to classify them in many different ways. The simplest method is to make a rough-and-ready distinction between bulbous and non-bulbous species; the latter often have rhizomes, but not all.

Cultivation Among the best-known bulbous irises are the Dutch, Spanish and English sorts, the Dutch coming into flower first and the English last. In colder areas, Spanish irises should be lifted after flowering and replanted in late October or November, lest they make too much leaf growth which can be damaged in winter. In cold areas, it is better to purchase new bulbs every year.

Nearly all non-bulbous irises are hardy. They are best transplanted soon after flowering, or in early autumn. These irises may also be transplanted in spring, but they will then produce fewer flowers during the first year and those that do appear may be short-stemmed and small. *I. cristata* and *I. pumila* are particularly suited to rock gardens. The rest, with the exception of *I. pseudacorus*, make good border plants. Many irises in this section also look very attractive when grouped around ponds. It is also possible to create special iris gardens with successively flowering plants from late winter to late summer. Many gardeners like to enhance a concentration of irises by adding lupins and brooms.

The earliest iris: *Iris reticulata*

I. kaempferi, the Japanese iris, needs special care. It is best grown in shallow water, but will also thrive in permanently damp ground. The plants are not fully hardy and in cold areas are best grown in 1ft (30cm) containers filled with a rich, acid soil mixture. The containers are placed in the pool or pond in April. In winter the containers are buried in the ground to a depth of 1ft (30cm).

Soil Most irises need a well-drained position in fertile soil—the bulbs tend to rot in standing water. It is a mistake to believe that all irises like moist soil. Only *I. kaempferi*, *I. pseudacoris*, *I. sibirica* and *I. laevigata* prefer a moist site.

Propagation Bulbous irises may be propagated by offsets or separating congested clumps after the foliage has died down in summer. Non-bulbous irises are generally propagated by division of the clumps or rhizomes. Species can also be grown from seed, but cultivars will not come true to type.

The most important bulbous irises are:
Iris bakeriana
From Mesopotamia, this is an early bloomer, 6in (15cm) high, bearing sky-blue flowers with dark blue and white falls in February–March.
Iris bucharica
Originally from Bukhara, USSR, this plant has leafy stems that grow to a height of about 16in (40cm). The creamy-white flowers, with dark yellow blotches on the lowermost petals, grow in the leaf axils and emerge in late April. This species does best in a sheltered sunny, well-drained position at the foot of a wall.
Iris danfordiae
A small, bright yellow iris, very suitable for rock gardens, that bears fragrant flowers in February–March.
Iris graeberiana
An iris from central Asia that grows to a height of 18in (45cm). Pale mauve flowers with light blue falls are borne in March and April. The flowers are about

The bearded iris 'Eleanor's Pride' combined with purple *Hesperis* and *Genista*

Iris sibirica likes a wet position

$2\frac{1}{2}$ in (6 cm) across with from four to six borne on a single stem.

Iris histrioides
From Asia Minor, this iris produces blue flowers in March; the leaves come out later than the flowers.

Iris × hollandica hybrids
○ ◑ ⬡ ⬯ ⬟ ⬢ ⊗

Dutch iris. It has somewhat smaller flowers than the Spanish iris but blooms roughly a month earlier, in May. There are numerous cultivars in several colours including 'Golden Harvest', which has golden-yellow flowers with a touch of orange; 'Imperator', dark blue; 'Professor Blaauw', which is ultramarine; and 'Wedgewood', with light blue flowers.

Iris orchioides
From central Asia, a plant growing to a height of 1 ft (30 cm). The golden yellow flowers are borne in April and May, four to a stem. It is not a hardy iris and is best cultivated in pots.

Iris regeliocyclus hybrids
○ ◑ ⊜ ⬡ ⬯ ⬟

Attractive crosses raised by Tubergen of Haarlem and botanically related to *I. stolonifera*. These plants need well-drained, fertile soil and dislike too much rain. The large, very beautiful flowers come out in May. Protect the

The native *Iris pseudacorus*

Iris germanica 'Rippling Waters'

Bulbous Dutch hybrids

Iris pumila for the rock garden

plants in winter. To propagate, lift them in July and store in not too dry sand for two months, then divide and replant. There are numerous cultivars and colours.

Iris reticulata
○ ◑ ⊜ ⬯ ⬟

From the Caucasus and Persia, this 6 in (15 cm) high iris is highly recommended for the rock garden or the front of the border. Large, bluish-mauve flowers appear in March–April. 'Cantab' is light blue with a gold spot; 'J S Dijt' is reddish-purple with an orange spot, it is a vigorous plant; 'Joyce' is sky blue with an orange stripe in the centre; and 'Wentworth' has deep violet flowers.

Iris tingitana
A native of northwest Africa that grows up to 2 ft (60 cm) high. The flowers are pale blue with a patch of yellow on the falls. They appear during April and May, two or three to a stem. It is not a hardy plant and requires a very hot summer if it is to flower the following year.

Iris xiphioides
○ ◑ ⊜ ⬡ ⬯ ⬟ ⬢

English iris, originally from southern France. It grows to a height of 20 in (50 cm) and in early to midsummer bears flowers that are larger and fuller

Iris kaempferi hybrids

than those of the Dutch and Spanish irises; like them, the English iris is good for cutting.

Iris xiphium
○ ◑ ⬡ ⬯ ⬟ ⊗

Spanish iris. A plant growing 20–28 in (50–70 cm) high and flowering in early summer. Numerous cultivars are available in all sorts of colours. Plants should be protected in winter.

The most important non-bulbous irises are:

Iris bulleyana
From western China, reaching a height of 2–3 ft (60–90 cm). The flowers are lilac with lemon falls having deep blue veins and spots. They appear, two to a stem, in June. The plant is believed to be a natural hybrid of *I. forrestii*, which it resembles.

Iris chrysographes
A native of southwest China attaining a height of $1\frac{1}{2}$–2 ft (45–60 cm). The flowers are $2\frac{1}{2}$ in (6 cm) across and dark blue or maroon with golden veins on the falls. The flowering period is June. There are many varieties that have a paler colour and also one that is almost black.

Iris cristata
◑ ⬡ ⬟ ⬢ ⬢ ⊗

A perennial from eastern North America reaching a height of about 6 in (15 cm). Flowering period in late spring to early summer, it bears lavender flowers with a white crest, tipped with orange. The leaves are 6–8 in (15–20 cm) long. This species requires fairly moist ground and a semi-shaded position.

Iris foetidissima
○ ◑ ⬡ ⬢ ⬢ ⬢ ⊗

Stinking iris, gladdon or gladwyn, from southern and western Europe. A plant $1\frac{1}{2}$–$2\frac{1}{2}$ ft (45–75 cm) high with an unpleasant smell, prized for its seed-pods which split open to reveal showy scarlet seeds.

Iris germanica
Purple flag. A plant from central and southern Europe that grows to a height of 1–2 ft (30–60 cm) and flowers in late spring to early summer. It does not like too much moisture. There are hundreds of hybrid cultivars in all sorts of colours and shades generally listed as bearded hybrids. Most catalogues list purple flags in their bearded iris section, dividing them into tall, intermediate and dwarf groups. The first two groups include 'Ambassadeur', violet-bronze and purple blooms; 'Blue Rhythm', pure blue; 'Empress of India', light blue; 'Nel Jape', apricot with cobalt yellow and a striking orange beard; 'Ola Kala', dark yellow; 'Zambia', bronze with violet-red and yellow stripes; 'Amethyst Flame', amethyst purple; 'Christmas Time', white with red beard; 'Desert Song', pale yellow; 'Harbor Blue', mid-blue; 'Olympic Torch', bronze-yellow; 'Prince Indigo', deep violet-blue. The dwarfs include: 'Blue Frost', pale blue; 'Bright White', pure white; 'Orchid Flare', mauve-pink; and 'Veri Bright', yellow and brown.

Iris kaempferi
From Japan, a plant that grows 2–3 ft (60–100 cm) high and flowers in midsummer. Numerous cultivators are available in many colours. The shape of the flower is flatter than in other perennial irises, and the blooms are very large. The leaves are thin, narrow and bright green.

Iris laevigata

Closely resembling *I. kaempferi*, this plant grows 1½–2ft (45–60cm) high with smooth, unribbed leaves. Blue flowers are borne in midsummer.

Iris pseudacorus

○ ◑ ⊛ ⊗

Yellow flag. Excellent for shallow ponds, this plant will also grow on drier sites. Yellow flowers appear May–June.

Iris pumila

○ ◑ ⊛ ⊗

From central and south-eastern Europe, this attractive plant grows 4–6in (10–15cm) high and is very suitable for the rock garden and for the edge of the border.

Iris sanguinea

○ ◑ ⊛ ⊛ ⊗

A plant from Korea and Japan that strongly resembles *I. sibirica*, but is shorter and has larger blue flowers, borne in clusters of 2–3 from late spring to early summer.

Iris sibirica

○ ◑ ⊛ ⊛ ⊗

From Europe and Siberia, this iris grows to heights of 2½–3ft (75–100cm), has well-branched stems and bluish leaves, wine-red at the base. It thrives at the edges of ponds but also does well on drier ground. In early summer it

Jasminum nudiflorum in December

produces blooms in either blue, violet-purple, lilac or white.

Jasminum
Oleaceae
Jasmine

A genus of deciduous and evergreen shrubs. Those that do not require greenhouse treatment grow best in sheltered positions. The most hardy is *J. beesianum*; *J. nudiflorum* is also fairly hardy, but the flowers are susceptible to damage from cold winds.

Soil Any ordinary garden soil is adequate. When jasmine is grown against a house wall, however, large planting holes should be dug and filled with good soil.

Propagation The shrubs may be raised from cuttings, by layering or from seed. Sow under glass in a warm position; the seeds take several weeks to germinate.

Jasminum beesianum

○ ◑ ⊛ ⊛ ⊗

A slender twining climber from western China that requires light soil and a warm position. Flowering from late

Chinese juniper, *Juniperus chinensis* 'Pfitzeriana Aurea'

spring to midsummer, it bears small, velvety red blooms.

Jasminum humile

○ ◑ ⊛ ⊛ ⊗

Yellow or Italian jasmine. A partially evergreen shrub, best with its waving stems against a wall or support. The leaves are made up of 3–7 leaflets, the end one the longest, up to 2in (5cm). The bright yellow flowers are fragrant in the form 'Revolutum' and are usually about ¾in (2cm) across. They open from late summer into autumn.

Jasminum nudiflorum

○ ◑ ⊛ ⊛ ⊛ ⊛ ⊗

Winter-flowering jasmine. A shrub growing 10ft (3m) or more high, from northern China. It is usually positioned against walls, where its winter flowers and shining green branches are seen to best advantage. The bright yellow flowers are susceptible to damage from cold winds and are borne singly in the leaf axils of last season's leaves, from November to April. The flowers are particularly striking when grown against *Hedera* (ivy), and it also makes a most attractive shrubbery plant. Branches in bud will bloom indoors and will continue flowering for some time when kept in a vase.

Jasminum officinale

○ ⊖ ⊛ ⊛ ⊛ ⊗

Common white jasmine. A twining climber from the Himalayas and Persia, naturalized in southern Europe, this is capable of reaching heights up to 30ft (10m). Flowering from midsummer to autumn, its blooms are white and sweetly scented. It prefers a sheltered position and soil that is not too dry. 'Affine' has attractive white and pink flowers.

Jasminum × stephanense

○ ◑ ⊛ ⊗

This hybrid was bred in France using the species *J. beesianum* and *J. officinale*. It also occurs in the wild both parents being found in the same area of China. In most respects it blends the characters of its parents having small, soft pink flowers and leaves which can be undivided or have 5–7 leaflets. The flowers are about 3in (8cm) across and appear in June.

Juniperus
Cupressaceae
Juniper

A popular genus of shrubs and trees. *J. communis* and *J. sabina* do well even in dry and poor soil, and both will tolerate a great deal of shade. *J. virginiana*, which makes a glorious ornamental tree, requires slightly moister and richer soil.

Propagation Plants are grown from

seed when ripe and from cuttings taken in September or October.

Juniperus chinensis

○ ◑ ⊖ ⊛ ⊛ ⊛ ⊙ ⟁

Chinese juniper, from China and Japan. A dioecious tree growing up to 75ft (23m) high, or a shrub. The scale-like leaves grow in whorls of 2–3, each scale having two white stripes on the upper side. The cones are brown with a white bloom and appear in the spring. Well-known cultivars, some of which may be of hybrid origin, are 'Blaauw', a compact shrub with feathery branches and greyish-green leaves, growing up to 4½ft (1.3m) high; 'Blue Cloud', a low, spreading shrub with greyish-blue leaves; 'Fairview', a quick grower with bright green leaves and a pyramidal habit; 'Hetzii', a 4½–7ft (1.3–2.1m) high shrub with bluish-grey to green foliage and wide-spreading branches; 'Keteleeri', a 15–30ft (5–9m) high columnar shrub with bluish-green to green leaves and

Juniperus horizontalis 'Douglasii'

Juniperus virginiana 'Canaertii'

Juniperus squamata 'Wilsonii'

Juniperus communis 'Compressa'

berry-like cones with a blue-white bloom; 'Old Gold', a small golden-yellow shrub, useful for containers; 'Pfitzeriana', a wide-spreading shrub with stout branches and green leaves, recommended for cultivation as a specimen plant; 'Pfitzeriana Aurea', which resembles the latter but has golden-yellow foliage that turns bronze in winter; 'Pfitzeriana Glauca', which has grey, glaucous leaves; 'Plumosa', an irregularly shaped, spreading shrub which grows to a height of 6ft (2m) and has plume-like sprays of green, scale-like leaves; 'Plumosa Albovariegata', which has sprays of deep green foliage speckled white; and 'Stricta', which is an erect pyramidal shrub with blue-green juvenile foliage. It reaches a height of 5ft.

Juniperus communis

○ ◐ ⊖ ⊜ ⊛ ☉ ⊕ ⊗ ▥

Common juniper, from Europe, northern Asia, North Africa and North America. A dioecious shrub (male and female flowers borne on separate plants) reaching a height of 15ft (5m). It has a columnar habit when planted on good soil, but can be more wide-spreading and bears a larger number of needle-shaped leaves when grown on poorer soil. The branches have wings and conspicuous axillary buds, the needles have broad white stripes on the upper surface, and the cones a bluish bloom; flowering takes place in spring. Cultivars include 'Depressa Aurea', which has a vase-shaped habit, and produces golden yellow leaves and young shoots during early summer; 'Hibernica', a compact form with a columnar habit and bluish-green leaves; 'Hornibrookii', a dwarf with a creeping habit and green foliage turning bronze in winter, excellent for rock gardens and for growing on banks; 'Pyramidalis', a conical bush with prickly green leaves covered with a waxy bloom; 'Repanda', a carpet-forming dwarf, reaching a height of 1ft (30cm) and a spread of up to 4½ft (1.3m), with foliage that is green underneath and has silver stripes on top; and 'Suecica', which is often confused with 'Pyramidalis' but has a more columnar habit.

Juniperus horizontalis

○ ◐ ⊖ ⊜ ⊛ ⊕ ⊘ ⊖

Creeping juniper. A prostrate, slow-growing shrub with very long branches. In height it reaches only 1ft (30cm), but develops a spread of up to 10ft (3m). 'Douglasii' has a spread of 6–10ft (2–3m) and steel-blue foliage turning purple in winter; 'Glauca' has glowing bluish foliage with a waxy bloom and is most suitable for rock gardens and use as ground cover; 'Plumosa', compact and prostrate in form, has grey-green leaves turning purple in winter; 'Prostrata' is a dull green creeper with a spread of 12ft (4m) and a height well below 1ft (30cm); and 'Wiltonii', which strongly resembles 'Glauca', is sometimes sold under that name.

Juniperus sabina

○ ◐ ⊖ ⊜ ⊛ ⊛ ☉ ⊕

Savin. From southern and central Europe and Asia, *J. sabina* is generally grown as a prostrate shrub, more rarely as an erect shrub, reaching up to 10ft (3m) high with almost rectangular branches. The leaves, often absent, are small and bluish-green and give off a disagreeable smell when rubbed between the fingers. The cones are bluish-black and have a waxy bloom; flowering occurs in spring. Well-known cultivars include 'Blue Danube', a tall shrub with grey-blue foliage and wide-spreading branches; 'Erecta', which is a medium-sized shrub with ascending branches; 'Hicksii', a 3–4½ft (1–1.3m) high vigorous shrub with wide-spreading branches and greyish-blue foliage turning purple in winter; and 'Tamariscifolia', a low-growing shrub, 2½–3ft (75–100cm) high with a spread of 3–6ft (1–2m) and with bluish-green foliage.

Juniperus squamata

A semi-prostrate shrub, 10in (25cm) or more high. Tiny leaves are borne in whorls of 3 and are blue-white on top, and green underneath. The cones measure ¼in (6mm) across and are black. 'Blue Star' has a dense habit with bluish-white leaves and is most attractive; 'Meyeri' is erect, eventually forming a large shrub with bluish-green leaves.

Juniperus virginiana

○ ◐ ⊖ ⊜ ⊛ ⊛ ☉ ⊕

Pencil cedar. A tree up to 100ft (30m) high, or a large shrub. The thin branches are clothed in tiny leaves, bluish-white on top. The cones are ovate, brownish-purple and bloomy, and flowering occurs in spring. Cultivars include 'Burkii', with blue foliage turning purple in winter and a slender conical habit; 'Canaertii', a very vigorous conical tree with dark green foliage; 'Glauca', with a columnar habit and a height of up to 15ft (5m); 'Grey Owl', with silvery-grey foliage and spreading branches; and 'Sky-rocket', with a very narrow columnar habit and bluish-green leaves.

Kalmia
Ericaceae

Ornamental plants for the shrubbery or for growing in woodland. They need a well-drained but not dry soil which should ideally be liberally enriched with peat or leaf-mould. On fairly moist soil, these plants will tolerate full sunlight; elsewhere they do better in more shaded positions.
Propagation By layering or from seed sown under glass.

Kalmia angustifolia

○ ◐ ◑ ⊜ ☉ ⊛ ☉ ⊕

Sheep laurel. A shrub that grows up to

Sheep laurel, *Kalmia angustifolia*

3ft (1m) high, preferably in a shady position. The branches are downy at first, later smooth, and the leaves have a leathery texture. From early to mid-summer pink flowers are borne in clusters. 'Rubra' bears dark pink flowers.

Kalmia glauca, see *K. polifolia*.

Kalmia latifolia

Calico bush or mountain laurel. A spring-flowering shrub up to 10ft (3m) high with smooth branches and somewhat leathery leaves, dark green on top and lighter underneath. Rose-red flowers are borne in clusters. Plants can be forced, giving an attractive indoor shrub which can later be planted outside. 'Myrtifolia' is a very low-growing form with pink flowers.

Kalmia polifolia

◑ ◐ ☉ ⊛ ☉

Syn. *K. glauca*. A small shrub, just 20in (50cm) high, with leathery leaves. Small pink flowers are borne in terminal clusters in May–July.

Kerria
Rosaceae
Jew's mallow

A one-species genus, the plant being a handsome ornamental shrub. One of its

Kerria japonica

most striking features is its green winter wood.
Cultivation Prune if required by cutting back flowered shoots after flowering. In very cold areas, kerrias are best grown against walls or fences.
Soil Kerrias like well-drained, not too heavy soil and a sunny position.
Propagation Plants are easily grown from rooted suckers.

Kerria japonica

○ ◐ ◑ ◐ ☉ ⊛ ☉

Bachelors buttons, from Japan and east Asia. A shrub reaching a height of 10ft (3m) with hairless green branches and buds. The leaves are 2in (5cm) long and sharply pointed, while the double yellow flowers appear May–June, sometimes as early as April, and usually come back into second flower either in late summer or, more commonly, in autumn. The long flowering period makes it an excellent addition to any border; it also looks most attractive when grown against a sunny wall. *K. japonica* var. *simplex* has single flowers; in catalogues it is generally listed as *K. japonica* and the double cultivar as 'Pleniflora' ('Flore-Pleno'). 'Picta' ('Argenteo-variegata') has leaves edged with white, smaller flowers.

'The Rocket', a hybrid red-hot poker

Kniphofia
Liliaceae
Torch lily, Red-hot poker

A genus of hardy herbaceous perennials giving magnificent and long-lasting cut flowers.
Soil Kniphofias like rich, slightly moist garden soil and a sunny position. Water freely during dry spells. The soil should be well drained.
Propagation The cultivars are raised in spring by division. Species can be grown from seed at the same time.

Kniphofia galpinii
A neat, slender, late-flowering species, 2 ft (60 cm) high, that bears spikes of orange-yellow flowers from September to October.

Kniphofia hybrids
These bloom more profusely than either of the species listed here. The flowers come in colours ranging from white through yellow to orange-red. 'Alcazar' is garnet coloured; 'Express' bears spikes of yellow and red flowers as early as June; 'Corallina' is short stemmed and has coral-red flowers; 'Royal Standard' is bright scarlet in the bud and golden-yellow when fully out; 'The Rocket' ('Saturnus') has very large orange spikes and is exceptionally tall.

Kniphofia uvaria
Red-hot poker. A South African plant growing 2½–4 ft (75–120 cm) high and producing orange-red flower spikes of tubular flowers, the open ends pointing downwards. These appear in late summer or early autumn. This plant makes an excellent focal point.

Koeleria
Gramineae

A genus of attractive grasses not often seen in gardens.
Soil They thrive in any well-drained soil, particularly an alkaline one.
Propagation Plants are grown from seed or by division.

Koeleria glauca

Koeleria glauca
From Europe and Russia, a plant with narrow blue-green blades of grass that grow up to 1 ft (30 cm) long. Flowers appear in dense spikes in early to midsummer.

Koelreuteria
Sapindaceae

A little-known genus of attractive flowering trees well suited to medium-sized gardens.
Soil Any ordinary, well-drained, fertile soil is suitable. A sunny position is required.
Propagation Grow from seed, sown in pots under glass in spring. The seed is long-lived.

Koelreuteria paniculata
From China, Korea and Japan, a tree or shrub that grows up to 16 ft (5 m) high with pinnate leaves up to 16 in (40 cm) long. Yellow flowers are borne in midsummer in terminal panicles followed in autumn by bladder-shaped, green, red flushed fruits, each containing three black seeds.

Kolkwitzia
Caprifoliaceae

A genus containing just one species, closely related to *Weigela* but much more ornamental. The flowers, which are borne in corymbs, appear on short lateral twigs.
Soil Ordinary garden soil is adequate.
Propagation Grow from seed or from cuttings taken in midsummer and overwintered in a cold frame.

Kolkwitzia amabilis
Beauty Bush, a 6 ft (2 m) high upright shrub with arching branches and peeling bark. In late spring and early

The lovely autumn colour of *Koelreuteria paniculata*

Kolkwitzia amabilis

summer it produces pink flowers with a yellow throat in large corymbs. The flower stems are covered with bundles of white hair. 'Pink Cloud' bears masses of bright pink flowers, and 'Rosea' is similar.

Laburnum
Leguminosae
Golden chain tree

A genus of popular garden shrubs with poisonous leaves and fruits that are dangerous for children and also for chickens and other domestic animals. The plants are most attractive when planted behind blue or white lilacs.
Cultivation Laburnums require no pruning but may, if necessary, be thinned out in spring. After transplantation they may not make any new growth for a whole year; this applies in particular to older shrubs. However, as long as the wood under the bark remains green, it will probably resume growth next spring. After flowering, plants should be dead-headed to encourage flower production the following year.
Soil Any ordinary garden soil is suitable.
Propagation Species are grown from seed sown in spring in open ground. Cultivars are generally grafted on to the rootstocks of *L. anagyroides* or, less often, *L. alpinum*, to produce half-standards or standards.

Laburnum alpinum
Scotch laburnum. A tree that grows up to 25 ft (8 m) high, with a spread of 10–12 ft (3–4 m). Flowering takes place in early summer, when attractive yellow flowers are borne in elongated racemes.

Laburnum anagyroides
Syn. *L. vulgare*. Common laburnum. A tree or shrub growing up to 25 ft (8 m) high with a spread of 0–12 ft (3–4 m). Its yellow flowers, borne in fairly short racemes, appear from late spring to early summer, about 10 days before those of *L. alpinum*. 'Pendulum' is a very beautiful flowering tree with weeping branches.

Laburnum vulgare, see *L. anagyroides*.

Laburnum × *watereri*
The most attractive of all laburnums, this is a cross between *L. alpinum* and *L. anagyroides*, remarkable for its very long racemes that can grow to 16 in (40 cm) long. 'Vossii' has even longer inflorescences, up to 20 in (50 cm).

Lamiastrum
Labiatae

A genus now distinct from *Lamium* but still often treated under that name. The method of cultivation is the same.

Lamiastrum galeobdolon

○ ◑ ⊞ ⊞ ⊞ ⊛ ⊗ ⊖

Yellow Archangel. A rampant evergreen perennial originating in Europe that reaches a height of about 10 in (25 cm). It is most frequently sold in the 'Variegatum' form, which has silver-flushed foliage. Flowers are borne in whorled spikes in early to midsummer.

Lamium
Labiatae
Dead nettle

A genus of herbaceous perennials for the wild garden. Because of its overly rampant habit, this plant is not completely satisfactory as ground cover.
Soil Any not too dry garden soil in either a sunny or shaded position.
Propagation Plants are raised by division of the roots or cuttings in summer.

Laburnum × watereri 'Vossii' in front of a beech

Lamiastrum galeobdolon, golden archangel

Lamium garganicum

A native of southern Europe, growing to a height of 6 in (15 cm). Useful as ground cover or as a border plant, it bears red or pink flowers in June and July. This plant grows best in a moist, shady site.

Lamium maculatum

○ ◑ ⊞ ○ ⊗ ⊗ ⊖

A plant growing up to 1 ft (30 cm) high that produces green leaves with a cen-

Lamium maculatum

tral silver stripe in winter. Pink-purple flowers are borne in dense clusters. Varieties include 'Album', which bears white flowers; 'Aureum', with golden leaves; and 'Roseum', which has pink flowers.

Lamium orvala

○ ◑ ⊗ ○ ⊛ ⊗

This robust and handsome species comes from central Europe. In a moisture retentive soil the erect, square-sectioned stems can reach 3 ft, but are generally less. The triangular ovate coarsely toothed leaves range from 2–6 in (5–15 cm) long and are attractive in themselves. In summer the $1\frac{1}{4}$–$1\frac{3}{4}$ in (3–4.5 cm) long hooded, red-purple flowers open in the upper leaf axils.

Laburnum flowers

Female flower and a ripe cone of *Larix decidua*

Larix kaempferi in the autumn

Larix
Pinaceae
Larch

A genus of fast-growing, deciduous conifers, to be planted as specimen trees or in groups in an open position.
Soil Any well-drained soil will do.
Propagation Plants are grown from seed sown in spring.
Pests Aphids may feed on leaves and stems, and sawfly larvae attack the tips of shoots.

Larix decidua
○ ❋ ⊕
Syn. *L. europaea*. European larch, from northern Europe. A tree that grows to heights of 65–85 ft (20–26 m) with a spread of 15–25 ft (5–8 m). It has an erect stem and a pyramidal crown, and the leaves turn an attractive shade of yellow in autumn.
Larix europaea, see *L. decidua*.
Larix kaempferi
Syn. *L. leptolepis*. Japanese larch. More attractive than *L. decidua*, this tree reaches up to 80 ft (25 m) high with a spread of 20–35 ft (7–10 m). It has a tall, broad crown with stout branches and 1¾ in (4 cm) long bluish-green leaves, set

spirally. The young branches are reddish-brown and so are easily distinguished in winter from those of *L. decidua*, which are yellowish when young. 'Pendula' is a tall elegant tree with long weeping branches.
Larix leptolepis, see *L. kaempferi*.

Lathyrus
Leguminosae
Sweet pea

A genus of hardy annuals, sub-shrubs and herbaceous perennials. The most popular species, *L. odoratus*, is an annual climber yielding masses of beautiful flowers for cutting, and is also excellent for covering fences or palings. The more flowers are cut, so impeding seed formation, the more new flowers the plant will produce.
Cultivation The simplest way to grow sweet peas is to sow them outside in March–April. Flowers can be obtained earlier by sowing the seeds in pots in autumn and overwintering the plants in a cold frame. Alternatively sow in February–March under glass, hardening off the seedlings and then transferring them to the flowering position. Plants intended to provide cut flowers are best supported with twiggy sticks or trained on wires or nets. If large flowers are wanted, all side shoots and tendrils should be removed and the plants tied to canes. Sweet peas tend to exhaust the soil on which they grow fairly quickly, hence it is best to move them from one part of the garden to another each year.
Soil Although *Lathyrus* grows in almost any kind of soil, it will produce unusually large numbers of long-stemmed flowers on fertile and cool garden soil that is neither too dry nor too moist. To keep the soil cool during the warmer months, it is advisable to cover the ground with well-rotted farm-yard manure or straw. For best results, trench or double-dig the soil in autumn, incorporating well-rotted manure in the lower spit. The soil may then be left over the winter for the clods to be broken up by the frost.

Propagation Usually from seed, though species may also be propagated by division or cuttings of basal shoots.

Annual species include:
Lathyrus odoratus
○ ☉ ⊛ ☺ ⊗
Sweet pea, from southern Italy and Sicily. A plant growing up to 10 ft (3 m) high with smooth, angular stems and pairs of ovate leaflets, each leaf stalk ending in a tendril. The flowers appear in small clusters at the end of 6 in (15 cm) stems; the flowering period varies according to the time of sowing. There are countless cultivars, including the large 'Spencer' group, and the earlier-flowering 'Cuthbertson' cultivars with their large flowers of good texture, available in nearly every colour. More recent are the 'Galaxy' cultivars, the 12–20 in (30–50 cm) high 'Bijou', and the 3 ft (1 m) 'Knee-hi'. Refer also to any good catalogue.

Perennial plants include:
Lathyrus latifolius
◐ ⌃ ○ ⊛ ☺ ⊗
Everlasting pea, from Europe. A plant that grows up to 10 ft (3 m) high and flowers from midsummer to autumn. The flowers are not as beautiful as those of the annual species; the colour is usually lilac-pink but there are also rose and white sorts.
Lathyrus vernus
Syn. *Orobus vernus*. A European non-climbing species that has a woody crown and grows 8–16 in (20–40 cm) high. Purple and blue flowers, fading to blue-green, are borne in clusters of 3–8 from April to June.

Laurus
Lauraceae
Laurel

The laurels are evergreen shrubs or small trees, one of which is grown for aromatic leaves which are used in cookery.
Soil Moderately fertile garden soil.

Annual sweet pea, *Lathyrus odoratus* cultivar

Propagation Plants are grown from ripe seed or from cuttings.

Laurus nobilis
○ ◑ ⊛ ○ ⊘ ⊛ ✿ ▥
Bay laurel, from the Mediterranean. In cultivation it usually grows 6–10 ft (2–3 m) high, but much more in the wild. Its glossy, oval leaves are the bay leaves used by cooks. The flowers are insignificant. The plant is not hardy where winters are severe and is often grown as a tub plant, given protection in winter. It withstands clipping and can make an effective hedge.

Lavandula
Labiatae
Lavender

A genus of attractive shrubs with grey-green foliage whose flowers compare favourably with most others in the mixed border. Older plants tend to become thin bottomed unless they are cut back directly after flowering. Lavender is justly prized for its scent, and people still observe the old country custom of hanging sachets of dried lavender flowers inside wardrobes.
Soil Although lavender will grow on poor and fairly dry soil, it needs full sun and a well-drained fertile rooting medium.
Propagation Plants are raised from cuttings taken in September.

Lavandula angustifolia
○ ⊖ ⌃ ⚙ ⊛ ⊗ ⊗
Syn. *L. officinalis*. Common lavender, from southern Europe. A plant growing to a height of approximately 2 ft (60 cm) and flowering in early to mid-summer, when blue flowers are borne in long spikes. Cultivars include 'Alba' with white flowers; 'Hidcote', a 1–2 ft (30–60 cm) plant with violet blooms; and 'Loddon Pink', which is like a pink-flowered 'Hidcote'.
Lavandula officinalis, see *L. angustifolia*.
Lavandula spica, see *Lavandula angustifolia*.

A path edged with *Lavandula angustifolia* 'Hidcote'

The snowflake, *Leucojum vernum*

Lavatera
Malvaceae
Mallow

This genus includes a particularly splendid annual herbaceous plant and a vigorous sub-shrub.

Soil Any well-drained fertile soil is suitable, preferably one that is not too rich.

Propagation The annual species is sown directly in the flowering position in late April and thinned to 20 in (50 cm) apart. The perennial sub-shrub is propagated from cuttings taken in spring. The cuttings will quickly develop into stout specimens and flower the same year.

Lavatera olbia

○ ○ ⊛ ⊕ ⊕ ⊗

A vigorous sub-shrub from southern France reaching a height of 6 ft (2 m). It has a very long flowering period, from July to November, producing large pink blooms. Cut flowering stems will usually keep in water for at least 14 days, during which time nearly all the buds will open. This plant looks at its best in the border. It is usually cut back to ground level by winter frost and if

Lavatera trimestris 'Tanagra'

not is best pruned to 1 ft (30 cm)

Lavatera trimestris

○ ⊖ ☉ ⊛

An annual from southern Europe that is a popular border plant. Growing to a height of about 3 ft (1 m), it flowers from midsummer to autumn, producing large pink flowers with dark veins. 'Alba' has white flowers; 'Tanagra' has large, deep rose flowers; and those of 'Loveliness' and 'Splendens' are crimson-pink.

Leontopodium
Compositae
Edelweiss

A genus of hardy herbaceous perennials, including the alpine edelweiss, that make interesting small plants for the rock garden.

Soil All species like well-drained soil that is not too rich. In rich soil edelweiss tends to lose its attractive silvery-grey colour. The more sunlight, the better the colour.

Propagation Sow seeds February–March in trays or pots containing two parts potting compost to one part sand, and place in a cold frame. Prick out into trays and plant out towards the end of May or early June. The plants will come into flower the following year. All species can also be propagated by division.

Leontopodium alpinum

○ ⊖ ⊖ ⊛ ○ ⊕ ⊗ ⊗

Edelweiss. A hardy plant from the European Alps, growing up to 8 in (20 cm) high and producing yellowish flowers surrounded by woolly white bracts in summer. The leaves are covered with woolly white hair, especially underneath.

Leontopodium souliei

A plant 4–10 in (10–25 cm) high with dense woolly foliage. The flower heads are set close together surrounded by silvery-white bracts. 'Mignon' forms hummocks 3–4 in (7.5–10 cm) high and bears silvery-white flowers in early to midsummer.

Edelweiss, *Leontopodium alpinum*

Leucojum
Amaryllidaceae
Snowflake

A genus of bulbous plants that look particularly attractive at the edge of ponds.

Soil A heavy, fertile and moist soil is required. *L. vernum* may be grown on somewhat drier soil.

Propagation Plants may be divided every few years, or grown from seed sown as soon as it is ripe.

Leucojum aestivum

○ ⦾ ⊗ ⌃ ⌃ ⊛ ⊕ ◎

Summer snowflake. A bulbous perennial from central and south-eastern Europe to the Caucasus, reaching 12–20 in (30–50 cm) high. In late spring to early summer, white flowers appear with green-tipped petals. Summer snowflakes should be planted in autumn 8–10 in (20–25 cm) apart, at a depth of 4–6 in (10–15 cm), or slightly deeper on dry soil. Transplant and divide the bulbs every three years, preferably after flowering.

Leucojum vernum

○ ⦾ ⦾ ⌃ ⊕ ◎

Spring snowflake, from central and southern Europe. Growing 4–14 in (10–35 cm) high, this plant flowers in early spring, when nodding white flowers with green tips appear. Plant them in early to mid-autumn at a depth of 3 in (7.5 cm) and about 4 in (10 cm)

Leucojum aestivum, summer snowflake

apart; they are hardy and may be left undisturbed for years.

Leycesteria
Caprifoliaceae

Medium-sized shrubs remarkable for their robust, hollow stems. Only one species is completely hardy in areas of moderate to hard frosts.

Soil Any reasonable fertile garden soil is adequate.

Propagation Grow from seed in spring or from cuttings in late summer and autumn.

Leycesteria formosa

○ ⦾ ○ ⌃ ⊕ ⊛

Himalayan honeysuckle. A plant that grows 5–8 ft (1.5–2.4 m) high and flowers from midsummer to early autumn. The arching stems carry pairs of narrow oval leaves and spikes of funnel-shaped white flowers flushed with purple and surrounded by purple bracts. In autumn, purplish berries add to the attraction of this easily grown shrub.

Liatris spicata is a very useful border plant

Liatris
Compositae

Blazing star, Gayfeather, Snakeroot. Very attractive, hardy, tuberous herbaceous plants suitable for the borders, lawns, banks, etc. Plant them in groups for the best effect.
Soil The species described here prefer a slightly moist but well-drained soil.
Propagation Plants are raised by division or from seed sown in March or April in a cold frame or greenhouse.

Liatris pycnostachya

○ ⊖ ◐ ⓨ ⊥ ⊗

A plant growing 3–5 ft (1–1.5 m) high that bears light purple flowers from July to autumn. It thrives on dry soil, unlike most other species.

Liatris spicata

○ ◐ ⓨ ⊥ ⊗

A perennial herbaceous plant from North America reaching a height of 3 ft (90 cm) or more. Purple-red flowers are borne in spikes in midsummer and start to bloom from the top. 'Kobold' has shorter stems and broad, very dense flower spikes.

Ligularia
Compositae

A large genus often listed under *Senecio*.
Soil Ligularias thrive on moist, boggy soil in a sunny position. They are exceptionally attractive when planted in groups around pools, and they also make very handsome and ornamental specimens.
Propagation Plants are raised by division in spring.

Ligularia clivorum, see L. dentata.
Ligularia dentata

○ ◑ ⊗ ◐ ⓨ ⊥ ⊗

Syn. *L. clivorum, Senecio clivorum.* A herbaceous perennial from China and Japan reaching heights of 3–5 ft

(1–1.5 m). Flowering from midsummer to autumn, it produces dark orange-yellow blooms with a dark brown centre in large, loose clusters. The leaves are heart-shaped, toothed, and glossy green in colour. 'Othello' has orange-red flowers, and leaves that are dark red underneath.

Ligularia × hessei

A cross between *L. dentata* and *L. wilsoniana* that resembles both parents and bears short, yellow flower heads.

Ligularia przewalskii

A plant growing 5 ft (1.5 m) high, with jaggedly lobed and toothed leaves. The small yellow flower heads are borne on very long, narrow spikes.

Ligularia stenocephala

From China and Japan, this 3–6 ft (1–2 m) plant produces large triangular leaves and long spikes of yellow flowers on a purple stem. 'The Rocket', a finer plant than the original species, is the form commonly grown in gardens.

Ligularia veitchiana

A 6 ft (2 m) high plant with very large heart-shaped leaves and pyramidal, bright yellow spikes.

Ligularia wilsoniana

A plant strongly resembling *L. veitchiana* except that its spikes are cylindrical rather than pyramidal.

Ligustrum
Oleaceae
Privet

A very well-known garden shrub including *L. ovalifolium*, one of the most popular evergreen hedging plants.
Soil Plants thrive in any garden soil. When transplanting privets care must be taken not to let the sun shine on the roots. This is bad for all plants, but *Ligustrum* is particularly sensitive to it.
Propagation Take 12 in (30 cm) hardwood cuttings, strip off the leaves and bury vertically up to 8 in (20 cm) deep in freshly dug fertile garden soil. Set out in rows 4–6 in (10–15 cm) apart.

Ligustrum amurense

○ ◐ ◐ ◐ ◐ ⊛

A very hardy shrub that grows up to 8 ft (2.4 m) high. It has oval leaves, and creamy-white flowers appear in early to midsummer.

Ligustrum delavayanum

○ ◐ ◐ ◐ ◐

Syn. *L. ionandrum, L. pratii.* A semi-evergreen shrub of medium size bearing flowers in dense panicles that is most suitable for hedges in warmer parts of the country.

Arrangement for a moist shady corner, including the yellow *Ligularia stenocephala*

Ligularia dentata likes moist ground

Ligustrum × ibolium
A cross between *L. obtusifolium* and *L. ovalifolium*, this shrub is hardier than the latter parent, and its twigs, undersides of leaves and inflorescences are covered with fine down.

Ligustrum ionandrum, see *L. delavayanum*.

Ligustrum japonicum
○ ◑ ◐ ◉ ⊛
A semi-evergreen shrub up to 5 ft (1.5 m) high that bears flowers in 4–6 in (10–15 cm) panicles in midsummer. 'Rotundifolia' has twisted, leathery and somewhat tougher leaves than the species.

Ligustrum lucidum
◑ ◐ ◉ ◑ ⊛ ⊛
An evergreen shrub from China attaining a height of up to 10 ft (3 m) or more, with dark green, leathery leaves and masses of mostly white flowers in 6–8 in (15–20 cm) panicles. One of the most attractive privets, it will tolerate a great deal of shade, but needs protection from cold winds.

Ligustrum obtusifolium
○ ◑ ◐ ◉ ⊕ ⊛
A spreading shrub up to 10 ft (3 m) high with very hairy, overhanging branches, and 1–2 in (2.5–5 cm) long, ovate leaves, hairy underneath. White flowers are borne in nodding panicles.

Ligustrum ovalifolium
○ ◑ ◐ ◉ ⊛ ⊛ ☺ ◑
A semi-evergreen shrub from Japan, up to 6 ft (2 m) high, sometimes more. Frequently used as a hedging plant, it has oval, hairless leaves and bears white flowers in 4 in (10 cm) panicles, followed by black fruits. 'Aureum' has yellow or variegated yellow leaves, and 'Argenteum' has white-edged leaves.

Ligustrum prattii, see *L. delavayanum*.

Ligustrum quihoui
○ ◑ ◐ ◉ ⌃ ⊛
An elegant, 5 ft (1.5 m) high shrub from China, semi-evergreen, with branches that are sometimes spinous. The leaves stay green deep into autumn, and small white flowers are borne in elongated panicles in September.

Ligustrum sinense var. **stauntonii**

Syn. *L. stauntonii*. A wide-spreading, robust shrub producing flowers in dense sprays in midsummer.

Ligustrum stauntonii, see *L. sinense* var. *stauntonii*.

Ligustrum × vicaryi
○ ◑ ◐ ◉ ⊛
A cross between *Ligustrum ovalifolium* 'Aureum' and *L. vulgare*, with a spreading and compact habit. It differs from the latter parent in having golden-yellow foliage that turns to green.

Ligustrum vulgare
○ ◑ ◐ ◉ ⊛ ⊛
Common privet. A native of Europe that flowers in summer with the white flowers borne in small panicles. 'Lodense' is a dwarf form, with brown leaves in winter, and 'Viride' has dark green leaves that turn brown in autumn and winter. All are partly evergreen;

Ligustrum sinense var. *stauntonii*

A privet hedge (*Ligustrum ovalifolium*)

their leaves, bark and shiny black fruits are all poisonous.

Lilium
Liliaceae
Lily

A very attractive genus of bulbous plants including many glorious species for the garden and for cutting. Lilies look splendid in the border when interspersed with herbaceous perennials and thrive in shaded positions.

Cultivation Lilies may be left undisturbed for several years. The young growths of some species are sensitive to late frost, and it is advisable to cover them when frost is forecast. *L. candidum*, the Madonna lily, should be planted in late summer or early autumn. For early cut flowers, other species should also be planted in autumn.

Soil All lilies thrive on rich, well-drained garden soil. They do best if their roots are kept cool by other plants. The sun must never be allowed to shine directly on the soil above the roots, especially if that soil is lacking in humus. The bulbs should be planted at a depth of 8 in (20 cm), but not quite so deep on moister ground. The soil on top should be very fertile, since some lilies make roots just above the bulb. They should be transplanted every 4–5 years.

Propagation Lilies can be propagated in various ways:

(a) From seed. This method is only applicable to wild species, because cultivars do not come true from seed. Seeds should be sown in autumn as soon as they are ripe, in pots protected against the frost, and kept fairly moist. Some species germinate quickly, others very slowly.

(b) By division. Many species increase naturally by producing new bulbs. Lift the plants in early spring, divide and replant. Small bulblets should be set out in nursery beds and left for a few years.

(c) From bulbils produced in the leaf axils. These bulbils may be detached and planted out in nursery beds.

(d) From scales. This method can be used with nearly all garden forms. Detach several scales from one of the bulbs, preferably in autumn or spring (it is not necessary to lift the bulbs for this purpose). Insert the scales into boxes containing equal parts of peat and sand. Provide a bottom heat of 10–13°C (50–55°F). Tiny bulbs should eventually appear on the scales, and can then be potted separately.

Pests and diseases Viruses and fungi may attack lilies if growing instructions are not followed carefully.

Lilium amabile
◑ ◐
A Korean lily which can reach almost 3 ft (90 cm) in height in good soil. The nodding flowers are bright red, the petals rolled back revealing deep brown anthers. It flowers in summer. Not recommended for picking because of its unpleasant smell.

Lilium auratum
◑ ◐ ⌃ ◉ ⓨ ☺ ⊕ ⊗
Golden lily. A herbaceous perennial from Japan and Korea reaching heights of 1–6 ft (30 cm–2 m), according to where it is grown. In August, sometimes earlier, it bears large white flowers with a golden yellow band and with numerous red-purple or wine-coloured spots on the inner surface. *L. auratum* var. *platyphyllum* is hardier than *L. auratum* and bears masses of very large flowers up to 1 ft (30 cm) across. 'Crimson Queen' has very large, bright red flowers.

Lilium brownii
A lily from China that flowers in early to mid summer. The large and fragrant flowers are pure white inside and flushed wine-red on the outside. Plants vary in height from 16–50 in (40–120 cm). *L. brownii* var. *colchesteri* generally has rose-purple outer petals, often with a touch of green. The innermost petals have a pink central stripe and a bright yellow edge. *L. brownii* is a very large-flowered species and requires protection in severe winters. It has the less attractive attribute of dying quite suddenly in summer. To prevent this, it should be planted at depths of 6–10 in (15–25 cm) in loose, very well-drained soil, and surrounded with clean sand.

Lilium bulbiferum
◑ ⌃ ⓨ ⊗
Syn. *Lilium aurantiacum*. Orange lily. A European lily which can exceed 3 ft (90 cm) in height. The 3 in (7.5 cm) long

orange-red, cup-shaped flowers are held erect, blooming in summer.

Lilium canadense
Canada lily. A plant that thrives in semi-shade and bears red to orange-yellow, pendent, bell-shaped flowers, covered with purple to brown spots, in early to midsummer. *L. canadense* var. *flavum* has golden-yellow flowers with brown spots, and the very beautiful 'Superbum' has scarlet-orange spots.

Lilium candidum
Madonna lily. A herbaceous perennial from southern Europe and the Near East that grows 3–5 ft (1–1.5 m) high and bears pure white, fragrant flowers in early to midsummer. Sometimes difficult to establish, it should be planted in early autumn, certainly not later than September. It is also prone to attack by 'lily disease' (botrytis). The winter spores of this fungus appear on the leaves as brown spots that turn white in spring. The only remedy is to destroy all the affected leaves, living or dead. Madonna lilies should be transplanted before autumn when the new leaves develop. Plant in August on rich, well-drained loam, and in a semi-shaded position.

Lilium chalcedonicum
Scarlet Turk's Cap. A striking lily from Greece, the nodding, bright orange-red flowers with strongly recurved petals. They are carried on strong, 4 ft (1.3 m) stems.

Lilium davidii var. willmottiae
Syn. *Lilium willmottiae*. From central China, this easily cultivated, extremely hardy, and highly recommended plant grows 3–6 ft (1–2 m) high and bears deep orange-red or apricot-coloured flowers, spotted with black, in clusters of up to 25 blooms. 'Unicolour' has orange-red, unspotted flowers.

Lilium elegans, see *L. maculatum*.

Lilium hansonii
A plant that deserves to be more widely known than it is, *L. hansonii* flowers in early summer with orange or saffron blooms having a red glow.

Lilium henryi
Growing up to 6 ft (2 m) high, this plant is easily cultivated on any soil, even calcareous types. It flowers from late summer to early autumn, producing pendent, orange flowers with small black spots and recurved petals.

Lilium hybrids
Many hybrids, especially among those raised in the United States, have exceptionally large flowers and glorious colours, and have partly ousted the botanical species. These hybrids are usually grouped into nine divisions, as follows: (1) Asiatic hybrids. These include *Lilium × hollandicum*, among which are 'Apricot', with its apricot-coloured flowers, and 'Darkest of All', with dark red flowers; Golden Chalice hybrids and Mid-Century hybrids, among them 'Destiny', which has yellow flowers spotted with brown, 'Enchantment', with cherry-red flowers, and 'Joan Evans', which is bright yellow; and the Rainbow and Harlequin hybrids. Most are sturdy and beautiful garden plants.

(2) Martagon hybrids. Plants in this group are derived from crosses between *L. martagon* (Turk's cap lily) and *L. hansonii*.

(3) Candidum (Madonna lily) hybrids. These are not often seen in gardens.

(4) American hybrids. Raised by crossing various lilies originating in America, they may be obtained in all sorts of colours.

(5) Longiflorum hybrids. Not generally available, plants in this group are also disease prone.

(6) Trumpet and Aurelian hybrids. A very large division with various subsections, it includes such well-known Aurelian hybrids as 'African Queen', with apricot-coloured flowers, and 'Black Dragon', whose blooms are white inside and purple-brown on the outside.

(7) Oriental hybrids, i.e. crosses between *L. auratum*, *L. japonicum*, *L. speciosum* and others. Particularly attractive are 'Imperial Crimson', 'Empress of India' and 'Magic Pink'.

(8) Various hybrids and forms not listed in any other hybrid division, including a host of Russian crosses not generally available.

(9) All true species and their cultivars.

Lilium lancifolium
Syn. *L. tigrinum*. Tiger lily, a hardy and easily cultivated herbaceous perennial from China and Japan that grows 2–3 ft (60–100 cm) high and flowers in mid to late summer. Racemes carry up to 25 bright red or orange-red flowers with numerous black spots. 'Plenum' has double flowers. Tiger lilies prefer semi-shade to full sun, and should be planted in autumn or spring.

Lilium longiflorum
Easter lily, from Japan. A perennial reaching heights of 2–3 ft (60–90 cm), it produces fragrant, pure white flowers, either singly or several to the stem, in early to midsummer. This lily is often

Lilium auratum, golden-rayed lily

The hybrid 'Empress of India'

Lilium regale

'Enchantment' is an Asiatic hybrid lily

'Shuksan', a Bellingham hybrid

used for bridal bouquets. It is excellent for indoor cultivation in pots but can also be planted out in a sheltered position. Plant in spring and cover well in winter.

Lilium maculatum
Syn. *L. elegans*, *L. thunbergianum*. A species that usually covers many hybrids. Plants grow 1–2 ft (30–60 cm) high and bear large flowers, either singly or in small clusters, varying from pale orange-yellow to crimson, in early to midsummer. This plant requires sandy loam and a semi-shaded position. Plant the bulbs to a depth of 4–5 in (10–25 cm), and leave undisturbed for at least 3 years.

Lilium martagon
Turk's cap lily, a native of Europe. A hardy perennial plant growing 1½–3 ft

Lilium candidum, Madonna lily

The beautiful 'African Queen' is an Aurelian hybrid

(45–100cm) or more high, in good soil. The flowers, borne in clusters of up to 50, are rose-purple and waxy in the species, white and violet in the cultivars. Plant in autumn.

Lilium monadelphum

From the Caucasus, a plant growing 2–5ft (60–150cm) high with deep yellow flowers borne 2–10 to the stem. The petals are strongly recurving and the yellow-tipped stamens generally widen into a tube at the base. In *L. monadelphum* var. *szovitsianum*, which is the most common variety, the tips of the anthers are brownish while the base is not enlarged. *L. monadelphum* thrives in loam and semi-shade, and should be planted at a depth of 6in (15cm).

Lilium pardalinum

○ ◐ ⊚ ⊕ ⊖ ①

Panther lily. A plant bearing flowers that are yellow in the centre with large brownish-red dots, and bright red at the recurved tips. It is easily grown in almost any garden soil. Lift every three years, divide and replant.

Lilium pomponium

A plant growing 18–30in (45–75cm) high and bearing pendent, bright red flowers with black spots in clusters of up to 6. It prefers sandy soil enriched with humus, and should be planted to depths of 6–8in (15–20cm).

Lilium pumilum

Syn. *L. tenuifolium*. A plant from northern China growing to heights of 1–3ft (30–100cm). Though small, dainty and fairly short-lived, it is the most elegant scarlet-flowering form. Plant it 4in (10cm) deep in light, sandy and fairly moist soil.

Lilium pyrenaicum

○ ◐ ① ⊚ ⊕

Yellow Turk's cap or Pyrenean lily. A strong growing lily from southwest France, reaching 2–4ft (60–120cm) with greenish yellow petals which are spotted with black and recurved in the typical Turk's cap fashion. It flowers in early summer. The flowers have an unpleasant smell at close quarters.

Lilium regale

From western China, a very easily cultivated plant growing 16–60in (40–150cm) high and flowering in mid to late summer. The funnel-shaped flowers are fragrant and rose-purple on the outside, yellow inside. Plant the bulbs in spring.

Lilium speciosum

From Japan, this lily grows 20–60in (50–150cm) high. In mid to late summer it bears white flowers, shaded with crimson and with red spots on the upper side in clusters of 3–20. Cultivars also come in other colours. *L. speciosum* var. *rubrum* has rose-red flowers, and *L. speciosum* var. *album* has white flowers. Plant in lime-free soil in spring.

Lilium superbum

◑ ⊚ ⊕ ⊗

A stately North American species which can reach 6ft (2m) in height. The narrow leaves are carried in whorls and the nodding flowers have strongly recurved petals up to 4in (10cm) long. Usually they are orange, shading crimson at the tips with dark red spotting. They can also be pure yellow or yellow with red spots.

Lilium tenuifolium, see *L. pumilum*.

Lilium × testaceum

◐ ⊚ ⊕ ⊗

Nankeen lily. This lily is a cross between *L. candidum* and *L. chalcedonicum*. In height it ranges from 3–5ft (1–1.8m). The apricot yellow, pink flushed flowers have the petals reflexed. The flowers open in summer.

Lilium thunbergianum, see *L. maculatum*.

Lilium tigrinum, see *L. lancifolium*.

Lilium willmottiae, see *L. davidii* var. *willmottiae*.

Limnanthes
Limnanthaceae

A genus of annuals from North America which need an open, sunny site.
Soil Any moderately fertile soil.
Propagation Sow seeds where the plants are to flower either in autumn for the following late spring or in spring for a summer display.

Limnanthes douglasii

○ ⊙ ⊕

Meadow foam. A bright summer annual full of flowers, each one an inch (2.5cm) across with a wide yellow centre and a narrow white edge. They almost cover the deeply cut leaves. The whole plant is rarely more than about 6in (15cm) high.

123

Sea lavender, *Limonium sinuatum*, in mixed colours

Linaria
Scrophulariaceae
Toadflax

This genus includes a number of plants that grow wild in Europe and particularly the Mediterranean region, and also many garden annuals and perennials. Perennial linarias make attractive wall and rock plants and will thrive in partial shade.

Soil It will grow in any ordinary garden soil providing there is good drainage.

Propagation Annual species are sown in the open at the end of April, and thinned to 6in (15cm) apart. Perennial species can be propagated by division or basal stem cuttings in spring; a few also from root cuttings. Seed may be sown in pots under glass in spring.

Linaria alpina

A hardy perennial from the Alps that reaches 2–6in (5–15cm) and is generally grown as an annual or a biennial. The flowers are violet-purple with orange-yellow spots and appear in summer, and the leaves are smooth and bluish-green. The stems creep across the ground and then curl up to produce attractive mats. It is not difficult to cultivate, and is also self-seeding. Sow seeds in summer in pots of seed compost, and overwinter in a cold frame, watering sparsely.

Linaria maroccana hybrids

○ ◑ ✦ ⊙

A summer-flowering annual growing 8–24in (20–60cm) high. Flowers occur in various shades, but all have a yellow throat. 'Fairy Bouquet' is never taller than 8in (20cm), while 'Northern Lights' can reach a height of 24in (60cm).

Linaria pilosa

Strongly resembling the *L. maroccana* hybrids, this species is hairier and has smaller flowers with shorter spurs.

Linum
Linaceae
Flax

A genus of annual and perennial plants, many of which are suitable for the garden. Many are native to the Mediterranean region, among them the common flax, which is grown for its fibre. Most perennial species require a warm, sheltered position and must be covered in winter.

Linaria maroccana 'Fairy Bouquet'

Limonium
Plumbaginaceae
Sea lavender

A genus formerly known as *Statice*. The most popular garden forms are annuals, which may also be used in dried flower arrangements.

Soil Limoniums thrive in any well-drained garden soil.

Propagation Sow seeds from the end of February at a temperature of 13–16°C (55–61°F), prick out into pots, harden off slowly and plant out in late spring in a sheltered position.

Limonium sinuatum

○ ✦ ⊙ ℗ ⊗

From the Mediterranean and S. Portugal, an annual to biennial plant reaching heights of 16–24in (40–60cm) and bearing clusters of purple flowers in summer. There are several cultivars with pink-red, lavender-blue and yellow flowers.

Limonium suworowii

From western Caucasus, Iran, C. Asia. An annual which reaches 20–28in (50–70cm). Rose-pink flowers are borne in plume-shaped panicles.

Liquidambar styraciflua, sweet gum, in the autumn

Soil A fairly dry soil in full sun is needed.

Propagation Perennials and annuals are easily grown from seed. Sow perennials in April in a cold frame and prick out the seedlings into nursery rows. Grow on until October and then transfer to the flowering position. Sow annuals *in situ* in spring.

Linum flavum

A sub-shrubby perennial from south-eastern Europe that reaches a height of about 16 in (40 cm). Clusters of golden-yellow flowers are borne in summer.

Linum grandiflorum

A hardy annual reaching a height of about 16 in (40 cm). The flowering period is summer to late autumn or the first sharp frost. The flowers of the species are in shades of red; pale pink in 'Roseum', bright red in 'Rubrum' (*Linum rubrum*).

Linum perenne

A sturdy perennial from Europe and North America reaching 16–24 in (40–60 cm) with erect leafy stems. Sky-blue flowers with darker veins are borne in branched clusters.

Linum perenne, blue flax

Linum rubrum, see *L. grandiflorum* 'Rubrum'.

Liquidambar
Hammamelidaceae
Sweet gum

A genus of wide-spreading trees with attractive autumn foliage.

Soil It thrives in any reasonably moist fertile soil, and can be grown by the waterside.

Propagation Sow seeds in autumn; these may take a long time to germinate. Propagation by layering in spring is also possible.

Liquidambar styraciflua

A tree from North America, where it can attain heights of up to 150 ft (45 m); in Britain it reaches 80 ft (24 m) or more. The leaves are large, palmate, with 5–7 indented and pointed lobes, and turn to shades of red, purple and yellow in autumn. The branches have corky outgrowths.

A ten-year-old specimen of *Liriodendron tulipifera* 'Fastigiata' in the autumn

Liriodendron tulipifera 'Aureomarginata' in the spring

Liriodendron
Magnoliaceae
Tulip tree

A genus of hardy flowering trees that look particularly imposing when planted as specimens; on a large lawn for example. Older trees are difficult to transplant; move younger ones in spring when the buds begin to swell.

Soil A fairly moist but well-drained fertile loam is preferred.

Propagation Sow the seeds, of which only a small percentage will germinate, when ripe in trays containing sandy soil and place in a cold frame.

Liriodendron tulipifera

A tree from North America where it can reach a height of 135 ft (40 m) but which in Britain can reach 120 ft (36 m) with a spread of up to 60 ft (18 m). In midsummer the large, tulip-like yellow-green flowers with orange spots are borne; these attract bees. The 4-lobed, saddle-shaped leaves turn butter-yellow in autumn.

Liriope
Liliaceae
Lily turf

Evergreen perennials with narrow, almost grass-like, leathery leaves and spikes of small bell-shaped flowers.

Soil Any well-drained but humus-rich soil is suitable, preferably in shade.

Propagation By seed sown when ripe or by division in spring.

Liriope exiliflora

Similar to the more familiar *L. muscari*, this plant has a mat-forming habit and more slender, looser flower spikes.

Liriope muscari

From China, Formosa (Taiwan) and Japan, a plant growing 15 in (45 cm) high, possibly more. Dense clumps of arching leaves with spikes of lavender flowers appear in autumn. The flowers are bell-shaped and usually 3–5 in (8–12 cm) long. 'Majestic' has longer violet flower spikes.

Lithodora
Boraginaceae

Attractive rock plants, the best known of which have attractive true blue flowers and make a welcome addition to any garden. Although these plants are small shrubs, they are usually listed in catalogues of perennial plants.

Soil A well-drained soil is needed, in a sunny position.

Propagation Grow by division, from cuttings or from seed. Young plants are generally overwintered in pots in a well-ventilated cold frame.

Lithodora diffusa

Lithodora diffusa

Syn. *Lithospermum diffusum, Lithospermum prostratum*. An evergreen sub-shrubby plant from southern Europe with spreading prostrate stems that grow no higher than 2–6 in (5–15 cm). Flowering in late spring to early summer, it bears dark blue flowers with reddish-violet stripes. The most popular cultivar is 'Heavenly Blue', with masses of sky-blue flowers. The flowering period can be protracted, sometimes lasting until early autumn. Use a neutral to acid soil.

Lobelia
Campanulaceae

A genus including several well-known annuals that make useful summer bedding plants and are also often used for edging and in hanging baskets or containers. In addition there are several perennial species that deserve a greater popularity.

Cultivation Annuals: If annual lobelias are dead-headed they will continue blooming until the first frost, especially if they are in fertile soil.

Lobelia erinus 'Kaiser Wilhelm'

Lobelia fulgens 'Queen Victoria'

Perennials: Some are not fully hardy, and must be protected against frost in winter, preferably in a well-ventilated cold frame.

Soil A rich, moist soil is required.

Propagation Annuals: Sow during February or early March in seed trays at a temperature of 16–18°C (61–64°F). Prick out the seedlings and replant in small clumps 1–2 in (2.5–5 cm) apart. As soon as the clumps touch one another again, they are placed in separate pots in a frame. Amateurs who have no frame or greenhouse may sow the seeds at the beginning of April behind a light, southern window in a warm room.

Perennials: These are grown by division in spring, stem cuttings in late spring or early summer, or root cuttings in winter.

Lobelia erinus

○ ◐ ☉ ⊛

An annual to perennial plant from South Africa, usually grown as an annual and reaching a height of 3–12 in (7.5–30 cm). From early summer to autumn it bears flowers in shades of sky-blue, pale blue and white, purple or white. There are several cultivars, and generally they are divided into three groups.

(a) Compact forms. In catalogues these are usually listed under *L. erinus compacta*. They grow to a height of 4 in (10 cm) and are suitable for edging. 'Cambridge Blue' has sky-blue flowers; 'Crystal Palace' is Oxford-blue; 'Mrs Clibran', deep violet; 'Rosamond', red; and 'White Lady' is a most attractive white form.

(b) Taller forms. The term tall must not be taken too literally, for the height of these lobelias is no more than 8–10 in (20–25 cm). They are usually listed in catalogues under *L. erinus*. There are cultivars with white, light blue, dark blue, purple or blue flowers, all with a white eye.

(c) Trailing forms. These are usually listed in catalogues under *L. erinus pendula*. 'Sapphire', bright blue with a white eye, is one of the best in this group. Others have white, rose-pink and purple-red flowers. 'Hamburger' is cornflower-blue and has a white eye.

Lobelia cardinalis

○ ◐ ◌ ◌ ⊛

A herbaceous perennial, not reliably hardy, that reaches heights of 2–4 ft (60–100 cm). From midsummer to early autumn it bears flowers that usually are scarlet or, more rarely, rose-red or light pink. 'Queen Victoria' has beautiful crimson to bronze leaves and pyramidal spikes of bright scarlet flowers that have an orange glow. It is an extraordinarily beautiful garden plant and not hard to grow. A few plants should be overwintered in a cold frame.

Lobelia fulgens

Cardinal flower. A perennial plant from Mexico reaching 2–3 ft (60–100 cm) and flowering in late summer to autumn, when dark crimson to scarlet blooms appear.

Lobelia × gerardii

Syn. *L. vedrariensis*. A cross between *L. cardinalis* and *L. syphilitica* that grows 3–4 ft (1–1.2 m) high and bears purple flowers in long spikes from midsummer to early autumn. There are several cultivars in shades of red and purple.

Lobelia vedrariensis, see *Lobelia × gerardii*.

Lobularia
Cruciferae
Sweet alyssum

Generally listed in catalogues under *Alyssum maritimum*, this is an attractive plant for the edge of the border.

Soil Any well-drained garden soil is suitable.

Propagation Sow seeds outdoors in spring, thinning out the more compact types to 4 in (10 cm) apart and the taller ones to 6–8 in (15–20 cm) apart.

Lobularia maritima

○ ○ ⊛ ⊗

Syn. *Alyssum maritimum*. A hardy annual 4–12 in (10–30 cm) high and flowering from late spring to early autumn. The species is not cultivated, but improved cultivars include the small compact white-flowered 'Little Dorrit', the carpet-forming 'Snow Carpet', the rose-red 'Rosie O'Day' and the attractive 'Violet Queen'. All remain in flower for a considerable period.

Lonicera
Caprifoliaceae
Honeysuckle

A varied genus of evergreen and deciduous flowering shrubs and climbing plants. Climbing honeysuckles may be grown on old trees or against walls, trained against pergolas or summer-houses, or grown on banks and slopes. The vigorous *L. caprifolium* and *L. periclymenum* are particularly suited to all these purposes. For covering low fences, etc., it is better to use some of the less vigorous cultivars of *L. sempervirens*. All these climbers eventually grow thin-bottomed, and they must either be cut back or grown behind shorter plants. Although climbing honeysuckles will tolerate shade, they flower more freely in sunny positions; *L. periclymenum* is particularly tolerant of shade.

Soil Honeysuckles are not very demanding plants, but it pays to enrich the soil with decayed manure or other sources of humus.

Propagation Honeysuckles are easily propagated from softwood or hardwood cuttings. The former should be taken in July–August and the latter in September–October. Climbing species can also be propagated by sowing seed when ripe.

Lonicera nitida

Lonicera periclymenum 'Serotina'

Climbing species include:

Lonicera × americana

○ ◐ ⊛ ⊛

This hybrid between *L. caprifolium* and *L. etrusca* is a deciduous climber which can reach 28 ft (9 m) in a suitable position. The flowers are yellow with a red-purple flush and are carried in whorled spikes at the end of the branchlets in summer.

Lonicera × brownii

◐ ◐ ⊛ ⊛ ⊛

A cross between *L. hirsuta* and *L. sempervirens*. This climber is fairly sensitive to frost but well worth growing; it will flower in shady positions. The best-known forms are 'Punicea', with orange-red flowers, and 'Fuchsioides', which has dark red flowers.

Lonicera caprifolium

○ ◐ ◐ ⊛ ⊛

Goat-leaf honeysuckle. A deciduous climber with creamy aromatic flowers appearing in mid- to late summer.

Lonicera etrusca

○ ◐ ⊛

A partially evergreen climber from the Mediterranean which can reach 32 ft (10 m). The leaves are broadly oval and hairless, those on the flowering stems perfoliate. The fragrant cream flowers darken to yellow as they age. They open in summer.

Lonicera × heckrotii

A cross between *L. × americana* and *L. sempervirens*, a deciduous climber which often develops a shrubby habit. The leaves are dark green on top and bluish-green underneath. Flowers, borne in whorls from early summer to early autumn, are purple outside and light yellow within. 'Goldflame' has flowers that are orange-red on the out-

Mixed colours of *Lobularia maritima*, better known as *Alyssum maritimum*

The graceful and vigorous *Lonicera* × *brownii* 'Punicea'

side and golden-yellow inside.

Lonicera japonica
○ ◐ ◐ ⬙ ⬙ ⬙ ⬙ ⬙

Japanese honeysuckle, a very hardy, semi-evergreen climbing plant from Japan. From early summer to early autumn it bears creamy white flowers, ageing yellow sometimes purple tinted.

Lonicera periclymenum
○ ◐ ◐ ◐ ◐ ⬙ ⬙

Woodbine, honeysuckle. A hardy plant from the Mediterranean that flowers in mid to late summer, producing large clusters of fragrant yellow flowers. This vigorous species is very tolerant of shade. 'Belgica' has flowers that are violet-purple on the outside and yellowish inside, and appear from late spring to early summer and often once more in early autumn. 'Serotina' may be grown both as a solitary plant and also in groups or for ground cover. If it is used as a shrub, it should be pruned from time to time. The flowers, violet-purple to purple-red outside and pale yellow inside, are borne from midsummer to autumn, followed by red berries.

Lonicera × tellmanniana
◐ ◐ ◐ ⬙

A cross between *L. tragophylla* which is deciduous and *L. sempervirens*, an evergreen species. It blends the characters of its parents being partially evergreen. The flowers, which are carried in clusters at the ends of the stems, are a bright coppery-yellow flushed deeper on the outside. They open in summer.

Lonicera tragophylla
◐◐◐◐

A deciduous climber from China which is more bushy and less ranging than many other climbing species, reaching

only about 16ft (5m). It is very tolerant of shade. The bright yellow, unscented flowers are large, reaching 3½in (9cm) in length and are carried in dense spikes at the ends of the shoots.

Lonicera sempervirens
○ ◐ ◐ ⬙ ⬙

Trumpet vine. An evergreen or partly deciduous climbing shrub from the southern United States. One of the best honeysuckles, it has a very long flowering period, from late spring to late summer, bearing yellow and scarlet flowers that are followed by scarlet berries. 'Sulphurea' has yellow flowers.

Evergreen shrubs include:

Lonicera fragrantissima
◐ ◐ ◐ ◐ ⬙

A partially evergreen shrub from China, growing up to 6ft (2m) high, that may be trained as a wall shrub. It is unusual in that, during mild weather, the creamy-white flowers will open from late autumn to March.

Lonicera nitida
◐ ◐ ◐ ◐ ⬙ ⬙

An evergreen shrub from western China that grows up to 6ft (2m) high with downy branches and small, leathery, oval leaves, light green underneath and glossy green on top. The tiny flowers are whitish and slightly fragrant, but insignificant and hidden by foliage. They appear from late spring to early summer, followed by violet berries. 'Baggeson's Gold' has rich yellow leaves in summer, yellow-green at other times; 'Ernest Wilson' has a broad habit and was formerly the cultivar most extensively used for hedging, but in Britain 'Yunnan' is now the most popular, being more robust, bushy

and vigorous.

Lonicera pileata
◐ ◐ ◐ ⬙ ⬙ ⬙

A dwarf horizontal-branching shrub from China that grows to a height of 24in (60cm), rarely to 3ft (1m). Its branches are covered with short hairs, and the elliptical leaves are bright green on top. White to pale yellow, fragrant flowers are borne in spring, followed by translucent purple berries.

Semi-evergreen shrubs include:

Lonicera korolkowii
◐ ◐ ◐ ◐ ⬙

From Turkestan, a plant growing up to 8ft (2.4m) high with greyish-blue foliage, white flowers and red berries.

Lonicera ledebourii
◐ ◐ ◐ ◐ ⬙

Syn. *L. involucrata*. A shrub from California that grows up to 5ft (1.5m) high and has highly ornamental flowers and fruits. The yellow flowers are surrounded by orange-red bracts and appear in late spring to early summer and are followed by purple berries in midsummer to early autumn. The leaves are dark green and downy on the veins beneath.

Lonicera morrowi

A wide-spreading shrub, up to 10ft (3m) high with downy branches and white, later yellow, flowers followed by red berries.

Lonicera × purpusii
◐ ◐ ◐ ⬙

A beautiful cross between *L. standishii* and *L. fragrantissima*. It has leathery leaves, and the flowers appear as early as December–March; they are fragrant and creamy-white, and are sometimes followed in early May by red fruits.

Plant in a sheltered position.

Lonicera syringantha
◐ ◐ ◐ ⬙

This plant bears fragrant lilac flowers in late spring to midsummer.

Lonicera tatarica
◐ ◐ ◐ ◐

An erect shrub from southern Russia that grows up to 10ft (3m) high and bears rose-red flowers in late spring to early summer, followed by coral-red berries. The best-known cultivars are 'Alba', with fairly large white flowers; 'Arnold Red', with purple-red flowers; 'Hack's Red', purple-pink, not quite so tall; 'Rosea', with soft pink flowers; and 'Zabelii', which has dark rose flowers.

Lonicera xylosteum

A native of Europe, this erect, bushy shrub grows up to 10ft (3m) high and flowers from late spring to midsummer. Yellowish-white to white flowers are followed by red berries.

Lunaria
Cruciferae
Honesty

The main attraction of honesty is its flattened silvery seed pods (siliquas), which make excellent indoor decorations. The plant itself is also attractive when in flower.

Soil Honesty grows in any garden soil that is neither too poor nor too dry.

Propagation Sow seeds from late spring to early summer outside in a nursery bed. Transplant in summer and move to the flowering position, keeping plants 16in (40cm) apart, in early autumn or the following spring.

Lunaria annua

Lunaria annua
○ ◐ ◐ ⬙

Syn. *L. biennis*. A European biennial that grows 1–3ft (30–100cm) high and flowers in late spring to early summer. 'Alba' has white, and 'Purpurea' dark pink flowers; while 'Variegata' has irregularly shaped white-edged leaves.

Lunaria biennis, see *L. annua*.

Lupinus
Leguminaceae
Lupin

A genus of annuals, herbaceous perennials and sub-shrubs.

Soil Lupins thrive in any well-drained but not dry humus-rich soil.

Cultivation Annual lupins are very suitable for planting in large groups, particularly when some temporary and inexpensive infilling is needed, for instance when it is too late to plant shrubs in a new garden. They also make a fine show in beds or borders, and are excellent for cutting. Nurseries have raised many splendid new strains of lupins, and the perennials among them can be propagated by division. Catalogues of herbaceous perennials usually list them in full by name and colour.

Propagation Annuals: These may be grown from seed like peas, i.e. in small drills 8–12 in (20–30 cm) apart according to size. Two to three seeds are placed in each hole in spring and the strongest seedling is preserved.

Perennials: These are sown in spring in a seed bed and transplanted to another bed as soon as the seedlings have produced a few leaves. Plant them 8 in

Annual *Lupinus hartwegii* hybrids

Perennial *Lupinus polyphyllus* hybrids are easy to cultivate

(20 cm) apart. If the seeds are sown early enough, the seedlings will flower during the first autumn and the most attractive can then be picked out for transplantation to a new flowering position for the following year. Cultivars do not come true from seed and should be propagated by division from cuttings taken in spring. Tree lupins are propagated by the same methods as the other types; also by cuttings in summer.

Annual lupins include:

Lupinus angustifolius

○ ◑ ○ ☺

Blue lupin. A downy plant that grows 2½–3 ft (75–100 cm) high and bears blue flowers. It is grown for green manure.

Lupinus cruckshanksii

○ ◑ ⊛ ○ ⊛ ⊗

Syn. *L. mutabilis* var. *cruckshanksii*. Probably the most attractive of the annual species, it grows 3–6 ft (1–2 m) high and in early to midsummer produces large flowers with light blue standards that later turn violet, and light pink keels.

Lupinus hartwegii hybrids

Late-flowering annuals from Mexico that reach a height of 2½ ft (75 cm), and from midsummer to autumn bear blue

flowers with white, later reddish, standards. Cultivars are available in white, sky-blue, and pink with red.

Lupinus mutabilis

A plant that grows 3–5 ft (1–1.5 m) high and flowers from midsummer to autumn, producing white blooms with a yellow standard that turns violet.

Lupinus mutabilis var. **cruckshanksii**, see *L. cruckshanksii*.

Lupinus nanus

○ ⊖ ○ ⊙ ⊛

An excellent lupin for planting in groups and also for edging, it grows 8–12 in (20–30 cm) high, and produces blue flowers with violet markings in early to midsummer. There are many varieties in a host of different colours.

Lupinus pilosus, see *L. varius* ssp. *orientalis*.

Lupinus varius ssp. *orientalis*

○ ⊖ ⊛ ○ ⊛

Syn. *L. pilosus*. A plant that grows 20–30 in (50–75 cm) high, its stems covered with white hair, and bears flesh-coloured flowers in summer. Cultivars are available in white and pink.

Herbaceous perennials include:

Lupinus polyphyllus hybrids

○ ◑ ⊛ ⊗ ⌒ ○ ⊛ ⊗

A North American lupin that grows to a

height of 3 ft (1 m) and in summer bears blue and white flowers. There are numerous cultivars. For growing from seed, the Russell strain is particularly recommended and will yield glorious plants in numerous good colours. 'Chandelier' produces golden-yellow flowers; those of 'My Castle' are red; and 'The Governor', blue and white.

Shrubby lupins include:

Lupinus arboreus

○ ◑ ⌒ ⊛ ⊗

Tree lupin. A shrub from California that grows up to 6 ft (2 m) high. In Europe it is generally more compact and is grown as a sub-shrub. The flowers are sulphur-yellow. Lilac- to blue-flowered forms are sometimes available. 'Snow Queen', a very beautiful shrub with white flowers, is not reliably hardy, and should be given some protection.

Lychnis
Caryophyllaceae
Campion

A genus of annuals and perennials with highly ornamental flowers, useful in the border.

Soil Any ordinary well-drained garden soil will do.

Propagation Species are grown from seed in spring. Cultivars are propagated from cuttings taken in spring.

Lychnis alpina

◑ ○ ⊛ ⊗

Syn. *Viscaria alpina*. A perennial herbaceous plant from the Alps that grows 2–5 in (5–12.5 cm) high, forming a tuft from which the flowers rise on viscous stems. Deep rose flowers appear in dense clusters in summer.

Lychnis × arkwrightii

◑ ⌒ ⊛ ○ ⊛ ⊗

A cross between *L. haageana* and *L. chalcedonica*, which grows 12–16 in (30–40 cm) high. If grown from seed the flowers, which appear in summer, will range from rose to orange, carmine to scarlet. It is advisable to propagate the most beautiful plants by division. This campion is not completely hardy and is best grown as a biennial: sow in pots, place in a cold frame from April to July, and move to the flowering position the following spring.

Lychnis chalcedonica

◑ ○ ⊙ ⊛ ⊗

A perennial herbaceous plant that grows up to 3 ft (1 m) high, is sturdy,

Lysichiton camtschatcensis

The colour of *Lychnis coronaria* makes it difficult to combine with other flowers

vigorous and has an erect habit. Bright scarlet flowers are borne in summer in dense flattened heads above the bright green leaves. It is a beautiful border plant which, because of its clean red colour, looks very well in combination with blue flowers, such as late-flowering blue larkspurs. It is easily grown from seed sown under glass in spring.

Lychnis coronaria
Syn. *Agrastemma coronaria*. From southern Europe, a biennial to perennial plant reaching 1–2 ft (30–60 cm). From late spring to midsummer it bears flowers that are crimson-magenta in the parent form, white in 'Alba', and crimson in 'Altrosanguinea'. It is a sturdy plant with greyish leaves, and is most suitable for planting in the border or in front of shrubs; it is also recommended as an edging plant. *L. coronaria* thrives in any well-drained soil, and can be propagated from seed or by division. Set out 8–10 in (20–25 cm) apart.

Lychnis flos-jovis
Syn. *Coronaria flos-jovis*. Originally from the sunny slopes of the Alps, it is a perennial but is often grown as a biennial, and grows up to 24 in (60 cm) high. Rose-red to light purple flowers are borne in loose rounded inflorescences from late spring to midsummer. This species requires a very sunny position and dry calcareous soil. Propagation can be by division or from seed. The leaves are silvery-grey.

Lynchis × haageana
A hybrid growing to 1 ft (30 cm) high with lanceolate, mid-green leaves that are often flushed with purple. It bears red or orange flowers, 2 in (5 cm) across, in early summer.

Lychnis viscaria
Syn. *Viscaria vulgaris*, *L. viscaria* ssp. *viscaria*. A herbaceous perennial from the Mediterranean that grows 1½ ft (45 cm) high and looks well at the front of borders. From late spring to early summer it bears rose-red to purple flowers; those of 'Splendens' are carmine; 'Plena' has double flowers; and 'Albiflora' has white flowers.

Lysichiton
Araceae

Particularly striking bog plants that look well in a partly shady position at the side of pools.
Soil A very fertile and moist soil is needed.
Propagation Plants may be grown from seed sown as soon as it is ripe. Since the plants usually take a few years before they begin to flower, propagation by division is generally preferable.

Lysichiton americanum
Yellow skunk cabbage, from North America. A plant growing 20–28 in (50–70 cm) high with dark green leaves 16–24 in (40–60 cm) long. In early spring to early summer flowers appear: these consist of fleshy greenish-yellow spikes up to 20 in (50 cm) high enclosed in golden-yellow spathes.

Lysichiton camtschatcensis
A plant that strongly resembles the yellow skunk cabbage but is a little smaller, has a white spathe and flowers a few weeks later.

Lysimachia
Primulaceae
Loosestrife

A genus of herbaceous perennials for the border. *L. nummularia* provides excellent ground cover.
Soil All species like moist garden soil.
Propagation Plants are raised by division in spring.

Lysimachia clethroides
A herbaceous perennial plant from eastern Asia that reaches 24–32 in (60–80 cm). In summer it bears small flowers set close together in long arching spikes. This is one of the most attractive lysimachias for the border, the leaves turning from mid-green to red or orange in the autumn.

Lysimachia nummularia
Moneywort, creeping Jenny. A quick-growing perennial plant from Europe found on moist pasturelands. It has a low, creeping habit, with short-stemmed, almost circular, bright green leaves, and in early to midsummer bears single golden-yellow flowers in the leaf axils. It is recommended for semi-shaded positions, beside ponds or in moist places on the northern side of the rock garden.

Lysimachia punctata
A spreading perennial, downy in all parts, growing up to 3 ft (1 m) high. The erect stems are densely covered with citron-yellow flowers borne in summer in the leaf axils. It can be invasive in rich soils.

The white flowers in the centre are *Lysimachia clethroides*

Moneywort, *Lysomachia nummularia* makes good ground-cover for moist sites

Lythrum
Lythraceae

Perennial plants that will thrive in partial shade and sun. The flowers are more beautiful if kept out of bright sunlight, and plants may be grouped with striking effect in large clumps at the front of the shrub border.

Soil Ordinary garden soil is adequate, preferably on the moist side.

Propagation *L. salicaria* can be grown from seed. Cultivars do not come true from seed and must be propagated from cuttings (in spring) or by division.

Lythrum hybrids

◑ ◐ ⊛ ◎ ⓨ ⊕

Cultivars of uncertain origin that flower from early summer to early autumn. 'Brightness', 4ft (1.2m) high, has large cherry-red flowers; 'Morden's Pink', 5ft (1.5m), has deep rose flowers; 'Robert', 2½ft (75cm) high, has salmon-pink flowers; and those of 'The Beacon', 3ft (1m) high, are carmine.

Lythrum salicaria

Purple loosestrife. A herbaceous perennial native to river banks, ditches and marshes, where it can grow 3–4½ft (1–1.3m) high. Masses of purple-red flowers are borne in long spires from midsummer to early autumn.

Lythrum virgatum

A herbaceous perennial similar to *L. salicaria* but more slender, reaching heights of 24–30in (60–75cm) and flowering from midsummer to early autumn, when purple-pink flowers are borne in graceful spires.

Macleaya
Papaveraceae
Plume poppy

Majestic ornamental plants that are seen to best advantage when planted in small groups at the back of large borders or in beds. They must be kept carefully in check, however, or they can be invasive.

Magnolia kobus

The plume poppy, *Macleaya cordata*

Lythrum salicaria combined with grasses

Soil Plant in deep loamy soil.

Propagation By division, from root cuttings and from seed.

Macleaya cordata

○ ◑ ◐ ⊛ ◎ ⓨ ◔

Syn. *Bocconia cordata*. A herbaceous perennial from China and Japan that grows to heights of 6–10ft (2–3m). Flowering in mid- to late summer, it bears pyramidal plumes with no petals but with white sepals surrounding the 24–30 ornamental white stamens. The leaves are deeply lobed and blue-green in colour. It is often confused in gardens with the similar *M. microcarpa*, the flowers of which have buff-pink sepals. 'Coral Plume' has pink flowers.

Magnolia
Magnoliaceae

Magnolias make glorious flowering shrubs in gardens and parks. The flowers of many species appear before the leaves.

Cultivation Spring-flowering species should be sheltered from cold winds and frost, or the blooms may be damaged. Magnolias are particularly attractive when planted as solitary specimens on the lawn, especially near water. When transplanting magnolias, make sure that the fleshy roots are as little damaged as possible.

Soil Magnolias like fertile, loamy soil. Poorer soils should be enriched with leaf-mould at planting time.

Propagation Plants are raised by layering or grafting under glass. Growing magnolias from seed is not difficult, but it takes many years for them to reach flowering size. The seeds do not remain viable for more than six months, and must therefore be sown as soon as they are ripe. Use pots containing a well-drained compost and place in a cold frame.

Magnolia campbellii

○ ◑ ⊛ ⊛ ◎ ○ ⓨ

A handsome tree-like species from the

Magnolia liliiflora flowers late

Himalayas which can reach 65ft (20m) in cultivation and far more in the wild. The broadly oval leaves are glaucous beneath, up to 10in (25cm) long. The large, erect flowers which measure 10in (25cm) across open before the leaves in spring. They are usually pink though they can be white or red. *M.c. mollicomata* has mauve-pink flowers. Several hybrids have been raised between this and the true species.

Magnolia conspicua, see *Magnolia denudata*.

Magnolia denudata

○ ⊛ ⊛ ◎ ⓨ ⊕

Syn. *M. conspicua* and *M. yulan*. A 6–12ft (2–4m) high shrub from China and Japan with oval leaves and creamy-white flowers.

Magnolia grandiflora

○ ◐ ○ ⊛ ⓨ ◔ ⊛

A tree from the south-eastern United States that grows 70ft (23m) high in the wild, but only up to 30ft (9m) in cooler areas. The large, oblong, leathery leaves are glossy above and reddish-brown and downy beneath. The wide, creamy-white, fragrant flowers can measure up to 10in (25cm) across.

Magnolia kobus

A tall shrub from Japan, where it also grows as a tree up to 30ft (9m) high.

lime tolerant and is probably a hybrid with *M. wilsoniana*.

Magnolia × soulangiana

○ ⊗ ⊛ ⊛ ⊕

A cross between *M. denudata* and *M. liliiflora*, and the source of the most attractive hybrids. The undersides of the leaves are often hairy, and the flowers are of various colours. 'Alba Superba' has pure white flowers; 'Alexandrina' has dark rose, early flowers, white outside; 'Lennei' has broad-petalled flowers, purple outside, white inside; 'Lennei Alba' has the same form but the flowers are pure white; and 'Speciosa' has flowers stained purple at the base.

Magnolia × soulangiana 'Nigra', see Magnolia liliiflora 'Nigra'.

Magnolia stellata

Syn. *M. kobus* var. *stellata*. A Japanese shrub that grows up to 6 ft (2 m) high and, apart from *M. soulangiana* hybrids, is the most commonly seen magnolia. Flowers are white and star shaped and appear March–April. They may turn brown unless they are protected from night frosts. 'Rosea' has pink buds and rose-white flowers. Both species and cultivar are slow-growing, and highly recommended for smaller gardens where the star-shaped flowers

Magnolia stellata 'Rosea'

Magnolia × soulangiana

Magnolia liliiflora 'Nigra'

The white flowers appear in spring before the leaves; the fruits are scarlet.

Magnolia kobus, var. stellata, see M. stellata.

Magnolia liliiflora

Syn. *M. obovata*. A wide-spreading shrub with short, hairy grey buds and purple, fragrant flowers in greenish sepals. 'Nigra' has smaller, dark purple flowers, blooms later than the species and flowers a second time in summer.

Magnolia obovata, see Magnolia liliiflora.

Magnolia parviflora, see M. steboldii.

Magnolia sieboldii

○ ⊗ ⊛ ⊛ ⊛ ⊕

Syn. *M. parviflora*. A wide-spreading shrub that grows up to 15 ft (5 m) high, and flowers in early summer. The flowers are small, bowl-shaped and white with conspicuous red stamens. This plant is not tolerant of lime.

Magnolia sinensis

○ ⊕ ⊛ ⊛ ⊛ ⊛

A large shrub or small tree from China usually less than 20 ft (6 m) tall. The oval leaves are bright green above and white hairy beneath. The pendant white flowers are up to 4 in (10 cm) wide and open in summer with the leaves. *M. × highdownensis* is similar and very

can be set off to great advantage in early spring. 'Royal Star' is similar except that it has larger flowers with more petals.

Magnolia × thompsoniana

A cross between *M. tripetala* and *M. virginiana*. A large, wide-spreading shrub, with leaves that are up to 10 in (25 cm) long, and glossy above and bluish-white underneath. The creamy-white flowers appear in early to midsummer.

Magnolia wilsoniana

○ ⊕ ⊛ ⊛ ⊛

A Chinese species which is very similar to *M. sinensis* but has narrower, dull green leaves which are brown-hairy beneath.

Magnolia yulan, see Magnolia denudata.

Mahonia
Berberidaceae

A genus of ornamental shrubs, all of which have attractive evergreen foliage.
Soil Mahonias thrive on moist but not wet soil. Shelter from cold winds will ensure good blooming of those that flower in winter. In sunny positions, the leaves turn a glorious brownish-red in autumn.
Propagation Plants are raised by layering, or from seeds sown in pots in autumn and kept in a cold frame.

Mahonia aquifolium

Syn. *Berberis aquilifolium*. Oregon grape. An early spring-flowering suckering shrub that reaches up to 6ft (2m) high, but is slow-growing. Yellow flowers are borne in dense racemes and are followed by blue berries. The leaves are green, glossy, ovate, sharply indented, and turn bronze in winter. Recommended cultivars include 'Atropurpurea', which has reddish-purple leaves in the winter; 'Dart's Distinction', which is floriferous, has

Mahonia × media 'Charity'

very small leaves, is not very wide-spreading and so is excellent for hedging; and 'Moseri', with light green leaves that quickly turn copper-red.

Mahonia bealei

Syn. *Berberis japonica* var. *bealei*. An upright, evergreen shrub that grows up to 3ft (1m) high. The leaves are sharply toothed, and light green in colour, yellowish at the base. Flowers are borne in 4in (10cm) racemes in March and April, followed by blue berries.

Mahonia japonica

Syn. *Berberis japonica*. A plant growing up to 3ft (1m) high with deep to yellowish-green leaves and bearing pendulous racemes of sulphur-yellow flowers in February and March. 'Charity' is a hybrid with *M. lomariifolia* and sometimes blooms as early as January–February; its flowers

Malus sargentii a spreading tree

The vigorous *Malus floribunda*

are borne in 1ft (30cm) long, light yellow racemes.

Mahonia lomariifolia

A palm-like plant growing 6ft (2m) high that looks very well in groups. The spiny leaves are up to 2ft (60m) long and the bright yellow flowers are borne in large central clusters in winter. It needs a sheltered site and can be cut to ground level in severe winters.

Malus
Rosaceae
Crab apple

A large genus of shrubs or trees. In this book only the most popular flowering crab apples are described.
Cultivation It is advisable to prune

The fruits of crab apple trees are often edible

flowering crabs lightly every few years, a treatment that will be amply rewarded with better flowers and more fruit.
Soil Flowering crabs thrive in any well-drained garden soil.
Propagation Flowering crabs, like apple trees, are propagated by budding or grafting on to seedling rootstocks. The species may also be grown from seed.
Diseases Some species and cultivars are particularly sensitive to apple scab. Because it is no longer possible to associate many cultivars with particular species, we have set out all the sorts described in alphabetical order.

Malus 'Aldenhamensis'

A small tree that grows to a height of 10ft (3m), and is recommended for smaller gardens. The leaves are purple, and masses of large, deep vinous-red flowers appear in late spring, followed by beautiful reddish-purple fruits.

Malus 'Almey'

A free-flowering small tree up to 18ft (6m) high, with purple leaves turning to bronze. The single flowers are large and lilac-red with a white central star. Red fruits are borne in autumn.

Malus × atrosanguinea

The result of a number of crosses, often listed under *M. floribunda* var. *atrosanguinea*. A small tree resembling *M. floribunda* but with crimson flowers that turn paler, and glossy green leaves. The greenish-yellow fruits with a red cheek are shed fairly early.

Malus 'Butterball'

A very attractive newer cultivar with small green leaves, soft pink flowers and golden-yellow fruits.

Malus 'Calocarpa'

A small, spreading tree with green leaves, small white flowers, and attractive fruits that turn red very late in the season but remain on the tree until December. See also under 'Golden Hornet' and 'Professor Sprenger'.

Malus 'Cheal's Weeping'

A weeping tree with drooping branches and purple-bronze leaves, producing large, bright lilac-red single flowers.

Malus coronaria

A small, thorny shrub or tree with large green leaves turning orange-red in autumn. The best cultivar is 'Charlottae', but only older specimens flower freely. Flowering takes place from late spring to early summer, when semi-double blooms with a rose tint appear. The fruits are green and inconspicuous.

Malus 'Dorothea'

A highly recommended small tree or shrub with slim branches and green foliage. The semi-double large flowers remain pale crimson throughout their life and are followed by yellow fruits.

Malus 'Echtermeyer'

A weeping form with single, rose-crimson flowers. See also under 'Cheal's Weeping'.

Malus 'Eleyi'

A slow-growing, densely branching tree with large, purple, glossy leaves that later turn bronze. Masses of single, light wine-red flowers are borne, and very decorative purplish-red fruits.

Malus floribunda

A very attractive, highly recommended shrub or tree from Japan that grows 10–18ft (3–6m) high with long drooping branches clothed in green leaves. It produces masses of pale pink flowers fading to white, and its small, yellowish-green fruits remain on the tree until late autumn.

Malus 'Golden Hornet'

A spreading tree with green leaves and very small white flowers. The main attractions are the bright yellow fruits, which are retained until the onset of winter.

Malus 'Gorgeous'

This tree resembles 'Golden Hornet' but has red fruits.

Malus 'Hillieri'

A moderately sized, upright shrub with green leaves and masses of small white flowers. The yellow and red fruits drop off very early.

Malus 'Hopa'

A quick-growing tree up to 16ft (5m) high with spreading branches. The

Fruits of *Malus sargentii*

Malus 'Lemoinei'

Malus 'Kingsmere'

leaves are light purple, turning almost green, and the flowers are single and dark purple-red.

Malus 'John Downie'
A vigorous tree with deep green leaves and single white flowers. The main attractions are the bright orange-red apples, which appear in large numbers in autumn, and are suitable for preserves.

Malus 'Lemoinei'
A vigorous tree with dark purple foliage. Older specimens bear masses of single, dark rose-purple flowers that do not fade with age. The dark fruits are not very conspicuous.

Malus 'Liset'
A small tree with shiny purple leaves. Even young trees bear masses of single, very attractive red flowers, followed by dark purple fruits. It is highly recom-

mended, and particularly suitable for smaller gardens.

Malus 'Makamik'
A tree growing up to 16ft (5m) high with a rounded crown. It resembles *M.* 'Almey' and *M.* 'Hopa', except that its flowers are a darker pink.

Malus 'Mary Potter'
○ ✤ ⓨ ❀ ⊥
A small shrub with overhanging branches that may be used as ground cover. The leaves are green, the flowers white, and masses of deep red fruits are retained until early winter.

Malus × micromalus
○ ✤ ⓨ ⊥
A cross between *M. baccata* and *M. spectabilis*, this tree grows up to 16ft (5m) high, with erect branches and green leaves. Single, deep pink flowers appear in spring. The yellow fruits do

not last long.

Malus 'Neville Copeman'
A fairly recent addition bearing masses of conspicuous bright orange apples, $1-1\frac{1}{2}$in (2.5–3.8cm) across, in autumn. The tree is fast-growing and has a wide, open crown. The green leaves are shaded purple and the flowers are light purple.

Malus 'Professor Sprenger'
○ ❀ ⓨ ⓩ ❀ ⓛ
A small tree with green foliage turning golden-yellow in autumn. The white flowers are followed by attractive orange apples which usually remain on the tree until December.

Malus 'Profusion'
○ ❀ ⓨ ❀ ⓛ
A fast-growing tree with coppery-crimson young leaves. The single, very large flowers are flushed wine-red and change colour slightly as they fade; the fruits are ox-blood red. 'Liset' is a generally favoured cultivar.

Malus 'Red Siberian'
○ ❀ ⓨ ⓨ
This tree is less attractive than *M.* 'Gorgeous', which it resembles, because the fruits are not retained for as long.

Malus sargentii
○ ❀ ⓨ ❀ ⓛ
A shrubby species that grows up to 6 ft (2 m) high and has a spread of up to 25 ft (8 m). The thorny branches have green leaves that turn to orange-yellow in autumn. Masses of white, fragrant flowers appear in May, followed by small, dark red fruits. This makes a most attractive specimen shrub for a large lawn.

Malus × scheideckeri
A cross between *M. floribunda* and *M. prunifolia*. It is an erect shrub with pink flowers, is highly sensitive to apple scab and has been almost completely supplanted by 'Hillieri'.

Malus sieboldii
A shrub or small tree up to 12 ft (4 m) high with glossy green leaves turning an attractive shade of yellow in autumn. White flowers appear at the end of May, followed by yellow fruits that last to the end of October.

Malus 'Van Eseltine'
○ ❀ ⓨ ❀
A small shrub having a distinctive columnar habit and green leaves. Very large, double flowers are borne in a most attractive shade of pink. The fruits, yellow-green with a touch of red, are not very conspicuous.

Malus 'Wintergold'
A small round-headed tree with glossy green leaves and white, pink-budded flowers. Its bright yellow, $\frac{1}{2}$in (12mm) fruits are retained until December.

Malva
Malvaceae
Mallow

Attractive perennial and annual plants for borders and flower beds.
Soil Mallows grow in any ordinary well-drained soil in a sunny situation. They are excellent plants for poor soils since they are easily grown and long-lived.
Propagation Annuals are sown in the flowering position in spring. Thin out, at first to 6 in (15 cm) apart and later 10–12 in (25–30 cm). Perennials are sown May–July in seed beds, pricked out into nursery rows and planted in the flowering site the following year.

Malva alcea
○ ○ ⓨ
A herbaceous perennial from Europe that grows $2\frac{1}{2}-3$ft (75–100cm) high with wide-branching stems, and bears masses of mauve-pink flowers, 2 in (5 cm) across, from early summer to early autumn.

Malva moschata
○ ⊖ ○ ⓨ
A herbaceous perennial from central and southern Europe that reaches 1–2 ft (30–60cm) high, and is an attractive and sturdy border plant. Flowering from midsummer to early autumn, it produces pink to rose-purple blooms. *M. m.* 'Alba' has pure white flowers.

Matteuccia
Aspidiaceae

Probably the most attractive of all garden ferns, it will tolerate a great deal of shade but prefers a sheltered position.
Soil A rich moisture-retaining soil is needed. Poorer soils should have organic material added at planting time.
Propagation Plants are raised by division in spring.

Matteuccia struthiopteris
○ ❀ ⊖ ○
Syn. *Struthiopteris germanica.* A funnel-shaped fern whose outer, infertile fronds resemble those of the male fern but are slightly arched, like ostrich feathers. The fertile fronds are less than half as large.

Matthiola
Cruciferae
Stock, Gilliflower

A genus of annual, biennial and perennial herbaceous plants and sub-shrubs, mostly grown as annuals for bedding or cut flowers. They may also be grown as pot plants.
Soil These plants like a well-manured garden soil containing lime.
Cultivation and propagation Stocks may be divided into four main groups; the spring-flowering or Brompton stocks, the summer-flowering or Ten-week stocks, the autumn-flowering or Intermediate (or East Lothian) stocks, and the winter-flowering stocks. Here we deal with summer-flowering stocks, and also with all-double stocks.

The mallow, *Malva alcea*

Matteucia struthioperis is one of the most beautiful garden ferns

Summer-flowering stocks
These plants must be sown towards the end of February at a temperature of 13–15°C (55–59°F) under glass, or in spring in a sheltered site outdoors. Protect the young seedlings from bright sunlight. Seedlings grown under glass are planted out as soon as they are strong enough to handle. Water regularly during dry spells. Examples of summer-flowering stocks include the 'Excelsior' plants, up to $2\frac{1}{2}$ft (75 cm) high and particularly suitable for cutting, though they require staking; 'Giant Imperial', growing up to 2 ft (60cm); 'Giant Perfection', up to $2\frac{1}{2}$ft (75cm); and 'Mammoth', an 18 in (45cm) type. All are available in mixtures or separate colours.

All-double stocks
A group of stocks that has been developed for the specific purpose of producing double forms. The seedlings themselves will not all bear double flowers, but their colour indicates which particular individuals will, for when they are grown at a maximum temperature of 12°C (53°F), some will be green and the rest light green to yellow. The green individuals will produce single flowers, the yellow individuals, double. Experience has shown that it pays to lower the temperature for 8 to 10 days to 2–4°C (36–39°F) as soon as the seed leaves are fully developed. It is also advisable to keep the temperature at 10–12°C (50–54°F) for the first 10–12 days after potting up. For double cultivars the best results are obtained if they are kept at a temperature that is 3–4 degrees higher than that used to grow ordinary 'Excelsior' stocks.

Matthiola incana
○ ◑ ○ ⓨ ❀
A hardy biennial or short-lived perennial of bushy habit from the Mediterranean. It grows 12–24in (30–60cm) high and, according to the strain, flowers in summer, autumn or winter. The flowers are borne in pyramidal spikes, mostly fragrant, and come in all shades and colours including white, pink, red, blue and yellow.

Meconopsis
Papaveraceae

A genus of hardy herbaceous perennials and biennials with poppy-like flowers.
Cultivation and Soil It does well in semi-shade and in a light fertile soil; it must be watered liberally in summer but may die in moist sites during the winter.
Propagation Sow seeds in spring in a cold frame. Prick out the seedlings into individual pots, harden off and plant out, making sure not to damage the rootball. Plants of some species may also be propagated by division.

Meconopsis betonicifolia
◑ ❀ ❀ ○ ○ ❀
Himalayan blue poppy from Tibet and China. Flowering from early to mid summer, it bears blue flowers, roughly 4 in (10cm) across and slightly nodding. The plants grow $2\frac{1}{2}-3\frac{1}{2}$ft (75–100cm) high.

Meconopsis cambrica
○ ◑ ○ ⓨ ❀
Welsh poppy, a self-seeding plant suitable for borders and larger rock

Stock (*Matthiola incana*)

gardens that grows 1ft (30cm) high and produces yellow flowers from early summer to autumn.

Meconopsis grandis
○ ⊗ ⊛ ⊙ ⊙ ⊘

From Nepal and Tibet, a plant that grows 2½–3ft (75–100cm) high and flowers from late spring to early summer, producing dark blue, 5in (12.5cm) wide, saucer-shaped flowers.

Meconopsis horridula
○ ⊙ ⊙

Syn. *M. prattii*. Like many of the genus, this fine poppy usually dies after flowering. It produces long-oval rosette leaves up to 10in (25cm) in length, covered with spiny bristles. The flowering stem can reach 3ft (1m) in height, carrying 4–8 petalled pale blue, light purple or white flowers in summer.

M. integrifolia
○ ⊙ ⊙

Lampshade poppy. The long narrow rosette leaves are softly hairy, while the 6–36in (15–90cm) stems carry 1–2 long stalked flowers up to 4in (10cm) across, the 6–8 rounded petals being yellow.

Meconopsis napaulensis
○ ⊙ ⊙

Satin poppy, syn. *M. wallichii*. Stems and leaves of this species are bristly or softly hairy, the hairs silky white in some forms, golden in others. The rosette leaves are deeply lobed and up to 20in (50cm) long. The stems can reach a magnificent 6½ft (2m) when well grown, the top third made up of branches of flowers, each 2–3in (5–7.5cm) wide. They are nodding on long stalks and are red, pink, purple, blue or white. They open in summer. Fresh seed must be sown each year as the rosettes, which take 2–3 years to reach flowering size, die afterwards.

Meconopsis prattii, see *Meconopsis horridula*.

Meconopsis quintuplinervia
Harebell poppy, from China and Tibet. A plant growing 1ft (30cm) high with rosettes of softly hairy leaves and solitary, nodding, lavender-blue flowers borne on slender, wiry stalks.

Meconopsis regia
○ ⊙ ⊙

Rather similar to *M. napaulensis* but with narrowly oval rosette leaves and a slightly shorter flowering stem, usually to 5ft (1.5m). The yellow flowers are 2–3in (5–7.5cm) wide and open in summer.

Meconopsis wallichii, see *Meconopsis napaulensis*.

Menyanthes
Menyanthaceae

A fairly uncommon marsh plant that will tolerate water to a depth of 12in (30cm).

Soil Any moist, preferably wet soil is suitable.
Propagation Grow from suckers or division in spring.

Menyanthes trifoliata
○ ○ ○ ⊜ ○

From Asia and Europe, a plant growing 6–16in (15–40cm) high with trifoliate leaves that incline upwards. Star-shaped, white or flesh-coloured flowers appear in late spring to early summer.

The blue *Meconopsis betonicifolia*

Mesembryanthemum
Aizoceae

Two species that strongly resemble each other are here discussed together, although, to be more correct, *M. criniflorum* should be described as *Dorotheanthus bellidiflorus*.

Soil A calcareous soil is needed.
Propagation Sow from January onwards at a temperature of 15°C (59°F) under glass. Prick out into peat pots, harden off slightly in April and plant out when in flower, at the end of May.

Mesembryanthemum criniflorum
○ ⊜ ○ ⊙ ⊗

Livingstone daisy. Syn. *Dorotheanthus bellidiflorus*. A profusely flowering little plant, 2–4in (5–10cm) high, that in midsummer produces blooms in many bright colours. The leaves and stems are covered with gem-like papilli.

Mesembryanthemum crystallinum
○ ⊜ ○ ⊙

A well-known annual that is usually sold as a bedding plant. Leaves and stems are covered with crystal-like papilli, the flowers are white to lemon.

The gnarled stem of a 30-year-old *Metasequoia glyptostroboides*

Mesembryanthemum crystallinum

A young *Metasequoia glyptostroboides*

Metasequoia
Taxodiaceae
Dawn redwood

This tree from China was not rediscovered until 1945. At the time the genus was only known in fossil form, but to everyone's astonishment trees were found still growing in a remote area of China. Since then, this conifer has been introduced to western Europe, where it grows quickly and is very hardy.

Soil It needs a fertile soil which must always be moist.
Propagation Grow from seed when obtainable, otherwise from tip cuttings taken in June and July or heel cuttings in October and November.

Metasequoia glyptostroboides
○ ⊛ ⊛ ⊕

Syn. *Sequoia glyptostroboides*. A tree growing up to 120ft (36m) high in the wild and having a spread of up to 40ft (12m) when fully grown. It bears a superficial resemblance to *Taxodium*. The leaves are light green and opposite, dropping off in autumn together with the short shoots. The cones are small and globular.

Bogbean, *Menyanthes trifoliata*

The yellow flowers are those of a *Mimulus* hybrid

Mimulus
Scrophulariaceae
Monkey flower

A genus of most rewarding garden flowers for planting in large groups in or near the front of the border.

Cultivation Monkey flowers are not reliably hardy, though they will survive most normal winters. It is worth while growing a few specimens in a frost-free frame, which should be aired whenever possible. In that way it will always be possible to propagate enough plants from cuttings or by division to provide masses of large flowers by late spring. If the plants are lifted after flowering, divided and transplanted, if necessary even in the same bed, they will come back into flower soon afterwards. Because they are so easily grown and flower so profusely and for so long, these plants are a valuable addition to any garden, and should be more popular than they currently are. Most nurseries offer a number of attractive cultivars.

Soil These plants do best in fairly moist soil, or even beside pools, and are tolerant of light shade.

Propagation All species are easily raised from seed. Sow seeds in spring in a cold frame or greenhouse. Barely cover the seeds with compost and press down gently. In late spring plant out at distances of 10–12 in (25–30 cm) apart. Plants may also be propagated from cuttings or by division.

Mimulus cardinalis
○ ◐ ⊗ ⊙ ⑦ ⊗

A perennial plant from North America,

sometimes grown as an annual, that reaches a height of 18 in (45 cm), sometimes more. Flowering is from summer to autumn, 10–12 weeks after sowing, when scarlet-red blooms appear.

Mimulus cupreus

A herbaceous perennial plant, often raised as an annual, that grows 10–12 in (25–30 cm) high. From early summer to autumn it produces copper-red to copper-orange flowers, fading to yellow. There are numerous cultivars.

Mimulus hybrids
○ ◐ ⊗ ⊗ ○ ⑦ ⊗

Syn. *M.* × *tigrinus*. The origins of these plants cannot be determined with accuracy, but certainly involve crosses with *M. guttatus* and *M. luteus*. Attractive hybrids in numerous colours are cultivated today, among them 'Major Bees', a 12 in (30 cm) plant with yellow flowers spotted rust; 'Orange Glow', 8 in (20 cm) high, is orange-red.

Mimulus luteus

Monkey flower or musk. A herbaceous perennial from North America that grows to a height of 1 ft (30 cm) and more. It flowers from midsummer to early autumn if sown outside, or from late spring to midsummer if over-wintered in a frame. The most popular cultivar is 'Tigrinus Grandiflorus', with yellow flowers splashed with brown or rust.

Mimulus moschatus
◐ ◐ ⊗ ⊗ ○ ⑦ ⊗ ⊖

Musk. This plant used to be much grown and loved for its scent, which has now disappeared completely. Less attractive than the other species listed above, it is cultivated in the same way as *M. luteus* and bears small yellow flowers from late spring to autumn.

Miscanthus sinensis 'Zebrinus'

Miscanthus
Gramineae

A genus of giant grasses suitable for the garden, alongside streams and around ponds and pools. Most species are hardy and perennial.

Soil Ordinary, moist garden soil is adequate.

Propagation Plants are raised by division or from seeds sown in pots at a moderate temperature. The soil must be very moist and the pots kept lightly shaded until the seedlings emerge.

Miscanthus sacchariflorus

Syn. *Imperata sacchariflora*. A perennial plant growing well over 6 ft (2 m) high and flowering in late summer, but only if the weather is warm. The florescence has a feathery delicate appearance and is mid-green with pale green ribs. 'Variegatus' has its leaves striped white.

Miscanthus sinensis

Syn. *Eulalia japonica*. A perennial plant from China and eastern Asia growing well over 3 ft (1 m) high. Attractive cultivars are 'Gracillimus', with very narrow leaves and a narrow white midrib; 'Zebrinus', with white cross-banding on the leaves; 'Giganteus', a 10 ft (3 m) high plant having broad leaves that droop gracefully at the tip. Sometimes listed under *M. japonicus*, it does not usually flower in Britain, but may do so in early autumn.

Molucella
Labiatae

A genus of four species, one of which is cultivated as a border plant or for cutting.

Soil Any well-drained garden soil will do.

Propagation Plants are raised from seed sown in the open in late spring, or earlier under glass in colder areas.

Molucella laevis
○ ○ ⑦ ⊗

Bells of Ireland; shell plant. Originally from the Middle East, it grows up to 18 in (45 cm) high and is cultivated for its flower spikes, which are made up of many small white flowers, each held within a large, pale green, shell-like calyx. They are pleasantly fragrant and the spikes dry well for winter decoration indoors.

Bergamot hybrids

Monarda
Labiatae
Bergamot

Attractive, sturdy, upright plants for the border. The flowers have a sweet aroma when rubbed between finger and thumb.

Soil A moist, rich garden soil is required.

Propagation By division.

Monarda didyma
○ ◐ ⊗ ⊖ ○ ⑦ ⊗

Oswego tea, bee balm or sweet bergamot. A perennial plant from North America that grows to heights of 2–3 ft (60–100 cm) and flowers from midsummer to early autumn. The scarlet flowers are combined with reddish bracts and are borne in dense whorled heads. 'Cambridge Scarlet' is a brighter coloured cultivar and the commonest monarda in cultivation.

Monarda fistulosa
○ ◐ ⊗ ⊖ ○ ⑦ ⊗

A plant growing 2½–3 ft (75–100 cm) high that bears purple flowers in small numbers. It generally resembles *M. didyma* but grows in drier positions.

Monarda hybrids
○ ◐ ⊗ ⊖ ○ ⑦ ⊗

Crosses between *M. didyma* and *M. fistulosa* that include many attractive forms such as 'Adam', with cyclamen-red flowers, 28 in (70 cm) high; 'Croftway Pink', which has soft pink flowers and grows 32 in (80 cm) high; and 'Prairie Night', which has dark purple flowers and reaches a height of 32 in (80 cm).

Morus
Moraceae
Mulberry

A genus of deciduous trees with spikes of tiny flowers followed by small rounded fruits that are fused together and look rather like loganberries.

Soil A well-drained, fertile but not too dry soil is required.

Propagation Grow from seed, or from hardwood cuttings taken in autumn.

Morus nigra
○ ○ ⊛ ⊗

Black mulberry, from western Asia. A broad-headed, deciduous tree growing up to 33 ft (10 m) high with broadly oval leaves, tiny catkins of greenish flowers and very dark red, juicy fruits.

Familiar garden plants including several compact forms suitable for growing in pots.

Soil These plants thrive on rich garden soil. On moisture-retaining soil they may be given a sunny position, otherwise it is best to plant them in partial shade. *M. palustris* requires moister ground than the other species.

Propagation Sow seeds thinly in boxes or seed beds outdoors in late June or early July. The soil must be kept just moist, using a fine rose. As soon as the seedlings are large enough to handle, prick out into nursery rows. Move young plants to the flowering position in autumn, not later than mid-October, or in spring, planting the more vigorous types 10in (25cm) apart and the less vigorous 6in (15cm) apart.

Myosotis alpestris

Alpine forget-me-not. A neat cushion-forming plant 4–6in (10–15cm) tall with a profusion of bright blue flowers. Several cultivars are available under this name which are mainly compact forms of *M. sylvatica*.

Myosotis dissitiflora

A biennial or perennial plant 1ft (30cm) high, which blooms in spring to early summer, bearing deep blue, very attractive flowers. Protect plants from severe spring frosts. Cultivars include 'Oblongata', which has a compact habit, yellow-green leaves and very large flowers, and 'Perfecta', which has large, deep blue flowers.

Myosotis palustris

Water forget-me-not. An aquatic plant reaching a height of 9in (23cm). Blue flowers appear from June–August.

Myosotis scorpioides, see *M. palustris*.

A white grape hyacinth, *Muscari botryoides* 'Album'

Muscari
Liliaceae
Grape hyacinth

Easily grown, completely hardy bulbous plants that thrive in any garden soil provided it is not too moist.

Cultivation Plant in large clusters from September to December at a depth of about 2in (5cm) and 2in (5cm) apart. They are very suitable for the rock garden (particularly if combined with white saxifrage), for the front edge of the border, and for cutting. Grape hyacinths may be left undisturbed for 3–4 years. The white form is less vigorous and weaker than the blue or purple and should be planted in well-drained soil not later than October. It also needs some winter protection.

Soil Any ordinary garden soil will do, provided it is not too wet in winter.

Propagation Propagation is from offsets planted 1–2in (2.5–5cm) deep in August or at the beginning of September. If planted out too late, they may remain dormant.

Muscari armeniacum

A plant that resembles *M. botryoides*, although the flowers do not protrude so obviously above the leaves, and are darker and larger. 'Blue Spike' has double, pale blue flowers.

Muscari aucheri

Syn. *M. tubergenianum*. This is a more recently introduced species: its leaves lie flat on the ground and it has inflorescences up to 3in (7.5cm) long, lighter in the upper part. The flowers are bright blue.

Muscari botryoides

A species from Europe and the Near East, the most popular of all grape hyacinths, it reaches 6–8in (15–20cm) and flowers in early spring. The species bears blue or violet-blue flowers; those of 'Album' are pure white, and of 'Carneum' soft pink.

Muscari comosum

Nurseries usually offer the cultivar 'Monstrosum' ('Plumosum') (feather hyacinth), which has amethyst inflorescences in the shape of plumes consisting exclusively of sterile branched filaments.

Muscari tubergenianum, see *M. aucheri*.

Forget-me-nots in an attractive urn

Large-cupped narcissi are heralds of the spring

Cyclamineus narcissi 'February Gold'

(1) Trumpet narcissi or daffodils

○ ◐ ◇ ◈ ⊛ ⊗

Large, robust flowers with long trumpet-shaped cups, growing 16–20 in (40–50 cm) high. 'Beersheba' is pure white; 'Dutch Master', pure yellow; 'Golden Harvest', deep golden-yellow; 'Magnet', white with a bright yellow trumpet; 'Mount Hood', white all over; and 'Trousseau', white with a yellow trumpet that turns rose.

(2) Large-cupped narcissi

In this group the cup is longer than the petals but not as long as that of the trumpet types. This division includes 'Carlton', soft yellow; 'Flower Record', yellow with a red cup; 'Fortune', golden-yellow with a very large red cup; 'Mrs R. O. Backhouse', white with a beautiful pink cup; 'Scarlet Elegance', dark yellow with a bright orange-red cup; and 'Semper Avanti', cream with a bright orange cup.

(3) Small-cupped narcissi

These have very small cups and petals in a different colour. The group includes 'Barrett Browning', white with a pure orange cup; 'Birma', golden-yellow with a fierce red cup; 'Edward Buxton', light yellow with a bright orange cup; 'Pomona', white with an apricot-coloured to greenish cup,

Myosotis sylvatica

○ ◐ ≋ ⊙ ⊛ ⊗

This is the common native forget-me-not, a biennial to perennial plant growing 6–20 in (15–50 cm) high. Blue flowers appear in late spring to early summer. There are many cultivars, most of them 4–12 in (10–30 cm) high, and bearing flowers in white, pink, light blue, royal-blue and deep indigo-blue. The dwarf cultivars are sometimes listed under *M. alpestris*.

Narcissus
Amaryllidaceae
Daffodil

Familiar bulbous plants for the garden and indoors, they are also excellent for cutting. The magnificent flowers may be stored in a refrigerator immediately after cutting.

Cultivation Daffodils are easy to grow and may be left undisturbed for years. Because they are known to be strong, however, people tend to treat them unreasonably, planting them in dense shade, not feeding them enough, or mowing the lawn too early and cutting off the leaves in the process. As a result of such maltreatment the flowers may

deteriorate and eventually disappear altogether, particularly on dry, poor soil under shrubs or close to a privet hedge. Those who want to enjoy their daffodils for a long time are advised to choose more satisfactory sites and feed the plants every year with artificial (not natural) fertilizer. If daffodils do deteriorate, they should be replaced with new plants which must then be better fed. Late planting is another common error; early October should be the deadline. Plant 3–4 in (7.5–10 cm) deep and 5 in (12.5 cm) apart. Daffodils grow best in full sunlight and fairly moist soil.

Soil Daffodils like a deep, well-drained but not-too-dry, fertile soil, rich in humus.

Propagation After the daffodils have been established for a few years, they may be lifted in summer when the foliage has died down. Plant some of the old and some of the younger bulbs in the same site and move the rest to another part of the garden. Species can also be grown from seed, but it takes several years before seeds give rise to flowering bulbs. Cultivars do not come true from seed.

The Royal Horticultural Society has grouped these plants in the following divisions:

Short-cupped narcissi combined with *Scilla sibirica*

sometimes with an orange-red edge; and 'Verona', pure white throughout.

(4) Double narcissi
This group includes 'Inglescombe', soft yellow; 'Irene Copeland', snow-white with an orange centre; and 'Texas', yellow with an orange centre.

(5) Triandrus narcissi
○ ◐ ◈ ◈ ◉ ⊛ ⊗
The result of a number of crosses, these have small, ornamental flowers, 1–6 per stem, with back-swept petals, and short, small cups. They grow 6–12in (15–30cm) high. 'April Tears' is soft yellow with a slightly darker cup; 'Silver Chimes' is white with a soft yellow cup; and 'Thalia' is shining white throughout.

(6) Cyclamineus narcissi
Like the previous group, these are the result of a number of crosses. The petals are swept back and the cup is narrow and elongated. They grow 6–10in (15–25cm) high, and flowers appear early, sometimes from the beginning of March. 'Dumplings' is white with a yellow cup, and 'February Gold' has yellow petals with an orange-yellow cup.

(7) Jonquil narcissi
○ ◐ ◈ ◈ ◉ ⊛ ⊗
Narcissi with clusters of small, finely scented flowers. They are slightly sensitive to frost and moist soil, and so are best placed in sheltered sites. There are single and double sorts. Fairly new is the butter-yellow 'Trevithian', which

Jonquil narcissi with flowers in clusters

Narcissus poeticus 'Actaea'

Miniature narcissus 'W. P. Milner'

Tazetta narcissi in front of scillas

is exceptionally hardy and does not need special protection.

(8) Tazetta narcissi
Also known as Poetaz narcissi, these are bunch-flowered narcissi with fairly large blooms borne 5–6 per stem. They include 'Cheerfulness', a double white; the very early 'Cragford', pure white with an orange cup; 'Geranium', white with an orange cup; and 'Scarlet Gem', with golden-yellow petals and a bright red corona.

(9) Poeticus narcissi
Narcissi with narrow strap-shaped leaves, that grow 18in (45cm) high. A particularly attractive strain is 'Actaea', which is white with a small, flattened orange cup edged with bright red.

(10) All species, wild forms and wild hybrids
○ ◐ ◈ ◈ ◉ ⊛ ⊗
This division includes *N. asturiensis* (syn. *N. minimus*), the smallest of all narcissi, up to 4in (10cm) high with yellow flowers; *N. bulbocodium*, syn. *Corbularia bulbocodium*, the hoop petticoat; *N. minor* var. *conspicuus* and *N. lobularis*, the earliest-flowering narcissus, which blooms as early as February, grows 6in (15cm) high and has white petals with a golden-yellow cup; *N. triandrus*, including 'Peeping

Triandrus hybrid 'Silver Chimes'

Nemesia 'Compacta Blue Gem'

Tom', which is 14in (35cm) high, deep yellow with long narrow petals and an elongated cup, and is suitable as a pot plant; and 'W.P. Milner', a small-trumpet narcissus with sulphur-yellow flowers. All these plants are extraordinarily attractive and should be tried in the rock garden.

(11) Miscellaneous narcissi
This group covers any not falling in the previous divisions, among them the recently introduced Collar and Split-corona groups.

Corbularia bulbocodium
○ ◐ ◐ ⊛ ◈ ◈ ◉ ⊛
Syn. *Narcissus bulbocodium*. Hoop petticoat, found by Mediterranean shores. Growing to a height of 4in (10cm), its tiny yellow flowers are very striking provided other plants are not allowed to overshadow it. The bulb offsets must be planted in very shallow soil at a depth of about 1in (2.5cm), preferably in groups of 12–15.

Nemesia
Scrophulariaceae

A genus of exceptionally attractive flowering plants in many colours. If they are dead-headed after the main flowering period is over, they will come back into flower in late summer.

Soil Light, sandy soil is required.

Propagation Sow thinly in late March under glass at a temperature of 16°C (61°F). Prick out into boxes in good time so that the plants do not grow spindly. Seeds may also be sown outdoors at the beginning of May and later thinned to 6–8in (15–20cm) apart. The plants will then flower somewhat later. The usual flowering period, varying according to the method of cultivation, is from the end of June to August.

Nemesia strumosa
○ ○ ⊙ ⊛ ⊗
Nemesias are often sown in mixtures to produce striking combinations. Thus 'Compacta Blue Gem' may be most effectively combined with the white 'Compacta Edelweiss', and both planted in front of the taller 'Prins Van Oranje'. Other cultivars include 'Suttonii', 12–16in (30–40cm) high, with flowers in yellow, red, white, blue and various mixtures of these colours. The smaller cultivars, which are sold as 'Compacta' and grow 8–10in (20–25cm) high, have large flowers.

Nepeta × faassenii may be used as an edging plant

Love-in-a-mist, *Nigella damascena*

Nothofagus antarctica

Nepeta
Labiatae
Catmint

Very attractive edging plants for sunny and fairly dry positions. The plants remain in flower for a long time and if those established for a year are dead-headed they will come back into flower later in the season.

Cultivation Nepetas are hardy and will grow in both sun and partial shade, though growth is more compact in sun. Nepetas do not like being transplanted in autumn; they should be moved in spring, or if necessary in summer.

Soil Any ordinary, well-drained garden soil will do.

Propagation Plants are raised by division, discarding sections with a woody root stock; from cuttings rooted in a cold frame in spring and also from seed sown in spring.

Nepeta × faassenii

○ ⊖ ⊙ ○ ○ ⊙, ⊗

A cross between *N. mussinii* and *N. nepetella*. A compact hybrid perennial plant that flowers from late spring to midsummer and, if dead-headed, will come into flower again in autumn. Lavender-blue flowers are borne in whorls, and the foliage is greyish-green. Since this hybrid is generally propagated by vegetative means and does not produce seeds, it remains in flower for a very long time. It is often confused with the species *N. mussinii*, a comparatively rare plant in gardens. 'Six Hills Giant' is a cultivar with larger flowers and long stems up to 20 in (50 cm) high.

Nepeta macrantha, see *N. sibirica*.
Nepeta mussinii, of gardens, see *N. × faassenii*.

Nepeta sibirica

○ ⊖ ○ ⊙ ⊙ ⊗

Syn. *Dracocephalum sibiricum*, *N. macrantha*. A highly recommended plant that reaches a height of 30 in (75 cm), and has erect stems clothed in dark blue flowers from midsummer to early autumn.

Nerine
Amaryllidaceae

A genus of 20–30 bulbous plants, several of which are grown as greenhouse plants or in the open in mild regions. One species is hardy where soils are not deeply frozen in winter.

Soil A well-drained, fertile soil is required.

Propagation Raise by offsets or seed, which must be sown as soon as it is ripe, usually in May.

Nerine bowdenii

○ ⓘ ⊕ ⊙ ○ ⊙ ⊙

From South Africa, a plant growing 1–1½ ft (30–45 cm) high, its glossy, strap-shaped leaves appearing from early summer until autumn. The trumpet-shaped, rosy-pink flowers are borne in early to mid-autumn in clusters of 6–12 at the top of sturdy, erect stems. 'Fenwick's Variety' is a deeper pink and is more vigorous.

Nicotiana
Solanaceae
Tobacco plant

In gardens we mainly see the annual forms with flowers whose glorious fragrance is most apparent in the evening. It is best planted close to a summerhouse or garden seat, where it may be savoured to the full.

Soil A rich, well-drained soil is required, in a warm, sunny site.

Propagation Sow from March onwards under glass at a temperature of 18°C (64°F), or in April in a cold frame. Prick out into pots, harden off, and plant out in May 10–12 in (25–30 cm) apart.

Nicotiana alata

○ ⊕ ⊙ ⊙ ⊙ ⊗

A tender perennial plant from S. America grown as an annual and attaining about 3 ft (1 m) high. In summer it bears scented flowers with long tubes, greenish outside with violet stripes, and white inside; the flowers only open at night unless planted in shade.

Nicotiana × sanderae

A cross between *N. alata* and *N. forgetiana*. A perennial grown as an annual, reaching 30 in (75 cm) high. If sown early in the year under glass it will flower in early summer and remain in bloom until autumn. Two of the best-known cultivars are 'Crimson Bedder' and 'White Bedder', both 18 in (45 cm) high. Also popular are the so-called 'Daylight Hybrids', which have flowers that stay open in daylight, although not during rain.

Nigella
Ranunculaceae

Annual flowering plants for the garden, including the popular *N. damascena*, love-in-a-mist. Nigella are best grown in small groups in the border. The smaller cultivars make excellent edging plants, the double sorts good pot plants, and the flowers are very good for cutting.

Soil Ordinary fertile garden soil is adequate.

Propagation Plants are easily grown from seed. Sow in the flowering site during March, cover thinly with soil and thin the seedlings to 9 in (23 cm) apart.

Nigella damascena

○ ○ ⊙ ⊗

Love-in-a-mist. An annual plant that grows up to 18 in (45 cm) high and flowers 8–10 weeks after sowing with

The yellow green flowers in the centre are *Nicotiana alata*

light blue or white blooms. The foliage is very finely divided. The most attractive cultivar is 'Miss Jekyll', with large, bright blue double flowers. Also recommended is the more recent 'Persian Jewels', with flowers in shades of purple, blue and pink.

Nothofagus
Fagaceae
Southern beech

A small genus of ornamental, fast-growing evergreen and deciduous trees or large shrubs from South America and Australasia. The species described is completely hardy and takes up little room because of its columnar habit. It is exceptionally decorative, especially in winter.

Soil Plants require an acid soil.
Propagation Grow from imported seed, by layering, or from cuttings taken in summer.

Nothofagus antarctica
○ ◑ ⌀ ❋ ⊞
A tree that does not grow taller than 18 ft (6 m) in European gardens. It has thin, downy twigs and oval, asymmetrical leaves up to 1 in (2.5 cm) long, and the trunk and primary branches are sometimes curiously twisted.

Nymphaea
Nymphaeaceae
Water lily

Cultivation Water lilies like quiet, sheltered ponds and a sunny position. If there is too little sun they will not come into flower. They must have at least 8 in (20 cm) of water, and some species prefer much more, up to 3 ft (1 m).
Soil Plant in baskets of rich loam or good garden soil mixed with bone-meal. Alternatively plant direct into the mud bottom of a natural pond.
Propagation Plants are generally propagated by division in spring. Hardy species may also be grown from seed, but this is rarely done (hybrids do not, of course, come true from seed). The seeds must be kept in water since otherwise they quickly deteriorate. Sow in early spring when the water temperature is not higher than 10°C (50°F). Some seeds will germinate after three weeks; the rest may remain dormant for a year before germinating.

Nymphaea alba
○ ⊗ ○ ⊛
Common white water lily, from Europe. 'Rosea' has crimson flowers and is not quite as robust as the species. 'Rubra' has rose-red flowers. All are hardy.

Nymphaea hybrids
Numerous beautiful hybrids are offered by nurseries. The following are particularly suitable for shallow water: 'Aurora', which has orange-yellow flowers turning dark red; 'Froebelii', a dwarf with star-shaped crimson flowers; 'Laydeckeri Purpurata', a compact plant with very beautiful wine-red flowers; 'Pygmaea Alba', a dwarf with white flowers; 'Rose Arey', which has deep rose flowers; and 'Sioux' with copper-coloured flowers, red at the edges. 'Aurora' and

The beautiful hybrid water lily 'James Brydon'

'Pygmaea Alba' need about 5 sq ft (1.5 sq m) of water surface, the rest about 10 sq ft (3 sq m).

The following are recommended for deeper ponds, with a minimum depth of 20 in (50 cm): 'Colonel A. J. Welch', which has large, deep yellow flowers and needs 25 sq ft (8 sq m); 'Colossea', with very large, orange-red flowers, needing 20 sq ft (7 sq m); 'Escarboucle', with large, dark red flowers, 50 sq ft (15 sq m); 'Gladstoniana', a vigorous grower with extremely large white flowers, 50–100 sq ft (15–30 sq m); 'Marliacea Albida', with large, aromatic white flowers, 20 sq ft (7 sq m); 'Marliacea Chromatella', with large pale yellow flowers and leaves with brown spots, 20 sq ft (7 sq m).

Nymphaea odorata
From North America, a hardy plant

The copper-coloured water lily 'Sioux'

The white hybrid 'Virginalis' is only suitable for larger ponds

with white flowers 5–6 in (12.5–15 cm) across. Specially recommended are *N. o.* 'Gigantea', which bears larger white flowers; *N. o.* 'Rosea', with bright red flowers, and *N. o.* 'Rubra', which has very beautiful dark red flowers.

Oenothera
Onagraceae
Evening primrose

The taller species of *Oenothera* look most beautiful when planted between young shrubs or as highlights in the border, where they remain in flower for a long time. The more compact forms are highly suitable for the rock garden and the front of the border.

Soil Any ordinary, well-drained soil is suitable.

Propagation Plants are raised by division or from seed. To obtain flowers in the same year, the seeds of annuals should be sown in early April in a cold frame. Otherwise sow in the flowering position in spring or summer. Biennials should be sown outdoors June–July, or March–April in a cold frame to produce flowers that same year; such plants do not overwinter well. Do not sow too close together.

Annuals:
Oenothera biennis
This plant is an annual when sown early, and a biennial when sown in summer or autumn. It grows to heights of 1½–5 ft (30 cm–1.5 m) and bears yellow flowers in early summer, midsummer or early autumn.

Oenothera drummondii
An annual or biennial usually growing 1½–2 ft (45–60 cm) high, although *O. d.* var. *nana* is shorter. From early summer to autumn, straw-coloured flowers with a touch of green appear; these measure 3 in (7.5 cm) across.

Perennials:
Oenothera fruticosa
A plant that grows 12–20 in (30–50 cm) high and in summer bears numerous bright yellow flowers in terminal clusters on slender stems. 'Youngii' has very attractive golden-yellow flowers, and those of 'Yellow River', 12 in (30 cm) high, are canary-yellow.

Oenothera missourienses
A plant that grows 6–8 in (15–20 cm) high and is strongly recommended for the rock garden. The very large golden-yellow flowers appear July–October.

Oenothera perennis
A compact perennial or biennial with small yellow flowers, suitable for the border or the rock garden.

Olearia
Compositae
Daisy bush

A large genus of evergreen shrubs with daisy-like flowers. Several will stand moderate frost, but few will survive the continuous day-and-night frost of northern winters.

Soil A well-drained, moderately fertile soil is required.

Propagation Grow from cuttings taken in late summer.

Oenothera fruticosa

Onopordium arabicum

Olearia × haastii
A hybrid of *O. avicennifolia* and *O. moschata* found in the wild in New Zealand. Growing 3–8 ft (1–2 m) high it is a rounded shrub, densely covered with leathery, dark green leaves which are white-felted beneath. In midsummer the bush is covered with clusters of white flowers.

Olearia macrodonta
Growing 3–10 ft (1–3 m) high with a spread of 6–10 ft (2–3 m), this shrub remains attractive all year round with its large, toothed and very shiny leaves, silvery-felted beneath. Its white flowers open in early to midsummer.

Onopordum
Compositae

A genus of annual, biennial and perennial herbaceous plants including one thistle-like plant frequently seen in gardens, where it is usually grown as a stately, impressive, silvery biennial.

Soil It will grow in almost any well-drained soil in a sunny site.

Propagation Sow the seeds in a shaded nursery bed in early summer and transfer to the flowering site in early autumn.

Onopordum nervosum
Syn. *O. arabicum*. A plant growing up to 8 ft (2.4 m) high with elliptical leaves that are irregularly indented, spinous, borne on short stems or sessile, and covered with silvery down; the stems

Ornithogalum umbellatum

are winged and spinous. Light purple flowers open late summer to early autumn. Dead-head the flowers before the seeds ripen or they will spread throughout the garden.

Ophiopogon
Liliaceae
Lily turf

A genus of tufted plants with grassy leaves, many of which are hardy only in areas where frosts are not severe. Those described here will survive low temperature but not continuous freezing.
Soil This should be well-drained but rich in humus.
Propagation Grow from seeds or by division.

Ophiopogon japonicus
A Japanese plant that grows 4–8 in (10–20 cm) high, it is mat-forming and spreads by underground stems. The small white to lilac flowers are borne in clusters and followed by conspicuous, dark blue fruits.

Ornithogalum
Liliaceae
Star of Bethlehem

Exotic and native bulbous plants, suitable for informal gardens and for cutting.
Soil A normal, fairly well-drained garden soil is adequate.
Propagation Sow seeds as soon as they are ripe in a cold frame. Alternatively, lift the bulbs, remove the bulbils and grow them for one or two years in nursery rows until they are ready to produce flowers.

Ornithogalum arabicum
A plant from the Mediterranean region where it flowers as early as May. In Britain it flowers a month later. It is not reliably hardy and requires a very sunny, sheltered position, ideally at the

The royal fern in the autumn. The yellow leaves belong to hostas

foot of a south wall. The white flowers are borne on stout flower stems 1–2 ft (30–60 cm) tall.

Ornithogalum balansae
From Asia Minor, a hardy dwarf growing to a height of 4 in (10 cm) and producing masses of star-shaped white flowers in early spring.

Ornithogalum nutans
A nodding species, ideal for naturalization, it grows up to 1 ft (30 cm) high, and bears pale green flowers with a silky sheen in late spring.

Ornithogalum thyrsoides
Chincherinchee. A bulbous plant from Cape Province, South Africa. Its fleshy leaves are carried almost erect, and the white flowers are borne in late summer in clusters up to 1 ft (30 cm) high. Plant the bulbs at the end of April; they are not hardy and should therefore be lifted fairly early. Plant 5–6 in (12.5–15 cm) apart in a sunny, sheltered position.

Ornithogalum umbellatum
Star of Bethlehem. A hardy bulbous plant that grows 4–12 in (10–30 cm) high and in spring produces flowers that are white on top, green underneath, with white stripes. The flowers open at about 11.00 in the morning. The plant is especially recommended for growing under trees, where it may be left undisturbed for many years. Plant at a depth of 3 in (12.5 cm), and about the same distance apart.

Osmunda
Osmundaceae
Royal fern

A genus of large ornamental ferns which are particularly attractive in spring, when the fronds unfurl, and again in autumn when they colour.
Soil A moist or very wet soil is needed, rich in humus.
Propagation Sow spores directly they are ripe; alternatively, divide the multiple crowns in spring.

Osmunda cinnamomea
Like all other osmundas, this fern makes masses of coarse, fibrous roots. Growing 20–60 in (50–150 cm) high, its fertile inner fronds appear before the sterile outer fronds. They are densely covered with spores, which give them a cinnamon colour, whence the name.

This species is not as popular in gardens as *O. regalis*.

Osmunda regalis
Flowering fern, royal fern. Found universally except in Australasia, this plant grows 28–40 in (70–100 cm) high and has large, bright green, doubly pinnate fronds with yellowish-green, elongated pinnae. The name "flowering fern" arises because the fertile fronds in the centre are covered with masses of spores and turn brown when the latter are shed. 'Gracilis', which is often listed as *O. r. var. gracilis*, comes from North America, is smaller than the species and more graceful.

Pachysandra
Buxaceae

A genus of evergreen creeping plants including one species that looks particularly fine when grown as an edging plant or as ground cover. The plant will always stand out even if the soil is fairly dry and the site heavily shaded.
Soil Plant on humus-rich, not-too-dry soil.
Propagation Division is the simplest method, but this plant may also be grown from cuttings taken in autumn and placed in a cold frame; they may take a very long time to root.

Pachysandra terminalis
A sub-shrub from Japan with leathery, deep green leaves that remain on the stem in winter. It takes several years to reach its maximum height of 1 ft (30 cm). Flowering in spring, when it bears clusters of off-white blooms. 'Variegata' has variegated white leaves. 'Green carpet', a recent addition, is very slow-growing and has shorter branches and smaller leaves than the species.

The royal fern, *Osmunda regalis*, slowly unrolling its leaves

Paeonia
Paeoniaceae
Peony

A genus of herbaceous perennials and shrubs with strikingly beautiful flowers, of which there is space here to describe only the most common. The herbaceous perennials are easily grown, and particularly suitable for borders; they are also excellent for cutting. The shrubby species are more of a challenge to the amateur.

Cultivation and propagation
Herbaceous perennials: Perennial peonies should be planted or transplanted from late summer to early autumn when the foliage is dying back. The soil must be fertile and moist but not wet, and the plants should be left

Paeonia mlokosewitschii

undisturbed for 5–10 years at a time. Peonies should only be transplanted when, despite good care and adequate feeding, there are clear signs of deterioration. Then the crowns should be lifted, the older sections cut off and discarded, and the younger ones replanted. In this process, which is also the best way of propagating the plant, it should be remembered that each section of the crown must have an eye, since otherwise no new growth will be made.

Shrubby or tree species: The young growth of these is sensitive to frost and they should therefore be planted in sheltered positions shaded from the morning sun after night frosts. Increase by layering, cuttings or grafting on to herbaceous rootstocks. Root formation on cuttings and layers may take a long time.

Soil A fertile, moist but well-drained garden soil is needed.

Diseases Peony wilt (*Botrytis paeoniae*) attacks shoots, leaves and flower buds. If the attack occurs in spring, the bases of the stems may rot, and the stems will fall over. If it occurs later in the year, it may be confined to the buds or flowers. Later on the stems may become covered with black spots, but by that time they will have become woody and will no longer fall over. The affected parts eventually become covered with a grey coating; the stems are often brown at the base.

Treatment Do not walk among healthy plants if contact has been made with infected specimens. Remove as many of the infected old stems as possible in autumn and burn them. In spring, soon after the leaves have expanded, treat with Bordeaux mixture,

Paeonia hybrid 'May Morning'

thiram or zireb, and repeat after an interval of 2–3 weeks.

Paeonia albiflora, see *P. lactiflora*.
Paeonia arborea, see *P. suffruticosa*.
Paeonia delavayi
○ ◑ ◐ ◉ ⊛ ⊗
An easily cultivated, hardy shrub from China that grows up to 3 ft (1 m) high. Small, dark purple-red flowers appear in midsummer.

Paeonia lactiflora
○ ◑ ◐ ◉ ⊗
Syn. *P. albiflora*, *P. sinensis*. This species is the main parent of the many cultivars offered as peony hybrids. Since many hundreds have been named (though not all clearly distinct), it is hard to do justice to even the most attractive in the space available. The best known include 'Duchesse de Nemours', 2½–3 ft (75–100 cm) high, white; 'Festiva Maxima', pure white; 'Marie Lemoine', white, sometimes with a red edge; 'Lady Alexandra Duff', large double, pale pink; 'Monsieur Jules Elie', dark pink with a silvery sheen; 'Sarah Bernhardt', deep rose; 'Solange', double, waxy-white flushed buff-salmon to mid-yellow; 'Shirley Temple', double, pale pink ageing white; 'The Moor', single, maroon-crimson; 'Whitleyi Major', single, pure white; and 'White Wings', which is single and white with a striking yellow centre.

Paeonia lutea
◑ ◐ ◉ ⊛ ⊗
From China and Tibet, this shrub grows 4–8 ft (1.2–2.4 m) high and has a similar spread. The leaves are light green and deeply cut, and fragrant, bowl-shaped yellow flowers appear in early summer. *P. l. ludlowi* is the Tibetan form and has larger, finer flowers up to 5 in (13 cm) across.

Paeonia mlokosewitschii
A Caucasian plant that grows up to 2 ft (60 cm) high. The single lemon-yellow flowers appear in spring, followed by attractive seedpods.

Paeonia officinalis
A plant growing 1½–2 ft (45–60 cm) high that flowers as early as late spring. In

the species the flowers are red and the stamens yellow. There are a great many cultivars, few of which are cultivated nowadays because their stems are too weak. Most nurseries still offer 'Alba Plena', white with pink-red buds; 'Rosea Plena', dark purple-rose; and 'Rubra Plena', which has crimson flowers with lighter shadings.
Paeonia sinensis, see *P. lactiflora*.

Paeonia suffruticosa
○ ⊜ ◈ ⊛ ⊗ ⊘
Syn *P. arborea*. A deciduous shrub from China and Japan that grows 2–6 ft (60 cm–2 m) high, and in late spring to early summer bears white to pink flowers, up to 1 ft (30 cm) across, with a magenta blotch at the base of each petal. This species has given rise to numerous cultivars.

Papaver
Papaveraceae
Poppy

Poppies may be divided into three large groups: annuals; herbaceous perennials; and alpines grown as annual, biennials or perennials.

Papaver orientale

One of many garden varieties of *Papaver somniferum*, the opium poppy

Cultivation It is widely believed that poppies must be grown in the full sun, when in fact they can tolerate a great deal of shade. If they are to be used for cut flowers, they should be cut in the morning, just when they have begun to show colour. If the bottom of the stem is flattened or crushed with a small hammer, the flowers will keep longer in water. Perennial poppies are not highly recommended for the border, because shortly after flowering the foliage dies, leaving gaps. However, the gaps may be easily filled with annuals. Poppies make very attractive edging plants for the shrubbery for the back of the lawn.

Soil Poppies thrive in most well-drained types of soil.

Propagation Annuals: Always sow in the flowering position, later thinning out to 12–16 in (30–40 cm) apart. If the

The annual *Papaver rhoeas*

The Iceland poppy, *Papaver nudicaule*

seeds are sown in early spring, the flowers will appear in summer and autumn; if they are sown in autumn, flowers will appear in late spring to early summer.

Perennials: Cultivars are propagated from root cuttings taken from late autumn to early spring, and may also be raised by division in spring.

Annual species include:

Papaver glaucum
○ ◐ ⊖ ⊙ ⊗

Tulip poppy, a plant similar to *P. somniferum* growing 20 in (50 cm) high. Scarlet flowers up to 4 in (10 cm) across, tulip shaped and with black spots at the base, appear in summer. The two outer petals are larger than the inner ones.

Papaver pavoninum
Peacock poppy. Growing 16–32 in

(40–80 cm) high, it blooms in summer with flowers measuring 1–2 in (2.5–5 cm) across, and scarlet in colour with a dark, eye-shaped heart.

Papaver rhoeas
○ ◐ ◉ ⊖ ⊙ ⊗ ⊗

Field or corn poppy, from Europe and Asia. A 1–2 ft (30–60 cm) high plant that from late spring to early summer bears bright red flowers in the wild species; cultivars, both single and double, flower in white, pink, scarlet, scarlet and white, crimson and white, and slate grey. The cultivars do not come true from seed. The old double types such as *P. r.* 'Ranunculiflorum' and *P. r.* 'Japonicum' are rarely seen in modern gardens, having been widely replaced with the large-flowered, single or double 'Shirley' strains.

Papaver somniferum
○ ◐ ◉ ⊖ ⊙ ⊗ ⊗

Opium poppy, from the Middle East. Growing up to 3 ft (1 m) high, these summer-flowering poppies are much larger than those of *P. rhoeas*. Colours range from pure white through red to dark purple, but there is no yellow or clear blue. Carnation-flowered types have fringed petals. The species not only yields opium but also the much less habit-forming poppy seed used by pastry cooks.

Perennials include:

Papaver alpinum
○ ◐ ◉ ⊖ ⊙ ⊗ ⊗

Alpine poppy. A mound-forming perennial that grows 4–8 in (10–20 cm) high with hairless stems. The leaves are bluish-green, and the solitary flowers are white or orange.

Papaver bracteatum
A perennial plant from the Caucasus, Turkey and Iran that flowers in late spring to early summer and is in every respect somewhat larger than and very similar to *P. orientale*, of which it is sometimes considered a variety. The scarlet to blood-red flowers, which have 2 bracts beneath, measure up to 8 in (20 cm) across.

Papaver nudicaule
○ ◐ ⊖ ⊖ ⊙ ⊗

Iceland poppy. A perennial generally grown as a biennial that reaches heights of 1–1½ ft (30–45 cm). The flowering period depends on the method of cultivation and may be in summer or autumn. The best time to sow for flowering the following summer is June–July. Seed sown in March–April will produce flowers that autumn. Seeds germinate within a week and retain their vitality for 3–4 years. Very attractive are 'Gibson's Orange' with tangerine flowers, 16 in (40 cm) high, and 'Cardinal' 16 in (40 cm) high, which has pure red flowers. The 'Kelmscott' strain bears very large flowers in a range of colours.

Papaver orientale
○ ◐ ◉ ⊖ ⊙ ⊗ ⊗

Oriental poppy, from Armenia and the Caucasus. A 2–3 ft (60–100 cm) high plant that flowers in late spring to early summer, and sometimes again in autumn. The blooms are large, up to 6 in (15 cm) across, and mostly carry a black blotch. See comment also under *P. bracteatum*. Attractive cultivars are 'Goliath', scarlet, 3 ft (1 m); 'Marcus Perry', scarlet, 3 ft (1 m); 'Mr Perry', pink, 3 ft (1 m); 'Orange Glow', orange, 3 ft (1 m); 'Perry's White', satin white, 2½ ft (75 cm); and 'Storm Torch', orange-scarlet, 2½ ft (75 cm).

The virginia creeper *Parthenocissus tricuspidata* can easily cover the whole house

Virginia creeper in the autumn

Parahebe
Scrophulariaceae

Low-growing sub-shrubs, with stems that root and form mats.

Soil Any well-drained garden soil will do.

Propagation Plants are raised from cuttings.

Parahebe catarractae
○ ◐ ◉ ⊙ ⊗ ⊛

From New Zealand, this very variable species, growing 6–12 in (15–30 cm) high, is usually mat-forming, with small, leathery, pointed leaves and abundant white to lilac flowers. These are marked with conspicuous faint veining, either pink or purple in colour. 'Delight' has lilac flowers with rich purple veining.

Parahebe lyalii
○ ◐ ◉ ⊙ ⊗ ⊗

From New Zealand, a mat-forming plant with very small oval oblong leaves and white flowers that are lilac to purple flushed and veined. The plant grows 4–6 in (10–15 cm) high.

Parrotia
Hamamelidaceae

A genus of trees containing only one species, grown for its resplendent autumn foliage.

Soil Any moderately fertile soil is adequate.

Propagation Plants are raised by layering, from cuttings or from seed.

Parrotia persica
○ ◐ ◉ ⊙ ⊛ ⊛ ⊙

A tree from Iran and the USSR that grows 25–50 ft (8–15 m) high and is prized for the yellow, orange and red tints that cover its large, oval to oblong leaves in autumn. The bark of older specimens flakes away, showing pink to buff colouring beneath.

Parthenocissus
Vitaceae
Virginia creeper

A genus of beautiful deciduous climbers particularly attractive in autumn thanks to their brightly coloured foliage.

Cultivation Virginia creepers will grow on any wall. After planting, they should be cut back to just above ground level, so that new tendrils can form and attach themselves directly to the wall (with sticky discs). If the old tendrils are left to do the job, the young plants may be pulled away by high winds. Virginia creepers are astonishingly vigorous and fast-growing, and will completely cover a house front up to 30 ft (9 m) high.

Soil Dig a large planting hole, and fill with good garden soil and compost or leaf-mould, well-rotted manure, peat or other suitable material.

Propagation Plants are raised from hardwood cuttings taken in November.

Parthenocissus henryana
Syn. *Vitis henryana*. Chinese virginia creeper, a self-clinging climber with

Paulownia in flower

angled stems and fairly thick leaves consisting of 3–5 leaflets, mostly with white veins, and dark blue berries.

Parthenocissus quinquefolia
Syn. *Ampelopsis quinquefolia*. The true virginia creeper, a self-clinging climber with yellow-green branches. The leaves are made up of 5 coarsely ser-rated leaflets that turn bright red in autumn. 'Engelmannii' is one of the most popular house creepers; it grows very quickly but is coarser and less attractive than *P. tricuspidata* 'Veit-chii'.

Parthenocissus tricuspidata
The original species is rarely seen in gardens, but the cultivar 'Veitchii' (Syn. *Vitis veitchii*) is one of the most attractive self-clinging creepers.

Paulownia
Scrophulariaceae

Young specimens of *P. tomentosa* are often damaged by frost, especially in exposed gardens, but once the plant has survived for several years it will become perfectly hardy.
Soil The soil must contain some lime, which should be added to sandy soil in the form of ground limestone or chalk. The soil should also be well drained and fairly rich.
Propagation Grow from seed in spring or cuttings taken in midsummer.

Paulownia imperialis, see *Paul-ownia tomentosa*.
Paulownia tomentosa
○ ◑ ⊗ ⊛ ⊙ ⊛ ⊥
Syn. *P. imperialis*. A tree or shrub from China and Japan that flowers in late spring. The flower buds, however, begin to form late the previous summer and may be damaged by severe winter frosts. The foxglove-shaped flowers are large and lavender-blue and are borne on erect panicles. The very large leaves, up to 1 ft (30 cm) long, unfurl after the flowers.

Pelargonium
Geraniaceae
Geranium

A genus of mainly tender sub-shrubs, suitable for growing indoors, in green-houses and for summer bedding. Zonal pelargoniums are frequently known as geraniums and should not be confused with the genus *Geranium*. The plants range in height from 2–6 ft (1–3 m), depending on the variety.
Propagation Pelargoniums are gener-ally propagated from tip cuttings over-wintered in a frost-proof place. More recently the introduction of F_1 hybrids has also made it possible to grow pel-argoniums from seed. 'Carefree' hy-brids in various shades of red, pink, salmon-pink and scarlet, and also in white, were raised in the United States; the first European F_1 hybrids are called 'Sprinter' and range from orange to scarlet. Plants sown in late January may flower as early as April, but usually need the touch of a professional gar-dener. Amateurs should sow the seeds at a temperature of 16–18°C (61–64°F) in peat pots and not harden off the seedlings until the end of April. The plants will then come into flower in about the middle of June. Seeds are very expensive and the choice of cul-tivars is still very small, so that the old method of overwintering cuttings taken August–September to flower in May is likely to be with us for quite some time to come.

Peltiphyllum peltatum

Peltiphyllum
Saxifragaceae
Umbrella plant

A genus of one attractive flowering and foliage plant for moist and sunny or shaded positions.
Soil A moist, fairly rich soil is needed.
Propagation Grow by division or from seed.

Peltiphyllum peltatum
○ ◑ ◍ ⊗ ○ ⊛ ⊛ ⊥
A North American plant that grows $1\frac{1}{2}$–3 ft (45–100 cm) high and flowers in spring, before the leaves unfurl. Masses of purple-pink flowers are borne on long stems. The green leaves are large, shield shaped and glossy, turning red in autumn.

Pennisetum
Gramineae

A genus of annual and perennial grasses of great ornamental appeal.
Soil Any ordinary garden soil is usually adequate. It should be well drained and not too heavily manured. Pennisetums must be watered regularly, and amply during prolonged dry weather.
Propagation Plants are raised by div-ision or seeds in spring.

Pennisetum alopecuroides
○ ◑ ◍ ⊗ ○ ⊛ ⊛ ⊥ ⊗
From E. Asia to Australia, a plant growing to 3 ft (90 cm) or more high with linear, gracefully arching leaves. The inflorescences, resembling old-

Pelargonium growing in pots during the summer

Pennisetum alopecuroides

fashioned candle-snuffers, do not appear until late summer or early autumn, and continue to look attractive until winter. This species is not reliably hardy.

Pennisetum orientale
A clump-forming plant with gracefully arching stems and with leaves 2–3 ft (60–90 cm) long. The inflorescences are like squirrels' tails and are often rose tinted.

Penstemon
Scrophulariaceae

This genus includes several very attractive perennial border plants that, unfortunately, are not reliably hardy. The snapdragon-like flowers are borne on graceful stems and keep for a long time in water, which makes them excellent for cutting.

Soil Penstemons like humus-rich, well-drained soil. They are intolerant of wet conditions. Plant in a sunny position.

Propagation Penstemons can be propagated by division, from cuttings and from seed. See also under *Penstemon* hybrids.

Penstemon hybrids

Penstemon barbatus
○ ⌒ ⌒ ○ ⊗ ⊗
Syn. *Chelona barbata*. A perennial from Mexico north to the mountains of Utah that will grow to heights of 2–5 ft (60–150 cm) and flowers from early summer to autumn. Tubular, crimson flowers are borne on long racemes. This is the hardiest garden species, but it, too, requires some protection in hard winters.

P. davidsonii menziesii
○ ⌒ ⌒ ○ ⊗ ⊗
A perennial from the north-western United States that grows 4–10 in (10–25 cm) high, and in midsummer produces pale violet-purple flowers, 1–2 in (2.5–5 cm) long. This species is highly recommended for the rock garden.

Penstemon × gloxinioides, see *Penstemon* hybrids.

Penstemon hartwegii
Syn. *P. gentianoides*. Not a reliably hardy plant, unlike the hybrids raised from it; see *Penstemon* hybrids.

Penstemon heterophyllus
A Californian species, becoming woody at the base. It is from 1–2 ft (30–60 cm) in height and the long narrow leaves are green or blue-green. The 1½ in (4 cm) long flowers range from blue to purple.

Penstemon hirsutus
A perennial plant with glandular hairs. It grows 8–28 in (20–70 cm) high, and in summer bears clusters of flowers with reddish-mauve petals. The leaves are mid-green and lanceolate.

Penstemon hybrids
○ ⌒ ⌒ ○ ⊗
Syn. *P.* × *hybridus*, *P.* × *gloxinioides*. This is the penstemon usually sold by florists. The group includes a number of crosses between *P. hartwegii*, *P. cobaea* and others. Flowering from summer to autumn, the blooms come in a great variety of colours and shades.

The crimson berries of *Pernettya mucronata*

The stiff and finely branching habit of *Perovskia atriplicifolia*

Gardeners distinguish between compact types growing 12–16 in (30–40 cm) high and taller ones. They not only make attractive garden plants, particularly when seen in large groups, but the more compact types also make valuable pot plants. They thrive on fairly moist soil and, on drier ground, should ideally be planted in such a way that they are lightly shaded during the middle of the day. None of these hybrids are reliably hardy. They are easily grown from seed, unless a particular colour is required, when they should be grown from cuttings. The cuttings root very quickly in late summer and must be overwintered in a cold frame. Pot up February–March into fairly large pots and plant out in the middle of May. Seedlings are generally raised as biennials, i.e. under glass, and allowed to flower the following year. Among the best-known types are 'Schoenholzeri' (syn. 'Firebird'), large, dark red, and 'Sweet Chiffon', which is available in various pastel shades. 'Sensation', with large flowers in various colours, is highly recommended for annual cultivation. Sow in April in boxes at 13–18°C (55–64°F), prick out into pots and plant out towards the end of the month. Penstemons grown as biennials are more floriferous than those grown as annuals.

Penstemon menziesii, see *P. davidsonii menziesii*.

Pernettya
Ericaceae

A genus of hardy, evergreen shrubs for the garden and for indoor cultivation. The fruiting branches make attractive winter decoration.

Cultivation Plant male forms close to females to ensure fruiting.

Soil These sub-shrubs are related to heathers and must be grown in lime-free soil, preferably in moist, peaty loam.

Propagation Cultivars can only be propagated from suckers removed in autumn or winter, or by cuttings in late summer or autumn. The species are easily grown from seed.

Pernettya mucronata
○ ⌒ ⌒ ⌒ ※ ⊗ ⊗
A beautiful, low-growing, evergreen shrub from Chile that grows 20–24 in (50–60 cm) or more high and has small, glossy, dark green leaves. Attractive white, pink or red fruits, the size of marbles, are borne from late summer until winter. The white urn-shaped flowers appear May–June. Cultivars include 'Crimsonia', with large crimson berries; 'Lilian', light purple; 'Pink pearl', light pink; 'Signal', deep red; 'Snow White', white with pink dots; and 'Wintertime', which has pure white berries.

Perovskia
Labiatae

Beautiful, completely hardy, aromatic border plants for sunny positions. Perovskias thrive on dry ground. It is not advisable to transplant the older specimens.

Soil A well-drained, light soil is required.

Propagation Plants are raised from seed or from 3 in (7.5 cm) long cuttings of lateral shoots with a heel taken in mid- to late summer.

Perovskia atriplicifolia
○ ⊖ ⌒ ○ ⊗ ⊗
A herbaceous border plant or semi-shrub of erect habit from the Himalayas. It grows to a height of 3–4½ ft (1–1.5 m) and flowers late summer to early autumn, bearing violet-blue flowers in long panicles. The leaves are grey-green.

Petunia
Solanaceae

Glorious annual herbaceous plants for window boxes, tubs, hanging baskets, beds and the edges of the border. The flowers appear in summer and last for a long time, particularly if occasionally fed with liquid (artificial) fertilizer. Flowers are available in white, yellow, rose, violet, mauve, red, blue and bi-coloured, and in a variety of different shapes. Some are single, others double, some have smooth edges, and others are toothed or fringed.

Cultivation Petunias thrive best in sheltered sunny sites, but are surprisingly tolerant of a British summer.

Soil A humus-rich, well-drained soil is preferred.

Propagation Generally they are grown from seed, but certain cultivars can also be propagated from cuttings taken in summer. This used to be the practice with the double sorts, but nowadays gardeners prefer the recently developed doubles, a large percentage of which come true from seed. Sow from the middle of February (for very early flowering) until May. Up to April

A striped Petunia hybrid

Not all the hybrids of *Philadelphus* are scented

the seeds must be sown at a temperature of 15°C (59°F) under glass. The seedlings are pricked out into peat pots, hardened off and planted out (after April the seeds may be sown in the flowering position). Seeds sown in February will produce flowers in May; seeds sown in March will give flowers in June, etc.

Petunia hybrids

○ ◑ ⊛ ⊙ ⊗

Originally raised from crosses between *P. axillaris*, *P. inflata* and *P. violacea*, they have since been repeatedly inter-bred. The numerous cultivars can be subdivided into several groups, most of which are cultivated almost exclusively in the form of F₁ hybrids. Nearly all are more floriferous, weather-resistant and more shapely than the original types.

Group 1 *Multiflora*. Bushy plants growing 6–12 in (15–30 cm) high, with flowers 2 in (5 cm) across.

Group 2 *Grandiflora*. Plants similar in size to Group 1 but with fewer and larger flowers which measure 3–4 in (7.5–10 cm) across. Single and double strains are available, and both Groups 1 and 2 include types with carnation-like flowers.

Group 3 *Nana compacta*. Dwarf plants 6 in (15 cm) high with flowers measuring 2 in (5 cm) across.

Group 4 *Pendula* varieties. Plants with a long trailing habit that bear flowers measuring 2 in (5 cm) across.

It is difficult in a book of this kind to give even a brief summary of the cultivars available because every year nurserymen introduce new improvements. When crossing petunias they pay particular attention to weather resistance, but unfortunately their most beautiful products are not always the hardiest, and vice versa. In fact many F₁ hybrids have garish colours that reduce their appeal. Most new strains have come from the United States, and the striped and star-shaped among them have proved to be particularly popular. There are various colour combinations in the *Multiflora* and *Grandiflora* groups. The small-flowered cultivars are the sturdiest; next come the large-flowered sorts, while the double-flowered are the least resistant.

Petunias are highly suitable for growing in pots and barrels

Philadelphus
Saxifragaceae
(Philadelphaceae)
Mock orange

Popular flowering shrubs with a most attractive fragrance. The various species and strains differ considerably in habit, and care is needed when planting.

Cultivation Philadelphus is very tolerant of shade. Old plants tend to grow thin bottomed and bear smaller flowers, and regular pruning is advisable. All old wood should be thinned out after flowering.

Soil It does well in any ordinary garden soil.

Propagation Plants are raised from cuttings, which can be taken in summer or winter.

Philadelphus coronarius

○ ◐ ⊕ ⊘ ⊛

A shrub from Europe and S. W. Asia that grows up to 10ft (3m) high. The white flowers have a lovely fragrance and appear in late spring to early summer.

Philadelphus grandiflorus, of gardens, see *P. pubescens*.

A *Philadelphus* hybrid

Philadelphus hybrids

Plants raised from various unspecified crosses and also from crosses with *P. coronarius*, *P. cymosus* and *P. lemonei*. Catalogues usually place these together. Most hybrids have peeling branches and large, often double, flowers. Some of the best cultivars are 'Avalanche', arching habit and a profusion of blossom; 'Belle Etoile', a robust shrub with single white flowers flushed maroon at the centre; 'Dame Blanche', a low shrub with creamy-white fringed, semi-double flowers; 'Innocence', a low shrub with variegated yellow leaves and white, semi-double flowers; 'Lemonei', with single, white, fragrant flowers; 'Manteau d'Hermine', a low shrub with large, pure-white, double flowers; 'Sybille', large flowers, the basal half of each petal stained rose-purple; and 'Virginal', a robust shrub whose flowers are semi-double, white and fragrant. It should be remembered, however, that not all cultivars are fragrant.

Philadelphus microphyllus

○ ◐ ⌃ ⌃ ⓦ ⊘ ⊕ ⊗

A not-so-hardy shrub reaching heights of 3–4ft (1–1.2m) and producing fragrant white flowers in early to mid-summer. See also *P. × purpureomacu-*

The annual *Phlox drummondii*

latus hybrids.

Philadelphus pubescens

○ ◐ ⓦ ⓦ ⊘ ⊕ ⊗

Syn. *P. grandiflorus* of gardens. A shrub from North America that grows 15ft (5m) high and in midsummer produces large, fairly flat, white flowers.

Philadelphus × purpureomaculatus

A group of hybrid shrubs 4–5ft (1.2–1.5m) high that has oval leaves and small clusters or solitary white flowers, about 1in (2.5cm) across, with a wine-red blotch at the base.

Phlomis
Labiatae

Mainly low-growing shrubs and sub-shrubs that have densely hairy foliage.

Soil Any well-drained soil in a sunny site will do.

Propagation Plants are grown from cuttings in autumn or from seed sown in spring.

Phlomis fruticosa

○ ○ ⓦ ⊘ ⓦ ⊘ ⊛

Jerusalem sage, which comes from the Mediterranean. A useful, grey-leaved

Phlox paniculata hybrids

shrub that reaches heights of 3–4ft (1–1.2m) and flowers in late spring to mid-summer. It produces whorls of yellow tubular flowers above the leaves, and is hardy in all but severe winters.

Phlox
Polemoniaceae

A genus of herbaceous perennials, annuals and sub-shrubs with unusually bright flowers. *P. drummondii* is a well-known and favourite annual; *P. amoena*, *P. divaricata* and *P. subulata* make excellent spring-flowering perennials, while *P. paniculata* is the ever-popular summer- and autumn-flowering border phlox.

Soil While phlox will make do with poor soil, it will only produce large flowers in well-dug ground kept adequately moist and enriched every year with fertilizer.

Propagation Grow annual species from seed sown in a warm frame in February and March, in a cold frame in April, or in the flowering position in May, thinning the seedlings to 6in (15cm) apart. Plants from seeds sown in a frame should be set out in late May

in soil that is fertile but has not been recently treated with fresh stable manure. Choose a sunny position and space out at 6–8in (15–20cm) apart. The seedlings are intolerant of cold, and seed sown in a warm frame produces the best plants. Perennials may be propagated by division, from cuttings or from seed.

Phlox amoena

○ ◐ ⊜ ⌃ ○ ⓨ ⊗

A perennial from North America that grows 6–12in (15–30cm) high and in late spring to early summer bears purple, light red or white flowers. This species needs well-drained soil, and is best planted on slopes or in the rock garden.

Phlox arendsii hybrids

○ ◐ ⊘ ○ ⊗

Perennials that are raised from crosses of *P. divaricata* var. *laphamii* and *P. paniculata* hybrids, and show mixed characteristics. They grow to a height of 16–24in (40–60cm).

Phlox canadensis, see *P. divaricata*. *Phlox decussata*, see *P. divaricata* hybrids.

Phlox divaricata

○ ◐ ○ ⓨ ⊗

A perennial from North America that reaches 6–10in (15–25cm), occasionally more. In late spring to early summer it bears violet to lavender flowers. It likes a fairly moist soil and is suitable for rock gardens and the front of borders.

Phlox drummondii

An annual from Texas that grows 8–20in (20–50cm) high and has a very long flowering period that begins 8–10 weeks after sowing. Flowers are red in the species and in different colours in the cultivars and look well when sown in mixtures. Catalogues usually list the species together with three groups of cultivars, namely Stellaris, syn. Cuspidata, which has star-shaped flowers and includes the popular 'Twinkle', with its variously coloured flowers; the large-flowered Grandiflora group, up to 12in (30cm) high, and the floriferous Nana Compacta group up to 9in (23cm) high.

Phlox paniculata hybrids

○ ◐ ○ ⓨ ⊗

Syn. *P. decussata*. A perennial from North America that reaches a height of 2–4ft (60–120cm) and flowers from midsummer to early autumn. This is the most popular phlox for the border or shrubbery, and comes in a large variety of colours and sizes and different flowering periods. When combining the various colours, care should be taken to separate groups with orange and scarlet flowers from groups with pink, purple and violet flowers; the white strains can be used to form a transition between the two groups.

Phlox subulata

○ ◐ ○ ⓨ ⊗ ⊖

Moss or mountain phlox. A perennial from North America reaching 2–6in (5–15cm) high that is suitable for the rock garden and as ground cover. Flowering from spring to early summer, it bears small purple-pink flowers with a dark centre in clusters of 2–4. From the many cultivars we recommend 'G. F. Wilson', gentle lavender-blue; 'Moerheimii', which has pink flowers; 'Temiscaming', with magenta-red flowers; and 'White Delight', pure white. All grow 4in (10cm) high.

Phlox subulata, a perennial for the rock garden

Phyllitis scolopendrium, hart's tongue

Physostegia
Labiatae
Obedient plant

Late but long-flowering plants for the border that are also excellent for cutting.
Soil They thrive in fertile, well-drained soil that must be kept moist, especially in summer.
Propagation Plants are raised by division or seeds.

Physostegia virginiana

○ ⌒ ⌒ ○ ⊙ ⊗

Obedient plant. A perennial plant from North America reaching heights of 2–4ft (60–120cm), and from midsummer to early autumn producing light rose-purple flowers with four vertical rows to each spike. The best cultivars are the very hardy 'Rose Bouquet', 3ft (1m) high, with rose-pink flowers; 'Summer Snow', 28in (70cm) high, with snow-white flowers; and 'Vivid', a $1\frac{1}{2}$–2ft (45–60cm) plant with bright deep lilac-pink flowers.

Picea
Pinaceae
Spruce

A genus of evergreen coniferous trees widespread across the Northern Hemisphere. There are many cultivars, including dwarfs for the rock garden. *P. abies* and *P. glauca* make good, if rather broad, hedges and windbreaks. For ways in which this genus differs from *Abies*, see under the latter.
Soil Spruces thrive in preferably acid to neutral, moist soil.
Propagation Raise from seed sown in spring. Cultivars may be grafted, or grown from cuttings.
Pests and diseases Spruces are attacked by many pests and diseases but perhaps the worst enemies are spruce adelgids (conifer gall lice and conifer woolly aphids); some secrete a white waxy substance, others form galls, and all stunt and weaken the trees, often causing premature leaf fall.

Picea abies

○ ⬭ ⬭ ⬭ ⚘ ⊛ ⌖

Syn. *P. excelsa*. Norway spruce or Christmas tree, a tree native to Europe that grows up to 60ft (13m) or more

Phytostegia virginiana 'Summer Snow'

Phyllitis
Aspleniaceae

A genus of ferns suitable for growing indoors as well as in the garden.
Soil Plant in humus-rich soil containing lime. It will also grow on walls.
Propagation By division or spores in spring.

Phyllitis scolopendrium

◗ ◐ ⊛ ⌒ ○ ⊘ ⊛

Syn. *Asplenium scolopendrium, Scolopendrium vulgare*. Hart's-tongue. A fern native to Europe that has strap-shaped fronds up to 16in (40cm) long and 2in (5cm) wide; these are pointed at the tip, heart-shaped at the base, leathery and glossy green. They remain green in winter and stay on the plant until they are replaced with fresh fronds in spring. There are many cultivars, but those with branched or crested fronds are less vigorous. 'Crispum' has frilled frond margins and 'Cristatum' has the tips of the fronds divided into crests and tassels.

The compact form of the Norway spruce, *Picea abies* 'Compacta', can attain an enormous spread

high with a spread of 20ft (7m). The hairless branches are reddish-brown and resinous, and bear brown, non-resinous buds; the needles, 1in (2.5cm) long, grow in two distinct rows on the underside of the branches; they are pointed and shiny dark green in colour, though on poorer soil may take a yellowish tinge. There are numerous cultivars, and of the taller kind the attractive 'Inversa' compels mention: growing 30–60ft (9–18m) high, its branches are first depressed against the stem, and later creep across the ground. More compact cultivars include 'Clanbrassiliana', a dense, flat-topped bush about 3ft (1m) high; 'Compacta', with a broad conical habit; 'Gregoryana Veitchii', a cushion-forming version; 'Maxwellii', which has a broad conical habit and orange-brown branches; 'Merkii', which has a broad pyramidal habit; 'Nidiformis', growing 3ft (1m) high with a similar spread, its shape suggesting the presence of a nest in the centre; 'Ohlendorfii', with very short light green needles and a pyramidal habit; 'Procumbens', 3ft (1m) high and up to $4\frac{1}{2}$ft (1.3m) wide, with horizontal branches; and 'Repens', a low, wide-spreading bush that makes excellent ground cover.

Picea pungens 'Koster'

Picea alba, see *P. glauca*.
Picea breweriana
Brewer's weeping spruce. An exceptionally beautiful spruce from South-West Oregon capable of reaching a height of 100ft (30m) and a spread of up to 20ft (7m). Curtains of branchlets, covered with blunt, flattened needles, are suspended from spreading branches. This species likes a great deal of moisture.
Picea engelmanii
Engelmann spruce. A not very well-known but extremely attractive conical conifer with greyish-blue needles that give off an unpleasant aroma when rubbed between the fingers. The attractive reddish-green cones later change to light brown. *P. e.* 'Glauca' has steel-blue needles.
Picea excelsa, see *P. abies*.
Picea glauca
○ ◑ ◐ ⊖ ⟳ ⊛ ✳ ⊥

Syn. *P. alba*. The white or Canadian spruce, growing up to 80ft (25m) high with a spread up to 16ft (5m). The long, thick branches are hairless, reddish-brown and slightly glaucous. The forward-lying bluish-green needles give off an unpleasant pungent smell when bruised. This is a very hardy species useful for planting in cold,

Picea breweriana can be distinguished by its curtains of shoots

windy positions. *Picea g. albertiana* 'Conica' has a perfect conical shape, seldom exceeds 6ft (2m), and has light green needles, while 'Echiniformis' is a very small, spherical shrub with short, bluish-green needles.
Picea hondoensis, see *P. jezoensis* var. *hondoensis*.
Picea jezoensis
○ ◑ ◐ ⌒ ⟳ ⊛ ✳ ⊥

Yezo spruce. A medium-sized to large tree, up to 80ft (25m) high and spreading to 18ft (6m), that originated in Japan and China. It has a broadly pyramidal habit and produces its cones very early. The cultivar usually seen is *P. jezoensis* var. *hondoensis* (syn. *P. hondoensis*), which has a broadly conical habit. This tree is not reliably hardy.
Picea mariana
Syn. *P. nigra*. Black spruce. A tree from northern U.S.A. and Canada of narrowly conical habit which can grow to a very great height. 'Nana', a dwarf version, is only 12–16in (30–40cm) and is very slow-growing and suitable for rock gardens. It has a globular shape, greyish-blue needles and is most attractive.
Picea nigra, see *P. mariana*.
Picea omorika
○ ◑ ◐ ⟳ ⊛ ✳ ⊥

Syn. *Pinus omorika*. Serbian spruce, a tree from Yugoslavia, where it can attain heights of over 100ft (30m). In gardens it rarely exceeds 90ft (27m) and a spread of 15ft (5m). The branches are densely covered with brownish hair, and the needles are blunt with broad white bands on the underside. The cones are bluish-black. 'Nana', $4\frac{1}{2}$ft (1.3m) high, has its needles arranged in whorls.

Picea orientalis
○ ◑ ◐ ⟳ ⊛ ✳ ⊥

Oriental spruce, from Asia Minor. A slow-growing tree reaching a height of 75ft (23m) and a spread of 18ft (6m), with branches covered in short hairs and cones that turn from purple when young to brown. The needles are short, blunt and dark green. This densely branched species is very wind-resistant, and makes an attractive specimen tree, though it tends to outgrow most gardens. A smaller cultivar is 'Aurea', up to 30ft (9m) high; its young branches are golden yellow, and later turn green.

Picea pungens
○ ◑ ◐ ⟳ ⊛ ✳ ⊗

Colorado spruce, from south-western United States. A tree growing to a height of 100ft (30m) with a spread of

Picea glauca albertiana 'Conica'

Picea omorika, the Serbian spruce

18ft (6m). Fairly fast-growing, it has hairless, shiny orange-brown branches and sharp, bluish-green needles. The best-known cultivar, usually grown as a specimen tree, is 'Glauca', the blue spruce, a conical tree with glaucous needles capable of reaching up to 60ft (18m). 'Globosa', a dwarf cultivar that grows up to 4ft (1.2m) high and has a spread of up to 3ft (1m), bears glaucous needles and is suitable for the rock garden; 'Hoopsii' is an excellent small to medium-sized conical tree with silvery-blue needles; 'Koster', another conical tree, can reach a height of 30ft (9m), and has bluish-green needles; 'Moerheim' resembles the last but has longer needles, and 'Prostrata', though it grows no taller than 3ft (1m), has a spread of up to 15ft (5m) and blue needles.

Picea sitchensis

○ ◐ ⊗ ⊛ ⊛ ⊕

Sitka spruce. A quick-growing tree from the north-western United States with a height of up to 100ft (30m) and a spread of 18ft (6m). It has hairless, yellowish-brown branches, pointed, non-resinous cones, and very sharp needles borne in whorls.

Pieris
Ericaceae

A genus of hardy evergreen flowering shrubs with flower panicles that form in autumn. Several species have attractive red-tinged buds which make them stand out in winter. The young leaves may also be red or bronze, and so add to the striking appearance of these shrubs.
Soil Pieris thrives on well-drained but not dry lime-free soil enriched with acid leaf-mould or peat.
Propagation Raise from seeds sown in a cold frame. *P. japonica* may be propagated from cuttings taken in late summer.

Pieris floribunda

○ ◐ ⊗ ⊛ ⊛

Syn. *Andromeda floribunda*. A spring-flowering evergreen shrub from North America reaching a height and a spread of up to 3ft (1m). White flowers are borne in erect panicles. This early, profusely flowering and very hardy plant is most suitable for smaller gardens.

Pieris formosa var. forrestii

○ ◐ ⊗ ⊛ ⊛

A shrub from western China that flowers in spring and grows up to 4½ft (1.3m) high. The bright red young foliage is extremely attractive, especially in the cultivars 'Wakehurst' and 'Jermyns'. 'Forest Flame' is an exceptionally hardy hybrid with the next species.

Pieris japonica

○ ◐ ⊗ ⊛ ⊛ ⊕

Syn. *Andromeda japonica*. Unlike *P. forrestii*, this shrub has drooping pan-icles and more divergent branches. It grows slightly taller, and is more attractive in bloom.

Pinus
Pinaceae
Pine

A well-known genus of evergreen conifers easily identified by their long needles arranged in groups of 2, 3 or 5.
Soil Pines like a neutral to acid soil, but most species will tolerate some lime and a fair degree of drought.
Propagation Grow the species from seed sown in spring. Cultivars should be propagated by grafting or from cuttings.

Pinus austriaca, see P. nigra.
Pinus cembra

○ ⊗ ⊖ ⊛ ⊛ ⊕

Arolla pine, Swiss stone pine. A tree that in the wild grows up to 100ft (30m) high, with a spread of 24–30ft (8–9m), but in gardens is rarely taller than 40ft (12m). Young shoots are clothed in orange-brown hairs, and the cones are pointed and resinous, while the needles come in groups of five and are 2–5in (5–12.5cm) long with bluish-white stripes. This species, although it will put up with less favourable conditions, generally requires a great deal of space and grows best in loamy, not too heavy, fairly moist soil.

Pinus densiflora

○ ⊖ ⊖ ⊛ ⊛ ⊕

Japanese red pine. A slow-growing tree with an umbrella-shaped crown that reaches heights of 75–100ft (23–30m). 'Umbraculifera' has a height and spread of up to 10ft (3m) and dark green, twisted needles.
Pinus excelsa, see P. wallichiana.
Pinus griffithii, see P. wallichiana.
Pinus maritima, see P. pinaster.

Pinus mugo

○ ⊖ ⊖ ⊛ ⊛ ⊛

Syn. *P. montana*. Mountain pine. A tree reaching heights of 15–30ft (5–9m), or, more usually, a lower-growing shrub with hairless brown branches, reddish-brown, resinous buds and very dark green needles. Especially recommended for the smaller garden are ssp. *mugo* and ssp. *pumilio*, both with a prostrate habit. *Pumilio* will grow to a height of 5ft (2m) and has a spread of up to 10f (3m).

Pinus nigra

Syn. *Pinus austriaca*. Black or Austrian pine. A tree growing up to 120ft (40m) high, with a spread of up to 25ft (8m). It has hairless, yellow-brown branches; light brown resinous buds, and dark green 4–6in (10–15cm) prickly needles, borne in pairs. It is the best pine for windy places. *Pinus nigra* var. *maritima*, the Corsican pine, has bright green needles and a less dense form. 'Pygmaea' is a very slow grower, reaching a height of 10ft (3m) and has dull green needles which turn yellow in the winter.

Pinus omorika, see Picea omorika.
Pinus parviflora

○ ⊖ ⊛ ⊛ ⊕

Japanese white pine. A tree that grows

Pieris japonica 'Variegata

Pieris forrestii which is vulnerable to late spring frosts

A well grown pine makes a fine background for the garden

pointed and somewhat resinous, and the glossy dark blue-green needles are borne in groups of 5. This tree is especially recommended for city parks as it is very resistant to atmospheric pollution. It likes fairly moist soil, and grows vigorously, but does not usually live to a great age. 'Radiata' (syn. 'Nana') is a dwarf form.

Pinus sylvestris

○ ⊖ ✳ ⚘

Scots pine. A tree that grows up to 100ft (30m) high with a spread of up to 30ft (9m), and an umbrella-shaped crown. The branches are hairless and yellowish-grey, the buds are oblong-ovoid and non-resinous, and the needles are bluish-green. This species is extensively planted in afforestation schemes. Compact types include 'Aurea', up to 18ft (6m) high, a slow-growing tree that is green in summer and bright gold-yellow in winter; 'Beuvronensis', 3ft (1m) high with a spread of up to 10ft (3m), a well-known dwarf pine, very compact during its first two years, and 'Watereri', a spherical, bluish-grey tree that grows up to 20ft (7m) high.

Pinus wallichiana

○ ⊖ ✳ ✳ ⚘ ⊥

Syn. *P. excelsa* and *P. griffithii*. Bhutan pine. One of the most beautiful of all the pines, it grows up to 80ft (25m) high with a spread of up to 20ft (7m). It has hairless, glaucous branches and conical, resinous buds. The needles are 5–7in (12.5–18cm) long and have white stripes.

Pittosporum
Pittosporaceae

Most of the members of this genus are suitable only for light, frost-free areas, but the species described here will withstand all but those winters having continuous night-and-day frost.
Soil Any well-drained garden soil.
Propagation Raise from cuttings in summer, or from seed.

Pittosporum tenuifolium

○ ○ ⚙ ✳ ⊛ ⚘ ▥ ⊗

From New Zealand, a tree growing up to 30ft (9m) high that is cultivated for its wavy edged, glossy, light green leaves, set off by the purple-black stems. Small brownish-purple fragrant flowers are followed by black-seeded fruits. A number of forms with variegated or suffused leaves are grown.

Long needles of *Pinus wallichiana*

up to 45ft (14m) high with a spread of up to 18ft (6m). It has hairless or downy branches, ovoid, slightly resinous buds and bluish-green needles in groups of 5 that are very twisted and densely crowded on the branchlets. 'Glauca' makes an attractive specimen tree with glaucous-blue foliage.

Pinus peuce

○ ⊖ ✳ ⚘

Macedonian pine. A tree with a narrowly conical habit that grows to a height of 60ft (18m) with a spread of 18ft (6m), and has hairless branches with ovoid buds. The needles are greyish-green and grow in groups of 5.

Pinus pinaster

Syn. *P. maritima*. Maritime pine. A tall tree with an umbrella-shaped crown and hairless, brownish-red branches. The needles are 4–8in (10–20cm) long, prickly, dark green and borne in pairs.

Pinus pumila

○ ⊖ ✳ ⊛

Dwarf Siberian pine, from northeastern Siberia and Japan. A shrub growing 10ft (3m) high with a similar spread and bluish-green needles. It is suitable for rock and heather gardens. 'Blue Dwarf' and 'Glauca' both have blue needles.

Pinus strobus

○ ⊗ ✳ ⚘ ⊥

Weymouth pine. A tree growing up to 125ft (38m) high with a conical habit and a spread of up to 30ft (9m). It later develops a rounded head. The buds are

Pinus mugo in autumn

London plane in the winter

Platanus
Platanaceae
Plane

A genus of hardy deciduous trees eminently suitable for planting in city parks and avenues, and easily recognized by their peeling bark.

Soil Planes thrive on moist loam, but will make do with poorer soils.

Propagation Raise from seed, by layering or from cuttings taken in late autumn. Only a very small proportion of the seeds will germinate.

Platanus × acerifolia, see *P. × hispanica*.

Platanus × hispanica

○ ◑ ❋ ⊕ ⊕

Syn. *P. × acerifolia* and *P. × hybrida*. London plane. A cross between *P. occidentalis* and *P. orientalis*. A well-known tree with flaking bark, it reaches a height of 100ft (30m) and has a spread up to 60ft (18m). It has hairless branches, reddish buds, and large palmate leaves 5–10in (12.5–25cm) long with 3–5 toothed, pointed lobes, smooth or downy underneath. It is tolerant of polluted atmospheres, and therefore eminently suitable for parks and streets in large cities.

Platanus × hybrida, see *P. × hispanica*.

Platanus occidentalis
Buttonwood or American sycamore. This species differs from *P. × hybrida* in having shallowly lobed leaves; it is also far more difficult to cultivate in Britain.

Platanus orientalis
Oriental plane. This tree has very deeply lobed leaves and is fairly common.

Platycodon grandiflorum 'Mariesii'

Platycodon
Campanulaceae
Balloon flower

A genus containing one species of beautiful border plants with large, bell-shaped flowers. They strongly resemble the more common *Campanula*.

Soil Any fertile, well-drained, but not dry soil is suitable.

Propagation Plants are raised from basal cuttings, division, or seed sown outdoors in April.

Platycodon grandiflorum
◑ ○ ⊛

A plant from China and Japan growing 1–2ft (30–60cm) high that from midsummer to early autumn produces blue or white flowers, sometimes semi-double.

In the autumn and winter, planes are loaded with fruit

Polemonium caeruleum

Ground-covering *Polygonum affine*

Polygonum amplexicaule, a late-flowering border plant

Polygonatum multiflorum

Polemonium
Polemoniaceae

A genus of herbaceous perennials including many beautiful blue flowers for the border. Plants are self-seeding and may become a nuisance if unchecked.
Soil A fairly rich, loamy soil is needed.
Propagation Cultivars are grown by division, and the species from seed.

Polemonium caeruleum
Ⓘ Ⓢ Ⓞ Ⓣ

Jacob's ladder, Greek valerian. A plant from Europe and North America that grows 1–3 ft (30–100 cm) high and bears beautiful sky-blue flowers in summer.

Polemonium reptans
Ⓘ Ⓘ Ⓞ Ⓣ

A North American plant with a creeping rootstock growing 4–8 in (10–20 cm) high. The blue flowers, smaller than in the last species, appear from spring to early summer.

Polemonium × richardsonii
Ⓘ Ⓢ Ⓞ Ⓣ

Probably a cross between *P. caeruleum* and *P. reptans*, this plant grows 16 in (40 cm) high and has a creeping rootstock. Large, sky-blue flowers are borne in spring, and often reappear in early to midsummer. Of the cultivars, 'Blue Pearl' is 10 in (25 cm) high with pure blue flowers.

Polygonatum
Liliaceae
Solomon's seal

Herbaceous perennials suitable for shady borders and for planting under deciduous trees and between shrubs.
Soil A peaty soil is required, which should not be too dry.
Propagation Plants are raised by division of the roots.

Polygonatum commutatum
Ⓘ Ⓘ Ⓞ Ⓐ Ⓣ

Syn. *P. canaliculatum*. Giant Solomon's seal, a plant of erect habit from North America that grows up to 3 ft (1 m) high. The leaves are fairly large and oval, and the flowers, which appear in late spring to early summer, are white and borne in groups of 2–8.

Polygonatum multiflorum
A European wood plant, growing 20–36 in (50–100 cm) high with rounded, drooping stems. It bears white flowers with green dots in clusters of 2–5. The plant in cultivation is generally of hybrid origin and correctly should be called *P. × hybridum*.

Polygonum
Polygonaceae
Knotweed

A fairly widespread genus of hardy annuals and herbaceous perennials. The genus also used to include various climbers now classified as *Bilderdykia*.
Soil A rich, moist garden soil is preferred.
Propagation Annual species are raised from seed sown in autumn or in April in the flowering position. Thin out to 6 in (15 cm) apart, the taller varieties to 16 in (40 cm). Perennials may be grown from seed, but are usually propagated by division.

Annuals include:
Polygonum capitatum
Ⓞ Ⓘ Ⓞ Ⓣ Ⓢ

A 4–6 in (12–15 cm) high creeping plant from Northern India with reddish stems, and masses of red flowers throughout the summer. This plant is really a perennial but since it is not hardy, must be grown as an annual. It can also be overwintered under glass, away from frosts. It is attractive in the rock garden or in hanging baskets.

Polygonum orientale
Ⓞ Ⓘ Ⓘ Ⓞ Ⓢ

A plant from China and Japan, where it grows, in moist places, to a height of 3–10 ft (1–3 m). Its flowering period is July until autumn. The flowers are in spikes, pink to scarlet or white, depending on the variety. A quick-growing plant, it may be used as an annual for rapid cover, but is not very ornamental except in autumn.

Perennials include:
Polygonum affine
Ⓞ Ⓘ Ⓞ Ⓣ Ⓢ Ⓢ

A 1 ft (30 cm) high plant with a mat-forming habit originally from the Himalayas, that makes very good ground cover in sunny or semi-shaded sites. Rose-pink flowers are borne in dense, erect spikes from late summer to early autumn. 'Darjeeling Red' is slightly taller and bears masses of crimson flowers.

Polygonum amplexicaule
Ⓘ Ⓢ Ⓞ Ⓣ

A beautiful border plant for moist sites that grows up to 5 ft (1.5 m) high. Masses of crimson flowers are borne in spikes from midsummer until autumn.

Polygonum bistorta
Snakeweed. A European plant growing 1–3 ft (30–90 cm) high and flowering from late spring to late summer. With its pink blooms, it is an attractive perennial plant near ponds, etc. 'Superbum' is taller and more robust than the species.

Polygonum campanulatum
A perennial plant, 2–3 ft (60–90 cm) high, somewhat woody at the base, that in summer is overladen with white, pink-tinted flowers. The leaves are lanceolate and covered with ash-grey hairs underneath.

In the foreground: *Polygonum bistorta*

The attractive *Polystichum setiferum*, soft shield fern

Polystichum
Aspidiaceae

A genus of ferns suitable for growing both indoors and in the garden.
Soil A humus-rich, non-acid soil is best, preferably containing some chalk.
Propagation The ferns are self-propagating by means of spores, and may also be divided in spring.

Polystichum acrostichoides
◑ ◐ ⊗ ⊗ ◯ ⊛
Christmas fern. A North American plant that grows 3 ft (1 m) high. Its deeply cut fronds keep their rich glossy green colour through the winter in all but the coldest regions. Where frosts are severe, it may need protection.

Polystichum aculeatum
◑ ◐ ⊗ ◯ ⊛ ⊗
Syn. *P. lobatum*. Hard shield fern. A plant with stiff, 1–3 ft (30–90 cm) long lanceolate fronds, pinnate or bipinnate, with deeply cut pinnules. These ferns retain their attractive, glossy green colour throughout the winter. They grow best in the wetter parts of Britain.

Polystichum angulare, see *P. setiferum*.

Polystichum lobatum, see *P. aculeatum*.

Polystichum setiferum
◑ ◐ ⊗ ⊗ ◯ ⊛ ⊗
Syn. *P. angulare*. Soft shield fern. Resembling *P. aculeatum*, it has softer, duller green fronds. Probably the most attractive cultivar is 'Acutilobum' ('Proliferum'), which has finely divided pinnules creating plumey fronds.

Pontederia
Pontederiaceae

A genus of aquatic perennials including one hardy species with exceptionally beautiful flowers suitable for growing in ornamental pools.
Soil It likes loam covered with 6–15 in (15–38 cm) of water.
Propagation Plants are raised by division in spring.

Pontederia cordata
◯ ◐ ⊗ ⊗ ◯ ⓨ
Pickerel weed. A hardy, herbaceous, summer-flowering perennial for shallow pools or swampy sites, with creeping rhizomes and heart-shaped bright green leaves that protrude above the water on 2–3 ft (60–100 cm) long stems. The purple-blue flowers are borne in erect spikes.

Populus
Salicaceae
Poplar

A genus of fast-growing deciduous trees making excellent screens and windbreaks. The best type for hiding undesirable views is *P. nigra* 'Italica'; *P. × berolinensis* is another: it comes into leaf 14 days earlier but also sheds its leaves before the other.
Soil Most poplars will thrive in any type of soil, but some need moist sites.
Propagation Plants are very easily propagated from hardwood cuttings; even older branches will root if they are sawn off and pushed into the ground.

Populus alba
◯ ◐ ⊖ ⊖ ⊛
White poplar. A tree growing up to 100 ft (30 m) high with a spread of 30–45 ft (9–14 m). Sometimes it is grown as a shrub by annual pruning. It has downy branches and broadly ovate, shallowy lobed leaves, dark green and almost hairless on top, and white and woolly underneath, especially when

Pontederia cordata, pickerel weed, an exceptionally attractive aquatic plant

young. 'Nivea' is distinguished by its downy white branches, while 'Pyramidalis' has an almost columnar habit.

Populus balsamifera
Syn. *P. tacamahacca*. Balsam poplar, Ontario poplar, Balm of Gilead. A large, erect-branched tree, grown mainly for the fragrance of its leaves, that has round, hairless and purple-brown branches with large sticky buds.

Populus × berolinensis
Berlin poplar. A cross between *P. laurifolia* and *P. nigra* 'Italica'. This resembles the Lombardy poplar but is more columnar and has straighter stems. The downy shoots are greenish when young but quickly turn grey; the leaves are elongated and pointed, often slightly wavy, bright green on the upper side and greenish-grey beneath.

Populus × canadensis
◯ ◐ ⊗ ⊛ ⊗
Syn. *P. euramericana*. Raised by crossing *P. deltoides* and *P. nigra*, these plants are known collectively as hybrid black poplars. Well-known types include 'Gelrica', a quick-growing, wind-resistant plant with erect stems that later turn whitish-grey and deep green leaves on reddish stalks; 'Robusta', also vigorous and erect, with dark green leaves on red stalks; and 'Zeeland', the most common variety, which is vigorous, with dark green leaves on green stalks.

Populus candicans, see *P. balsamifera*.

Populus × canescens
◯ ◐ ⊗ ⊛ ⊗
Grey poplar. A medium-sized tree that sometimes forms thickets. The leaves are heart-shaped and covered with greyish down underneath when young, then turn mostly hairless and brownish-green.

Populus deltoides
◯ ◐ ⊗
Cottonwood. A large tree with a pyramidal crown, suitable for lining streets and avenues. See also *P. canadensis* hybrids.

Populus lasiocarpa
A medium-sized tree generally of

156

Populus canadensis hybrids assume an attractive yellow shade in the autumn

rather gaunt habit when mature. The twigs are olive-green, the buds somewhat sticky. The leaves are very large, oval, pointed, and hairy along the conspicuous veins.

Populus nigra

○ ◑ ⊖ ⊗ ✳ ⊕ ▥

Black poplar. A spreading tree with round, greenish-grey twigs and sticky brownish-green buds. The leaves are ovate to rhomboid. The best-known cultivar is 'Italica', the Lombardy poplar, a columnar tree with angular twigs and rhomboid leaves. This species makes an excellent tall hedge and a very good windbreak, and also a fine specimen tree. It is resistant to winds from the sea. See also *P.* × *berolinensis* and *P.* × *canadensis*.

Populus simonii

◖ ◑ ⊖ ✳ ✳ ▥

Of the many cultivars, 'Fastigiata' is the best known. It is a small, columnar tree, with pale green, oval leaves, and makes an excellent windbreak.

Populus tremula

○ ◑ ⊖ ✳ ✳ ▥

Aspen. A medium-sized tree, often planted as a shrub to hide unsightly objects. It is excellent for parks and also for planting under larger trees.

Populus trichocarpa

Black cottonwood, Western balsam poplar. A large tree with a pyramidal crown, greyish-brown, angular branches and ovate, pointed leaves that are pale and net-veined beneath. It is suitable for parks.

Portulaca
Portulacaceae
Purslane

A genus of many frost-tender annuals and perennials, one of which is widely grown.

Soil Any well-drained garden soil in sun will do. The plants should only be watered when they start to wilt.

Propagation Grow from seed sown either under glass in March or in the flower bed in April–May.

Portulaca grandiflora

○ ☉ ⊛

Sun plant, from South America. A low tufted annual that grows 6–9 in (15–23 cm) high and bears large, buttercup-like flowers in summer in a range of colours from purple to yellow.

Potentilla
Rosaceae
Cinquefoil

This genus supplies the gardener with glorious, unusually floriferous herbaceous perennials and shrubs for the border and rock garden.

Soil Any garden soil will do, but particularly when enriched with humus and lime. The shrubs are deep rooted and can survive periods of drought fairly easily.

Cultivation The perennials are used a great deal in rock gardens and herbaceous borders. The shrubby species flower for a long time and are therefore eminently suitable for mixed or shrub borders, especially in small gardens. The tips of dead flowering shoots should be regularly removed.

Propagation The perennials are propagated from seed or by division. The shrubby cultivars are propagated from cuttings taken in late summer and autumn.

Perennials include:

Potentilla ambigua

Sometimes known as *Potentilla cuneata*, this Himalayan species is a very dwarf growing, tufted perennial with 1 in (2.5 cm) wide golden flowers in summer.

Potentilla atrosanguinea

○ ◑ ○ ⊗

A Himalayan plant that grows 16–24 in (40–60 cm) high, and in summer bears dark crimson flowers. 'Gibson's Scarlet' is a hybrid with dazzling brick-red flowers, which make a striking contrast with the bright green leaves.

Potentilla aurea

○ ◑ ○ ⊗ ⊗

From the Alps and Pyrenees, a 4–8 in

(10–20 cm) high plant that is suitable for the rock garden. In summer it bears small saffron-yellow flowers.

Potentilla fragiformis

A clump forming species growing to 10 in (25 cm) tall. The leaves are silky beneath and the small, golden-yellow flowers are borne in clusters.

Potentilla hybrids

Crosses between *P. argyrophylla* and *P. atrosanguinea*. Cultivars include 'Yellow Queen', which has golden-yellow, double flowers, and 'Fireball', with bright red, double flowers.

Potentilla nepalensis

From Nepal and the Himalayas, a plant that grows 16–24 in (40–60 cm) high. Flowering from summer to autumn, it produces cerise to scarlet blooms. Particularly recommended is 'Miss Willmott', which has cherry-pink flowers with deeper pink centres.

Potentilla nitida

From southern Europe and the Alps, a 2–4 in (5–10 cm) plant with silvery, silky leaves that in midsummer bears soft pink, usually solitary flowers.

Potentilla palustris

○ ◑ ⊗ ⊗

Syn. *Comarum palustre*. Marsh cinquefoil. Occasionally found in the wild, it is suitable for wet sites in the garden.

Potentilla nepalensis 'Miss Willmott'

Its beautiful little red flowers resemble those of the strawberry plant. It thrives on acid peaty soil.

Potentilla recta

○ ◑ ○ ⊗ ⊗

A plant that grows 1–2 ft (30–60 cm) high with bright green foliage and bears sulphur-yellow flowers from early to midsummer. 'Warrenii' has a more vigorous habit.

Potentilla × tonguei

A cross between *P. anglica* and *P. nepalensis*. Syn. *Potentilla × tormentillo-formosa*. An attractive rock plant with long, partly prostrate stems and compound leaves with 3 or 5 toothed leaflets. Salmon-orange flowers with a brown centre appear in summer.

Potentilla × tormentillo-formosa,
see *P.* × *tonguei*.

Shrubby species include:

Potentilla fruticosa

○ ◑ ◑ ◑ ◑ ▥

A shrub up to 3 ft (1 m) high with peeling twigs and small pinnate leaves with 3–7 narrow leaflets. The flowers are yellow in the species and appear from early summer to early autumn. Some of the best known of the countless cultivars are: 'Abbotswood', white, up to 3 ft (1 m) high, a wide-spreading plant with bluish-green leaves; 'Arbuscula' ('Elizabeth'), a dwarf shrub particularly suitable for growing on banks and as ground cover, with greyish-green leaves and yellow flowers; 'Farreri', growing 1–3 ft (30–100 cm) high, a bushy shrub with small green leaves and small, dark yellow flowers; 'Klondike', up to 3 ft (1 m) high, with very large golden-yellow flowers; 'Primrose Beauty', 3 ft (1 m) high, with spreading branches and very large, bowl-shaped, soft yellow flowers with a somewhat darker centre; 'Sunset', orange to brick-red, but fading in hot sun; and 'Tangerine', which grows 20–28 in (50–70 cm) high and twice as broad, with light orange flowers fading to yellow when exposed to the full sun.

Potentilla fruticosa is often used for low, loose hedges

Primula
Primulaceae

A genus of perennial plants including many beautiful garden species. It is not always easy to find the right place for them, and in the wrong position they do not do well.

Soil Most primulas like fairly moist soil, but alpine species need well-drained sites especially in winter, or they will soon rot. A mixture of clay and humus usually brings good results.

Propagation Most species can be divided directly after flowering, or grown from seed sown in February in pots of seed compost covered with moist moss and sheets of glass and kept in a shady position. The seed compost should be adequately moist. Prick out the seedlings when they are large enough to handle and plant out in the flowering position.

Primula acaulis, see *P. vulgaris*.
Primula auricula
Alpine auricula, from the European Alps. A plant which grows 3–6 in (7.5–15 cm) high that flowers April–June, bearing mostly bright yellow, often fragrant blooms. Crosses between *P. auricula* and *P. hirsuta* are the basis of garden auriculas, also known as *P. × pubescens*. There are numerous sorts in countlesss shades. *P. auricula* demands a calcareous soil and not too sunny a position. It may also be planted between stones in rockeries and on walls; otherwise grow as specified above.
Primula beesiana
A moisture-loving perennial plant belonging to the Candelabra group. Flowers are borne in whorls ascending the stem. Growing 2 ft (60 cm) high, it flowers from early to midsummer bearing lilac-purple blooms with a dark yellow eye. Growing instructions are as for *P. vulgaris*.
Primula bulleyana
A perennial plant growing up to 3 ft

Primula bulleyana hybrids in orange and pink

Primula pulverulenta

Primula denticulata

A pretty coloured *Primula vulgaris* hybrid

Primula vialii

(1 m) high, common in moist pastures, beside brooks and in mountain crevices. In summer it produces reddish-orange to chrome-yellow flowers. Particularly attractive are the hybrids with *P. beesiana*. They flower in every shade of yellow, orange, pink, red, mauve and violet. Of special importance are the Dutch 'Moerheimii' hybrids and the English 'Ipswich' hybrids.
Primula denticulata
A perennial plant reaching 6–8 in (15–45 cm) high and flowering March–April, before the leaves come out. The blooms appear in dense globular heads, pale lilac in the species and white in 'Alba'. 'Juno' is quick-growing and has large, bright lilac flowers. Sow in trays or pots in early spring, place in a cold frame and bed out later. 'Cache-meriana' resembles the species but is powdery-white, as though covered with a substance such as flour; its leaves come out in spring at the same time as the flowers; these are violet with a small yellow eye, and are borne in globular heads.
Primula farinosa
Bird's-eye primula. A perennial plant

found throughout Europe that grows up to 8 in (20 cm) high with powdery leaves and light or dark purple flowers with a deep yellow throat. I is highly recommended for the rock garden though rather difficult to grow; it prefers cool, moist soil but dislikes water-logged ground in winter.
Primula florindae
Himalayan cowslip. An unusually late-flowering, hardy primula, native to Tibet, that grows 20–28 in (50–70 cm) high and flowers from mid- to late summer. The nodding to pendent blooms are sulphur-yellow, fragrant, and borne 40 or more to a head.
Primula frondosa
A perennial plant from Bulgaria that strongly resembles *P. farinosa* but is less sensitive and hence more suitable for growing outdoors. It flowers in spring.
Primula gracilipes
A plant with a reputation for being difficult, but very successful in a cool, shady place where the soil never dries out completely. The 4 in (10 cm) leaves are wavy and toothed and the pinky-mauve flowers, each 1–1½ in (2.5–3 cm) across, are freely borne in spring and earlier in a mild winter. Best divided every third year.
Primula × helenae, see *P. juliae* hybrids.
Primula hirsuta
A plant from the Alps and Pyrenees that is tolerant of semi-shade, even at very high altitudes. Growing 6 in (15 cm) high, it flowers in April, bearing pink, sometimes lilac, more rarely white, blooms. It dislikes overly moist conditions after flowering. The green parts of the plant are very sticky and covered with glandular hair.
Primula japonica
A perennial plant from Japan that grows up to 20 in (50 cm) high and flowers from early to midsummer, bearing red, pink, white or violet blooms. A very attractive Candelabra type, it is slightly more difficult to cultivate than most, and likes a clay soil. On lighter soils, plant in semi-shade. Young plants are best covered with bracken in winter; overly dry soil in winter or early spring does more damage than frost.
Primula juliae
This species from the Caucasus and Asia Minor forms a flat mat of creeping stems, 2–4 in (5–10 cm) high. An attractive rock plant, it flowers March–April, bearing red-purple blooms. The many cultivars are perhaps better described as *P. juliae* hybrids (syns.

Primula veris, cowslip, grows wild on limy soil

Polyanthus in various colours

Primula vialii

Syn. *P. littoniana*. A perennial plant from south-western China that grows up to 2 ft (60 cm) high with violet-purple, red-calyxed flowers borne in spikes. Often grown as a biennial, it demands a humus-rich, moist soil and a semi-shady position. The soil must not be allowed to become waterlogged in winter.

Primula vulgaris

Syn. *P. acaulis*. Primrose. A perennial plant from Europe, widespread in woods and on meadows, that grows 2–6 in (5–15 cm) high and flowers March–April, bearing light yellow blooms with a darker eye. The names of the cultivars are generally based on the colour of the flower: 'Alba' is white; 'Caerulea', blue; 'Lutea', yellow; and 'Rubra', red. These plants are best grown in cool, fertile garden soil in the semi-shade of shrubs, etc.

Primula warschnewskiana

A delightful, mat-forming perennial from Afghanistan. It spreads slowly by means of stolons and in spring is covered with a profusion of $\frac{1}{2}$ in (1.5 cm) wide, rose pink flowers, each with a yellow centre. They are carried on stems up to 2 in (5 cm) high before the leaves expand to their full length of $2\frac{3}{4}$ in (7 cm).

P. × *pruhoniciana*, P. × *helenae* and P. × *juliana*). These include 'E. R. James', salmon-pink; 'Pearl White', ivory; 'Praecox', red, early-flowering; and 'Wanda', purple—all with sessile inflorescences. Others are 'Enchantress', violet; 'Garden Delight' orange-rose; and 'Mrs MacGillavry', purple-rose—all with short-stemmed inflorescences.

Primula littoniana, see *P. viallii* hybrids.

Primula × pruhoniciana, see *P. juliae* hybrids.

Primula × pubescens, see *P. auricula*.

Primula pulverulenta

A perennial plant from Yunnan that grows up to 32 in (80 cm) high, and in early to midsummer bears red flowers with a darker eye.

Primula rosea

A perennial plant from the north-western Himalayas that flowers in spring, bearing rose-pink blooms, and demands partial shade and moist soil. Recommended cultivars include 'Grandiflora', coral-pink and quick-growing, and 'Micia Visser de Geer', dark red and very early-flowering. For propagation, see under *P. denticulata*.

Primula sieboldii

A particularly attractive species from Japan with pale green, oval leaves having prominent rounded teeth. Bright rose-purple flowers are borne on stiff stems from late spring to early summer. There are countless beautiful cultivars, most of them originating in Japan. Their colours include white, pink, red and purple.

Primula × tommasinii

Syn. *P.× polyantha*. Polyanthus. Some of the most popular old-fashioned garden primulas, these perennials from Europe grow 3–12 in (7.5–30 cm) high and flower in spring, sometimes again in late summer. The flowers come in various shades and colours. For cultivation, see under *P. vulgaris*.

Primula veris

Cowslip. A clump-forming perennial plant from Europe that grows 4–10 in (10–25 cm) high and flowers in spring. The blooms are deep yellow in the wild species, and light yellow to orange-red and brownish in the cultivars. More tolerant of sun and drought than most other primulas, it thrives in grassland provided this is not mowed too early.

Primula florindae flowers exceptionally late

Prunella × webbiana

Prunella
Labiatae
Self-heal

Perennial plants with attractive short flower spikes resembling small baskets that are eminently suited for the front of borders and rock gardens.

Soil A not-too-dry but well-drained soil is needed.

Propagation Raise by division in spring.

Prunella grandiflora

○ ◑ ◍ ⊕ ⊗

A perennial plant from Europe, 6–10 in (15–25 cm) high, that flowers in midsummer to early autumn. Violet blooms are borne in dense terminal spikes.

Prunella × webbiana

A cross between *P. grandiflora* and *P. hastifolia* (*P. grandiflora pyrenaica*) that resembles *P. grandiflora* except that its leaves are shorter and the spikes more compact. It grows 8 in (20 cm) high and flowers, according to type, between spring and early autumn. 'Loveliness' is pale violet; 'Pink Loveliness' is clear pink; and 'White Loveliness', pure white.

Prunus
Rosaceae

A large and widespread genus of trees and shrubs including ornamental almonds, ornamental plums and other ornamental garden shrubs, all grown for their beautiful flowers. In addition, there are some species that are very useful for planting under larger trees. The evergreen species, the laurels, make valuable windbreaks and thrive nearly everywhere.

Cultivation Most species, including the Japanese standard specimen trees, are wind-resistant. Unfortunately these grafted garden forms are not very long-lived, having an average life-expectancy of 40 years. Pruning is seldom necessary except with *P. triloba* and *P. glandulosa*.

Soil Most species thrive in ordinary garden soil, preferably enriched with humus and a little lime.

Propagation Most species can be propagated from seed or from cuttings taken in summer; laurels are easily grown from cuttings taken in winter. Cultivars are propagated by grafting, generally on to rootstocks of *P. avium*.

Prunus × yedoensis bears flowers on the old wood

Prunus laurocerasus in flower

Prunus persica 'Klara Meyer'

Prunus triloba

Evergreen species include:

Prunus laurocerasus

◑ ◯ ⊛ ◍ ⊗

Syn. *Laurocerasus officinalis, Cerasus laurocerasus*. Cherry laurel or common laurel, a vigorous shrub that can tolerate a great deal of shade and is often used for hedging, although these can soon grow out of control. In late spring, white flowers appear in axillary racemes. The reddish fruits turn black. Cultivars include 'Otto Luyken', growing up to 3 ft (1 m) tall, a compact, particularly hardy shrub with dark green, elongated leaves; and 'Zabeliana', a very hardy 3 ft (1 m) shrub with a spread of up to 10 ft (3 m) and lanceolate, green, slightly glossy leaves. It makes excellent ground cover and is also useful for breaking the regular outline of a border or bed.

Prunus lusitanica

◑ ◠ ⊛ ◍ ⊛ ⊗

Syn. *Cerasus lusitanica*. Portuguese laurel. This grows up to 10 ft (3 m) high but must be shaded from the morning sun, or else it may be badly damaged after night frosts. White flowers are borne in erect, long, slender racemes. Plant in a sheltered position.

The most common deciduous species

and crosses include:

Prunus × 'Accolade'

○ ◯ ⊛ ⊕ ⊘ ⊙

A cross between *Prunus sargentii* and *Prunus subhirtilla*. A small tree to 16 ft (5 m) or more in height, the bright pink, semi-double flowers carried in drooping clusters. The foliage often colours well in autumn.

Prunus × amygdalo-persica.

○ ◍ ⊛ ◍ ⊗

A cross between *P. dulcis* (*amygdalus*) (almond) and *P. persica* (peach).

Prunus avium

○ ⊛ ◍ ⊗

Syn. *Cerasus avium*. Gean, wild cherry. An attractive tree with a pyramidal habit, up to 45 ft (13.5 m) high, flowering April–May. The flowers are white in pendulous clusters, the dark red fruits may be bitter or sweet. 'Plena' has drooping double flowers.

Prunus × blireana

○ ◯ ⊛ ⊕ ⊘ ⊙

A cross between *Prunus cerasifera* 'Pissardii' and *Prunus nume* 'Alphandii'. A large shrub, sometimes a small tree to 16 ft (5 m). The young leaves open a coppery red, becoming green as they age. The double pink flowers usually open on the bare stems in late March or April

Prunus serrulata 'Shirotae'

Prunus serrulata 'Kiku-Shidare-Sakura' a weeping form of the Japanese cherry

Prunus mahaleb

○ ⊕ ✳ ⊙ ◎

Syn. *Cerasus mahaleb*. St Lucia cherry. A shrub or small tree which provides the rootstock on to which morello cherries are usually grafted. White flowers from April to May are followed by black fruits. Almost circular leaves.

Prunus mume

○ ○ ✳ ⊙

Japanese apricot. In spite of its name, this 20–32 ft (6–10 m) tree is a native of China and Korea. The almond-scented flowers are pale pink and often over an inch (2.5 cm) across. They are borne in March and April before the leaves.

Prunus nana, see Prunus tenella

Prunus 'Okame'

A cross between *Prunus campanulata* and *Prunus incisa*. A compact shrub up to 10 ft (3 m) high with small, single, carmine-rose flowers combined in groups of 3 and set close along the twig. This resembles *Prunus subhirtella* 'Fukubana'.

Prunus padus

○ ⊕ ⊙ ◎

Syns. *Padus avium* and *Cerasus padus*. Bird cherry. A large, wide-spreading shrub flowering April–May. The flowers are white in drooping racemes, the fruits black. Suitable for planting beneath tall trees and in woods. 'Colorata' is a small tree or large shrub with coppery-purple foliage and pink flowers from April to May. 'Watereri' has conspicuous racemes of white flowers up to 8 in (20 cm) long.

Prunus persica

○ ○ Syn. *Amygdalus persica*. Peach. Includes 'Klara Mayer', a large shrub with a spread of more than 15 ft (5 m) and double peach-pink flowers, which

Prunus cerasifera

○ ⊕ ✳ ⊙ ⊛ ⊙ ⊥

Cherry plum. A small tree or shrub from the Caucasus and western Asia with green, sometimes spiny, twigs. It produces single white flowers 1 in (2.5 cm) across in early spring. The yellow or reddish fruits look like small plums. There are several cultivars including particularly 'Atropurpurea' (syn. *Prunus pissardii*), an erect shrub or small tree with a rounded crown and reddish-purple leaves. If the early flowers are not destroyed by night frosts, they are followed by wine-red sweet fruits; 'Hollywood' (syn. 'Trailblazer') first has green and then red-purple leaves and bears small white flowers, followed by red, edible plums. 'Nigra' resembles 'Woodii' but has larger leaves; 'Rosea' is a very attractive wide-spreading shrub, with bronze-coloured leaves that later turn dark green, and masses of salmon-pink flowers; 'Woodii' has purple leaves and red flowers.

Prunus cerasus

Syn. *Cerasus vulgaris*. Sour cherry. A tree with red, sour fruit. There are several cultivars, including ornamental trees with double flowers and fruit trees with single flowers. The following make particularly good ornamental cherries: 'Rhexii' with double, pure white sessile flowers for long periods in May, and 'Semperflorens', All Saints cherry, with double white flowers intermittently throughout the spring and the summer. *Prunus cerasus* var. *austera* is the Morello cherry. Sour cherries are smaller than the sweet cherries, growing to 15 ft (5 m) high.

Prunus davidiana

○ ◑ ○ ✳ ⊘

David's peach. A small, slender tree 16–24 ft (5–7 m) in height, carrying a profusion of small, pink flowers in late winter before the leaves. In a mild year they can open in February. 'Alba' has pure white flowers.

Prunus dulcis var. dulcis

Syn. *Prunus amygdalis* var. *sativa*. Common almond. It has been grown in England since the sixteenth century, but it rarely produces good nuts in the British climate. It has small pink flowers and lanceolate leaves. There are several cultivars, including: 'Alba', which is white flowered, and 'Roseoplena' with double pale pink blossoms.

Prunus glandulosa

○ ⊕ ⊙

Chinese bush cherry, a shrub up to 4½ ft (1.3 m) which flowers in May. 'Albiplena' has large double white flowers, and 'Sinensis' double pink flowers appearing in May.

Prunus × hillieri

○ ◑ ○ ✳ ⊙ ⊘

A cross between *Prunus sargentii* and an uncertain species. It makes a spreading tree to 32 ft (10 m). The young leaves are bronze at first and also colour well in autumn. The pink flowers open in spring. 'Spire' is a slender cultivar with a spread of never more than 10 ft (3 m).

Prunus incisa

Fuji cherry. A dense shrub up to 10 ft (3 m) high with thin, greyish-brown twigs. The leaves are hairy along the lower veins. Masses of single white flowers with a purple-red calyx and throat appear in late March to early April. See also under 'Okame'.

Adult specimen of *Prunus × yedoensi*

is particularly recommended for the ornamental garden.

Prunus pissardii, see *Prunus cerasifera* 'Atropurpurea'.

Prunus pumila

○ ◑ ⊛ ⊛

Sand cherry. A 3ft (1m) high, erect shrub with thin, reddish-brown twigs. The leaves, which point upwards, are greyish-green turning an attractive red in the autumn. It bears white flowers towards the end of April and early May followed by black fruits.

Prunus sargentii

○ ◑ ⊛ ⊛ ⊛ ⊛

Syn. *Prunus serrulata* var. *sachalinensis*. Judged the most attractive species of all. A small tree or shrub with bronze leaves when young and dark pink flowers, 2–4 to a cluster, it turns a glorious orange-red in the autumn.

Prunus serotina

○ ◑ ⊛ ⊛ ⊛

Syn. *Padus serotina*. A beautiful tree or large shrub with olive-green twigs covered with bright light-coloured lenticels. The leaves are rather leathery. White flowers in drooping racemes are produced May–June. The fruits are black, and sweet or bitter. Likes moist soil.

Prunus cerasifera 'Nigra'

Prunus serrula

○ ◑ ⊛ ⊛

A 32ft (10m) tree from China with a highly decorative trunk, the bark reddish brown with a high gloss. The $\frac{1}{2}$–$\frac{3}{4}$in (1.5cm) white flowers open after the 2–4in (5–10cm) slender leaves and are rather hidden by them. The tree is however worth growing for its bark alone.

Prunus serrulata

○ ◑ ⊛ ⊛ ⊛

Japanese flowering cherry. Probably the best known of all the ornamental cherries. The young foliage is reddish or bronze, the flowers are mostly double and the trees rarely bear fruit. There are numerous cultivars, of which only the most attractive are listed (in alphabetical order). In general, these plants can be ordered as shrubs, half-standards or standards.

'Amanogawa' is a very unusual, columnar, Lombardy poplar-like cherry bearing soft pink, semi-double flowers from the end of April. It is highly recommended for smaller gardens. 'Hokusai', a wide-spreading shrub with semi-double pale pink blossoms, flowers in late April and early May, is also used as a street tree. 'Jo-nioi' is a strong-growing cherry with masses of

white, single flowers in May. 'Kiku-shidare-sakura', often wrongly described as 'Cheal's Weeping' cherry, is a very attractive tree with drooping branches and masses of deep pink semi-double flowers in early April. It is best grown as half-standard or standard, when the arching branches can be shown to best advantage. 'Kanzan' is one of the most common ornamental cherries with dark pink, double flowers. It is often planted in streets. 'Shimidsu-sakura' (syn. 'Shogetsu') is a 10ft (3m) high tree with a broad, flattened crown and masses of 2in (5cm) wide double white flowers in clusters of 3–6 from April to the middle of May. 'Pink Perfection' resembles 'Kanzan' but has brighter rosy-pink flowers. 'Shirofugen' (syn. 'Alborosea') is a wide-spreading shrub with white double flowers in mid-May fading to pink. 'Shirotae' (syn. 'Mount Fuji') is a small shrub with slightly drooping branches and masses of 2in (5cm) wide semi-double or single flowers from the beginning of April to May. 'Tai Haku' is a robust shrub with pure white, single flowers set off by dark bronze foliage. 'Ukon' is a robust shrub with yellowish-white, semi-double flowers and bronze-brown leaves. The colour

Prunus serrulata 'Kanzan' (shrub form) in front of an elegant Dutch house

of its flowers makes it a most unusual cultivar.

Prunus serrulata var. ***sachalinensis***, see *Prunus sargentii*

Prunus spinosa

○ ◑ ⊛ ⊛

Blackthorn or Sloe. A thorny shrub up to 12ft (4m) high with hairy twigs, white flowers and fruits like small damsons, with a bluish bloom at first, later shining black. 'Plena' is a double-flowered cultivar; 'Purpurea' has deep purple leaves.

Prunus subhirtella

○ ◑ ⊛ ⊛ ⊛ ⊗

Spring cherry. A shrub or tree with hairy young twigs. Its leaves are ovate, 2–4in (5–10cm) long, on hairy leaf stalks. The flowers are small and pink, with a hairy throat, and the fruit black. The species is uncommon, but there are several popular cultivars, including 'Autumnalis', a small tree or shrub with brown twigs, and semi-double white, faintly pink-flushed flowers. It starts to flower as early as November, and continues throughout mild winters with a final flush in spring. 'Autumnalis Rosea' has light pink flowers. More attractive still is 'Fukubana', a bushy shrub, 6–10ft (2–3m) high, with masses of dark pink flowers from April to May.

'Pendula' is a weeping form with small pink flowers. Though most floriferous, it has a very short flowering period in early April.

Prunus subhirtella hybrids

These hybrids are crosses between *Prunus subhirtella* and *Prunus sargentii* or *Prunus* × *yedoensis*. 'Accolade' (dark pink), 'Hally Jolivette' (pale pink) and 'Pandora' (pink) seem to have a very promising future.

Prunus tenella

Syns. *Prunus nana*; *Amygdalus nana*. Dwarf Russian almond. A small, ornamental shrub with greyish-brown stems. The flowering period is April. The flowers are pink, 1–3 to a cluster set along the entire stem. 'Fire Hill' has bright rose-red blossoms. This dwarf only reaches heights up to 4½ft (1.3m). It is suitable for larger rock gardens and smaller gardens.

Prunus triloba

An ornamental almond with double pink flowers resembling small roses borne March–April. The flowers are short stemmed and distributed evenly over the branches. Most attractive as a small tree on the lawn, where the branches should be cut back hard immediately after flowering (down to 6in (15cm) from the base in order to preserve a good shape. If they are cut back too late they will not flower in the following year. May be trained against walls. Flowering branches are often sold by florists in the early spring.

Prunus × yedoensis

Believed to be a cross between *Prunus speciosa* and *Prunus subhirtella*. May grow to a height of 30 ft (10 m). The bark is smooth, though the young twigs are covered with down. The bright green leaves turn yellow and red in the autumn. Flowers are bluish-white and almond scented, the fruits black, the size of peas, but not freely produced. 'Ivensii', a weeping form with white flowers is generally smaller in all its parts. 'Shidare Yoshino', has an attractive shape with its branches arching over and the shoots hanging down. The flowers are a pale pink.

Pseudosasa
Gramineae

The commonest bamboos grown in Europe. It is often found in large thickets on old country estates.
Soil Plant in any ordinary soil that does not dry out. Best on moist sites.
Propagation By division.

Pseudosasa japonica

○ ◑ ⊗ ⊛ ⊛ ⊛ ⊛ ⊕

Syns. *Bambusa metake*; *Arundinaria japonica*. A fairly tall bamboo 6–10 ft (2–3 m) with brown stems, covered with bristles. The leaves are 4–10 in (10–25 cm) long and up to 2 in (5 cm) wide and bluish-green underneath. Suitable for large ponds and ditches: rather invasive in moist soil and not suitable for the small garden.

Pseudotsuga
Pinacea
Douglas fir

A genus of quick-grown conifers that can stand up to a great deal of wind, widely used in commercial forestry.

Pseudosasa japonica, the bamboo most commonly cultivated in the British Isles

A branch of *Pseudotsuga menziesii* 'Glauca'

Highly recommended for planting to the rear of larger gardens.
Soil Douglas firs need moisture-retentive but well-drained soil.
Propagation Grow from seed in the spring.

Pseudotsuga douglasii, see *Pseudotsuga menziesii*.

Pseudotsuga menziesii

○ ⊛ ⊛ ⊛ ⊛ ⊕

Syn. *Pseudotsuga douglasii*. Oregon Douglas fir. A tree up to 270 ft (79 m) high in its North American home. The needles are about 1 in (2.5 cm) long, in horizontal ranks. The twigs make excellent winter decorations, because they retain their needles for a very long time. *Pseudotsuga menziesii* var. *glauca* is the blue Douglas fir, with bluish-green needles, which is often planted as a specimen tree. Its needles smell of turpentine when touched. 'Fletcheri' is an attractive slow-growing dwarf form eventually up to 6 ft (2 m) high with a spread of up to 10 ft (3 m), and bluish-green, soft needles.

Pulmonaria
Boraginaceae
Lungwort

Herbaceous perennials for borders in semi-shady positions and for planting under deciduous trees and between shrubs.
Soil Moist, humus-rich garden soil is needed.
Propagation By division.

Pulmonaria angustifolia

◑ ◑ ⊛ ○ ⊛

Syn. *P. azurea*. Blue cowslip. Found in woods on clay in northern and western Europe, it grows 8–12 in (20–30 cm) tall, has hairy stems and elongated, lanceolate leaves on winged leafstalks. The flowers are first red, later violet-blue. 'Azurea' turns gentian-blue. Flowering period is March–April.
Pulmonaria azurea, see *P. angustifolia*.

The lungwort, *Pulmonaria rubra*

Pulmonaria rubra
Soft-haired perennial plants from the Balkans, 12–16 in (30–40 cm) high with light green, oblong to oval leaves. Flowering period March–April, flowers red.

Pulmonaria saccharata
Bethlehem Sage. Has oval narrowly to elliptic leaves, conspicuously spotted with silver-white and narrowing down to winged stalks. Flowering period April–May. Flowers first red, later violet to blue.

Pulsatilla
Ranunculaceae

Hardy herbaceous perennials with hairy, fern-like leaves and anemone-like flowers that come out very early in the spring. The flowers, nodding at first and later erect, have a hairy ruff of narrow leaf segments. The seeds are surrounded with masses of filaments that lend these little plants an even more attractive appearance.
Soil They need moisture-retaining but well-drained garden soil.
Propagation From seeds, sown as soon as they are ripe.

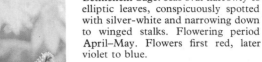

The pasque flower, *Pulsatilla vulgaris*

Pulsatilla alpina

○ ◑ ⊝ ⊙ ○ ⊕ ⊗

Syn. *Anemone alpina*. Herbaceous perennials native to the Alps, Dolomites and Apennines. They will not do well at lower altitudes unless they are grown on lime-free soil and tended with the utmost care. They have large white flowers covered with yellowish hair June–August. 'Sulphurea' has large, sulphur-yellow flowers.

Pulsatilla halleri ssp slavica

Syn. *Anemone slavica*. A perennial plant from the Balkans and the Alps, growing up to 12 in (30 cm) high, flowering July–August. The very hairy leaves come out after the dark violet flowers. Must be tended in the same way as the last species.

Pulsatilla vulgaris

○ ◑ ⊝ ⊙ ○ ⊕ ⊗ ⊗

Syn. *Anemone pulsatilla*. Pasque flower. A perennial plant found in most of Europe. Flowering in April, its height is about 6 in (15 cm); 16 in (40 cm) when in fruit. This is the species commonly offered by nurseries. The bright violet flowers, which are very large in comparison to the plant, are bell-shaped, first horizontal, later erect. 'Alba' is white; 'Rubra' is red; and 'Mrs Van der Elst' is pure pink.

Puschkinia
Liliaceae

A genus of small, hardy bulbs which may be left undisturbed for years at a time. They are suitable for the rock garden and for edging, either in the sun or in semi-shade.

Soil They thrive in ordinary, well-drained garden soil.

Propagation Grow from seed sown immediately it is ripe, or from offsets lifted with the bulbs when the leaves die down.

Puschkinia scilloides

○ ◑ ◐ △ ◉ ◎

A bulbous plant from the Caucasus, about 10in (25cm) high. Wedgwood-blue flowers in clusters, slightly bigger and lighter in colour in *P. scilloides* var. *libanotica*. Plant the bulbs September–October, at a depth of 2in (5cm), and the same distance apart. Hardy, they may be left untouched for years and are suitable for rock gardens and for edging. 'Alba' is a white cultivar.

Puschkinia scilloides var. *libanotica*

Pyracantha
Rosaceae
Firethorn

A genus of slow-growing but extremely vigorous flowering shrubs useful for growing against walls. The glossy leaves are highly ornamental, as are the beautiful flowers in May and the fruits in the late summer. The berries are great favourites of blackbirds.

Cultivation Firethorns, especially when grown as shrubs, may sometimes refuse to bear fruit. This may be the fault of the species or cultivar chosen, but may also be the result of too vigorous growth. In that case it may help to prune the roots with a spade at some distance from the stem. If grown as wall plants, support with trellis or wires. Tie in vigorous growths.

Soil Improve the soil near the wall with humus.

Propagation From cuttings taken in the late summer or from seed gathered and sown in the autumn.

Diseases Although pyracantha scab does occur in Britain and occasionally is bad, in general this is not a disease to worry about.

Pyracantha 'Orange Glow'

Pyracantha coccinea

○ ◑ ◐ ◈ ◉ ◎ ⊗

Syn. *Cotoneaster pyracantha*. A shrub from southern Europe and the Near East; 3–6ft (1–2m) high as a shrub, but much taller when trained against a wall. The flowering period is May–June, with white flowers resembling those of the hawthorn. Leaves are leathery and dark green, persisting during the winter. Berries (the main attraction) are round, bright red, scarlet, orange or yellow.

'Orange Giant' is a cultivar with large, bright orange berries as early as August. It is very hardy but unfortunately susceptible to scab. 'Lalandii', bears a profusion of deep orange berries but is sensitive to scab. 'Golden Charmer' is a densely branching shrub, hardy and unaffected by scab. It bears a profusion of orange-yellow berries which look best against red brick walls. 'Orange Charmer' bears deep orange berries from the middle of September, and is also resistant to scab. 'Orange Glow' is probably the most attractive Pyracantha. The berries are deep red at first then turn deep orange. They remain on the shrub from the end of September to the end of December. Birds are not attracted to them because they are hard and tough. Most ornamental when trained against walls or grown as a free-standing shrub. 'Watereri' bears masses of relatively small scarlet berries.

Pyracantha crenulata var. rogersiana, see Pyracantha rogersiana
Pyracantha rogersiana

○ ◑ ◠ ◎ ◈ ◉ ◎

Syn. *Pyracantha crenulata* var. *rogersiana*. 'Flava' bears small yellow berries and is scab resistant.

Pyracantha augustifolia

○ ◑ ◎ ◈ ◉ ◎ ◎

From China, growing 6–12ft (2–4m) high. It has a spreading and bushy habit with narrow, dark green leaves, grey felted beneath. The flat-topped clusters of white flowers are followed by orange-yellow berries.

Pyrus
Rosacea
Ornamental pear

A genus of deciduous trees including the common pear and a number of small- to medium-sized ornamental species with green to silvery-grey leaves and clusters of white flowers.

Soil Any reasonably fertile garden soil.

Propagation From seed or by grafting on to *Pyrus communis*.

Pyrus amygdaliformis, see *Pyrus spinosa*.
Pyrus salicifolia

○ ◈ ◉

Willow-leaved pear. A tree with drooping grey and spiny branches, it flowers profusely and produces pear-shaped fruits. 'Pendula', a smaller tree with weeping branches, is the most attractive cultivar.

Pyrus spinosa

○ ◑ ◈ ◉ ◎

Syn. *Pyrus amygdaliformis*. Grows up to 18ft (6m) tall, it occasionally has spiny branches. Leaves are very variable in shape, silvery underneath. White flowers appear in May, followed by 1in (2.5cm) yellow-brown fruits. Not very common in gardens.

Pyrus calleryana

○ ◑ ◐ ◈ ◉ ⊕

From China. Grows to 33ft (10m). A flowering pear with the added attraction of good autumn colour. 'Bradford' is taller and has a round head; 'Chanticleer' is conical in outline and useful where space is limited. All are resistant to fire blight.

Pyrus salicifolia 'Pendula'

Quercus pontica in the autumn

Quercus
Fagaceae
Oak

A very large genus of deciduous and evergreen trees and shrubs frequently planted along roads, in parks and in larger gardens. Here we can only discuss the most common, smaller species, the use of this genus in smaller 2,000–10,000 sq ft (186–930 sq m) to medium-sized 10,000–45,000 sq ft (930–4,180 sq m) gardens being severely restricted.

Soil Oak trees grow in any garden soil provided it is not too dry.

Propagation Grow from seed (acorns). Cultivars must be grafted on to seedling stocks of the species.

Quercus borealis, see Quercus rubra
Quercus cerris

◑ ◐ ◈ ◉

Turkey oak. A tree with a broad, pyramidal crown and downy branches. Leaves very variable, the upper sides rather rough, and brown in autumn. 'Pendula' is a weeping variety with deeply indented leaves.

Quercus conferta, see Quercus frainetto.

The flowers of the most beautiful of grey trees: *Pyrus salicifolia* 'Pendula'

Quercus robur, the English oak

Autumn foliage of *Quercus pontica*

Quercus frainetto, the Hungarian oak

Quercus frainetto
Syn. *Quercus conferta*. Hungarian oak. A large tree with a broad, irregular crown and grey to olive-green branches. The leaves are deeply lobed with 6–10 lobes.

Quercus ilex
Evergreen oak, Holm oak. A large tree with fissured bark and evergreen leaves. The young leaves are holly-like; older leaves generally entire and leathery. It does not thrive in very cold areas.

Quercus ilicifolia
Bear oak. A wide-spreading shrub up to 10 ft (3 m) high. The branches are covered with greyish hair. The leaves are dull green, downy underneath.

Quercus libani
Lebanon oak. An attractive tree 25 ft (8 m) high or more with a fairly small crown. highly recommended for smaller gardens. Although originating from the Lebanon, the acorns will ripen in western Europe. The glossy green leaves are margined with triangular teeth.

Quercus palustris
Pin oak. An attractive dense-headed tree with slender rust-coloured glossy branches. The leaves, which are sharply lobed to various depths, have a glorious red autumn colour.

Quercus pedunculata, see *Quercus robur*.

Quercus petraea
Syns. *Quercus sessiliflora* and *Quercus sessilis*. Sessile oak. It resembles *Quercus robur* but has more pointed and larger buds, and leaves that are light green underneath and not auricled at the base. Another distinguishing mark is the attachment of the acorns: they are sessile in *Q. petraea* but suspended on slender stalks in *Q. robur*.

Quercus phellos
Willow oak. A native of North America, this is one of the most graceful and ornamental of oaks. Its name derives from the shape of its leaves which are unlobed and lanceolate.

Quercus pontica
Armenian oak. A small tree or tall shrub from the Caucasus with indented, oval leaves.

Quercus robur
Syn. *Quercus pedunculata*. Common oak, English oak. A widely distributed oak with a broad, irregular crown. The branches are grey to olive-green, the bluish-green leaves have 3–7 pairs of rounded lobes, ear shaped at the base, and hairless underneath. There are a great many varieties with differences in habit, leaf shape and leaf colour. The acorns are suspended from long, slender stalks, singly or in groups. 'Concordia' is a smallish tree with golden-yellow leaves; 'Fastigiata' has a columnar habit; 'Pendula' (syn. 'Weeping oak') is small to medium sized with pendulous branches.

Quercus rubra
Syn. *Quercus borealis*. Red oak. Grows up to 80 ft (25 m) tall, spreads up to 40 ft (12 m) with a broad open crown. The branches are glossy and dark grey. Leaves, which are 3–6 in (7.5–15 cm) long, are very variable but rarely indented to more than half their depth. They turn a glorious red colour in the autumn.

Quercus sessiliflora, see *Quercus petraea*.

Quercus sessilis, see *Quercus petraea*.

Quercus × turneri
Turner's oak. A fairly short semi-evergreen tree with a dense oval crown. The leaves are leathery with 4–8 pairs of shallow lobes; the veins hairy underneath. It is one of the few oaks that is suitable for smaller gardens.

Quercus rubra, red oak, in the autumn

Ranunculus acris 'Multiplex'

Reseda odorata, 'Machat'

Yellow spikes of *Rheum alexandrae*

Ranunculus
Ranunculaceae
Buttercup

A genus of annuals and herbaceous and tuberous-rooted perennials. They are not as popular in gardens as they used to be. This list ignores the annuals and distinguishes between tuberous-rooted and herbaceous species.

Cultivation Tuberous-rooted perennials: Commercial growers distinguish between French, Persian, Peony-flowered and Turban groups, all of which have semi-double or very double compact flowers. Turbans are best planted in the spring and covered well during the winter. French and Persian ranunculi may be planted equally well in the autumn or in the spring; those planted in the autumn are best protected in the winter and will, of course, come into flower much earlier. Plant at distances of 3–4in (7.5–10cm) apart. The site may be in partial shade but must be sheltered from the wind, or else the long, hollow stems tend to collapse. Always dead-head, and lift plants annually when the leaves turn yellow. If they are to be replanted in the spring, they must be stored in an airy and frost-free place in the winter.

Soil Tuberous-rooted and herbaceous ranunculi do best in well-drained, but not dry, fertile soil. Set the tops of the tuberous roots about 2in (5cm) deep.

Propagation Tuberous-rooted plants can be propagated by division, which is simple enough since the plants must be lifted once every year in any case. Herbaceous perennials can be propagated by division or from seed.

Tuberous-rooted ranunculi:
Ranunculus asiaticus
From the Middle East. Heights 6–12in (15–30cm). The small tubers are shaped like claws or fangs. Flowering period is June–August.
Ranunculus bulbosus
Native to northern and central Europe, it grows 12–20in (30–50cm) high. Flowering period is April–August. 'Pleniflorus' bears 1in (2.5cm) wide, very densely filled, golden-yellow flowers with a greenish centre from May to June.

Herbaceous perennials:
Ranunculus aconitifolius
Perennial plant from southern and central Europe reaching heights of 16–24in (40–60cm). Bright white flowers May–June. 'Flore Pleno' has double white flowers.
Ranunculus acris
Common buttercup. The single species has been superseded by the double-flowered 'Flore Pleno' ('Multiplex'). Flowering throughout the summer, it is an excellent border plant growing 20–32in (50–80cm) high.
Ranunculus aquatilis
Common water crowfoot, from Europe. An aquatic plant with white flowers, growing a few inches above the water surface. Flowering period is from May to August. The submerged leaves are very finely divided into thread-like segments; the floating leaves are rounded and lobed. The white flowers have a yellow centre. Suitable for ponds.
Ranunculus lingua
Greater spearwort. From Europe and Asia, it grows 24–32in (60–80cm) high. Flowering period is June–August. The flowers are golden-yellow, to 2in (5cm) across. Ideal as a marginal plant.
Ranunculus repens
Creeping buttercup. It is widespread in meadows and a weed of gardens. 'Pleniflorus', which has double flowers, grows as vigorously as the wild form and is easily naturalized.

Reseda
Resedaceae
Mignonette

A good old-time cottage garden flower still popular in British gardens.
Soil Fertile, well-drained but not dry garden soil.
Propagation Sow thinly from March to April in the flowering position.

Reseda odorata
An annual, sometimes perennial, plant from N. Africa, 10–15in (25–38cm) high. It is grown for the sweet scent of its flowers, which appear from June to autumn. The flowers are yellow-white with red or golden-yellow stamens. The best cultivar is 'Machet', with red-tinged flowers in dense cylindrical spikes.

The hybrid rhododendron 'Mrs. Furnival'

Rheum
Polygonaceae
Ornamental rhubarb

Several ornamental rhubarbs are suitable for the garden.
Soil Rich, moist garden soil is needed.
Propagation By division of old plants between November and February. Each segment must have a dormant crown bud. Or by seeds in spring.

Rheum alexandrae
Herbaceous perennial from Tibet reaching a height of 28–36in (80–100 cm). The basal leaves are mid-green and borne on short stalks. Erect flower spikes with graceful cream-coloured bracts resembling candles. The flowers are inconspicuous.
Rheum palmatum
An 8ft (2.4m) perennial from China with very large, almost circular, deeply cut leaves, each with 3–5 veins. Small red flowers in erect panicles bloom May–June. *Rheum palmatum* var. *tanguticum* has less deeply cut leaves, usually flushed red.

Rhododendron
Ericaceae

A genus of evergreen and deciduous trees and shrubs including many gorgeous garden plants, azaleas among them (see below).

Many of the hundreds of species in this genus have been crossed to yield a veritable profusion of hybrids and garden strains. Here, we shall try to follow a practical system of classification, although that is a very difficult task, since very few gardeners agree on the correct nomenclature. We have space to discuss a very limited sample only.

Cultivation Most rhododendrons are intolerant of cold, drying winds and bright sunlight. All spring-flowering rhododendrons must be protected from the morning sun, since young growths and buds are easily damaged by sudden thaws after frosts. Rhododendrons do not do as well near trees that take too much moisture out of the ground.

It should be clear by now that the site on which rhododendrons are planted has to be very carefully chosen. It should afford shelter both from the early morning sun and the fierce midday sun but may admit direct sunlight in the afternoon and evening, for such light will not harm the plant. Rhododendrons should not, moreover, be planted in dense shade, and in dry areas every plant should be placed in a small hollow so that rainwater can run down towards the root.

Rhododendrons and azaleas require no regular pruning but should be dead-headed as soon as possible to encourage bud formation. It may also become necessary to shorten the odd straggly branch; this should preferably be done shortly before or during the flowering period. The cut branches make a fine show in large vases. What pruning has to be done must never be left too late—if the plants are allowed to become too straggly it is almost impossible to cut them back so as to restore their optimum shape. Many

Rhododendron repens hybrid

The Japanese garden in Westphalia Park, Dortmund, Germany, is a sea of pink in the spring when the azaleas come into bloom

amateurs make the serious mistake of planting rhododendrons, and particularly the large-flowering types, too closely together—most tend to spread sideways rather than grow upwards, and overcrowding is the inevitable result. Vigorous large-flowered species should be planted at least 6ft (2m) apart; even then it is surprising how quickly adjacent plants will touch one another on correctly prepared soil. People in a hurry may plant them closer together, perhaps 4ft (1.2m) apart, but they will have to remove two out of every four plants as soon as the branches touch. The remaining plants will then be 8ft (2.4m) apart. More attractive groups should, however, be planted closer together.

Soil Rhododendrons like humus-rich moist soil and a humid atmosphere. Most species do not tolerate chalky or limy soil or hard water. Those which do will be singled out in the separate entries.

If the soil is not peaty or naturally rich in humus, then it must first be improved with peat, manure or leaf-mould. Preparing the soil may prove more costly than buying the plants. It is best to remove poor soil to a depth of 12in (30cm), and to fill the hole with a mixture of three parts peat, one part well-rotted leaf-mould, two parts ordinary garden soil (the soil that has been dug up) and one part well-rotted cow manure.

Rhododendrons raised on humus-rich, sandy soil will tolerate transplantation much better than plants raised on peat. If the soil for peat-raised plants is not carefully improved, they may often be pulled out after a few years with great ease, so little root has the plant made outside the original root ball.

Propagation The main method of propagation is by saddle grafting. This must be done in a greenhouse and is a job for experts. Many cultivars can also be grown from cuttings, but some species and cultivars are not easy. Amateurs will do best with layering rhododendrons, which must be done in spring. It takes at least 18 months before the stems are fully rooted.

Pests and diseases Rhododendrons are attacked by leaf hoppers, which puncture the buds and introduce bud blast disease; vine and clay-coloured weevils; whiteflies and rhododendron bugs. Azaleas are attacked by azalea gall, bud blast disease, suckers and whiteflies. In what follows we shall describe several rhododendron species

and hybrids, and then various azaleas divided into groups.

Rhododendron arboreum

A handsome evergreen tree which thrives best in areas with a moist atmosphere. It grows to about 20ft (6m) in Britain, larger in the wild, its leaves from 4–8in (10–20cm) long deep green above and brown to silvery hairy beneath. The flowers are red, up to 2in (5cm) long; opening in late winter and early spring.

Rhododendron augustinii

A 6ft (2m) high shrub with oblong, dark green leaves, scaly underneath and with bristles along the central ribs. The flowers are borne in groups of 3–4 and are broadly funnel shaped, lavender blue to mauve with yellow or green-spotted throats. The most attractive cultivars are 'Blue Diamond', with 2in (5cm) dark purple, later violet-blue, flowers in mid-April to early May, and 'Blue Tit', with bright lavender-blue flowers in late April.

Rhododendron barbatum

An evergreen shrub from the Himalayas, rarely above 16ft (5m) in Britain,

though far more than this in the wild. The narrowly oblong leaves are 4–9in (10–24cm) long and the 1½in (4cm) wide flowers are dark red.

Rhododendron calendulaceum

Flame azalea. A deciduous shrub much used in azalea hybridizing. It is a native of south eastern USA and reaches a height of 10ft (3m). The funnel-shaped flowers are a bright orange or scarlet.

Rhododendron campylocarpum

This handsome Himalayan species makes a shrub from 3–10ft (1–3m) tall, the leaves dark and shining above, blue-green and matt below. The large bell-shaped flowers are up to almost 3in (7.5cm) wide and are a bright yellow, sometimes flushed with red at the base and on the reverse of the petals, showing in bud.

Rhododendron campylogynum

A low growing shrub from China, rarely above 2ft (60cm) though occasionally specimens may exceed this. The 1in (2.5cm) leaves have inrolled margins. In the summer the plant carries pinkish-red to purple bell-shaped flowers each ¾in (2cm) across. In the variety myrtilloides, the flowers are a dark red-purple

Rhododendron 'Marinus Koster'

and the whole bush rarely exceeds 1 ft (30 cm) in height.

Rhododendron catawbiense

A species not now grown much, but the parent of many hardy hybrids. Flowering period May–June. The flowers are lilac with olive-green dots. It can tolerate a fair amount of shade and is evergreen. See also under *Rhododendron* hybrids.

Rhododendron cinnabarinum

◐ ⊛ ✿ ⍟ ✦

Reaching 6½ ft (2 m) in height, this Himalayan species has lustrous grey-green leaves. These contrast well with the funnel-shaped orange-red flowers which are up to 2 in (5 cm) long. It flowers in May–June. *R. cinnabarinum blandfordiaeflorum* is red with a yellow interior. It flowers at the same time as the species.

Rhododendron dauricum

◐ ⊛ ✿ ⍟ ✦

A very attractive 6 ft (2 m) high shrub from south-east Asia. The leaves are shed in the spring, so that the shrub is green in winter and summer. Each leaf is 1–2 in (2.5–5 cm) long; the flowers are pink, broadly funnel shaped, 1–1½ in (2.5–4 cm) wide. Flowering period is January to March, and it is exceptionally hardy.

Rhododendron falconeri

◐ ⊛ ✿ ⍟ ⊛ ✦

A large shrub or small tree to 23 ft (10 m) or more in its native Himalayas, but usually half this in Britain. The stems and the undersides of the 6–12 in (15–30 cm) long leaves are covered with rusty-brown hairs while the 2 in (5 cm) wide flowers are pale creamy-yellow with a purple marking at the base.

Rhododendron fargesii

◐ ⊛ ✿ ⍟ ✦

A native of China, this large shrub or small tree will reach 10 ft (3 m) in height. The oblong leaves are 2–3½ in (5–9 cm) long, shining above, blue-green, glaucous beneath. The pale pink to mauve flowers are 2¼ in (6 cm) wide and often spotted with purple inside.

Rhododendron ferrugineum

◐ ⊛ ✿ ⍟ ✦

The alpine rose of Switzerland. A small, compact evergreen shrub about 2–3 ft (60–90 cm) high which flowers in July. The flowers are small and rose-pink. It is highly recommended for the rock garden. 'Album' has white, and 'Coccineum' crimson-pink, flowers. It will tolerate some chalk or lime.

Rhododendron flavum, see Rhododendron luteum.

Rhododendron forrestii

○ ◐ ✿ ⍟ ✦

A low growing species rarely reaching 1 ft (30 cm) in height, with oval leaves, up to 1½ in (4 cm) long, glossy green above and with a purplish flush beneath. The bright, shining crimson flowers are

bell-shaped but not freely borne. *Repens* is a prostrate form without the purple coloration beneath the leaves.

Rhododendron hippophaeoides

◐ ⊛ ✿ ⍟ ✦

A small evergreen shrub. The leaves are ½ in (1.25 cm) long, set close together, spatulate, with greyish scales underneath, sweetly scented when they unfurl. Lilac flowers appear in April and May. The plant is fairly wide spreading and grows 2–3 ft (60–100 cm) high. It thrives in semi-bog conditions, hence avoid the common mistake of assigning this plant to too dry a spot in the rock garden.

Rhododendron hirsutum

Often described as a hairy variety of *Rhododendron ferrugineum*. Slow-growing, and of compact habit, it grows up to 20 in (50 cm) high. It will tolerate calcareous ground. An evergreen shrub with hairy twigs. The salmon-pink flowers appear in June and July.

Rhododendron hybrids

◐ ⊛ ✿ ⍟ ✦ ⊛

Crosses between many species have given rise to the numerous attractive and fairly large rhododendrons that have become so prevalent in our gardens. Many catalogues list them as "large-flowered rhododendron hybrids". For cultivation, see p. 167. The following deserve special mention:

Flowering period January–March: 'Nableanum', rich rose, flushed white.

Flowering period March–April: 'Dr. Stocker', milk-white, marked brown-crimson; 'Lady Primrose', pale yellow; 'Peter Koster', light red.

Flowering period May–June: 'Beefeater', geranium-red; 'Britannia', crimson; 'Goldsworth Pink', rose-pink to white; 'Hawk', sulphur-yellow; 'Lady Roseberry', deep and light pink; 'Loderi King George', large white; 'Purple Splendour', purple-blue.

Flowering period June–July: 'Furnival's Daughter', which is light rose-pink with dark markings; 'Goldsworth Orange', pale orange and apricot; 'Gomer Waterer', white flushed mauve with mustard-yellow blotch; 'Jutland', geranium-red; 'Polar Bear', white; 'Romany Chal', cardinal-red; 'Souvenir of Anthony Waterer', salmon-pink, yellow blotch.

Rhododendron impeditum

◐ ⊛ ✿ ⍟ ✦ ⊛

A dwarf shrub, slow-growing, 1–3 ft (30–90 cm) tall with very small leaves. Light purple-blue flowers are borne in May. It is a very suitable shrub for rock gardens.

The azalea 'Christopher Wren'

A Knap Hill-Exbury azalea

The early-flowering Japanese azalea 'Fedora'

Rhododendron luteum

◐ ⊛ ✿ ⍟

Syn. *Rhododendron flavum*. A very hardy but deciduous shrub, the parent of many crosses. Grows up to 6 ft (2 m), with a densely branching form. The leaves are lanceolate, hairy at first, turning yellow-red in the autumn. The golden, strongly fragrant flowers appear shortly before the leaves unfurl.

Rhododendron minus

◐ ⊛ ✿ ⍟ ⊛

Syn. *Rhododendron punctatum*. Dense, evergreen shrub with fairly thick, blue, later brown, leaves covered with dense, reddish-brown scales underneath. Purple-pink flowers with large green spots appear in June. Suitable for rock gardens.

Rhododendron mucronulatum

◐ ⊛ ✿ ⍟ ⊛

A handsome deciduous shrub which may flower as early as January in mild winters, though the flowers may then be destroyed by later frosts. The broadly funnel-shaped flowers are purple-pink.

Rhododendron neriiflorum

An evergreen shrub from China growing to 8 ft (2.5 m) high. Purple-pink flowers are borne in December–February.

Rhododendron ponticum

◐ ⊛ ✿ ⍟ ⊛

The most commonly seen rhododendron in the British Isles, it resembles *Rhododendron catawbiense* but has oblong leaves, light green underneath. The flowers are lilac-pink to magenta from May to June. 'Imbricatum' is a compact, slow-growing shrub with overlapping leaves and purple flowers.

Rhododendron × praecox

◐ ⊛ ✿ ⍟ ⊛

A cross between *Rhododendron ciliatum* and *Rhododendron dauricum*, it is an attractive evergreen flowering shrub. Dark pink flowers with a touch of lilac appear from February to April. It is splendid in combination with yellow crocuses or *Erica carnea*. Perhaps the most rewarding of the smaller rhododendrons, though it sometimes flowers so early as to suffer from late frosts.

Rhododendron punctatum, see Rhododendron minus.

Rhododendron racemosum

An evergreen shrub 3–5 ft (1–1.5 m) high with leaves distributed very evenly over the branches. Foliage is dull green on top, silvery-grey underneath and covered with dark brown scales. The flowers, which are in shades of pink, appear in March or April. It is sensitive to late frosts but will usually recover.

Rhododendron × praecox

A *Rhododendron williamsianum* hybrid

Rhododendron repens hybrids

An important group of small, early-flowering shrubs producing masses of blooms. 'Elizabeth' has salmon-pink flowers; later-flowering are 'Baden-Baden', scarlet; 'Carmen', dark red; 'Elizabeth Hobbie', bright red; 'Salute', bright red, and 'Scarlet Wonder', ruby-red.

Rhododendron viscosum

Syn. *Azalea viscosa*. Swamp honeysuckle. A deciduous shrub, 4½–6ft (1.5–2m) high, with oval, dark green leaves, bluish-green underneath. The flowers are white or pink from July to August. Thrives in moist positions.

Rhododendron williamsianum

A shrub, 2–5ft (60–150cm) high with a 1–2in (2.5–5cm) long bright green, small, heart-shaped leaves. The branches spread out horizontally so that the shrub has a globular habit. The bell-shaped flowers, 1–2in (2.5–5cm) long and pale pink, appear towards the end of April. Some of the best modern cultivars are: 'April Glow', early flowering with rose-red flowers; 'Bow Bells', with soft coral-red flowers in May–June; 'Karin', early-flowering, deep pink; 'Linda', rose-red and late flowering; 'Tibet', with pink buds and white flowers from May to June.

Rhododendron yakushimanum

An evergreen shrub up to 3ft (1m) high with a globular habit. Young shoots are covered with silvery hair. The leaves are 2–4in (5–10cm) long, hard and leathery. Masses of apple-blossom pink, later white, flowers appear in May.

Rhododendron yedoense

A deciduous shrub with narrow, pointed leaves, downy on the top and hairier underneath. Double rose-lilac flowers with purple spots appear April–May.

Azaleas

Azaleas, which are now officially classified as rhododendrons, can be divided into the following six groups:

Japanese hybrid azaleas

This group includes a series of small semi-evergreen and evergreen shrubs 20–60in (50–150cm) high originating from numerous crosses. They are often sub-divided into large- and small-flowered varieties, although a careful distinction on these lines can no longer be made. All varieties named below are hardy.

Early (first half of May) with large flowers: 'Fedora', deep pink; 'Kathleen', dark pink; 'Lilac Time', deep lilac; 'Vuyk's Scarlet', deep scarlet. Flowering in the second half of May: 'Beethoven', orchid-purple; 'Mother's Day', carmine, double flowered; 'Palestrina', ivory-white.

Early with small flowers: 'Addy Wery', deep vermilion; 'Aladdin', geranium-red; 'Campfire', deep red; 'Favourite', deep rosy-pink; 'Hino de-ro-taka' deep crimson. A number of these, such as 'Blaauw's Pink', which is salmon-pink, may also flower in late May.

Knap Hill-Exbury azaleas

This group is of greater importance than the first. It includes many fairly new and exceptionally beautiful crosses raised in England. The varieties named below are all reliably hardy. Second half of May: 'Ballerina', white; 'Balzac', deep orange-red; 'Gibraltar', deep orange; 'Persil', white with a yellow spot; 'Pink Delight', deep pink with a yellow spot; 'Strawberry Ice', light pink; and 'Sylphides', soft pink. Slightly later: 'Basilisk', light yellow; 'Klondyke', golden-yellow. Still later (June): 'Cecile', deep pink; 'Fireball', deep orange; 'Golden Sunset', deep yellow; 'Royal Command', vermilion; 'Satan', deep red; and 'Sun Chariot', golden-yellow.

Occidentale hybrids

Raised from various crosses with *Rhododendron occidentale*, a small shrub with fragrant, white or red flowers flushed yellow. The best-known cultivars include: 'Exquisitum', light pink with a yellow flush; 'Irene Koster', pink with a yellow flush; 'Magnificum', creamy-white with a pink flush; and 'Pink Cloud', pink. All are very hardy. Flowering period is the second half of May or later.

Ghent hybrids

Their flowering period is the second half of May or slightly earlier, and the flowers are fragrant and small. 'Coccinea Speciosa' is orange; 'Corneille', is double pink; 'Fanny' is dark purple-rose; and 'Nancy Waterer' is golden-yellow.

Rustica hybrids

These are all double varieties and flower in late May and early June. 'Aida', is pink with a touch of lilac; 'Freya' is salmon-yellow; 'Norma' is rose-red; 'Phebe' is sulphur-yellow; and 'Velasquez' is creamy-white with a touch of pink.

Mollis azaleas

An attractive group of selections of *R. japonicum* crossed with *R. molle* to produce a wide range of exceptionally beautiful plants with flowers of more intense colours, with a very short flowering period in April or May. Some of the best-known varieties are: 'Christopher Wren', which is orange-yellow; 'Dr. M. Oosthoek', orange-red; 'Frans van der Bom', which is salmon-orange; Hamlet', salmon-orange; 'Hortulanus H. Witte', orange-yellow; 'Koningin Emma' ('Queen Emma'), salmon-pink; 'Koster's Brilliant Red', orange-red; 'Mrs Peter Koster', deep red; 'Salmon Queen', salmon-pink; 'Spek's Orange', orange-red; 'Spinoza', orange with a touch of pink.

Rhus
Anarcardiaceae
Sumach

A genus of deciduous and evergreen shrubs, trees and climbers. Several species are suitable for planting in groups in large gardens, but *Rhus glabra* 'Dissecta' (syn. *Rhus glabra laciniata*) is specially recommended as a specimen tree for the smaller garden, where its glorious autumn foliage will make an exceptional show.

Soil They will grow in any soil, even if dry. Sumachs are also tolerant of chalk.
Propagation Usually from suckers or root cuttings, but also stem cuttings in late summer and from seed sown when ripe and placed in a cold frame.

Rhus cotinus, see Cotinus coggygria.
Rhus glabra

Smooth sumach. A deciduous shrub or small tree from North America reaching a height of 10ft (3m). The branches are hairless, sometimes with a bluish bloom. The composite leaves with 11–31 leaflets, each 4in (10cm) long and 2in (5cm) wide are pointed, hairless and bluish-green underneath. The flowers are green in dense panicles, which remain on the stem in the winter. The red autumn colour is very beautiful. An added attraction is the clusters of rosy-red fruits in erect spikes.

Rhus × pulvinata

A cross between *Rhus glabra* and *Rhus typhina*, a hybrid blending the characters of both parents. The young twigs are slightly hairy, later bare. Leaves are bluish-green underneath, with inflorescences covered with thick hair.

Rhus trichocarpa

A small tree native to China, Japan and Korea, growing to a height of 10–15ft (3–5m) with a spread of about 10ft (3m). It has pinnate leaves that turn bright scarlet in autumn and small inconspicuous flowers borne on panicles in June. The fruits are yellow and suspended in clusters.

Rhus typhina

Stag's horn sumach. A shrub or small tree from North America reaching a height of 15ft (5m). The greenish-yellow flowers open June–July. Resembles *R. glabra* but the branches are covered with velvety red-brown hair. Also has male and female flowers on separate plants.

Rhus typhina 'Laciniata' with deeply incised leaflets

Ribes sanguineum

Ribes sanguineum 'Splendens'

Ribes
Saxifragaceae
Flowering currant

A genus of flowering and fruiting shrubs including the edible currants and the gooseberry, which are not covered in this book. The flowering types are often used to fill poorer sites, as they can tolerate a fair amount of shade.

Soil Any ordinary garden soil is adequate.

Propagation Hardwood cuttings taken in October and November root very easily.

Ribes alpinum
○ ◐ ◒ ◒ ❀ ▥

A shrub from northern and central Europe and Siberia reaching heights of 3–6ft (1–2m). The flowering period is April–May. Yellowish-green, inconspicuous flowers are borne in erect racemes. The berries are dark red and sweet. The leaves have an attractive yellow-gold autumn colour. It is very suitable for planting under deciduous trees and good for hedging.

Ribes aureum
○ ◐ ◒ ❀ ❀

Golden or buffalo currant. A shrub from North America, up to 6ft (2m) high. Bright yellow, fragrant flowers bloom from April to May. It has attractive red autumn foliage, but does not grow in the shade. Brilliant yellow flowers appear in April.

Ribes floridum, see *Ribes americanum*.

Ribes sanguineum
○ ◐ ◒ Ⓨ ⊗

A shrub from California north to British Columbia, up to 10ft (3m) high. Rose-red flowers April–May are followed by blackish-blue berries. This is probably the most popular flowering currant. Some of the best cultivars are: 'Atrorubens', compact habit, dark red flowers; 'Brocklebankii', leaves golden-yellow; 'King Edward VII', deep crimson flowers; 'Pulborough Scarlet', large scarlet racemes; 'Splendens', crimson flowers in large and long racemes.

Ricinus
Euphorbiaceae
Castor oil plant

This tropical shrub is usually treated as a half-hardy garden annual grown from seed, but it can also be grown in pots and tubs, overwintered in a heated greenhouse or warm room, and allowed to develop into a very large specimen. When grown as an annual, it makes a most attractive foliage plant for use in formal bedding schemes, for planting in groups at the back of the border or in a solitary position. On fertile soil it can reach a height of 8ft (2.4m) within a year of being planted.

Soil Grow in any well-drained fertile soil. Plant out in late May to June in a sunny place, after the soil has been dug over and enriched with organic matter, and water regularly in dry weather.

Propagation Sow seeds in March, one to a pot, and keep at about 18°C (65°F) or just above. As soon as the seedlings are large enough to handle, they must be moved to larger pots. If smaller plants are preferred, the seeds should be sown outdoors during the second half of May. Depending on the size and shape of the garden, plant at distances of 2½–6ft (75cm–2m) apart.

Ricinus communis
○ ❀ ◒ ◒ ⊕

From Africa, it grows up to 5ft (1.5m) when grown as an annual. A quick-growing, wide-branching plant with mid-green palmate leaves. The flowers are inconspicuous. 'Gibsonii' (small with red leaves), 'Cambodgensis' (dark purple leaves and stems) and 'Zanzibariensis' (leaves green, whitish veined) are amongst the best cultivars.

The leaves of *Ricinus communis*, the castor oil plant

Robinia pseudoacacia

Robinia pseudoacacia 'Frisia'

Robinia
Leguminosae
False acacia

A genus of beautiful flowering trees and shrubs of which the best known is *Robinia pseudoacacia*.
Cultivation The branches of all species snap off easily in high winds. This is a particularly grave problem with *Robinia hispida* and *R. kelseyi*, which should therefore be trained against walls.
Soil Well-drained, ordinary garden soil is needed.
Propagation Species can be grown from suckers, root cuttings, layers and seed. Cultivars can also be grafted on to seedlings of *Robinia pseudoacacia*.

Robinia hispida
○ ⊜ ❀ ⑩ ⑨ ⊕
Rose acacia. A shrub from China and Japan, up to 6ft (2m) high. Branches are spineless, first red and covered with bristly hair, later olive-green with red stipples. The leaves are made up of 9–13 leaflets; they are ½–1½in (1–4cm) long, round to oval, spiky and hairless. It flowers in June and often again in late summer. The flowers are borne in

dense racemes, pink to rose-pink. A very attractive plant, particularly at the back of the smaller shrub or mixed border. It is essential to shelter it from the wind.
Robinia kelseyi
From the SE United States. One of the most attractive of all robinias, it requires shelter from the wind and grows up to 10ft (3m). It is easily trained against a wall. The flowers are lilac-pink, in 2in (5cm) inflorescences, on the previous year's shoots. The flowering period is May.
Robinia luxurians
○ ❀ ⑩ ⊕
A strong growing shrub or small tree to 33ft (10m). The pale rose to white flowers open in June and often again later.
Robinia pseudoacacia
○ ⊜ ❀ ⑧ ❀ ⊕
Common or false acacia; black locust. A tree 80ft (25m) high or more with an umbrella-shaped crown. The branches are green to reddish-brown and hairless. It has strong, large spines. The leaves are made up of 9–19 leaflets in number, 1–2in (2.5–5cm) long, ovate and spinous. The flowering period is June. The flowers are white, sometimes pink, fragrant with a yellow stain at the

base of the standard and borne on pendulous racemes, about 8in (20cm) long. The young leaves, inner bark and seeds of this tree are poisonous. The best-known cultivars are: 'Bessoniana', a small- to medium-sized tree with a decorative rounded crown, and branches almost entirely devoid of spines; 'Frisia', a smaller tree with yellow leaves and red spines; 'Inermis', a small tree with thornless twigs; 'Semperflorens' with flowers produced intermittently from June to September; 'Tortuosa', a small tree or shrub with contorted branches; 'Umbraculifera' an old-fashioned tree with a rounded head that never flowers; 'Unifoliola', a spineless tree with leaves reduced to a single large leaflet or to groups of 3–5 leaflets. Because the leaves do not come out until late April or May, *Robinia pseudoacacia* may be transplanted very late in the spring (the best planting time), and is suitable for planting in places where no shade is desired in May, but welcomed later in the year, for instance in front of south-facing windows.
Robinia viscosa
Clammy locust. A tree up to 30ft (9m) high with sticky, olive-green twigs having few spines. Hairless leaflets, 13–25 to the leaf, about 1in (2.5cm)

The pink flowers of *Robinia hispida*

long, oval, sometimes slightly hairy underneath, have rudimentary spines. The flowering period is June, often later. The flowers are light pink. Because of its small size, this tree is more suitable for smaller gardens than *Robinia pseudoacacia*.

Rodgersia
Saxifragaceae

A genus of hardy herbaceous perennials reminiscent of shrubs.
Cultivation A partially shaded site sheltered from strong winds is needed to grow these plants to perfection.
Soil Humus-rich soil that is always moist but not too wet is needed.
Propagation Mostly by division but also from seed.

Rodgersia aesculifolia
◑ ⑩ ⊗ ⊕ ○ ⊛
A 5ft (1.5m) high species from China, with glossy bronze leaves similar to those of the horse-chestnut. White flowers in 2ft (60cm) long panicles appear in June–July. The whole plant is covered with brownish hair.
Rodgersia pinnata
This resembles the last species, except that the centremost of the 5–9 leaflets is always long stemmed while the rest is sessile. The small flowers are pink and white. 'Superba' has bronze-coloured leaves and pink flowers.
Rodgersia podophylla
A herbaceous perennial from China, 3–5ft (1–1.5m) high. Leaves are palmate, divided, first bronze-coloured, later green. Sprays of cream-coloured flowers from June to July.
Rodgersia purdomii
Probably only a form of *Rodgersia pinnata* but has somewhat smaller leaves. White flowers in large inflorescences in June and July.
Rodgersia sambucifolia
A perennial plant from China with pinnate leaves. White flowers in small inflorescences appear in July and August.

The brown leaves of *Rodgersia podophylla*

Rosa
Rosaceae
Rose

The rose is without doubt the most beloved and popular of all garden shrubs, and one that is versatile as no other: bedding schemes, ground cover, wall climbers, hedges, specimen trees, mixed borders—the rose lends itself readily to all these purposes.

Where should roses be bought? The number of roses on offer to the gardener is enormous and, needless to say, there is a great deal of chaff among the wheat. In particular, it would be quite wrong to assume that the nurseryman with the most beautiful catalogue invariably supplies the best roses. The gardener would do well to visit some of the leading rose gardens at home and abroad to see roses growing and assess their beauty and quality. The commercial ones will supply catalogues in which he can mark the roses of his choice and later order them from the comfort of his armchair.

Soil Roses demand well-drained, rich garden soil and are tolerant of lime. Before planting, it is advisable to dig a hole 2–3 ft (60–100 cm) deep. If this should go below the water table, then a 4 in (10 cm) layer of rubble should be placed at the bottom of the hole and a minimum of 2 ft (50 cm) of soil laid on top of it. Poor, sandy soils can be improved with peat, litter, clay, leaf-mould or compost. Roses like fertile soil and must be fed regularly, preferably with cow manure that has been thoroughly mixed with the soil. Lime [4 lb (2 kilos) of ground limestone per 100 sq ft (9.3 sq m)] should be applied a few weeks later and raked in. Roses may be left undisturbed until they begin to deteriorate, anything from 10 to 20 or more years. If it is intended to construct another rose bed in the same position, the earth should be completely replenished to depths of 1½–2 ft (45–60 cm).

Planting Roses are best planted in the autumn, except on moist ground, when they should be planted in the spring. Plant at a depth such that the bud union comes to lie 1 in (2.5 cm) below soil level. To prevent the roots from drying out in the sun or wind, it is advisable to wrap in polythene sheeting or cover them with wet sacking until they can be planted. The roots should not be pruned beyond the careful removal of any broken or damaged sections. The stem may be cut back very hard before or after planting. The previous year's stems of shrub or standard roses are pruned back to some 2–3 buds—more buds should be left in the autumn than in the spring. Climbers should be cut back to within 2 ft (60 cm) of the ground. Plant rose bushes 14–18 in (35–45 cm) apart, depending on their vigour; climbers should be planted 10–12 ft (3–4 m) apart; standards 32–40 in (80–100 cm) apart. Standard roses should be secured to sturdy stakes positioned before the roses were planted.

Pruning Rose bushes should be pruned back severely every year. In the autumn only the soft tips are removed; in the spring, when the winter frosts are past, the dead wood and then all weak or damaged shoots are removed. The remaining branches should be cut back to 3 or 5 buds from the base depending on the nature of the plant—vigorous

Rosa 'Prima Ballerina' (Hybrid tea)

plants should be allowed to retain a few buds more than weak ones. Standard roses should be pruned like rose bushes, summer pruning being usually confined to dead-heading. Too much pruning in the summer may weaken a rose; at least one complete (mostly quintuple) leaf must be left on each stem. Dead flowers should be removed with at most one-third of the stem; better still no more than 6 in (15 cm) at the tip should be cut off, the rule being that the cut should be made immediately above the uppermost complete leaf.

Climbers must be pruned differently. These roses produce long branches that have to be tied carefully, for during their first year they are very soft and snap off easily. During the second year, there appear short lateral shoots, which bear flowers. During the third year these lateral shoots may have grown long, in which case they will only bear flowers at their tips and the plant will look bare in the middle. To prevent this happening, the lateral shoots should be cut back to 3 or 5 buds in the spring. Climbers are therefore pruned in much the same way as shrub roses, provided that the main framework branches are treated as the main stem. When climbers are well fed they will produce a number of long vigorous shoots in the summer. This enables the gardener to remove some of the main framework branches that may have lost their vigour, thus rejuvenating the plant and keeping it in good heart and good flower.

Miniature roses are pruned in the same way as rose bushes. Species roses require little pruning other than the removal of straggly growths and dead wood.

Feeding Well-rotted manure is still the best rose fertilizer, and is indeed used in most leading rose gardens. Mulching is best done in spring after pruning. It is not advisable to dig a great deal between roses. In the summer after the first flowering period, roses should be given a dressing of dried blood, hoof and horn or bone-meal or a proprietary

rose fertilizer. Many gardeners attribute their success with roses to this particular treatment. If the ground is deficient in lime, it is advisable to apply some ground limestone. Ideally the soil should be slightly acid, having a pH of 6.5.

Propagation Species roses can be grown from seed or propagated from cuttings, a method that can also be used with miniature roses, old-fashioned roses and old-fashioned climbers. Modern roses, too, can be successfully grown from cuttings, but the resultant plants usually lack vigour. Growers accordingly prefer to propagate roses by budding. To follow their example, the amateur should acquire a number of rootstocks and insert growth buds of the desired cultivar into them.

Pests and diseases Though commercial growers do their utmost to raise resistant strains, roses are nevertheless prone to attack by many diseases and parasites, of which aphids, mildew and black spot are the best known. Bad siting (too much shade, too dry, or too wet) and lack of fertilizer greatly encourage disease and pests. If the buds are seen to be covered with greenfly in the early summer, it is not generally necessary to rush for the spray gun—within a few days natural enemies (ladybirds, spiders and birds) will have made the same discovery and slaughter will follow on a massive scale. Even a shower or a good dousing with the hose can get rid of a great many aphids. In obstinate cases, the plants should be sprayed with not too toxic an insecticide, preferably one with a pyrethrum base, which is a natural poison. Other enemies of the rose, such as rust, caterpillars, leaf-rolling sawflies, chafer beetles and red spiders may safely be ignored—well-sited and well-fertilized roses are not seriously threatened by them. If yellow discolorations appear between the veins of the leaf, the plant is probably suffering from magnesium deficiency. The cure is an application of Epsom salts at 1 oz per sq yd (30 g per sq m), or a proprietary preparation.

Classification of roses Here we shall

Climbing rose on a pergola

Rosa multiflora

Rosa pimpinellifolia 'Frühlingsanfang'

not be using the method of classification based on botanical characters. Most amateurs are not really interested in the finer botanical details, and those who are can consult a host of standard works devoted to the subject. Just for the record, we would point out that *Rosa chinensis*, *Rosa odorata* and several other species are the parents of the Bourbon roses, the Noisette roses, the Tea roses and the Hybrid Teas. Of all these hybrids, only the Hybrid Teas, which are very common, are still cultivated. *Rosa multiflora* is the parent of the Polyantha roses and hence of the Floribundas, and of many modern climbers. For practical reasons we shall divide roses into the following groups: Hybrid Teas; Floribundas; Climbers; Miniature or Dwarf roses; Standard roses; and Species roses.

Rosa 'Kathleen Ferrier' a modern shrub

Hybrid Tea roses

○ ⌒ ⍾ 🐝 🦋 ⊥ ⊗

Every yellow rose used to be called a tea rose, but ever since the advent of the Hybrid Tea this description has had to be dropped, for Hybrid Teas come in all possible colours with the exception of pure blue. Hybrid Teas can be distinguished by their unusually large, beautiful and often fragrant double flowers, borne singly. Long-stemmed cultivars make particularly good cut flowers: most roses sold by florists are Hybrid Teas, generally grown under glass. In recent years, Floribundas have begun to oust Hybrid Teas in popularity, particularly in public places, because they flower much more profusely and over a longer period. Amateur gardeners need not necessarily follow suit, since there is no need to fill beds with roses of the same type. Indeed, there is nothing more beautiful than a wide selection of Hybrid Teas, with two or three specimens of each type, gaps in the collection being filled gradually with new acquisitions.

Hybrid Teas produce their first and richest show of blooms in July, and continue to produce flowers, though less profusely, until October. However, the flowering period and profusion differ from one cultivar to the next, and the height, too, varies from 2ft (60cm) to 5ft (1.5m). Below, we shall list some of the best-known, strongest, and most beautiful Hybrid Teas. Needless to say this is no more than a random selection; it would be impossible to present an exhaustive list in a book of this type.

'Blessings', soft coral-pink, 3ft (1m); 'Chicago Peace', yellow and salmon-pink, 4ft (1.2m); 'Criterion', cerise, 3½ft (1m); 'Dame de Coeur', scarlet, 3ft (1m); 'Duke of Windsor', orange-vermilion, very fragrant, 2½ft (75cm); 'Eden Rose', deep pink, scented, 3½ft (1m); 'Ena Harkness', crimson-scarlet, inclined to droop, 2½ft (75cm); 'Ernest Henry Morse', cherry-red, sweetly scented, 3ft (1m); 'Grandpa Dickson' ('Irish Gold'), yellow, 3ft (1m); 'Michele Meilland', soft pink, fragrant, 2½ft (75cm); 'Miss France', orange-red

A bright floribunda rose

2½ft (75cm); 'Mullard Jubilee' ('Electron'), deep rose-pink, 2½ft (75cm); 'Papa Meilland', dark crimson, beautiful fragrance, 2½ft (75cm); 'Pascali', white, 3½ft (1m); 'Peace', yellow with flushes of pink, extremely well known, faintly scented, 4ft (1.2m); 'Pink Peace', deep pink, sweetly scented, 3½ft (1m); 'Prima Ballerina', cherry-pink, richly scented, 3ft (1m); 'Rose Gaujard', white flushed carmine, with buds of an unusual shape, 3½ft (1m); 'Silver Lining', rose with silver, very fragrant, 2½ft (75cm); 'Super Star', ('Tropicana'), vermilion, popular as a cut flower, fragrant, 3ft (1m); 'Uncle Walter', scarlet, 6ft (2m); 'Virgo', the most attractive of the pure white hybrids, but only a moderate grower, 2ft (60cm); 'Wendy Cussons', cerise-scarlet, strongly fragrant, 3ft (1m).

Floribunda roses

○ ⍾ 🐝 🦋 ⊗

Modern Floribundas are mainly derived from crosses between the Dwarf Polyantha and Hybrid Tea roses. The flowers may be single, semi-double or double and are borne in terminal clusters. Floribundas have been hybridized with Hybrid Teas and it is now sometimes difficult to decide which is which. The largest-flowered cultivars are now officially known as Grandifloras. Floribundas may be grown in separate beds or in shrub borders and look well

in private gardens no less than in public parks. They should always be planted in fairly large numbers, preferably all of the same kind. They are much more floriferous than Hybrid Teas, and also flower for much longer periods. Some cultivars are particularly good for cutting. The selection given below is once again far from exhaustive, but is based on personal experience and preference.

'Allgold', buttercup-yellow, semi-double, 2½ft (75cm); 'Chinatown', yellow, very fragrant, double, 5ft (1.5m); 'City of Belfast', vermilion-scarlet, double, 2½ft (75cm); 'Europeana', deep crimson, semi-double, 2½ft (75cm); 'Fervid', scarlet, single, 3½ft (1m); 'Fresco', orange with yellow, double, 2½ft (75cm); 'Jan Spek', yellow, double, 2ft (60cm); 'Lilli Marleen', scarlet-red, single, 2½ft (75cm); 'Olala', crimson-scarlet, double, 3ft (1m); 'Paprika', bright geranium-red, semi-double, 2½ft (75cm); 'Pernille Poulsen', salmon-pink, double, 2½ft (75cm); 'Queen Elizabeth', clear pink, double, 5ft (1.5m); 'Red Gold', golden-yellow and pink, semi-double, 3ft (1m); 'Sarabande', orange-red, single, 2½ft (75cm); 'Saratoga', white, double, 2½ft (75cm); 'Scarlet Queen Elizabeth',

A modern *Rosa gallica* hybrid

bright scarlet, double, 4ft (1.2m); 'Iceberg', pure white, double, 4ft (1.2m); 'Sunday Times', bright pink, double, 2ft (60cm).

Climbers

○ ⍾ 🐝 🦋 ⍾ ⊖ ⊗

Among climbers and ramblers we distinguish cultivars with large double flowers (derived from Hybrid Teas) and more floriferous sorts with single or semi-double flowers. Some may reach heights of 18–30ft (6–9m); others are much shorter. Climbers are not really perpetual flowerers—modern types may be repeat-flowering but the main flowering period in summer is nevertheless by far the most important. Nurseries would seem to have ignored the improvement of climbers. A great deal of further research could be done into their flowering properties, colours and hardiness.

Ramblers are suitable for growing over pergolas, arbours, pillars and fences. Climbers are best trained against walls, but it is important to leave a gap, preferably 4in (10cm) wide, because roses need a great deal of air. Hence they should be attached to trellises or wires. Some ramblers make excellent ground cover on slopes and banks. Some of the best cultivars of climbers and ramblers are: 'Danse de Feu', dark foliage, vivid red double, 10ft (3m); 'Dortmund', red, single, 8–10ft (2.4–3m); 'Handel', cream and

pink with interesting markings, semi-double 8–10ft (2.4–3m) high; 'Leverkusen', pale yellow, double, 10ft (3m); 'Mermaid', single, yellow with amber red stamens, 25ft (8m); 'New Dawn', pale pink, double, 7–12ft (2.2–4m); 'Parkdirektor Riggers', crimson, single, 12ft (4m); 'Paul's Scarlet Climber', crimson, very popular cultivar, double, 10ft (3m); 'Pink Perpétue', semi-double, coral pink, 8ft (2.5m); 'Solo', dark red, double, 7ft (2.2m).

Miniature roses

Very compact 6–12in (15–30cm) shrubs that produce otherwise perfectly normal but small flowers. Most cultivars are repeat-flowering and completely hardy, but can also be grown indoors in pots or window boxes, a method strangely enough not much practiced today. Recommended cultivars are: 'Baby Faurax', lavender purple, 1ft (30cm); 'Coralin', salmon-red, 1ft (30cm); 'Little Flirt', red and yellow bicolour, 1–1.3ft (30–40cm).

Standard roses

○ ⌒ ⍾ 🐝 ⊥ ⊗

Standard roses are not a separate race, but are simply bush roses budded to the top of a 2–5ft (60cm–1.5m) high stem, so that they look like small trees. If the scion is a rambler the result is a weeping standard, an extraordinarily beautiful plant that makes an outstanding specimen tree.

Standard roses have fallen out of favour somewhat in recent times, which is a pity, for although they require more care than other roses and are more expensive, they have a unique appeal, and a line of standard roses along one or both sides of the front path is as striking a sight in the modern garden as ever it was in our grandfathers' day.

If suckers are sent up from the rootstock they should be removed at once for they greatly weaken the rest of the plant. Standard roses should be pruned and tended in the same way as rose bushes; weeping standards in the same way as climbers. There is no point in listing cultivars since, in principle, every shrub or climbing rose can be budded on to a standard rootstock.

Species roses

Under this heading we include all wild roses as well as natural crosses between two species. Most flower early, in May–June, usually with single blooms. There is no repeat flowering but some species produce beautiful hips in the autumn. Species roses, which can quickly grow to a fair height, are usually planted in parks, or used as specimen plants or in groups and as hedging plants in the garden. The most important, in alphabetical order, are:

Rosa alpina, see *Rosa pendulina*.

Rosa banksiae

○ 🐝 ○ ⍾ 🐝 🐝

Banksian rose. A climbing rose which remains evergreen in mild winters. Against a sheltered wall it can reach 23ft (7m), its purple-tinted, slender stems without prickles. The leaves are made up of 3–5 leaflets and the white or yellow fragrant flowers are up to 1in (3cm) across. They are followed by small and rounded red hips. 'Normalis' is the single white form; 'Lutescens' single yellow; 'Alba Plena' double white and 'Lutea' double yellow.

Rosa canina

○ ◑ ◐ ◐ ◐

Dog rose. Frequently used as a root-stock for modern roses, and is suit-able for hedging. Flowering period is June–July, with pink flowers in groups of two or more. Hips are oval. There are several cultivars, with heights up to 10ft (3m).

Rosa carolina

○ ◑ ◉ ◎

The best-known variety is 'Alba', a beautiful, compact and spherical shrub. The hips which follow the white flowers last for a long time.

Rosa centifolia

○ ◑ ◉ ⊗

Cabbage or Provence rose. A large shrub with bright green shoots and fairly large and broadly toothed leaflets. Pink flowers appear in June–July. Varieties include 'Blanche Moreau', with double white flowers; 'Fantin-Latour', a particularly attractive sort with pink flowers; 'La Noblesse', soft red; and 'Petite de Hollande', light pink, pompon flowered.

Rosa chinensis

○ ○ ◑ ◉

Monthly or China rose. This scramb-ling shrub rose grows 6–10ft (2–3m) in height. The leaves are a shining green

Rosa nitida in the autumn

with 3–5 leaflets. The 2in wide (5cm) flowers are red, pink or white. The cultivar 'Minima' (often called *Rosa roulettii*) is only 6–12in (15–30cm) high and has double flowers. It has been used in hybridization to produce the minia-ture roses.

Rosa cinnamomea, see *Rosa pendulina*.

Rosa damascena

Damask rose. A large shrub covered with hooked spines and prickly bristles. Leaflets are oval, elongated and hairy underneath, and are found on spinous stalks. Flowering period is June–July with large red or bluish flowers in groups of 5–10. The flower stalks are covered with glandular bristles. 'Trigintipetala' has semi-double flowers and is heavily scented. Attar of Roses is derived from this plant. 'Versicolor' ('York and Lancaster') has semi-double flowers with white and red stripes.

Rosa ecae

○ ○ ◑ ◉ ⊛

A prickly, dense shrub up to 3ft (1m) in height. A native of Afghanistan it has small leaves, each with 5–11, rounded, leaflets and bright yellow flowers. These are borne singly in May and June and are up to 1in (2.5cm) across.

Hips of *Rosa moyesii*

Rosa eglanteria, see *Rosa rubiginosa*.

Rosa elegantula

○ ◑ ◐ ◉

Syn. *Rosa farreri*. A suckering shrub to 4½ft (1.5m) with bristly stems which are red when young. The small, oval leaflets are 7–11 to a leaf and the pink flowers are up to an inch (2.5cm) wide. *Persetosa*, the threepenny bit rose is smaller with deeper coloured flowers.

Rosa filipes

○ ◑ ◐ ◉ ⊛

A climber reaching at least 20ft (6m), often more, the strong stems with curved prickles. The cream, sometimes pink flushed flowers are 1in (2.5cm) across and are carried in large clusters, which cascade from the branches. They are followed by bright red, rounded hips. 'Kiftsgate' is a strong growing, free flowering form that is excellent for growing over a tree, which it will cover with blossom.

Rosa foetida

Syn. *Rosa lutea*. A large shrub with prickly stems. Leaflets are oval, doubly toothed and hairy underneath. They are shed very early on in the summer. Single bright yellow flowers, 2–2½in (5–6cm) across, solitary or in small clusters, appear in June. They have an unpleasant scent. The best-known varieties are: 'Bicolor', with coppery red flowers, yellow on the outside, appearing as early as April; 'Lawrence Johnston', a climber with single yellow flowers; and 'Persiana' ('Persian Yellow') with bright golden-yellow double flowers.

Rosa gallica

○ ◑ ◐ ◉ ⊛

French rose. A large suckering shrub with greyish-green hairless stems and

spines and bristles that break off very easily. The leaves are fairly thick and hairy underneath. Solitary rose-red flowers, 2–3in (5–7cm) across, appear June–July. It has orange hips. The best-known cultivars—all of hybrid origin—are 'Cardinal de Richelieu', violet-red; 'Complicata', 4½ft (1.3m), single, pure pink flowers in May fol-lowed by red hips in the autumn; 'Constance Spry', bright rose; 'Scarlet Fire', 6ft (2m), scarlet-crimson flowers followed by pear-shaped hips.

Rosa glauca, see *R. rubrifolia*.

Rosa × harisonii

Syn. *Rosa* 'Harison's Yellow'. A hybrid reaching 3–7ft (1–2m). In June and July it is covered with bright yellow, semi-double flowers which contrast with the dark green, shining foliage.

Rosa helenae

○ ◑ ◐ ◉ ⊛

A climbing shrub reaching 13–20ft (4–6m) with clusters of fragrant white flowers to 1½in (4cm) across. They are followed by oval, orange-red hips.

Rosa lutea, see *Rosa foetida*.

Rosa moschata

○ ◑ ◉ ⊗

Autumn musk rose. A shrub reaching a height of 3–12ft (1–4m). Musk scented. White flowers, 2in (5cm) across, in clusters of up to 10, are followed by brown hips.

Rosa moyesii

○ ◑ ◉ ◎ ⊗

A shrub 6–10ft (2–3m) high with arch-ing branches. The numerous thorns are short and straight, the leaflets oval and pointed, with the central rib covered with hair. Flowering period is June, with 2–4 dark red 2in (5cm) flowers per cluster. The large orange-red to crim-

son hips are flask shaped. It makes a very good solitary plant. Cultivars in-clude 'Geranium', 4½ft (1.3m), scarlet; 'Margaret Hilling', pink 'Nevada', 6ft (2m), large white flowers; 'Sealing Wax', light pink.

Rosa multiflora

○ ◑ ◉ ◎ ⊗

Syn. *Rosa polyantha*. Polyantha rose. A semi-evergreen shrub from China and Japan. The stems are greenish-brown, with few spines. The foliage has up to 9 leaflets. The small white flowers, borne in profuse clusters appear June–August. Small, brownish hips follow.

Rosa nitida

○ ◑ ◉ ◎ ⊗

A low suckering shrub 16–24in (40–60cm) with spines set closely to-gether, and glossy leaflets. It flowers in June and July, with solitary rose-pink 2in (5cm) flowers. Hips are red and spherical. Makes a good flowering shrub and an excellent hedging plant.

Rosa omeiensis

○ ○ ◑ ◉ ⊗

Represented in gardens mainly by *pteracantha*, with large, triangular, crimson, translucent thorns and small fern-like foliage. The small, pure white flowers come out in April. Height 6ft (2m).

Rosa pendulina

Syn. *Rosa cinnamomea* and *Rosa alpina*. Alpine rose. A very hardy, 4½–6ft (1.3–2m) high shrub with hairless branches and solitary, single, magenta-pink flowers in May–June. The 1in (2.5cm) wide scarlet hips are elongated to bottle shaped.

Rosa pimpinellifolia

Syn. *Rosa spinosissima*. Scots or burnet rose. A fairly low but very dense suckering shrub. The stiff stems are covered with spines and bristles. Flowering period is May–June, with white, sometimes pink or yellow blooms, followed by black hips. Well-known hybrid cultivars include 'Frühlingsduft', double yellow, scented flowers; 'Frühlingsgold', single, yellow, scented; 'Frühlingsmorgen', semi-double, pink; 'Frühlingsschnee', semi-double, white, scented; 'Marigold', golden-yellow, large, scented, very floriferous.

Rosa polyantha, see *Rosa multiflora*.

Rosa primula

○ ◐ ⑪ ⑨ ⊛

A 6–10ft (2–3m) tall shrub with prickly brownish-red stems and leaves divided into 7–13 leaflets. These have a distinctive fragrance if they are crushed. The 1½in (4cm) wide flowers open a primrose-yellow, fading almost to white. The rounded hips are dark red.

Rosa rubiginosa

○ ⑪ ⑨ ⑨ ⑩ ⊗

Syn. *Rosa eglanteria*. Sweet briar. A large shrub with a spicy fragrance and dense thorny branches. Leaflets are oval, rather blunt, and smooth underneath. Pink flowers 1–2in (2.5–5cm) across in groups of 1–5, bloom in June–July. It makes an almost impenetrable hedge that remains pungently fragrant even when the shrub is not in flower. 'Amy Robsart' is rich pink; 'Goldbush' is up to 6ft (2m) high with masses of orange-yellow flowers followed by orange hips in the autumn; 'Lady Penzance' is coppery-yellow and 'Lord Penzance' has fawn-yellow flowers; 'Meg Merrilies' has crimson flowers and orange-red hips.

Rosa rubrifolia

○ ⑨ ⑪ ⑨ ⊗

Syns. *Rosa ferruginea*, *Rosa glauca*. A compact shrub with drooping branches covered with a purple bloom. The spines are few and almost straight, the leaves bluish-green, shot with red. The flowering period is June–July, with 2½in (5cm) flowers followed by red hips.

Rosa rugosa

○ ⑨ ⑪ ⑨ ⊛ ⑩ ⊗

Ramanas rose. A wide-spreading shrub with thick and very prickly stems, flowering from May to August. The flowers are solitary or in small clusters, red or white. The hips are large, red and apple shaped. A very rewarding garden shrub, also suitable for hedging and planting on slopes. Well-known cultivars, mostly of hybrid origin, include 'Alba', white flowers; 'Frau Dagmar Hagstrup', pink, more compact, larger hips; 'F. J. Grootendorst', 3ft (1m), bright crimson flowers with fringed petals; 'Hansa', purple-red flowers, attractive hips; 'Pink Grootendorst', pink; 'Sarah van Fleet', pink, double; and 'Snow Dwarf' ('Schneezwerg'), white, double.

Rosa spinosissima, see *Rosa pimpinellifolia*.

Rosa virginiana

A shrub up to 4ft (1.2m) high forming a thick mass of shoots from the base. Bright cerise-pink flowers, single or in groups of three, come from June to August. 'Alba' has white blooms. The glossy green leaves change to yellow and scarlet in autumn. Round red hips, which birds do not eat, appear in autumn. It is suitable for hedging.

Rosa villosa

○ ⑪ ⑨ ⑩

Syn. *Rosa pomifera*. Apple rose. A 3–6ft (1–2m) erect shrub with large, deep

pink flowers 1½–2½in (4–6.5cm) across. They are followed by dark red, bristly hips. 'Duplex', Wolley Dod's rose, has semi-double flowers.

Rosa wichuriana

○ ◐ ⑪ ⑨ ⊛

Memorial rose. A partially evergreen climber which has been used in hybridizing to produce the familiar rambling roses, and also features in the parentage of some climbers. It can reach 13ft (4m) in height and has dark, shining green leaves and 1½–2in (4–5cm) white flowers which are very fragrant. The dark red hips are oval.

Rosa willmottiae

○ ⑪ ⑨ ⑩

This dense shrub is 4½–10ft (1.5–3m) tall with elegant blue-green leaves and a profusion of purplish-rose flowers, each over 1in (2.5cm) across. They are followed by orange-red hips.

Rosa xanthina

○ ⑪ ⑨ ⑩

A tall, arching shrub from 6–13ft (2–4m) in height. The leaves are divided into 7–13, almost rounded leaflets and the golden-yellow flowers are up to 1½in (4cm) across. The form usually cultivated is semi-double, the truly wild, single form being known as *Rosa xanthina spontanea*.

Rosa 'Schneewittchen' (Floribunda)

Rosmarinus
Labiatae
Rosemary

Familiar culinary plants from which oil is distilled for perfumery.
Soil Any well-drained garden soil.
Propagation By cuttings in summer to early autumn.

Rosmarinus officinalis

○ ⑪ ⑨ ⊛ ⑩

From Europe and S.E. Asia. Heights 6–7ft (2m), less than this in cooler climates. It flowers from April to September. The narrow grey-green leaves are white beneath. 'Fastigiatus' ('Miss Jessup's') is erect and stiff. The plant is not tolerant of wetness at the roots and can be cut back by severe frost.

Rubus
Rosaceae
Bramble

A very large genus of mainly scrambling, prickly shrubs, some of which are

cosmopolitan weeds, but others attractive ornamental plants.
Soil Any well-drained garden soil.
Propagation Cuttings or tip layering in late summer; division in autumn or spring.

Rubus calycinoides

○ ◐ ⑪ ⑨ ⊛ ⑩ ⊖

Syn. *R. fockeanus*. From Taiwan. Height 1ft (30cm). The stems are low, arching and rooting, with glossy green leaves showing grey-white beneath. The white flowers are followed by scarlet fruits. A useful ground cover.

Rubus tricolor

○ ⑪ ⑨ ⑪ ⑨ ⊛ ⑩

From China. Height 6in (15cm). A prostrate plant which will scramble through shrubs or lie on the ground, making good ground cover. The dark green leaves are felted grey-white beneath and the white flowers are up to ¾in (2cm) across. The red fruits are pleasant to eat.

Rubus × 'Tridel'

○ ⑪ ⑨ ⑪ ⑨

A hybrid between *Rubus deliciosus* and *Rubus trilobus*. Heights 6–8ft (1½–2½m). Flowering in May. The form 'Benenden' is usually seen. This has white flowers up to 2¾in (7cm) across,

Rosa 'Dainty Bess' (Hybrid tea)

centred with a boss of bright yellow stamens. The plant is sterile.

Rudbeckia
Compositae
Coneflower

A genus of hardy annuals and herbaceous perennials that make striking additions to the border. They can also be used as bedding plants.
Soil Ordinary fertile garden soil.
Propagation Sow annuals at the end of March in a greenhouse or frame. Alternatively sow in situ in April. Prick out the seedlings and plant out at distances of 12–16in (30–40cm) apart. Perennials are best propagated by division of the roots in late winter.

Annuals include:
Rudbeckia bicolor, see *Rudbeckia hirta* var. *pulcherrima*.

Rudbeckia hirta

○ ⊖ ⑨ ⊙ ⑨ ⊗

Black-eyed Susan. North America. Heights 1–2ft (30–60cm). Flowering period is August–September, with 2–3in (5–7cm) flowers with golden-yellow ray petals and a deep purple

Rosa 'Blessings' (Hybrid tea)

Rosa moyesii hybrid 'Nevada'

The annual *Rudbeckia hirta* var. *pulcherrima*

Rudbeckia fulgida var. *sullivantii*

central cone. Space young plants 12 in (30 cm) apart each way. This is a very attractive annual, especially when planted near blue flowers. 'Gloriosa' and 'Double Gloriosa' have very large golden-yellow to dark brown flowers.
Rudbeckia hirta* var. *pulcherrima
Syns. *Rudbeckia bicolor*, *Rudbeckia serotina*. Differs very little from the last species. Flower heads are somewhat larger and ray petals are banded or suffused maroon. ·Cultivars include: 'Golden Flame', 12 in (30 cm), golden-yellow with a brownish-red centre; 'Autumn Forest' ('Herbstwald'), 2 ft (60 cm), orange to copper coloured; 'My Joy', 2 ft (60 cm), orange-yellow with a black centre. To obtain a profuse and early show of flowers, gardeners often grow these plants in the shade in June, prick out the seedlings and plant them out in the flowering position in September.
Rudbeckia serotina, see *Rudbeckia hirta* var. *pulcherrima*.

Herbaceous perennials include:
Rudbeckia fulgida* var. *speciosa
○ ◑ ⊗ ⊛ ⊙ ⓨ ⊗
Syns. *Rudbeckia newmanii*, *Rudbeckia speciosa*. A glorious and very sturdy perennial for the border, long and profusely flowering with orange-yellow ray petals. It likes a moist site, flowering August–October. Height 2 ft (60 cm).
Rudbeckia fulgida* *sullivantii
A 24 in (60 cm) plant, thinly covered

with hair. The ray petals are 1–2 in (2.5–5 cm) long. 'Goldsturm' has saffron-yellow flowers with a black centre, borne in July–October.
Rudbeckia laciniata
North America. Height 6–7 ft (2–2.2 m). Flowering period is July to September, with flowers in attractive shades of yellow. The double cultivars are the most popular. They will tolerate a great deal of shade and like moist soil. Specially recommended are 'Golden Glow', 6 ft (2 m), densely filled golden-yellow flowers; 'Goldquelle', 3 ft (1 m), very sturdy, deep yellow semi-double flowers from September to October.
Rudbeckia newmanii, see *Rudbeckia fulgida* var. *speciosa*.
Rudbeckia nitida
◑ ⊗ ○ ○ ⓨ ⊗
A 3½–4 ft (1–1.2 m) high plant similar to *R.laciniata* with dark yellow recurved ray petals. Flowers July–September. 'Autumn Sun' ('Herbstsonne') with large golden-yellow flowers is particularly attractive. Height 7½ ft (2.4 m).
Rudbeckia purpurea, see *Echinacea purpurea*.
Rudbeckia speciosa, see *Rudbeckia fulgida* var. *speciosa*.
Rudbeckia sullivantii, see *Rudbeckia fulgida* var. *sullivantii*.

Ruscus
Ruscaceae (Liliaceae)
Butcher's Broom

A small genus of low-growing, rhizomatous shrubs. There are separate male and female plants, both being needed for fruiting.
Soil Any ordinary garden soil.
Propagation By division in spring.

Ruscus aculeatus
◑ ● ○ ⊛ ⊛ ⊛
Found from W. Europe to S. W. Asia and growing 1–3 ft (30–90 cm) high. Flowers March to April. A tufted shrub with small, dark green, spine-tipped leaf-like cladodes. These are in reality modified stems and carry the small greenish-white flowers.

Ruta
Rutaceae
Rue

Only one member of this genus is commonly seen, formerly much grown as a flavouring herb but its strong, rather bitter flavour is not now widely appreciated and the plant is grown for its decorative foliage.
Soil Any well-drained soil.
Propagation From seed in spring or cuttings in late summer.

Ruta graveolens
○ ○ ⊛ ⊛
From S. Europe. Heights 1½–2½ ft (40–80 cm). The deeply divided leaves are blue-green and the yellow flowers are borne in clusters from June onwards.

Sagina
Caryophyllaceae
Pearlwort

Herbaceous perennials sometimes used in carpet bedding. They should be pressed down from time to time.
Soil Not too dry.
Propagation By division.

Sagina pilifera, see *Sagina subulata*.
Sagina subulata
○ ◑ ⊗ ⊙ ⊛ ⊛
Syn. *Sagina pilifera*. Pearlwort. A perennial plant native to Europe, heights 1–3 in (2.5–7.5 cm). The flowering period is July–August, with white flowers like small stars protruding above the very fine, light green foliage. Do not plant in full sun, as the yellow-leaved 'Aurea' and variegated forms may scorch.

Sagina subulata 'Aurea

Sagittaria sagittifolia

Sagittaria
Alismataceae
Arrowhead

A genus of attractive plants suitable as marginals for small ponds.
Soil Needs fertile soil covered by 4–16 in (10–40 cm) of water.
Propagation By division of the root-

Catkins of *Salix hastata* 'Wehrhahnii'

Twisted branches of *Salix matsudana* 'Tortuosa'

Salix sachalinensis 'Sekka'

stock in the spring. Species may also be grown from seed sown immediately they are ripe in pots stood in water.

Sagittaria sagittifolia

○ ◐ ⊗ ○ ⊘

Common arrowhead. Native perennial found in ponds and slow-flowing streams, growing 12–28 in (30–70 cm) high. Flowering period is June–July/August, with erect whorled racemes of white flowers tinted purple.

Salix
Salicaceae
Willow

A well-known genus of deciduous trees and shrubs found throughout the temperate regions of the world. Male and female catkins are borne on separate plants and are attractive to bees.

Soil Most willows like fairly moist rooting medium, but some species will thrive on dryer soil.

Propagation Very easy from hardwood cuttings taken in the autumn or early winter.

Salix acutifolia

○ ◐ ⊗ ◍ ⓨ ⊥

A broad, picturesque tree up to 15 ft (5 m) high. The very slender, drooping, damson-coloured shoots are covered with a white bloom. The pointed leaves are at least six times as long as they are wide. The catkins—only the male form is grown—are golden-yellow.

Salix alba

○ ◐ ⊗ ✳ ○ ⊥

White willow. A tree up to 40 ft (12 m) high with a spread of up to 25 ft (8 m). The branches are hairy, olive to tan in colour, and drooping at the tips. Leaflets are covered with silky hair on both surfaces; later they are smooth on top. The catkins appear with the young leaves in April to May. 'Chermesina' (Scarlet willow) is a tall shrub with conspicuous orange-scarlet branches in the winter.

Salix × chrysocoma

Syns. *Salix alba* 'Vitellina Pendula', *Salix alba* 'Tristis'. Height 65 ft (20 m). Flowers in April. A broad-headed tree with long, pendulous branchlets and yellowish twigs. The leaves are long and narrow, and golden catkins open with the young leaves. 'Sepulcralis' is a hybrid with brownish twigs and the branchlets do not hang so completely vertically.

Salix × sepulcralis, see *Salix × chrysocoma* 'Sepulcralis'.

Salix amygdalina, see *Salix triandra*.

Salix caprea

Common sallow, Goat willow. A tree or shrub 10–30ft (3–9m) high with a spread of 10–18ft (3–6m). The male has large yellow catkins, the female, known as 'pussy willow', has silvergrey catkins. The branches are at first covered with greyish hair, later smooth. Leaves are elongated, oval, irregularly toothed, sometimes entire, with their undersides covered with a net of veins clothed in greyish hairs. 'Pendula' (Kilmarnoch willow) has drooping branches and is propagated by grafting on to the top of a common sallow stem of the desired height. Grown on its own roots from cuttings it stays prostrate.

Salix cinerea

Grey sallow. A shrub 6–20ft (2–6m) tall and with a similar spread. The branches are usually covered with greyish hair, rarely smooth. Leaflets are obovate, irregularly toothed, sometimes entire, with their undersides grey and downy. Catkins appear March–April. 'Variegata' has leaves with white and yellow spots.

Weeping willow, *Salix × chrysocoma*

Salix daphnoides

Violet willow. A tree up to 30ft (9m) high or more with a spread of 24ft (7.5m), which also occurs as a shrub. The shoots are violet, overlaid with a white bloom. Large and attractive catkins are borne in March–April. The attractive leaves are bluish-green underneath.

Salix elaeagnos

Syn. *Salix incana*. Hoary willow. A shrub of dense, bushy habit with reddish-brown stems. Thrives on moist soil. 'Angustifolia' has very narrow rolled-up leaves. Very attractive when planted in groups.

Salix fragilis

Crack willow. A tree up to 60ft (18m) high or more with a spread of up to 30ft (9m). Branches are yellow, angular and fragile. The undersides of leaves are pale green or bluish-green. Flowering period is April–May.

Salix hastata

A native of Switzerland. A small shrub, 2½ft (75cm) high, with oval leaflets and large silvery-grey catkins March–April. Very attractive when planted in groups, it is also suitable for heather and rock

Fine examples of pollarded willows, *Salix alba* in the spring

gardens. 'Wehrhahnii' is the most common cultivar, producing an abundance of small catkins.

Salix incana, see *Salix elaeagnos*.

Salix matsudana 'Tortuosa'

An attractive, medium-sized tree with twisted branches and leaves, from China. It is excellent in parks.

Salix pentandra

Bay willow. A tree up to 30ft (9m) high, with a spread of up to 20ft (7m). Branches are yellow, hairy when young. The glossy, ovate leaves are pleasantly aromatic when crushed. Catkins 2in (5cm) long appear in May.

Salix purpurea

Purple osier. A shrub with a height and spread of 12ft (4m). Branches are red to yellow and the narrowly oblong leaves are often in opposite pairs. Small catkins appear March–April. 'Eugenei' is an erect small tree, bearing grey-pink catkins earlier than those of the original species. 'Gracilis' ('Nana') is a dwarf form that makes a useful low hedge on damp sites. 'Pendula' may be grown either as a small weeping tree or else as a creeping shrub.

Salix repens

Creeping willow. A small shrub, rarely taller than 3ft (1m) and with at least the same spread. The branches are at first covered in down, later smooth and brown. The leaflets are oval to lanceolate, entire, their underside generally hairless but sometimes covered in silky down. Small catkins appear in April. It is attractive beside ponds in small gardens, or on steep banks of larger pools, where it prevents erosion.

Salix sachalinensis 'Sekka'

A large, wide-spreading shrub with curiously fasciated (flattened and recurved) stems and masses of elongated catkins. The branches are often used in floral decorations.

Salix × smithiana

A cross between *Salix cinerea* and *Salix viminalis*. A vigorous, tall shrub. Young branches are covered in grey down. The large, oval, grey leaves are covered with woolly hair underneath. Silver-white, later pink, catkins are produced before the leaves in spring.

Salix triandra

Syn. *Salix amygdalina*. Almond-leaved willow. A small tree or large shrub, which produces catkins in April and May. The serrated lanceolate leaves are bluish-grey underneath.

Salix viminalis

Common osier. A large shrub with yellowish branches and elongated 4–9in (10–23cm) long leaves. The branches are very pliable and are used in basket-making.

Salvia
Labiatae

The name salvia usually suggests the bright red flowers that adorn so many gardens. However, this genus also contains many attractive plants in different colours.

Soil Fertile garden soil is adequate.

Propagation Annual salvias are sown in early to mid spring under glass.

Perennial salvias can also be propagated from seed, but it is much easier to divide them.

Grown as annuals or biennials are:

Salvia farinacea

A sub-shrub from Texas, 24–32in (60–80cm) high. Blue flowers appear from May to October. 'Blue Bedder' is deep blue; 'Royal Purple' is dark violet. Sow at the end of February and in March in a warm frame or greenhouse. Harden off and plant out when fear of frost has passed.

Salvia horminum

Syn. *Salvia viridis*. From Spain, growing to 20in (50cm). Large red or violet bracts, and lilac or violet flowers from June to August. 'White Swan' is a recommended white-bracted variety. Sow in April in a cold frame and plant out after mid-August to flower the following year.

Salvia sclarea

Clary, from the Mediterranean. Height up to 5ft (1.5m). Bluish-white flowers in August. A culinary herb but also excellent in borders. Generally grown as an annual, but may also be treated as a biennial.

Salvia splendens

A sub-shrub from Brazil, where it attains heights of 4½–5ft (1.3–1.5m). Grown as an annual it rarely exceeds 12in (30cm). Scarlet flowers from summer to autumn. Sow February–March at a temperature of 64°F (18°C). Prick out the seedlings into boxes, harden off in a cold frame and plant out in May. The leaves will turn dark if the soil is too poor. This is one of the most popular bedding salvias, although its fierce red colour is very difficult to combine with other plants. Pink and white cultivars may be used instead.

The most common perennial salvias include:

Salvia officinalis
○ ◐ ○

Sage. A well-known culinary herb from southern European uplands. A sub-shrub, up to 2 ft (60cm) high, it is matted with greyish-green hairs. It has fragrant, finely wrinkled leaves and violet-blue or white flowers borne in spikes May–June. 'Purpurascens' has flushed purple leaves; 'Tricolor' has white-, pink- and purple-tinted leaves, whilst 'Icterina' is gold variegated. Grown as a herb but also excellent in borders and rock gardens. Sage has the additional advantage that it attracts bees.

Salvia patens
○ ◐ ◇ ◇ ◉

A perennial plant, 24–32 in (60–70 cm) high. It flowers from August to September, with blooms widely spaced on slender stems. It is not very hardy. Treat the tuberous roots like those of dahlias in cold areas.

Salvia × superba

A cross between *Salvia nemorosa*, *Salvia pratensis* and *Salvia villicaulis*. A densely branched perennial plant, 3 ft (1m) high or more, with downy stems. Flowering period June–September, with small violet-purple flowers in erect branched spikes. 'Lubeca', 18 in (45 cm) high, has dark violet-blue flowers. A sturdy border plant that will also do well on poorer soil. The terminal spikes come into flower before the lateral spikes.

Sambucus
Caprifoliaceae
Elder

The common elder is a true pioneer, for whenever a shrubbery is to be started in an awkward spot, elders will help to prepare the way. Elders are deciduous and are either shrubs or trees.
Soil Elders will grow on almost any soil. They are also very shade tolerant. Those with golden flowers prefer a sunnier position.
Propagation From cuttings taken in the late autumn, early winter. Leafy cuttings may also be taken in summer and placed in a propagating frame.

The white flowers of *Sambucus nigra*, common elder

Salvia × superba, a vigorous plant

The biennial *Salvia horminum*

The annual *Salvia splendens*

Sambucus canadensis
○ ◐ ◑ ◐ ◉ ◉ ◉

American or sweet elder. A shrub 8–12 ft (2.5–4m) high and with about the same spread. Grows rapidly. The branches are bare, yellowish-grey and often downy. The buds are brown, and the pinnate leaves are usually made up of 7 lanceolate leaflets, with a silken sheen underneath. The white flowers are grouped in large, flattened heads, and purple-black berries follow. Highly recommended is 'Maxima', which bears larger flowers in heads up to 14 in (35 cm) across in July and August, followed by dark purple berries. Leaves turn purple-red in the autumn. 'Rubra' has red fruits.

Sambucus nigra
◑ ◑ ⊖ ◉ ◉ ◉

Common elder. A native of Europe, it is a shrub or small tree up to 18 ft (6m) high, sometimes taller. Grey, hairless branches with greenish-brown buds. There are generally 5 oval, pointed, toothed leaflets, light green underneath, to a composite leaf. The flowers are yellowish-white; berries black. Flowering period is normally June–July, but often is as early as May. Well-known cultivars are: 'Aurea', with golden-yellow leaves; and 'Laciniata',

with finely divided leaves, from which this plant derives its name of fern-leaved elder. It is very wind-resistant and tolerant of shade, and hence eminently suitable for growing under deciduous trees.

Sambucus racemosa
○ ◑ ◑ ◐ ◉ ◉ ◉ ◉

Red-berried elder. A shrub about 12 ft (4m) high and with the same spread, from Europe. Flowers are produced as early as April–May. The branches are hairless and light brown. The brown buds are set fairly close together. Pinnate leaves are usually made up of 5 to 7 ovate-lanceolate and deeply cut leaflets. Flowers are grouped in yellowish-white conical heads, with red berries following. 'Plumosa' has finely cut leaflets, bronze to brown when young. 'Plumosa Aurea' also has finely cut leaflets, first bronze coloured, later golden-yellow, and looks very attractive in the autumn.

Santolina
Compositae
Cotton lavender

A small genus of shrubs with finely cut aromatic foliage.
Soil Any well-drained garden soil is suitable.
Propagation By cuttings in late summer.

Santolina chamaecyparissus
○ ○ ◑ ◉ ◉ ◉ ◉

Syn. *Santolin incana*. From the Mediterranean, this plant grows to heights of 15–24 in (40–60 cm). Flowering period July–August, it is a distinctive small shrub forming hummocks of grey-white leaves. The button-shaped, lemon-yellow flowers are borne singly. The bushes are best trimmed in spring to maintain a compact habit.

Clary, *Salvia sclarea*, a herb that also looks at home in the border

Saponaria ocymoides 'Splendens'

Saponaria
Caryophyllaceae

Perennial plants for the border, the rock garden, and raised beds.

Soil Fertile soil; if grown in rock gardens, then the soil must be well drained.

Propagation Species can be grown from seed, but it is preferable to divide them.

Saponaria ocymoides
○ ⊖ ⊖ ⊗ ⊗

A perennial plant from the Alps, with prostrate stems 1 ft (30 cm) long. Flowering from May to July, but if sown under glass in early spring it will bloom during the summer. Flowers are rose-red and fragrant. It is recommended for rock gardens, for growing on walls and as an edging plant, and is also very good as ground cover. 'Splendens' has dark pink flowers. 'Rubra compacta' is neater and much more compact; better suited for the smaller rock garden.

Saponaria officinalis
○ ⊖ ○

Soapwort. Native of Europe, grows 20–32 in (50–80 cm) high. Flowering period is July–September, the flowers flesh coloured to rose-red, 'Plena' has double flowers. Very invasive and not recommended for the herbaceous border.

Saxifraga
Saxifragaceae

A large genus including numerous species, hybrids and cultivars particularly suited to the rock garden.

Cultivation Many species form large cushions that eventually become bare in the centre. They should then be divided and transplanted, preferably immediately after flowering.

Soil Most saxifrages thrive on fairly light soil. Those with a moss-like appearance (Dactyloides section) prefer slightly moister and shadier sites. Those forming large silvery rosettes (Euazoonia section) tolerate dry spells fairly well and prefer a sunny position.

Propagation Mossy species are easily divided. Rosette-forming species can be increased by the removal of non-flowering rosettes, which are inserted in sandy soil and treated as cuttings. Saxifrages are divided into sixteen sections, but most cultivated sorts belong

in the following sections:

Dactyloides (mossy) section including *Saxifraga × arendsii* hybrids, *S. hypnoides* and *S. trifurcata*.

Kabschia and Engleria sections with small silver rosettes, including *Saxifraga burseriana*.

Euazoonia section with large silver rosettes, including *Saxifraga cochlearis*, *S. cotyledon*, *S. longifolia* and *S. paniculata*.

The remaining sections include *Saxifraga cortusifolia*, *Saxifraga × geum*, and *S. umbrosa*.

Saxifraga aizoon, see *S. paniculata*.
Saxifraga burseriana
A perennial from the eastern Alps. Cushion-forming, its white flowers appear March–May, one to each 1 in (2.5 cm) stem. It requires light, fertile soil generously mixed with rubble, and a site out of direct sun.

Saxifraga cochlearis
◑ ◑ ○ ⊛ ⊗

A perennial from the Maritime Alps, with rosettes of narrow leaves in hummocks. Flowers 4–16 in (10–40 cm) high, white with red spots. Flowering period is June–July. It thrives on calcareous soil enriched with a little humus, and likes a shady position.

Saxifraga umbrosa 'Variegata'

Saxifraga cortusifolia
◑ ◑ ◑

A perennial from Japan, green only in the summer. Height 4–16 in (10–40 cm). It has white flowers, with the two upper petals being considerably longer than the three lower. Flowering period is September–October. It thrives in shade.

Saxifraga cotyledon
○ ◑ ○ ⊗ ⊛ ⊗ ⊗

A perennial from the Pyrenees and northern Europe, growing 16–24 in (10–40 cm) high. It has large, strap-shaped, leathery leaves which are 2–3 in (5–7.5 cm) long and ¼–½ in (1–1.5 cm) wide. Flowering period is May–June, with white flowers in large, plume-like sprays. The petals are often stippled blood-red. Only the strongest 2- to 4-year old plants produce flowers. One of the most attractive saxifrages for the rock garden, best in a vertical crevice or dry wall.

Saxifraga × geum
◑ ◑ ○ ⊗ ⊗

A cross between *Saxifraga hirsuta* and *Saxifraga umbrosa*. A perennial blending the characters of both parents, and occurring naturally in the Pyrenees and various parts of western and central Europe. Small white flowers are borne on 6–12 in (15–30 cm) stems. It likes a shady position and does best in humus-rich woodland soil.

Saxifraga hypnoides
Mossy saxifrage. From north-western Europe, a cushion-forming perennial 4–12 in (10–30 cm) high, with 3–7 white flowers per stem. The sepals are covered with glandular hair. Flowering period is May–June.

Saxifraga longifolia
◑ ◑ ○ ⊛

A perennial from the Pyrenees. The leaf rosettes are large and flat, and up to 6 in (15 cm) across. The flower stems are 10–20 in (25–50 cm) high, and hairy. White flowers are grouped in large plume-like panicles, appearing in June. It grows in shady positions, especially in crevices of limestone rocks.

Saxifraga paniculata
Syn. *Saxifraga aizoon*. A perennial

Mossy saxifrage hybrids combined with blue grape hyacinths

Scabiosa caucasica

Scabiosa atropurpurea

from the mountains of Europe and N. America, 6–10 in (15–25 cm) high. The flowers are white with purple-red spots, numerous on branching stems. This plant is cushion forming, with rosettes of narrow, toothed, thick leaves, 1–2 in (2.5–5 cm) long, ¼ in (½ cm) wide at the tip. It grows best in a calcareous soil.

Saxifraga umbrosa
◑ ◑ ○ ⊗

A mat-forming plant native to Europe. Heights 12–16 in (30–40 cm). Appearing in June, the flowers are white with red dots, in large clusters. 'Clarence Elliott' and 'Walter Ingwersen' are much more compact than the species and have rose flowers; 'Variegata' has its leaves splashed with yellow. The plant under this name so commonly known as London pride is *S. × urbium*, a hybrid between *S. umbrosa* and the similar *S. spathularis*. It is more vigorous and floriferous than either parent.

Scabiosa
Dipsacaceae
Scabious

A genus of annuals and herbaceous perennials, of which the species listed below produce exceptionally attractive cut flowers which keep in water for a long time.

Soil Scabious grows in any fertile, well-drained garden soil.

Propagation *Scabiosa atropurpurea* and other annual species: Sow the seeds under glass in early March or *in situ* in late April. Thin out the seedlings, spacing the smaller cultivars 6–8 in (15–20 cm) apart and the taller 12 in (30 cm) apart. Plants sown under glass are often larger and flower earlier than those sown outdoors providing they are transplanted carefully.

Scabiosa caucasica and other perennial species are best increased by division in the spring or in the summer, but preferably not in the autumn because of the wintering problem. They can also be grown from seed, but the resulting plants vary in flower colour.

Hybrid bluebells

Scilla mischtschenkoana

Schizanthus wisetonensis hybrids

Scabiosa atropurpurea

○ ◑ ◔ ○ ◑ ⑳ ⊗

Sweet scabious. An annual from southern Europe, sometimes grown as a biennial. Flowering period is June–October, with dark crimson, velvety flowers. Catalogues usually distinguish between tall (36 in/1 m), medium-sized (24 in/60 cm), small (18 in/45 cm) and dwarf (8 in/20 cm) cultivars, most sold in mixtures or separate colours, including white, salmon, rose, red-purple, lavender and blue. All are very easily cultivated, the taller mainly for cut flowers, the shorter for borders and rock gardens, where their late flowers make them stand out.

Scabiosa caucasica

A perennial from the Caucasus, 20–32 in (50–70 cm) high. Flowering period is June–September, with beautiful lavender-blue flowers. Some well-known cultivars are: 'Clive Greaves', rich mauve, large flowered; 'Miss Willmott', white, semi-double; 'Moerheim Blue', deep violet-blue; 'Staffa', deep violet-blue. Highly recommended for cutting and also for the border. Not very floriferous, but the colour of the flowers is magnificent.

Schizanthus
Solanaceae
Butterfly flower

Attractive annual plants with small orchid-like flowers.
Soil Rich, well-drained soil is needed.
Propagation Sow in early spring in a cool, airy greenhouse or in a frame kept at 61°F (16°C). Prick out, harden off, and plant out at the end of May or the beginning of June.

Schizanthus × wisetonensis

○ ◑ ◔ ⊗

Reputedly originally crosses between *Schizanthus pinnatus* and *Schizanthus abtusus grahamii*, they are annual to biennial plants from Chile, mostly 12–16 in (30–40 cm) high, though some cultivars grow to a height of 3 ft (100 cm). Clusters of flowers occur in a wide range of colours including crimson, lilac, purple, pink, violet and white. Nurseries usually offer mixed seeds.

Scilla
Liliaceae

A genus of bulbous plants including many species that are eminently suitable for naturalization.
Cultivation Plant the bulbs immediately upon arrival because they dry out very easily. They may be left undisturbed for years, even in the lawn, provided that it is not mown before the leaves are completely dead.
Soil Any moist but well-drained soil.
Propagation From offsets lifted as the leaves die down, cleaned and replanted. The bulbs will flower a year or two later. They may also be propagated from seeds ideally sown when ripe.

Scilla bifolia

○ ◑ ◔ ◠ ◐ ⑳ ⊗

From southern Europe and Turkey. A small, early-flowering species (March–April) with small, mauve-blue flowers in clusters. Each bulb usually has two leaves only, hence the Latin name.
Scilla companulata, see *Scilla hispanica*.

Scilla hispanica

Syns. *Scilla companulata* and *Endymion hispanicus*. A perennial from Spain and Portugal, 10–14 in (25–35 cm) high. Flowering period is May–June. The flowers appear in pyramidal clusters, bell shaped, short stemmed and outward facing, in a variety of colours ranging from white through pink to blue. The species is rare in cultivation, being represented by hybrids with *S. non-scripta*. They are identified by the pendent flowers, which are much wider than those of *S. non-scripta*. The following are hybrid cultivars: 'Excelsior' is deep blue with large bells; 'La Grandesse' is pure white; 'Rose Queen' is pink. Plant in August–September at a depth of 3–4 in (7.5–10 cm) and the same distance apart.

Scilla mischtschenkoana

Syn. *Scilla tubergeniana*. This plant flowers at the same time as snowdrops. It resembles *Scilla sibirica*, but its porcelain-blue flowers come out earlier.

Scilla monophylla

A native of Spain, Portugal and Morocco, this plant grows to a height of 8–12 in (20–30 cm). It bears single leaves and blue flowers which appear in May–June. The flowers, which are bell-shaped, are $\frac{1}{4}-\frac{1}{2}$ in ($\frac{1}{2}$–1 cm) long and are borne in racemes in groups of between five and twenty.

Scilla non-scripta

Syn. *Scilla nutans*, *Endymion non-scriptus*. English bluebell; Wild hyacinth. Native to W. Europe, including Great Britain. Heights 8–12 in (20–30 cm). They have numerous narrowly bell-shaped, blue, fragrant flowers on stems that are reflexed at the tips until all the flowers have opened. There are also white and pink cultivars.
Scilla nutans, see *Scilla non-scripta*.

Scilla peruviana

Cuban lily. A native of Italy, Algeria and Malta, growing to a height of 9–12 in (25–30 cm). It bears blue flowers which are star-shaped in racemes containing up to a hundred each. The flowering period is May and June.

Scilla sibirica

○ ◑ ◔ ◠ ◐ ⑳ ⊗

A perennial from central and southern Russia. 4–8 in (10–20 cm) high. Flowering period is March–April, the flowers brilliant blue or white. The most beautiful cultivar is 'Spring Beauty', which is dark blue. It may be left undisturbed for years, and is suitable for rock gardens, borders, and growing in lawns.
Scilla tubergeniana, see *Scilla mischtschenkoana*.

Scilla hispanica

Sedum spectabile 'Brilliant' in fruit

Sedum
Crassulaceae

Most of the cultivated species in this genus are hardy perennials suitable for growing in rock gardens.

Soil Sedums will grow in soil too dry to sustain most other plants. Some sorts will also do well, and indeed grow more robust, in moister sites.

Propagation Sow *Sedum caeruleum* in March, and germinate at a temperature of 15°–18°C (59°–64°F). When the seedlings are large enough to handle, prick them out into pans and later move to 3 in (7.5 cm) pots. Plant out 6–8 in (15–20 cm) apart in late May. Alternatively sow *in situ* in April. Sow the seeds of *Sedum hispanicum* in the flowering position in April or in the autumn. They will seed themselves in subsequent years.

All perennial sedums can be increased by division, from stem cuttings taken in the summer, and also from seed.

Sedum acre

Biting stonecrop. A perennial from Europe, Asia and North Africa, up to 6 in (15 cm) high. The flowering period is June–July, with deep yellow flowers. The very small, oval, overlapping and conical, yellow-greenish leaves are mostly set in 2–3 rows. The plant is evergreen and mat-forming.

Sedum aizoon

A perennial from Siberia, China and Japan, growing to 12–16 in (30–40 cm). The flowering period is June–July, the flowers golden-yellow. Leaflets are bright green, toothed, lanceolate, on short stalks or sessile; 2 in (5 cm) long, $\frac{1}{2}-\frac{3}{4}$ in (1 cm) wide. It is suitable for rock gardens and borders.

Sedum album

White stonecrop. Native of Europe, including Great Britain, it is perennial, up to 8 in (20 cm) high, and evergreen. Flowering period is June–July, the flowers numerous and white. Leafy creeping stems carry erect flower stalks. The leaves are very fleshy, fairly even above but spherical beneath. This plant is mat-forming. *Sedum album* var. *murale* has purple-flushed stems and leaves, and pink flowers. It is suitable for rock gardens and walls, and also as ground cover.

Sedum caeruleum

An annual from the W. Mediterranean, 4–6 in (10–15 cm) high, which flowers within 10–12 weeks of sowing. The flowers are numerous, pale blue, later violet-blue. Very attractive in rock gardens and as an edging plant, it requires a dry, sunny position.

Sedum ewersii

A perennial from the Himalayas to Mongolia, 6–7 in (15–17 cm) high, flowering July–August. The flowers are purple-pink in dense clusters. The leaves are fleshy, almost round, sessile, bluish-green, $\frac{1}{2}-\frac{3}{4}$ in (1–1.5 cm) wide, and slightly pink at the edges. It is completely hardy and excellent for edging.

Sedum floriferum

'Weihenstephaner Gold' is a 6 in (15 cm) high, mat-forming plant with dark green leaves and bright golden-yellow flowers appearing June–August. It is evergreen.

Sedum glaucum, see *Sedum hispanicum*.

Sedum hispanicum

Syn. *Sedum glaucum*. An annual to biennial plant from the Swiss Alps to Asia Minor, 6–10 in (15–25 cm) high. Flowering in June, it has white to light rose flowers in flattened heads. The fleshy leaves, $\frac{1}{2}-1$ in (1–2.5 cm) long and $\frac{1}{10}$ in (0.23 cm) across, are bluish-green, sometimes with a reddish tint.

Sedum hybridum

A perennial from E. and C. Siberia, Mongolia, reaching a height of 4 in (10 cm). Masses of golden-yellow flowers appear July–August, sometimes with a first flush as early as May. It makes good ground cover, even in shaded positions.

Sedum kamtschaticum

A perennial 6–10 in (15–25 cm) high, flowering June–September. The flowers are orange-yellow in loose clusters. The dark green, glossy, obovate to spatular, toothed leaves are about 2 in (5 cm) long. 'Variegatum' has yellow variegated leaves. It requires a sunny position and humus-rich soil.

Sedum lydium

A perennial from Asia Minor, up to 4 in (10 cm) high, mat-forming. Flowering period is June–July, the flowers white, in small, flattened clusters. The cylindrical leaves are bright green, flushed red at the tips.

Sedum pluricaule

A 3–4 in (7–10 cm) high, mat-forming plant with bluish-green leaves and pinkish-purple flowers which appear in June–August.

Sedum reflexum

Reflexed stonecrop. A perennial from western Europe, 6–12 in (15–30 cm) high. Golden-yellow flowers open in July. The leaves are fleshy, greyish, sometimes with a reddish tint, linear, pointed and sessile.

Sedum roseum

Syn. *Sedum rhodiola, Rhodiola rosea*. Rose root. A circumpolar species of tufted habit from a semi-woody above-ground rootstock. Stems erect 6–12 in (15–30 cm) tall, with blue-grey leaves and small clusters of yellow to greenish-yellow flowers from late spring to summer. The dried roots are fragrant.

Sedum spathulifolium

A perennial plant from California to British Columbia, with crowded rosettes of grey-blue, often red-tinted fleshy, spatulate leaves. The flowering period is June–July. Heights are 2–4 in (5–10 cm). A very attractive rock plant that should be sheltered from the rain to prevent the bluish bloom from being washed off. 'Capa Blanca' has silver-white leaf rosettes; 'Purpureum' has larger, purple-red leaf rosettes with a silvery bloom when young, and yellow flowers.

Sedum album 'Coral Carpet'

Biting stonecrop, *Sedum acre* 'Majus'

Sedum telephium in fruit in autumn

Sedum spectabile

A perennial from China and Korea (much cultivated in Japan), 12–20 in (30–50 cm) high. Flowering period is August–September, the flowers rose-red with a touch of violet. 'Brilliant' has bright red flowers in dense, flat clusters. The large greyish blue-green leaves, 3 in (7.5 cm) long and 2 in (5 cm) wide, are almost sessile, slightly toothed to entirely obovate. Highly recommended for the front of the border, it attracts butterflies.

Sedum spurium

A mat-forming perennial from the Caucasus, 3–6 in (7.5–15 cm) high. The flowers, which appear August–September, are rose-red to purple-pink in large flat umbels. Leaflets $\frac{1}{2}-\frac{3}{4}$ in (1–1.5 cm) wide, dark green, short stemmed, obovate to wedge-shaped, crenate to toothed at the tip. 'Coccineum' has ruby-red blooms; 'Greenmantle' is fast-growing and makes good ground cover; leaves bright green, rarely flowers; 'Schorbuser Blut' has crimson flowers and grows about 8 in (20 cm) high.

Sedum stevenianum

A mat-forming plant from Asia Minor

Sedum cyaneum 'Rosenteppich'

The common houseleek, *Sempervivum tectorum*, in flower

with very thin stems and very fleshy, spoon-shaped leaves, 2 in (5 cm) long. The flowers are pink outside, white inside, and appear in summer.

Sedum telephium

○ ◐ ○ ⊕

Orpine, Livelong. A perennial plant reaching 12–16 in (30–40 cm) high. Found in woods throughout Europe, including Great Britain. Flowering period is July–August, with purple-red 4 in (10 cm) wide semi-spherical heads. *S. t. maximum* (*S. maximum*) is taller and more robust, with greenish or yellowish flowers. *S. t. maximum* 'Atropurpureum' has dark red-purple leaves and pinkish flowers—a handsome border plant.

Sempervivum
Crassulaceae
Houseleek

This genus includes a number of rosette-forming plants that often form dense carpets.

Cultivation These are attractive plants for the rock garden, dry walls, paths, balconies and window boxes. All species are completely hardy. They need a sunny site to thrive and flower well. The rosettes die down soon after the flowers have faded but leave many offsets behind.

Soil Will thrive even under the most unfavourable conditions providing the soil is well drained. *Sempervivum tectorum* is sometimes seen on unglazed roof tiles, generally planted there because of the old superstition that houseleeks protect the house from lightning and cholera. They will not survive in moist sites.

Propagation Propagate by division and from young suckers. Houseleeks may also be grown from seed, but unless the seeds are of known origin they are likely to give rise to hybrids. Germination is within two weeks of sowing. The seeds remain viable for about three years.

We shall only list the best known of the many species of this genus.

Sempervivum arachnoideum

○ ◐ ⊖ ○ ⊛ ⊗

Cobweb houseleek. From the mountains of Europe, this is one of the most attractive species. It forms small rosettes that seem to be covered with white cobwebs. This attractive webbing tends to disappear if the plant is grown in the shade. Flowering period is July–August, the flowers rose-red and ¾ in (2 cm) across.

Senecio bicolor, a well-known bedding plant

Sempervivum marmoreum

Syn. *Sempervivum schlehanii*. Forms 2–4 in (5–10 cm) flat rosettes, with purple-red 1 in (2.5 cm) flowers in August. 'Rubrifolium' ('Rubicundum') has crimson flushed leaves.

Sempervivum ruthenicum, see *Sempervivum zeleborii*.

Sempervivum schlehanii, see *Sempervivum marmoreum*.

Sempervivum tectorum

Common houseleek. A native of the mountains of Europe. It forms large rosettes, with obovate dark green leaves often purple-brown tipped. Flowering period is July–August, the flowers pink to red-purple and star shaped.

Sempervivum zeleborii

Syn. *Sempervivum ruthenicum*. Eastern Europe. The rosettes are only 1¼ in (3 cm) across, and greyish-green in colour. The flowers are greenish-yellow, 5–8 in (12.5–20 cm) high. The several cultivars include 'Alpha', pink; and 'Triste', with copper-coloured rosettes and pink flowers. The flowering period is usually July.

Senecio
Compositae

A large genus, most cultivated species of which have now been reclassified as *Ligularia*. The undermentioned annual and shrubby species are the only plants that still come under the old heading.

Soil Ordinary garden soil that is not too moist.

Propagation Sow from February under glass. *Senecio elegans* may be sown outdoors from late March to the end of April.

Senecio bicolor

○ ◐ ○ ◉

Syn. *Senecio cineraria*, *Cineraria maritima*. Growing 8–16 in (20–40 cm) high. An evergreen sub-shrub, usually grown as an annual, with deeply indented grey leaves. Popular cultivars include: 'Candicans', 'Diamond' and 'Silverdust', the latter only 8–12 in (20–30 cm) high. Excellent as bedding plants, they combine well with ageratums, lobelias and other blue flowers.

Senecio cineraria, see *Senecio bicolor*.

Senecio clivorum, see *Ligularia dentata*.

Senecio elegans

Heights 12–24 in (30–60 cm). An annual that may also be cultivated as a biennial. Flowering July–October, the purple flowers have a yellow centre. Cultivars come in a host of separate colours, but it is best to buy mixed seeds to produce a range of soft colours. If the flowers are dead-headed after the first flowering, new shoots will develop and continue to bear flowers until late in the autumn.

Senecio × **'Dunedin Hybrids'**

○ ○ ⊛ ⊕ ○ ⊛

Syn. *Senecio greyi* and *Senecio laxifolius* of gardens. A group of hybrids derived from New Zealand species. 'Sunshine', to 3 ft (1 m) high, flowers from June to

Sidalcea malviflora

September. A rounded shrub, with the stems and the undersides of the oval leaves white felted, and the upper surfaces green. The yellow, daisy-like flowers are about 1 in (2.5 cm) across and borne in loose clusters.

Sidalcea
Malvaceae

A genus of attractive herbaceous perennials for the border with a sturdy, pyramidal habit.

Soil This plant will grow in any garden soil, providing it is well drained but not too dry.

Propagation From seeds and by division. Cultivars do not come true from seed.

Sidalcea malviflora

○ ⊛ ○ ⊗

Perennial plants, 24–32 in (60–80 cm) high, with leafy stems and flowers in terminal spikes. Flowering period is June–August. The best-known cultivars are 'Brilliant', a bright shining red; 'Elsie Hugh', which is satin-pink; 'Loveliness', shell-pink; 'Mr. Lindbergh', dark crimson.

Silene
Caryophyllaceae
Campion

A large genus of herbaceous plants, many species of which occur in the wild or have been naturalized. The annual and biennial species are usually grown in borders and beds, and the perennial species in borders or rock gardens.

Soil Any ordinary, well-drained garden soil is suitable.

Propagation *Silene armeria* is best grown as a biennial, sown in June and wintered in a frost-free place. It is also possible to sow the seeds early in the year. *Silene pendula* can be treated as an annual or as a biennial. *Silene coeli-rosa* is always sown outdoors in April and the seedlings thinned out to 8–12 in (20–30 cm) apart.

Perennial species are increased by division and also grown from seed in the spring.

Annuals and biennials:
Silene armeria
○ ☉ ☻

An annual or biennial plant naturalized throughout the world. Height 12–20 in (30–50 cm), with stems sticky at the top, and leaves oval to lanceolate, smelling slightly of cabbage. The pink flowers are grouped in clusters, flowering July–September.

Silene coeli-rosa
Rose of Heaven or viscaria. Also listed in catalogues under *Agrostemma*, *Lychnis* and *Viscaria*. Heights up to 2 ft (60 cm). Oblong and sharply pointed leaves, and flowers pink with a darker eye. Flowering June–September. 'Alba' has white and 'Azurea' azure flowers. Nurserymen often supply mixed seeds.

Silene pendula
○ ☉ ☻ ⊛

Growing 8–16 in (20–40 cm) high, with stems shortly prostrate but with long, erect tips. The leaves are oblong, rather pointed, and the flowers pink, in one-sided clusters. Flowering period is May–August. Once the flowers have faded, the calyx becomes inflated. Cultivars are compact or tall and may also be double or single. 'Bijou' is medium-sized and has double flowers. 'Compacta', cushion-forming to about 8 in (20 cm) tall; 'Peach Blossom' is compact, with particularly attractive double flowers; 'Ruberrima', flowers ruby-red.

Perennial species include:
Silene acaulis
○ ⊘ ○ ☻ ⊛

A cushion-forming perennial from the Alps, 2 in (5 cm) high. Flowering period is May–August, when the flowers come in an attractive shade of pink. 'Albiflora' is white. At lower altitudes the plant does not flower as profusely as it does at higher altitudes, but is nevertheless a rewarding addition to any rock garden.

Silene schafta
A tufted perennial plant, 4–6 in (10–15 cm) high, from the Caucasus. Flowering period August–September. The flowers are fairly large and vary in colour from pink to rose-magenta. They are ¾ in (2 cm) across, and are borne in July–October. The leaves are very small and light green.

Sisyrinchium
Iridaceae
Blue-eyed grass

A genus of herbaceous perennials with sword-shaped leaves and small, colourful flowers, each lasting one day only, but borne very freely.

Soil Any well-drained soil.

Propagation By division from autumn to spring, or from seed sown in autumn or spring.

Sisyrinchium bermudianum
○ ○ ○ ☻

From Bermuda, this is a plant growing 1 ft (30 cm) tall, flowering in May or June. Erect stems carry violet-blue, star-shaped flowers with a yellow eye. It needs some protection where frosts are severe.

Sisyrinchium brachypus
○ ○ ☻ ⊛

Now considered only a form of *Sisyrinchium californicum*. From the western USA, it grows to 6 in (15 cm). Flowers June–September. A tufted plant with bright green iris-like leaves. The starry, deep yellow flowers are borne on branched stems and are ¾ in (2 cm) across.

Sisyrinchium striatum
○ ◐ ○ ☻

From Chile, growing to 2 ft (30 cm) tall, it flowers from June to August. An erect, clump-forming plant with iris-like leaves and pale yellow, starry flowers carried in dense spikes. 'Variegatum' has white-margined leaves and is not as hardy as the true species.

Skimmia
Rutaceae

A genus of attractive small evergreen shrubs, grown not only for their red berries but also for the beautiful flower buds that grace these plants throughout the winter. The young leaves may suffer during severe frost unless the plants are sheltered by trees or taller shrubs.

Soil Ordinary well-drained but not too dry soil, preferably enriched with humus at planting time.

Propagation From seeds that must be sown immediately they are ripe. Cuttings may be taken in the summer, but they root slowly. The plants may also be divided. This is best done in October.

The annual *Silene armeria*

Skimmia japonica, flowers and fruits

The *Solidago* hybrid 'Lemore'

The rose of heaven, *Silene coeli-rosa*

The brilliant red berries of *Skimmia × foremanii* persist throughout the winter

Skimmia × *foremanii*

○ ◐ ⬙ ⬗ ✾ ⊛

A cross between *Skimmia japonica* and *Skimmia reevesiana*. It grows more vigorously than *Skimmia japonica*, and has purple-brown stems. The flowers are white in loose panicles, the berries dark red.

Skimmia fortunei, see *Skimmia reevesiana*.

Skimmia fragrans, see *Skimmia japonica*.

Skimmia japonica

A popular, slow-growing, evergreen shrub, about 4ft (1.2m) high, suitable for small gardens. Flowering period is May and June, with white to yellowish flowers. Male and female flowers are often found on separate plants. 'Foremanii' ('Veitchii') is a vigorous female clone; 'Fragrans' is free-flowering; and 'Rubella' is a red-budded cultivar, both being male.

Skimmia reevesiana

○ ◐ ⬙ ✾ ⊛ ⊛

Syn. *Skimmia fortunei*. A less hardy, compact shrub, often grown as a pot plant. The leaves are 2–4in (5–10cm) long and dark green. The whitish flowers are dioecious and appear May–June, followed by red berries.

Solidago
Compositae
Golden rod

Vigorous perennial plants for the border or for naturalization. The nomenclature of the various species and cultivars still causes some confusion among gardeners.

Soil Will grow in any soil, but care must be taken from time to time to lift the plants and fertilize the soil underneath the rootballs.

Propagation Divide and use the outer parts of the clumps for propagation.

Solidago canadensis

○ ◐ ⬙ ⬗ ⊗

Naturalized in many parts of western Europe, but originally from Canada and northern USA. Heights 2½–4ft (75–120cm). Flowering period is July–September. The plant has a creeping rootstock, lanceolate leaves and flowers in large, pyramidal, plumose heads.

Solidago hybrids

Raised from crosses of *Solidago canadensis* with various other species. A few of the most attractive hybrids are: 'Golden Dwarf', 10in (25cm), golden-yellow, flowering August–September; 'Goldenmosa', height 2½ft (75cm), sprays of deep yellow, fluffy flowers in August–October; 'Laurin', 12in (30 cm), golden-yellow, flowering August–September; 'Lenmore', 2ft (60cm), spherical plumes of soft primrose-yellow flowers August–September.

Solidago virgaurea

Golden Rod. A native of Europe, 32–4cin (80–100cm) high, with downy stems carrying rosettes of elongated and indented basal leaves; the upper leaves being pointed and sessile. it flowers July–August, with bright yellow terminal flower heads.

Sorbaria
Rosaceae

A genus of shrubs that come out very early in spring, though young shoots

The *Solidago* hybrid 'Golden Wings'

Sorbaria sorbifolia

may be damaged by severe night frosts.
Soil No particular soil requirements.
Propagation Rooted suckers are removed in the spring or autumn and grown in a nursery bed for a year before planting out in the permanent position. This shrub may also be increased from cuttings taken in late summer under glass or in autumn outside.

Sorbaria aitchisonii

○ ◐ ⬙ ⬗

The species with the largest flower clusters. A 10ft (3m) high shrub with hairless, brownish-red branches. Pinnate leaves made up of 13–21 leaflets,

2–3in (5–7.5cm) long, pointed, less than ½in (1cm) wide, serrate, hairless. The flowering period is June–July, with white flowers in large plume-like panicles.

Sorbaria arborea

A wide-spreading shrub with large flowers and grey twigs. The leaves are 2–3in (5–7.5cm) long, 1¾in (1–1.5cm) wide, and are covered with hair underneath, but later are often hairless. Flowering period is July–August, the flowers being white. This is the tallest sorbaria (a good 12ft/4m high).

Sorbaria sorbifolia

Syn. *Spiraea sorbifolia*. A shrub up to

6ft (2m) high. Flowering June–July, it carries white flowers in long, pyramidal plumes. The branches are erect and downy, but sometimes hairless. The pinnate leaf is made up of 13–21 leaflets 2–4in (5–10cm) long, lanceolate and pointed with about 20 lateral ribs. The leaflets are hairless underneath.

Sorbus
Rosaceae

A genus of hardy ornamental trees and shrubs, frequented by birds, most attractive during the flowering period, and particularly decorative when in fruit. The trees do not grow too tall and are easily accommodated in medium-sized gardens.

Soil Any well-drained but not dry garden soil will do. A sunny or lightly shaded site is best.

Propagation Propagate from seed that has been stored in sand for a year and planted out in a seed bed in the autumn.

Sorbus americana

○ ◐ ⬙ ⊛

A tree from north America, up to 25ft

Unfurling buds of *Sorbus aria*

(8m) high or more and with a spread of 15–22ft (5–7.5m). It flowers in June, with greyish-white flowers larger than those of *Sorbus aucuparia*. The fruits, by contrast, are smaller, though very numerous and a brighter red. The branches are reddish-brown and hairless, the buds elongated, sticky and dark brown. Leaflets are 11–17 in number, 2–3in (5–7.5cm) long, pointed and sharply toothed. The underside of the young leaf is slightly hairy. The most attractive cultivar is 'Belmonte', with a compact habit and attractive orange-red fruits in large, densely packed bunches from August to September.

Sorbus americana decora, see *Sorbus decora*.

Sorbus aria

Whitebeam. A tree up to 30ft (9m) high and with a spread of up to 25ft (8m). White, sometimes pale red flowers appear in May. The fruits are ovoid, scarlet, often turning to brownish-red. The branches are silky grey and sometimes hairless. Buds are green and sticky, and leaves oval, doubly toothed, 2–5in (5–12cm) long and silky white underneath. The best cultivars are: 'Lutescens', with an erect habit and leaves that are creamy-white when young;

Attractive fruits of *Sorbus hupehensis* 'November Pink'

Flowering mountain ash

'Magnifica', a robust tree with a conical crown, very large, dark green leaves, silky white underneath, and small orange-red fruits; and 'Majestica', which resembles the last except that its leaves are dull green on top and greenish on the underside. All prefer calcareous ground.

Sorbus aucuparia
Mountain ash, Rowan. A tree up to 30ft (9m) high or more and with a spread of up to 22ft (7.5m). Flowering period is May. It has off-white flowers and conical, pea-sized red fruit no more than ½in (1cm) across, appearing from the end of July to the end of September. The hairy twigs are hairless later. The buds are hairy. Pinnate leaves consist of 1–2in (2.5–5cm) long leaflets sharply or weakly pointed, entire at the base. Their undersides may be slightly covered with bluish hair. The best cultivars are: 'Edulis', a large tree with a columnar habit, dull green leaves and large, orange-red, edible (but sour) fruits; 'Fastigiata', a slow-growing, columnar shrub with bluish-green leaves and large, deep red fruits that are not retained for very long, takes up very little space because of its narrow habit. A very attractive tree, but susceptible to apple canker; 'Xanthocarpa' bears yellow fruits, as do 'Pendula' and 'Pendula Variegata', which has variegated yellow leaves.

Sorbus decora
Syn. *S. americana decora*. A small tree or shrub with a loose, open habit and pinnate, dark green leaves. The large scarlet fruits are borne in bunches measuring 5–8in (12–20cm) across and are very conspicuous from July to October. Excellent for smaller gardens and streets.

Sorbus discolor
A very small tree from northern China, with pinnate leaves. The fruits are white or yellow to orange-yellow. A cultivar under this name with red autumn leaves and glowing orange fruits is 'Embley'.

Sorbus hupehensis
'November Pink'. An exceptionally beautiful, fairly large cultivar, with a picturesque crown, and pinnate, bluish-green leaves. The fruits are rose-white spotted with red, later soft pink all over, and are retained until November.

Sorbus intermedia
Syn. *Sorbus suecica*. Swedish whitebeam. A native of northern Germany, Sweden and Norway, this tree grows up to 25ft (8m) high with a spread of up to 20ft (7m). Resembles *Sorbus aria* but is smaller. The flowers are white, the leaves grey and hairy beneath. Fruits are round, orange-red with yellow flesh, and appear August–September.

Sorbus lombarts hybrids
A fairly new group, still lacking a proper name and resulting from crosses between *Sorbus aucuparia*, *Sorbus discolor* and *Sorbus prattii*. Their most characteristic feature is the colour of the fruit, which ranges from bright red through chamois to pure pink, depending on the cultivar. There are also forms with pure white fruits. Highly recommended.

Sorbus prattii
A moderately tall shrub from western China with white fruits

Sorbus reducta
From Burma and China this grows 1–2ft (30–60cm) high. The pinnate leaves of this dwarf shrub turn red-purple in autumn, while the clusters of small white flowers in May and June are followed by pink-tinted fruits.

Sorbus sargentiana
From China. Growing to heights of 25–35ft (8–10m), it flowers in May. A handsome species which carries large, deep red-brown sticky buds in winter. The pinnate leaves turn rich red in autumn and the clusters of white flowers can be up to 6in (15cm) across. They are followed by scarlet fruits which ripen in August–September.

Sorbus suecica, see *Sorbus intermedia*.

Sorbus × thuringiaca
A cross between *Sorbus aria* and *Sorbus aucuparia*. The best-known form is 'Fastigiata', a tree with a dense, compact head, lobed and toothed leaves and deep red, large fruits from August to October.

Sorbus vilmorinii
From China. Height 8–9ft (2.5–3m). Flowering in June. Of spreading habit, this species has very finely dissected leaves, each made up of 11–31 leaflets. The loose clusters of white flowers are followed by red fruits, which vary from red to white with a pink flush.

Spartium
Leguminosae
Spanish broom

A genus containing only one broom-like shrub which is hardy except where severe or continuous frosts are experienced.
Soil Any well-drained garden soil is adequate.
Propagation Should be grown from seed.

Spartium junceum
An erect shrub from the Mediterranean, height 8–12ft (2.5–4m), flowering from June to August, with dark green stems and small narrow leaves which fall in summer. The pea-shaped flowers are bright yellow and are carried in spikes at the end of the twigs.

Spiraea
Rosaceae

A genus of hardy deciduous flowering shrubs that make no special demands, although they like a sunny position.
Cultivation Spiraeas should be pruned for good shape and large flower heads. Shrubs that flower on shoots of the previous year, e.g. *Spiraea × arguta*, *S. nipponica*, *S. prunifolia*, *S.*

Spiraea japonica 'Anthony Waterer'

Spiraea thunbergii

Spiraea veitchii

thunbergii, S. trilobata and S. × vanhouttei, should be thinned out in the winter. Untidy specimens of S. arguta and S. thunbergii should also be pruned immediately after flowering. Those which flower in the summer or the autumn, e.g. S. albiflora, S. bullata and S. bumalda hybrids, should always be pruned in the spring.

Soil Good fertile garden soil is needed.

Propagation Most garden types are best increased from cuttings of half-ripe lateral shoots, but they may also be propagated by layering, from hardwood cuttings taken in October, and from rooted suckers.

Spiraea albiflora
A dwarf, 20 in (50 cm) high shrub with white flowers borne in dense terminal corymbs June–August, on the current season's shoots.

Spiraea × arguta
Bridal wreath or Foam of May. A cross between Spiraea × multiflora and Spiraea thunbergii. A highly ornamental shrub up to 6 ft (1.8 m) high, with white flowers in April along the shoots of the previous year. It has graceful, slender, drooping, slightly angular branches. It is one of the most attractive spring-flowering spiraeas. Dead flowering shoots should be removed.

Spiraea bullata
A dwarf shrub up to 16 in (40 cm) high and eminently suitable for edging. The leaves are small, dark green and crinkled. The flowers are dark pink, in flat-topped clusters. Flowering period is June and July.

Spiraea bumalda hybrids
Dwarf shrubs up to 3 ft (1 m) high, flowering July–September. The flowers are generally red, in profuse umbels on broad flattened terminal panicles on the current year's shoots. The stems are striped and often strongly peeling. The bare leaves are ovate-lanceolate. For the most attractive and largest flowers, the shrub should be cut back every spring to within 3 in (7.5 cm) of ground level, and only the strongest shoots allowed to develop. 'Anthony Waterer' has small often white-spotted leaves and violet-red flowers. It can tolerate a fair amount of shade and is most suitable for the front of borders. 'Froebelii' has broader leaves and deep red flowers.

Spiraea cantoniensis
Syn. Spiraea reevesiana. Height 5 ft (1.5 m). Rhomboidal leaves and white flowers in rounded clusters, flowering in June.

Spiraea chamaedryfolia
Syn. Spiraea flexuosa. A native of Europe, 4½ ft (1.3 m) high, flowering in May or June. The flowers are white, borne in corymbs, while the branches are hairless, greyish brown and later peeling. Leaves are 2 in (5 cm) long, obovate, toothed above the middle, hairless and bright green underneath. A profusely flowering shrub that will tolerate a great deal of shade.

Spiraea flexuosa, see Spiraea chamaedryfolia.

Spiraea japonica
A shrub from Japan and China that grows to 3 ft (1 m). Pink flowers in large flattened heads come in summer. The branches are purple-brown, round, hairless and slightly flaking; the leaves 1–3 in (2.5–7.5 cm) long, ovate-lanceolate, pointed, doubly toothed, light or bluish-green and somewhat hairy underneath. 'Little Princess' is 20 in (50 cm) high with hairy twigs, small leaflets and 1 in (2.5 cm) wide clusters of rose-crimson flowers; 'Macrophylla' has very large, bullate leaves and very small inflorescences. All should be pruned close to ground level in the spring.

Spiraea latifolia
A 3 ft (1 m) shrub with hairless, angular branches and white or pale rose flowers in broad conical panicles June–August.

Spiraea nipponica
A wide-spreading shrub growing up to 4½ ft (1.3 m) high with slightly drooping branches. The small, ovate, dark green leaves are bluish-green underneath. The flowers are white and borne in semi-spherical umbels on last year's wood May–June.

Spiraea reevesiana, see Spiraea cantoniensis.

Spiraea thunbergii
A shrub from China and Japan up to 6 ft (2 m) high, flowering from March to May, the flowers being white, grouped in sessile clusters all along last year's wood. Branches are reddish-brown and somewhat hairy, the leaves 1 in (2.5 cm) long, linear-lanceolate, pointed, hairless, sharply toothed and light green. In cold winters and on draughty sites the tips sometimes freeze up.

Spiraea trilobata
This small shrub reaches a height of 3 ft (1 m). It has arching branches, and more or less circular bluish-green leaves. The flowers are white in crowded umbels, and appear May–June.

Spiraea × vanhouttei
A shrub up to 4½ ft (1.3 m) high. This plant is a cross between Spiraea cantoniensis and Spiraea trilobata. Flowering period is April–May. White flowers are borne in dense umbels. The branches are reddish-brown and hairless, the leaves 1–2 in (2.5–5 cm) long, obovate, mostly lobed and rounded at the foot. Excellent for loose hedges, it requires little pruning, although dead flowering shoots must be cut back vigorously after flowering.

Spiraea veitchii
A shrub from central and western China, up to 6 ft (2 m) high, with drooping branches. Numerous white flowers in large umbels appear in July.

Stachys
Labiatae

A genus including numerous herbaceous perennials suitable for the border and the rock garden.

Soil Stachys does well on dry soil, provided it contains no lime.

Propagation By division, but also from seed.

Stachys grandiflora
Syns. Betonica macrantha and Betonica grandiflora. Heights 1½–2½ ft (45–75 cm). Flowering period is June–August, with flowers 1–2 in (2.5–5 cm) long and lilac-pink. The leaves are elongated and heart shaped.

Stachys grandiflora

Stachys lanata, see *Stachys olympica.*

Stachys olympica
○ ◐ ⊖ ○ ◉

Syn. *Stachys lanata*. Lamb's tongue. A perennial plant covered with white silvery hairs. It grows 12–28 in (30–70 cm) tall with attractive greyish leaves that help to set off blue flowers in, for example, *Viola cornuta* or *Campanula carpatica*. Inconspicuous flowers are borne in woolly spikes. Flowering period is June–August. 'Siver Carpet' is a non-flowering, silvery-grey, ground-covering plant.

Stipa
Gramineae
Feather grass

A genus of particularly attractive grasses, with handsome feathery plumes that make excellent winter decorations.

Soil Dry, light, alkaline soil is required.

Propagation From seed.

Stipa pennata
○ ⊖ ⊙ ○ ◉ ⊗

From Europe. Growing 16–34 in (40–90 cm) high. Leaves are very

Stokesia laevis

narrow and stiff, with flowers in silvery-white plumes, from June to August.

Stokesia
Compositae
Stokes' aster

A plant with glorious blue flowers that are becoming increasingly popular.

Soil Normal, well-drained garden soil is adequate, and it will tolerate long dry spells.

Propagation By division or from root cuttings taken in September and over-wintered in a cold frame.

Stokesia laevis
○ ○ ⊙ ◉ ⊗

A plant from southern Carolina, growing to heights of 12–16 in (30–40 cm). Flowers are slightly reminiscent of cornflowers, and appear from July to September. It is not completely hardy.

Stranvaesia
Rosaceae

A small genus of evergreen trees and shrubs, one of which is hardy in all but continental climates, though it may lose its leaves after prolonged frosts.

Soil Any fertile, well-drained but not completely dry soil will do.

Propagation By cuttings in summer or from seed.

Stranvaesia davidiana
○ ◐ ◖ ⊛ ⊗ ⊛ ⊛

From China, this tree reaches 10–35 ft (3–10 m), flowering in June. The narrow leaves are red tinted when young and during cold weather, making it a feature in winter. The white flowers are followed by clusters of red berries in autumn. 'Fructoluteo' has yellow fruits.

Symphoricarpos
Caprifoliaceae
Snowberry

These are vigorous shrubs that will tolerate a great deal of shade and are

Symphoricarpos albus var. *laevigatus*

therefore suitable for planting under deciduous trees. The most attractive features are the berries, which may remain on the shrub throughout the winter.

Soil These shrubs make hardly any demands on the soil.

Propagation From suckers and by division. Ordinary species can also be grown from seeds sown outdoors in the autumn.

Symphoricarpos albus var. laevigatus
○ ◐ ◖ ⊛ ⊛ ⊙ ⊙ ⊗

A broad, low-suckering shrub with hairless branches and leaves. Pink flowers are followed by white berries up to ¾ in (1.5 cm) across in terminal and axillary clusters, which stay from summer to November–December. This snowberry is often sold under the name of *Symphoricarpos racemosus*. It is suitable for planting under deciduous trees and in other shaded places. 'Constance Spry' is a denser shrub with very large, pure white berries.

Symphoricarpos × chenaultii

A cross between *Symphoricarpos microphyllus* and *Symphoricarpos orbiculatus*. Resembles *Symphoricarpos orbiculatus* except that the undersides of

Symphoricarpos × chenaultii 'Mother of Pearl'

the leaves are more hairy, the flowers are grouped in small spikes and the berries are larger and darker. It is suitable as a hedging plant. 'Hancock' is a compact but wide-spreading shrub from Canada, very suitable for ground cover. Exceptionally attractive berries are produced by: 'Magic Berry', a compact, bushy shrub with ⅓ in rose-pink berries; 'Mother of Pearl', an attractive cultivar with ½ in marble-like berries; 'White Hedge', with ½ in (1 cm) white berries in erect clusters.

The shrubs with the most attractive berries are often listed as *Symphoricarpos × doorenbosii* (*Symphoricarpos rivularis* and *Symphoricarpos × chenaultii*).

Symphoricarpos orbiculatus

Indian currant or Coral berry. A dense, bushy shrub from North America, a good 3 ft (1 m) high. Flowering period is August–September, with pink flowers in axillary clusters forming large plumes. The fruits are red, the branches brown, hairless and often flaking. The buds are small and hairy, the leaves 1–2 in (2.5–5 cm) long, ovate, blunt, bluish-green underneath and slightly hairy, though not lobed. 'Variegatus' has smaller leaves, irregularly margined in yellow. It requires a sunnier position.

Symphoricarpos racemosus, see *Symphoricarpos albus*.

Symphoricarpos rivularis

Syn. *S. albus laevigatus* Similar to *S. albus* but leaves and berries larger, the latter more profusely borne.

Syringa microphylla flowering in the summer

The purple, single-flowered *Syringa vulgaris*

Single-flowered cultivar of *Syringa*

Syringa
Oleaceae
Lilac

The exceptionally attractive cultivars of *Syringa vulgaris* have replaced the species almost entirely. The magnificent flowers with their wonderful scent are among the most memorable features of gardens in May. But attractive though they undoubtedly are, it is a grave mistake to cram too many lilacs into a small garden, not least because lilacs tend to grow larger than expected, crowding out other plants for the remainder of the year. It is probably best to plant them in a small group, say a white and a purple or blue lilac in front of a laburnum.

Cultivation The common lilac, *Syringa vulgaris*, will grow in neglected parts of the garden and is therefore commonly used for masking ugly corners, such as the compost heap.

Lilacs require little pruning; at most they should be trimmed back, preferably during the flowering period when the flowering shoots can be used as cut flowers in the house. The plant should be dead-headed after flowering. Plants that have grown thin bottomed and straggly may be cut down to within 2 ft (60 cm) of the ground in the winter.

After planting, it is advisable to apply a mulch of well-rotted manure, but the manure must not be put directly on to the roots. In the spring, what manure remains on the surface can be worked lightly into the upper layer of the soil. Care should be taken not to damage the roots; they lie very close to the surface.

Lilacs root very easily and can therefore be transplanted from autumn to the early spring without too many problems.

Soil Lilacs thrive in any fertile, not too dry, humus-rich soil.

Propagation Cultivars may be grown from summer cuttings under glass or budded in August on to seedlings of *Syringa vulgaris* or rooted cuttings of privet.

Pests and diseases Lilacs may be attacked by caterpillars of the lilac leaf miner, by scale insects and by lilac blight.

Syringa patula

Syn. *Syringa palibiniana*, *Syringa valutina*. Korean lilac, from Korea and Japan. It grows to 10 ft (3 m), flowering in May. The small, oval leaves are hairy on both sides and the lavender to pink flowers are borne in numerous spikes. It is slow-growing and a good lilac for the smaller garden.

Syringa × chinensis

Rouen lilac. A cross between *Syringa × persica* and *Syringa vulgaris*, which grows 8–10 ft (2.5–3 m) high. Purple flowers in broad pyramidal panicles are borne in May.

Syringa josikaea

Hungarian lilac, growing 10–12 ft (3–4 m) high. The flowering period is June–July, with dark violet flowers in narrow, pyramidal panicles. The branches are olive green and hairless, the buds brownish-red. Leaves are 2–4 in (5–10 cm) long, ovate, pointed, finely ciliate, almost bare and bluish-green underneath.

Syringa microphylla

A small shrub, 3–4½ ft (1–1.3 m) high, with small leaves, ½–2 in (1–5 cm) long, greyish green underneath. This species is not often seen in gardens, where its place has been taken by 'Superba', a cultivar with dark pink flowers borne in loose plumes from late May often until October.

Syringa reflexa

Very late-flowering (June), with large drooping panicles of pink flowers, somewhat lighter inside. Highly recommended because of its late flowering and distinctive habit.

Syringa × swegiflexa

A cross between *Syringa reflexa* and *Syringa sweginzowii*. A robust shrub with pink flowers in cylindrical panicles, flowering in June.

Syringa vulgaris

Common lilac. A shrub from Hungary, the Balkans and the Near East, reaching heights of 8–20 ft (2.5–7 m). Flowering in May, colours are lilac, blue, white, red and various intermediate shades, single and double. It is the basis of countless cultivars, with names and types that differ from one catalogue to the next.

The best are: Purple, single: 'Andenken an Ludwig Spaeth', 'G. J. Baardse'; purplish-red, double: 'Charles Joly', 'Mrs Edward Harding' and 'Paul Deschanel'; Rosy-purple, lilac and violet, single: 'Madame Charles Souchet' and 'President Lincoln'; double blooms with the above colours: 'Katherine Havemeyer', 'Leon Gambetta' and 'Olivier des Serres'; white, single: 'Mont Blanc'; double: 'Madame Lemoine', 'Miss Ellen Willmott' and 'Monique Lemoine'.

Tagetes tenuifolia

Tamarisk, *Tamarix tetrandra*

F₁-hybrid of *Tagetes patula*

Tagetes
Compositae
Marigold

A genus of very sturdy annuals and herbaceous perennials, including *Tagetes patula*, French marigold, which is mainly grown from seed. Garden-lovers should also try *Tagetes tenuifolia* 'Pumila', a small cultivar that flowers for an extremely long time and in great profusion. Both single- and double-flowered types are available.

Soil Marigolds are not choosy and will tolerate fairly dry and poor conditions. The taller sorts, however, require somewhat better and moister soil.

Propagation Sow in March under glass at 18°C (64°F), prick out the seedlings into boxes and harden off in a cold frame. Plant out in late April or in May. The plants may even be moved while in flower provided the rootballs are left intact. The distance apart depends upon the size: the smallest should be set out 8–10 in (20–25 cm) apart; the medium sized 10–14 in (25–35 cm) apart, and the tallest 14–18 in (35–45 cm) apart. Do not allow crowding and if necessary thin out to the distances given above.

Tagetes erecta

African marigold. An annual plant from Mexico, 18–30 in (45–80 cm) high, with curiously aromatic foliage. The green stems carry flower heads 3–4 in (7.5–10 cm) across, mainly yellow or orange-yellow. There are numerous cultivars, nearly all of them double and some possessing unscented foliage. Chrysanthemum-flowered types include: 'Orange Fantastic', bright orange, 28 in (80 cm), and 'Glitters', canary-yellow, 26 in (75 cm); dwarf forms include 'Spun Gold', golden-yellow and 'Spun Yellow', canary-yellow, both 12 in (25 cm) high.

Carnation-flowered cultivars include: 'Burpees Gold', bright orange, 26 in (75 cm), early-flowering, and 'Hawaii', deep orange, 22 in (55 cm), both scentless. Dwarf carnation-flowered cultivars include: 'Mr Moonlight', canary-yellow, 10 in (25 cm) high. The introduction of F₁ hybrids has greatly improved uniformity. Of these, 'Double Eagle' is light orange and 'Doubloon' is canary-yellow; both are 2½ ft (75 cm) high. The so-called Jubilee series reaches a height of 12 in (45 cm). The Ladies series includes such plants as 'First Lady', primula-yellow, and 'Orange Lady', orange, both 12 in (30 cm) high and mainly used for bedding. Still more compact varieties (10 in/25 cm high) include 'Apollo', bright orange and 'Moonshot', primula-yellow. Both have large, globose flowers.

Tagetes patula

French marigold. An annual from Mexico, flowering from July to autumn. The flowers are on longer stems and are smaller than those of *Tagetes erecta*, but they are just as attractive. The species has crimson-brown to golden-yellow flowers, but varieties come in a host of different colours. They are divided into tall 24–30 in (50–75 cm) types, which are not very common; compact types (12–14 in/30–35 cm) in the so-called 'Nana' group; and even smaller types (8 in/20 cm) in the 'Lilliput' group. In the 'Nana' group, 'Belinda', golden-yellow with a brownish-red centre; 'Oriania', deep orange; and 'Red Brocade', mahogany-red, are especially recommended.

A recently introduced group has flowers up to 12 in (30 cm) across and is known as 'Gigantea'. It includes 'Bolero', mahogany with a golden-yellow edge, and 'Fiesta', chestnut-red with a yellow edge.

Well-known cultivars in the 'Lilliput' group are 'Lemon Drop', bright yellow, and 'Sunkist', orange. The so-called 'Petite' forms are improvements of the latter. F₁ hybrids are available although not yet very widely.

The so-called 'Nugget' series, height 12 in (30 cm), is exceptionally floriferous. Special mention should also be made of 'Gold Seven Star', golden-yellow, and 'Red Glow', reddish-brown and yellow.

Finally, there is the Simplex group of small, single-flowered marigolds. They appeal particularly to those who find double flowers too artificial. 'Naughty Marietta' attains a height of 12 in (30 cm) and bears golden-yellow flowers with a brown spot. 'Eliza' is a bright rust-red colour.

Tagetes signata, see *Tagetes tenuifolia*.

Tagetes tenuifolia

Syn. *Tagetes signata*. Bush marigold. An annual from Mexico, 24–28 in (50–60 cm) high. Compact cultivars are not more than 1 ft (30 cm) high. Flowering period is June to autumn, within about three months of sowing. The flowers are single, star-shaped and

Swamp cypress. Note the knee-like growths from the roots of the specimen, left

Glorious autumn colour of the swamp cypress, *Taxodium distichum*

In the spring, the swamp cypress also buds on older wood

golden-yellow. 'Pumila', 8–12 in (20–30 cm) high, is exceptionally attractive and floriferous. Two other well-known varieties are 'Orange Gem', pure orange, and 'Paprika', brownish-red. These plants have a fairly wide spread and can cover an area of 12 in (30 cm). If they are planted too close together and grow too spindly they may be safely trimmed down since they will quickly come back into flower.

Tamarix
Tamaricaceae
Tamarisk

A genus of flowering shrubs with feathery sprays of foliage, superficially resembling a cypress. The flowers are borne in fluffy spikes.

Tamarisks may be planted as specimen plants or in bold groups in parks or large gardens; they also form sturdy windbreaks near the sea.
Soil Tamarisks thrive in any well-drained garden soil. They are tolerant of salt in the soil and will grow in almost pure sand. They are not, however, tolerant of lime.
Propagation Readily increased from hardwood cuttings in the autumn or early winter.

Tamarix parviflora
○ ◑ ◍ ⊗
Syn. *Tamarix tetrandra purpurea*. A shrub from eastern Europe and Turkey, up to 15 ft (5 m) high, with arching purple-brown branches. The flowering period is May. The deep pink flowers are borne on the previous year's growth.
Tamarix ramosissima
○ ◑ ◍ ⊗
Syn. *Tamarix pentandra*. A robust, tall shrub with bluish-green leaves and light pink flowers in large flowery heads. Flowering period is July–September. 'Pink Cascade' has bright pink flowers in long, slender and drooping racemes; 'Rubra' has deep rose-red flowers.
Tamarix tetrandra
○ ◑ ◠ ◍ ⊗
A shrub from the Balkans, 10 ft (3 m) high. It has pink flowers from April–May, with young foliage. Not quite as hardy as the last two species.
Tamarix tetrandra purpurea, see *T. parviflora*.

Taxodium
Taxodiaceae
Swamp cypress

A genus of deciduous conifers for the larger garden. Older specimens established in fertile, moist soil develop peculiar growths from the roots, which are known as knees or pneumatophores and help to supply the plant with oxygen.
Soil As their vernacular name suggests these ornamental trees do best in very moist soil.
Propagation From cuttings in late summer in a cold frame, or from imported seed.

Taxodium distichum
○ ⊗ ❋ ⊕
Tall, pyramidal tree from swamps and river banks in eastern North America. Garden specimens reach heights of 75 ft (22 m) or more and have a spread of 25 ft (8 m). Leaves and secondary branchlets

Old *Taxus* wall

Taxus baccata 'Semperaurea'

Taxus cuspidata

○ ◑ ▦ ◉ ⊛ ⊛ ◎ ⊛

Japanese yew. It resembles *Taxus baccata* and is listed in some catalogues as a variety of it. It differs in having pointed bud scales and thicker leaves that come to a sudden point. 'Nana' is a dwarf clone with ascending branches and a loose habit. It is very slow growing. The leaves are short and radially arranged.

Taxus × media

○ ◑ ▦ ◉ ⊛ ◎ ⊛

A cross between *Taxus baccata* and *Taxus cuspidata*. Cultivars include 'Hatfieldii', a dense, compact shrub with short dark green needles. With its many erect branches, it resembles *Taxus baccata* 'Fastigiata'. 'Hicksii' grows more vigorously and has a broad columnar habit. 'Hillii' strongly re-

Taxus baccata can be pruned into almost any shape

are shed in the autumn. The linear leaves on shoots over one year old are up to ¾in (1.5cm) long, light green with two bright lines underneath, and are borne in two flattened ranks.

Mature trees flower in the spring. Male and female flowers are borne separately on the same tree; the male flowers are loose purplish catkins about 4in (10cm) long, the female flowers are tiny, developing into cones 1in (2.5cm) across, ripening purple-brown.

Taxus
Taxaceae
Yew

A genus of long-lived conifers found in Europe, Asia and North America. In England some species are thought to be more than a thousand years old. All larger specimens are hollow. Even very old trees continue to grow, but slowly. Young trees do not grow very much faster, which explains why yews are no longer popular as hedging plants—gardeners say that they plant yews for their children, not for themselves. This claim is not entirely true, however: a yew will grow from 2½ft (75cm) high to 6½ft (2m) high in 6–8 years, sometimes less in fertile soil.

The yew, which is poisonous in all its parts, is exceptionally easy to shape, and hence is a favourite subject for topiary work. In Britain there are many splendid examples of this art. Yews stand up extremely well to the wind and are very tolerant of shade. If they are allowed to grow undisturbed they will develop into robust trees with a good crown. All yews have male and female

flowers borne on separate plants.
Soil Yews will grow in all types of soil, including chalky, provided they are well drained but not too dry. An annual dressing of decayed manure, leaf-mould or peat and a general fertilizer is recommended.
Propagation The common yew is almost invariably increased from seed, which explains the slight differences between individual shrubs. All cultivars must be propagated from cuttings taken in the late autumn in a cold frame since they do not come true from seed.

Taxus baccata

○ ◑ ▦ ◉ ⊛ ⊛ ◎ ▦

Common yew. The leaves are ¾–1¼in (1–1.5cm) long, dark green and glossy. The fruits have a red aril (fruit coat) and resemble berries. It can reach a height of 60ft (18m), but in gardens rarely grows to beyond 30ft (9m), with a spread of 12–18ft (4–6m).

Nurseries offer numerous attractive cultivars with some special and many common features. The most popular are:
Narrowly columnar shape: 'Fastigiata', Irish yew; 'Fastigiata Aureomarginata', Golden Irish yew, having leaves with yellow margins; 'Standishii', slow-growing, like a small golden Irish yew and ideal for the small garden.
Weeping forms: 'Dovastoniana' has a pyramidal habit with spreading branches, drooping at the tip; 'Dovastoniana Aurea' with the same habit and variegated yellow leaves.
Other shapes: 'Adpressa' is a wide-spreading, densely branching shrub with short, fairly wide leaves;

'Repandens' is very wide-spreading and semi-prostrate, providing good ground cover in shade.
Yellow forms: 'Semperaurea' is a broad, densely branching shrub with bright yellow needles; 'Washingtonii' has a compact habit and yellowish-green needles that turn bronze in the winter; 'Lutea' has fruits with orange-yellow (instead of red) arils.

Taxus cuspidata 'Aurescens', a golden yew

Loose flower sprays of *Thalictrum dipterocarpum*

Thalictrum aquilegifolium

sembles 'Hicksii' but has smaller and darker green needles. All are good for hedging.

Thalictrum
Ranunculaceae
Meadow-rue

These are elegantly attractive herbaceous perennial plants with ferny leaves and fluffy or airy inflorescences. They are suitable for planting in a solitary position or in small groups.
Soil Fertile, moist garden soil is needed. It is tolerant of shade.
Propagation The best method of propagation is by division. The species can also be increased from seed but the seedlings are slow to develop.

Thalictrum aquilegifolium
○ ◑ ◌ ○ ⓨ ◎ ⊗

A herbaceous perennial from Europe, Siberia and Japan, growing to heights of between 16–60 in (40–150 cm). The flowering period is May–July, with fluffy panicles of small flowers with attractive yellow or purple stamens. 'Album' has white stamens while, 'Atropurpureum' has purple stamens and stems covered with a purple bloom.

Thalictrum chelidonii
○ ◑ ◌ ◌ ⊗

A 3–5 ft (1–1.5 m) tall species for a cool, moist position. It has deeply divided leaves and branched panicles of lilac flowers each $\frac{1}{2}-\frac{3}{4}$ in (1.5–1.8 cm) wide.

Thalictrum dipterocarpum
A perennial from central China, growing up to 6 ft (2 m) high. The flowering period is summer. The flowers are fairly large, lilac, with yellow anthers in airy sprays, and the foliage is most attractive. A single branch in a cutglass vase makes a beautiful talking point. Even better for cutting is 'Hewitt's Double'. In the border, it is prone to wind damage. Staking should be done early to avoid damaging the loose inflorescences.

Thalictrum minus
○ ◑ ◌ ○ ◌ ◎ ⊗

Lesser meadow-rue. A perennial from Europe and Siberia, up to 60 in (1.5 m) high. Inconspicuous flowers appear May–June. Grown chiefly for its very attractive ferny foliage, it is rather invasive in some soils. *T. m. arenarium* is smaller, growing to 8 in (20 cm) tall.

Thuja
Cupressaceae
Arbor-vitae

A popular genus of conifers for the garden. *Thuja occidentalis*, which will stand up to strong winds, is often used for hedging. When the foliage of these plants is rubbed between the fingers, it gives off a characteristic sweetly aromatic scent. For the differences between *Thuja* and *Chamaecyparis* see under the latter.
Cultivation Like all conifers, these plants must be transplanted with a good rootball. Many species change colour in the winter or after transplantation, but this will correct itself either in the spring or after the plants have become established.
Soil Thujas will thrive in any ordinary well-drained, but not dry, fertile soil.
Propagation Species may be increased from seed. Cultivars, however,

must be propagated from cuttings, or by grafting. Amateurs will do best with cuttings taken in the late autumn.

Thuja gigantea, see *Thuja plicata*.
Thuja occidentalis
○ ◑ ❀ ◈ ◌

American arbor-vitae or White cedar. A pyramidal tree from North America, up to 60 ft (18 m) high with a spread of 12–18 ft (4–6 m) and an open crown. It will tolerate a great deal of pruning and hence is very suitable for hedging. Branches are flattened and densely intertwined, and the scales slightly glossy, yellowish-green, never white underneath. This species has a particularly strong scent when the leaves are bruised. Some well-known cultivars are:

Dwarf types: 'Globosa' has a rounded shape and a compact habit. The branches are nearly vertical. 'Hoveyi' is an oval dwarf with bright green scales. 'Little Gem' has a globular, slightly flat-topped habit, and dark green foliage. 'Recurva Nana' is more conical but with branchlets noticeably recurved at the tips, and bright green leaves. It is excellent for low, spreading hedges. 'Rheingold' is a compact, broadly conical bush with bronzy-gold leaves in winter.

Taller types: 'Pyramidalis compacta' is an attractive bright green columnar plant, excellent for taller hedges. 'Rosenthalii' has a columnar habit and dark green foliage, and grows fairly slowly. 'Wareana' has a conical habit with short, thickened sprays of bright green foliage, and grows fairly quickly. 'Wareana Lutescens' is more compact and has yellow leaves, bright at first, darker later.

There are also numerous more recent introductions, including 'Danica' and 'Hetz Midget', up to 2 ft (60 cm) high and with a spread of up to $2\frac{1}{2}$ ft (75 cm). The foliage is green in the summer and brownish in the winter. 'Skogholm' resembles 'Rosenthalii' but does not share its tendency to become choked in the centre. 'Smaragd' ('Emerald'), 12–30 ft (4–9 m) high, has a conical

A *Thuja occidentalis* hedge

habit and bright green leaves.
Thuja orientalis
○ ◑ ◌ ❀ ❀

Chinese arbor-vitae. A tall shrub with a dense oval habit, several cultivars of which are highly suitable for the rock garden. 'Aurea Nana', a dwarf globular bush of dense habit, has bright green leaves that turn bronze-yellow in the winter. 'Elegantissima' has a dense columnar habit, and yellow foliage turning golden-bronze. 'Meldensis' forms a dense globe to 18 in (45 cm) wide, with sea-green foliage turning purple in winter.

Thuja plicata
○ ◑ ❀ ❀ ◌

Syn. *Thuja gigantea*. Western red cedar. A fast-growing, very tall conifer with a pyramidal habit. The small branches are generally erect and very evenly spaced. The scales are glossy green in the species, but dark green and very shiny in 'Atrovirens'. An attractive park tree for the larger garden. 'Zebrina' has green leaves banded with creamy-yellow.

Thuja standishii
Japanese arbor-vitae. This tree reaches great heights in Japan but is usually grown as a medium-sized tree in Europe. Loosely spreading branches; yellow-green foliage with white stripes or spots on the underside.

Thuja orientalis 'Aurea Nana'

Thymus
Labiatae
Thyme

A genus which includes not only culinary herbs but also valuable dwarf shrubs for the rock garden.

Soil Any ordinary well-drained soil is suitable.

Propagation By division, from cuttings and from seed.

Thymus × citrodorus
○ ◑ ⊖ ⌃ ⌘ ⊛ ⊗

A cross between *Thymus pulegioides* and *Thymus vulgaris*. Lemon thyme. A small lemon-scented shrub, 4–10 in (10–25 cm) high, with erect shoots covered with hairs. The leaves are hairless. Light pink flowers in terminal clusters appear July–August. 'Silver Queen', with dark green, white-edged leaves, is a particularly attractive cultivar. 'Aureus' has yellow-flushed leaves and is very aromatic.

Thymus praecox arcticus
○ ◑ ⊖ ⌃ ⌘ ⊛ ⊗

Syn. *Thymus serpyllum*, *T. drucei*. Wild thyme. A mat-forming plant with hairy flower stems. Leaves, which are up to $\frac{1}{4}$ in (0.5 cm) long, are oval, blunt, and ciliate at the base. The flowering period is June–August, the flowers dark pink in nearly spherical terminal clusters. 'Coccineus' has crimson flowers.

Thymus vulgaris

Common or garden thyme. A strongly scented spreading shrub up to 12 in (30 cm) tall, with shoots clothed in short hairs. Very useful as a culinary herb. Light mauve flowers appear May–July.

Wild thyme, *Thymus arcticus* 'Coccineus'

Tiarella cordifolia makes good ground-cover

Tiarella
Saxifragaceae

A genus of low-growing perennials with attractive small flowers suitable for planting under trees and in cool, shady positions in the rock garden.

Soil Garden soil that should never become too dry is necessary.

Propagation From seeds and by division of the roots or by separating the rooting stolons.

Tiarella cordifolia
◑ ◑ ◯ ◯ ⊗ ⊖

Foam flower, from North America. It has green, sometimes purple-mottled leaves on long stems, maple like in appearance. Flowers are white, small and appear in foamy clusters May–June. The foliage turns an attractive bronze in the autumn. It forms wide mats, which make good ground cover.

Tigridia
Iridaceae

A genus of bulbous plants that must be planted close together in bold groups to make any kind of show. Visitors to the garden will be pleasantly surprised if they are given a few buds and told to put them in water. If the buds have been cut just before they are ready to open, they will look spectacularly beautiful the next day. The flowers come in a variety of very attractive colours.

Cultivation Lift them every year, dry, and protect from frost, except in sheltered south-facing borders, where the plants may be left undisturbed for several years. Replant March–May, 5–6 in (12–15 cm) apart, at a depth of 3 in (7.5 cm).

Soil Rich, well-drained soil in full sun is needed.

Propagation From offsets when dormant.

Tigridia pavonia
○ ⌘ ⊗

Tiger flower. A bulbous plant from Mexico, 10–18 in (25–45 cm) high. Flowering period is August–September, when individual flowers open for one day only, but the flowers are so beautiful that few plant-lovers would willingly omit them from their gardens. The leaves are sword-shaped, like those of the iris. The flowers have three large plain and three small, sometimes spotted, petals, all radiating from a spotted and cup-shaped base. 'Alba' is white with crimson spots; 'Canariensis' is yellow with a red-spotted centre; 'Lutea Immaculata' is yellow all over; 'Speciosa' is scarlet with yellow and red-spotted centres.

Tilia
Tiliaceae
Lime

A genus of deciduous ornamental trees whose size makes them more suitable for growing in parks and squares than in private gardens.

Soil Ordinary, well-drained garden soil is adequate.

Propagation From seed, which takes 6 months to 2 years to germinate.

Tigridia pavonia

Cultivars must be increased by layering, grafting or from cuttings placed in a mist propagator in summer.

Diseases Many limes are attacked by aphids and become sticky as a result. *T. cordata*, *T. × euchlora* and *T. tomentosa* are "clean" limes, less badly affected in this way.

Tilia americana
○ ⊛ ⌖

American lime. A tree to 60 ft (18 m) high or more, with a spread of up to 30 ft (9 m). The branches are hairless and brownish-red in colour. Leaves 4–8 in (10–20 cm) long, very broad, tapering to a very short point and are asymmetrical. They are hairless except for minute axillary tufts on the underside.

Tilia cordata

Small-leaved lime. A tree up to 90 ft (27 m) high, sometimes taller, with a spread of up to 35 ft (11 m). The branches are first covered with a fine down, later hairless and are olive green. The leaves are 1–2 in (2.5–5 cm) long, heart-shaped, dark green above, and pale green with brown axillary tufts beneath.

Tilia × euchlora

A cross between *Tilia cordata* and *Tilia dasystyla*. A tree up to 60 ft (18 m) high with a spread of up to 30 ft (9 m). Leaves are glossy green and deeply toothed. Light yellow flowers appear June–July. It attracts bees, but the nectar has a narcotic effect on them.

Tilia × europaea

Syn. *Tilia vulgaris*. A cross between *Tilia cordata* and *Tilia platyphyllos*. Common lime. A tree up to 135 ft (40 m) high, with a spread of up to 40 ft (12 m).

Tilia platyphyllos

A lime in front of an old house in Baarn, Holland

Lime blossoms

The branches are hairless and often drooping. Leaves are 2–4in (5–10cm) long, broadly ovate or rounded, obliquely heart-shaped at the base, sharply toothed, dull green on top, with axillary tufts underneath. 'Pallida' has bright green leaves and reddish branches and buds towards the autumn.

Tilia petiolaris
Pendant silver lime. A tree of uncertain origin, possibly a hybrid. It reaches 100ft (33m) or more with a narrowly erect head and pendant branches. The long stalked, dark green leaves are whitish beneath and the pale yellow flowers are fragrant. The nectar is attractive to bees, but as with some other limes, it has a narcotic effect upon them.

Tilia platyphyllos
Broad-leaved lime. A tree up to 100ft (30m) high with a spread of up to 40ft

(12m). The branches are olive-green to brownish-red. Leaves are 2–5in (5–10cm) long, roundish-ovate, with a short, pointed tip. The tops are dull green, the undersides light green and hairy, especially along the veins. There are various forms of the tree, with erect or compact habits, and also with differently shaped leaves, some of them yellow.

Tilia tomentosa
Silver lime. A tree up to 45ft (13m) high with a spread of up to 36ft (10m). The branches are erect and covered with greyish-green hair. The buds are blunt. The leaves are 2–5in (5–10cm) long, round, with a short point. They have a green upper side which is hairy at first but later almost completely bald, and are covered with silvery down underneath.

Trachymene
Hydrocotylaceae

A genus containing both annuals and perennials, one of the former being grown for summer bedding and as a pot plant.

Soil Any well-drained soil is adequate.
Propagation These plants are grown from seed.

Trachmene coerulea

○ ⊙ ⊗

Syn. *Didiscus coerulea*. From Australia. Blue Lace Flower. Growing 1½–2ft (45–60cm) tall and flowering from July onwards, it is an attractive annual with deeply divided leaves and rounded clusters of tiny, light blue flowers.

Tradescantia hybrid

Trollius cultivar 'Etna'

Tropaeolum peregrinum canary creeper

Tsuga heterophylla 'Conica'

Tradescantia
Commelinaceae

A genus of very long-flowering perennial plants, each flower of which blooms for one day only.
Soil Fairly moist, rich garden soil is needed.
Propagation These plants are propagated by division.

Tradescantia × andersoniana

Syn. *Tradescantia virginiana* of gardens. Trinity flower; spiderwort. A race of cultivars derived from *T. virginiana*, *T. ohiensis* and *T. subaspera*, growing to a height of 20–24 in (50–60 cm) and flowering from June to September. The leaves are grass-like but broader. Of the several cultivars the following deserve special mention: 'Weguelin', very large, sky-blue flowers; 'Innocence', pure white; 'Leonora', deep violet-blue with a yellow centre; 'Osprey', white with violet-blue stamens; 'Purple Dome', rich purple; and 'Rubra', deep rose-red.

Trollius
Ranunculaceae
Globeflower

Very attractive perennial plants for cutting and the border. The flowers are formed of yellow sepals, which surround the small tongue-shaped petals or honey leaves (nectaries).
Cultivation If the seeds are sown in the spring, the flowers may appear in autumn. Plants given a semi-shaded position will produce flowers of a better colour and remain in flower longer than those planted in the sun.
Soil Ordinary moist garden soil is adequate. Flowers intended for cutting should be given a dressing of fertilizer each spring.
Propagation Propagate by division or from seed when ripe.

Trollius ledebourii (of gardens)

A perennial plant 24–40 in (60–100 cm) high, densely branching. The flowering period is May–July, with orange-yellow flowers. It is suitable for borders. 'Golden Queen' has exceptionally attractive, large, orange-yellow semidouble flowers with dark orange pistils, flowering in late June.

Trollius europaeus

A group of nasturtiums, *Tropaeolum majus*, in flower

A perennial from Europe, 20–28 in (50–70 cm) high. Flowering period is May–June; though sometimes there is a second flush in the autumn. The flowers are large, light yellow and globose. The 5–10 "honey leaves" are as long as the stamens. This plant grows very vigorously.

Trollius × cultorum (hybrids of catalogues)

These are crosses between *Trollius asiaticus*, *Trollius chinensis* and *Trollius europaeus*. They are similar to *T. europaeus*, but more robust with larger flowers. The best orange-coloured cultivars are: 'Etna', 'Goliath', 'Orange Princess' (the most attractive of all) and 'Prichard's Giant'. The best of the yellow sorts are: 'Canary Bird', 'Earliest of All' (very early flowering), 'Goldquelle' and 'Lemon Queen'.

Tropaeolum
Tropaeolaceae
Nasturtium

A genus of well-known annual and herbaceous perennials, most of them climbers. In recent years, however, many compact bedding cultivars in a wide range of shades have been added.

For these see *Tropaeolum majus*.
Soil These plants, especially the compact cultivars, do not like soil that is too rich, in which they tend to produce foliage at the expense of flowers.
Propagation Raise the annual species in April under glass and plant out in early May; alternatively sow in the flowering position in late April or early May, 12 in (30 cm) or more apart. Propagate the herbaceous perennials by division of the rootstock, and the tubers in the same way as potatoes.

Tropaeolum canariense, see Tropaeolum peregrinum.

Tropaeolum majus

Nasturtium. Annuals with a trailing and climbing habit, the many dwarfs among which are usually referred to as *Tropaeolum majus nanum*. Both groups include double- and single-flowered cultivars and also plants with dark, variegated, yellow or wavy leaves. Flowers come in red, pink, salmon, orange yellow and shades intermediate between these.

Tropaeolum peregrinum

Syn. *Tropaeolum canariense*. Canary creeper. A climbing plant from Peru,

6–10 ft (2–3 m) high, with five-lobed, kidney-shaped leaves. The flowering period is July–September, the flowers being solitary, dotted with red, and irregular in shape. It has green spurs, arched at the tip. Very suitable for growing on dead trees and on walls.

Tropaeolum tuberosum

A tuberous plant from Peru. In cold areas tubers can be planted in situ in April, choosing a sunny, sheltered site, ideally against a south-facing wall. The stems, which can grow to a height of 10 ft (3 m), need the support of netting or twiggy sticks. The small orange flowers appear from July to October. Lift the tubers after frost kills the leaves in the autumn and store in a dry place. In sheltered places the tubers may be mounded over with soil or peat or replanted 4–6 in (10–15 cm) deep in the growing-site.

Tsuga
Pinaceae
Hemlock, hemlock spruce

A genus of evergreen conifers, most of which grow very tall. However, dwarf forms exist.
Soil Any soil types except those rich in lime.
Propagation The species can be grown from seed. Cultivars must be increased from cuttings taken in the summer.

Tsuga canadensis

Eastern hemlock. A tree from North America which grows 60–100 ft (18–30 m) high, with a spread of up to 20 ft (7 m). The branches are yellowish-brown and hairy. The buds are light brown and pointed. The leaves are $\frac{1}{4}-\frac{3}{4}$ in (0.5–1.5 cm) long, narrowing towards the tip, with white stripes and green margins underneath. 'Albospica' is slower growing and more compact with creamy-white tips to its shoots. 'Pendula' is a shrubby, weeping form.

Tsuga heterophylla

Western hemlock. A tall, slender tree from western North America, growing up to 100 ft (30 m) high. It resembles *Tsuga canadensis*, having brown branches and blunt, greyish-brown buds. The leaves are blunt, of even width, with broad white stripes underneath but no green margins, and glossy green on top. It stands up well to sea winds, and makes a good hedging plant that stands regular clipping.

Tulipa
Liliaceae
Tulip

A genus of hardy bulbs introduced to western Europe from Turkey in the mid-sixteenth century. From 1623 to 1636 tulipmania swept Holland, the bulbs fetching enormous prices.

Cultivation Because the flowers are present in the bulb when it is bought, tulips will bloom in even the worst sites, but if they are to flower again the following year they must be given a sunny position and a fertile soil. Moreover the leaves must be allowed to die naturally. But even if these demands are met, the flowers usually deteriorate from one season to the next, so that many gardeners do not think that any except the most valuable tulip bulbs are worth saving.

Tulips are planted from October to December at depth of 3–4 in (7.5–10cm). It is most important to make sure that the planting depth is even, especially in flower beds, so that all the plants come into flower more or less simultaneously. For bedding, bulbs should be about 4–6 in (10–15 cm) apart, unless they are to be interplanted with other bedding plants, when a much wider distance is desirable. Like all flowering bulbs, tulips must not be fed with fresh manure.

If attractive tulips are required, they should not be allowed to grow in the same spot for more than two successive years, or else the disease known as "tulip fire" may occur, producing scorch marks and spots on the leaves,

Tulipa greigii 'Charmeuse'

Darwin-tulip 'Black Swan'

Parrot-tulip 'Orange Favourite' with forget-me-nots in the background

and possibly attacking the flowers as well. If tulips are required for years in a particular border, say for interplanting, then the old positions should be carefully marked and the plants changed about in successive years, or else lifted immediately they have stopped flowering. They should then be dead-headed, planted in rows in, say, the kitchen garden, and the strongest replanted the following year. To disinfect the ground, and to destroy the tulip fire fungus, it is best to apply a dressing of quintozene (Botrilex) to the soil according to the maker's instructions just before planting. Tulips should be grown on very well-drained soil—if rainwater cannot run off quickly, the roots are likely to rot.

Propagation Tulips are usually increased from offset bulbs, which are kept dry and replanted in the autumn. It is advisable to grow them for the first year in a sunny nursery bed.

The most popular garden tulips have been bred from wild species, of which several are still grown today.

Tulipa acuminata

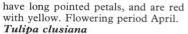

Not a true species, but a sport or mutant of *T. gesneriana*. The flowers have long pointed petals, and are red with yellow. Flowering period April.

Tulipa clusiana
From Afghanistan. White with pink flowers in April, height 8–12 in (20–30 cm).

Tulipa eichleri
From Iran to Tadjikistan. Flowers, which appear in March–April, are vermilion with pointed petals having yellow, black blotched bases.

Tulipa gesneriana
From Turkey. Dull crimson-scarlet blooms with an olive-black and yellow basal blotch within. White and yellow forms are known. This is considered to be the basic species from which the modern tulips have descended.

Tulipa marjolettii
Of unknown origin, probably a hybrid of *T. gesneriana*. The flowers are yellow on the inside, red-purple tinted on the outside, flowering in May to a height of 24 in (60 cm).

Tulipa praestans
A tulip from central Asia. The leaves are broad and greyish-green. There are 2–5 flowers per stem, fiery red.

Tulipa pulchella var. *violacea*
From Iran, it grows to a height of 8 in (20 cm). Magnificent violet flowers with a yellow centre appear in April.

Tulipa praestans 'Fusilier'

Tulipa kaufmanniana hybrid

Cottage-tulip 'Maureen'

A semi-double early tulip

Triumph-tulip 'Orange Wonder' with blue grape hyacinths

Tulipa maximowiczii

The fringed Triumph tulip 'Aleppo'

Tulipa tarda

Syn. *Tulipa dasystemon*. Native to Turkestan, with star-shaped yellow flowers with white tips, several to a stem. Height is 8 in (20 cm), the flowering period March–April.

Listed below are the most important garden varieties, fitted into 14 divisions, including *T. kaufmanniana*, *T. fosteriana* and *T. greigii*.

(1) Single early tulips
Single flowers on 6–12 in (15–30 cm) stems, flowering outdoors in April.

(2) Double early tulips
Large double peony-shaped flowers, up to 4 in (10 cm) across, on 8–12 in (20–30 cm) stems, flowering in April.

(3) Mendel tulips
Raised from crosses between single early and Darwin tulips, they resemble the last division, but flower towards the end of April. Rounded flowers are borne on rather fragile 12–18 in (30–45 cm) stems.

(4) Triumph tulips
Raised from crosses between single early tulips and late-flowering varieties. The petals are matt and often have edges of a different colour. Very sturdy stems grow up to 18 in (45 cm) high. Flowering period is the end of April.

(5) Darwin hybrids
Raised from crosses between Darwin tulips and *Tulipa fosteriana*. The flowers are very large; the stems 24–28 in (60–70 cm) long. Flowering period is the end of April to the beginning of May.

(6) Darwin tulips
The flowers are very glossy and have almost square bases. The stems are 24–32 in (60–80 cm) long. The flower-

Tulipa turkestanica

ing period is May.

(7) Lily-flowered tulips
These are tulips with waisted flowers and pointed petals that bend out. The stems are roughly 18–24 in (45–60 cm) long. The flowering period is May.

(8) Cottage tulips
Also known as Single Late-flowering tulips, 14–26 in (35–65 cm) tall, they flower from the end of April to May.

Tulipa saxatilis

(9) Rembrandt tulips
These are Darwin tulips, except that the petals are affected by a virus that produces broken colours. Heights are 24–28 in (60–70 cm). The flowering period is May.

(10) Parrot tulips
These are tulips with often bicoloured petals, twisted and irregularly fringed. Heights are 24–28 in (60–70 cm), the flowering period May.

(11) Double late tulips
Showy flowers resembling double peonies, on very fragile stems, 20–24 in (50–60 cm) tall. They flower latest of all, in May.

(12) Tulips mainly derived from *T. kaufmanniana*. These are compact plants with broad leaves and elongated flowers, generally bicoloured. They grow 8–12 in (20–30 cm) tall, flowering in early April.

(13) Tulips mainly derived from *T. fosteriana*. The flowers are mostly red, sometimes yellow, growing 12–18 in (30–45 cm) tall, flowering in early April.

(14) Tulips mainly derived from *T. greigii*. These are easily recognized by the broad, striped leaves. They have a compact habit, growing 8–12 in (20–30 cm) high, flowering in early April.

A fine hybrid Darwin-tulip

Flower heads of the reedmace

Typha
Typhaceae
Reedmace

A genus of perennial aquatics, mistakenly described as bullrushes. Their brown, mace-like flower heads make them extremely decorative in the autumn.

Soil They will grow in any moist to wet soil. A water depth from 4 in (10 cm) is tolerated by the smallest species, and 2 ft (60 cm) or more by the largest.

Propagation They are propagated by division in the spring.

Typha angustifolia

○ ◐ ⊗ ⊗

Lesser reedmace. A native perennial plant, 4–10 ft (1.2–3 m) high. Flowering

period is July–August. Male and female inflorescences are usually $1-3\frac{1}{2}$ in (2.5–9 cm) apart. The leaves are $\frac{1}{8}-\frac{1}{4}$ in (0.25–0.5 cm) wide.

Typha latifolia
Great Reedmace. A native perennial; commoner than the last, 5–10 ft (1.5–3 m) high. The flowering period is July–August. Male and female inflorescences are usually contiguous, the leaves $\frac{1}{2}-\frac{3}{4}$ in (1–2 cm) wide.

Typha minima
Dwarf reedmace. A perennial plant 14–30 in (35–75 cm) high with ovoid inflorescences on slender stems; flowering May–June. Suitable for small ponds.

Ulmus
Ulmaceae
Elm

The elm has been much less popular of late, for fear of Dutch elm disease. It is now claimed, however, that immune plants have been developed.

Soil Any ordinary, well-drained but not wet soil will suit.

Propagation The species can be grown from seed; cultivars are usually propagated by grafting or layering.

Elms can also be increased by summer cuttings under mist propagation conditions.

Ulmus carpinifolia, see U. minor.
Ulmus glabra

○ ◐ ⊛ ⊕

Syn. *U. montana, U. scabra*. Wych or Scotch elm. A tree with hairy dark brown young shoots and obovate leaves $\frac{1}{2}-\frac{2}{3}$ in (0.5–1.5 cm) long, unequal at the base, rough to the touch above. The leaf stems are $\frac{1}{8}$ in (0.25 cm) long. *U. g.* 'Camperdownii' is pendulous, with branches forming a rounded head. 'Exoniensis', also known as 'Fast igiata', (Exeter elm) has a more or less columnar head and jaggedly toothed leaves. 'Pendula' also has a weeping habit but is a smaller tree with an almost flat-topped crown.

Ulmus × hollandica
A cross between *Ulmus glabra* and *Ulmus minor*. Resembles the wych elm but has almost hairless branches. Leaf stalks are $\frac{1}{5}-\frac{2}{3}$ in (0.4–0.5 cm) long. 'Commelin' is a disease-free selection with spreading branches, dark grey branchlets and oval leaves measuring 3 by 4 in (7.5 by 10 cm), covered underneath with short hairs. 'Dampieri' has a

Ulmus × hollandica 'Wredei'

This tree, *Ulmus Glabra* 'Horizontalis' strongly resembles the weeping wych elm

Vaccinium corymbosum in the autumn

columnar habit with leaves pressed to the stems. 'Wredei' has yellow-suffused leaves and a pyramidal habit.

Ulmus parvifolia

From China and Japan. Chinese Elm. Grows eventually to 60ft (18m). A graceful tree which retains its long elliptical leaves in mild winters. An added attraction is the grey bark, which flakes to show red-brown beneath. It appears to be resistant to Dutch elm disease.

Ulmus minor

Syn. *Ulmus carpinifolia*. Smooth-leaved elm. A large native tree, 60–100ft (18–30m) high, with hairless buds and branches. Oval to oblanceolate leaves, 2–4in (5–10cm) long, doubly toothed. As in all the species discussed here, the leaves are hairless on top and bare underneath. 'Cornubiensis' (*Ulmus stricta*) (Cornish elm) is of dense habit and conical when young, broadening with age.

Ulmus procera

Syn. *U. campestris*. English elm. This tree resembles the smooth-leaved elm but generally has hairy twigs and 1–3in (2.5–7.5cm) long oval leaves, rough on top and somewhat downy underneath. The habit too is more dense, the head of branches forming a broad crown. 'Argenteo-variegata' has the leaves splashed and striped silvery-grey; 'Louis van Hantle' has golden-yellow foliage.

Vaccinium
Ericaceae
Bilberry, Blueberry, Cranberry or Whortleberry

A genus of attractive shrubs that will thrive in sunny or partially shaded sites.
Soil Bilberries only do well on moist, acid soil. Before planting, dig in plenty of peat and acid leaf-mould.
Propagation Grow from seed, by layering or by division.

Vaccinium corymbosum

Swamp or high-bush blueberry. This shrub, which grows to a height of 6ft (2m), comes from the eastern part of North America. The leaves are 1–3in (2.5–7.5cm) long. The rosy-white flowers are borne in long racemes, which appear in May or June. It has blue berries with a somewhat white, waxy bloom. The fruits are good to eat, which explains why there are several cultivars grown commercially for their berries. These include particularly: 'Berkeley', light blue; 'Bluecrop', light blue; and 'Concord', blue, a very good cropper.

Many English gardens are stocked with glorious *Verbascum* hybrids

Verbascum bombyciferum is felted with white hairs

Vaccinium vitis-idaea

Cowberry, mountain cranberry. Native to Europe, it grows best in sandy, woodland soil, attaining a height of 1ft (30cm) only. The leaves are small and dull green. Scarlet berries are borne in pendulous racemes. It makes excellent ground cover.

Verbascum
Scrophulariaceae
Mullein

Most species of this large genus of herbaceous plants are cultivated as biennials. They have large and conspicuous cylindrical flower spikes mostly with yellow flowers, and look most spectacular when planted in bold groups near shrubs or along the edges of woods or as solitary plants.

Catalogues usually list hybrids in several colours and shades, most of which are suitable for borders. They reach a height of 3–4½ft (1–1.3m) and flower from June to August.
Soil Any ordinary, well-drained garden soil will do.
Propagation Grow from seed. Biennial cultivation gives the best re-

The mullein, *Verbascum chaixii* 'Pyramidale' with Veronica in the foreground

sults, hence sow in June. Hybrids are increased by division or from root cuttings.

Verbascum bombyciferum

○ ◐ ☉ ⍟ ⊡

A plant from Turkey growing up to 6ft (2m) tall, with downy grey leaves in rosettes. Long yellow flower spikes covered with white hair appear in July.

Verbascum chaixii

○ ◐ ◉ ⍟ ⊡

A biennial with reddish-brown stems, leaves which are often deeply indented, and yellow flowers with a purple centre. 'Pyramidale' is larger and has more densely branching stems.

Verbascum densiflorum

Syn. *Verbascum thapsiforme*. A biennial growing 3–7ft (1–2m) high with yellowish-grey, matted stems. The leaves, most noticeably the topmost, narrow down towards the stalks. Yellow flowers 2in (5cm) in diameter appear June–September. Both the leaves and the stems are covered with yellow hairs.

Verbascum hybrids

○ ◐ ◉ ⍟

These are raised from various crosses, *V. phoeniceum* (purple mullein) being a primary parent. Some well-known cultivars are 'Blushing Bride', white with a cream centre, 3ft (1m); 'Cotswold Queen', salmon-coloured bronze with shades of lilac, 3ft (1m), 'Gainsborough', sulphur-yellow, 3ft (1m); 'Hartleyi', biscuit-yellow shaded purple; 'Pink Domino', soft lilac-rose, 3ft (1m); 'Royal Highland', apricot and yellow, 3ft (1m). Flowering period June to August.

Verbascum nigrum

○ ◐ ◉ ⍟

Dark mullein. A biennial to perennial plant from Europe, Siberia and the Caucasus, up to 4ft (1.2m) high. The flowering period is June to September. Flowers bright yellow with a purple centre, in fairly long, slightly branching spikes.

Verbascum phoeniceum

Purple mullein. Biennial to perennial plant from southern and central Europe, 16–32in (40–80cm) high. Flowering period is from June to August. The flowers are violet-purple in long, erect spikes.

Verbena
Verbenaceae

A genus of annual and also of perennial herbaceous plants, most of which are treated as annuals, including *Verbena bonariensis* and *Verbena rigida*, two of the most attractive species.
Soil These plants do well in any fertile, well-drained soil.
Propagation Sow the seeds of all species under glass, from the end of January onwards. All the species listed are cultivated as annuals, with the exception of the two mentioned above.

Verbena aubletia, see Verbena canadensis.

Verbena bonariensis

○ ⌃ ⌄ ⍟ ⊗

A perennial plant from South America and South Africa, about 4½ft (1.3m) high, sometimes less. Flowering period is July–October, with lavender-blue flower heads. The stems bear few leaves. It makes an attractive border plant not only because of its long flowering period but also because there are so few other lavender-blue plants that look so splendid, especially in the autumn, in combination with yellow-flowering or foliage plants. It is almost hardy in sheltered sites.

Verbena canadensis

○ ☉ ⍟ ⊗

Syn. *Verbena aubletia*. A perennial plant from North America that is mostly grown as an annual, reaching 16in (40cm) high. Flowering period is summer and autumn, with reddish purple-mauve, occasionally white flowers. 'Drummondii' has lilac-blue flowers. It will grow on poorer soil.

Verbena hybrida

○ ☉ ⍟

Syn. *Verbena × hortensis*. The most commonly grown verbenas. The flowers are white, pink, bright to dark red and violet, in flattened heads, the stems semi-erect. A very attractive plant for window boxes or alongside rows of shrubs. If sown in March, these plants will flower from June to the first frosts. Sow in small pots, planting out in late May to early June in a sunny spot, about 12in (30cm) apart. Catalogues usually distinguish between two groups of verbena hybrids: Grandiflora', 12–15in (30–40cm) high, and the more spreading 'Compacta', which is 9–12in (23–30cm) high.

Verbena peruviana

○ ☉ ⍟ ⊗

Syn. *Verbena chamaedrifolia* and *Verbena chamaedryoides*. A half-hardy perennial of spreading almost matforming habit, growing 4in (10cm) high, with oblong-lanceolate leaves. The flowers are bright scarlet, borne in short terminal spikes June–September.

Verbena rigida

○ ⌃ ⌄ ⍟ ⊗

Syn. *Verbena venosa*. A perennial plant, it is a smaller version of *Verbena bonariensis*, 12–20in (30–50cm) high, with small purple flowers in large clusters.

Verbena venosa, see V. rigida.

Veronica longifolia

Veronica teucrium

Veronica
Scrophulariaceae
Speedwell

A genus of annual and perennial herbaceous plants for borders and rockeries, good also for wild gardens. The flowers are usually borne in terminal or lateral racemes. Veronica used to include the

Annual *Verbena* hybrids

Verbena bonariensis

genus hebe, which is shrubby and evergreen.

Soil Ordinary garden soil that should be well drained, especially in the case of the rock plants of this genus.

Propagation Plants are generally divided in the spring. The rock plants can also be increased from cuttings taken in summer and seed under glass in spring.

Veronica armstrongii, see *Hebe armstrongii*.

Veronica buxifolia, see *Hebe buxifolia*.

Veronica cupressoides, see *Hebe cupressoides*.

Veronica filiformis
○ ◑ ⊘ ⊝ ⊖

A perennial plant from Turkey and the Caucasus, growing to a height of 1 in (2.5 cm). Flowering period is April–May, the flowers sky-blue. It quickly forms a dense mat, and can be used as a grass substitute. Very invasive and not suitable for the rock garden.

Veronica gentianoides
○ ◑ ⊛ ⊘ ⊝ ○ ⊖

A perennial plant from the Crimea and the Caucasus, 10–14 in (25–35 cm) high, flowering May–June. Flowers are blue in terminal racemes. 'Variegata' has white-edged leaves.

Veronica incana
○ ⊜ ⊘ ○ ⊛

Syn. *V. spicata incana*. A perennial plant from eastern Europe, 10–16 in (25–40 cm) high, having very attractive densely grey-white hairy lanceolate, toothed leaves. The combination of grey leaves and deep blue flowers in long terminal racemes is most pleasing. Flowering period is late summer, and it is suitable for borders and the rock garden.

Veronica longifolia
○ ◑ ◐ ○ ⊛

A perennial plant, native to Europe and Asia, common in meadows, 20–40 in (50–100 cm) high. The white cultivar has the sturdiest stems. The amethyst-blue flowers are borne from June to August in numerous axillary clusters. 'Exaltata' grows to 4 ft (1.2 m) tall with clear pale blue flowers.

Veronica pinguifolia, see *Hebe pinguifolia*.

Veronica prostrata
○ ⊜ ⊘ ⊘ ○ ⊛

Syn. *Veronica rupestris*. A perennial plant from southern Europe, growing 3–6 in (7.5–15 cm) high. It has a creeping habit, but with erect flowering stems. Flowering period is May to July. The lilac-blue flowers are borne in short, dense, axillary racemes. There are also pink and white cultivars, called 'Rosea' and 'Alba' respectively. 'Coerulea' is dark blue.

Veronica rupestris, see *Veronica prostrata*.

Veronica spicata
○ ⊘ ⊘ ○ ⊛

A perennial plant from Europe and Siberia, 8–16 in (20–40 cm) high. Flowering period July–August, with sky-blue flowers in dense 4 in (10 cm) racemes. Some well-known cultivars are: 'Barcarolle', rich pink; 'Blue Fox', lavender-blue; 'Heidekind', dark rose-red, floriferous, 8 in (20 cm); 'Romily Purple', dark violet-blue, 2 ft (60 cm); 'Snow White', pure white.

Veronica teucrium
○ ⊘ ⊘ ○ ⊛

Syn. *V. austriaca teucrium*. A perennial plant from central and southern Europe, growing 10–16 in (25–40 cm)

high. The lanceolate to ovate leaves are sometimes lobed. Flowering period is June and July, the flowers being blue in axillary racemes. Attractive varieties for rock gardens and borders include 'Royal Blue', 12 in (30 cm), dark blue, most floriferous; 'Shirley Blue', 8 in (20 cm), violet-blue.

Viburnum
Caprifoliaceae

A genus of deciduous and evergreen shrubs, including several most attractive garden species. A few come into flower in the autumn and continue to bloom on the naked wood in the winter. There are very great differences in habit and flower shape and colour, so

The evergreen *Viburnum davidii* in flower

Viburnum rhytidophyllum, another evergreen species

that these plants are suitable for various purposes. Some are particularly prized for their fruits.

Soil Most viburnums thrive in any fertile garden soil, though some make special demands (see under the separate headings).

Propagation Cuttings are taken in the late summer, or layering is practised in spring. Species can also be propagated from seed sown when ripe, though some may take 1½ years to germinate.

Viburnum × bodnantense
○ ◑ ⊛ ⊛ ○

A cross between *Viburnum farreri* and *Viburnum grandiflorum*. A very popular cultivar is 'Dawn', a shrub up to 7½ ft (2 m) high. Its rose-white flowers may come as early as November, but the normal flowering period is February–

Viburnum × burkwoodii

Viburnum opulus 'Compactum'

April. A recent addition is 'Charles Lamont', a 6 ft (2 m) high shrub with large, dark pink flowers which are red when in the bud. Flowering period is November–January.

Viburnum buddleifolium
○ ◑ ⊛ ⊛ ○

A very tall (10 ft/3 m), semi-evergreen shrub with dull green, downy foliage. Creamy-white flowers in clusters are borne May–June. The fruits change to red, later black.

Viburnum × burkwoodii
Cross between *Viburnum carlesii* and *Viburnum utile*. A medium-sized semi-evergreen shrub with arching branches and 2–4 in (5–10 cm) oval leaves, slightly toothed, dark green and glossy on top, downy white underneath. The fragrant flower heads are first pink then white, and appear April–May, exceptionally as early as the autumn. 'Chenault' comes into flower about two weeks earlier in the spring.

Viburnum × carlcephalum
Cross between *Viburnum carlesii* and *Viburnum macrocephalum*. A rounded shrub up to 6 ft (2 m) high with broad oval leaves, dark green on top and downy underneath. The spherical flower heads are first slightly pink, then white, and have a glorious scent. It is excellent for small gardens.

Viburnum carlesii
○ ◑ ⊛ ⊛ ○

A low shrub up to 4½ ft (1.3 m), from Korea. Flowering period is April–May, the flowers first pink and later white, with a glorious scent. Flowers ½ in (1 cm) across, in 3 in (7.5 cm) heads with a waxy bloom. There are new forms that are highly recommended, very fragrant and with pink flowers that pale as they fade; among them 'Aurora', 'Charis' and 'Diana'.

Viburnum davidii
○ ◑ ⊘ ⊛ ⊛ ⊛ ⊝ ⊖

An attractive small, dome-shaped shrub, growing to 3 ft (1 m) or more, flowering May–June, though sometimes as early as the previous September. White flowers in seven-rayed cymes are followed by blue berries in August.

Viburnum plicatum 'Mariesii' after flowering

Viburnum farreri

○ ◑ ◍ ⊛ ⊚

Syn. *Viburnum fragrans*. An erect shrub from northern China, up to 10ft (3m) high. It often flowers as early as February–April, sometimes even the previous November. The flowers are borne in small terminal and lateral clusters, and are light pink and fragrant. 'Candidissimum' is a cultivar with pure white flowers, while 'Nanum' (syn. 'Compactum') is a dwarf form which is unfortunately not very free flowering.

Viburnum fragrans, see *V. farreri*.

Viburnum lantana

◑ ◑ ◍ ⊛ ⊚

Wayfaring tree. A broad, erect shrub, it is densely covered in star-shaped scales. The poisonous leaves are slightly hairy on top and densely hairy underneath. The cream-coloured flowers, which are also covered with hairs, appear May–June. There are red fruits that later turn black, and appear July–September. It likes calcareous soil, and will tolerate some shade. Not for small gardens because it grows too vigorously and because there are much more attractive smaller species.

Viburnum macrocephalum

◑ ◍ ⊛ ⊛ ⊚

A shrub from China and Japan, 6ft (2m) high. Large, white, slightly scented flowers appear May–June. It is fairly hardy and semi-evergreen.

Viburnum opulus

○ ◑ ◍ ⊚

Guelder rose. A native shrub 12ft (4m) high. Flowering period is May, with large white flower clusters surrounded by sterile florets. Later there are magnificent red berries. 'Compactum' is a small shrub of dense habit with large, bright red berries. 'Notcutt' is a vigorous shrub with clusters of large, bright red berries. 'Roseum' (syn. *Viburnum opulus* 'Sterile') has infertile florets in the shape of snowballs. It is particularly tolerant of shade, but likes a moist position.

Viburnum plicatum

○ ◑ ◍ ⊛ ⊚ ⊙

Japanese snowball. A broad, fairly tall shrub from Japan, flowering May–June. Sterile white florets are grouped in spherical, globular heads. 'Lanarth' and 'Rowallane' are similar, having a less obviously tiered habit of growth and are very free-flowering. 'Mariesii' grows to a height of about 4½ft (1.3m) and has a spread of 10–12ft (3–4m). Sterile and fertile white florets in flat heads appear in May or June. It makes a superb specimen plant.

Viburnum rhytidophyllum

○ ◑ ◍ ⊛ ⊚ ⊙

A vigorous shrub from western China which can attain a height of almost 12ft (4m). The leaves are evergreen. The white flowers appear over several months. The berries are first red, later black. It grows best with protection from north and east winds.

Shrubby form of *Viburnum plicatum*

Vinca
Apocynaceae

A genus of sub-shrubs and herbaceous perennials.
Cultivation *Vinca minor* is chiefly planted for ground cover. *Vinca major* may also be used for this purpose but is more commonly seen as a trailing shrub in pots, raised beds, on walls, etc.
Soil Ordinary fertile garden soil is adequate.
Propagation Propagation is by division and from cuttings.

Vinca difformis

Rather similar to *Vinca major*, this species loses its leaves in cold winters. The blue-mauve petals are almost diamond-shaped and expand in autumn and early winter.

Vinca major

◑ ◑ ◍ ⊛ ⊛ ⊚ ⊛ ⊜

Greater periwinkle. A semi-shrub from France, southern Europe and North Africa. The non-flowering stems are prostrate, and about 2½ft (1m) long. The flowering stems are more erect and only about 12–16in (30–40cm) long. Flowering period is March–June, the flowers being light blue. 'Variegata' ('Elegantissima') has creamy-white-edged leaves.

Vinca minor

◑ ◑ ◍ ⊛ ⊛ ⊚ ⊜

Lesser periwinkle. A sub-shrub from central Europe, 20–24in (50–60cm) high. A very sturdy plant for shaded positions such as north-facing banks and under deciduous trees. Flowering period is April to September, sometimes shorter, depending on the cultivar and season. 'Bowles Variety' bears large blue flowers until the autumn. 'Multiplex' bears double plum-purple flowers. 'Variegata' has creamy-white variegated leaves and blue-purple flowers, 'Alba' has white flowers, and 'Rubra' has red flowers. 'Atropurpurea' has deep plum-purple flowers.

Vinca major 'Variegata' before the flowers have begun to droop

Vinca minor, lesser periwinkle

A double form of *Viola odorata* sweet violet

Viola × wittrockiana

Viola
Violaceae
Pansy

A genus of annual, biennial and perennial herbaceous plants that are found in most gardens.

The biennials are valued as particularly early-flowering bedding plants. The perennials are much less floriferous and hence more suitable for borders and rock gardens.

Soil The biennials like fertile, not too dry soil; the perennials require well-drained soil, especially in the winter.

Propagation Biennials: Sow during the second half of July or at the beginning of August. This pansy must not be allowed to develop too strongly before the winter, and it is best to make two sowings. If the autumn turns out to be cool, then the first series of seedlings is selected for further cultivation; if the autumn is warm, the second series is used. Smaller plants winter much better than the larger. Since the seeds must be sown in the summer, it is best to choose a seed bed that is protected from the midday sun, since otherwise it is difficult to keep the top layer of the

Viola 'White Perfection'

soil moist. If the top layer of the soil dries out, the seeds will not germinate. Water regularly with a fine rose or spray. Transplant the seedlings 3–4 in (7.5–10 cm) apart in nursery rows as soon as they are large enough to handle. Move the flowering position before mid-October, and set out 8–12 in (20–30 cm) apart. Alternatively, over-winter the plants in the nursery row.

Perennials: These may be increased by division but also from cuttings taken in the summer. Species may also be grown from seed.

Viola cornuta

A perennial plant, 6–12 in (15–30 cm) high, from the Pyrenees, Switzerland and the Atlas mountains. Flowering period May to July; if transplanted immediately the plant will produce a second flush in the late summer. Flowers are light violet in the species; cultivars come in many colours and sizes, for which it is best to consult a good catalogue.

Well-known sorts are: 'Amethyst', soft amethyst-blue; 'Blue Perfection', light blue; 'Bullion', golden-yellow; 'Hansa', blue-violet, richly flowering; 'Purple Bedder', dark purple, large flowered; 'White Perfection', pure white.

Viola cucculata

A small perennial species from North America with broad, kidney-shaped deep green leaves 2–3½ in (5–9 cm) wide. The ¾ in (2 cm) wide violet flowers open from May to July. *Albiflora* with white flowers is sometimes grown.

Viola gracilis

A perennial from the Balkan Peninsula, 4–6 in (10–15 cm) high. The flowering period is April–July, the flowers large and violet. Garden hybrids come in several colours. Treat this plant as *Viola cornuta*; it dislikes too much moisture in the winter.

Viola labradorica

A low, mat-forming species from northern North America and Greenland, reaching only 4 in (10 cm) in height. In the form 'Purpurea', which is most commonly grown, the leaves have a distinctive deep purple suffusion. The pale purple flowers open in April and May.

Viola odorata

Sweet violet. A perennial plant from Europe and Asia, 4–8 in (10–20 cm) high. Flowering period March and April, but cultivars also flower later and earlier. The flowers are blue or violet, occasionally pink, white, yellow or red. The best-known variety is 'The Czar', which is violet-blue and fragrant. Sweet violets spread by means of easily rooting runners. They thrive in shady places, provided the ground is not too sandy or dry. Often forced and sold in bunches.

Viola tricolor

Heartsease. A well-known biennial, 6–12 in (15–30 cm) high. Flowering period May–September. Various crosses have led to the development of *Viola × wittrockiana*, the garden pansy, of which glorious plants can now be grown from seed. The old division (according to V. B. Wittrock) was as follows:

(a) 'Maxima', large single-coloured flowers, including the Dutch giants.

(b) 'Hiemalis', as above, but earlier flowering. Now even pansies in other divisions may flower as early as November.

(c) 'Trimardeau', in which the three lower petals have a dark spot with a brighter edge, and the two upper petals are single coloured. This group includes the Swiss giants.

(d) 'Odier', in which the flowers have a rather angular shape, and all the petals having a dark spot. No longer cultivated.

(e) 'Cassier', like the previous group, but with the spots having a brighter edge. No longer cultivated.

(f) 'Bugnot', like the previous group, but with dark lines radiating out from the spots towards the edges of the petals.

(g) 'Germania', with petals having a crinkled or wavy edge.

Crossings between these divisions have led to the emergence of all sorts of new cultivars that can no longer be clearly subdivided. Catalogues still list Dutch and Swiss giants, and often mention 'Hiemalis' and 'Trimardeau' types as well. Attempts to produce even earlier-flowering garden pansies have provided such cultivars as 'Primavera'.

F₁ hybrids are also becoming increasingly popular. At present they are mainly used to produce summer-flowering plants. In that case they should be sown in December under glass. 'Sunny Boy', golden-yellow, and 'Blue Boy', blue, are two well-known selections.

Glorious autumn foliage of *Vitis coignetiae*, an ornamental vine

Waldsteinia
Rosaceae

A genus of creeping plants including several that are highly recommended for ground cover and shaded positions. They are as good as the much more popular pachysandra.
Soil Waldsteinias thrive in any moderately fertile garden soil.
Propagation By division

Waldsteinia geoides

A creeper from south-east Europe, 2–10 in (5–25 cm) high. A sturdy plant with creeping rhizomes and heart- and kidney-shaped leaves. Golden-yellow flowers appear in groups of 3–8 in April–May.
Waldsteinia sibirica, see *Waldsteinia ternata*.

Waldsteinia ternata

Syn. *Waldsteinia sibirica*, *Waldsteinia trifolia*. A creeping perennial, 6–10 in (15–25 cm) high, with evergreen, leathery leaves and hairy suckers. Yellow flowers appear in May.
Waldsteinia trifolia, see *Waldsteinia ternata*.

Flowers of *Waldsteinia ternata*

Vitis
Vitaceae
Grape vine

A genus of climbing shrubs including the wine grape.
Cultivation Grape vines thrive in sunny, sheltered positions, such as a south-facing wall. For plentiful fruit, it is essential to prune the plants carefully. They are easily trained against a wall or a pergola, for instance in a U-shape. Every year a layer of laterals is added, allowing optimum leaf development and maximum light reception. The flowers (and hence the grapes) are borne on lateral shoots. Unwanted shoots should always be rubbed out.
Soil Dig a large planting hole in front of the wall, ideally 5 ft × 1½ft × 3 ft deep (1.5 m × 0.5 m × 1 m) and fill it with compost, peat, well-rotted cow manure, leaf-mould and rich loam. Grapes like lime but will absorb it from the wall.
Propagation One-year-old growths can be layered in the autumn. In the early spring it is also possible to grow vines from hardwood cuttings, each with a bud. Cut the wood carefully lengthwise and place the half with the bud flat on a pan of sandy soil, and root at a temperature of 13–16°C (55–61°F).

Vitis coignetiae

Japanese crimson glory vine. Branches and tendrils are covered with rust-red down. Leaves are 4–8 in (10–20 cm) wide, 3–5 lobed, brownish-red underneath and covered in cobwebby down, turning an attractive colour in autumn. An excellent climber.

Vitis vinifera

Grape vine, wine grape. A climbing plant with very long tendrils and large, light green lobed leaves. Inconspicuous flowers are followed by grapes that will only ripen in sheltered positions or warm summers. Recommended vines for wine-making include 'Riesling Sylvaner', with tawny-yellow grapes, and 'Siegerrebe' with large golden grapes of fine muscat flavour, both ripening in October.

The *Weigela* hybrid 'Rosabella'

Wisteria sinensis, Chinese wisteria

Flowers of Wisteria floribunda

Weigela
Caprifoliaceae

A genus of hardy deciduous and richly flowering shrubs.

Soil Ordinary, well-drained fertile soil is adequate.

Propagation Grow from cuttings taken in June and July or in October.

Weigela florida

An erect, fairly large shrub with yellow-brown branches, having two parallel lines of hairs running along their entire length. The leaves are covered with hairs along the central rib only. Flowering period May–July, the flowers being dark pink, lighter inside. 'Variegata' is a dwarf shrub with creamy-white-edged leaves and light pink flowers. 'Foliis Purpureis' grows no higher than 36in (90cm) and has purple-flushed leaves and pink flowers.

Weigela hybrids

Numerous crossings have led to the appearance of attractive cultivars of which the best are: Red: 'Bristol Ruby', 'Eva Supreme' and 'Newport Red'. Pink: 'Abel Carriere', 'Ballet', 'Boskoop Glory', 'Conquete', 'Feerie' and 'Rosabella'. White: 'Candida'.

Weigela middendorffiana

Syn. *Calyptrostigma middendorffiana* and *Macrodiervilla middendorffiana*. A wide-spreading shrub up to 5ft (1.5m) high with greyish-brown twigs having two lines of hairs. Leaves ovate-lanceolate, pointed, bright green, sessile, hairy along the ribs. Flowering period April–July. Flowers sulphur-yellow with orange spots on the inside.

Wisteria
Leguminosae

A genus of quick-growing climbing shrubs that must be supported. In very severe winters the flower buds may be damaged by frost unless protected by south- or west-facing walls. Some plants are not as floriferous as they might be, and if this is not the fault of the particular cultivar chosen, flowering may sometimes be encouraged by avoiding nitrogen-rich fertilizers.

Soil Any garden soil that is not too poor, but wisterias do best in moist, rich, medium loam.

Propagation By layering, from nodal cuttings taken from the base of the current year's wood in summer. Seeds may be sown under glass in spring.

Wisteria floribunda

A climbing shrub from Japan. The branches have grey stripes. Flowering period is May–July, with flowers in drooping violet racemes, but white in 'Alba'. 'Issai' is exceptionally attractive and floriferous; its light blue inflorescences are up to 10in (25cm) long. 'Macrobotrys' has up to 3ft (1m) long blue inflorescences; 'Rosea' bears lilacrose flowers.

Wisteria sinensis

A climbing plant from China with blue-violet flowers, mostly in dense racemes. This plant strongly resembles the last species. The roots and bark are poisonous.

Yucca
Agavaceae

A genus of evergreen shrubs and small trees most of which are not frost hardy. The species described below are mostly hardy in all but the coldest districts. Highly recommended for planting in groups in the lawn. These plants also look attractive when scattered about the border.

Soil Well-drained garden soil, preferably on the calcareous side, is desirable.

Propagation Grow from rooted suckers removed in the spring.

Yucca filamentosa

Adam's needle. A species with stiff, upright, narrow, bluish-green leaves carrying 2–3in (5–7.5cm) long curly threads at the edges. The flowers are yellowish-white, drooping in plume-like panicles up to 6ft (2m) high. The flowering period is July–August.

Yucca flaccida

A plant from Carolina, North America, growing 3–6ft (1–2m) tall. It strongly resembles *Yucca filamentosa* and is often confused with it, but the leaves are less rigid and have straight marginal threads. The flowering period is July–September, with large, bell-shaped, creamy-white flowers.

Yucca glauca

A smaller species than most, only 3ft (1m) tall in flower with slender, erect leaves with white threads at the edges. The cream flowers open in July and August.

Yucca gloriosa

Spanish dagger, palm lily. Native to south eastern USA. This species is easily recognized by its stiff, dark green leaves which are up to 2½ft (75cm) long and do not bend downwards. The flowering stem which can reach 3–6½ft (1–2m) in height, carries a close panicle of large, bell-like white flowers which are sometimes tinged with pink. They open from August to September.

Yucca recurvifolia

Similar to *Yucca gloriosa* in general shape, this species which comes from the same area of the USA, is distinguished by its softer leaves. They are held erect at first, but later the lower ones become recurved. 'Variegata' has a yellow band down the centre of the leaf. All Yuccas can be grown in pots, but need root room to flower.

Yucca gloriosa does not flower until it is about five years old

Zinnia angustifolia 'Lilliput'

Zinnia
Compositae

A genus of extremely attractive annual and perennial herbaceous plants and sub-shrubs. The taller ones are excellent for cutting and the more compact make good bedding plants.

Soil Zinnias do best in humus-rich, not-too-dry soil in a sunny position.

Propagation Sow the seeds in late March in a heated greenhouse. As soon as the seedlings touch one another, prick them out very gently into peat pots, carefully avoiding damage to the tender roots. Plant out in the second half of May, 8–20in (20–50cm) apart, depending on the height. Young seedlings are often attacked by flea beetles. Water them during dry spells.

Zinnia elegans

The most popular garden zinnia. An annual plant from Mexico, 1–3ft (30–100cm) high, garden forms slightly less. The flowering period is from June to July until the first frosts. Cultivars fall into the following groups (all double flowered):

(1) *Plena*. Height 28in (70cm). Flowers 3–4in (7.5–10cm) across.

(2) *Early Wonder*. Height 20in (50cm). Flowers 3in (7.5cm) across, early-flowering.

(3) *Lilliput or Pompom*. Height 16–28in (40–70cm). Flowers 1–2in (2.5–5cm) across.

(4) *Dahlia-flowered giants*. 36in (1m). Flower heads 4–6in (10–15cm) diameter, resembling dahlias.

(5) *Californian giants*. Height 36in (1m). Flowers 4–6in (10–15cm) across, petals overlapping like tiles.

(6) *Scabiosa flowered*. Height 32in (80cm). Flowers up to 3in (7.5cm) across, resembling scabious.

(7) *Cactus flowered*. Height 32–36in (80–100cm). Flowers 3–4in (7.5–10cm) across. Petals are slightly recurved as in cactus dahlias.

(8) *Uniflora*. Height 32–36in (80–100cm). Flowers 3–4in (7.5–10cm) wide, one to each stem.

(9) *Tom Thumb*. Height 12in (30cm). Flowers 4–6in (10–15cm) across. Some forms are even smaller.

(10) *Thumbelina*. Height 6in (15cm). A new strain with masses of small flowers. For choice of colours consult a good catalogue.

PROPAGATION

Propagating your own plants is not only most enjoyable but in many cases easier than you might think. So try to sow your own plants, take your own cuttings and do your own root-dividing. Indeed, in some cases, propagation is the only way to raise rare plants.

There are two types of propagation, generative or sexual, from seed; and vegetative or asexual propagation from cuttings, layering, division and grafting. With vegetative propagation we always obtain plants that are exactly like the parent plant, but plants raised from seed may bear flowers differing from the parent in colour and habit.

Sexual reproduction

All plants that produce viable seeds can be grown from seed in theory, but this method of reproduction is not necessarily the best or the most reliable. Thus an apple tree or a large-flowered rose grown from seed is likely to prove a disappointment. Both these plants will only do well if grafted on to a special rootstock.

If you use seeds of the popular F_1 hybrids (for instance, of petunia) you will discover that the descendants are considerably less attractive than the parents. This is because F_1 hybrids must be crossed anew every time and, since you do not own both parent plants, you cannot hope to produce really good F_1 offspring.

If you sow iris seeds, you will also notice that the descendants have flowers whose colour differs markedly from that of the parents. Generally, too, they are less attractive, but it can happen that a real marvel occurs by chance, which is, after all, how all the most beautiful irises have been raised. Most natural species and a large number of crosses will come true from seed. It does not always matter very much if a plant does not come completely true from seed, as can happen with *Taxus baccata*, a favourite hedging plant. The small differences in colour rarely clash; on the contrary the large masses of green are enhanced by the slight variations.

Although seeds always look dead they are fully alive. We can even demonstrate that seeds breathe. Seeds differ greatly in viability: some will germinate after a thousand years, others will lose their power soon after ripening.

Seeds need moisture, oxygen and warmth to germinate. Some will only germinate in the light and should therefore remain uncovered.

Sowing medium The correct sowing medium must be used to sow seeds successfully. Various seed composts are available, the best known being the John Innes seed and potting composts. But the keen amateur may prefer to make his own seed compost. The original formula used by the John Innes Institute consisted of 2 parts (by volume) sterilized loam, 1 part peat and 1 part sand, with $1\frac{1}{2}$oz of superphosphate and $\frac{3}{4}$oz ground chalk or limestone added per bushel (except for lime-hating plants). Many firms offer alternatives in the form of loamless mixtures of peat, sand, vermiculite and nutrients in suitable proportions.

There are also special seed pellets, and various proprietary substances such as Perlite (an expanded mineral substance consisting of small white granules) which do the same job.

Tests have shown that the germinating percentage varies with the acidity of the sowing medium. Acid-loving plants germinate appreciably better in acid soil and chalk-loving plants thrive in a calcareous medium. The calcium content of the soil can be increased by adding $\frac{1}{2}$oz of ground limestone to each pint of seed compost.

Heated propagators Many seeds, particularly those of tropical plants, will only germinate at a temperature of 20–30°C (68–86°F). Because such high temperatures do not occur constantly either in the garden or in the house, the seed tray has to be heated. This used to be done with the help of horse manure, which produced the necessary warmth by fermentation in a so-called hotbed. Now small electrically heated propagators that will fit most window ledges can be bought.

It is also possible to heat large propagating frames. The floor of the propagator is lined with a layer of polystyrene foam (e.g. Styropor), which should be slightly convex so that all excess moisture can run off at the sides. To the top of this insulating slab attach a 240-volt heating cable with plastic insulation tape. The loops of the cable are placed 4 in (8 cm) apart, so as to increase the temperature of the seed compost by approximately 10 degrees. No thermostat is needed.

Once the cable has been taped down everything is covered with a 2 in (5 cm) layer of river sand, which will keep even the most obstinate cable in place. The sand has the additional function of acting as a heat distributor. If the cable were in direct contact with the peat, the latter would be burned to cinders in no time at all. Make sure that the plug is in a dry place. If the cable is too long then let it run a little way across the ground. It should never be rolled up.

You can use your propagator to sow seeds in the open from the beginning of February. In severe frost the frame should be covered with a straw mat. Later on, when the outside temperature rises, the glass on top of the frame can open gradually. The frame should be sheltered from the sun because newly germinated plants scorch very easily. The seeds are sown in pots or, more usually now, in handy plastic seed trays that can be placed directly on the heated sand. Fill the trays with seed compost and press the compost down well. Distribute the seeds evenly; be particularly careful not to sow them too close together. Put a little river sand in a sieve and shake it over the seeds until they are just covered with sand. This treatment should be omitted for plants that only germinate in the light. Place the seed tray in water and allow the soil to become saturated from beneath. When the covering sand turns a dark colour the water has reached the top, which means that no more watering will be required until the seedlings have broken through.

Sowing in a cold frame If you do not have a heated frame you cannot sow until a month later, about the middle of March. The seeds are sown in the same way, except that all the heat must now come from the sun. Everything proceeds more slowly than it does in a heated frame, but for many plants this is no disadvantage because they develop quickly. As soon as the seeds have germinated, the frame should be aired slightly in the daytime, for instance by placing a brick under the lid or, in the case of sliding aluminium frames, by sliding the pane open a crack. Make absolutely sure that the frame is closed again at night, for the weather is still very treacherous. During severe frosts place a straw mat over the frame. Water the seedlings every day—the ground dries out quickly in small frames.

Pricking out Young seedlings bear two seed leaves followed by two true leaves. Once the latter have appeared, the seedlings can be pricked out into boxes, say 2 in (5 cm) apart, or into plastic or peat pots. Keep the frame closed for a few days after pricking out.

Sowing in the open Seeds can be sown in the open from April onwards, after the danger of night frosts is past. They can be broadcast, sown in straight rows, or grown in clusters. The two last methods are to be preferred, because germinating plants can be confused with germinating weeds; since weeds do not grow in orderly rows, it is easier to identify the seedlings by their regular spacing.

To prevent seedlings drying out in the upper layer of the soil, you can make little drills and fill them with humus (see illustration). Once they have germinated, the seedlings should generally be thinned out. The distance apart depends on the future size of the plant, and is usually specified in the A–Z section.

Sowing biennials Biennials, or perennials grown as biennials, are usually sown from May to June, depending on the species. Because the weather is often hot and dry at this time, it is best to choose a shaded seed bed and to water it regularly. The plants can also be grown in plastic propagators; in either case, the seedlings should be pricked out and allowed to grow until the beginning of September. Then the plants must be moved to their final flowering position.

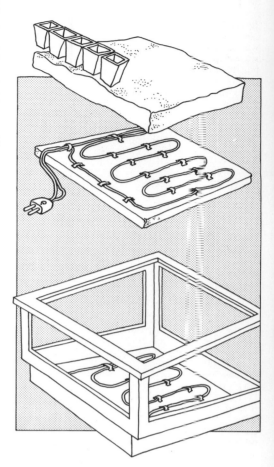

A heated frame. The cable should be covered with 2 in (5 cm) of sharp sand.

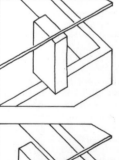

Frame with a hinged lid can easily be aired with the help of a brick.

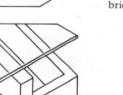

To cut ventilation place the brick sideways.

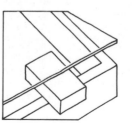

For even less ventilation the brick should be laid flat.

Sometimes it is advisable to protect the plants during the winter. This is best done by covering them with bracken or litter.

Special techniques The seeds of some plants, e.g. *Aconitum*, *Helianthemum*, *Meconopsis* and *Primula*, will germinate better when they are first exposed to some frost. Because in our fitful winters it is impossible to guarantee frost, the following method is preferable.

Use ordinary plastic trays with seed compost, sow the seed evenly and cover it slightly. Wrap the trays in aluminium foil and place them in the freezing compartment of the refrigerator or into a deep-freeze for 14 days. Next allow the trays to thaw outside, or—if the weather has meanwhile started to freeze—leave them frozen outside. Then remove the foil and place the trays in a cold frame, but one that is frost-proof. In general the results will be very good.

Seeds with a hard coat are often soaked in water for 24 hours before they are sown. Such seeds may also be scratched with a very fine file, but care has to be taken not to damage the germ.

The seeds of various shrubs may be stratified, i.e. they are layered in moist sand for close on a year, during which time bacteria and moisture gradually break down the seed coat. The seeds can then be sown in the normal way.

Vegetative propagation

Most amateurs are happy to grow their flowers from seed, but many are afraid of trying their hand at vegetative (asexual) propagation. This is a great pity since, with the exception of grafting, vegetative propagation calls for very little expertise, takes up very little time, and almost always gives good results.

Here we shall be discussing methods of vegetative propagation in order of increasing difficulty.

Division The division of plants gives exceptionally good results. The method is chiefly used with perennials with several growth buds, and with shrubs having woody crowns. The best time to divide plants is from March to April (the sooner after the frosts the better), but many plants, irises chief amongst them, can also be divided in September.

Whether or not a plant should be divided depends to some extent on its habit. In fact, the answer is obvious once you have lifted the plant. With older herbaceous perennials it is best to discard the centre of the clump, which has few or no growth buds, and to replant the outer, more vigorous parts. In principle you can take as many sections as you like, provided each has at least one leafy bud and roots on each portion. The story is told of a shrewd nurseryman who bought in perennial plants from his colleagues, split them into three, and then undercut his competitors. This method turned him into a millionaire in record time.

You are unlikely to aim at becoming a plant millionaire, but when you see that such plants as *Cotoneaster dammeri*, *Pachysandra terminalis* or *Waldsteinia ternata*, which are far from cheap to buy in the shops, can be made to produce hundreds of descendants within a few years by simply being cut up and replanted, then it is difficult indeed to resist having a try at such easy propagation yourself.

Small, surface-rooting plants, including the leaves if necessary, should be covered with earth. A plant will always try to grow upwards out of the ground, but when it is planted near the surface of the soil it quickly gets too dry.

Tuberous plants, too, can be propagated by division. To be sure of what you are doing, it is best, in the case of dahlias for instance, to wait until the buds have begun to swell. Then the tubers can be cut into as many sections as you like provided that each part has at least one bud. Bulbous plants often produce offsets, which can be removed and planted separately in a nursery bed. The small bulbets will begin to flower within a few years.

Some shrubs will send up suckers which can be separated from the parent plant and moved elsewhere, to produce new shrubs or trees where you want them. Others, such as strawberries, send out runners which can be cut off to establish new plants.

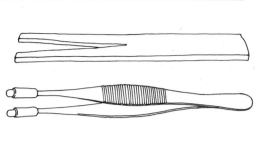

Young seedlings first produce two seed leaves (cotyledons) followed by two ordinary leaves. As soon as the latter have grown a little, the seedlings can be pricked out either into another seed bed at greater distances apart or into pots.

Handle the tender plants with the utmost care, using a notched piece of wood or a padded pair of tweezers.

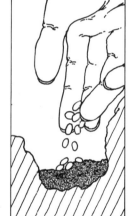
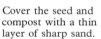

Sowing in the open is much more effective if you have first drilled a small hole.

Fill the hole with weed-free compost and place the seed on top.

Cover the seed and compost with a thin layer of sharp sand.

Finally water well, taking care not to wash the seed away.

When clumps of perennial plants are too tough to pull apart by hand, a spade will often help.

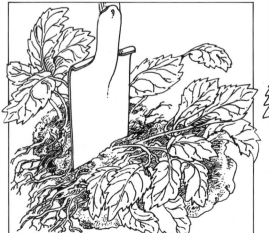
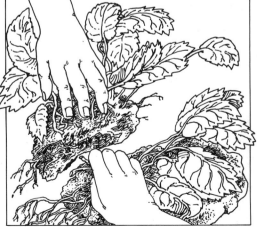

Layering Many shrubs and some herbaceous perennials (e.g. carnations) can be propagated by layering: a growing (and supple) branch of the plant is bent over until it touches the ground, a small slit being made at this point on the underside of the branch and kept open with a small stone. Next a hollow is made in the ground and some sharp sand placed in it. The sharp sand is worked into the slit, the layer lowered into the hollow and kept in place with a hoop. Layering should be done in the autumn; the newly formed plant can be severed and planted.

A related method is known as stooling. A stool is a mother plant that is cut back to encourage it to produce shoots, which are earthed up and induced to root.

Cuttings There are various methods of propagating plants from cuttings. With herbaceous perennials it is possible to take stem as well as root cuttings. With shrubs we distinguish between softwood or greenwood cuttings taken in late spring, and hardwood cuttings taken in the winter. The various methods are described below.

Herbaceous perennials and bulbous plants
Many perennial plants can be propagated from semi-hard cuttings, which, depending on the species, can be taken in the spring, in the summer or in the autumn.

The growing medium is the same as that used for seeds. It must be airy, water-retaining and not too rich. It can be bought ready-made, but you can make it yourself by mixing peat and sharp sand with a little potting compost. It is also possible to grow cuttings in pure peat, in pure sharp sand or in Perlite. To avoid loss of the hormone powder which is generally applied to the wounds, it is best first to make a hole in the mix with a pencil.

The cuttings should be grown in a cold frame, if possible equipped with a soil warming device. Cover with glass and also protect from the sun. After some weeks the roots should have formed. The plants are then lifted, possibly topped, and potted up separately. Leave in the frame for some time. If the cuttings are taken in the summer or autumn, the plants must be overwintered in a frost-proof frame.

Many members of the poppy family, some anemones and several other herbaceous perennials can be propagated from root cuttings taken in the autumn. Lift the plants, cut the roots into 2in (5cm) long pieces and place them in a small frame or tray of cutting compost under glass. The cuttings will begin to shoot in the spring, when they can be planted out.

Bulbs can be propagated from offsets or bulbils, but some bulbs, e.g. lilies, can be propagated by the careful detachment of healthy, undamaged scales.

Softwood cuttings of shrubs Softwood cuttings are taken in June, July or August from the current year's shoots. Many deciduous and evergreen shrubs and conifers, above all species with long twigs, lend themselves to this method of propagation.

Two to 6 inch-long (5–15cm) shoot tips are cut off just below a bud and the basal leaves removed. Often it is helpful to take a cutting with a heel, that is together with a small section of bark from the main branch. The upper leaves should be left on the shoot, otherwise the cutting will die. The cuttings are then dusted with hormone rooting powder and allowed to root; after which they should be potted up as soon as possible.

Because the leaves of cuttings transpire, but for lack of roots cannot take up water, it is essential to restrict evaporation as much as possible. To that end cover with glass and mats, and water frequently. Cuttings that will not root easily are best grown by mist propagation, enveloped in a fine mist-like spray of water to reduce transpiration. It is advisable that this is done in conjunction with a soil-warming device. Although mist propagation is really professional work, amateurs are taking to it in growing numbers, and if they grow many cuttings they will certainly recover the cost of the equipment fairly quickly.

Heathers are particularly easy to grow from softwood cuttings. The tip should be about 2in (5cm) long and the basal leaves should be removed. Often the tips are still too tender in August, in which case it

Dahlias and other tubers can be divided into numerous parts, each of which must have at least one eye.

When layering, bend a supple shoot and lay it in a trench filled with cutting compost. Make a cut in the shoot and tie it down well. Start in the autumn and lift the layer 12 months later.

Another method of layering that often yields a whole series of new plants is earthing up. The shrub is cut back hard in the winter, causing it to send up shoots from the base. Before that happens the whole plant is almost buried under a mound of cutting compost. The hard-pressed shoots will then begin to root at their bases. In the spring, but preferably in the following autumn, the rooted sections can be severed and replanted.

Tuberous plants such as begonias and dahlias can be divided in the spring, and allowed to sprout in March in a warm frame. As soon as the shoots are 2in (5cm) long, they should be cut off, preferably with a piece of tuber attached.

Four-inch (10cm) tips are cut just beneath a leaf axil, and the lowermost leaves removed. It often helps to leave a heel attached to the cutting. Treat with hormone powder.

Hardwood cuttings are buried in sharp sand in the autumn, and then covered as protection from frosts.

After the winter calluses will have formed over the wounds.

The sections are placed into frost-free ground where they quickly take root.

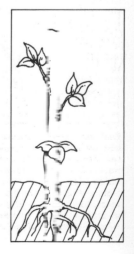

is better to take cuttings from under a flower. The cuttings should then be planted in a propagator containing pure peat, at a depth of ½in (1cm) and ½in apart. Cover with glass no more than 1in (2cm) above the cuttings. Protect against frost during the first winter. No rooting powder or soil-warming devices are needed.

Hardwood cuttings Hardwood cuttings are even simpler to take than softwood cuttings. The method is particularly suited to shrubs with stout and sturdy branches. Choose straight shoots of the previous year and cut them into 4–8in (10–20cm) long segments just as soon as the leaves have been shed in October and November.

The cuttings must be kept cool in the winter but protected from frost. This is best done in V-shaped trenches covered with litter, but the cuttings can also be packed in plastic bags and stored in a refrigerator at a temperature of just above freezing point.

In the early spring the cuttings are moved to a cold frame, where they will root very quickly.

Grafting Now we come to a considerably more difficult method of propagation. Grafting is the joining of the rooting system and main stem of one plant (stock or rootstock) to a shoot of another plant (scion) so that they grow together and form one plant. It is mainly used for propagating shrubs, the aim being to give the weaker scion a more solid stem with a better rooting system. Grafting is also used to obtain long, straight, standard trees (e.g. apples and ornamental cherries). The scions or grafts are usually taken in the autumn, bundled together and set vertically in sand near a north-facing wall, or else stored in a refrigerator. They can be grafted on to the rootstock next spring. There are various types of grafts, of which the following are the most important:
Splice grafting is a very simple method that is used when the scion and rootstock are roughly the same thickness. Both are cut diagonally and tied together with raffia. The stock must still bear some leaves so that the plant can assimilate food substances. When the scion has taken, all the lateral branches of the stock are cut away.
Crown or rind grafting is used whenever the rootstock is much thicker than the scion. The scion is cut obliquely at the base and the resulting wedge is pushed under the bark of the stock so that the exposed inner surfaces touch. It is important that the cambium layers of both are in close contact, otherwise the two parts will not grow together. The two cut surfaces are tied together with raffia and the whole covered with grafting wax. In this way, fruit trees can be made

to bear scions of other species, or various species can be grown on a single trunk. Crown grafting is usually performed at the end of the dormant season.

Budding Budding is the easiest form of grafting and is a quick method of increasing the stock of ornamental shrubs and trees such as roses and crabapples. The work is done in the summer. Instead of using a whole scion, a single bud only is needed, as illustrated below.

Evergreen cuttings The propagation of evergreen trees and shrubs from stem cuttings is a traditional and valuable method. Evergreen cuttings are taken from stems of very ripe wood, that is, almost hard wood. They cannot be regarded as hardwood cuttings as they are not leafless and are not fully dormant because of their evergreen habit.

In winter, prune the parent plant from which the cuttings are to be made. This will encourage the development of strong, vigorous, fast-grown shoots that have the required high capacity to produce roots.

Prepare the soil in a cold frame by digging thoroughly and mixing in grit, peat and sand. Evergreen cuttings taken in late summer should be 4–6in long, although their length must be related to

the normal size of the plant and the amount of annual growth. Cuttings from dwarf *Hebe*, for example, may be only 1½in long. Take a heel with the cutting if it is to be propagated in unsterilized soil in a cold frame or polythene tunnel. Leave on the cutting any terminal bud that may have set. If, however, growth is continuing, cut out the soft tip with a knife. Strip any leaves off the bottom third to half of the cutting. Make a shallow vertical wound about 1in long in the bottom of the stem of plants such as *Daphne*, *Elaeagnus* and *Magnolia grandiflora* that are difficult to root. Dip the base of the cutting in a rooting hormone powder of ripewood strength.

To make more economical use of space, reduce the size of large leaves by cutting off up to half of each leaf-blade with a sharp pair of scissors. Plant the cutting up to its leaves. Allow the leaves of cuttings to touch but not to overlap.

Label the cuttings and water them with a dilute solution of fungicide. Close the lid of the cold frame as tightly as possible. Shade the frame until light intensity and day length decreases during the autumn.

Leave the cuttings *in situ* for the whole growing season. Transplant in autumn, taking considerable care when lifting the cuttings as many evergreen plants produce fairly thick, fleshy and brittle roots.

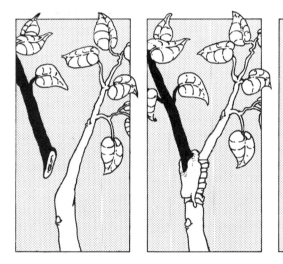

In grafting, the scion and the stock are cut at a slant and then tied together.

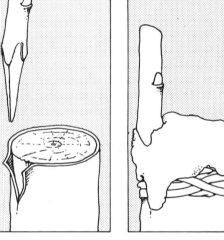

This method is known as crown grafting. It is essential to bring the cambium layers into close contact with each other.

Budding a rose. Take an 8–15in (20–40cm) long, healthy scion stem in full bloom, and snap off all the thorns cleanly. Cut off and discard the soft tops and the leaves, leaving ½in (1cm) of the leaf stalks. The stem thus treated, which will probably yield 4–6 good buds, must be preserved in moist moss, for it tends to dry out quickly. The buds together with the remaining leaf stalk must now be sliced out with a sharp knife.

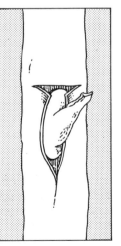

Make a T-shaped cut in the bark of the neck of the rootstalk, which should be straight and even.

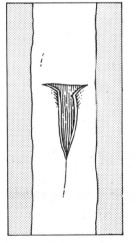

Quickly place the bud in the cut. If it does not fit, trim off the surplus bark of the bud. Work fast or the bud will dry out.

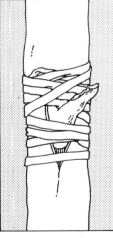

When everything is in place bind the bud firmly to the stock with raffia. If the leaf stalk drops off within a week, it is safe to assume that the graft has been successful.

The following spring cut the whole shrub just above the implanted bud, whereupon the latter should send up a leaf. Budding is not simple but well worth the trouble.

Herbaceous border plants by colour

In the herbaceous border, plants have to be grouped by colour, height and flowering period and that is why this information has been arranged in distinct tables. Not all the border plants listed in this book are here, only the most important ones. Moreover it would have been too cumbersome to name all the races of, say, a blue bearded iris. Thus *Irish germanica* hybrids are the only bearded irises listed under "blue", and the reader is advised to consult a good catalogue or garden-centre for the best available blue races.

As far as the colours themselves are concerned, the list is rough and ready and may pose problems when it comes to, say, red. Thus crimson and cherry-red have not been separated, though they clash very badly. A completely accurate colour code would prove too complicated and too unwieldy. In creating a border, the reader would do well to combine the listed flowers with ornamental grasses, foliage plants and ferns. The mixed border is usually made up of shrubs and conifers. For their colours, see below.

White and cream

	Height	*Flowering*
Primula juliae hybrids	2–4 in (5–10 cm)	March–April
Primula elatior hybrids	3–12 in (8–30 cm)	March–May
Phlox subulata	4 in (10 cm)	April–June
Iris pumila	4–6 in (10–15 cm)	April–May
Arabis caucasica	4–8 in (10–20 cm)	May
Cerastium	4–8 in (10–20 cm)	June
Saxifraga arendsii hybrids	6–8 in (15–20 cm)	May
Aster alpinus	6–10 in (15–25 cm)	June–July
Alyssum saxatile	6–12 in (15–30 cm)	April–May
Viola cornuta	6–12 in (15–30 cm)	May–July
Aster dumosus hybrids	6–15 in (15–40 cm)	Sept.–Nov.
Primula denticulata	6–18 in (15–50 cm)	March–April
Dianthus plumarius	10–15 in (25–40 cm)	July–Aug.
Iberis sempervirens	12 in (30 cm)	May–June
Lychnis viscaria	12–15 in (30–40 cm)	May–June
Bergenia cordifolia	12–18 in (30–50 cm)	April–May
Iris germanica	1–2 ft (30–60 cm)	May–June
Platycodon grandiflorum	1–2 ft (30–60 cm)	July–Sept.
Stachys grandiflora	15–27 in (40–70 cm)	June–Aug.
Anemone vitifolia	15–30 in (40–80 cm)	July–Aug.
Aquilegia caerulea	15–30 in (40–80 cm)	May–June
Campanula persicifolia	1¼–3 ft (40–100 cm)	June–Aug.
Tradescantia andersoniana	15–30 in (50–80 cm)	June–Sept.
Erigeron hybrids	15–30 in (50–80 cm)	June–Aug.
Scabiosa caucasica	15–30 in (50–80 cm)	June–Sept.
Chrysanthemum lacustre	1½–3 ft (50–100 cm)	June–Sept.
Anemone japonica hybrids	1½–3¼ ft (50–100 cm)	Aug.–Oct.
Campanula lactiflora	1½–3¼ ft (50–100 cm)	June–Aug.
Aster novi-belgii	1½–5 ft (50–150 cm)	Sept.–Nov.
Campanula latifolia	1½–5 ft (50–150 cm)	July–Aug.
Astilbe japonica	2 ft (60 cm)	May–June
Gillenia trifoliata	2–2½ ft (60–70 cm)	June–July
Aster ericoides	2–3¼ ft (60–100 cm)	Sept.–Nov.
Astilbe arendsii	2–3¼ ft (60–100 cm)	Sept.–Nov.
Dictamnus albus	2–3¼ ft (60–100 cm)	June–July
Polygonum campanulatum	2–3¼ ft (60–100 cm)	May–June
Phlox paniculata	2–4 ft (60–125 cm)	July–Sept.
Iris sibirica	2½–3¼ ft (60–100 cm)	May–June
Centranthus ruber	2¾ ft (100 cm)	July–Aug.
Papaver orientale	2¾ ft (80 cm)	May–June
Gypsophila paniculata	3¼ ft (1 m)	June–July
Lupinus polyphyllus hybrids	3¼ ft (1 m)	June–Aug.
Verbascum hybrids	3¼ ft (1 m)	June–Aug.
Cimicifuga racemosa	3¼–5 ft (1–1.5 m)	June–July
Aruncus dioicus	3¼–6½ ft (1–2 m)	June–July
Delphinium hybrids	3¼–6½ ft (1–2 m)	June–July
Chrysanthemum serotinum	5 ft (1.5 m)	Sept.–Oct.
Cimicifuga simplex	5 ft (1.5 m)	Sept.–Oct.
Rodgersia aesculifolia	5 ft (1.5 m)	June–July
Cimicifuga dahurica	6½ ft (2 m)	Sept.–Oct.
Macleaya cordata	6½–10 ft	July–Aug.
Rheum palmatum	8 ft (2.5 m)	May–June

Yellow

	Height	*Flowering*
Primula elatior	3–12 in (8–30 cm)	March–May
Sedum hybrids	4 in (10 cm)	July–Aug.
Iris pumila	4–6 in (10–15 cm)	April–May
Sedum floriferum	6 in (15 cm)	June–Aug.
Alyssum saxatile	6–8 in (15–20 cm)	April–May
Viola cornuta	6–8 in (15–20 cm)	May–June
Adonis amurensis	8–12 in (20–30 cm)	Feb.–April
Buphthalmum salicifolium	8–24 in (20–60 cm)	June–Aug.
Potentilla hybrids	8–24 in (20–60 cm)	June–Aug.
Doronicum orientale	10 in (25 cm)	April–May
Geum hybrids	1 ft (30 cm)	June
Mimulus hybrids	1 ft (30 cm)	June–Oct.
Hemerocallis middendorffii	1–1½ ft (30–45 cm)	May–June
Oenothera fruticosa	1–1½ ft (30–45 cm)	June–Aug.
Inula ensifolia	1–2 ft (30–60 cm)	July–Aug.
Solidago hybrids	1–2 ft (30–60 cm)	Aug.–Sept.
Iris germanica	1–2 ft (30–60 cm)	May–June
Anthemis tinctoria	1–2½ ft (30–80 cm)	June–Aug.
Primula bullesiana hybrids	1½ ft (50 cm)	April–July
Aster linosyris	15–24 in (40–60 cm)	Sept.
Coreopsis lanceolata	15–24 in (40–60 cm)	June–Aug.
Rudbeckia fulgida var. *sullivantii*	15–24 in (40–60 cm)	July–Sept.
Aquilegia caerulea	15–24 in (40–60 cm)	May–June
Centaurea macrocephala	15–36 in (40–90 cm)	July–Aug.
Alchemilla mollis	1½ ft (50 cm)	June–Aug.
Doronicum orientale	1½ ft (50 cm)	April–May
Trollius europaeus	15–27 in (40–70 cm)	May–June
Primula florindae	15–27 in (40–70 cm)	July–Aug.
Trollius hybrids	1½–3 ft (50–100 cm)	May–June
Helenium autumnale	1½–6 ft (50 cm–2 m)	Aug.–Oct.
Hemerocallis hybrids	2–2½ ft (60–80 cm)	July–Aug.
Lysimachia clethroides	2–2½ ft (60–80 cm)	June–Aug.
Aster ericoides	2–3 ft (60–90 cm)	Sept.–Nov.
Echinacea purpurea	2–3 ft (60–90 cm)	Aug.–Oct.
Helenium bigelovii	2–4 ft (60–120 cm)	July–Sept.
Rudbeckia laciniata	2–8 ft (60 cm–2.5 m)	July–Sept.
Achillea clypeolata	2½ ft (70 cm)	July–Sept.
Rheum alexandrae	2½–3 ft (70–90 cm)	May–June
Coreopsis verticillata	2¾ ft (80 cm)	May–June
Lysimachia punctata	3 ft (90 cm)	June–Aug.
Achillea filipendulina	3 ft (90 cm)	July–Aug.
Coreopsis grandiflora	3 ft (90 cm)	July–Aug.
Lupinus polyphillus hybrids	3 ft (90 cm)	June–Aug.
Verbascum hybrids	3 ft (90 cm)	June–Aug.
Rudbeckia nitida	3–4 ft (90–120 cm)	July–Sept.
Heliopsis helianthoides	3–4 ft (90–120 cm)	July–Sept.
Ligularia × *hessei*	3–5 ft (1–1.5 m)	July–Sept.
Helenium hybrids	3–6½ ft (1–2 m)	Aug.–Sept.
Helianthus decapetalus	3–6½ ft (1–2 m)	Aug.–Oct.
Ligularia przewalskii	5 ft (1.5 m)	July–Sept.
Inula magnifica	5–6 ft (1.5–1.8 m)	July–Aug.
Helianthus atrorubens	6½ ft (2 m)	Aug.–Oct.
Ligularia veitchiana	6½ ft (2 m)	July–Sept.

Golden-yellow, orange and orange-red

	Height	*Flowering*
Primula × *tommainii (polyanthus)*	3–12 in (8–30 cm)	March–April
Inula orientalis	1 ft (30 cm)	July–Aug.
Mimulus hybrids	8 in (20 cm)	June–Oct.
Geum hybrids	1 ft (30 cm)	June
Geum coccineum	1–1½ ft (30–50 cm)	June–Aug.
Primula bulleyiana hybrids	15 in (40 cm)	June–Aug.
Inula orientalis	1½–2¼ ft (50–70 cm)	July–Aug.
Helenium hoopesii	1½–2½ ft (50–80 cm)	May–June
Trollius hybrids	1½–3 ft (50–90 cm)	May–June
Rudbeckia fulgida var. *speciosa*	2 ft (60 cm)	Aug.–Oct.
Hemerocallis	2–2½ ft (60–80 cm)	July–Aug.
Alstroemeria aurantiaca	3–4 ft (90–120 cm)	June–Aug.
Hemerocallis fulva	2–4 ft (60–120 cm)	June–July
Phlox paniculata hybrids	2–4 ft (60–120 cm)	Aug.–Sept.
Kniphofia hybrids	2–4 ft (60–120 cm)	Aug.–Sept.
Papaver orientale	3 ft (90 cm)	May–June
Chrysanthemum rubellum	2–2½ ft (60–75 cm)	Sept.–Oct.
Trollius chinensis	3 ft (90 cm)	May–July
Heliopsis helianthoides	3–4 ft (90–120 cm)	July–Sept.
Ligularia dentata	3–5 ft (90–150 cm)	July–Sept.
Helenium hybrids	3–6½ ft (90 cm–2 m)	July–Aug.

Red, crimson, pink and rose-red

	Height	*Flowering*
Primula juliae hybrids	2–4 in (5–10 cm)	March–April
Sedum spurium	3–6 in (8–15 cm)	Aug.–Sept.
Primula elatior	3–12 in (8–30 cm)	March–April
Phlox subulata	4 in (10 cm)	April–June
Iris pumila	4–6 in (10–15 cm)	April–May
Geranium subcaulescens	4–8 in (10–20 cm)	June–Sept.
Dianthus gratianopolitanus	4–10 in (10–25 cm)	May–June
Dianthus plumarius	6 in (15 cm)	June–Aug.
Geranium sanguineum	6–10 in (15–25 cm)	May–Aug.
Dianthus deltoides	6–12 in (15–30 cm)	June–Sept.
Aster dumosus hybrids	6–15 in (15–40 cm)	Sept.–Nov.
Dicentra formosa	8–12 in (20–30 cm)	June–Oct.
Sedum telephium	8–15 in (20–40 cm)	July–Aug.
Veronica spicata	8–15 in (20–40 cm)	July–Aug.
Geranium endressii	10–12 in (25–30 cm)	June–Aug.
Geranium 'Russell Prichard'	1 ft (30 cm)	June–Sept.
Geum hybrids	1 ft (30 cm)	June
Polygonum affine	1 ft (30 cm)	Aug.–Sept.
Saponaria ocymoides	1 ft (30 cm)	May–July
Bergenia cordifolia	1–1½ ft (30–50 cm)	April–May

	Height	Flowering
Lychnis viscaria	1–1½ft (30–50cm)	May–June
Sedum spectabile	1–1½ft (30–50cm)	Aug.–Sept.
Astrantia major	1–2ft (30–60cm)	June–July
Malva moschata	1–2ft (30–60cm)	July–Sept.
Iris germanica	1–2ft (30–60cm)	May–June
Polygonum bistorta	2–3ft (30–60cm)	May–Aug.
Gypsophila paniculata	15ft (40cm)	June–Sept.
Primula bulleyiana hybrids	15ft (40cm)	April–July
Potentilla hybrids	15ft (40cm)	July–Aug.
Armeria pseudarmeria	15–24in (40–60cm)	May–June
Geum chiloense	15–24in (40–60cm)	June–Aug.
Potentilla atrosanguinea	12–18in (30–45cm)	June–Aug.
Potentilla nepalensis	12–18in (30–45cm)	July–Sept.
Stachys macrantha (grandiflora)	1–2ft (30–60cm)	June–Aug.
Heuchera hybrids	1½ft (45cm)	May–July
Saponaria officinalis	1½–3ft (50–90cm)	July–Sept.
Anemone japonica hybrids	1½–3ft (50–90cm)	Aug.–Oct.
Aster novi-belgii	1½–5ft (50–150cm)	Sept.–Nov.
Aster amellus	2ft (60cm)	Aug.–Sept.
Astilbe japonica	2ft (60cm)	May–June
Chelone obliqua	2ft (60cm)	June–Sept.
Heuchera hybrids	2ft (60cm)	May–June
Hemerocallis hybrids	2–3ft (60–90cm)	July–Aug.
Kniphofia hybrids	2ft (60cm)	Sept.–Oct.
Sidalcea hybrids	2–3ft (60–90cm)	June–Aug.
Papaver orientale	2–3ft (60–90cm)	May–June
Anemone hupehensis var. *japonica*	2–3ft (60–90cm)	Aug.–Sept.
Aquilegia hybrids	2–3ft (60–90cm)	June–Aug.
Astilbe arendsii	2–3ft (60–90cm)	June–Aug.
Physostegia virginiana	2–4½ft (60–150cm)	July–Aug.
Physostegia virginiana	2–4½ft (60–130cm)	July–Aug.
Phlox paniculata hybrids	2–4½ft (60–130cm)	July–Sept.
Monarda hybrids	2½–3ft (75–90cm)	July–Sept.
Iris sibirica	2½–3ft (75–90cm)	June
Centranthus ruber	3ft (90cm)	July–Aug.
Chrysanthemum rubellum	3ft (90cm)	Sept.–Oct.
Malva alcea	3ft (90cm)	June–Sept.
Campanula lactiflora	3ft (90cm)	June–Aug.
Lychnis chalcedonica	3ft (90cm)	June–Aug.
Lupinus polyphyllus hybrids	3ft (90cm)	June–Aug.
Verbascum hybrids	3ft (90cm)	June–Aug.
Lythrum hybrids	3–4ft (90–120cm)	June–Sept.
Helenium hybrids	3–5ft (90–150cm)	July–Aug.

Purple

	Height	Flowering
Aubrieta hybrids	2–4in (5–10cm)	April–May
Primula juliae	2–4in (5–10cm)	March–April
Phlox subulata	2–6in (5–15cm)	April–June
Silene schafta	4–6in (10–15cm)	Aug.–Sept.
Iris pumila	4–6in (10–15cm)	April–May
Verbascum hybrids	4in–4½ft (10–125cm)	July–Sept.
Aster alpinus	6–10in (15–25cm)	June–July
Viola cornuta	6–12in (15–30cm)	May–June
Aster dumosus hybrids	6–15in (15–40cm)	Sept.–Nov.
Aster sedifolius	2–3ft (60–90cm)	Aug.–Sept.
Dianthus plumarius	10–15in (25–40cm)	July–Aug.
Astilbe chinensis var. *pumila*	1ft (30cm)	July–Oct.
Geranium meeboldii	12–15in (30–40cm)	June–July
Anemone tomentosa	1–1½ft (30–50cm)	Aug.–Sept.
Aster tongolensis	1–1½ft (30–65cm)	May–June
Bergenia cordifolia	1–1½ft (30–50cm)	April–May
Verbena rigida	1–1½ft (30–50cm)	July–Oct.
Iris germanica	1–3ft (30–90cm)	May–June
Primula bulleyiana hybrids	15in (40cm)	April–June
Geranium platypetalum	1–2ft (30–60cm)	June–Aug.
Stachys macrantha (grandiflora)	1–2ft (30–60cm)	June–Aug.
Aquilegia vulgaris	1–3ft (30–90cm)	May–June
Thalictrum aquilegifolium	2–3ft (60–90cm)	May–July
Liatris spicata	1½ft (45cm)	Aug.–Sept.
Tradescantia × andersoniana hybrids	1½–2ft (45–60cm)	June–Sept.
Erigeron hybrids	1½–3ft (45–90cm)	July–Aug.
Aster novi-belgii	1½–5ft (50–150cm)	Sept.–Nov.
Aster amellus	2ft (60cm)	July–Sept.
Monarda hybrids	2–3ft (60–90cm)	June–July
Sidalcea hybrids	2–3ft (60–90cm)	July–Aug.
Aster sedifolius	2–3ft (60–90 cm)	Aug.–Sept.
Astilbe arendsii	2–3ft (60–90cm)	June–Aug.
Dictamnus albus	2–3ft (60–90cm)	June–July
Echinacea purpurea	2–3ft (60–90cm)	July–Aug.
Phlox paniculata hybrids	2–4½ft (60–130cm)	July–Sept.
Lythrum hybrids	3–4ft (90–120cm)	June–Sept.
Lupinus polyphyllus hybrids	3ft (90cm)	June–Aug.
Delphinium hybrids	3–6½ft (1–2m)	June–Sept.
Acanthus mollis	4ft (1.2m)	June–July
Acanthus spinosus	4–5ft (1.2–1.5m)	July–Aug.
Verbena bonariensis	5ft (150cm)	July–Oct.
Thalictrum dipterocarpum	6½ft (2m)	July–Sept.

Violet

	Height	Flowering
Aubrieta hybrids	2–4in (5–10cm)	April–May
Primula juliae hybrids	2–4in (5–10cm)	March–April
Iris pumila	4–6in (10–15cm)	April–May
Aster × alpellus	6in (15cm)	June–July
Campanula portenschlagiana	6in (15cm)	June–Sept.
Aster alpinus	6–10in (15–25cm)	June–July
Prunella grandiflora	6–10in (15–25cm)	June–Aug.
Viola cornuta	6–12in (15–30cm)	May–June
Primula denticulata	6–18in (15–45cm)	March–April
Pulmonaria angustifolia	8–12in (20–30cm)	March–April
Veronica spicata	8–28in (20–70cm)	July–Aug.
Campanula glomerata	10–24in (25–60cm)	June–Aug.
Bergenia × schmidtii	12–15in (30–40cm)	Feb.
Nepeta × faassenii	1–1½ft (30–45cm)	May–Aug.
Iris germanica	1–2 ft (30–60cm)	May–June
Aster amellus	15in (40cm)	July–Sept.
Tradescantia andersoniana hybrids	1–2ft (30–60cm)	June–Aug.
Aster farreri	1½ft (45cm)	May–June
Aconitum fischeri	1½–2ft (45–60cm)	Aug.–Sept.
Erigeron hybrids	1½–3ft (45–90cm)	July–Aug.
Salvia × superba	1½–3ft (45–90cm)	June–Sept.
Scabiosa caucasica	1½–3ft (45–90cm)	June–Sept.
Phlox paniculata hybrids	1½–4ft (45–120cm)	July–Aug.
Aster novi-belgii	1½–5ft (45–150cm)	Sept.–Nov.
Aster cordifolius	2–5ft (60–150cm)	Aug.–Oct.
Aster novae-angliae	2–7½ft (60–250cm)	Sept.–Oct.
Aster × frikartii	2ft (60cm)	Aug.–Sept.
Iris sibirica	2–3ft (60–90cm)	June
Lupinus hybrids	3ft (90cm)	June–July
Acanthus mollis	3ft (90cm)	June–Aug.
Eryngium × zabelli	3ft (90cm)	June–Sept.
Delphinium hybrids	3–5ft (90–150cm)	June–July
Aconitum carmichaelii	5–6½ft (1.5–2m)	Aug.–Oct.

Blue

	Height	Flowering
Aubrieta hybrids	2–4in (5–10cm)	April–May
Veronica prostrata	3–6in (8–15cm)	May–June
Iris pumila	4–6in (10–15cm)	April–May
Aster alpinus	6–10in (15–25cm)	June–July
Phlox divaricata	6–10in (15–25cm)	May–June
Viola cornuta	6–12in (15–30cm)	May–June
Aster dumosus hybrids	6–15in (15–40cm)	Sept.–Nov.
Campanula carpatica	6–12in (15–30cm)	June–Sept.
Aster yunnanensis	8–12in (20–30cm)	May–July
Pulmonaria angustifolia	8–12in (20–30cm)	March–April
Veronica spicata	8–15in (20–40cm)	July–Aug.
Veronica incana	10–15in (30–40cm)	July–Aug.
Veronica teucrium	10–15in (30–40cm)	June–July
Campanula garganica	6in (15cm)	May–June
Campanula lactiflora	1ft (30cm)	June–Aug.
Brunnera macrophylla	1–1½ft (30–45cm)	April–May
Stokesia laevis	12–15in (30–40cm)	July–Sept.
Iris germanica hybrids	1–3ft (30–90cm)	May–June
Platycodon grandiflorum	1–2ft (30–60cm)	July–Sept.
Aquilegia caerulea	1–2ft (30–60cm)	May–June
Aquilegia vulgaris	1–2ft (30–60cm)	May–June
Campanula persicifolia	1–3ft (30–90cm)	May–June
Geranium meeboldii	1½ft (45cm)	June–July
Tradescantia andersoniana hybrids	1½–2ft (45–60cm)	June–Sept.
Scabiosa caucasica	1½–3ft (45–90cm)	June–Sept.
Echinops ritro	1½–3ft (45–90 cm)	July–Sept.
Anchusa italica	1½–4½ft (45–120cm)	June–Aug.
Campanula latifolia	1½–5ft (45–150cm)	July–Aug.
Aster amellus	2ft (60cm)	July–Sept.
Campanula lactiflora	2–4ft (60–120cm)	June–Aug.
Aquilegia hybrids	2–3ft (60–90cm)	June–Aug.
Veronica longifolia	2ft (60cm)	July–Aug.
Iris sibirica	2–3ft (70–90cm)	June
Nepeta sibirica	3ft (90cm)	July–Aug.
Eryngium planum	3ft (90cm)	June–July
Echinops banaticus	3ft (90cm)	July–Aug.
Aconitum × arendsii	3–4ft (90–120cm)	Sept.–Oct.
Aconitum napellus	3ft (90cm)	June–Aug.
Lupinus polyphyllus hybrids	3ft (90cm)	June–Aug.
Delphinium hybrids	3–6½ft (1–2m)	June–July
Aconitum × cammarum	4–5ft (120–150cm)	June–Aug.

Grey foliage plants

	Height
Anaphalis triplinervis	8–12in (20–30cm)
Veronica incana	10–15in (25–40cm)
Anaphalis margaritacea	1–2ft (30–60cm)
Stachys olympica	1–2½ft (30–75cm)
Artemisia ludoviciana	2–3ft (60–90 cm)
Artemisia 'Silver Queen'	2½–3ft (75–90cm)
Salvia officinalis	2ft (60cm)
Perovskia atriplicifolia	3–5ft (90–150cm)

Annual plants by colour

Herbaceous annuals come in much the same colours as perennial border plants. Because of the vast number of races and varieties we only list species, and the reader is once again advised to consult a good catalogue.

The flowering periods are not shown—most annuals are in bloom from May to the end of August. For further details see the A–Z section.

White and cream

Mesembryanthemum criniflorum 2–4in (5–10cm)
Lobelia erinus 3–12in (8–30cm)
Lobularia maritima 4–12in (10–30cm)
Begonia semperflorens 6–15in (15–40cm)
Dianthus chinensis 6–18in (15–50cm)
Ageratum houstonianum 8in (20cm)
Nemesia strumosa 8–10in (20–25cm)
Callistephus chinensis 8–12in (20–30cm)
Iberis amara 8–12in (20–30cm)
Verbena hybrids 8–12in (20–30cm)
Pelargonium hybrids 8–15in (20–40cm)
Petunia hybrids 8–18 in (20–50cm)
Impatiens balsamina 8–24in (20–60cm)
Linaria maroccana hybrids 8–24in (20–60cm)
Antirrhinum majus 8–32in (20–80cm)
Scabiosa atropurpurea 8–36in (20–90cm)
Godetia × hybrida 12–15in (30–40cm)
Schizanthus wisetonensis 12–15in (30–40cm)
Chrysanthemum frutescens 1–3ft (30–90cm)
Zinnia elegans 1–3ft (30–90cm)
Arctotis hybrids 1–1½ft (30–50cm)
Celosia argentea 1–2ft (30–60cm)
Chrysanthemum carinatum 1–2ft (30–60cm)
Chrysanthemum parthenium 1–2½ft (30–80cm)
Matthiola incana 1–2½ft (30–80cm)
Delphinium ajacis 1–3¼ft (30–90cm)
Helichrysum bracteatum 1–3ft (30–90cm)
Nicotiana × sanderae 1½ft (45cm)
Heliotropium arborescens 1½–2ft (45–60cm)
Salvia argentea 1½–2ft (45–60cm)
Clarkia unguiculata 2ft (60cm)
Centaurea moschata 1½–2½ft (45–70cm)
Callistephus chinensis 10–18in (25–45cm)
Cleome spinosa 3–4ft (90–120cm)
Cosmos bipinnata 3ft (90cm)
Lavatera trimestris 3ft (90cm)
Papaver somniferum 3ft (90cm)
Silene coeli-rosa 3ft (90cm)
Lupinus mutabilis 3–6ft (1–2m)
Malva verticillata 3–6ft (1–2m)
Polygonum orientale 3–10ft (1–3m)
Centaurea americana 6½ft (2m)
Lathyrus odoratus 6½ft (2m)

Yellow

Reseda odorata 6–12in (15–30cm)
Gazania hybrids 8in (20cm)
Tagetes patula 8in (20cm)
Coreopsis bigelovii 8–15in (20–40cm)
Petunia hybrids 8–20in (20–50cm)
Linaria maroccana hybrids 8–24in (20–60cm)
Antirrhinum majus 8–32in (20–80cm)
Chrysanthemum multicaule 10in (25cm)
Helipterum humboldtianum 10–15in (25–40cm)
Rudbeckia hirta var. *pulcherrima* 1ft (30cm)
Tagetes tenuifolia 1ft (30cm)
Tagetes patula 12–15in (30–40cm)
Nemesia strumosa 12–15in (30–40cm)
Zinnia angustifolia 12–15in (30–40cm)
Adonis aestivalis 1–1½ft (30–50cm)
Calendula officinalis 1–2ft (30–60cm)
Chrysanthemum segetum 1–2ft (30–60cm)
Eschscholzia tenuifolia 1–2ft (30–60cm)
Rudbeckia hirta 1–2ft (30–60cm)
Senecio elegans 1–2ft (30–60cm)
Chrysanthemum coronarium 1–3ft (30–90cm)
Chrysanthemum frutescens 1–3ft (30–90cm)
Zinnia elegans 1–3ft (30–90cm)
Arctotis hybrids 1½ft (45cm)
Chrysanthemum carinatum 1½–2ft (45–60cm)
Celosia argentea 1½–2ft (45–60cm)
Hibiscus trionum 1½–2ft (45–60cm)
Calceolaria scabiosifolia 1–2ft (30–60cm)
Chrysanthemum parthenium 1½–2½ft (45–75cm)
Matthiola incana 1½–2½ft (45–75cm)
Helichrysum bracteatum 1½–3ft (45–90cm)
Tagetes erecta 1½–2½ft (45–75cm)
Coreopsis tinctoria 1¾ft (50cm)
Lupinus luteus 2ft (60cm)
Tagetes patula 2–2½ft (60–75cm)
Amberboa moschata 2½ft (75cm)
Cosmos sulphureus 3ft (90cm)
Helianthus annuus 3–6½ft (1–2m)
Hibiscus manihot 3–6½ft (1–2m)
Tropaeolum peregrinum 3–10ft (1–3m)

Orange

Begonia semperflorens 6–15in (15–40cm)
Mimulus cupreus 8–10in (20–25cm)
Nemesia strumosa 8–12in (20–30cm)
Pelargonium hybrids 8–15in (20–40cm)
Antirrhinum majus 8–32in (20–80cm)
Dimorphotheca aurantiaca 10in (25cm)
Eschscholzia californica 1–2ft (30–60cm)
Zinnia elegans 1–3ft (30–90cm)
Helichrysum bracteatum 1–3ft (30–90cm)
Tagetes erecta 1½–2½ft (45–75cm)
Coreopsis basalis 1¾ft (50cm)
Rudbeckia hirta var. *pulcherrima* 2ft (60cm)
Calendula officinalis 2–2½ft (60–75cm)
Euphorbia heterophylla 3ft (90cm)
Cosmos sulphureus 3ft (90cm)
Papaver somniferum 3ft (90cm)
Lathyrus odoratus 6½ft (2m)

Red, pink and rose-red

Mesembryanthemum criniflorum 2–4in (5–10cm)
Lobelia erinus 3–12in (8–30cm)
Polygonum capitatum 4–6in (10–15cm)
Verbena peruviana 6in (15cm)
Silene pendula 6–8in (15–20cm)
Begonia semperflorens 6–15in (15–40cm)
Dianthus chinensis 6–20in (15–50cm)
Celosia argentea 6–24in (15–60cm)
Gazania hybrids 8in (20cm)
Callistephus chinensis 10–18in (25–45cm)
Clarkia concinna 8–12in (20–30cm)
Verbena hybrids 8–12in (20–30cm)
Centranthus macrosiphon 8–15in (20–40cm)
Convolvulus tricolor 8–15in (20–40cm)
Pelargonium hybrids 8–15in (20–40cm)
Petunia hybrids 8–20in (20–50cm)
Phlox drummondii 8–20in (20–50cm)
Impatiens balsamina 8–24in (20–60cm)
Linaria maroccana hybrids 8–24in (20–60cm)
Antirrhinum majus 8–32in (20–80cm)
Scabiosa atropurpurea 8–36in (20–90cm)
Salvia splendens 1ft (30cm)
Godetia × hybrida 12–15in (30–40cm)
Nemesia strumosa 12–15in (30–40cm)
Schizanthus wisetonensis 12–15in (30–40cm)
Adonis aestivalis 12–15in (30–40cm)
Gaillardia pulchella 1–1½ft (30–45cm)
Helipterum manglesii 1–1½ft (30–45cm)
Silene armeria 1–1½ft (30–45cm)
Anchusa capensis 1–2ft (30–60cm)
Eschscholzia californica 1–2ft (30–60cm)
Papaver rhoeas 1–2ft (30–60cm)
Zinnia elegans 1–3ft (30–90cm)
Tropaeolum majus 1–6ft (30cm–2m)
Linum grandiflorum 15in (45cm)
Arctotis hybrids 1½ft (45cm)
Chrysanthemum carinatum 1½–2ft (45–60cm)
Matthiola incana 1½–3ft (45–90cm)
Delphinium ajacis 1½–3ft (45–90cm)
Helichrysum bracteatum 1½–3ft (45–90cm)
Mimulus cardinalis 1½ft (45cm)
Gypsophilia elegans 1½ft (45cm)
Papaver glaucum 1½ft (45cm)
Limonium suworrowii 1½–2½ft (45–75cm)
Clarkia unguiculata 2ft (60cm)
Amberboa moschata 2½ft (75cm)
Nicotiana × sanderae 2½ft (75cm)
Callistephus chinensis 2½–3ft (75–90cm)
Cleome spinosa 3–4ft (90–120cm)
Cosmos bipinnatus 3ft (90cm)
Lavatera trimestris 3ft (90cm)
Papaver somniferum 3ft (90cm)
Silene coeli-rosa 3ft (90cm)
Helianthus annuus 3–6½ft (1–2m)
Polygonum orientale 3–10ft (1–3m)
Centaurea americana 6ft (2m)
Impatiens glandulifera 6ft (2m)
Lathyrus odoratus 6ft (2m)
Ipomoea purpurea 13ft (4m)

Purple

Iberis umbellata 6–15in (15–40cm)
Dianthus chinensis 6–20in (15–50cm)
Petunia hybrids 8–20in (20–50cm)
Impatiens balsamina 8–24in (20–60cm)
Antirrhinum majus 8–32in (20–80cm)
Scabiosa atropurpurea 8–36in (20–90cm)
Godetia × hybrida 12–15in (30–40cm)
Schizanthus × wisetonensis 12–15in (30–40cm)
Zinnia elegans 1–3ft (30–90cm)
Verbena canadensis 12–15in (30–40cm)
Matthiola incana 1½–2½ft (45–75cm)
Helichrysum bracteatum 1½–2½ft (45–75cm)
Arctotis grandis 2–2½ft (60–75cm)
Centaurea moschata 2½ft (75cm)
Cleome spinosa 3–4ft (90–120cm)
Papaver somniferum 3ft (90cm)
Centaura americana 6½ft (2m)
Lathyrus odoratus 6½ft (2m)
Cobaea scandens 10ft (3m)

Violet

Lobularia maritima 4–12in (10–30cm)
Lupinus nanus 8–12in (20–30cm)
Dimorphotheca annua 8–15in (20–40cm)
Petunia hybrids 8–20in (20–50cm)
Impatiens balsamina 8–24in (20–60cm)
Linaria maroccana hybrids 8–24 in (20–60cm)
Antirrhinum majus 8–32in (20–80cm)
Godetia × hybrida 12–15in (30–40cm)
Schizanthus × wisetonensis 12–15in (30–40cm)
Verbena tenuisecta 1–1½ft (30–50cm)
Zinnia elegans 1–3ft (30–90cm)
Matthiola incana 1½–2½ft (45–75cm)
Heliotropium arborescens 1½–2ft (45–60cm)
Celosia argentea 2ft (60cm)
Nicotiana alata 3ft (90cm)
Papaver somniferum 3ft (90cm)

Blue

Lobelia erinus 3–12in (8–30cm)
Sedum caeruleum 4–6in (10–15cm)
Ageratum houstonianum 8–18in (20–45cm)
Nemesia strumosa 8–10in (20–25cm)
Callistephus chinensis 8–12in (20–30cm)
Convolvulus tricolor 8–15in (20–40cm)
Dimorphotheca annua 8–15in (20–40cm)
Linum narbonense 8–20in (20–50cm)
Petunia hybrids 8–20in (20–50cm)
Scabiosa atropurpurea 8–36in (20–90cm)
Anchusa capensis 1–2ft (30–60cm)
Centaurea cyanus 1–3ft (30–90cm)
Echium lycopsis 15in (40cm)
Nigella damescena 1½ft (45cm)
Cynoglossum amabile 2ft (60cm)
Limonium sinuatum 1½–2ft (45–60cm)
Matthiola incana 1½–3ft (45–90cm)
Anchusa italica 1½–3ft (45–90cm)
Lupinus hartwegii 1½–3ft (45–90cm)
Salvia farinacea 2–3ft (60–90cm)
Callistephus chinensis 10–18in (25–45cm)
Amberboa moschata 2½ft (75cm)
Ipomoea violacea 3–6½ft (1–2m)
Lathyrus odoratus 6½ft (2m)

Biennial plants by colour

Below are listed the most important biennials and plants usually cultivated as biennials. The qualifying remarks in the section on annual plants are also applicable here.

White and cream

Myosotis hybrids 4–12in (10–30cm)
Bellis perennis 6in (15cm)
Dianthus barbatus 6in (15cm)
Viola tricolor 6–12in (15–30cm)
Lunaria annua 1–3ft (30–90cm)
Salvia argentea 1½–2½ft (45–75cm)
Althaea rosea 10ft (3m)

Yellow

Viola tricolor 6–12in (15–30cm)
Cheiranthus cheiri 10–15in (25–40cm)
Oenothera drummondii 1½–2ft (45–60cm)
Verbascum chaixii 1½–3ft (45–90cm)
Oenothera biennis 1½–5ft (45–150cm)
Verbascum densiflorum 3–6½ft (1–2m)
Verbascum longiflorum 4ft (120cm)
Verbascum nigrum 4ft (120cm)
Althaea rosea 10ft (3m)

Red, pink and rose-red
Myosotis sylvatica 6–12 in (15–30 cm)
Viola tricolor 6–12 in (15–30 cm)
Dianthus barbatus 6–15 in (15–40 cm)
Dianthus chinensis 6–18 in (15–45 cm)
Penstemon hybrids 1–1½ ft (30–45 cm)
Dianthus caryophyllus 2 ft (60 cm)
Althaea rosea 10 ft (3 m)

Purple
Penstemon hybrids 1–1½ ft (30–45 cm)
Lunaria annua 1–3 ft (30–90 cm)
Salvia horminum 1½ ft (45 cm)
Digitalis purpurea 1½–4½ ft (45–140 cm)
Dipsacus sativus 3–6½ ft (1–2 m)
Onopordum bracteatum 8½ ft (2.5 m)
Althaea rosea 10 ft (3 m)

Violet
Viola tricolor 6–12 in (15–30 cm)
Verbascum phoeniceum 15–30 in (40–80 cm)
Campanula medium 2–3 ft (60–90 cm)
Campanula pyramidalis 3–4½ ft (90–140 cm)
Althaea rosea 10 ft (3 m)

Blue
Myosotis hybrids 6–12 in (15–30 cm)
Myosotis sylvatica 6–20 in (15–50 cm)
Myosotis dissitiflora 1 ft (30 cm)
Cynoglossum amabile 1½–2 ft (45–60 cm)
Meconopsis betonicifolia 1½–3 ft (45–90 cm)

Bulbs by colour

Below we distinguish between spring- and summer-flowering bulbs. Some tuberous plants usually treated as bulbs are also included.

A. Spring-flowering bulbs

White and cream

	Height	Flowering
Crocus chrysanthus	2–4 in (5–10 cm)	March–April
Hyacinthus orientalis	4–6 in (10–15 cm)	March–April
Galanthus nivalis	4–8 in (10–20 cm)	Feb.
Scilla sibirica	4–8 in (10–20 cm)	March–April
Ornithogalum umbellatum	4–12 in (10–30 cm)	April–May
Leucojum vernum	4–15 in (10–40 cm)	March–April
Erythronium revolutum	6 in (15 cm)	April–May
Ipheion uniflorum	6 in (15 cm)	April–May
Puschkinia scilloides	6 in (15 cm)	April–May
Muscari botryoides	6–8 in (15–20 cm)	March–April
Narcissus triandrus hybrids	6–12 in (15–30 cm)	March–May
Scilla hispanica	8–12 in (20–30 cm)	April
Tulipa clusiana	8–12 in (20–30 cm)	April
Tulipa, Double Early	8–12 in (20–30 cm)	April
Fritillaria meleagris	8–15 in (20–35 cm)	April–May
Narcissus, Double	1–1½ ft (30–45 cm)	March–May
Tulipa, Mendel and Triumph	1–1½ ft (30–45 cm)	April
Leucojum aestivum	1–1¾ ft (30–50 cm)	May–June
Ornithogalum arabicum	1–2 ft (30–60 cm)	May
Narcissus, Small-cupped	1½ ft (45 cm)	March–May
Narcissus, Large-cupped	1¼–1¾ ft (40–50 cm)	March–May
Iris bucharica	1–1½ ft (30–45 cm)	April
Narcissus, Trumpet	1½ ft (45 cm)	March–April
Tulipa, Double Late	1½–2 ft (45–60 cm)	May
Tulipa, Lily-flowered	1¾ ft (50 cm)	May
Tulipa, Darwin	2–2¾ ft (60–80 cm)	May

Yellow

	Height	Flowering
Crocus chrysanthus	2–4 in (5–10 cm)	March–April
Corbularia bulbocodium	4 in (10 cm)	April
Iris danfordiae	4 in (10 cm)	March
Narcissus, Miniature	4 in (10 cm)	March
Hyacinthus orientalis	4–6 in (10–15 cm)	March
Narcissus cyclamineus	6–10 in (15–25 cm)	March–April
Narcissus triandrus hybrids	6–12 in (15–30 cm)	March–May
Tulipa, Single Early	6–12 in (15–30 cm)	April
Tulipa tarda	8 in (20 cm)	March–April
Tulipa, Double Early	8–12 in (20–30 cm)	April
Tulipa kaufmanniana	8–12 in (20–30 cm)	April
Tulipa greigii	8–12 in (20–30 cm)	April
Allium moly	10 in (25 cm)	May–June
Erythronium tuolumnense	10 in (25 cm)	April
Narcissus, Jonquil	10–15 in (25–40 cm)	March–May
Narcissus, Double	1–1½ ft (30–45 cm)	March–May
Tulipa, Mendel and Triumph	1–1½ ft (30–45 cm)	April
Erythronium grandiflorum	6–12 in (15–30 cm)	April–May
Narcissus, Miniature	15 in (40 cm)	March
Narcissus, Tazetta and Small-cupped	15–18 in (40–45 cm)	March–May
Narcissus, Large-cupped	15–21 in (40–50 cm)	March–May
Narcissus, Trumpet	18–20 in (45–50 cm)	March–May
Tulipa, Double Late	1½–2 ft (45–60 cm)	May
Iris xiphium	2–2½ ft (60–75 cm)	June
Tulipa, Darwin hybrids	2–2½ ft (60–75 cm)	April–May
Tulipa, Darwin	2–2½ ft (60–75 cm)	May
Tulipa, Cottage	3 ft (90 cm)	April–May
Fritillaria imperialis	3 ft (90 cm)	April–May

Golden-yellow, orange and orange-red

	Height	Flowering
Crocus flavus	2–3 in (5–8 cm)	March–April
Crocus angustifolius	2–3 in (5–8 cm)	March
Hyacinthus orientalis	6–8 in (15–20 cm)	March–April
Tulipa, Single Early	6–12 in (15–30 cm)	April
Tulipa, Double Early	8–12 in (20–30 cm)	April
Tulipa kaufmanniana	8–12 in (20–30 cm)	April
Narcissus, Double	1–1½ ft (30–45 cm)	March–May
Tulipa, Triumph	1–1½ ft (30–45 cm)	April
Narcissus, Tazetta	1¼–1½ ft (40–45 cm)	March–May
Narcissus, Large-cupped	1¼–1¾ ft (40–50 cm)	March–May

Narcissus poeticus	1½ ft (45 cm)	March–May
Tulipa, Lily-flowered	1¾ ft (50 cm)	May
Tulipa, Darwin hybrids	2–2¼ ft (60–70 cm)	April–May
Lilium hansonii	2–5 ft (60–150 cm)	June
Tulipa, Cottage	3 ft (90 cm)	April–May
Fritillaria imperialis	3 ft (90 cm)	April–May

Red, crimson, pink and rose-red

	Height	Flowering
Hyacinthus orientalis	6–8 in (10–20 cm)	March–April
Iris reticulata	6 in (15 cm)	March–April
Muscari botryoides	6–8 in (15–20 cm)	March–April
Tulipa, Single Early	6–12 in (15–30 cm)	April
Allium karataviense	8–12 in (20–30 cm)	April–May
Scilla hispanica	8–12 in (20–30 cm)	May–June
Tulipa, Double Early	8–12 in (20–30 cm)	April
Tulipa kaufmanniana	8–12 in (20–30 cm)	April
Tulipa greigii	8–12 in (20–30 cm)	April
Fritillaria meleagris	8–15 in (20–40 cm)	April–May
Tulipa eichleri	10 in (25 cm)	March–April
Tulipa praestans	10–24 in (25–60 cm)	April
Tulipa, Mendel and Triumph	1–1½ ft (30–45 cm)	April
Tulipa fosteriana	1–1½ ft (30–45 cm)	April
Narcissus, Large-cupped	1¼–1¾ ft (40–50 cm)	March–May
Narcissus, Small-cupped	1½ ft (40 cm)	March–May
Tulipa acuminata	1½–1¾ ft (40–50 cm)	April
Lilium pomponium	1½–2½ ft (40–75 cm)	June
Tulipa, Lily-flowered	1¾ ft (50 cm)	May
Tulipa marjoletti	2 ft (60 cm)	May
Tulipa, Darwin hybrids	2–2½ ft (60–75 cm)	April–May
Tulipa, Rembrandt	2–2½ ft (60–75 cm)	May
Tulipa, Parrot	2–2½ ft (60–75 cm)	May
Tulipa, Darwin	2–2¾ ft (60–75 cm)	May
Tulipa, Cottage	3 ft (90 cm)	April–May

Purple

	Height	Flowering
Crocus tomasinianus	2–4 in (5–10 cm)	Feb.–March
Crocus chrysanthus	2–4 in (5–10 cm)	March–April
Tulipa, Single Early	6–12 in (15–30 cm)	April
Bulbocodium vernum	4–6 in (10–15 cm)	Feb.–April
Tulipa, Double Early	8–12 in (20–30 cm)	April
Tulipa, Triumph	1–1½ ft (30–45 cm)	April
Tulipa, Double Late	1½–2 ft (45–60 cm)	May
Tulipa, Lily-flowered	1¾ ft (50 cm)	May
Lilium martagon	2–5 ft (60–150 cm)	May–June
Tulipa, Darwin hybrids	2–2½ ft (60–75 cm)	April–May
Tulipa, Rembrandt	2–2½ ft (60–75 cm)	May
Tulipa, Parrot	2–2½ ft (60–75 cm)	May
Tulipa, Darwin	2–2¾ ft (60–80 cm)	May
Allium aflatunense	2½–3 ft (75–90 cm)	May–June
Fritillaria persica	2½–3 ft (75–90 cm)	May
Tulipa, Cottage	3 ft (90 cm)	April–May

Violet

	Height	Flowering
Crocus neapolitanus	3–4 in (7–10 cm)	Feb.–March
Crocus versicolor	2–4 in (5–10 cm)	March–April
Erythronium dens-canis	4–8 in (10–20 cm)	April–May
Iris reticulata	6 in (15 cm)	March–April
Tulipa, Single Early	6–12 in (15–30 cm)	April
Chionodoxa gigantea	6–8 in (15–20 cm)	Feb.–April
Tulipa pulchella var. *violacea*	8 in (20 cm)	April
Tulipa, Double Early	8–12 in (20–30 cm)	April
Tulipa, Double Late	15–24 in (40–60 cm)	May

Blue

	Height	Flowering
Crocus chrysanthus	2–4 in (5–10 cm)	March–April
Crocus neapolitanus	3–4 in (7–10 cm)	Feb.–March
Chionodoxa luciliae	4–6 in (10–15 cm)	March
Chionodoxa sardensis	4–6 in (10–15 cm)	March–May
Hyacinthus orientalis	6–8 in (15–20 cm)	April–May
Ipheion uniflorum	4–6 in (10–15 cm)	April–May
Iris bakeriana	6 in (15 cm)	Feb.–March
Iris reticulata	6 in (15 cm)	March–April
Iris regeliocyclus hybrids	6 in (15 cm)	May
Puschkinia scilloides	6 in (15 cm)	April–May

Muscari botryoides	6–8 in (15–20 cm)	March–April
Muscari armeniacum	6–10 in (15–25 cm)	April–May
Scilla sibirica	8 in (20 cm)	March–April
Scilla (Endymion) non-scripta	8–12 in (20–30 cm)	April–May
Scilla hispanica	8–12 in (20–30 cm)	May–June
Allium caeruleum	1½–2 ft (45–60 cm)	May–June

B. Summer-flowering bulbs

White and cream	*Height*	*Flowering*
Colchicum autumnale	6–8 in (15–20 cm)	Aug.–Sept.
Tigrida pavonia	10–18 in (25–45 cm)	Aug.–Sept.
Ornithogalum thyroides	1 ft (30 cm)	Aug.
Colchicum speciosum	8–12 in (20–30 cm)	Sept.–Oct.
Ornithogalum pyramidale	1–2 ft (30–60 cm)	June–July
Lilium longiflorum	2–3 ft (60–90 cm)	June–July
Lilium speciosum	2–4½ ft (60–130 cm)	Aug.–Sept.
Lilium auratum	2–6 ft (60–180 cm)	Aug.
Lilium candidum	2–5 ft (60–150 cm)	June–July
Gladiolus hybrids	3–5 ft (90–150 cm)	July–Aug.

Yellow	*Height*	*Flowering*
Tigrida pavonia	10–18 in (25–45 cm)	Aug.–Sept.
Lilium regale	1–5 ft (30–150 cm)	July–Aug.
Gladiolus hybrids	3–5 ft (90–150 cm)	July–Aug.
Lilium hybrids	3–5 ft (90–150 cm)	June–July

Golden-yellow, orange and orange-red	*Height*	*Flowering*
Crocus sativus	4 in (10 cm)	Sept.–Nov.
Lilium maculatum	1–2 ft (30–60 cm)	June–July
Crocosmia × crocosmiiflora	2–3 ft (60–90 cm)	June–Sept.
Lilium canadense	2–4½ ft (60–130 cm)	June–July
Gladiolus hybrids	3–4½ ft (90–150 cm)	July–Aug.
Lilium henryi	3–8 ft (1–2.5 m)	Aug.–Sept.

Red, crimson, pink and rose-red	*Height*	*Flowering*
Colchicum autumnale	6–8 in (15–20 cm)	Aug.–Oct.
Colchicum speciosum	1–1¼ ft (30–40 cm)	Sept.–Oct.
Allium schubertii	1–2 ft (30–60 cm)	June–July
Lilium longiflorum	1–3 ft (30–90 cm)	June–July
Gladiolus primulinus	1½–2½ ft (45–75 cm)	July–Sept.
Allium roseum	2 ft (60 cm)	June–July
Lilium auratum	2–6 ft (60–200 cm)	Aug.
Gladiolus hybrids	3–4½ ft (1–1 5 m)	July–Aug.
Lilium hybrids	3–4½ ft (1–1.5 m)	June–July

Purple	*Height*	*Flowering*
Crocus medius	4 in (10 cm)	Oct.–Nov.
Colchicum autumnale	6–8 in (15–20 cm)	Aug.–Oct.
Colchicum bornmuelleri	12–15 in (30–45 cm)	Aug.
Allium sphaerocephalon	1–1½ ft (30–45 cm)	July–Aug.
Iris xiphioides	1½ ft (45 cm)	June–July
Allium christophii	2 ft (60 cm)	June–July
Gladiolus hybrids	3–4½ ft (1–1.5 m)	July–Aug.

Violet	*Height*	*Flowering*
Crocus speciosus	4–5 in (10–12 cm)	Sept.–Oct.
Colchicum autumnale	6–8 in (15–20 cm)	Aug.–Oct.
Gladiolus hybrids	3–4½ ft (1–1.5 m)	July–Aug.
Allium giganteum	6 ft (2 m)	June–July

Tuberous-rooted and rhizomatous plants by colour

White and cream	*Height*	*Flowering*
Iris pumila	4–6 in (10–25 cm)	April–May
Anemone nemorosa	4–10 in (10–25 cm)	March–May
Convallaria majalis	6–10 in (15–30 cm)	May
Ranunculus asiaticus	6–12 in (15–30 cm)	June–Aug.
Dahlia hybrids	8 in–6½ ft (20 cm–2 m)	July–Oct.
Begonia × tuberhybrida	10–15 in (25–40 cm)	May–Aug.
Iris germanica	1–2 ft (30–60 cm)	May–June
Butomus umbellatus	1½–3 ft (45–90 cm)	May–Sept.
Polygonatum multiflorum	1½–3 ft (45–90 cm)	May–June
Iris sibirica	2½–3 ft (75–90 cm)	June
Artemisia dracunculus	3 ft (90 cm)	Aug.–Sept.
Polygonatum commutatum	3 ft (90 cm)	May–June
Eremurus himalaicus	3–6½ ft (1–2 m)	June

Yellow	*Height*	*Flowering*
Eranthis hyemalis	4–6 in (10–15 cm)	Feb.–March
Iris pumila	4–6 in (10–15 cm)	April–May
Eranthis cilicica	4–8 in (10–20 cm)	March–April
Ranunculus asiaticus	6–12 in (15–30 cm)	June–Aug.
Dahlia hybrids	8 in–6½ ft (20 cm–2 m)	July–Oct.
Begonia × tuberhybrida	10–15 in (25–40 cm)	May–Aug.
Corydalis cheilanthifolia	1 ft (30 cm)	May–June
Corydalis lutea	1 ft (30 cm)	June–Sept.
Iris forrestii	1¼ ft (40 cm)	June
Iris germanica	1–2 ft (30–60 cm)	May–June
Canna indica hybrids	1¼–2¼ ft (40–70 cm)	Aug.

Golden-yellow, orange and orange-red	*Height*	*Flowering*
Ranunculus asiaticus	6–12 in (15–30 cm)	June–Aug.
Dahlia hybrids	8 in–6 ft (20 cm–2 m)	July–Oct.
Begonia × tuberhybrida	10 in (25 cm)	May–Aug.
Iris germanica	1–3 ft (30–90 cm)	May–June
Canna indica hybrids	1¼–2¼ ft (40–70 cm)	Aug.
Eremurus stenophyllus	2–4 ft (60–120 cm)	June–July
Tropaeolum tuberosum	6½–10 ft (2–3 m)	Aug.–Sept.

Red, crimson, pink and rose-red	*Height*	*Flowering*
Convallaria majalis	6–8 in (15–20 cm)	May
Anemone nemorosa	6–10 in (15–25 cm)	March–May
Ranunculus asiaticus	6–12 in (15–30 cm)	June–Aug.
Anemone pavonina	8–12 in (20–30 cm)	Feb.–March
Dicentra formosa	8–12 in (20–30 cm)	June–Oct.
Dahlia hybrids	8 in–6½ ft (20 cm–2 m)	July–Oct.
Begonia × tuberhybrida	10 in (25 cm)	May–Aug.
Canna indica hybrids	1¼–2¼ ft (40–70 cm)	Aug.
Dodecatheon jeffreyi	2 ft (60 cm)	May–June
Iris sibirica	2½–3¼ ft (70–100 cm)	June
Dicentra spectabilis	3 ft (90 cm)	April–June
Eremurus robustus	3¼–6½ ft (1–2 m)	June–July
Eremurus elwesii	6½ ft (2 m)	May–June

Purple	*Height*	*Flowering*
Iris pumila	4–6 in (10–15 cm)	April–May
Iris cristata	6–8 in (15–20 cm)	May–June
Anemone nemorosa	6–10 in (15–25 cm)	March–May
Dahlia hybrids	8 in–6½ ft (20 cm–2 m)	July–Oct.
Corydalis nobilis	1¼ ft (40 cm)	April–June
Dodecatheon meadia	1¼–2 ft (40–60 cm)	May–June

Violet	*Height*	*Flowering*
Corydalis solida	6–10 in (15–25 cm)	April–June
Dahlia hybrids	8 in–6½ ft (20 cm–2 m)	June–Oct.
Iris germanica	1–2 ft (30–60 cm)	May–June

Blue	*Height*	*Flowering*
Campanula collina	6 in (15 cm)	July–Aug.
Iris germanica	1–2 ft (30–60 cm)	May–June
Iris sibirica	2½–3 ft (75–90 cm)	June

Deciduous shrubs by height

The shrubs in this table all have well-developed side-shoots so that there is no trunk. Trees including conifers are listed in a separate table. The reader is advised to consult the A–Z section for more detailed information.

Height up to 1½ ft (50 cm)	*Flowering*	*Flowers*	*Fruits*
Ceratostigma plumbaginoides	Sept.–Oct.	blue	—
Cotoneaster adpressus	May	pink	red
Cytisus albus	June–Aug.	white	—
Cytisus × kewensis	April–May	cream	—
Cytisus purpureus	June–July	white, purple	—
Genista hispanica	June–July	yellow	—
Genista lydia	June	yellow	—
Genista pilosa	May–June	yellow	—
Lavandula angustifolia	June–July	blue, violet red	—
Rosa, Miniature or Dwarf	June–Sept.	var. col.	—
Salix repans	April	yellow	—
Spiraea bullata	June–July	pink	—

Height 1½–4 ft (50–125 cm)	*Flowering*	*Flowers*	*Fruits*
Azalea, Japanese	May	var. col.	—
Azalea occidentale hybrids	May	var. col.	—
Berberis × media	—	—	—
Berberis wilsoniae	July	yellow	red
Caryopteris × clandonensis	Sept.–Oct.	blue	—
Caryopteris incana	Aug.–Sept.	violet	—

	Flowering	Flowers	Fruits
Ceanothus hybrids	July–Sept.	var. col.	—
Ceratostigma willmottianum	Aug.–Oct.	blue	—
Chaenomeles × superba	March–May	red	—
Cotoneaster conspicuus	May–July	white	orange
Cotoneaster horizontalis	June	red	red
Cotoneaster praecox	June	red	red
Cotoneaster sternianus	June	red	orange
Daphne × burkwoodii	May–June	white, pink	—
Daphne mezereum	March–April	pink	red
Deutzia gracilis	May–June	white	—
Deutzia × rosea	June–July	pink	—
Fothergilla gardenii	April–May	white	—
Fothergilla monticola	May	white	—
Fuchsia magellanica	July–Oct.	red	—
Genista tinctoria	June–Aug.	yellow	—
Hydrangea macrophylla ssp. serrata	July–Sept.	blue, red	—
Hypericum androsaemum	July–Sept.	yellow	black
Hypericum hookerianum	July–Oct.	yellow	—
Lonicera syringantha var. wolfii	May–July	pink	—
Potentilla fruticosa	June–Sept.	white, yellow	—
Prunus pumila	April–May	white	black
Prunus tenella	April	rose-red	—
Rhododendron mucronulatum	Jan.–March	purple	—
Rosa, Large-flowered	June–Sept.	var. col.	—
Rosa, Floribunda	June–Sept.	var. col.	—
Rosa carolina 'Alba'	July–Aug.	white	red
Rosa gallica	June–July	pink	orange
Rosa nitida	June–July	red	red
Rosa pimpinellifolia	May–June	var. col.	purple
Salix hastata	March–April	yellow	—
Spiraea bumalda, S. japonica	July–Sept.	red	—
Spiraea latifolia	July–Aug.	white	—
Spiraea trilobata	May–June	white	—
Symphoricarpos albus var. laevigatus	June–Sept.	pink	white
Symphoricarpos orbiculatus	Aug.–Sept.	pink	red
Weigela florida	May–July	red	—

Height 4–8ft (1.25–2.5m)

	Flowering	Flowers	Fruits
Azalea, Knap Hill, Exbury	May	var. col.	—
Azalea pontica hybrids	May	var. col.	—
Azalea rustica hybrids	May	var. col.	—
Azalea, Mollis	April–May	var. col.	—
Berberis aggregata	May–June	yellow	orange
Berberis dictyophylla, B. koreana	May	yellow	red
Berberis × mentorensis	—	—	—
Berberis × ottawensis	May–June	yellow	red
Berberis × rubrostilla	May	yellow	red
Berberis thunbergii	May–June	yellow	red
Berberis vulgaris	May–June	yellow	red
Callicarpa bodinieri	June–July	purple	purple
Chaenomeles × superba	—	—	—
Colutea orientalis	July–Sept.	red	cream
Cornus alba 'Siluvica'	May–June	yellow-white	white
Cornus stolonifera 'Flaviramea'	June–July	yellow	white
Corylopsis pauciflora, C. spicata	March	yellow	—
Corylus maxima 'Atropurpurea'	March	yellow	brown
Cotoneaster acutifolius	June–July	red	black
Cotoneaster dielsianus	June	white	red
Cotoneaster divaricatus	June	red	red
Cotoneaster franchetii	June	red	orange
Cytisus × praecox	April–May	var. col.	—
Cytisus scoparius	May–June	var. col.	—
Decaisnea fargesii	May–June	yellow	blue
Deutzia × hybrida	May–June	purple, red	—
Deutzia × kalmiiflora	May	red	—
Deutzia × lemoinei	May–June	white	—
Deutzia × magnifica	June	white	—
Elaeagnus commutata	—	—	—
Elaeagnus multiflora	April–May	yellow	orange
Enkianthus campanulatus	May	pink, white	—
Escallonia hybrids	June–July	white, red	—
Euonymus alatus	—	—	—
Exochorda × macrantha	May–June	white	—
Forsythia × intermedia	March–April	yellow	—
Fothergilla major	April–May	white	—
Hibiscus syriacus	Aug.–Oct	var. col.	—
Hydrangea aspera	July–Aug.	purple	—
Hydrangea aspera ssp. sargentiana	July–Aug.	violet	—
Hydrangea macrophylla	July–Sept	var. col.	—
Kerria japonica	May–June	yellow	—
Kolkwitzia amabilis	May–June	purple	—
Ligustrum japonicum	July–Aug.	white	—
Ligustrum quihoui	Sept.	white	—
Lonicera korolkowii	June	white	red
Lonicera ledebourii	May–June	orange	blue
Lonicera maackii	June	white	red
Lonicera × purpusii	Dec.–March	white	red
Magnolia liliiflora 'Nigra'	May	purple	—
Magnolia stellata	March–April	pink, white	—
Philadelphus hybrids	June	white	—
Prunus glandulosa	May	red, white	—
Rhododendron luteum	April–May	yellow	—
Rhododendron × praecox	March–April	pink	—
Rhododendron viscosum	July–Aug.	white	—
Ribes alpinum	April–May	yellow	red
Ribes americanum	April–May	yellow	black
Ribes aureum	April–May	yellow	purple
Ribes sanguineum	April–May	red	black
Robinia hispida	June	red	—
Rosa canina	June–July	pink	red
Rosa damascena	June–July	red	—
Rosa foetida	June	yellow	—
Rosa omeiensis	April	white	—
Rosa pendulina	May–June	red	red
Rosa rubiginosa	June–July	var. col.	orange
Rosa rubrifolia (glauca)	June–July	pink	red
Salix cinerea	March–April	yellow	—
Sorbaria sorbifolia	June–July	white	—
Spiraea arcuata, S. nipponica	May–June	white	—
Spiraea × arguta	April	white	—
Spiraea cantoniensis	June	white	—
Spiraea chamaedryfolia	May–June	white	—
Spiraea douglasii	July–Sept.	red	—
Spiraea prunifolia	April–May	white	—
Spiraea salicifolia	June–July	pink	—
Spiraea thunbergii	March–May	white	—
Spiraea × vanhouttei	April–May	white	—
Spiraea veitchii	July	white	—
Symphoricarpos × chenaultii	June–July	red	var. col.
Syringa × chinensis	May	purple	—
Syringa microphylla 'Superba'	May–Oct.	red	—
Vaccinium corymbosum	May–June	pink	blue
Viburnum × bodnantense	Feb.–April	red	—
Viburnum × carcephalum	April–May	white	—
Viburnum carlesii	April–May	white	—
Viburnum plicatum	May–June	white	—
Weigela hybrids	May–June	red, white	—

Height 8–15ft (2.5–5m)

	Flowering	Flowers	Fruits
Acer ginnala	—	—	—
Acer japonicum	May	red	—
Acer palmatum 'Dissectum'	May	yellow	—
Acer palmatum 'Ornatum'	May	yellow	—
Aesculus parviflora	June–Aug.	white	—
Aralia elata	Aug.–Sept.	cream	black
Buddleia alternifolia	June	violet	—
Buddleia davidii	June	var. col.	—
Colutea arborescens	May–Sept.	yellow	cream
Colutea × media	May–Sept.	orange	cream
Cornus florida	May	red	red
Cornus kousa	May–June	white	—
Cornus mas	March–April	yellow	red
Cornus nuttallii	May	white	—
Cornus sanguinea	—	white	red
Corylus avellana	March	yellow	brown
Cotinus coggygria	June–July	fawn	—
Cotoneaster watereri hybrids	June	white	red
Deutzia scabra	June–July	white, pink	—
Elaeagnus umbellata	—	—	red
Euonymus europaeus	—	—	pink
Exochorda racemosa	May–June	white	—
Hamamelis × intermedia	Dec.–Jan.	orange	—
Hamamelis japonica	Jan.	yellow	—
Hamamelis mollis	Dec.	yellow	—
Hippophae rhamnoides	April	orange	—
Holodiscus discolor	July–Aug.	white	—
Hydrangea arborescens	July–Aug.	white	—
Hydrangea paniculata 'Grandiflora'	July–Sept.	white	—
Ilex verticillata	—	—	red
Ligustrum obtusifolium	July–Aug.	white	—
Lonicera morrowii	May–June	yellow	red
Lonicera tatarica 'Alba'	May–June	white	red
Lonicera xylosteum	May–July	white	red
Magnolia × soulangiana	April–May	purple, white	—
Philadelphus coronarius	May–June	white	—
Philadelphus pubescens	July	white	—
Prunus × amygdalo-persica	March–April	pink	—
Prunus incisa	March–April	white	—
Prunus 'Okame'	April	red	—
Prunus sargentii	May	rose-red	—
Prunus spinosa	March–April	white	black
Prunus subhirtella	Nov.–March	pink, white	—
Pyrus spinosa	May	white	yellow

Rhus glabra	July–Aug.	green	red
Rhus typhina	June–July	yellow-green	red
Robinia kelseyi	May	red	—
Rosa moschata	Aug.–Oct.	white	—
Rosa moyesii	June	white-red	red
Rosa multiflora	June–Aug.	white	red
Salix acutifolia	March	yellow	—
Salix purpurea	March–April	yellow	—
Salix sachalinensis 'Sekka'	March–April	yellow	—
Salix triandra	April–May	yellow	—
Sambucus canadensis	June–July	white	black
Sambucus nigra	June–July	white	black
Sambucus racemosa	April–May	yellow	red
Sorbaria aitchisonii	June–July	white	—
Sorbaria arborea	July–Aug.	white	—
Sorbaria tomentosa	July–Aug.	white	—
Syringa josikaea	June–July	violet	—
Syringa reflexa	June	red	—
Syringa × swegiflexa	June	red	—
Tamarix parviflora	April–May	red	—
Tamarix pentandra	Aug.–Sept.	red	—
Tamarix ramosissima	July–Sept.	red	—
Tamarix tetrandra	April–May	red	—
Viburnum buddleifolium	May–June	white	black
Viburnum burkwoodii	April–May	white	—
Viburnum farreri	Feb.–April	pink	—
Viburnum lantana	May–June	white	black
Viburnum opulus	May	white	red
Weigela middendorffiana	April–July	yellow	—

Height 15–30 ft (5–10 m)

	Flowering	Flowers	Fruits
Acer negundo	April–May	yellow-green	—
Acer palmatum	May	yellow-green	—
Acer palmatum 'Atropurpureum'	May	yellow-green	—
Acer pensylvanicum	May	yellow-green	—
Amelanchier laevis	April–May	white	purple
Amelanchier lamarckii	April–May	white	black
Crataegus crus-galli	May	white	red
Crataegus laevigata	May	red, white	—
Crataegus monogyna	May–June	white	red
Elaeagnus angustifolia	—	—	yellow
Euonymus phellomanus	—	—	red
Laburnum alpinum	June	yellow	—
Laburnum × watereri	May–June	yellow	—
Lonicera × heckrottii	June–Sept.	purple, yellow	—
Prunus cerasifera	April	white, pink	yellow
Prunus cerasus	May	white	red
Prunus mahaleb	April–May	white	black
Prunus padus	April–May	white	black
Prunus persica	April	pink	—
Prunus serotina	May–June	white	black
Prunus serrulata	April–May	var. col.	—
Salix caprea	March–April	yellow	—
Syringa·vulgaris	May	var. col.	—

Evergreen shrubs by height

The most important evergreen shrubs are listed below; conifers will be treated separately. The colour of the flowers and the flowering period are only mentioned if the flowers are of ornamental value.

Height up to 1½ ft (50 cm)

	Flowering	Flowers	Fruits
Calluna vulgaris	Aug.–Sept.	var. col.	—
Cotoneaster dammeri	June–July	white	red
Cotoneaster salicifolius 'Parkteppich', 'Repens'	June–July	var. col.	—
Daboecia cantabrica	June–Oct.	var. col.	—
Daphne cneorum	May–June	pink	—
Dryas octopetala	July–Sept.	white	—
Erica carnea	Jan.–May	var. col.	—
Erica ciliaris	Aug.–Sept.	pink	—
Erica cinerea	June–Sept.	var. col.	—
Erica × darleyensis	April–May	var. col.	—
Erica tetralix	July–Sept.	white, red	—
Erica vagans	July–Sept.	white, red	—
Gaultheria procumbens	June	red	red
Hebe armstrongii	June–July	white	—
Hebe cupressoides	June–Aug.	white	—
Hebe pinguifolia	June–Aug.	white	—
Helianthemum hybrids	June–July	var. col.	—
Hypericum calcinum	July–Oct.	yellow	—
Kalmia polifolia	May–June	pink	—
Lithodora diffusa	May–June	blue, violet	—
Lonicera pileata	April–May	white	violet
Pachysandra terminalis	April–May	white	—
Pernettya mucronata	—	—	white

Rhododendron hirsutum	June–July	red	—
Rhododendron impeditum	May	purple, blue	—
Thymus citrodorus	July–Aug.	red	—
Thymus doerfleri	June–July	red	—
Thymus serpyllum	June–Aug.	white, purple	—
Vaccinium vitis-idaea	—	—	red
Viburnum davidii	May–June	white	violet
Vinca minor	April–Sept.	blue	—

Height 1½–4 ft (50 cm–1.25 m)

	Flowering	Flowers	Fruits
Berberis candidula	May	yellow	black
Berberis × frikartii	—	—	—
Berberis linearifolia	May	orange	—
Buxus microphylla	April	yellowish	—
Buxus sempervirens 'Suffruticosa'			
Cotoneaster microphyllus	May–June	white	red
Hebe odora	June–Aug.	white	—
Hedera colchica 'Arborescens'	Sept.	yellow-green	black
Hypericum × moserianum	July–Oct.	yellow	—
Kalmia angustifolia	June–July	red	—
Rhododendron ferrugineum	July	white, red	—
Rhododendron racemosum	March–April	purple	—
Rhododendron russatum	April–May	violet	—
Rhododendron williamsianum	April	white, red	—
Rhododendron yakusimanum	May	red	—
Skimmia × foremanii	May	white	red
Skimmia japonica	May–June	white	red
Vinca major	April–May	blue	—

Height 4–8 ft (1.25–2.50 m)

	Flowering	Flowers	Fruits
Aucuba japonica	—	—	red
Berberis buxifolia, B. hookeri	May	yellow	blue
Berberis darwinii	April–May	yellow	—
Berberis gagnepainii	May	yellow	black
Berberis × hybrido-gagnepainii	May	yellow	violet
Berberis julianae	May–June	yellow	blue

Height 4–8 ft (1.25–2.50 m)

	Flowering	Flowers	Fruits
Berberis stenophylla	May	yellow	blue
Camellia japonica	Feb.–June	white, red	—
Cotoneaster bullatus	May–June	red	red
Cotoneaster simonsii	June	white	orange
Elaeagnus pungens	—	—	—
Erica arborea var. *alpina*	May–June	white	—
Euonymus fortunei	—	white	—
Euonymus japonicus	—	—	—
Ilex glabra	—	—	black
Ligustrum amurense	June–July	white	—
Lonicera nitida	May–June	white	violet
Mahonia aquifolium	April–May	yellow	black
Mahonia bealei and *japonica*	Feb.–April	yellow	black
Osmanthus heterophyllus	Sept.–Oct.	white	purple
Pieris floribunda	March–April	white to pink	—
Pieris japonica	March–April	white	—
Prunus laurocerasus	May	white	—
Pyracantha coccinea	May–June	white	red, orange
Rhododendron augustinii	April–May	blue to purple	—
Rhododendron dauricum	Jan.–March	red	—
Viburnum macrocephalum	May–June	white	—

Height 8–15 ft (2.5–5 m)

	Flowering	Flowers	Fruits
Buxus sempervirens			
Cotoneaster salicifolius	June	white	red
Cotoneaster simonsii	June	white	red
Elaeagnus × ebbingei	—	—	—
Ilex aquifolium (variegated)	—	—	—
Ilex crenata	—	—	black
Kalmia latifolia	April–May	red	—
Ligustrum lucidum	July–Aug.	white	—
Prunus lusitanica	May	white	—
Pseudosasa japonica	—	—	—
Rhododendron catawbiense	May–June	purple	—
Viburnum rhytidophyllum	May–Aug.	white	black

Height above 15 ft (5 m)

	Flowering	Flowers	Fruits
Ilex × altaclarensis	—	—	orange
Ilex aquifolium	—	—	red

Climbers

The most important deciduous and evergreen climbing and wall shrubs are listed below. Many non-climbing shrubs are often used as wall shrubs but they are not listed here because this group is not clearly defined.

Aristolochia macrophylla, yellow-green flowers May–June, height 15–35 ft (5–10 m)

Bilderdykia aubertii, white flowers August–September, height 35–50ft (10–15m)

Campsis radicans, orange and yellow flowers July–September, height 15–35ft (5–10m)

Celastrus orbiculatus, orange fruits, height 15–35ft (5–10m)

Celastrus scandens, orange fruits, height 15–35ft (5–10m)

Clematis × durandii, violet flowers June–September, height 6–10ft (2–3m)

Clematis flammula, white flowers July–October, height 10–15ft (3–5m)

Clematis hybrids, flowers in various colours June–August, height 6–15ft (2–5m)

Clematis macropetala, blue or purple flowers May–August, height 6–12ft (2–4m)

Clematis montana, white or red flowers May–June, height 15–50ft (5–15m)

Clematis tangutica, yellow flowers August–October, white fruits, height 15–35ft (5–11m)

Clematis vitalba, white flowers June–August, white fruits, height 15–30ft (5–10m)

Clematis viticella, violet flowers July–August, height 6–12ft (2–4m)

Hedera colchica, dark glossy green or variegated leaves frequently stained or blotched, height 10–25ft (3–8m)

Hedera helix, various leaf shapes and forms of variegation, height 15–65ft (5–20m)

Hydrangea anomala ssp. *petiolaris*, white flowers in July, height 15–32ft (5–10m)

Jasminum nudiflorum, yellow flowers October–March, height 6–15ft (2–5m). (Stems need tying.)

Lonicera caprifolium, fragrant yellow flowers May–June, height 15–35ft (5–11m)

Lonicera periclymenum, purple flowers July–August, height 15–40ft (5–13m)

Lonicera sempervirens, red flowers May–August, red fruits, height 15–35ft (5–11m)

Parthenocissus henryana, blue fruits, height 15–40ft (5–13m)

Parthenocissus quinquefolia, blue-black fruits, height 30–50ft (10–15m)

Parthenocissus tricuspidata, blue fruits, height 30–60ft (10–18m)

Rosa, flowers in various colours June–August, height 6–20ft (2–6m)

Vitis coignetiae, blue fruits, 15–60ft (10–18m)

Wisteria floribunda, white or violet flowers May–July, height 15–35ft (5–11m)

Wisteria sinensis, blue flowers May–July, height 15–60ft (10–18m)

Conifers by colour

Green and dark green
Abies balsamea 'Nana' 1½–3ft (50–100cm)
Abies cephalonica 30–50ft (10–15m)
Abies homolepis 50–65ft (15–20m)
Abies nordmanniana >65ft (20m)
Cedrus deodara 50–65ft (15–20m)
Cedrus libani >65ft (20m)
Chamaecyparis lawsoniana 'Alumnii' 15–35ft (5–10m)
Chamaecyparis lawsoniana 'Filiformis' 15–35ft (5–10m)
Chamaecyparis lawsoniana 'Fraseri' 15–35ft (5–10m)
Chamaecyparis obtusa 'Filicoides' 3–5ft (1–2m)
Chamaecyparis obtusa 'Gracilis' 23–25ft (7–8m)
Chamaecyparis pisifera 'Filifera Nana' 1–2¼ft (30–70cm)
Chamaecyparis pisifera 'Plumosa' 25–50ft (8–15m)
Cryptomeria japonica 'Bandai-Sugi' 2½–5ft (75–150cm)
Cryptomeria japonica 'Viminalis' ('Dacrydioides') 6–15ft (2–5m)
Cryptomeria japonica 'Elegans' 25–50ft (8–15m)
Juniperus sabina 'Erecta' 6–10ft (2–3m)
Juniperus chinensis 'Plumosa' 3–6ft (1–2m)
Juniperus horizontalis 'Prostrata' 8–16in (20–40cm)
Juniperus virginiana 'Canaertii' 10–25ft (3–8m)
Larix decidua to 65ft (20m)
Picea abies 50–100ft (15–30m)
Picea abies 'Clanbrassiliana' 2½–4ft (75–120cm)
Picea abies 'Procumbens' 3–4½ft (90–140cm)
Picea breweriana >50ft (15m)
Picea omorika 50–80ft (15–25m)
Picea omorika 'Nana' 3–4½ft (1–1.5m)
Picea orientalis >100ft (30m)
Picea pungens >65ft (20m)
Picea sitchensis 65–150ft (20–45m)
Pinus densiflora >45ft (13m)
Pinus densiflora 'Umbraculifera' 6–9ft (2–3m)
Pinus mugo 10–30ft (3–9m)
Pinus mugo ssp. *pumilio* 3–6ft (1–2m)
Pinus nigra >65ft (20m)
Pinus nigra 'Pygmaea' 6–10ft (2–3m)
Pinus pinaster 65–100ft (20–30m)
Pinus ponderosa 65–120ft (20–37m)
Pinus strobus 65–120ft (20–37m)
Pinus sylvestris 'Beuvronensis' 2½–4ft (75–120cm)
Pinus wallichiana 65–100ft (20–30m)

Pseudotsuga menziesii 65–150ft (20–45m)
Taxodium distichum 45–100ft (13–30m)
Taxus baccata 20–40ft (7–12m)
Taxus × media 15–30ft (5–9m)
Tsuga canadensis 45–90ft (13–27m)
Tsuga heterophylla 45–90ft (13–27m)

Light green and grey-green
Araucaria araucana 45–100ft (13–30m)
Chamaecyparis lawsoniana 'Erecta Viridis' 15–35ft (5–11m)
Chamaecyparis lawsoniana 'Forsteckensis' 1–3ft (30–90cm)
Chamaecyparis nootkatensis 'Pendula' 30–50ft (9–15m)
Chamaecyparis obtusa 'Nana Gracilis' 3–10ft (1–3m)
Chamaecyparis pisifera 'Filifera' 10–20ft (3–7m)
Cryptomeria japonica 'Vilmoriniana' 1–2ft (30–60cm)
× *Cupressocyparis × leylandii* 40–90ft (12–27m)
× *Cupressocyparis × leylandii* 40–90ft 'Leighton Green' 40–90ft (12–27m)
Juniperus chinensis 'Blaauw' 2½–5ft (75–150cm)
Juniperus chinensis 'Fairview' 10–25ft (3–8m)
Juniperus chinensis 'Pfitzeriana' 3–10ft (1–3m)
Juniperus communis 'Hornbrookii' prostrate
Juniperus horizontalis 'Plumosa' 10–20in (0–50cm)
Metasequoia glyptostroboides 50–100ft (15–30m)
Picea glauca albertiana 'Conica' 3–8ft (1–2.5m)
Pinus peuce 40–65ft (12–20m)
Thuja plicata 65–120ft (20–37m)
Tsuga canadensis 'Bennett' 2–3ft (60–90cm)

Yellow-green, yellow and gold
Cedrus atlantica 'Aurea' 25–50ft (8–15m)
Chamaecyparis lawsoniana 'Lutea' 35–50ft (10–15m)
Chamaecyparis lawsoniana 'Stewartii' 35–50ft (10–15m)
Chamaecyparis nootkatensis 'Aurea' 35–65ft (10–20m)
Chamaecyparis obtusa 'Crippsii' 15–25ft (5–8m)
Chamaecyparis obtusa 'Tetragona Aurea' 10–25ft (5–8m)
Chamaecyparis pisifera 'Aurea' >65ft

(20m)
Chamaecyparis pisifera 'Filifera Aurea' 20–35ft (7–10m)
Chamaecyparis pisifera 'Plumosa Aurea' 15–35ft (5–10m)
Chamaecyparis pisifera 'Squarrosa Sulphurea' 25–50ft (8–15m)
Juniperus chinensis 'Pfitzeriana Aurea' 3–8ft (1–2.5m)
Juniperus chinensis 'Plumosa Aurea' 3–6ft (1–2m)
Junipera chinensis 'Plumosa Aureovariegata' 3–6ft (1–2m)
Juniperus communis 'Depressa Aurea' 6–12ft (2–4m)
Picea orientalis 'Aurea' 22–35ft (7.5–10m)
Pinus sylvestris 'Aurea' 15–20ft (5–7m)
Thuja occidentalis 50–65ft (15–20m)
Thuja orientalis 30–50ft (9–15m)
Thuja standishii 15–35ft (5–10m)

Grey, blue-green and silver-blue
Abies concolor 65–100ft (20–30m)
Abies grandis 65–150ft (20–45m)
Abies koreana 20–30ft (7–9m)
Abies lasiocarpa 40–50ft (12–45m)
Abies pinsapo 65–90ft (20–27m)
Abies pinsapo 'Glauca' 50–80ft (15–25m)
Abies procera 65–130ft (20–40m)
Abies procera 'Glauca' 65–120ft (20–37m)
Abies veitchii 45–75ft (13–23m)
Cedrus atlantica 65–120ft (20–37m)
Cedrus atlantica 'Glauca' 65–120ft (20–37m)
Cedrus atlantica 'Glauca Pendula' 10–30ft (3–9m)
Chamaecyparis lawsoniana 'Columnaris' 15–25ft (5–8m)
Chamaecyparis lawsoniana 'Elwoodii' 10–25ft (3–5m)
Chamaecyparis lawsoniana 'Fletcheri' 15–25ft (5–8m)
Chamaecyparis lawsoniana 'Minima Glauca' 1–3ft (30–90cm)
Chamaecyparis lawsoniana 'Pembury Blue' 25–45ft (8–13.5m)
Chamaecyparis lawsoniana 'Silver Queen' 35–50ft (10–15m)
Chamaecyparis lawsoniana 'Tharandtensis Caesia' 1½–3ft (0.5–1m)
Chamaecyparis lawsoniana 'Triomph van Boskoop' 25–50ft (8–15m)
Chamaecyparis lawsoniana 'Wisselii' 25–50ft (8–15m)
Chamaecyparis nootkatensia 'Glauca' 35–65ft (10–20m)

Chamaecyparis obtusa 'Pygmaea' 3–6ft (1–2m)
Chamaecyparis pisifera 'Boulevard' 5–15ft (1.5–5m)
Chamaecyparis pisifera 'Squarrosa' 25–50ft (8–15m)
Cryptomeria japonica 'Cristata' 10–25ft (3–8m)
Juniperus chinensis 'Hetzii' 5–15ft (1.5–5m)
Juniperus chinensis 'Keteleeri' 15–25ft (5–8m)
Juniperus chinensis 'Pfitzeriana Glauca' 3–10ft (1–3m)
Juniperus chinensis 'Plumosa Albovariegata' 2–4ft (60–120cm)
Juniperus communis 'Hibernica' 5–15ft (1.5–5m)
Juniperus communis 'Repanda' prostrate
Juniperus communis 'Suecica' 6–10ft (2–3m)
Juniperus horizontalis 'Douglasii' 8–18in (20–45cm)
Juniperus horizontalis 'Glauca' prostrate
Juniperus horizontalis 'Wiltonii' prostrate
Juniperus sabina 'Blue Danube' 2–5ft (60–150cm)
Juniperus sabina 'Hicksii' 3–4½ft (1–1.5m)
Juniperus sabina 'Tamariscifolia' 1½–3ft (45–90cm)
Juniperus squamata 6–15ft (2–5m)
Juniperus virginiana 'Burkii' 6–12ft (2–4m)
Juniperus virginiana 'Glauca' 10–25ft (3–8m)
Juniperus virginiana 'Grey Owl' 10–25ft (3–8m)
Juniperus virginiana 'Skyrocket' 10–20ft (3–7m)
Larix kaempferi 65–100ft (20–30m)
Picea engelmannii 45–90ft (13–27m)
Picea glauca 45–75ft (13–22m)
Picea mariana 'Nana' 1–1½ft (30–45cm)
Picea pungens 'Glauca' 45–75ft (13–22m)
Picea pungens 'Globosa' 2–4ft (60–130cm)
Picea pungens 'Koster' 25–45ft (8–13m)
Pinus cembra 25–45ft (8–13m)
Pinus parviflora 25–45ft (8–13m)
Pinus sylvestris 30–65ft (9–20m)
Pinus sylvestris 'Watereri' 6–15ft (2–5m)
Pseudotsuga menziesii 'Fletcheri' 3–6ft (1–2m)

Trees by height

By "tree" we mean all tall, woody, perennial plants having a well-marked trunk with few or no branches growing from the base. Sometimes it is difficult to distinguish trees from shrubs, in which case the shrubs may be listed in either or neither of the two groups. Coniferous trees are listed separately.

Only the most important characteristics are mentioned below. Look for the tree of your choice and then consult the text for more detailed information.

Height up to 15 ft (5 m)

Acer ginnala, yellow-green flowers in June; dark-green foliage turning red and yellow in the autumn

Acer japonicum, soft green or yellow leaves turning red in the autumn

Acer pseudoplatanus 'Brilliantissimum', foliage yellow and pink in spring, green in summer, yellow in autumn

Betula pedula 'Youngii', Young's weeping birch, green foliage

Elaeagnus angustifolia, silvery-green leaves, yellow fruits

Malus 'Aldenhamensis', purple flowers in May, purple-brown leaves

Malus 'Cheal's Weeping', weeping form, purple flowers, purple-brown leaves, red fruits

Malus coronaria, light red flowers May–June, green fruits

Malus 'Echtermeyer', weeping form, purple flowers in May, red fruits

Malus 'Eleyi', purple-red flowers in May, purple leaves, red fruits

Malus 'Hopa', purple flowers in May, light green leaves, red fruits

Malus 'Liset', red flowers in May, purple fruits

Malus × *micromalus*, light red flowers in early May, yellow fruits

Malus 'Professor Sprenger', white flowers in May, golden-yellow autumn colouring, orange fruits

Malus 'Red Sentinel', light red flowers in May, red fruits

Malus sargentii, a shrubby tree with white flowers in May, red fruits

Malus sieboldii, white flowers in late May, yellow autumn colouring, yellow fruits

Malus 'Van Eseltine', light red, double flowers in May, yellow fruits

Prunus subhirtella, white or light red flowers in April; various strains

Rhus glabra, beautiful red autumn foliage, red fruits

Rhus typhina, beautiful red autumn foliage, red fruits

Sorbus decora, green leaves, red fruits

Height between 15 and 35 ft (5–10 m)

Acer campestre, green leaves, yellow autumn colouring

Acer cappadocicum, dark green leaves, yellow autumn colouring

Acer cissifolium, green leaves, orange autumn colouring

Acer griseum, greyish-green leaves, golden-brown flaking bark, red colouring in the autumn

Acer pennsylvanicum, light green leaves, striped bark, yellow autumn colouring

Acer platanoides 'Crimson King', deep crimson-purple leaves

Acer platanoides 'Faasen's Black', dark red foliage

Acer platanoides 'Drummondii', light green leaves with a white band

Acer platanoides 'Globosum', dark green leaves, mop-shaped head

Acer platanoides 'Lorbergii', light green leaves

Acer pseudoplatanus 'Prinz Handjery', pink leaves tinged with yellow, yellow autumn colouring

Acer pseudoplatanus 'Worlei', orange-yellow in spring, light yellow in summer, yellow in autumn

Alnus incana 'Aurea', yellow-green leaves, reddish-brown catkins

Alnus incana 'Pendula', weeping form, reddish-brown catkins

Betula jacquemontii, peeling white bark

Betula medwediewii, yellow-grey bark

Carpinus betulus 'Purpurea', brown leaves turning green

Carpinus betulus 'Quercifolia', oak-leaf-shaped foliage

Carpinus betulus 'Variegata', leaves splashed creamy-white

Carpinus caroliniana, blue-green leaves turning orange-red in autumn

Carpinus japonica, green, heart-shaped leaves

Catalpa bignonioides, large light green leaves, white flowers June–July

Catalpa bignonioides 'Aurea', yellow leaves, white flowers June–July

Catalpa × *erubescens* 'Purpurea', brown leaves in the spring, white flowers June–July

Catalpa ovata, green leaves, white flowers July–August

Cercis siliquastrum, violet flowers April–May

Crataegus × *grignonensis*, white flowers in May, brownish-red fruits

Crataegus laevigata 'Gireoudii', white leaves mottled green

Crataegus × *lavallei*, white flowers May–June, red leaves in spring, orange fruits

Crataegus × *prunifolia* 'Splendens', white flowers in May, red fruits

Fraxinus excelsior 'Pendula', weeping form, yellow autumn colouring

Fraxinus ornus, white flowers May–June, yellow autumn colouring

Ilex × *altaclarensis*, dark green leaves, orange-red fruits

Ilex aquifolium, silvery and gold-mottled leaves, few fruits

Laburnum alpinum, yellow flowers in June, green leaves

Laburnum × *watereri*, yellow flowers May–June

Magnolia kobus, white flowers April–May, red fruits

Malus 'Almey', purple flowers in May, red fruits

Malus × *atrosanguinea*, red flowers in May, green leaves

Malus 'Butterball', crimson flowers in May, yellow fruits

Malus 'Calocarpa', white flowers in May, red fruits

Malus floribunda, bright red flowers with a pale blush, yellow fruits

Malus 'Golden Hornet', white flowers in May, yellow fruits

Malus 'Gorgeous', white flowers in May, red fruits

Malus 'John Downie', white flowers in May, orange fruits

Malus 'Lemoinei', red flowers in May, dark purple leaves, red fruits

Malus 'Profusion', red flowers in May, purple fruits

Malus 'Wintergold', bright red flowers in May, yellow fruits

Paulownia tomentosa, heliotrope flowers in May, very large leaves

Populus balsamifera, leaves with a balsamic odour, covered with white down on the underside

Prunus cerasifera 'Atropurpurea', white flowers in April, brown leaves, yellow fruits

Prunus cerasus, white flowers in May, red fruits

Prunus sargentii, bright red flowers in April, leaves bronze in spring, orange-red in autumn

Prunus serrulata, white or red, single or double flowers in April–May

Prunus subhirtella 'Autumnalis', white flowers from November onwards

Pyrus salicifolia, white flowers in April, grey foliage, brown fruits

Quercus robur 'Concordia', yellow leaves

Robinia pseudoacacia 'Frisia', yellow leaves

Robinia viscosa, bright red flowers in June

Salix caprea, large yellow catkins March–April

Salix daphnoides, large yellow catkins March–April, branches covered with a white bloom

Salix matsudana 'Tortuosa', twisted branches

Salix pentandra, yellow catkins in May

Salix triandra, yellow catkins April–May

Sorbus americana, white flowers in June, red autumn colouring, red fruits

Sorbus aria 'Lutescens', white flowers in May, greyish-white leaves turning green, orange fruits

Sorbus aucuparia, white flowers in May, red fruits

Sorbus hupehensis, grey-green leaves, white or pink flushed fruits

Sorbus intermedia, white flowers in May, red fruits

Ulmus glabra 'Camperdownii'

Ulmus × *hollandica* 'Wredei', densely borne golden-yellow leaves

Height between 35 and 50 ft (10–15 m)

Acer cappadocicum 'Rubrum', red leaves turning green

Acer negundo, soft green leaves

Acer negundo 'Auratum', yellow leaves turning a deeper yellow in the autumn

Acer negundo 'Aureovariegatum', spotted yellow leaves

Acer negundo 'Variegatum', white-edged leaves

Acer negundo var. *violaceum*, dark green leaves

Acer platanoides 'Schwedleri', leaves brownish-red in spring, green in summer, bronze in autumn

Acer pseudoplatanus 'Erectum', green leaves turning yellow in the autumn

Acer pseudoplatanus 'Leopoldii', leaves speckled yellow and pink, yellow in the autumn

Acer rubrum, dark green leaves turning red in the autumn

Aesculus × *carnea*, red flowers May–June, yellow leaves in the autumn

Aesculus pavia, red flowers May–June

Alnus cordata, dark green leaves

Alnus glutinosa 'Aurea', leaves yellow in spring, light green in summer

Betula costata, creamy-white bark

Betula pendula 'Tristis', weeping form, narrow symmetrical head

Catalpa speciosa, white and purple flowers June–July, attractive bark

Crataegus laevigata, white flowers in May, red fruits

Crataegus laevigata 'Paul's Scarlet', double red flowers in May

Crataegus pinnatifida var. *major*, red flowers May–June

Ilex aquifolium, dark green leaves, red or yellow fruits

Liquidambar styraciflua, dark green leaves turning crimson in the autumn

Prunus avium, white flowers April–May, dark red fruits

Quercus cerris, *Q. frainetto*, brown autumn foliage, brown fruits

Tilia tomentosa, bright yellow, aromatic flowers in July, leaves covered with white down underneath

Ulmus glabra, dark green leaves turning yellow in the autumn

Height between 50 and 65 ft (15–20 m)

Acer platanoides, bright green leaves turning yellow in the autumn

Betula lutea, amber-coloured bark

Betula ermanii, pinkish white bark

Betula nigra, reddish-brown bark

Betula pubescens, white bark

Carpinus betulus, green leaves

Corylus colurna, yellow-brown catkins in March, grey bark

Fagus sylvatica 'Zlatia', golden-yellow leaves in the spring turning yellow-green in late summer

Fraxinus americana, yellow and purple leaves in the autumn

Fraxinus excelsior 'Jaspidea', yellow leaves

Fraxinus pennsylvanica, violet leaves in the autumn

Gleditsia triacanthos, greenish flowers June–July, large thorns, yellow autumn foliage

Gleditsia triacanthos 'Sunburst', leaves yellow in spring, later yellow-green

Salix fragilis, yellow catkins April–May

Tilia americana, yellow-green flowers in July
Tilia cordata, yellow-green, fragrant flowers in July
Tilia × euchlora, bright yellow flowers June–July

Height above 65 ft (20 m)
Acer pseudoplatanus, bright green leaves turning yellow in the autumn
Acer saccharinum, leaves white underneath, red with yellow in the autumn
Aesculus hippocastanum, white flowers in May, yellow autumn foliage
Betula papyrifera, white bark shot with brown
Betula pendula, white bark shot with black
Fagus sylvatica, green leaves, various leaf shapes may occur
Fagus sylvatica 'Atropurpureum', dark purple leaves
Fraxinus excelsior, yellow autumn colouring

Ginkgo luloba, characteristic leaf shape, yellow autumn colouring
Platanus × hybrida, mottled bark, dark brown fruits
Populus alba, leaves silvery white underneath
Populus × berolinensis, leaves grey-green underneath
Populus × canadensis, leaves reddish in spring, yellow in autumn
Quercus robur, dark green leaves turning red in the autumn, brown fruits
Quercus rubra, autumn foliage red, brown fruits
Robinia pseudoacacia, fragrant white flowers in June
Salix alba, yellow catkins April–May
Salix alba 'Tristis', weeping form
Tilia platyphyllos, bright yellow flowers June–July
Tilia × vulgaris, fragrant, bright yellow flowers June–July
Ulmus hollandica, green leaves turning browny yellow in the autumn

Plants for dry ground

Below are listed a number of plants that demand, or will tolerate, dry positions. For further details consult the A–Z section.

A. Annuals and biennials
Adonis aestivalis
Arctosis, all species
Cheiranthus cheiri
Echium lucopsis
Gazania hybrids
Gypsophila, all species
Helipterum, all species
Iberis, all species
Lavatera trimestris
Lupinus luteus
Lupinus nanus
Lychnis coronaria
Mesembryanthemum, all species
Onopordum bracteatum
Papaver, all species

B. Bulbs, etc.
Allium, various species
Artemisia dracunculus
Aubrieta hybrids
Centranthus rubes

C. Perennials
Acaena buchananii
Acaena microphylla
Acaena novae-zelandiae
Achillea kellereri
Achillea chrysocoma
Achillea taygetea
Alyssum montanum
Alyssum saxatile
Anaphalis, all species
Anchusa, all species
Armeria, all species
Campanula caespitosa
Campanula carpatica
Campanula cochleariifolia
Centaurea dealbata
Centaurea hypoleuca
Centaurea macrocephala
Centaurea montana
Cerastium, all species
Coreopsis, all species
Dianthus, all species
Dictamnus albus
Echinops, all species
Eryngium, all species
Euphorbia cyparissias
Euphorbia epithymoides
Euphorbia myrsinites
Festuca, all species
Filipendula vulgaris
Gaillardia, all species
Gypsophila, all species
Helictotrichon sempervirens
Iberis, all species
Koeleria glauca
Leontopodium, all species
Linaria aequitriloba
Linaria alpina
Lychnis flos-jovis
Malva moschata
Nepeta, all species
Papaver, all species

Perovskia atriplicifolia
Phlox amoena
Salvia officinalis
Salvia pratensis
Saponaria, all species
Sedum, all species
Sempervivum, all species
Stachys, most species
Stipa pennata
Veronica incana
Veronica teucrium

D. Shrubs
Ceratostigma, all species
Cytisus decumbens
Dryas octopetala
Elaeagnus commutata
Elaeagnus umbellata
Genista hispanica
Genista sagittalis
Genista tinctoria
Helianthemum hybrids
Hippophae rhamnoides
Lavendula angustifolia
Robinia, all species
Tamarix parviflora
Thymus, all species
Yucca, all species

E. Trees (other than conifers)
Betula, some species
Fraxinus ornus
Gleditsia triacanthos
Rhus, all species

F. Conifers
Juniperus, all species
Pinus mugo
Pinus nigra
Pinus parviflora
Pinus peuce
Pinus pinaster
Pinus pumila
Pinus sylvestris

Plants for moist sites and aquatic plants

Below are listed a number of plants that demand, or will tolerate, moist sites. No distinction is made between such plants and true marsh plants or drifting aquatic plants. See the A–Z section for further details.

A. Annuals and biennials
Heracleum mantegazzianum
Mimulus, all species
Myosotis, all species

B. Bulbs, etc.
Artemisia lactiflora
Astilbe, all species
Butomus umbellatus
Narcissus bulbocodium
Crocosmia × crocosmiiflora
Dodecatheon, all species
Erythronium, all species

Euphorbia palustris
Fritillaria meleagris
Iris, various species
Mimulus, all species
Osmunda, all species
Ranunculus, some species

C. Perennials
Achillea filipendulina
Alchemilla mollis
Astrantia major
Athyrium filix-femina
Brunnera macrophylla
Buphthalmum salicifolium
Caltha palustris
Chelone barbata
Cimicifuga, all species
Dryopteris filix-mas
Eichhornia
Epimedium, all species
Filipendula, most species
Galium odoratum
Gentiana, some species
Gillenia trifoliata
Gunnera manicata
Helianthus salicifolius
Helleborus, most species
Hemerocallis, all species
Heuchera
Hippuris vulgaris
Hosta, all species
Kniphofia, some species
Ligularia, all species
Lysichiton, all species
Lysimachia, most species
Lythrum hybrids
Matteuccia struthiopteris
Meconopsis, all species
Menyanthes trifoliata
Monarda, various species
Nymphaea, all species
Peltiphyllum peltatum
Phlox arendsii hybrids
Polemonium caeruleum
Polygonum bistorta
Pontederia cordata
Potentilla palustris
Primula, many species
Pseudosasa japonica
Pulmonaria, all species
Ranunculus, all species
Rheum, all species
Rodgersia, all species
Rudbeckia, all species
Sagittaria sagittifolia
Sidalcea hybrids
Tradescantia andersoniana hybrids
Trollius, all species
Typha, all species

D. Shrubs
Cornus, various species
Daphne laureola
Hedera, all species
Hydrangea, all species
Magnolia, all species
Pieris, all species
Rhododendron, all species
Azalea, all species
Salix, all species

Vaccinium, all species
Viburnum opulus
Weigela middendorffiana

E. Trees (other than conifers)
Alnus glutinosa
Betula nigra
Cercidiphyllum japonicum
Koelreuteria paniculata
Populus, various species
Prunus, various species
Salix, all species

F. Conifers
Picea sitchensis
Pinus, some species
Metasequoia glyptostroboides
Taxodium distichum

Specimen plants

Below are listed a number of plants which, because of their impressive appearance, are eminently suitable for planting as specimens in solitary positions on the lawn or between smaller plants. See the A–Z section for further details.

A. Annuals and biennials
Althaea rosea
Heracleum mantegazzianum
Ricinus communis
Verbascum, various species

B. Bulbs etc.
Allium giganteum
Eremurus, all species
Fritillaria imperialis
Lilium, all species
Osmunda regalis

C. Perennials
Acanthus mollis
Aruncus, all species
Cortaderia selloana
Gunnera manicata
Lavatera olbia
Ligularia, all species
Lythrum hybrids
Macleaya cordata
Peltiphyllum peltatum

D. Shrubs
Aralia elata
Cornus, various species
Cotinus coggygria
Cotoneaster, various species
Decaisnea fargesii
Exochorda × macrantha
Fothergilla, all species
Hamamelis, all species
Hibiscus syriacus
Holodiscus discolor
Hydrangea, all species
Ilex, some species
Kolkwitzia amabilis
Magnolia, all species
Pieris japonica

Prunus triloba
Robinia, all species
Rosa, standards
Viburnum plicatum
Wisteria sinensis
Yucca, all species

E. Trees (other than conifers)
Acer, various species
Aesculus, various species
Alnus incana
Araucaria araucana
Betula, all species
Catalpa, all species
Cercidiphyllum japonicum
Cercis siliquastrum
Fagus sylvatica
Fraxinus, all species
Gleditsia triacanthos
Koelreuteria paniculata

Liriodendron tulipifera
Malus, all species
Paulownia tomentosa
Tilia, all species

F. Conifers
Abies koreana
Cedrus, all species
Chamaecyparis, all species
Cryptomeria japonica
× Cupressocyparis leylandii
Ginkgo biloba
Juniperus, tall species
Larix, all species
Metasequoia glyptostroboides
Picea, all species
Pinus, all species
Pseudotsuga menziesii
Taxodium distichum
Thuja plicata

Hedging plants

The plants listed below are suitable for compact and tall hedges. All can be pruned, though generally at the expense of flowers. For further details, see the A–Z section.

A. Shrubs
Berberis, various species
Buxus sempervirens
Cornus mas
Cotoneaster, various species
Crataegus monogyna and others
Elaeagnus, various species
Euonymus japonicus
Forsythia, various species
Ilex, various species
Ligustrum, various species
Lonicera, various species

Potentilla fruticosa
Prunus laurocerasus
Pyracantha coccinea
Rhododendron hybrids
Ribes, various species
Rosa, various species
Spiraea, various species
Symphoricarpos, various species

B. Trees (other than conifers)
Carpinus betulus
Fagus sylvatica

C. Conifers
Chamaecyparis lawsoniana
× Cupressocyparis leylandii
Juniperus, erect species
Taxus, baccata and × media
Thuja plicata
Tsuga heterophylla

INDEX

Daisy, shasta see *Chrysanthemum maximum*
Daisy bush see *Olearia*
Dawn redwood see *Metasequoia*
Deodar see *Cedrus deodara*
Dogwood see *Cornus*
Dogwood, common see *Cornus sanguinea*
Dogwood, red-barked see *Cornus alba*
Douglas fir see *Pseudotsuga*
Douglas fir, Oregon see *Pseudotsuga menziesii*
Dove tree see *Davidia*
Dusty Miller see *Centaurea cineraria*
Dutchman's breeches see *Dicentra spectabilis*
Dutchman's pipe see *Aristolochia*
Dyer's greenweed see *Genista tinctoria*
Edelweiss see *Leontopodium*
Elder, American see *Sambucus canadensis*
Elder, box see *Acer negundo*
Elder, common see *Sambucus nigra*
Elder, red-berried see *Sambucus racemosa*
Elder, sweet see *Sambucus canadensis*
Elm, Chinese see *Ulmus parvifolia*
Elm, English see *Ulmus procera*
Elm, Scotch see *Ulmus glabra*
Elm, smooth-leaved see *Ulmus minor*
Elm, wych see *Ulmus glabra*
Everlasting see *Helichrysum, Helipterum*
Feather grass see *Stipa*
Fern, flowering see *Osmunda regalis*
Fern, lady see *Athyrium filix-femina*
Fern, royal see *Osmunda*
Fescue, creeping see *Festuca rubra*
Fescue, red see *Festuca rubra*
Fescue, sheep's see *Festuca ovina*
Feverfew see *Chrysanthemum parthenium*
Filbert see *Corylus maxima*
Fir, Alpine see *Abies lasiocarpa*
Fir, balsam see *Abies balsamea*
Fir, blue Spanish see *Abies pinsapo*
Fir, Caucasian see *Abies nordmanniana*
Fir, giant see *Abies grandis*
Fir, grand see *Abies grandis*
Fir, Greek see *Abies cephalonica*
Fir, Korean see *Abies koreana*
Fir, Nikko see *Abies homolepis*
Fir, noble see *Abies procera*
Fir, Oregon see *Abies grandis*
Fir, red see *Abies procera*
Fir, silver see *Abies*
Fir, white see *Abies grandis, Abies concolor*
Firethorn see *Pyracantha*
Flag, purple see *Iris germanica*
Flag, yellow see *Iris pseudacorus*
Flame azalea see *Rhododendron calendulaceum*
Flax see *Linum*
Flax, New Zealand see *Phormium*
Fleabane see *Erigeron*
Floss flower see *Ageratum*
Flower-of-an-hour see *Hibiscus trionum*
Foam flower see *Tiarella cordifolia*
Foam of May see *Spiraea × arguta*
Forget-me-not, Alpine see *Myosotis alpestris*
Forget-me-not, common see *Myosotis sylvatica*
Forget-me-not, water see *Myosotis palustris*
Foxglove see *Digitalis*
Furze, needle see *Genista anglica*
Gean see *Prunus avium*
Gentian see *Gentiana*
Geranium see *Pelargonium*
Ghost tree see *Davidia*
Gilliflower see *Matthiola*
Gladdon see *Iris foetidissima*
Gladwyn see *Iris foetidissima*
Globeflower see *Trollius*
Glory of the snow see *Chionodoxa*
Goat's beard see *Aruncus dioicus*
Goat's beard, false see *Astilbe*
Golden chain tree see *Laburnum*
Golden rod see *Solidago virgaurea*
Golden tuft see *Alyssum saxatile*
Goldilocks see *Aster linosyris*
Gorse, Spanish see *Genista hispanica*
Granny's bonnet see *Aquilegia vulgaris*
Grape vine see *Vitis vinifera*
Handkerchief tree see *Davidia*
Harebell see *Campanula rotundifolia*
Hawthorn, common see *Crataegus monogyna*
Hazel see *Corylus avellana*

Hazel, Turkish see *Corylus colurna*
Heartsease see *Viola tricolor*
Heath see *Erica*
Heath, Cornish see *Erica vagans*
Heath, Dorset see *Erica ciliaris*
Heath, Irish see *Daboecia cantabrica*
Heath, St Dabeoc's see *Daboecia cantabrica*
Heath, tree see *Erica arborea* var. *alpina*
Heather see *Calluna vulgaris*
Heliotrope see *Heliotropium*
Hellebore see *Helleborus*
Hellebore, stinking see *Helleborus foetidus*
Hemlock, eastern see *Tsuga canadensis*
Hemlock, western see *Tsuga heterophylla*
Hogweed see *Heracleum*
Hogweed, giant see *Heracleum montegazzianum*
Holly, American see *Ilex opaca*
Holly, Chinese see *Ilex crenata*
Holly, common see *Ilex aquifolium*
Holly, Japanese see *Ilex crenata*
Holly, sea see *Eryngium*
Hollyhock see *Alcaea*
Honesty see *Lunaria*
Honey locust see *Gleditschia triacanthos*
Honeysuckle see *Lonicera*
Honeysuckle, goat-leaf see *Lonicera caprifolium*
Honeysuckle, Himalayan see *Leycesteria formosa*
Honeysuckle, Japanese see *Lonicera japonica*
Honeysuckle, swamp see *Rhododendron viscosum*
Hoop petticoat see *Corbularia bulbocodium*
Hornbeam, American see *Carpinus caroliniana*
Hornbeam, common see *Carpinus betulus*
Horse chestnut see *Aesculus*
Hound's tongue see *Cynoglossum*
Houseleek, cobweb see *Sempervivum arachnoideum*
Houseleek, common see *Sempervivum tectorum*
Hyacinth, grape see *Muscari*
Hyacinth, water see *Eichornia*
Hyacinth, wild see *Scilla non-scripta*
Inkberry see *Ilex glabra*
Iris, Dutch see *Iris hollandica*
Iris, English see *Iris xiphioides*
Iris, Spanish see *Iris xiphium*
Iris, stinking see *Iris foetidissima*
Ivy, common see *Hedera helix*
Ivy, Persian see *Hedera colchica*
Jasmine, common white see *Jasminum officinale*
Jasmine, Italian see *Jasminum humile*
Jasmine, winter-flowering see *Jasminum nudiflorum*
Jasmine, yellow see *Jasminum humile*
Joseph's coat see *Amaranthus tricolor*
Judas tree see *Cercis siliquastrum*
June berry see *Amelanchier lamarkii*
Juniper, Chinese see *Juniperus chinensis*
Juniper, common see *Juniperus communis*
Juniper, creeping see *Juniperus horizontalis*
Kingcup see *Caltha palustris* .
Knapweed see *Amberboa*
Knotweed see *Bilderdykia, Polygonum*
Laburnum, common see *Laburnum anagyroides*
Laburnum, Scotch see *Laburnum alpinum*
Lady's mantle see *Alchemilla*
Lamb's tongue see *Stachys olympica*
Larch see *Larix*
Larkspur see *Delphinium orientale Delphinium ajacis*
Laurel see *Laurus*
Laurel, cherry see *Prunus laurocerasus*
Laurel, common see *Prunus laurocerasus*
Laurel, mountain see *Kalmia latifolia*
Laurel, Portuguese see *Prunus insitanica*
Laurel, sheep see *Kalmia angustifolia*
Lavender see *Lavandula*
Lavender, sea see *Limonium*
Leopard's bane see *Doronicum*
Lilac, California see *Ceanothus*
Lilac, common see *Syringa vulgaris*
Lilac, Hungarian see *Syringa josikaea*
Lilac, Korean see *Syringa patula*
Lilac, Rouen see *Syringa × chinensis*
Lily see *Lilium*
Lily, African see *Agapanthus*
Lily, American trout see *Erythronium revolutum*
Lily, Canada see *Lilium canadense*
Lily, Cuban see *Scilla peruviana*

Lily, day see *Hemerocallis*
Lily, Easter see *Lilium longiflorum*
Lily, foxtail see *Eremurus*
Lily, glacier see *Erythronium grandiflorum*
Lily, golden see *Lilium auratum*
Lily, Madonna see *Lilium candidum*
Lily, Nankeen see *Lilium testaceum*
Lily, palm see *Yucca gloriosa*
Lily, panther see *Lilium pardalinum*
Lily, Peruvian see *Alstroemeria*
Lily, plantain see *Hosta*
Lily, Pyrenean see *Lilium pyrenaicum*
Lily, sword see *Gladiolus*
Lily, torch see *Kniphofia*
Lily, turf see *Liriope, Ophiopogon*
Lily, Turk's cap see *Lilium martagon*
Lily-of-the-valley see *Convallaria*
Lime, American see *Tilia americana*
Lime, broad-leaved see *Tilia platyphyllos*
Lime, common see *Tilia × europaea*
Lime, silver see *Tilia tormentosa*
Lime, silver pendant see *Tilia petiolaris*
Lime, small-leaved see *Tilia cordata*
Ling see *Calluna vulgaris*
Livelong see *Sedum telephium*
Loosestrife see *Lysimachia*
Loosestrife, purple see *Lythrum salicaria*
Love-in-a-mist see *Nigella damascena*
Love-lies-bleeding see *Amaranthus caudatus*
Lungwort see *Pulmonaria*
Lupin see *Lupinus*
Lupin, blue see *Lupinus angustifolius*
Lupin, tree see *Lupinus arboreus*
Lyme grass see *Elymus arenarius*
Maidenhair tree see *Gingko*
Mallow see *Lavatera, Malva*
Mallow, Jew's see *Kerria*
Maple, Canadian see *Acer rubrum*
Maple, field see *Acer campestre*
Maple, Japanese see *Acer japonicum Acer palmatum*
Maple, moosewood see *Acer pennsylvanicum*
Maple, Norway see *Acer platanoides*
Maple, paper bark see *Acer griseum*
Maple, red see *Acer rubrum*
Maple, silver see *Acer saccharinum*
Maple, snake bark see *Acer pennsylvanicum*
Mare's tail see *Hippuris vulgaris*
Marigold see *Calendula, Tagetes*
Marigold, African see *Tagetes erecta*
Marigold, bush see *Tagetes tenuifolia*
Marigold, corn see *Chrysanthemum segetum*
Marigold, French see *Tagetes patula*
Marigold, marsh see *Caltha palustris*
Masterwort see *Astrantia*
May see *Crataegus*
Meadow foam see *Limnanthes douglasii*
Meadow-rue see *Thalictrum*
Meadow-rue, lesser see *Thalictrum minus*
Meadow saffron see *Colchicum autumale*
Mespilus, snowy see *Amelanchier*
Mexican orange blossom see *Choisya*
Mezereon see *Daphne mezereum*
Mignonette see *Reseda*
Milfoil see *Achillea millefolium*
Milkweed see *Asclepias*
Mock orange see *Philadelphus*
Moneywort see *Lysimachia nummularia*
Monkey flower see *Mimulus*
Monkey puzzle tree see *Araucaria araucana*
Monkshood see *Aconitum*
Morning glory see *Ipomoea*
Mountain ash see *Sorbus aucuparia*
Mugwort, white see *Artemisia lactiflora*
Mulberry see *Morus*
Mulberry, black see *Morus nigra*
Mullein see *Verbascum*
Mullein, dark see *Verbascum nigrum*
Mullein, purple see *Verbascum phoeniceum*
Musk see *Mimulus moschatus*
Nasturtium see *Tropaeolum majus*
New Zealand bur see *Acaena*
Oak, American see *Quercus pontica*
Oak, bear see *Quercus ilicifolia*
Oak, common see *Quercus robur*
Oak, English see *Quercus robur*
Oak, evergreen see *Quercus ilex*

Oak, holm see *Quercus ilex*
Oak, Hungarian see *Quercus frainelto*
Oak, Lebanon see *Quercus libani*
Oak, pin see *Quercus palustris*
Oak, red see *Quercus rubra*
Oak, sessile see *Quercus petraea*
Oak, Turkey see *Quercus cerris*
Oak, Turner's see *Quercus × turneri*
Oak, willow see *Quercus phellos*
Obedient plant see *Physostegia virginiana*
Oleaster see *Elaeagnus*
Orpine see *Sedum telephium*
Osier, common see *Salix viminalis*
Osier, purple see *Salix purpurea*
Oswego tea see *Monarda didyima*
Ox-eye see *Buphthalmum salicifolium*
Pampas grass see *Cortaderia*
Pansy see *Viola*
Partridge berry see *Gaultheria procumbens*
Pasque flower see *Pulsatilla vulgaris*
Pea, everlasting see *Lathyrus latifolius*
Pea, sweet see *Lathyrus*
Peach see *Prunus persica*
Peach, David's see *Prunus davidiana*
Pear, ornamental see *Pyrus*
Pear, willow-leaved see *Pyrus salicifolia*
Pearl bush see *Exochorda*
Pearl everlasting see *Anaphalis*
Pearlwort see *Sagina subulata*
Peony see *Peonia*
Periwinkle, greater see *Vinca major*
Periwinkle, lesser see *Vinca minor*
Pheasant's eye see *Adonis*
Pine, Arolla see *Pinus cembra*
Pine, Austrian see *Pinus nigra*
Pine, Bhutan see *Pinus wallichiana*
Pine, black see *Pinus nigra*
Pine, dwarf Siberian see *Pinus pumila*
Pine, Japanese red see *Pinus densiflora*
Pine, Japanese white see *Pinus parviflora*
Pine, Macedonian see *Pinus peuce*
Pine, maritime see *Pinus pinaster*
Pine, Monterey see *Pinus radiata*
Pine, mountain see *Pinus mugo*
Pine, Scots see *Pinus sylvestris*
Pine, western yellow see *Pinus ponderosa*
Pine, Wyemouth see *Pinus strobus*
Pink see *Dianthus*
Pink, Cheddar see *Dianthus gratianopolitanus*
Pink, Indian see *Dianthus chinensis*
Pink, wild see *Dianthus plumarius*
Plane, London see *Platanus × hispanica*
Plane, oriental see *Platanus orientalis*
Poplar, balsam see *Populus balsamifera*
Poplar, Berlin see *Populus × berolinensis*
Poplar, black see *Populus nigra*
Poplar, grey see *Populus × canescens*
Poplar, Ontario see *Populus balsamifera*
Poplar, white see *Populus alba*
Poppy see *Papaver*
Poppy, Alpine see *Papaver alpinum*
Poppy, Californian see *Eschscholzia californica*
Poppy, corn see *Papaver rhoeas*
Poppy, field see *Papaver rhoeas*
Poppy, hareball see *Meconopsis quintuplinervia*
Poppy, Himalayan blue see *Meconopsis betonicifolia*
Poppy, Iceland see *Papaver nudicaule*
Poppy, lampshade see *Meconopsis integrifolia*
Poppy, opium see *Papaver somniferum*
Poppy, oriental see *Papaver orientale*
Poppy, peacock see *Papaver paroninum*
Poppy, plume see *Macleaya*
Poppy, satin see *Meconopsis napaulensis*
Poppy, tulip see *Papaver glaucum*
Poppy, Welsh see *Meconopsis cambrica*
Primrose see *Primula vulgaris*
Primrose, evening see *Oenothera*
Primula, bird's-eye see *Primula farinosa*
Privet see *Ligustrum*
Purple cone flower see *Echinacea*
Purslane see *Portulaca*
Quince, Japanese see *Chaenomeles speciosa*
Quince, Maule's see *Chaenomeles japonica*
Quince, ornamental see *Chaenomeles*
Red buckeye see *Aesculus pavia*
Red-hot poker see *Kniphofia*

Reedmace, dwarf see *Typha minima*
Reedmace, great see *Typha latifolia*
Reedmace, lesser see *Typha angustifolia*
Rhubarb, ornamental see *Rheum*
Rose, alpine see *Rosa pendulina*
Rose, autumn musk see *Rosa moschata*
Rose, burnet see *Rosa pimpinellifolia*
Rose, cabbage see *Rosa centifolia*
Rose, Christmas see *Helleborus niger*
Rose, damask see *Rosa damascena*
Rose, dog see *Rosa canina*
Rose, French see *Rosa gallica*
Rose, guelder see *Viburna opulus*
Rose, memorial see *Rosa wichuriana*
Rose, polyantha see *Rosa multiflora*
Rose, Provence see *Rosa centrifolia*
Rose, ramanas see *Rosa rugosa*
Rose, rock see *Helianthemum*
Rose, Scots see *Rosa pimpinellifolia*
Rose, sun see *Cistus*
Rosemary see *Rosmarinus*
Rose of heaven see *Silene coeli-rosa*
Rose of Sharon see *Hypericum calycinum*
Rowan see *Sorbus aucuparia*
Rue see *Ruta*
Rush, flowering see *Buomus umbellatus*
Sage see *Salvia officinalis*
Sage, Bethlehem see *Pulmonaria saccharata*
Sage, white see *Artemisia ludoviciana*
St John's wort see *Hypericum*
Sallow, common see *Salix caprea*
Sallow, grey see *Salix cinerea*
Savin see *Juniperus sabina*
Saxifrage, mossy see *Saxifraga hypnoides*
Scabious see *Scabiosa*
Scabious, sweet see *Scabiosa atropurpurea*
Sea pink see *Armeria maritima*
Self-heal see *Prunella*
Shadbush see *Amelanchier canadensis*
Shell plant see *Molucella laevis*
Shooting star see *Dodecatheon*
Slipperwort see *Calceolaria*
Sloe see *Prunus spinosa*
Smoke tree see *Cotinus*
Snakeroot see *Cimicifuga racemosa*
Snake's head see *Fritillaria meleagris*
Snakeweed see *Polygonum bistorta*
Snapdragon see *Antirrhinum*
Sneezewort see *Achillea ptarmica*
Snowball, Japanese see *Viburnum plicatum*
Spanish dagger see *Yucca gloriosa*
Spearwort, greater see *Ranunculus lingua*
Speedwell see *Veronica*
Spider flower see *Cleome spinosa*
Spiderwort see *Tradescantia × andersoniana*
Spindle tree see *Euonymus*
Spruce, black see *Picea mariana*
Spruce, Brewer's weeping see *Picea breweriana*
Spruce, Canadian see *Picea glauca*
Spruce, Colorado see *Picea pungens*
Spruce, Engelmann see *Picea engelmanii*
Spruce, Norway see *Picea abies*
Spruce, oriental see *Picea orientalis*
Spruce, Serbian see *Picea omorika*
Spruce, sitka see *Picea sitchensis*
Spruce, yezo see *Picea jezoensis*
Spurge see *Euphorbia*
Spurge, painted see *Euphorbia heterophylla*
Star of Bethlehem see *Ornithogalum*
Star of the veldt see *Dimorphotheca*
Stock see *Matthiola*
Stonecrop, biting see *Sedum acre*
Stonecrop, white see *Sedum album*
Strawberry tree see *Arbutus*
Sumach see *Rhus*
Sumach, smooth see *Rhus cotinus*
Sumach, stag's horn see *Rhus typhina*
Sunflower see *Helianthus*
Sun plant see *Portulaca grandiflora*
Swamp cypress see *Taxodium*
Sweet alyssum see *Labularia*
Sweet briar see *Rose rubiginosa*
Sweet gum see *Liquidambar*
Sycamore see *Acer pseudoplatanus*
Sycamore, American see *Platanus occidentalis*
Sweet sultan see *Amberboa moschata*
Sweet William see *Dianthus barbatus*

Tarragon, French see *Artemisia drectnculus*
Tassel flower see *Emilia flammea*
Teasel see *Dipsacus*
Tickseed see *Coreopsis*
Thistle, globe see *Echinops*
Thorn, Washington see *Crataegus pheenopyrum*
Thrift see *Armeria*
Thyme, common see *Thymus vulgaris*
Thyme, lemon see *Thymus × citrodorus*
Thyme, wild see *Thymus praecox articus*
Tiger flower see *Tigridia pavonia*
Toadflax see *Linaria*
Tobacco plant see *Nicotiana*
Touch-me-not, Himalayan see *Impatiens glandulifera*
Trinity flower see *Tradescantia × andersoniana*
Trumpet creeper see *Campsis*
Trumpet-flower, Chinese see *Incarvillea*
Tulip tree see *Liriodendron*
Turk's cap, scarlet see *Lilium chalcedonicum*
Turk's cap, yellow see *Lilium pyrenaeum*
Turtle head see *Chelone*
Umbrella plant see *Peltiphyllum*
Valerian see *Centranthus*
Valerian, red see *Centranthus ruber*
Vetch, crown see *Coronilla varia*
Vine, Japanese crimson glory see *Vitis coignetiae*
Vine, staff see *Celastrus*
Vine, trumpet see *Lonicera sempervirens*
Violet, dog's tooth see *Erythronium*
Violet, sweet see *Viola odorata*
Virginia creeper see *Parthenocissus*
Virginia creeper, Chinese see *Parthenocissus henryana*
Viscaria see *Silene coeli-rosa*
Wallflower see *Cheiranthus*
Wand flower see *Dierma*
Water crowfoot, common see *Ranunculus aquatilis*
Water lily see *Nymphaea*
Wayfaring tree see *Viburnum lantana*
Whortleberry see *Vaccinium*
Whitebeam see *Sorbus aria*
Whitebeam, Swedish see *Sorbus intermedia*
Willow, almond-leaved see *Salix triandra*
Willow, bay see *Salix pentandra*
Willow, crack see *Salix fragilis*
Willow, creeping see *Salix repens*
Willow, goat see *Salix caprea*
Willow, hoary see *Salix elaegnos*
Willow, violet see *Salix daphnoides*
Willow, white see *Salix alba*
Windflower see *Anemone*
Windflower, mountain see *Anemone blanda*
Windflower, snowdrop see *Anemone sylvestris*
Wine grape see *Vitis vinifera*
Winter aconite see *Eranthis hyemais*
Wintergreen see *Gaultheria procumbens*
Witch hazel, Chinese see *Hamamelis mollis*
Witch hazel, common see *Hamamelis virginiana*
Witch hazel, Japanese see *Hamamelis japonica*
Witch hazel, Ozark see *Hamamelis vernalis*
Woodbine see *Lonicera periclymenum*
Wormwood see *Artemisia absinthium*
Yarrow see *Achillea*
Yellow shrunk cabbage see *Lysichiten americanum*
Yew, common see *Taxus baccata*
Yew, Japanese see *Taxus cuspidata*

Acknowledgements

All photographs reproduced in this book were taken by the author with the exception of the following:
(tr = top right, cl = centre left, b = bottom, etc.)

Georges Lévêque 60 tl, 117 b, 132 tr, 154 b, 159 tl, 166 tr, 189 bl, 198 tr, 205 t, 208 t

Harry Smith 35 l, 89 tr

Wolfram Stehling 2, 9 tl, 11, 18 t, 41 br, 42 cl, 52 tl, 71 tl, 84 cl, 85 tl, 105 tc, 112 cl, 113 c, 117 tr, 119 tr, 122 tr, 122 cr, 122 br, 123 t, 133 t, 154 tl, 158 cr, 159 tr, 169 t, 197 b